FRANK HURTEE
DEC. 31, 1978

FURNITURE TREASURY
VOLUME III

FURNITURE TREASURY

(Mostly of American Origin)

BEING A RECORD OF DESIGNERS, DETAILS OF DESIGNS
AND STRUCTURE, WITH LISTS OF CLOCK MAKERS
IN AMERICA, AND A GLOSSARY OF FURNITURE
TERMS, RICHLY ILLUSTRATED

BY

WALLACE NUTTING

DRAWINGS BY

ERNEST JOHN DONNELLY

VOLUME THREE

MACMILLAN PUBLISHING CO., INC.
NEW YORK

Macmillan Publishing Co., Inc.
866 Third Avenue, New York, N. Y. 10022

Fourteenth Printing 1977

PRINTED IN THE UNITED STATES OF AMERICA

DIRECTIONS AND EXPLANATIONS

IN this volume, F. T., with a number, refers to the number under the picture in the author's 1st and 2nd vols. FURNITURE TREASURY.

The pictures in that two-volume work, which this volume may or may not accompany, are numbered consecutively from 1 through 5000, without reference to the volume, for the sake of greater simplicity. There are no page, no chapter numbers. Hence rapid consultation is feasible.

This volume is prepared to supplement the text of the former volumes, and to supply very full details, hitherto unavailable, on styles, dates, construction, origins; on great designers, on salient points regarding the entire broad field of articles of wood or iron used in American dwellings.

The author learned, after publishing FURNITURE TREASURY, that the public was desirous of fuller descriptions. In part this demand is justified. But in many instances the slight variations between two objects pictured call for no special comment. The effort, therefore, will be to supply every reasonable demand, but not to dwell on stories about owners, which stories, especially if extended, have no possible significance regarding the furniture itself, but have been so long used as padding in volumes on this subject that the reader is surprised by their absence.

This volume will not in any instance duplicate the material in the other volumes of FURNITURE TREASURY.

The only illustrations to appear here are sketches of construction of odd or rare objects, drawn, and included in the text to give the three volumes an even richer and definitive nature, though the 5000 illustrations in volumes one and two would seem to be a great plenty.

Particularly the author has taken advantage, on the subject of clocks, of publishing a list of American makers extending nearly to 1700, and thus more than doubling the number of his CLOCK BOOK, long since out of print, and of enlarging here and there the matter descriptive of the more eminent makers. It is beyond possibility to trace every clock maker's name, but hundreds of volumes have been searched to render this list as full as it is. In this particular the list given in the CLOCK BOOK is used as a basis, and that list, revised, is included in one alphabet with this. Only a few very eminent English makers are included.

I ought to state that the chair back on page 202 has motives added to the original as alternates if desired, namely, the fluting of the posts, the engrailing basing the splat, and the carving at the outside of the top of the splat above the acanthus leaf.

Mr. Ernest John Donnelly has supplied from my material the drawings.

The profound knowledge of Henry Wood Erving, our venerable and genial mentor, has been availed of when possible. Yet he is in no way to be held responsible for the volume, especially for any severities of statement. His well-known irenic temper, his wide experience as a collector for sixty years, and the incalculable amount of generous information he has given to a multitude of persons, strangers as well as friends, place a heavy debt, lovingly acknowledged, upon all American collectors and especially upon the author.

I feel embarrassed not to mention more kind helpers. To do so would be invidious, because I should surely omit some, but a further reason is that it is sometimes necessary to point out features not wholly worthy and I wish to make criticism impersonal as far as possible. It has seemed wiser to omit all names of owners.

The measured drawings have been done by Mr. J. S. Crytzer, and some are very beautiful, as the brass fixture showing the beehive.

I beg to assure everybody concerned that I am too old to entertain hard feelings, though some persons have given me cause. I have nothing but hope for all men, among whom, as an object of hope, I would like to be included.

Particularly for the very generous assistance of collectors I am altogether grateful.

WALLACE NUTTING.

FRAMINGHAM, MASSACHUSETTS
1933.

CONTENTS OF VOLUME III

FURNITURE TREASURY
(Mostly of American Origin)

AN OUTLINE OF CABINETMAKING

Civilization being reflected in furniture, the forms of furniture are indicative not only of the skill and imagination of those who created the forms, but they are a reflex of character. A stern age will produce heavy, simple furniture. An artistic age will express itself perhaps more generally through furniture than through any other medium, because for every piece of sculpture or painting there are many articles of furniture. In cottages where no other form of art except needlework and furniture existed, the seventeenth and eighteenth centuries exhibited articles of a high degree of taste and skill.

So the late eighteenth and early nineteenth centuries showed many finicky designs, frail, over-luxurious, trivial, and hastening to depravity.

The nineteenth century was the climax in the world's history of haste and thought-lessness in matters of decoration. Men were so absorbed in new inventions and the social and political upheavals concomitant with the coming in of machinery, that they esteemed too lightly the richer side of life. Even the furniture must be on the go, hence the glorification of the rocking-chair. Indeed, while that instrument which has barked so many shins and even caused death and encouraged profanity was invented before 1800, the nineteenth century may be called the rocking-chair age. The American, when his day's work was done, preferred to go rapidly back and forth, since, until the next day, he could no longer go forward. It is noticeable also that the decline of the cradle is coincident with the rise of the rocking-chair. In fact, a settee on rockers was invented so that mother and child could rock at once, one at either end of the settee.

Because also men had discovered many mechanical and chemical facts hitherto locked in darkness, they took a conceit to themselves that they must be "smarter" than their fathers. The fallacy lay in the fact that the more absorbed men grew in mechanics the less they knew or cared about beauty and taste. They deteriorated in almost everything except the knowledge of mechanics. If they could make a locomotive and their fathers could not, they presumed they could also make better furniture than their fathers. In shuffling off the cloak of darkness regarding natural sciences, they superficially supposed that all the knowledge of their fathers was defective, stupid, or false. They therefore neglected their valuable heritage and became barbarous, in the matter of the forms of things. It is necessary only to look at the decorations of 1840 to 1900 to be convinced of the appalling delinquency that had overtaken taste. Again, since they had made machines, they took a pride in doing everything by machine. The marvelous power of the human hand, which had really developed the human brain,

Engrailing under front rail of Chippendale chairs usually about ⅜ inch wide by 14 inches long, reaching to the brackets.

(3)

58

(4)

especially when using hand tools, was lost sight of, and individuality was lost, together with nicety of shape, accuracy of structure, and the charm invariably resultant from the skilful and loving human touch. It became a maxim in shops, as it is to this very day, "You can't afford to do it by hand." This spirit yet rules and largely ruins the age. There is no extensive manufactory of furniture where much work is done by hand, or where it is encouraged or even tolerated. Nemesis has overtaken furniture making. The extensive factories have, mostly, failed, and those that made the best furniture have failed most completely. The leading man in a concern widely boasting of its "reproductions" stated in the hearing of the writer that "finish was ninety-nine per cent important." So furniture is made with a lick and a go. A form was selected that could be managed by a machine. What nameless nightmares resulted witness the towering bed head of 1870. The mortise and tenon were wholly forsaken and the quick dowel substituted. In fact, the name "joiner" of old, given to a man who could unite by mortise, is totally inapplicable to the rank and file of woodworkers today. They pass no examination of a guild. They have no pride in their product. This system is subversive of character. Everything below the surface is rotten — if not the wood, the method. There is no possible objection to a machine for the work that a machine can do better than the hand, as is often true. But to omit or distort a feature because hand work is debarred is to enter on the path of deception and even theft of what is due to good materials. It is the murder of the finer attributes. And it will go merrily on, civilization dancing about its own open grave, until men repent, and insist on honest structure, the reflex of an honest man.

Since high achievement is the consequence of devoted study, it is not a marvel that taste deteriorated. How much attention was paid to it? Save the surface and you save nothing. We cannot paint on fog, or plate rot with gold, and the man who has no respect for his ancestors has none for himself.

Conceit, hurry, ignorance of past achievements, these have borne their natural fruits. What house is harmoniously furnished throughout? "If such there be," as the stranger clergyman said in praying for the children of an old maiden, I have not seen them. But voices are lifted up in the wilderness, even of the department stores where the clerk answers when asked what that piece of furniture is, "a hundred dollars." And he also informs his victim that all styles go together. And they do, the sheep and the goats, lame, halt and hollow, or stuffed with grass and moss, and suffering quite obviously from colic — overstuffed.

(On the opposite page is the finest portrait bust so far found in America, John Milton, on a Pennsylvania secretary.)

Carved middle slat on late Empire chairs and settees.

(5)

It is therefore that books on furniture are in demand, for the American, after all, is inquisitive, and he desires to know what all this talk of periods and antiques is about. Hence the haste of the merchant to lay a false mantle of style over every conceivable object and to claim the name Jacobean for jack.

Or, what is worse? Why, to "design" furniture. I am handed a card by a large and very respectable house, who enter themselves on it as "designers." But why design? I possess seven thousand pictures of old furniture, and have seen seven times seven thousand variations of these pictures. Is it likely that anybody can think of anything new *and* good? It may be new, but it looks as if born in the infernal regions to plague the glimpses of the moon. Nobody in a hundred years has brought forth anything new except monstrosities, or at least inelegancies, weak shapes, or mongrels. And mongrels greatly predominate. They are hash. It is as if a foot grew out of a face; or as if the skeletons of a dozen beasts had been set up, happy go lucky, by a child at play. Every furniture designer ought to be devoted to the past. There is no objection to his diverting himself with an effort after new forms, but an employer who pays him to do so knows little of the history of furniture.

Take Euclid, for example. How many new solutions have been added to the old in geometry? Lately a solution has been announced to one problem with which a hundred generations of mathematicians have wrestled in vain. The obvious forms of furniture, in their main outlines occur freshly in the morning of the world to students of the subject. But every age finds less and less that remains untried. That is often heralded as new which was discarded by the cabinetmakers of Nebuchadnezzar. And beeswax still remains the best final finish for furniture, as it was when Egypt was young. Human needs in the home are about what they always have been. Can any reader invert a curved line that has not been classified and experimented with? Perhaps, but serious men after they have visited museums, copy, and honest serious men admit that they copy. Has there been any change in the shape of a human back? We have them crooked and we have them straight. So of chair backs. The old "sleepy hollow" was crooked enough. And as to cupboards, the writer has tallied at least a thousand. Beds there are little and big, buried in feathers and hard as a rush couch on which I slept one night to learn what it was like. I knew in the morning — before

An excellent Chippendale chair back, the best features of which are the acanthus leaves and the molded ears. Date probably before 1765.

morning. There are bed heads of many of the animals, bedposts, fluted, reeded, bulbous, tenuous, straight, curved, and tortuous. I suppose it might be possible to make one more hideous than has been made. Who wants to try? Why? Because somebody is fool enough to pay him. Forms of great beauty ought to be cherished. The eye was made to enjoy them. Thousands of good bedposts have been designed. Try again. Certainly. But I will make this statement: show something designed in this generation, and I will show one better that is old.

But the pride of intellect arises and demands brusquely, "What do you mean, that this age is inferior in design?" "Precisely, that is what I mean, inferior in skill, taste, patience, knowledge, purpose." But if not, the constantly expressed shapes are limited. There can be only one circle. Why not try to invent another? A straight line will always seem such, despite Einstein. An equilateral triangle will never be changed by the infinity of a particle if this world stands billions of years more. These lines are the tools of the designer. He can't throw away his parabolas. A square is a square. Ovals have been drawn with every possible degree of elongation from a circle to a straight line as a limit. Furniture design in practice is an arrant humbug. There is plenty of good design. And nearly all of it is neglected. Lincoln's phrase should be modified: you can fool most of the people all the time. They are making furniture today in a certain southern state, and it is called southern furniture. Most of it is copied directly from English or American manuals, and the architects are swallowing the bait.

The history of furniture is fascinating because it is the most intimate of our permanent creations. A clock has a good deal of humanity. It has a face and hands, a waist, a hood, feet, a voice. And it has wheels in its head, and talks and strikes; it wags, and wears. A tasteful, thoughtful, loving person mayhap shaped it with grace; a good mechanic wrought its interior. Woods from far are worked into it. Several metals, several gums combine to complete it. It is a monument of skill and beauty. Many thousands of keen minds for a thousand years of invention have added to its perfection and charm. Fingers long since dust have wound and cared for it; were proud of it.

A Philadelphia Chippendale chair rail with a pierced rococo scroll and reeded splat. A highly approved design, well touched off by the dainty little foliage arising from the top of the reed openings at the sides of the splat top.

"When the old man died" it did not stop. Good clocks are still going, six, seven generations. But send it to the rummage sale and put up an electric clock that will stop the first time anything happens to the current, and has a hand made with a jackknife.

The way out from this shameful condition is in the cultivation of knowledge and taste in the buyer. A steady demand for fine and tasteful products can have but one result.

In a recent conversation with a young Jew, born in America of an old-world father of skill and taste, the writer said: "I presume you will go into cabinetmaking and carry on the traditions of your father?" "No," said he, "I think young Americans are not becoming cabinetmakers any more." So this young man sells antiques; for his *father* has abandoned bench work, is selling antiques, and grumbling because there is no good furniture made!

Under the circumstances this volume will at least record a thousand details of approved patterns of early date, and the available names of persons who have left their records or reputations for early work.

The natural growth of cabinetmaking was of course from the need of a receptacle to hold valuable belongings. That means a coffer, chest, box, trunk, all the same originally. As this receptacle was intended primarily for use in traveling, it must be strong. Four hundred six-horse vehicles were commandeered by Queen Elizabeth when she made a progress. Hence the old chests were much battered. At length the English in modern times called the traveling chest a box, and the English in America called it a trunk. No name should be connected with a chest with reference to its contents, except in an individual home, where one is set aside for a young lady, her hope chest; another for blankets and so forth. They were all the same pattern. Little chests were Bible boxes or desk boxes, though of course the little boxes were used for a multitude of purposes besides keeping Bibles.

In fact, they existed long before individuals had Bibles. The frame was omitted, usually, from the small chest, as unnecessary. Good larger chests always had frames, the board chests being for the poor man, or not intended to be transported.

The pineapple was used on door heads of dwellings long before it came into use on furniture. This is one of the instances that show how easy it is to go astray on style. The bedposts with pineapples are nineteenth century, and we believe also the clocks. Nos. 78 and 80 are good examples. No. 79 passes for a pineapple, but also suggests the pine cone from which I suppose the pineapple derived its name. (*Page 79.*)

The tastefully carved and shell-decorated skirt of a Queen Anne highboy. The spread of the central shell arranged to coincide with the bottom scroll is commendable. The two dainty side shells and the four whorls complete a decorative scheme which, while simple, is harmonious and pleasing.

Carving may be assigned a date as early as cabinetmaking. The oriental and the American Indian carved their receptacles as naturally as they breathed. Indeed, the carving of the totem pole by the Alaskan Indians probably was done, originally, on a standing tree. Who shall say who first carved love tokens on a beech? Obviously, the tree grew for this purpose.

Quite likely the first mortises and tenons were made like the truss on a trestle table frame — the tenon projected beyond the mortise and was pinned or wedged on the outside, and it was so found in early Egypt. Progress was so exceedingly slow, any wave of barbarism sweeping across a continent swept the race back and lost the early patterns as at Grand Rapids.

The ordinary seller of furniture has a poorer idea of how it should be put together than the people eight thousand years ago.

I once tried an experiment. I have an exquisite Queen Anne chair. In contour and carving it is near the apex of style and beauty as reached in 1720. The slip seat being completely worn out, I substituted a modern, machine-woven seat cover, a fine and handsome one. Then I set this chair as a bait. Probably a thousand women of education, those we call ladies, have examined it. Their eyes invariably turn directly to the seat. Most think it hand work, all admire it. The woman has yet to come who shall glance at the shape and ornamentation of the chair itself. We are living at the very climax of barbarism. This incident could not have occurred in the eighteenth century, nor in any century before, nor in any part of the earth, Kamchatka and Patagonia least of all. Properly speaking, there is no taste for art or beauty. The millionth man really loves good lines, and whatever following he has marks the fad.

Interior decorating is what it is for the same reason. Search for the woman. At a great art school — I use the name they give it — the huge class in interior decorating was set to submit graduation theses. With scarcely an exception they drew pictures of windows and passages the only feature of which was the hangings. As for the

A scroll on the top of the upper section of a secretary which is to be decorated on the center with a finial. The carving in this case is applied, and that is quite usual. Of course the foliage is inchoate with no attempt to be naturalistic, but it certainly is not sufficiently overdone to be offensive.

furniture, hang it! After several years' training in decorating there was not one graduate who knew good furniture from bad. How should she? There had been no effort to teach her (we know why). But the poor girl went out into the world and set up her sign and opened her shop, and installed her blue wood boxes, and there you are! And there you are likely to be for some time. There are several women who have good collections. They are widows. They inherited. But more of them sell. The greatest auction of antiques ever held was ordered by a widow. They seem not to want the furniture to remember their husbands by. They remember them too well.

Of late, just as soon as a few very rich men ceased to buy antique furniture everybody else ceased. The writer, though not rich, created a fad for court cupboards, buying them for about a thousand dollars apiece. Soon they were twenty-five thousand. One buyer paid twenty-seven thousand. I ceased to buy several years ago. More than one such cupboard has been sold or offered, lately, at less than five hundred dollars. You will say there is no sense in that. True. There is the same degree of sense as in buying stock at a premium of several hundred, at which price it paid one and a half percent, and in declining to buy it now at thirty, at which price it pays sixteen percent.

Business is done on sentiment, just as antiques are bought. There is nothing new in this situation, except perhaps, as the rustic said, "people grow fooler and fooler." That is, the pendulum of prices varies more widely from the reasonable, and taste varies in the same way. We may soon take to wearing rings in our noses again. But we are led by the nose so completely that no ring is needed. It is better to laugh at human vagaries than to storm. In fact, a laugh is more powerful than guns.

Nearly all collectors are men, as are nearly all great artists. In fact, men lead the fashions in dressmaking. Women are interested in fabrics, not furniture. They wear snuff-colored ill-fitting trousers in winter. It is said they do it to attract attention, but nobody would look twice.

Men make the great collections, though women now have half the money and control the other half. When as in a few years they actually possess most of the money, there is likely to be nothing really good wanted.

It is, to remedy this condition, probably of little use to try to lead taste. One brilliant friend of mine says preaching does no good. I think he is wrong, because I am a preacher. But it is more difficult to lead tastes than morals. A mountaineer philosophizing on the condition of his neighbors, said, "There ain't no leader, and they ain't none of us that will foller, and we *caint* be druv."

A carved base or skirt of a lowboy reaching completely to the bracket of the post. The partial opening above is the bottom drawer. This carving is in excellent taste in the manner in which the acanthus scrolls are connected.

The only notable exception I recall to this tirade is the far-shining example of Mrs. J. Insley Blair. Of course there are others.

How many collectors have bought pieces and kept them in their offices, or in out-buildings, until the purchases were finally noticed by the better, but less artistic half. "When did you get that?" "That? Why, I've had it a long time." And so it is finally sneaked into the house. I know a dear wife, to whom the husband said, "I have a secret, I have kept it from you for four months. Find it out. You have only to use your eyes." It was some time after that when she discovered he had substituted a fine antique chair for a shoddy modern one.

Of course, all these facts have been patent for years. They have been whispered behind the hand, but now it behooves all men everywhere to repent and rebel. I am getting old, and if I am shot at sunrise, one old fellow less will not be missed, and it is not a bad cause to die for. There have been worse.

Two out of the three great collectors were bachelors. That is why they collected.

Beneath it all there may be a reason. Women should be jealous of things, because persons, as Quinneys' has pointed out, are more important. So when an old chest comes between a man and his wife, of course the chest should go. Still, a man had better be driven to collecting than driven to drink. Collecting leaves him with his wits about him, and the man who has not a fad has nothing else, except possibly money, which will do him no good without a taste for something worth while.

It is the upholstery that pleases the ladies. If you wish to marry, merely say, "Madam, you are the best-dressed woman in town." If that is not effective, raise your bid and say the best dressed in the state. A man with a huge nose or scarcely any nose at all, and no chin, can get married by this recipe. Any little runt, even the

A decoration found on the center of the front rail of a Philadelphia chair attributed to Gillingham. Some chairs otherwise of this type have a straight rail or an incipient decoration at this point. A full development of the style, however, requires this carving. The raised bead extends to the brackets of the legs.

Prince of —— can marry if he just says, "My dear, what fine taste in the selection of your gown." You might just add, incidentally, "You are very handsome and don't remind me at all of an antique, and I see no evidence of more than minor restoration."

It would throw a ray of sunshine across my declining years, if at length the millionth woman, viewing my Queen Anne chair (named after a woman), should exclaim, "What style, what artistry!" The shape is really quite feminine. Its high ramped back graciously curving, its subtle charm indefinable, though one must admit the foot is somewhat stubbed for a Queen's.

In early cabinetmaking the matter of uniformity never arose. The matter of humanity was uppermost. Just as no two persons are alike, except twins, so no two pieces of furniture are alike, except chairs in sets, and even so, careful scrutiny detects a difference, as in twins.

No effort was made at interchangeability. There being no machine to enforce identical parts, a maker joyed in the slight variations incident to or sought for in hand work, just as no two musicians play even a masterpiece alike.

Especially in turning and carving was there variation. An architect recently called attention to a variation of a sixty-fourth of an inch in some hand turning being done for him! Why, the rule that the old-time turner used was not graduated less than a sixteenth of an inch, and no old turning that I have examined was even as close as that. About an eighth of an inch is as near as good old hand turning comes to a supposed template. It is doubtful if the calipers were applied in more than one place on a turning. The turner followed his eye. If the work looked right, it was right, because he was trained to use his eye instead of a gauge. The matter of entasis was considered only on long turnings. As the Parthenon columns show a swell of only three-

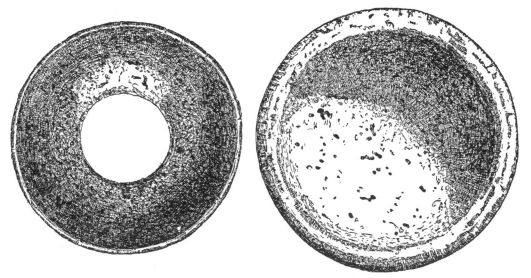

Bowls of burl or burr found in many kinds of wood, but more commonly maple or walnut, are highly decorative objects much neglected by furniture collectors. Placed on a large cabinet nothing could be better. The left piece is a strainer with a rim on the under side to which a piece of cloth may be tied. That on the right is the largest plain bowl that I happen to have seen.

quarters of an inch, obviously the matter of half a stretcher, perhaps five inches long, should have an entasis of one in somewhere about six hundred! Clearly an absurdity. The most a turner tried to do was to see that his work fulled rather than scanted, and so avoided a lean turning.

Carving on a pattern that is doubled, as most carvings of conventional patterns are, shows even at a casual glance, variations in the two sides, and variations also in the depth of the carving. The spirit of the work, its effectiveness, is what the carver sought, and what he usually achieved, though there was some poor work even of old. Hence arises the difficulty of discriminating between old carving and new. Two or three passes of a wire brush over good modern carving that is a fair imitation of the old impart an appearance which may deceive the keenest judges, and has done so in important cases that have come to the direct knowledge of the writer.

Why, then, if old work can be imitated to an extent that leaves careful examiners in doubt, is it important to know whether work is old or new? If the new work is as good as the old, there is only one point of superiority for the old — the sentiment connected with age. Of course, in practice the new is seldom as good as the old.

A matter of framing in which machine work usually fails is the abandonment of the best old method, whereby a stretcher was made perfectly flush, outside, with a leg. The old method is more expensive to finish because the surfaces must be exactly harmonized, which means hand sanding. Commercial work, therefore, sinks the stretcher a little below the surface of the leg. This detail is the quickest form of betrayal of new work. A person of any experience can detect it without coming near a chair. The slightest crack in a joint may enable the examiner to see that dowels rather than mortises were used. But where no bad joint appears one can generally see the continuing wood of the tenon entering the mortise, because nearly always the tenon on one side at least is flush with the surface of the piece on which it is cut. One cannot detect the draw bore pin without taking furniture apart. Then, if old, the pin is found

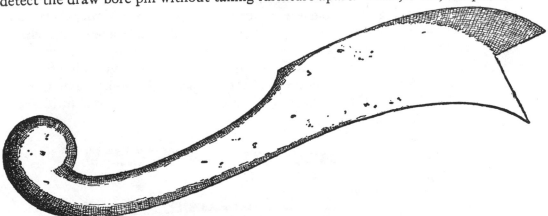

The arm of a chair may make it or break it in more senses than one. Above is the graceful arm of an early Chippendale chair, which is also used on the Georgian type. The chair which scrolls sidewise is earlier than the type which scrolls vertically. There is a thinning away of the arm on the inside, reaching its deepest curve about a third of the way from the back. The method of attachment to the post was by a very small, shallow, open mortise into which the arm was pinned.

(13)

to be crooked. Sad to say, to the champions of the draw bore, the pin is also either broken or weakened from the crook it must follow in being driven.

There will, with few exceptions, be twists in old posts, or warping, or irregularities not found in modern work.

Old glue can no longer be known, because new glue is colored dark to look old.

In all traces of saw scarfs on the unfinished sides, one should look for curved lines, the lines of the circular saw, unknown of old. Old chests, panels, or bottoms show the mark of the ax in shaping our finest specimens. Many points of importance were glanced at in Vols. I and II.

Houses are often dear to us. But how much dearer is grandfather's chair, then father's, then ours, then to be our sons' and grandsons'! How happy was I to find a chair from the family of Thomas Robinson, a founder of Guilford, whose father was the leader of the Pilgrims in Holland! Notable in ancestry, connection, design, used for ten generations and now reposing in a museum! Every portion reminiscent of a wonderful past, from the age of Cromwell to the age of Phillips Brooks. Is it a wonder that cultivated persons enjoy old furniture and wish to be near it and imitate it? It has a rich suggestion of fidelity, of romance. It ties the generations together and makes us one.

Anybody who sneers at collectors sneers at the work of good men who have left good monuments. This tangible arm their strong, skilful hands rested upon. Patriarch and sage, dreamer and doer, were upheld in weariness in this honest old wainscot. When we understand those men and do as good work and show as good taste we shall be worthy to enjoy their relics.

It is probable that the legs and feet of furniture in the very earliest times imitated the legs and feet of animals. This appears in the records of Mesopotamia and Egypt. In this sense the Directoire and early Empire periods revived the earliest known forms. Structurally such furniture presented difficulties unless it was done in bronze or some sort of metal. Overlaying with gold was practiced in the furniture of palaces, and even solid silver furniture was made. And then as now the rich copied the styles of the court, and these again were copied by the less rich until, debased in form and material, the result was as far from the original as the later Phyfe styles were from the days of 1790–1800. A truer motive lies behind the simpler styles which came into use in the houses of substantial English people, who, in forms like the turned furniture of

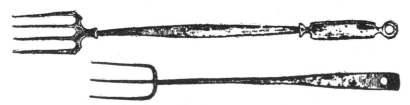

The bottom fork above is the daintiest and the lightest (all except the upper part of the handle being done in the round) that I have seen. The other one is also good. Our ancestors showed their taste in hardware even more than in their furniture.

our own Pilgrim period, sought for sense and stability rather than imitations of the natural world. The wealth and greater culture found in the church and monkish establishments gave a strong impetus to Gothic shapes, especially in church receptacles, as coffers, chests, cupboards, and credences.

The production of special forms is fostered by seclusion, enthusiasm, and study. The Gothic idea developed in the quiet of cloistered retreats and showed itself in the illuminated manuscripts, in sacred historical sculpture, in choir seats and shrines, as well as in the springing vaults of those enriched embodiments of art wedded to adoration which we associate with the word cathedral. It is for this reason that the earlier forms of furniture were massive, as was necessary in a setting of vast dimensions.

Furniture as we know it, in its better forms, arose with the rise of the middle class, and the necessary adaptations to a comfortable and ample home life were made. Except for a few examples, domestic furniture for our practical studies begins nearly about 1620. It is merely a coincidence that this date agrees with the beginning of American settlements from Great Britain.

The methods of good cabinetmaking were known to the ancients, though before the Gothic period the memory of many methods had been lost with the loss of the objects themselves. There was a guild of cofferers in the fifteenth century. It is impossible to see any betterment in the joiners' art as time went on, though there was

The English exercised far more skill and gave far more attention to stools than we did. The reason is largely to be found in the numerous window recesses which are common to stone and brick dwellings. Also, of course, it is to be reasoned that large wealth would show itself by bestowing care and rich decoration even upon minor pieces of furniture. The carved stool above with its central masque, apparently a portrait, and its lion's head on the knees corresponding to the lion's foot is an elaborate specimen in the Metropolitan Museum. The nulling around the slip seat completes the full decoration.

a wider degree of specialization. The advance from the heavy furniture of the middle ages to the dainty types of the year 1790 does not necessarily mean an advance in skill. Certainly the art of carving steadily declined from about 1700 to the wretched coarse work of 1830. It is true that rococo work often showed great skill, but it was not in the best taste. The nineteenth century did not bring more skill but worse taste.

In large centers of population there were always specialists in woodwork. The American combination of carpenter and joiner existed mostly in remoter districts, or on simple work. Skill when carried to a high degree of excellence always means specialization.

The present abandonment of the apprentice system makes for ignorance and clumsiness in construction. The trade schools, in seeking to remedy the lack, are not persistent enough in fundamentals. We find young men undertaking carving before they are able to do joining.

There is a lack of young American workmen in the cabinet shops which is disquieting at least to one who wishes to see the old American stock leading in all fields. The writer, after a considerable experience in the employ of hundreds of men, has come upon only two American born, of English blood, who really understand cabinetmaking. Both of these men were more than seventy years old and have now passed from the scene.

Americans lack the sense of the importance of fine work, and they lack the patience required to attain thorough mastery. The best shops are largely filled with Swedish workmen, with lesser numbers of Finns, Letts, Scotch-Irish, English, Germans, Italians.

There are good numbers of capable Russian-Jewish cabinetmakers, but they are largely engaged in shops as repairers of the antique, the repairs often being the major part of the piece. Great quantities of furniture made of old wood, or wood artificially aged, are produced in repair shops, and this condition will continue so long as human nature remains unregenerate, and so long as the collector remains credulous and superficial, as he will, except in rare instances.

There is not anywhere a sufficient demand for really good furniture to warrant manufacturers in producing it. That is a cold, incontrovertible fact which has been proved by many serious, honorable, persistent attempts to produce such furniture.

It is humiliating but none the less true that no amount of money can purchase in the shops furniture made in the best manner and applicable to all modern needs. That is, even a young millionaire couple cannot order and obtain a general supply of worthy ready-made furniture for a large house. It is still necessary to get the articles wanted, made. Even so there are many large American cities where no cabinet shops have sufficient good patterns. Mongrel is the only word to describe the products found or offered to be supplied. Without patterns, without experience, without taste, without ambition and, worst of all, without encouragement how is an order shop to succeed? A certain city in old America, a center of a quarter of a million persons — in fact, the city which by tradition, by considerable fine collections, and by ample wealth should be a natural center of exquisite cabinet work — has only one first-class repairer, and he is Hungarian! Of course, newer cities, even though they are larger, are yet worse provided.

The remarkable fireplace shown above has all the quality of an old-world setting, but it is located in southern New England. It is very broad and high, but its crowning merit is in the cupboard space above. The great chimney always draws in, slanting backward above the chimney tree, and thus a space shallow at the bottom and going broader at the top is left for cupboards usually closed by doors. In this case it is conveniently divided into three sections by plastered pillars into which a shelf is inserted. Wherever articles can be exposed as here to view a far more homelike and familiar background is supplied. It is to be noted that in the earliest fireplaces an independent shelf on the chimney tree is quite unusual, and that even in fine fireplaces of the period of 1760 also there is a heavy bolection molding, but no shelf. This fireplace has no crane, but a lug pole.

CABINETMAKING: STYLE AND PERIOD

Ladies looking at several exquisite pieces of furniture, some of which were unique masterpieces, perceived next to them a dilapidated Hitchcock chair of the cheapest pattern, and minus most of its paint. They exclaimed, "Isn't that a beautiful thing!" and they seriously meant it. Because there are such people, still at large, and "collecting," it is still important to point out:

1. That no furniture built after 1830 is worth having or classing as antique. This is not merely because of the date, but also because style blindness had by that time settled down, like a plague, so that people no longer "discerned the things that were excellent."

Many efforts have been made, none successful, to explain the cause of style blindness. It is sufficient, practically, to recognize its existence, and to seek the remedy.

It was seemingly impossible before the Revolution to erect a bad house. It was almost impossible after 1830 to erect a good house. Taste declined, whether owing to conceit, overemphasis or modernity, ignorance, haste, or machine products, no man can say precisely, though all these and other causes contributed. But back of all is the question, why? We must leave that to the philosophers. No one else is wise enough to answer it.

2. Quality in furniture is to be judged from its lines. If they are bizarre, or extreme, like the degraded Empire, they are to be avoided.

3. Quality must be judged by construction, that is, its putting together, its joints.

New furniture may be, usually is, bad because of being doweled rather than mortised, but the fact does not easily obtrude on the outside until use discloses weakness.

4. Quality in some sorts of furniture appears by the widths of its materials. Thus all commercial Windsor chairs are made with more than one piece in the seat. Unless the chair is painted it is easy to see where different strips come together. Old Windsor seats are made with one piece.

Cheap modern Windsors are also made with thin seats. Old seats are fully if not quite two inches thick in the thicker parts. Old Windsors because the seat was thick were deeply shaped. The process involves much hand labor, but is necessary to comfort. Sit for one hour in a modern Windsor and the result is almost torture. One may sit for hours in comfort on an old Windsor, the seat of which is often shaped an inch and an eighth in depth. No machine has been invented to do this. The machines in use made a shallow shape (ten a minute) in shallow seats.

The material of an old Windsor seat is in Pennsylvania usually poplar, white wood, or pine, and in New England usually pine. These woods are light in weight. A chair made in the usual modern heavy maple seat must, to be light, use thin material.

We now point out with emphasis some abuses to which the public have been subject in the way of reproduction. One is the making of a Windsor chair with a mahogany seat — a thing not known in the old time and not desirable now because it neither adds to the comfort, nor takes from the cost.

5. Quality in mahogany furniture is partly determined by weight. Light-weight mahogany is not only cheaper than maple, but it is brittle, slivery, and weak. Baywood passes in the furniture trade as mahogany, which it is not. All good mahogany is heavy, because strength and a close grain mean weight. This heavy mahogany costs

several times as much as baywood and is prohibitory in furniture sold at a low price. Any mahogany piece that impresses one as light weight, compared with known good old examples, should be declined. Further, cheap mahogany will not carve well.

6. Quality is maintained if an article retains its integrity of structure so as to be substantially what it was originally. Ten per cent of reconstruction has been named as the limit allowable, but that means restorations not of elements essential to the beauty or style.

7. It does not add to value that an article was bought from some notable person.

8. It does add to value that the article is rare; still more that it is unique. The quality of carving counts. Late carving is worthless because crude in design and execution, like late four posters.

9. The kind of wood makes for desirability. Mahogany is better than maple or cherry. The execution of the cabinetwork is important. So is the finish, if original.

10. But buyers should not suppose an article rare unless they have had a wide experience in collecting. A rather successful dealer used generally to assure his prey: "This piece is the only one of the kind." Pieces may be rare in one section and plentiful in another.

Clockwork jacks were much sought for till it was found many could be bought in England at a tenth of their value here.

A young lady, recently married, began to collect. Going into a repair shop in her own home town, she saw a good Windsor chair hanging high on the wall. "I'd like that chair," she said. "I should think you would," said the repair man, "your great-grandfather left it here about sixty years ago, but dad never got to it." Yet perhaps even this is not the record. No doubt when Pompeii was destroyed there was furniture in the shops awaiting restoration for a century or so. If Noah took any furniture into the ark, it needed fixing or was unlike any other. It certainly must have swelled in that long rain.

A cabinetmaker has a chair which he takes apart every two years, but it always gets loose in the joints. Baseboards on houses one hundred and fifty years old, if taken off and planed, will shrink. Furniture is always swelling or shrinking. In this respect it is no better than the human figure.

Repair men get to be dealers because jobs left them can't be paid for or cost more than the piece is worth (a common event), or because they are forgotten in old estates. The very names and uses of many old pieces are forgotten. Nobody knows what the pilgrim chest-on-frame was made for, and people "want to know." A huge burl bowl in my possession always elicits the question "what was it for?" I reply, a baby bath, and most believe it.

The zest of the collector consists largely in ferreting out the ramifications of style and the odd and curious uses of old furniture. The process enables one to reconstruct the setting of the olden time so that history becomes more realistic and particular in its references. Theatrical representations could well study to supply some of the minor decorative pieces of peculiar charm. A piece of furniture taken by itself is lonely and has slight significance. The placing is more important than the piece.

A brief glance at the matter of stairways is all that may be looked for in a work of this kind, yet the stair approaches in its rail construction to furniture. The specimen on page 19 is, we think, more beautiful than the unbroken straight run, and that it even rivals the single landing. There are here two landings, the second one being merely indicated by the corner of the panel on the upper left hand. The unusual newel post is shown with a central break and square. Inside the spiral elements of course is a copy of one of the spindles, and the cap is always in good specimens, as here, made with breaks and returns into the main rail. An amusing problem met the builder when he placed his balusters; his three each different repeated nicely until he reached the bottom step where, owing to the outward sweep, he required four and therefore repeated one of the patterns. An ideal scheme would have furnished a fourth pattern for this extra spindle, but that would be too much to ask.

The other stair shown is somewhat simpler, but both dwellings date about 1735. This is the height of the Georgian period and supplies us with more fascinating and dignified details than any later time. (*Page 122.*)

Fireplaces also are due to receive in a work like this merely a passing treatment. On this page at the right is a very simple example which gets its dignity from the generous panel above, which is, or should be, of one board.

On page 21 is a mantel almost identical with one known as a McIntire, yet this specimen is in Connecticut, which indicates, I believe, that architects use manuals. The fine break in the cornice doubles the effectiveness of the mantel and overmantel, making them an architectural unit.

Those old makers were no more bound to render a reason than a negro playing a melody. They just enjoyed doing things. It would be unreasonable to expect them to be reasonable, any more than a colt kicking up in a pasture. They made things sometimes to show how clever they were. They made them to puzzle people. They made them because some silly patron ordered them, just as some patrons do today.

But the creative urge was strong upon them, only, strange to say, they almost invariably wrought in good taste. Now when forms change they become uncouth; then they changed from grace to grace, until along about 1800–1820 men's minds at length grew barren of good ideas, and they ran to monstrosities increasingly, from the late Phyfe to the late Grand Rapids. At the same moment that they lost the knowledge of design they lost also the good sense to copy. There was a time here and abroad when to be old was enough to ban anything. Examples of priceless value were cut down, painted, degraded to the woodshed or the attic, or destroyed. A chest worth thousands of dollars was found in a Cape Cod poor house. Another entered in an estate inventory as "one old chest" was valued at ten dollars, but afterwards brought two thousand. A unique table found in an old attic was offered for almost nothing, but when the owner happened to be warned by a friend to investigate, she was able to sell for thirty-five hundred. A block-and-shell desk of unique pattern came into the hands of a bride. She saw a fine Goddard shell on the lid and said to the repairer, "Take that off, I don't like it." So said, so done. When, twenty years after, I saw the desk, I said, "Do you know what you have done? You have planed away five thousand dollars." Of course most good old specimens are destroyed, which goes to show how much of good there must have been, and how surrounded our fathers were by the creations of good taste. Now their heirs are impoverished as well as the remainder of the generation.

As to the periods when the cabriole leg was forsaken, a good thing was lost. If a straight leg has a carved fret, well, but such a leg costs more than the cabriole and is ornate rather than beautiful. No art conceals art like the early Georgian, or the simpler Queen Anne.

It bears the impress of style without seeming overdone.

Of course, oak is very desirable, especially for halls. It is too much for us to ask general admiration for oak. Its dignity and distinction are for the very few. Perhaps that is well, because the supply of American oak is small, and it gravitates to museums where already about half of the court cupboards are.

Oak imparts an impression to a hall of substantiality, of durability, continuance, family dignity. Since our halls are not used to sit in, it is of no consequence that a wainscot chair is uncomfortable. A chest in a hall dominates the house and is convenient and beautiful if of oak.

Looking-glasses of the earliest or the Queen Anne time, at any rate, are good in halls where they are very convenient for sly glances at guests. They also bring light into what is usually the darkest room in the house. A hall can well have several looking-glasses (of old no one said mirrors). Then a narrow table, and all is perfect.

In a later period (1730–1800) a long settee of the Windsor type is admirable both for style and shape, in the ordinarily narrow hall. One or more chairs of the same style and a narrow gate table may complete the setting.

But oak and mahogany hurt one another. Their backgrounds should be different, to begin with. The limit of range ought to be two contiguous periods as early Georgian and Chippendale, or Chippendale and Hepplewhite. It has been plausibly put forward that an old family continually occupying a dwelling for generations naturally gets in new furniture from time to time. Hence let us admit all sorts. But the fallacy here is that the old family supposedly furnished properly to begin with, and, if so, additions are only unnecessarily crowding. The best old families kept up their fine furniture. Different rooms at least should be set aside for the various types, thus avoiding a jumble.

In the dining room people seem obsessed in favor of sideboards, even when Chippendale or earlier furniture makes up the balance of the setting.

Far finer is the large Chippendale or Queen Anne side table, the true sideboard, the china being kept in cupboards, except what display of rare china or silver are desired on this table.

The taper leg (Hepplewhite) table is properly unpopular, as it is infested with a dozen to sixteen legs.

But the Chippendale two- or three-part table with central standards is far handsomer, and also is better than the commonly found Empire (Phyfe). The Queen Anne two- or three-part table is equally good.

A dining room in old oak is one of the rarest things known. I have never seen such a room, though there are several collectors who might have provided it. The court cupboard is the main piece. The refectory table would be proper, but it is avoided owing to the interference of the feet with the stretcher. Of old the feet rested on it! Now, however, the only practical substitute is a very old gate leg which, however, must be in walnut. If in oak, it is almost certainly English. The chairs may be any of the pilgrim century.

A maple and pine dining room with pine dresser is good (the oak dresser is always foreign) and long Connecticut light turned table or late maple gate leg and turned chairs of the 1710–40 period.

Dens are good in oak, walnut, or maple.

Chambers can still be furnished with a satisfactory setting in several styles, except that twin beds must be new. The fashion of cutting down an old bed and making a new to match it has happily gone out. The old bed in this case is never in good style. It is better to cling to the old large bed or frankly supply new twin beds.

The oak age is still possible in chambers with chests of drawers and chests, but the bed — in fact, all turned parts — are in earliest maple.

Walnut is difficult on account of the bed, though shopping in Pennsylvania or farther south may discover it.

Mahogany offers a wide field. Strangely, Chippendale beds, either with claw-and-ball feet or even with square molded base, are rare. The square base is recommended, however, as the more available for purchase. Then highboys and lowboys with chairs of the period, especially a wing, are indicated.

Instead of highboys early chests of drawers or chest-on-chests are excellent. The better have ogee feet; the simpler have plain bracket feet.

The Hepplewhite bed with spade foot is desirable, with the outsweeping French foot for the chests of drawers, and shield-back chairs. Practically all the beds placed in collectors' bedrooms are turned Sheraton, of course the least desirable style, partly in themselves, and partly because they call for Sheraton chests of drawers and chairs.

Looking-glasses are easy to get of any period except the oak. But it is better not to inquire too particularly whether they are English or American. Few know, and perhaps none, because the style was the same. You will, of course, be told that they are American. They are made up in vast numbers abroad or at home. With old wood for backs they require better advice than is available to detect the age.

Of course old prints and maps and early paintings are always good anywhere, and are also important in completing a real setting.

Very little attention is paid to hardware. It should match the period of the house, and very much that is good is still available.

In the simplest rooms rag or braided rugs are good.

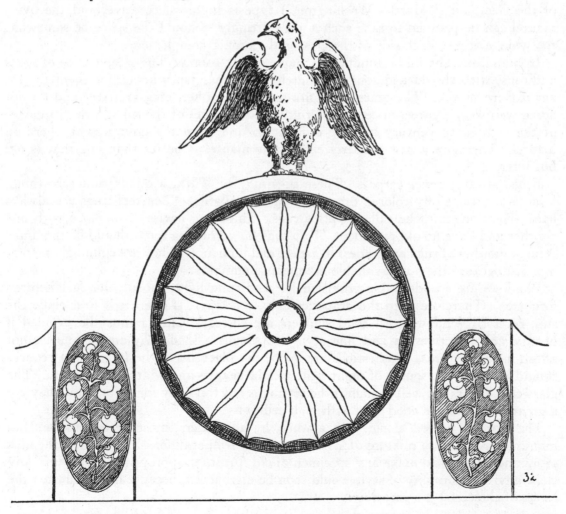

In a house confined to mahogany one can hardly go wrong in a hall, provided always that overcrowding, the common error of collectors, is avoided. A hall should have an air of space. But the walls will bear, if the background is plain paper, as it may well be, old maps, charts, or early pictures in addition to the looking-glasses.

Narrow modern floor boards do not contribute to an early atmosphere, whereas blocked or square paneled floors are excellent, unless brick or stone tiles are available.

The sitting or living room which has succeeded to the ancient parlor need not be furnished very differently on that account, with the simple proviso that a couple of comfortable chairs should be provided of the wing chair type, or "Sleepy Hollow" pattern. Plain walls, a few — one or two — large pictures, looking-glasses, wall cabinets for china, with or without a corner cupboard of the shell variety, may occupy the walls very well. It is to be noted that the Chippendale, still less a Queen Anne, glass horizontally long is rare, and it is better that the painting should be over the mantel unless the space accommodates itself to a vertically long glass. Such a glass of the Georgian ("Martha Washington") type is highly decorative, and the over-mantel can be planned to take such a glass fittingly. Should the space be somewhat too wide, a sconce each side of the glass is the proper complement.

Iron andirons should be confined to maple or oak rooms. The steeple type of brass andirons, with shovel and tongs to match, and brass jamb hooks for them to rest against are proper. The grate and "fire set" with poker, etc., are later and do not agree well with eighteenth-century furniture. A mantel of the middle third quarter of the eighteenth century is more difficult to find than the omnipresent Sheraton mantel. Therefore a new properly early style mantel is better than one that is old but later.

Rugs, always, never carpets. These rugs may be Turkish unless that rare thing, a large and tastefully colored drawn-in rug is available. "Scatter" rugs are always bad. They ought to be called spatter rugs. These are never harmonious with one another and have no old precedent. Two rugs for an oblong room should be the limit. A large number of rugs are restless in aspect and influence. They are cunningly recommended because they are available in immense numbers.

Windows are an admirable provision for admitting light, though this fact is often forgotten. Therefore keep the draperies light and lacy. If one needs to exclude the sun, recessed windows with solid shutters are correct. Clutter must be avoided if beauty and effectiveness and fine style are sought. Sheffield plate, if one cannot afford silver; or brass candlesticks are good, the plate being the later. But sconces should be the main source of night light to add beauty and width to the room. The glass chandeliers are well enough if the setting is not too early for them. But they are a great care, and are good only with high ceilings.

The word is passed along, with a wink, by all dealers, most decorators, and all manufacturers that a mixture of styles is proper. I must differ. The basis of the idea of mixing styles is to make any specimen of old furniture appropriate. Of course any clerk advising harmony of style would soon be discharged, because he has limited the range of choice for his customer.

Above is an English urn knife box inserted here because my other volumes omit them as not being American, though we cannot certainly say that none was made here. In these rich examples the cover lifts on a central shaft and is not intended to be removed completely. Such exquisite specimens would naturally be rare in America if existing at all as their construction is very expensive especially since they were almost invariably used as pairs.

The pilaster on the right is the detail of a quaintly carved capital on the pilasters of the best-known example of a shell-top cupboard, some years since removed from the now destroyed Jaffrey house in Portsmouth, New Hampshire.

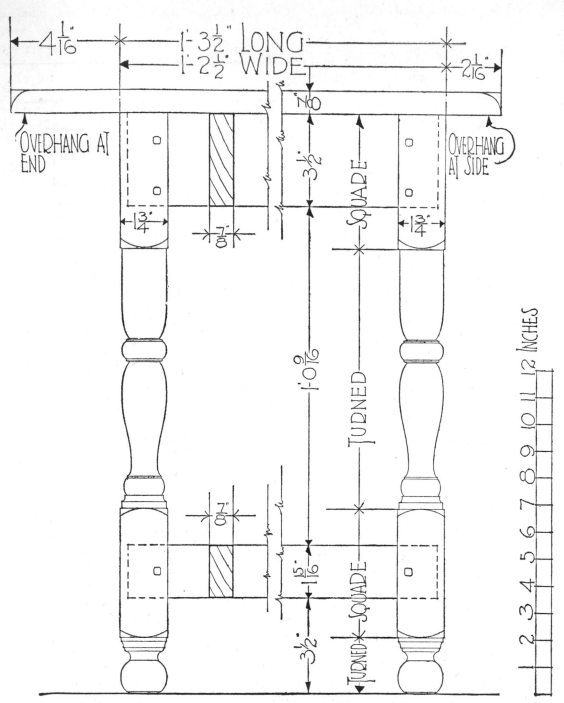

Just now there is much talk of coffee tables. None has been known to me of the old time. Recently I discovered this table in maple, pine top, the use of which, with its probable date 1690–1710, should exactly fit the requirements. Coffee tables ordinarily were of course round and a little higher, that is, tea tables, as we call them.

A mantel and fireplace not of the richer sort but of a description found on the Connecticut River in Massachusetts and Connecticut. It is effective and provides a shelf though more frequently the panel is continued without it on all four sides. This variation is a greater convenience. The capital rosette is a great favorite on Connecticut River work.

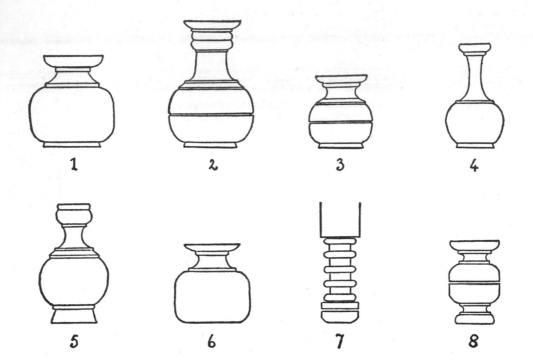

1   2   3   4

5   6   7   8

FURNITURE FEET

The saying regarding a horse, that if his feet and head are good, he is good altogether, holds true also of furniture. The stylistic features appear in the feet and the finials. If a piece of furniture is poorly described by a novice seeking information, it is necessary only to ask about the feet and finials, and, like the fossil, the entire outline can be fully seen by the eye of the sophisticated. If, for instance, one is shown a John Goddard clock finial or a bracket foot ending with a curled scroll on the inside, one knows at once that the piece is a Goddard block type, because his work is quite distinct. There is nothing else in the range of design comparable to these details.

A little knowledge of these subjects would save restorers, not to say reproducers, numerous humiliating mistakes. One sometimes sees, even in museums, and of course in collections, wrong restorations, and when the restoration of feet is attempted the ungainly turnings and "Spanish" feet often ruin the piece.

The growth of the styles of feet was anciently based on the imitation of the feet of quadrupeds, "dragons," and birds. Hence the Directoire and early Empire styles are merely revivals of Egyptian, Mesopotamian, and Greek forms. In the case of turned feet there is a simple principle of nearly uniform application: Where there is a square for the lower stretchers the turnings constituting a necking or stem just above and below that square are identical. In splicing feet or finials the joint should, if possible, occur at a V of the turning, so as not to show.

Practically, so far as our collections go, the earliest feet are either plain extensions of the stiles, or they are large balls.

Nos. 1 to 10 are on early oak chests and cupboards. Nos. 3 and 4 are somewhat lighter variants. They are all 17th century. No. 8 is very little later, on a one-drawer

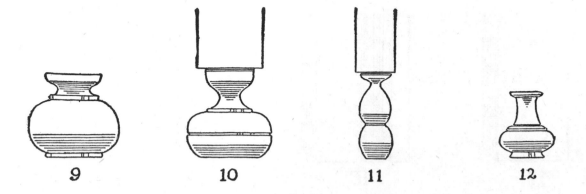

9   10   11   12

chest. No. 7 is dated about 1690, and occurs on an oak chest. No. 4 is called a turnip foot. Its lines have been thought graceful. Nos. 1, 2, and 6 are seen mainly on the heaviest early styles of cupboards or chests. No. 5 occurs on various chests of drawers or chests, but the design more properly harmonizes with the style of the William and Mary highboy and lowboy. No. 9 is a variation, probably not quite so early as No. 1. No. 10 shows by its bulbous character that it was generally attached to the stile above it by a dowel. In fact, nearly all the large ball feet were so attached. No. 11, on the other hand, being no larger than the post, is turned upon it. It is found on the lighter maple pieces. No. 12 is a much smaller foot, really a miniature of the big ball and occurs on a seventeenth-century desk box. A similar foot is sometimes found on Pennsylvania clocks of the eighteenth century. No. 13 is an agreeable variant on the Pennsylvania arched slat-back chairs. It is really a reduction or nearly so of No. 5, although No. 5 is of somewhat earlier use. It is turned in one piece with the leg. No. 14 is usually called a pear foot, and it appears in several other examples with variations, as No. 15 and No. 40. In some of the originals the base probably rounded down a bit farther. That is to say, the greater part of the flattening may be attributed to wear. This pear foot is the conventional construction on the butterfly tables and on leather-back chairs as seen in FURNITURE TREASURY. This foot is so obviously good, albeit simple, that we find it on cane chairs (F. T. 2046), tavern tables (F. T. 859, worn down, 856), folding gate tables (F. T. 939–949). It may be said to be the safest foot to use

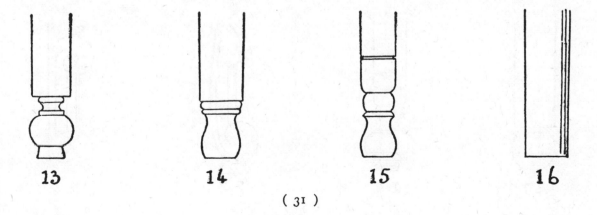

13   14   15   16

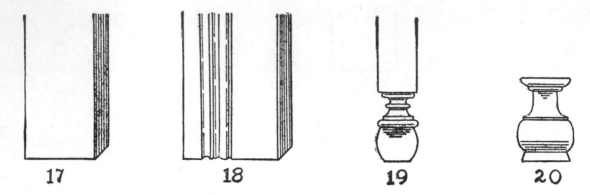

17   18   19   20

on any light turning if one is not sure of the style in restoration, but this form is seldom seen on very heavy turnings. Its diameter is from 1½ to 2¼ inches, and its length is sometimes pulled out into an attenuated pear shape. No. 15 is a somewhat elaborated pear foot, as seen on turned chairs of about 1690.

Nos. 16, 17, and 18 are numerously found on most of the seventeenth-century stile legs of oak chests. This is the simplest form of leg known, it being merely a continuance of the corner post of the frame. While No. 16 has a mold on one side, and No. 17 has no mold at all, No. 18 has the usual channel or shadow mold. In some of the catalogs this mold is described as cannelated, channel being an old equivalent of canal. This molding is quite common in horizontal sections as well as uprights, in seventeenth-century furniture, and is often painted black to assist its emphasis. In the earlier forms the section of this leg is never square, but about 1½ to 2 inches thick and 3 or more in width. When square it is smaller and verges into eighteenth-century practice. The contour of this channel mold will be shown elsewhere.

No. 19 is found on small oak or maple frames of the late seventeenth century. No. 20, suggesting No. 5, appears on smaller pieces of furniture. No. 21 is illustrated as the awkward effort of some early and more late makers who have attempted to construct the ball foot. Lacking a necking, it is without grace and cannot be recommended for good style.

No. 22 resembling No. 42 is the foot used on Pennsylvania chairs of the early eighteenth century, with their handsome arched slat back. It is important to observe

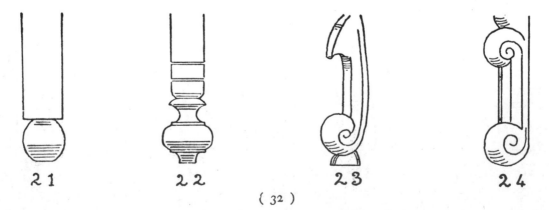

21   22   23   24

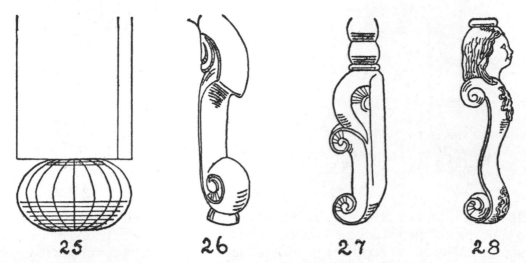

25 26 27 28

that the ball is turned larger than the post, and yet the foot is never doweled. To dowel a chair leg was against the traditions of the early day, and ought to be against those of the present day.

We now enter upon a highly specialized class of feet called the Flemish scroll. The relation between the cabinetmakers of Spain and the Netherlands was close. They had been under one government, and furniture often passed from one country to another, owing to transference of residence. It is probable that the so-called Spanish foot is a later outgrowth of the Flemish scroll. Some authorities consider the scroll when it turns inward on the foot to be more characteristic of England. When both scrolls, that of the foot and one above it, turn the same way they are called unilateral. They have not in that case so much brilliance or attraction as when the foot scroll turns outward, and the upper scroll inward. The fully developed Flemish foot gets away from the nearly straight line shown in Nos. 23 and 24 where the back of the leg is without grace. Reasons of economy of material often governed the old makers, as is true now. On No. 23 the wedge-shaped base or shoe appears, whereas it is absent on No. 24. The origin of this shoe is lost in obscurity. Whether it was a turner's stub left to be cut off and then seen to be attractive we can never know.

In No. 25 we inject a melon foot, which is merely a variant of the English bun foot.

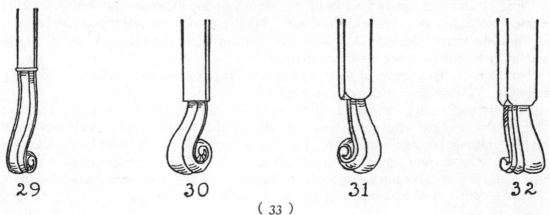

29 30 31 32

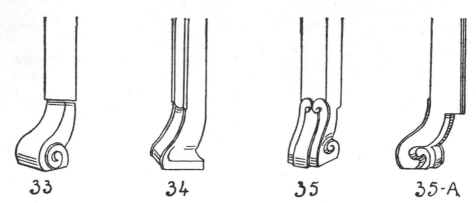

33 34 35 35-A

In Nos. 26, 27, and 28 we have variations of the Flemish scroll. It will be seen that the upper part of the scroll is cut away on Nos. 25 and 26, and the full development only is shown on No. 28. It is curious to observe the differences in modern taste regarding this foot. Some persons approve of it very highly, whereas others abominate it. Of course, dislike of it might arise from seeing it in a degraded form or from lack of familiarity with it in any form.

The Spanish foot is properly enough so-called because no one can say it did not originate in Spain, although it is so frequently found in the Netherlands as to have raised the question of origin. When this foot is properly constructed it is undoubtedly amongst the most beautiful for form; but when, as is usually the case, it is distorted or otherwise degraded it becomes ugly enough.

No. 29 shows an extremely attenuated example found on the leg of a harpsichord. No. 30 is very graceful indeed and retains its complete curvature, or very nearly so, at the base. In No. 31 there is no trace of wear whatever. The corners of the square above are cut off a little where the carving ceases. This adds to the grace of the foot. Very few specimens are in existence as graceful as Nos. 30 and 31. It is too much to hope to find them. No. 32 is the more usual form of the better foot as seen in America. The scroll is somewhat reduced in sweep, and there is a flattening more or less at the bottom. No. 33 is a coarse form from which the groovings have been omitted. No. 34 also is a form that cannot be commended because there is no break on the inside line, and the shape is somewhat crude.

Nos. 35 and 35A are two views of the same foot found on a table which actually came from Spain and is now in the South. Had it not lost something at the bottom, it would be nearly ideal, as an archaic example, owing to the attractive scroll on the outside where it joins the square of the post.

No. 36 is the bad dream of some artisan who was working from a faulty and foggy memory. (*Illustrations 36, 37, 38 on Page 36.*)

Nos. 37 and 38 are the graceful development of this foot with a cuff or wrister at the top where it joins the post. It is also peculiar that in this form it is always found on the cabriole leg as distinguished from other forms of the Spanish foot which are always on the straight leg. This form with the cuff is said to be peculiar to New Jersey, where the cuff is carved in one piece with the leg. The style has been found elsewhere with the cuff applied as a molding, which of course is not so good.

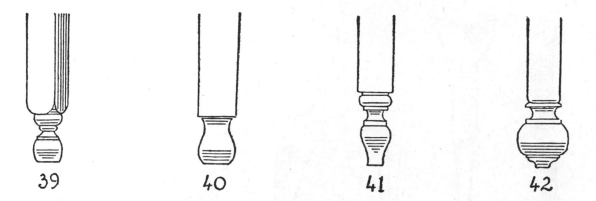

39   40   41   42

A peculiarity of the Spanish foot is its construction by means of two glued-on blocks for the outward sweep of the scroll. It is very difficult to work the leg except in this manner. Inexperienced collectors may be afraid of this glued-on foot. It is only in very rare instances that we find it in any other form, and in that case, of course, it is prized. Old specimens of Spanish feet have often lost one or both of the glued blocks, and it is necessary to restore them. Counterfeiters are always carving these feet on the square bases of old chairs. In this case they cut too deeply at the top, and of course the omission of the glue blocks results in a deformed foot, whose crudity is at once seen by the experienced.

No. 42 is one of the forms which appears on Pennsylvania chairs with four, five, and six backs. It would be more proper to use the term Delaware Valley. It is also found in a large form, best when bulbous, on the Pennsylvania day bed, a variety of the early Windsor type, before it separated from the Queen Anne style. This foot with a blunt arrow something like that terminating No. 41 also appears on the early type of Pennsylvania Windsor chairs.

We return in No. 39 to the turned foot. This is found on a three-legged table of small section and dates around 1700, the date also of No. 40, a form somewhat too plain, of the pear foot.

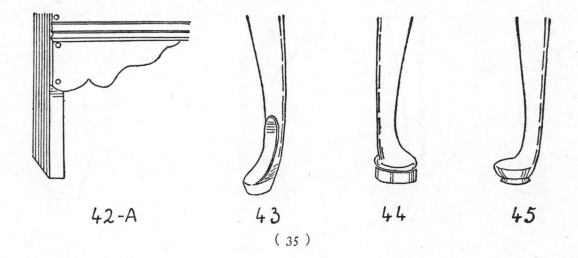

42-A   43   44   45

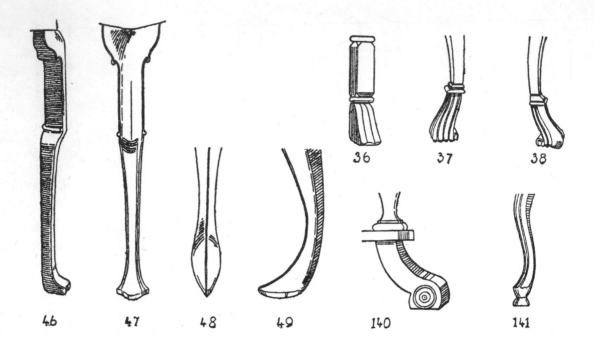

No. 41 is found on some butterfly tables and rarely on chairs. It has not a close analogy to the other styles and is hard to classify.

Nos. 43 to 70 are variants of the most popular-shaped foot from about 1710 to and even through the Chippendale period. Indeed, whenever economy or a taste for simplicity ruled, this foot was used. It was commonly called the Dutch foot, by which late Dutch is meant or Queen Anne. But long after her day the foot prevailed. It must of course appear as the termination of a cabriole, that is, a goat-shaped leg. This term cabriole does not at all accurately describe the gentle curves, but the name held

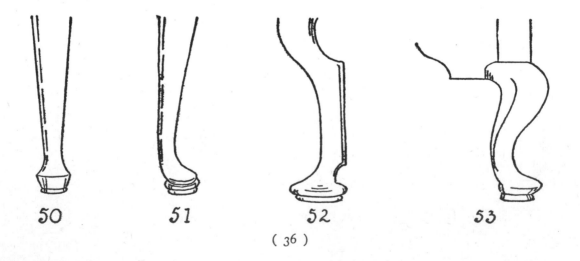

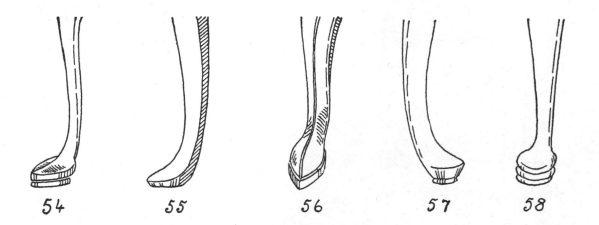

54   55   56   57   58

over from the quick angles between curves found in the scroll legs of 1690–1710. The leg is really an irregular ogee (cyma) curve.

The foot also goes appropriately under the name pad foot and, when well flattened, disc foot. If flat, with or without rudimentary toes, it is sometimes called a camel foot. It takes the place in simple furniture of the claw-and-ball foot which is used in more elaborate specimens.

When coming to a point it is often called the snake foot. In some examples, especially English, it may have a ridge or rib running along its center and continuing to the floor (No. 56).

No. 43 is a shape not recommended, it not being convincing in the somewhat crude outline. No. 44 has an unusually heavy and formless shoe, and the foot itself is somewhat stubby. No. 45 is the usual compact form of the foot with a slight good beveled shoe. Nos. 46 and 47 are side and front views of the legs belonging to a small corner table, of southern origin, and probably date from the fore part of the eighteenth century. Nos. 48 and 49 are the curious legs of a highboy attributed with all probability to John Goddard, and now in Newport. They are on a large piece and are effective. The extreme measurement between perpendiculars of the curve attains the astonishing dimension of five inches. This pointed or snake foot was used more or less by Goddard in the earlier part of his career. In fact, we have more examples of his work in the Queen Anne than in the Chippendale influence. Where he used the disc foot it was usually large. This large size may be called a stylistic mark of Goddard. No. 50 is thicker for its size than is usual, and does not require so much wood as a large disc. No. 51 is the termination of a leg, straight except at the bottom, of a country Dutch stand, dating about 1750. The style of turning was called country Dutch because the leg is not a true cabriole. The main turning was done on one axis, and then the foot was moved over a little in the lathe and turned off center. The result seen on many simple pieces is quaint and not objectionable.

No. 52 is an odd foot almost suggesting a hoof. It is found on a small table.

No. 53 is a very condensed Queen Anne foot found frequently on the shallow base frame of secretaries and high chests of drawers. It should be of course a unit with the

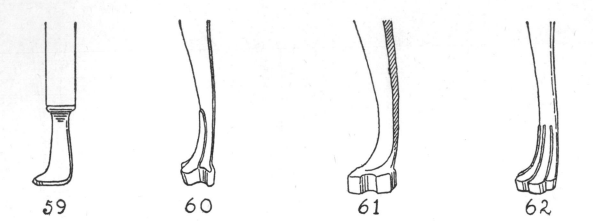

59 60 61 62

post above it. The term "bandy leg" often used with these short feet is really not properly confined to them but should apply as an alternate description to any Queen Anne furniture leg.

No. 54 is a pointed or snake foot with a shoe, and No. 55 is a slightly heavy specimen without the shoe. It will be seen that there is no distinct disc formed on No. 55.

No. 56 is one of three legs obtained from a lazy Susan or dumb-waiter and showing the rib running down the center. The piece from which it is taken is English.

No. 57 varies enough from previous examples to be worth showing. No. 58 has a kind of doubled shoe, so that with the disc above it almost suggests a pile of flapjacks and probably has one element too many for beauty.

No. 59 is a country-made foot on a composite chair, the base of which suggests a turned form of about 1710, whereas the back has ears like the Chippendale.

In No. 60 we reach a ribbed foot having sometimes three and sometimes four toes and called also a drake foot. In some specimens there is a grooving which runs up the leg for some distance, and either falling away to combine with the leg or ending in a raised or incised definite stop. This style of foot is more generally found in points south of New York. It was quite popular in Pennsylvania Queen Anne chairs and appears also on highboys. In No. 66 it is cleft in a somewhat crude, yet not unpleasing, form.

In No. 67 we have a more clearly defined large disc. Nos. 68, 69, and 70 are found in large or small forms on tripod tables and in their day achieved great popularity. This foot is not accompanied by carving on the knee above it. It would seem that such carving was reserved for the claw-and-ball foot almost exclusively.

In No. 42A (*Page 35*) we enter a very simple foot appearing on board chests which were usually in pine. They are found very commonly from 1690 to the middle of the eighteenth century.

No. 71 is a handsomely shaped pad or camel foot ribbed with stops at the top.

Nos. 72, 73, and 74 are found on somewhat pretentious chairs about 1720 to 1740 or 1750. Sometimes the claws grasp a ball, and sometimes they rest directly on the floor, as in No. 73. The name "dog foot" has often been applied to them. It is easy to see in Nos. 75 and 76 how slight variations may change the character of a foot. The

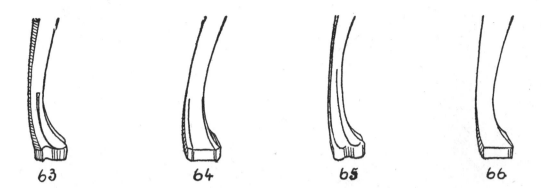

63   64   65   66

famous claw-and-ball foot did not by any means originate with Thomas Chippendale. He found it fully developed when he began his work, and, instead of being named for him, it should certainly be called early Georgian. The impression prevails in America that this foot connotes a Chippendale chair. Chippendale himself abandoned it about 1750 and, in his celebrated work issued for cabinetmakers at about that time, he does not show a solitary example of the claw-and-ball foot. By that period he had developed and popularized the straight leg, more or less decorated with Gothic motives or the Chinese fret.

No. 77 shows a foot where the quick outward turning at the ankle is lacking, so that the foot lacks the grace of the numbers immediately preceding.

No. 78 shows a form of the claw-and-ball foot as used on a tripod table, though the marked angular turning of the outer toe is not so pronounced as it might well be. This cabriole leg in its fine form runs from the foot horizontally for some distance or even drops a little. It should never sweep up directly in the ankle toward the hip.

Nos. 79, 80, and 81 are aspects of the claw and ball. The knuckles are best shown on No. 81. They should be quite marked and angular. The secret of this foot is found more in the curvature just above it than in the shaping of the foot itself. Good examples vary from the ball slightly flattened at the base as in No. 80 to a marked flattening as in No. 81. In fact, in many fine examples there is scarcely more than two-thirds of a ball.

No. 82 (*Page 211*) shows the full leg of a chair regarded diagonally and with the acanthus carving on the knee terminating in a spiral. This carving is not of the best character, consisting, as it does, of a rather crude imitation. The good proportions,

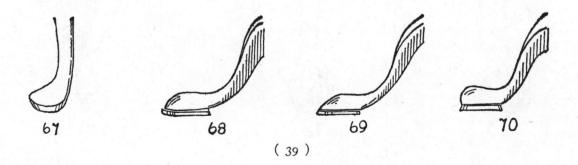

67   68   69   70

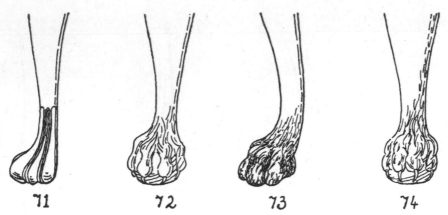

71   72   73   74

however, of the foot and the bracket are well shown. The brackets are always separate glue blocks. This is a necessity, for otherwise a stick of timber eight or ten inches wide would be required.

No. 83 is the huge condensed foot found almost nowhere else except on the oxbow-front walnut Queen Anne desks popularly but erroneously called Governor Winthrop desks. On the same desk the bracket foot is frequent and, in the author's estimation, more graceful. This claw-and-ball foot is so massive as to be almost clumsy, but a piece on which it stands should not be rejected on that account. The diameter of this specimen falls only an eighth of an inch short of five inches, and is seven and three-quarters inches high. Thus it requires a very heavy block of walnut or, rarely, mahogany.

No. 84 is the complete corner assembly of a rich Philadelphia lowboy or highboy. The acanthus curves are more realistically developed than in the previous example, and the carving is seen to be carried on to the frame. An unusual chamfered base occurs for the quarter column. This, instead of being fluted, is decorated with foliage carving. The style represents the heyday of the Philadelphia period.

In the series of feet Nos. 85–88 we have a number of variations of the hoof pattern: in No. 85 with realistic hair, in No. 86 with a scroll repeated on the knee, in No. 87 with a single scroll, and in No. 88 a somewhat poorer example. In Nos. 85 and 87 the hoof is divided so that it becomes a thoroughly cloven foot, whereas in the other

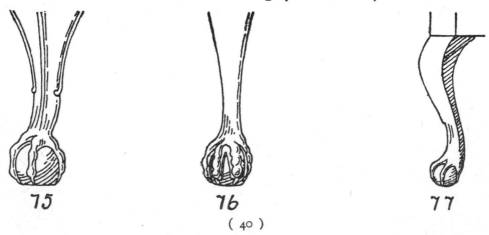

75   76   77

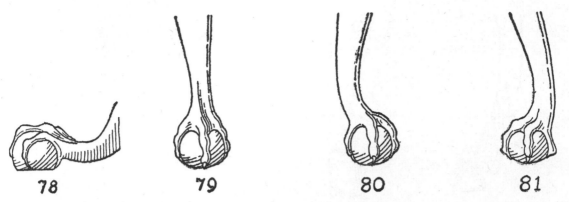

78   79   80   81

examples the resemblance is closer to a horse's foot. These feet did not become popular and, as the writer thinks, with good reason. Yet where found they are, of course, sought for, and they add value to a piece of furniture owing to their oddity. Examples of the human leg are found. Mostly they appear on tables. In No. 89 we have a bird's claw-and-ball foot, so called because the leg scales are brought into prominence. This form also is rare. In No. 90 appears the rat's ball-and-claw foot, the name applied to a long and narrow ball foot. This was not uncommon on small

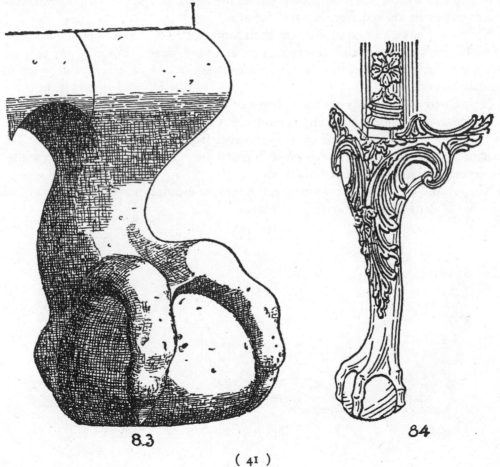

83   84

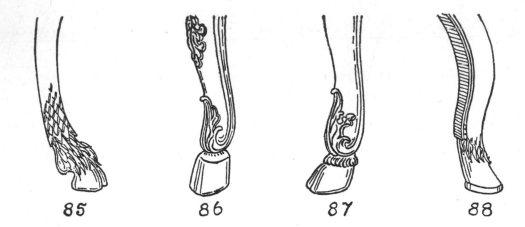

85   86   87   88

tables or even on sizable dish top tables, but one always suspects that the foot was made in this form to save wood. The full development of the ball in the round form requires a four-inch stick on a large tripod table. In spurious examples glue blocks are used to get the width, but one should shake his head at them. The attenuated ball here shown can be carved from a narrow form.

In No. 91 we have an extremely rare shell foot, not to be recommended because the junction of the leg scroll with the foot is exceedingly weak. Possibly for this reason the style was little used. It, however, seems to be an overdone attempt at grace which was not achieved.

In Nos. 92 to 96 inclusive we have forms of the French scroll of Louis XIV period. These appear on Chippendale chairs and are very graceful. One wonders at their rarity. Chippendale freely used carving motives from every land and clime. This to the writer's taste is one of his happiest borrowings. The foot is found on some few pieces traced to New York City makers.

In Nos. 95 and 96 we have a variant in the form of a dolphin foot, two views of which are given. It is of extreme rarity in America.

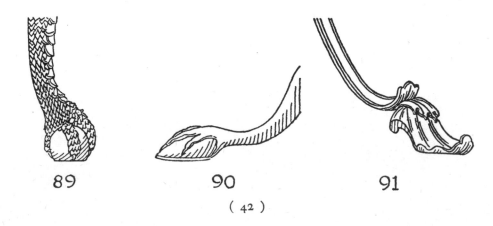

89   90   91

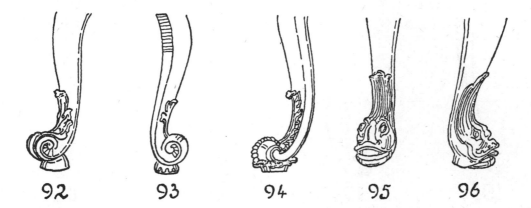

92 93 94 95 96

No. 97 is a somewhat more pronounced scroll of much grace.

In Nos. 98, 99, and 100 we have Chippendale examples of chairs more common in England than here, but strongly played up by Chippendale in his later career. In No. 98 appears the simplest form of this leg which is always vertical and of even size throughout. To taper it would be to degrade the style and shift by transition to the Hepplewhite period. The bracket about the base is of course applied, in fact, must be. It looks simple, but it is a fussy construction when well done and probably takes as much time as a claw-and-ball foot. The leg in this case is perfectly plain. In No. 99 we have a Chinese fret which we find to be incised on the leg. We mention this because the frets on highboys are often applied. We think, however, in the case of chairs they should always be cut from the solid. In No. 100 we have a combination of the molded, bracketed, or pedestal foot with carved incised panels above. All these straight-leg styles are to be included between the dates 1750 and 1780, or, in rare instances, 1785.

A feature of the straight Chippendale leg is that the inside corner is very generously chamfered away. The purpose was to give lightness of appearance. Of course the chamfer begins just below the frame, so that it does not at all weaken the chair. The neglect of this chamfer is a radical departure from style. It often cuts away a quarter to a third of the adjoining sides of the post.

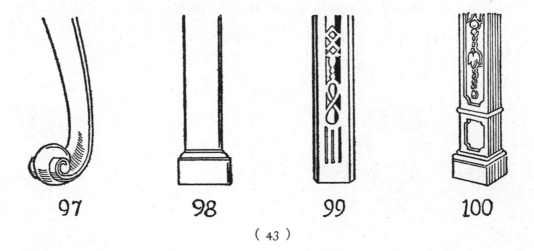

97 98 99 100

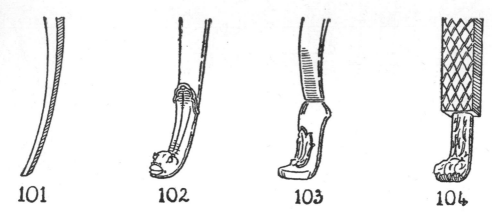

101   102   103   104

It seems necessary here to introduce a few special legs. In No. 101 we have what may be regarded as an inferior shaping of a back leg. The Chippendale and later chair leg should hold its size at the back as well as in front to the floor in almost every instance, and to taper it away on two sides is inferior construction indulged in by the uninitiated with the purpose of obtaining lightness of effect, which it does at the expense of style and strength.

No. 102 represents a variant of the dolphin foot. In this case it is in brass, and perhaps wisely so, as delicate carving on the floor is subject to too many accidents. No. 103 is a table foot perhaps to be classified as the Queen Anne period. Few would be distressed if it couldn't be classified at all. No. 104 is a very oddly carved foot, perhaps of the late Sheraton type. No. 105 is the leg on a tripod table of about 1800. The design can scarcely be approved. In No. 106 is the foot of a set of bed steps of the early nineteenth-century type. No. 107 is found on a glass cupboard of the Sheraton period. The truncated cone foot, No. 108, is not very appealing, but is included for a fuller survey. No. 109 is another bed-step foot of the same period as the other.

Returning to the straight Chippendale, leg No. 110 shows a grooved or molded leg, whereas No. 111 has merely a corner bead, and No. 112 is absolutely plain. All of these, of course, together with No. 113, have the chamfered inner corner. The moldings on Nos. 110 and 113 show in one case a repeated motive and in the other a continuous change, which affords a greater variety, but there is slight choice.

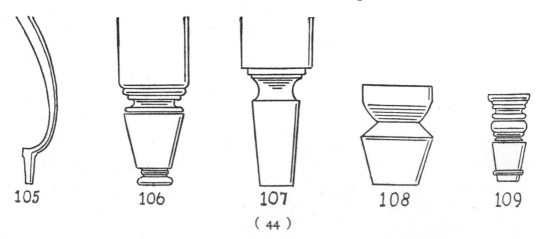

105   106   107   108   109

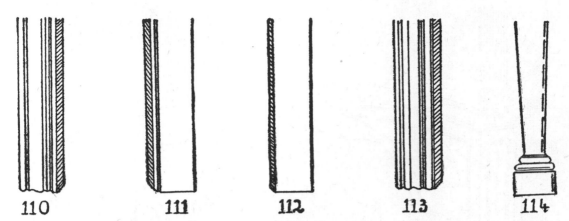

110   111   112   113   114

An important and totally distinct style of foot now presents itself, in No. 115, which is on a Queen Anne oxbow-front chest of drawers. It is called a plain bracket foot because it must be distinguished from the more refined and somewhat later curved or ogee bracket foot. While the plain bracket may appear on a very elegant piece of furniture, especially in England, the really fine examples in America have the ogee bracket. A simple variation is No. 116.

A special variant of much importance is the chamfered bracket foot as seen in No. 117 and following. It is used on serpentine fronts. A little more elaborate form is No. 118.

An ornate development of this foot on the serpentine front is No. 119, the first example we show of the ogee form, achieved as if a straight bracket foot of elastic material were pressed down to form the curves, but in this instance the inside curve of the bracket does not agree with the outside curve. This is a rare form, and, were it not so ornate and important, it would not be considered so good as the usual ogee.

No. 120 is a chamfered corner bracket of the simplest sort, but where the chamfer above the foot is fluted. No. 121 shows the chamfered ogee foot in a very large form

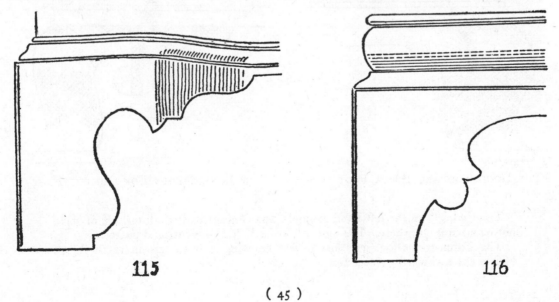

115   116

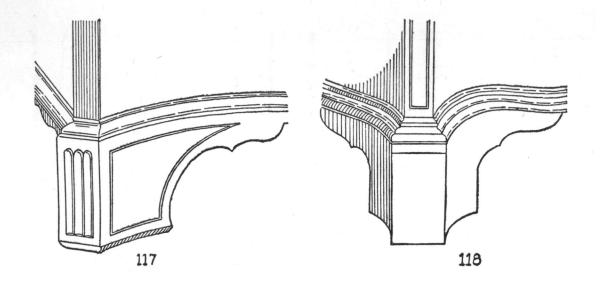

117   118

which to beginners seems clumsy, but it always appears on massive furniture. It will be seen here that the inward and the outward curves correspond to each other. No. 122 is a similar foot observed from a different angle, but with an inconclusive inside curvature. No. 123 is a lighter foot beneath a quarter column corner. One sees here the flat surface or fillet which terminates the foot quite generally in the ogee form. No. 124 is a stockier design found on a serpentine front.

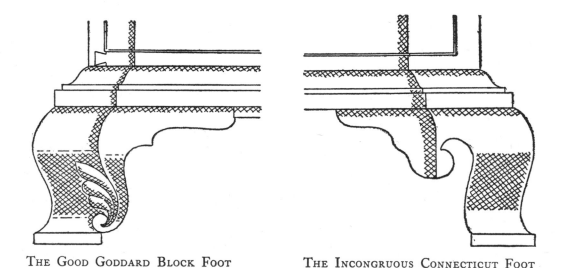

THE GOOD GODDARD BLOCK FOOT   THE INCONGRUOUS CONNECTICUT FOOT

The "wing" on the left-hand example was Goddard's little interlude of style not occurring elsewhere. The foot otherwise is his conventional pattern.

The Connecticut foot gets lost in not knowing how to terminate the block. Hence the awkward cutting across the scroll.

(46)

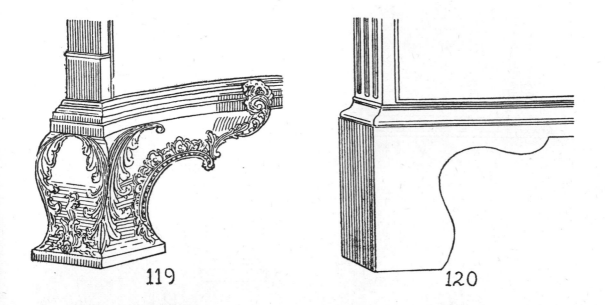

119   120

The claw-and-ball foot presumed by novices to be superior to the bracket foot is not so, either intrinsically or in connection with the furniture of which it forms a part. Most of the massive, rare, and very highly valuable American pieces have the bracket foot, and it was almost invariably used by Goddard, not only in Queen Anne style, but also in the Georgian. In fact, the bracket foot originates early in the eighteenth century in its finer forms and is a direct descendant of the stile leg with a supporting bracket of the latter part of the seventeenth century.

The above remarks are borne out by No. 125, which is a foot on a serpentine chest of drawers surmounted by a column set in front of a chamfered corner. That design is excellent, but a bracket foot would have been handsomer.

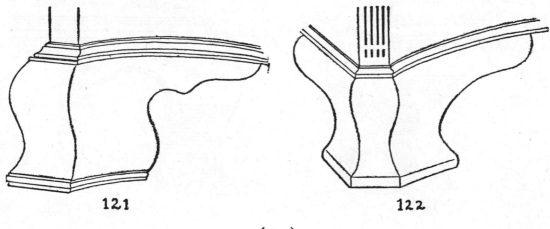

121   122

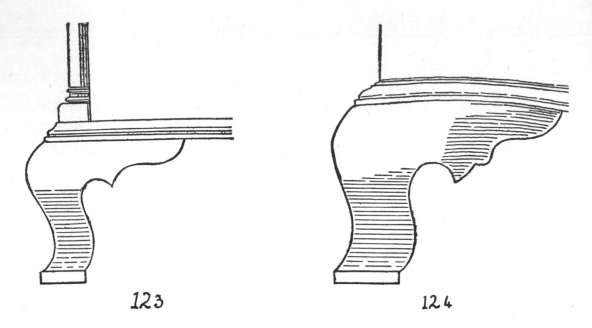

123   124

The most important class of furniture feet is that connected with the block front. This design requires more skill than any other foot in construction, and, when not adhered to precisely according to the best designs, it becomes of doubtful desirability. It prevailed for long from about 1750 to 1780 in the Goddard and Goddard imitation patterns. No. 126 while not attached to a block front has a scroll on the inside of the foot which first appears on Goddard furniture. The presumption in this case is that the foot is not a source of the scroll, but a copy of it, a little after it had become established.

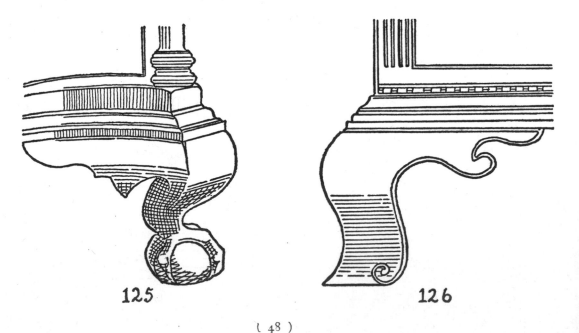

125   126

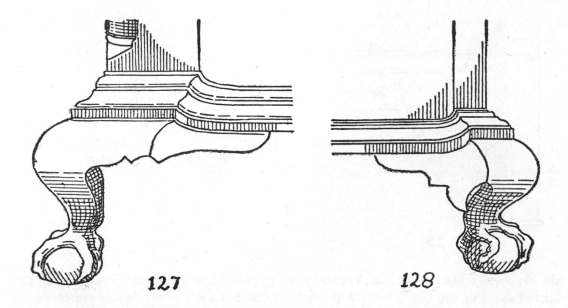

127   128

Designs of the block front using the claw-and-ball were either not made by Goddard or were tried by him and shortly rejected.

No. 127 shows the device by which the inside miter of the block is carried down on the foot bracket. It is not a thoroughly satisfactory design. The combination of the block front with a quarter column is of course the richest form of the development. No. 128 is a heavy example in which the block approaches nearer to the corner of the carcass. This involves a new problem in carrying down the line of connection between

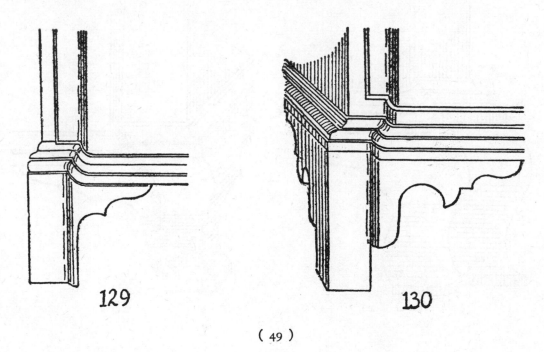

129   130

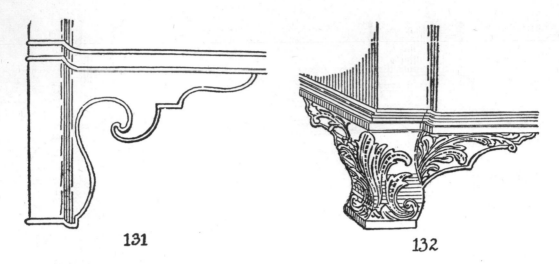

131 132

the bracket and the foot. Nos. 129 and 130 show Goddard's adaptation, or at least the former does, of the block front with straight bracket foot. This design appears on a good many plain block fronts where the block is carried up to the lid of the chest of drawers, and the lid is contoured to correspond with the top of the block. My own feeling is that this style was an adaptation of the block-and-shell design with an ogee foot carrying a scroll on the inside, and that the adaptation was in the interests of economy for customers who would not pay for the fully elaborated design. The somewhat narrow base of the bracket in No. 129 is inconclusive and disappointing and would seem to bear out this theory, which one cheerfully admits is only a theory.

It is to be observed that Goddard's brackets were rather simple, and that his

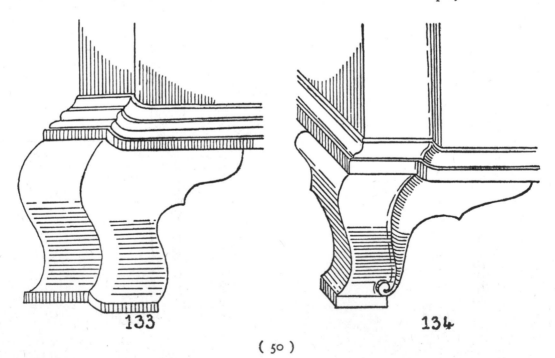

133 134

emphasis was mostly on the foot itself. Wherever the bracket is very much contoured, not to say contorted, we may decide with a good degree of probability, that the design is a Connecticut modification. Some believe that it was a design carried on by one of the Townsends in Connecticut, but search for data has so far been inconclusive. At any rate, the Rhode Island type, or more properly Newport type, showed greater restraint in the bracket contour. The emphasis was placed where it belonged — on the foot itself. No. 130 is a case in point where the bracket is not flamboyant, as it is usually found out of Newport, yet its attachment is a kind of an accommodation to design, not wholly satisfactory. In No. 131 is still another design of doubtful origin, but probably not Newport. No. 132 represents a richly carved ogee foot on a block front. Here again we see the difficulty of the designer in bringing his bracket to an end at the miter. It appears not to have any logical ending. No. 133 shows a heavy double foot on a block front. At once one is impressed by the feeling that the construction is too heavy. It either occurred before Goddard worked out the designs which follow, or it was the independent product of someone else. In No. 134 we have Goddard's perfect design. It varies very little from No. 136, in external contour, but the foot is wider in proportion to the length than in No. 136 because the block front does not approach so closely to the corner. The bracket on this No. 134 is extremely simple and commendable. It would seem that only Goddard dared to use this simple form. By this device of a light scroll at the base of the bracket he condensed the double foot of a preceding number into a single foot and obtained much grace and a fairly satisfactory termination of the mitered connection. In No. 137 there is a slight difference in the bracket, which is no improvement.

One sees in No. 138 how this work was done by memory at a distance. The connection of the bracket is much less satisfactory, and the shape of the scroll under it is a probable evidence of Connecticut origin.

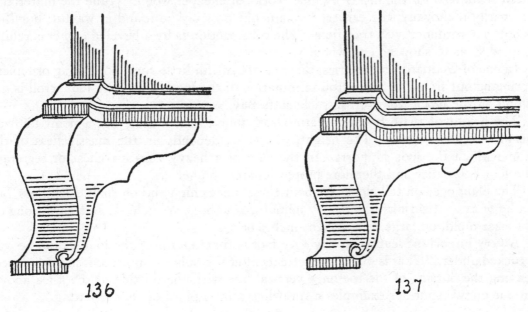

136   137

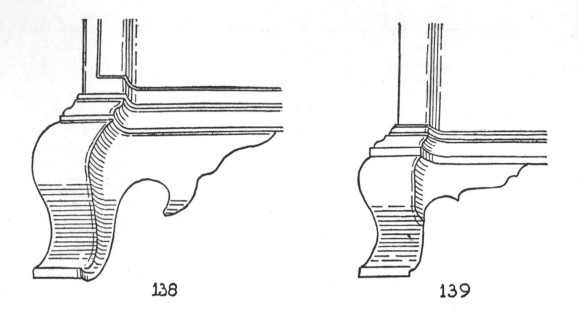

138   139

No. 139 is another unsatisfactory working out of the bracket. It was any way to stop it.

Neither of these feet is quite equal to Goddard's standard. Whether he made them before he devised his little scroll, as in No. 136, or whether these pieces were by his imitators is a nice question.

The back leg on these furniture cases is shaped on one face only, and the rear is left straight and plain. The leg is, of course, always attached to the carcass, and it is often reinforced on the inside by glue blocks of cheaper wood. While the material is ordinarily mahogany, the earliest forms might possibly be found in walnut, but that is not in accordance with traditions. The construction is by a beveled corner carefully splined so as to show no end wood.

In one of Goddard's secretaries, there is a beautiful little spur like a wing ornament springing out from the final scroll termination of the foot. The little foot scroll is not found on the block front of Massachusetts Bay.

The height of these brackets varies from four to six inches, but a point halfway between is more usual. The height, of course, depends on the massiveness of the frame which the foot supports. In the case of a heavy chest-on-chest or secretary the foot is broader and therefore proportionately higher.

The plain ogee on tall clocks is about three inches high and on shelf clocks less, but on knife cases it shrinks to a dainty miniature of about an inch. It stretches along on the base mold, on large pieces, eight inches or so.

A very important feature in any ogee foot is that the toe of the foot should be well "tucked under." That is, the curve retreats after the bulge as much as it had advanced, leaving the outside of the toe on a vertical line with the outside of the knee above. In one or two spurious examples a sprawling foot is proof of counterfeiting.

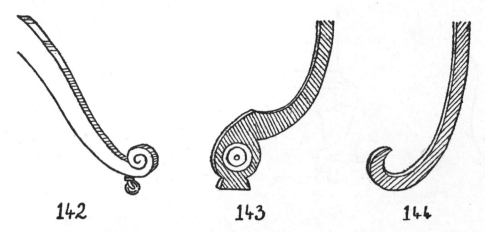

142   143   144

No. 140. This peculiar foot is found below the X stretcher of a slate-top table, and is quite effective. No. 141 is found on the foot of a so-called French Chippendale, Louis XV, but perhaps the construction is a little later. No. 142 shows a tripod foot on a dainty serving table of the period 1795–1815. Sometimes there is an inlay on the face of the leg. No. 143 is a tripod foot on a torchère. The buttons are attached. The period is probably about 1780. No. 144 is the somewhat crude scroll of a small stand, and it should be placed about 1810–20. (*Illustrations 140 and 141 on Page 36.*)

It has afforded the author much pleasure in getting together twelve feet found on tall clocks, Nos. 145–156. It will appear that these feet do not strictly follow their styles in date as found on heavier pieces of furniture. No. 145 is the peg or cone foot on a Pennsylvania clock. No. 146 is the straight form of the Hepplewhite "French" foot appearing in a heavy scroll in No. 153 (a Willard shelf clock), and in a scroll altogether too light in No. 154. One may say that the ogee foot prevailed in the best construction nearly altogether up to 1800, and in many fine examples up to 1820, although that date is a great deal later than the style as found on other furniture. No. 149 is a variant of No. 146, and No. 151 is a better form than No. 154 (an Isaac Brokaw).

No. 147 is a pure ball foot evidently copied from an early period, but put on a Bagnall clock (1740–50). No. 148 is the uninteresting foot found on a Pennsylvania clock. No. 152 is a variant not so good.

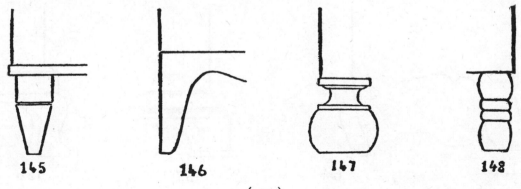

145   146   147   148

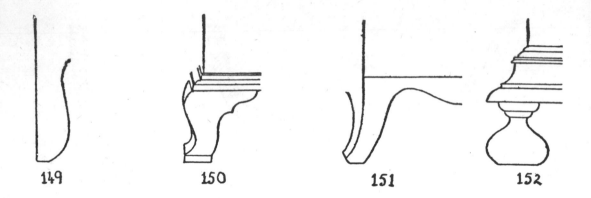

149   150   151   152

No. 150 is the best shape for a clock foot. It is a little daintier and more accurate than No. 156. One should observe that the foot extends beyond the frame of the clock, whereas in the Hepplewhite examples like No. 146 the line of the foot is an extension on the frame. No. 155 is a Thomas Harland straight bracket foot with a shoe. It is seen on some English clocks also. It is probably next best in style to Nos. 150 and 156.

With No. 157 we enter on the Hepplewhite style of chair legs. This particular type is called the spade foot. All these legs are built with a taper, and as a rule that taper is altogether on the two inside squares. The spade foot is a handsome device. It varies in style, being large or small. In No. 158 it is reduced. In No. 159 the Hepplewhite leg is shown in a perfectly simple taper which may or may not be inlaid. No. 160 shows an unusual square on the tapering foot which is probably to be counted as a sport. No. 161 is a molded taper and therefore somewhat more decorative.

It is the habit to ascribe square legs with taper to Hepplewhite and turned taper legs with or without decoration to Sheraton. However, Sheraton shows some square legs, and in this country the tendency was very strong to use square taper legs with Sheraton chair backs. The turned and reeded or otherwise decorated foot is far more common on secretaries and chests of drawers than on chairs in America. One wonders

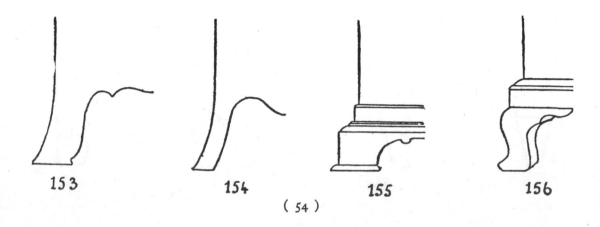

153   154   155   156

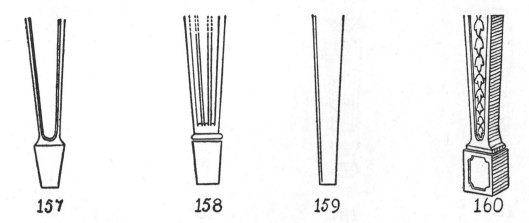

157   158   159   160

why this should be so, as the turned leg seems the more elegant. In Nos. 162 and 163, examples of turned Sheraton legs, we see one somewhat more attenuated than another. In Nos. 164 to 166 are later forms of the Sheraton, more commonly found on chests of drawers and desks in the simpler examples. Nos. 167 and 168 are reeded in the later style, showing a return of the reeding at the top, which is not so good as the reeds that stop against the turning.

Nos. 169 and 170 are still other variants of the reeded leg. No. 171 shows this leg terminated by a brass casting having a ball at the base. No. 172 is the style influenced by the French Empire having a brass animal foot. Nos. 173, 174, and 175 are late Sheraton legs, No. 174 being extremely slender and found on a stand. No. 175 (Page 164) is found on a straight-front late Sheraton chest of drawers. The length of the turned portion is 8¾ inches. The upper bulge is 1½ inches, and the ball is 1⅜ inches in diameter. No. 176 is a reeded foot surmounted by a reeded post on a Sheraton swell-front chest of drawers. No. 177 represents the slightly outswept leg of a Hepplewhite case, which is

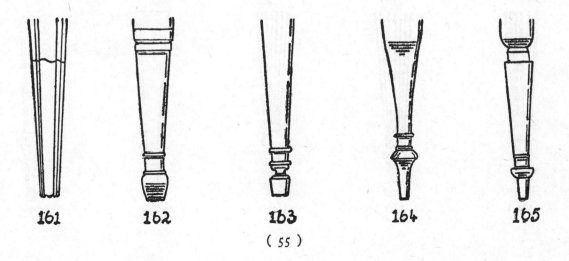

161   162   163   164   165

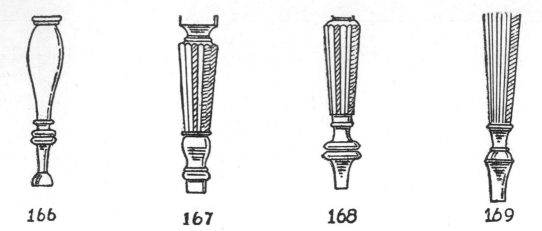

166   167   168   169

shown here last of all of that style because the author thinks the outward curvature is not the best style. In No. 178 we have the leg of a chair carved as an animal foot, with the hair above, which is attributed to Phyfe. The author could never become very enthusiastic over this style, as it seems as if it were stuck on to a leg above. The style being somewhat rare, however, and agreeable with a cult for it, has been very highly prized by New Yorkers.

In Nos. 179 to 182 we have the table legs of the period from 1800 to 1825, perhaps. In No. 179 the brass foot is attached to a cyma curved leg. The No. 180 is a variant from the simple curve of No. 181. Both have brass feet and are usually found on the side and dining tables of their period. No. 182 is a foot of much simplicity used indiscriminately by many makers from 1790 and forty years onward. If it terminates with a spade foot, the shape of which may be seen by a former description, it is attributed to the earliest date named. If, however, plain as here shown, it is generally later and is a favorite on many small and inexpensive stands. Nos. 183 and 184 are carved and plain legs respectively of the Sheraton period. The last is sometimes found as the back leg, poor because tapering, on chairs of late Sheraton type.

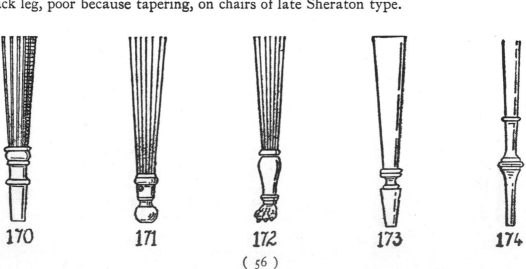

170   171   172   173   174

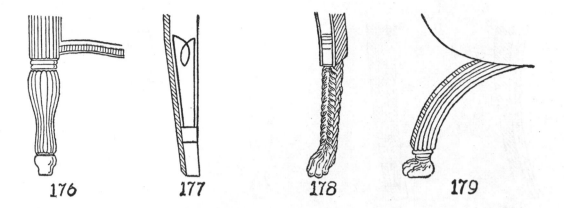

176   177   178   179

No. 185 is a leg found on some early patterns of late Sheraton chairs and settees verging toward the Hitchcock models. Nos. 186 and 187 are the bent-foot Hitchcock chair and settee styles, from 1830 on for some years. They are better than the usual Hitchcock model. Of course the curve was obtained by a steam or hot-water bending.

No. 188 is a foot found on some pieces which in other respects appear to be marked by Sheraton features, but it comes down from the Hepplewhite influence. Nos. 189 and 190 are late Empire patterns, the latter on a piece almost verging into a Victorian chest of drawers. No. 191 is a foot found on the pilasters of Connecticut clocks of 1830 and thereabouts and also as the degraded Empire type on sideboards.

It has seemed wise to treat as a unit the distinctive and peculiar sofa and settee legs of the Empire period. No. 192 is the most frequently found of the carved Empire sofa legs. Of course it is somewhat more elaborate than the common sofa. The clumsy foot, of course, has no possible reference to the fruit and foliage above, but the poor taste of the period swallowed the construction whole, and continues to do so among superficial collectors. No. 193 is the most elaborate foot that has come to the writer's attention. Why this fierce dragon was holding up a basket of fruit is not explained. The entire carving is done in a rich green gold.

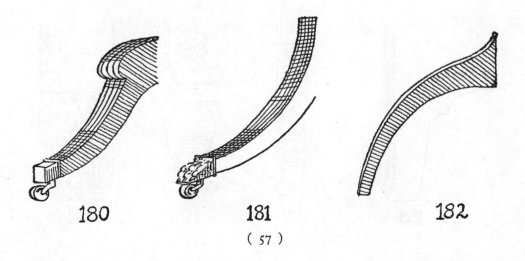

180   181   182

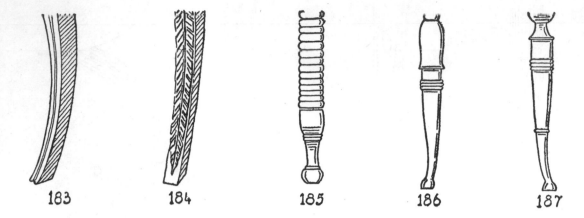

183   184   185   186   187

No. 194 is the usual simple foot on the Empire sofa. In almost all instances it runs from the right to the left, but in one or two examples it projects to the front. No. 195 is an elaboration of the same style with a decoration on the rail above the leg. No. 196 shows the conventional leg with the brass foot.

A series of bases for candlestands, mostly country made, perhaps, is of considerable interest. No. 197 is, however, the shoe on a trestle table. No. 198 is the base of a stand which, as those that follow, has the cross pieces halved into each other. The quaint and favorite method of notch carving on the edges of the bracket ends is noticeable. No. 199 is the simplest form of a stand base. No. 200 is an excellent form. No. 201 is rather decorative beyond its contemporaries. The standard or shaft is fluted and is set on as a diagonal. It probably dates among the early patterns, as it is in walnut, while all others are maple. No. 202 is a lighter form which concludes our X-base examples and closes our list of illustrations of feet.

The Adam brothers supplied designs which mix inextricably with Chippendale and Hepplewhite. In many cases the separation is only arbitrary. Makers borrowed from one another, or drew from the same original sources. Some of the most graceful light furniture, however, may be fairly attributed to Adam, or to copies of his designs.

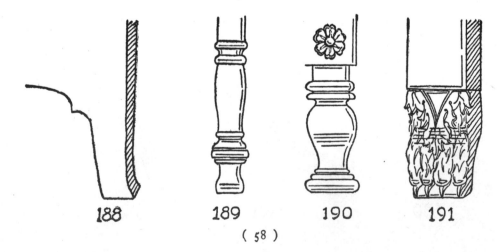

188   189   190   191

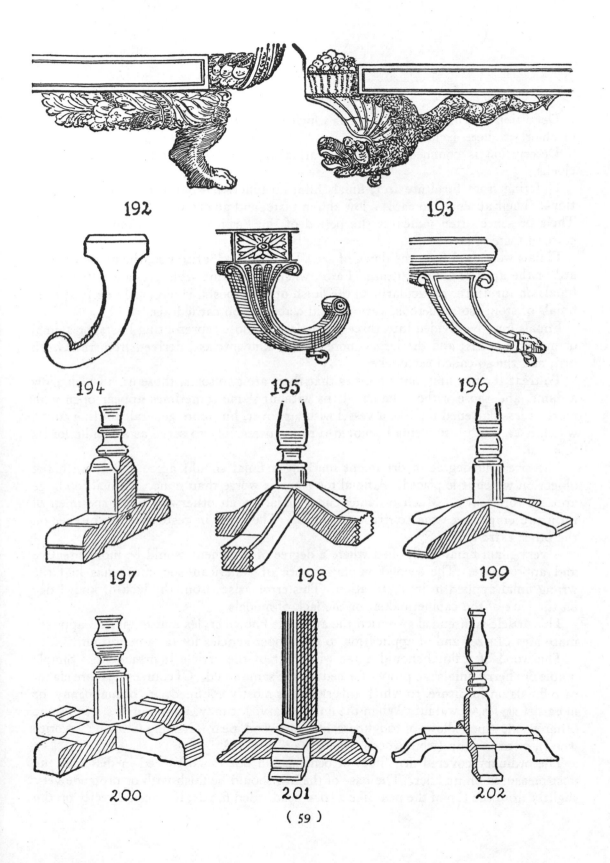

192

193

194

195

196

197

198

199

200

201

202

FURNITURE FINIALS

Definition and illustration of finials which are in one piece with a post, as of a bed or chair, are here excluded.

Description is confined to the decoration applied as crestings of furniture and clocks.

Differing from furniture feet, finials fulfil no function whatever except as decorations. Their absence indicates a low ebb in taste, and an exclusively utilitarian spirit. Their presence often indicates the period of the furniture they surmount, and the state of taste.

Finials were used from the dawn of art. They reached, of course, the highest standard at the apex of Greek culture. Later, when the Gothic style prevailed, the use of finials on furniture, particularly as the finish of chair posts, is obviously derived from finials of stone, so numerous, various, and elaborate on cathedrals.

Finials may be divided into three main classes: those representing busts, or animal or monster heads; and the larger more usually known class, derived from the Greek urn; and the so-called cartouche.

To treat the urn first, one observes that there are two sorts, those urns which show a flame, and those without flame. Urns without flame sometimes appear open with more or less flattened top like a vessel without cover, but more generally with a cover, which is carried up to a small pointed turning, ostensibly to serve as a handle for its removal.

The size and degree of ornament marking a finial should agree closely with the object on which it is placed. A finial too small is worse than none. A finial too large appears top heavy. Much ornament in a finial on an otherwise plain specimen of furniture emphasizes the contrast too much. The error in restoration is oftener on the other extreme.

A very plain finial is supplied where a degree of ornament would be more effective and appropriate. The second in importance of American specimens has had the wrong finial applied in its restoration. This error arises from the lack of knowledge on the part of the cabinetmaker, or the lack of models.

This article is intended to enrich the available known styles and to give an approximate idea of sizes and of application to the proper articles for ornamentation.

The wood of a finial should agree with that of the article it ornaments. Simple maple or cherry finials are proper for beds of the same wood. Of course the more elaborate finials on furniture, to which this sketch is mostly confined, are of mahogany, or in earlier styles, of walnut. When the finial is carved it may, as on mirrors, be of some other wood, which allows of toughness, like basswood, pear (Grinling Gibbons' favorite wood), or even tulip (whitewood), which may be gilded.

The ordinary covered urn finial of beds should not much exceed in diameter the post measured on its fillet. The base of the urn should be flush with or protrude very slightly from the top of the post like a cock bead. Bed finials, if placed directly on the

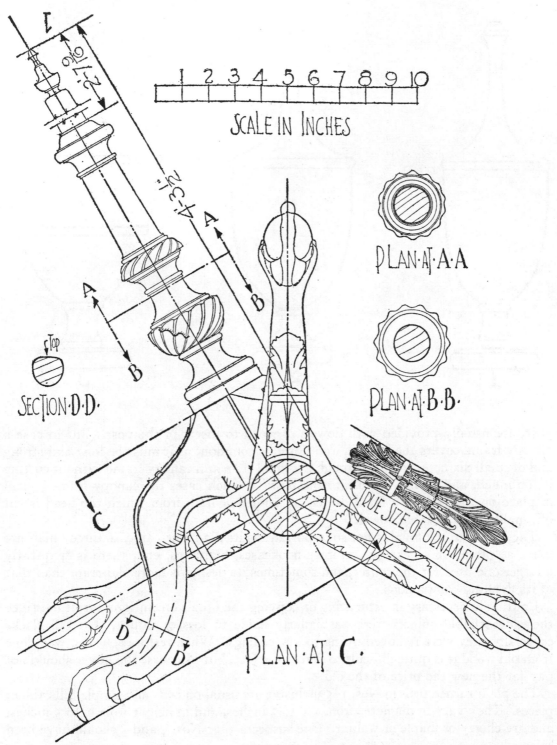

SCALE IN INCHES
1 2 3 4 5 6 7 8 9 10

PLAN·AT·A·A

PLAN·AT·B·B·

SECTION·D·D

TRUE SIZE OF ORNAMENT

PLAN·AT·C·

The above is a rich pole-screen. The screen proper is not shown, but should be rectangular and of any convenient size to fit needle-point.

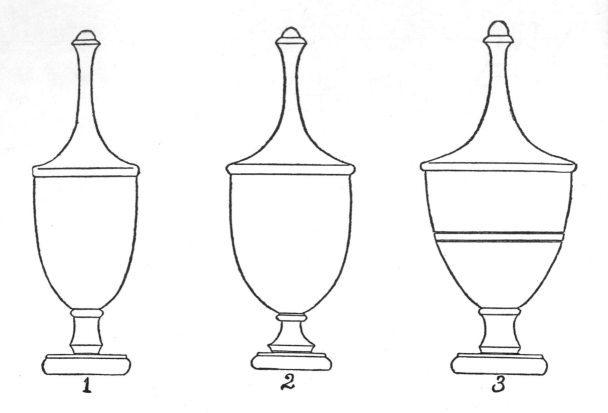

1   2   3

post, are usually provided with dowels of wood to insert in the post. But in case a canopy frame covers the bed, an iron dowel is common, as it must be long and strong and of small diameter to pass through the finial stem and canopy frame without cutting it too much, and thence down into the post. In such cases the canopy frame is held in place on the bed by a finial dowel. A tenpenny nail, from which the head is cut off, makes a serviceable dowel.

The height of the finial is not so important as its diameter. In case three finials are used, as often, on clocks or secretary-bookcases, highboys, etc., there is frequently a larger one used for the center, and sometimes its design is more elaborate than that of its flanking companions.

Caution is necessary in estimating or copying the finials on antique furniture, since these detachable objects were particularly liable to loss or injury. On tall clocks especially they were removed owing to low ceilings. When restorations are well done from old wood it is quite difficult to detect the fact, but of course the buyer should not pay for the new the price of the old.

The plain turned urns in Nos. 1–5 inclusive are usual on beds and simple tall cabinet pieces. They vary in diameter from 1¼ to 2 inches, and in height from 4 to 5 inches, and are cherry or maple or walnut. One suspects that Nos. 4 and 5 should have been spiraled.

Clock finials in the earlier styles were often in wood. It is very doubtful if brass

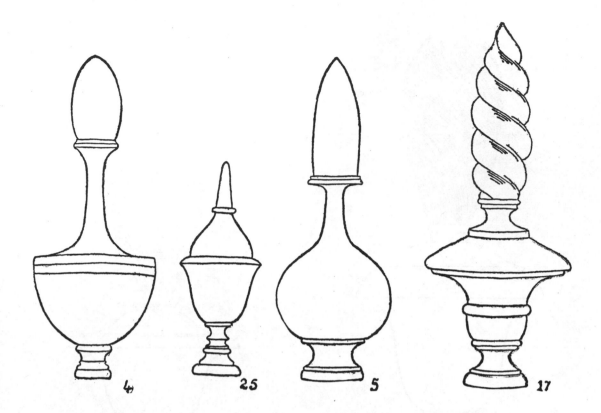

4   25   5   17

clock ornaments on American clocks ever reached the degree of taste and elegance achieved by the finials and other ornaments in wood. The highest degree of taste in clock finials was achieved by John Goddard and by the Philadelphia makers. Goddard clock cases are surmounted as a rule by dainty mahogany finials, fluted, and with spiral flames. Of course, flames represent the ancient burning of oil as incense or for other purposes. Goddard finials for his large pieces, like secretary-bookcases and chests-on-chests, were of somewhat similar pattern, but showed more generally as half than as full balls, and always fluted.

The Philadelphia flames did not spiral so much or so generally as the New England styles. In many cases they achieved a fine naturalness and especially an irregularity in the flame points. They were not so often fluted or reeded as the Goddard styles. Nos. 6 and 7 are among the better examples on large pieces, and Nos. 8 and 9 on clocks. The largest are 9½ by 3½ inches. No. 8 is 8 by 2½ inches, and No. 9 is 6 by 2 inches.

The finials left us by Eliphalet Chapin of Windsor, Connecticut, are mostly quaint, naïve, and attractive. A Chinese motive is noticeable on the two superb examples Nos. 10 and 11, the larger being the central, 8⅞ by 3¼ inches, the smaller 7¾ by 2⅜ inches are the flanking finials and are Chapin's masterpiece on a secretary owned by Mrs. Fuller, Suffield, Connecticut. The amazing incident in relation to this secretary is that it originally stood in the house in Suffield where it now is; that it was removed, and at length carried to California whence, by a peculiar chance, it was returned to its old home.

6   7

Maple finials are seldom carved. Pieces were made without finials in instances where their use would have improved the appearance greatly. Sometimes they were an afterthought and were omitted also at times where it had been the intention to use them. Some otherwise excellent pieces have ugly finials which, of course, may be a later replacement. The reader is warned that while we are able to classify finials as to their general origin and as to their appropriateness on a particular specimen of furniture, we wish to be careful to state that we are often at a loss as to the authenticity of these decorations. They are ordinarily removable by hand, for convenience in transportation. For this very reason they were sometimes never replaced as, being small, they were especially likely to be lost. Occasionally in modern times an owner destroys them from a false standard of taste. There is a large class of persons who are ashamed of decoration lest they be thought pretentious. This curious psychology is accountable for destruction or degradation of furniture.

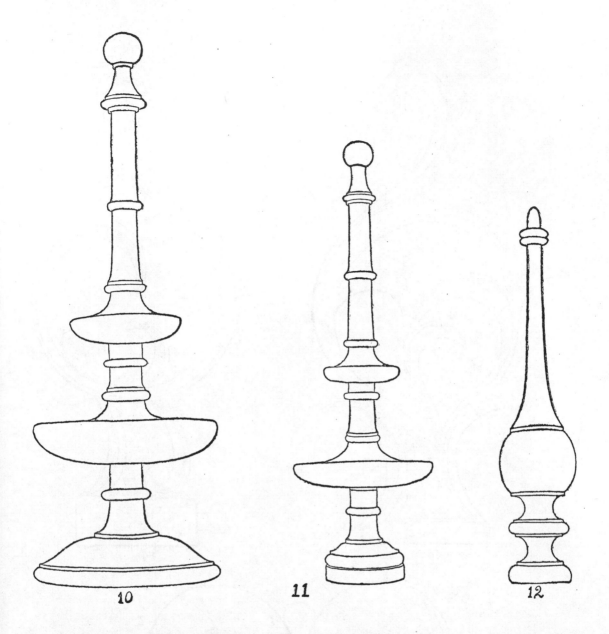

10   11   12

The limitations of knowledge on the part of the Chapins evidently left them, owing to the lack of examples for copying, largely to their own taste, and thereby led to the development of various, but always artistic, results. A unique result in American cabinetmaking.

Their finials were often reduced almost to decorative spikes like No. 12, which is 7 by 1½ inches. One openwork scroll, however, No. 13, which they used is quite different from any other pattern known. It is 11½ by 4¾ inches, and ½ inch thick. No. 14 is a variation of it.

The scroll on the base of a simple New England highboy.

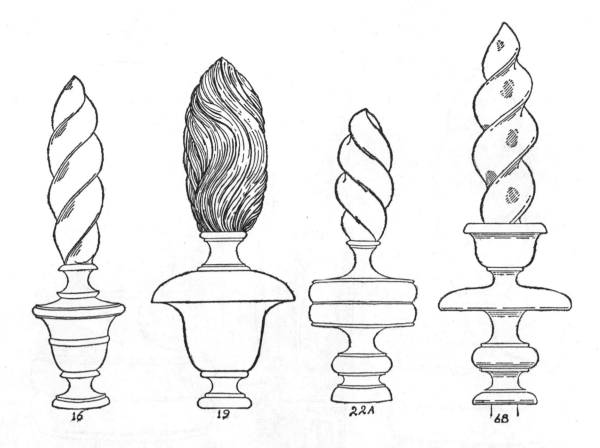

It was not often then or now that customers allowed the cabinetmaker to do his best. A few examples of paneled urns exist, as No. 15, the origin of which is not certain, but its grace is unquestioned. (*Page 69.*)

One feature deserves attention, from the proof it affords of the economy practiced by the cabinetmaker. When good mahogany was used the finials were often made in three parts and doweled together. Today the labor of fitting the parts would outweigh the value of the material. But this feature may, in a negative manner, help to determine the age of the finial. Goddard often separated the parts.

Practically without exception all forms of finials required a base, or plinth. Sometimes the finial itself was so turned as to afford a basal standard. But ordinarily a square plinth, plain, fluted or reeded was employed. At a late period of decline this plinth appeared too elongated and attenuated, as on some clocks and secretary-bookcases.

But without some base a finial loses beauty; its elements are lost in a squat shape like a cup, rather than like a goblet, as it should be, with at least a short stem.

Restoration of finials with a base too abbreviated is frequent, and loses the effect desired.

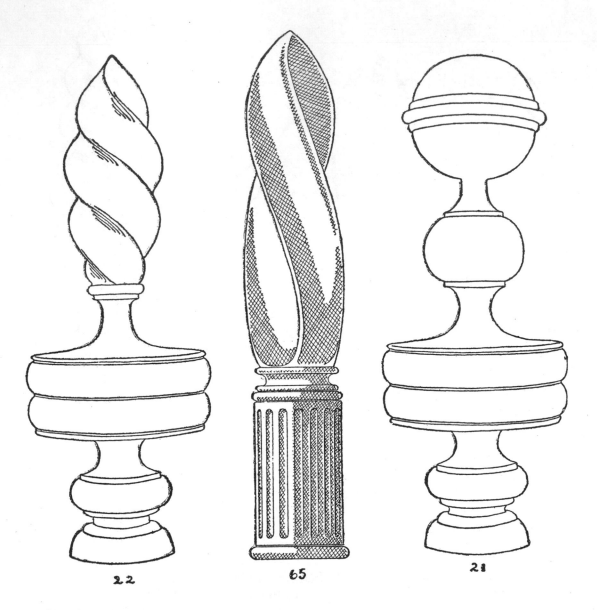

22 65 21

There is a class of flaming urns, seen on North Shore and other furniture as far south as Baltimore, covered by such examples as No. 16. They differ in height as proportioned to width. There is a variation in the number of grooves that form the spirals. They are all graceful. They are dated like most urns with flames 1750–1780. No. 16 is seen on New England highboys, 2⅛ x 7¾ inches, No. 17 on smaller pieces, 4¾ x 2 inches. It is one of the most graceful known. Their differences are no doubt sometimes caused by failure of memory. *(Page 63.)*

Again finials differ owing to an attempt at distinctiveness. No. 18 *(Page 71)* is like No. 4, but larger and in walnut. When the flame reverses or wavers in direction as in

15   71   42

No. 19 (*Page 67*) it offers an agreeable and naturalistic variation. Its size is 8¼ x 3¼ inches. The origin is probably Philadelphia. It has been used by way of restoration in New England, giving a bad effect.

There is a very small class of urns in which the flame seems to proceed, as in No. 20 (*Page 86*), from the top of the spindling handle of the urn cover. This seems illogical, and perhaps it is not classical, but no one can say it lacks grace.

There are a few urns which may classify as sports. No. 21 terminates in a large ball and occurs as a central ornament in conjunction with the flaming urn No. 22 (*Page 68*). It curiously follows no known shape or law. It is found on a Connecticut chest-on-chest. A small form is No. 22A. No. 24, ending in button-like form, is an amusing puzzle on a very rich Connecticut piece. (*Also 24A, Page 82*.)

The dainty little finial No. 25 (*Page 63*) is on a Sheraton china closet, size 2¾ x 1¹⁄₁₆ inches.

No. 26 is a large late finial, only one being used on a shelf clock. It is in wood. (*Page 75*.)

69

48

70

52

53

18   29   8   27

Another form very graceful, No. 50, is delicate. Yet neither of these can be explained, nor was it intended they should be, by reference to anything in nature. They represent a graceful imagination. (*Page 78.*)

An ornament like a wreath is shown in No. 51 (*Page 83*) found on a southern highboy. In this connection southern usually means Baltimore. The other details should probably assign this one to Philadelphia. No. 52 is a proud bird on a desk owned by Mr. Kindig of York, Pennsylvania. It is interesting, if for nothing else, for its rarity. It is possible this piece of furniture commemorates some successful political campaign. (*Page 70.*)

The owl being the bird of wisdom, No. 53 was felt to be a proper decoration for a bookcase. One appears on a large southern case owned by Aetna Life Insurance Company, Hartford. It varies in form from that shown. (*Page 70.*)

The eagle is late on furniture and is mostly more properly found on mirrors, though even there the pheasant and the heron or the dove are more usual. Nos. 54, 55, and 56 are specimens of three of these birds. (*Pages 79–81.*)

30   31   32   33

The Sheraton and Hepplewhite china cupboards often had brass finials of the same shape as is known in wood. No. 27 is a little lacking in grace. (*Page 71.*) The origin has not been determined by the writer. No. 28 is an urn in walnut found on a large secretary-bookcase. It has also been found with the top spiraled as a flame. (*Page 77.*) No. 29 suggests to the ribald a shaving brush, or shall we say a plume? (*Page 71.*)

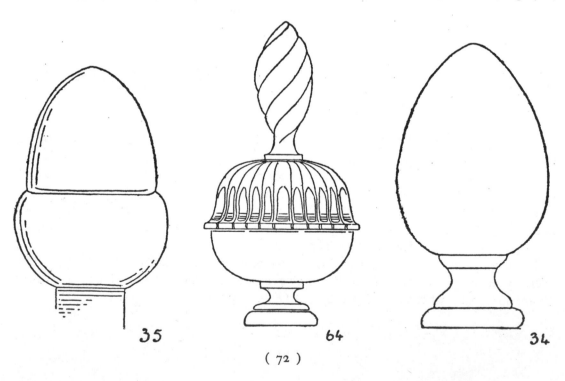

35   64   34

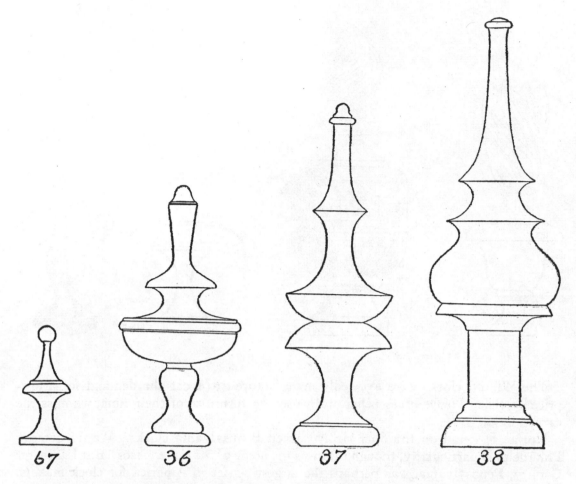

67   36   37   38

No. 57 is a decorative urn with flowers on a high, important piece. (*Page 82*.)

Busts, especially those of famous political or literary characters, were regarded as quite right on rich English specimens, but in America busts are rare.

Shakespeare is perhaps oftenest found. The altogether finest example ever seen is No. 58 on a secretary-bookcase, doubtless originating in Philadelphia, but found in Carlisle.

The splendid intellectual qualities of John Milton are well shown in Ernest John Donnelly's drawing of this bust, a highly creditable piece of work, but of course it is necessary to see the original to obtain the real effect of this carving, which Harry Wood Erving has said is a piece of sculpture. The author knows by sad experience that it is impossible to copy the original with any degree of satisfaction. In fact, the effort has been consigned to oblivion. The original stands about a foot high and probably was done without flanking companions. (*Page 4*.)

No. 59 is a Pilgrim worthy, a "John Winthrop." (*Page 83*.)

There is a considerable series of forms used at the intersections of cross-stretcher tables or highboys, as Nos. 60 and 61. The former is the more elegant form and is derived from a reversal of the leg turning, with appropriate modifications. (*Page 85*.)

9   45   39-A   40

The Willard clocks were avowedly manufactured to meet the demand for a low-priced article. Hence brass being much used on furniture of their time, we miss the carved finial.

No. 40 is found on the finer richly carved Pennsylvania clocks. We do not say Philadelphia particularly, though that was the home of the richer cases. But Lancaster County, Pennsylvania, was perhaps the largest center in America for clock makers. The finials, however, were ordinarily quite inferior, to meet the same broad demand for a low price that was encountered in New England.

The dainty finial No. 41, used on clock cases by John Goddard, and the larger style No. 42, both fluted on the urn, and with graceful flames, doubtless originated with Goddard or John Townsend and are altogether delightful. The larger examples about 8 x 3½ inches, were used on Goddard's tall secretary-bookcases and chests-on-chests. The larger examples are found in two sizes, varying about a quarter of an inch. The small clock finial is found with minor variations, some of them closely approaching a circle in the urn shape. We show what we regard as the more perfect forms. (*Page 76.*)

A John Townsend finial, No. 42A, is nearly the same, on a clock in the Metropolitan Museum. It is a proof that both these makers used not only similar small motives, but the same block-and-shell door. No. 43 is a massive finial suitable for a stair post. Its elaboration is such that it was used probably as a single central ornament. It probably belongs to Philadelphia. It is a very rich example surpassed only by those which follow. It belongs only on a large Chippendale style. (*Page 75.*)

Clock finials in brass, Nos. 30–33, are familiar. The first may be called a ball-and-spike pattern, the spike portion being a four-sided section. These finials are made in three or four parts, the top and bottom being held together by a rod running through all parts and a tightening nut. There is a close analogy between these and brass andirons. (*Page 72.*)

The eagle patterns are somewhat later. But the shape of these patterns shown, omitting the eagle, is preferable to the ball. No. 33 is frequent with slight variations on the famous pillar-and-scroll shelf clocks, made by Eli Terry and his imitators.

No. 34 is the best shape of the gilded ball used on the first banjo clocks by Simon Willard. A variation of it, showing the acorn in its condition before separating from the base, is known (No. 35). (*Page 72.*)

Nos. 36, 37, and 38 are of wood and are found as central ornaments on shelf clocks. No. 38 is 5½ x 1¹³⁄₁₆ inches. (*Page 73.*)

No. 39 is the well-defined ornament on the celebrated Thomas Harland tall clocks made at Norwich, Connecticut. A modification is known in which the flame is shorter, No. 39A. This maker followed early traditions. (*Pages 77 and 74.*)

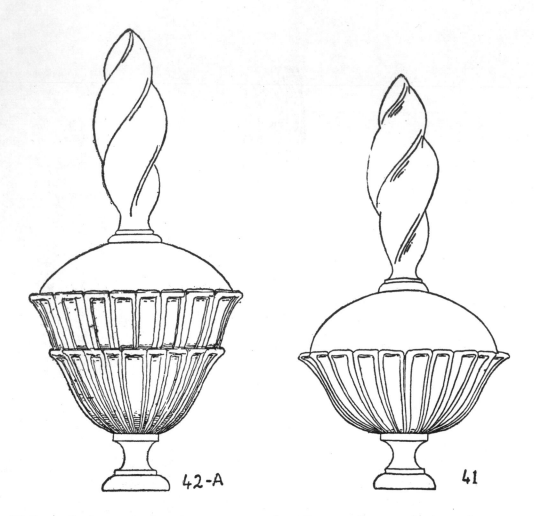

42-A   41

Slight variations, not important to record, and somewhat crude examples are now passed over in favor of some of the richer urns like Nos. 44 and 45 on Pennsylvania pieces. (*Pages 82 and 74.*)

While the inspiration of these is like most of our types English, the American examples have been somewhat specialized and show the personal skill of the American carver. They are really beyond the experience or the reach of most collectors.

A simpler, but still rich, urn is No. 46, on a Metropolitan Museum specimen. (*Page 82.*)

No. 47 (*Page 77*) is the large central urn of a highboy or chest-on-chest. It will be noted that these highly ornate urns are always on a broken arch top, which is also decorated by a pierced lattice. No. 48 is a beautiful and favorite New England pattern. (*Page 70.*)

The cartouche as seen in No. 49 has been copied from some old specimen. The author admits he knows but few that seem to be original, but more of them may be. A number of them have been examined. The work over a pulpit in Philadelphia is thought to have been the original inspiration of No. 50. The central portion like a kidney bean is characteristic. Variants of the top appear. (*Pages 82 and 78.*)

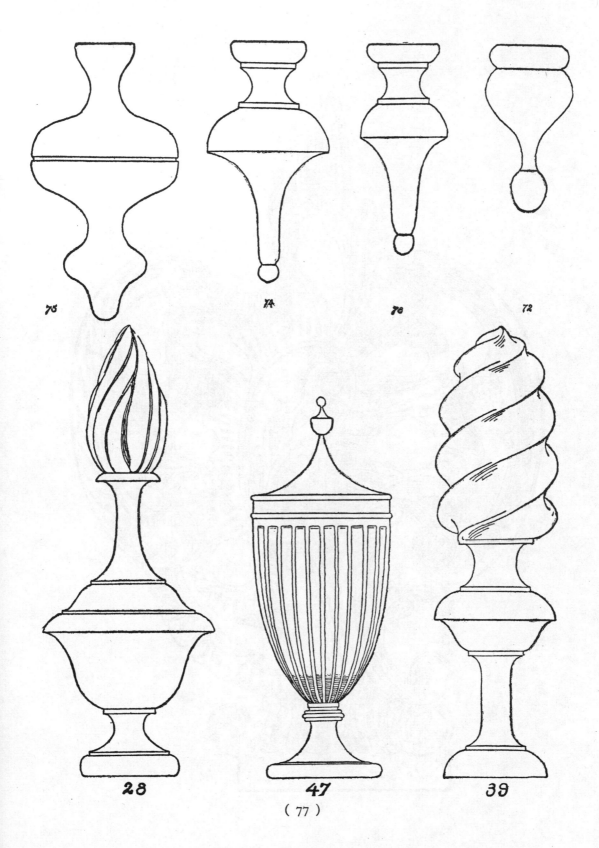

75   74   78   72

28   47   39

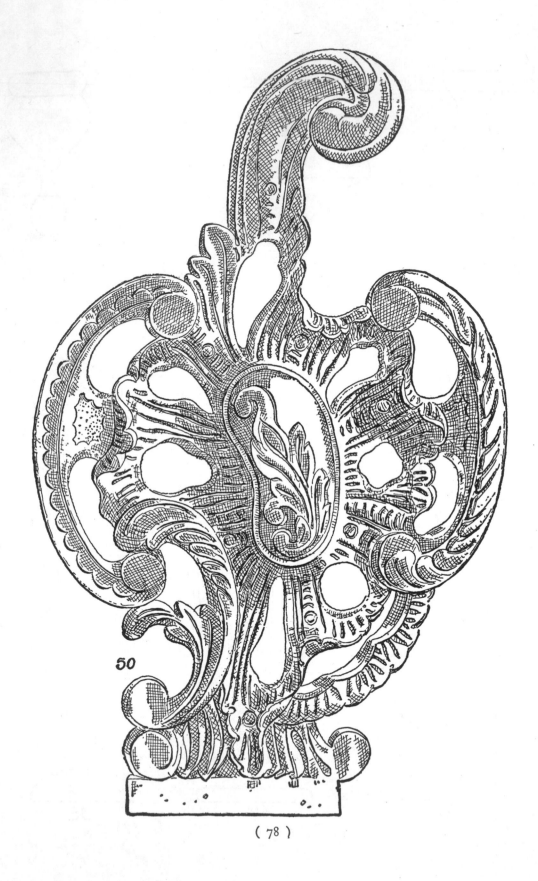

50

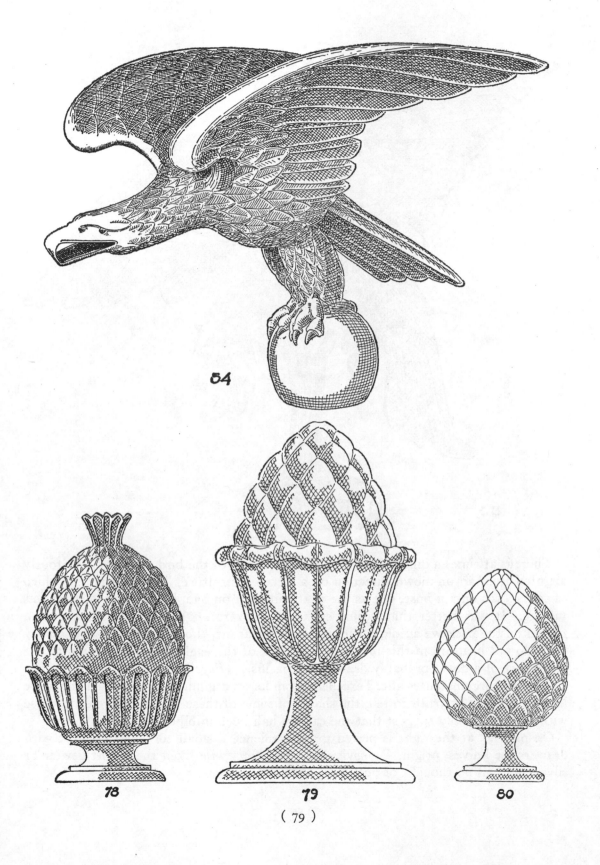

64

78 79 80

55

There is at times a difficulty in assigning the genus of the bird that has fortuitously alighted from an unknown direction on a piece of furniture, like Poe's raven, which of course was only a bust, but as the poet had been on one, he thought the bird was talking. It was better than seeing snakes, at any rate. Where the feathers seem ruffled on the neck we account a bird to be a pheasant, though the pheasants on my lawn do not head up in this manner. The lines of the eagle also often soften to the semblance of a dove; probably drawn by a pacifist. (*Page 79.*)

All these circumstances afford excellent room for an argument, or did when men were in their cups. But truth to tell, the shapes of some of these bipeds (we refer to those with feathers) really suggest that the carvers had been imbibing.

On page 75 at the right is placed for convenience a small corner spoon rack with drawers for knives, origin, Pennsylvania. The housewife liked the bright pewter or silver and had no thought of putting it out of sight.

56

No. 61 is found on the square intersections of Canadian tables. (*Page 85.*) No. 62 has a hollowed top like a shallow urn, and appears on a cross-stretcher lowboy. (*Page 141.*)

No. 63 is a cross-stretcher urn with carving. (*Page 85.*)

No. 64 is a dainty miniature clock finial, fluted. (*Page 72.*)

No. 65 might almost be called an auger (*Page 68*), its slender straightness being really a continuation of the same twist as that in the inserted corner column below it on the highboy upper section. No. 66 is a central vase finial with a large ball. (*Page 84.*)

No. 67 is a miniature on a Queen Anne shaving mirror post. No. 68 is a long spiral urn of New England origin, probably North Shore. (*Pages 73 and 67.*)

No. 69 is a banjo clock finial of odd construction, as if a pineapple had been separated from its foliage. (*Page 70.*)

No. 70 (*Page 70*) is a shelf clock finial of delicate, satisfactory design. It is an elaboration of the so-called ball-and-spike type. No. 71 is the side finial on a secretary of the early Chippendale period. (*Page 69.*)

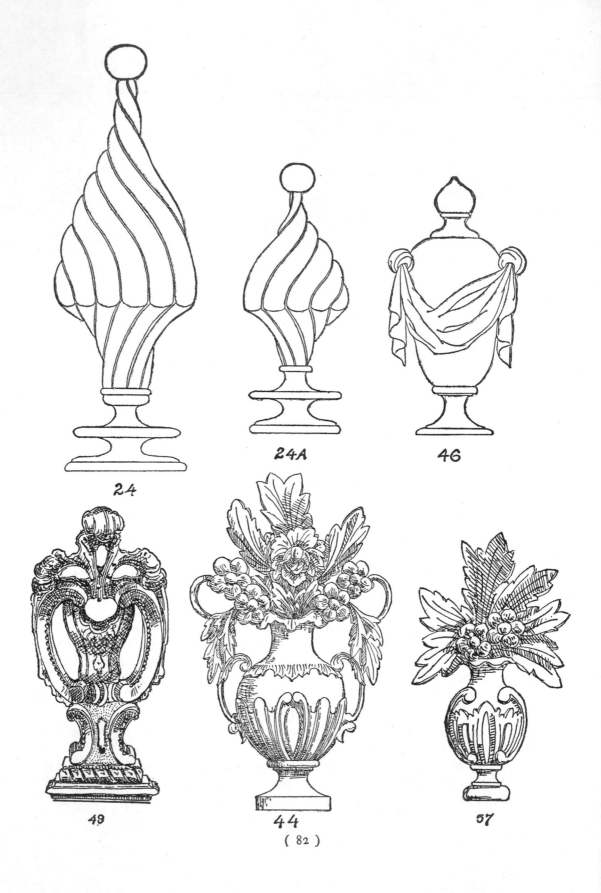

24

24A

46

49

44

57

51 59

DROPS

Drops are found on the main frame members of tables, highboys, and lowboys. They ceased to be used on lowboy and highboy frames when the Queen Anne skirt was abandoned. On tables their use ran through the entire oak period and the walnut period, but if the skirt is carved, it does not have drops. The drops seem to be a substitution for the richer decoration.

The shape of the drop, like that of the cross-stretcher urn, is often the condensation and a reverse of the finial.

No. 72 is a very small oak drop. Nos. 73–75 are oak drops increasing in size and are found on tables from the period of earliest turned types to 1690. (*Page 77.*)

Nos. 76 and 77 are very odd in shape and are found on tables. (*Page 141.*)

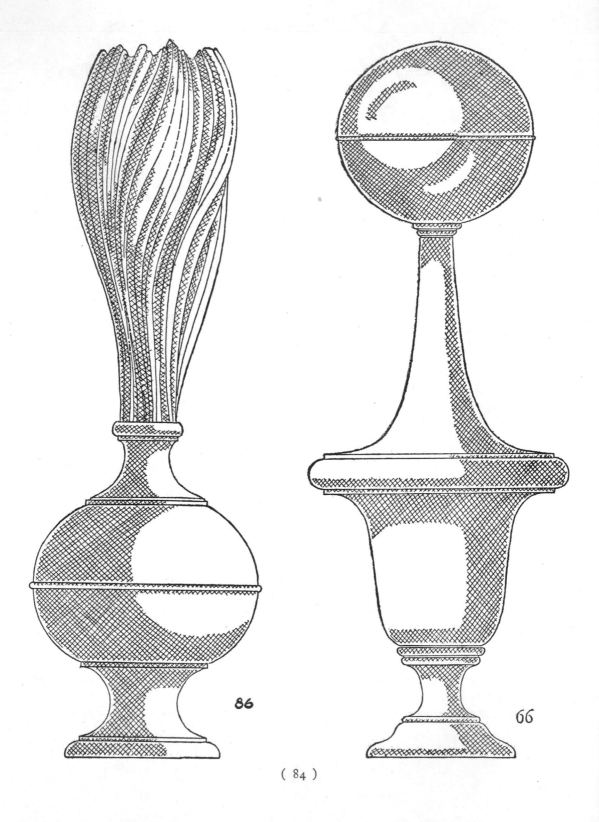

86

66

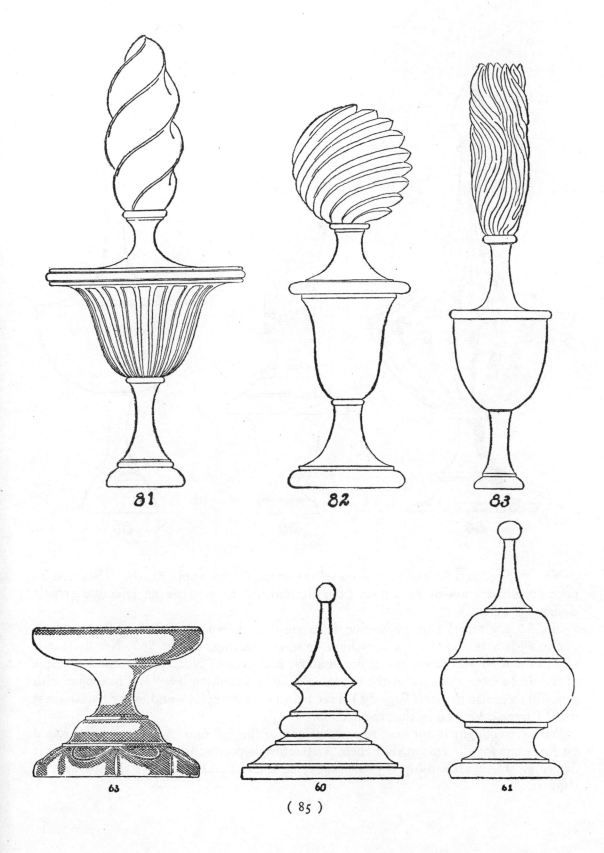

81 82 83

63 60 61

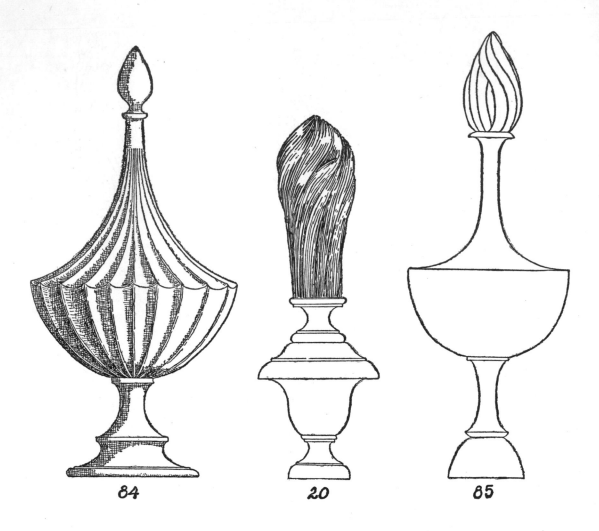

84   20   85

Nos. 78, 79, and 80 are variations of the graceful pineapple finials. They are an apposite illustration of variations from the natural to produce an effective artistic design. (*Page 79.*)

No. 81 is a fluted flame variation from another shown. No. 82 is a flaming ball.

No. 83 is attenuated for a very light or small cresting. (*Page 85.*) No. 84 stands alone on a high wall piece, and is fluted above and below. No. 85 is a second example of the flame from the neck of the cover. No. 86 is a striking large ball like a jar with graceful irregular flame. (*Page 84.*) It is found on a fine clock and is the handsomest finial I have ever seen in that connection.

We have thought it not best to attempt any of the full figures or other busts found on furniture for the reason that their satisfactory reproduction is impossible in a flat drawing. Their artisanship if good cannot be shown, and if bad we do not wish to show it.

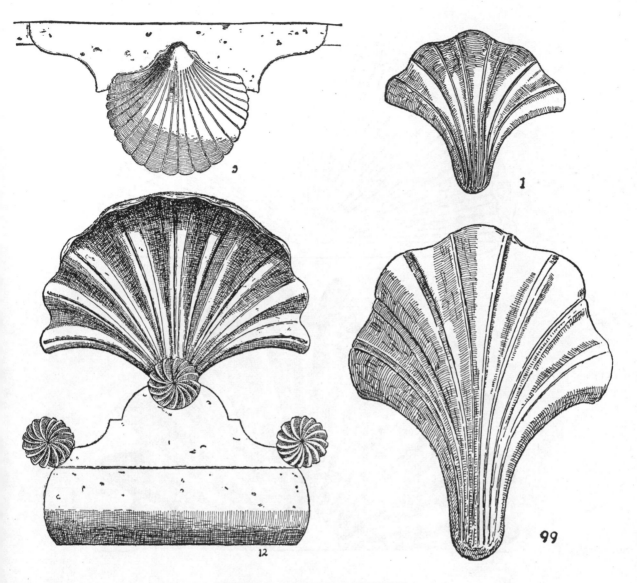

SHELLS AND ROSETTES

The shell, admired ever since men have loved beauty, acquired a peculiar significance at the time of the crusades. The palmer wore on his garments a shell as a token of his journey to the Holy Land. The shell thus added to its beauty a sentiment connected with age, distance, and religion.

Nevertheless, the shell seems not to have been adopted as a decorative feature of furniture until about the year 1700, though of course isolated examples to the contrary may have existed a long time before that. The shell reached its fullest development in the Queen Anne, the Georgian, and the Chippendale eras.

In the Queen Anne time the major part of the examples left to us are decorations on chairs. These shells are usually raised. They show the convex side, especially on the

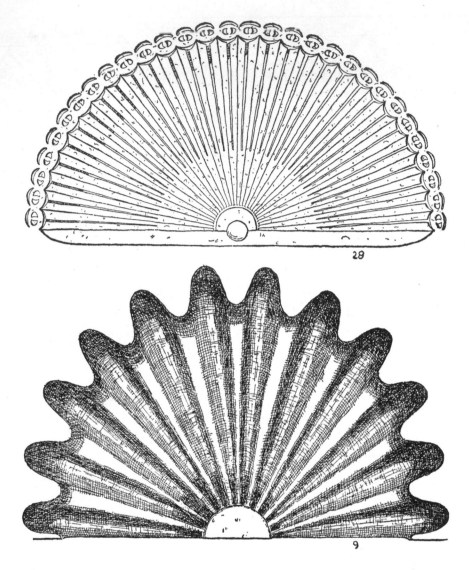

28

9

knees of chairs, though the concave side of the shell appeared sometimes on the chair back, but was commoner on the fine scrutoire or the bookcase above it.

By a shell we restrict the term here to such carvings as really suggest the object, and consider later those cheaper modifications which more properly are denominated fans.

The scallop is handsomer than the cockle shell, but both are used indifferently, as a rule omitting the purely naturalistic parts which contribute little to the beauty or offer difficulty in reproduction. The convex of the shell fitted admirably on the rounded hip of a chair leg, and seemed as if it grew there. In Nos. 1 and 2, particularly 2, the contour was a perfect decoration. There is a variety in treatment, the shell being either broad end up or broad end down. (*Pages 87, 108.*)

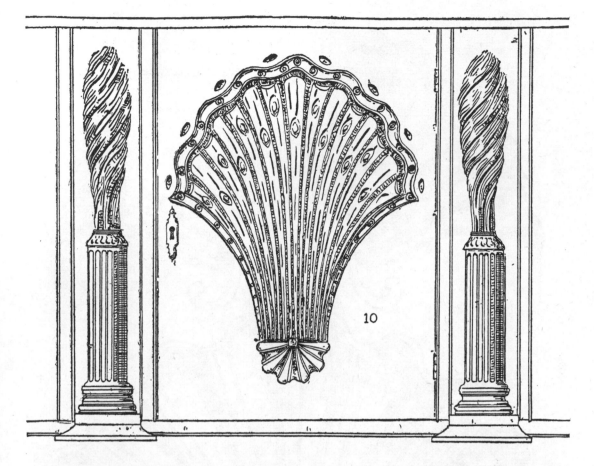

10

In No. 3, the scrolled skirt of a highboy or lowboy, we find three shells used, the central one following the conventional curve at the base which is often found without a shell. The small shells in this case greatly enhance the beauty of the piece by their contrast in style and size with the larger. The combination of the scrolls and whorls with the other elements has produced a handsome effect. (*Page 8.*)

No. 4 (*Page 11*) is one of the shells to which we have alluded as at the center of a seat rail. Under the heading "Cupboards" will be found illustrations of shells just described. The rarest and least satisfactory use of a shell is that in the decoration of a table foot.

On page 99, at the bottom, will be found at the center of the back rail the illustration of rococo ornament which is neither a shell nor, properly speaking, anything else. It is this mixture of odd motives which has probably caused critics to challenge rococo forms. They mean nothing, and a thing without meaning is always a thing without taste. In No. 5 is shown the excellent base ornament of a secretary. The objection to it is that it is close to the floor. Such ornaments are more effective and more appropriate if occurring at a higher level on a piece of furniture. (*Page 87.*)

In No. 6 we have the shell occurring on a base mold formed like a block. (*Page 105.*)

No. 7 (*Page 105*) is a highly conventional and elaborate shell of much beauty. Refer-

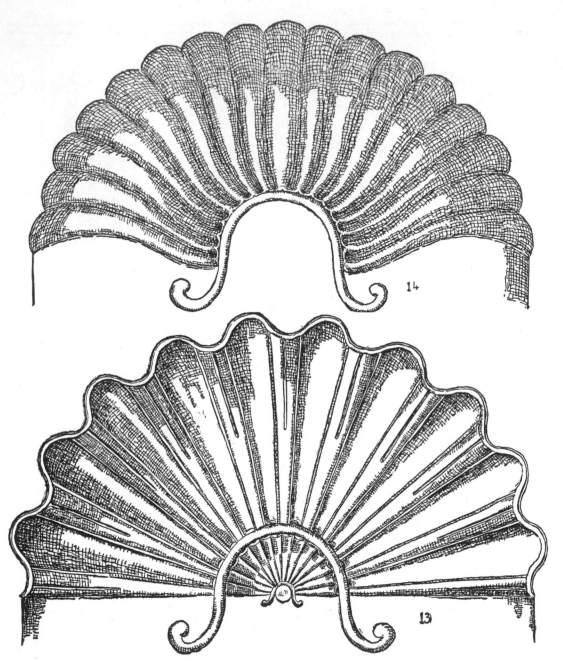

ence to the author's first and second volumes of FURNITURE TREASURY may be allowed to indicate the application and the appropriateness of many of these forms if the sections on high chests of drawers, highboys, lowboys, and walnut and Chippendale chairs are examined with care. In No. 8, on page 112, we have an ornament which should not perhaps be called a shell, but is found between the gooseneck or broken arches of a high cabinet. No. 9 is a more highly naturalistic shell than some of the others shown. Its radiates carry additional detail. (*Page 88.*)

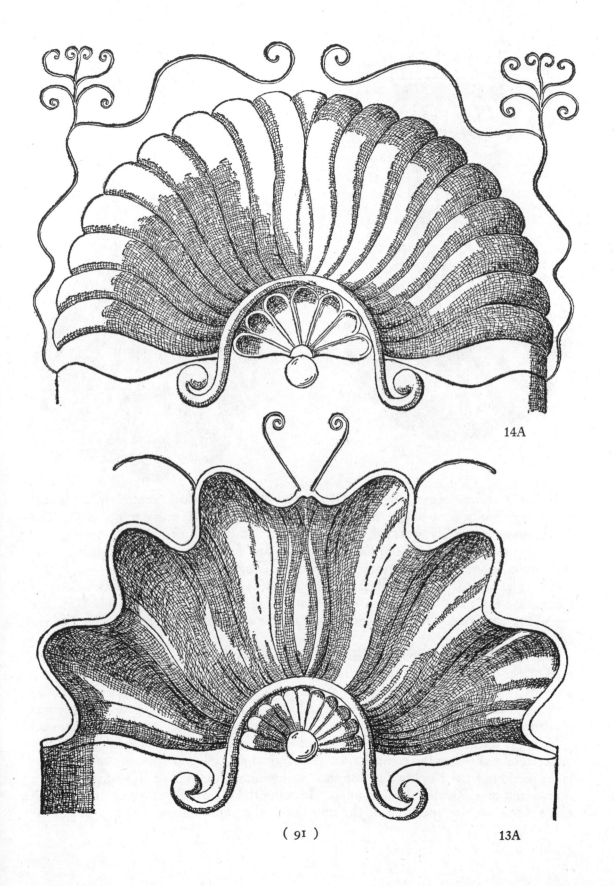

14A

13A

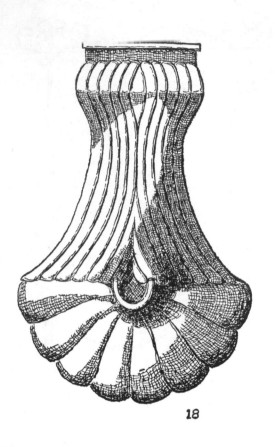

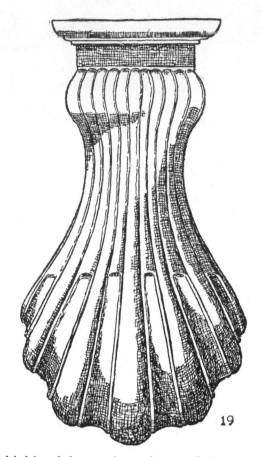

18

19

In No. 10 on a desk cabinet door is a most highly elaborated specimen. It is certainly beautifully done and terminated at the base by an additional minor shell. The flames show naturally spiraled, proceeding from fluted shafts and decorating the document doors at each side of the central shell and form altogether a cabinet decoration which is not surpassed in my observation. (*Page 89.*)

No. 11 (*Page 101*) shows a shell occurring in the spandrel between the two doors of a bookcase top. No. 12 is a combination of a shell with three rosettes on a bookcase top above the doors. The rosettes are spiraled as conventionally as possible, but are effective. (*Page 87.*)

No. 13 is the shell variously called concave, hollowed, intaglio, incised, and cut out, used on the center of a Connecticut high chest of drawers. The radiates are absolutely straight. The slight rim which is supposed to show the edge of the shell incidentally also supplies a stop against which the radiates terminate. The central bow-shaped element renders the entire shell suggestive of a butterfly. (*Nos. 13 and 14, Page 90.*)

No. 14 is the convex shell with curved radiates on the same piece of furniture. Curving certainly enriches the composition. The right-hand edge at the bottom shows the plain section of the block which the shell surmounted. A shell of this sort has never been found on a Rhode Island example. In using the word "never" here and through this volume we are speaking of the knowledge that has become public. Of course, private individuals may know of a good many things that have never come to public knowledge. Quite frequently someone comes out with the announcement that there has been found something that is listed as non-existent in the books. The discovery is always delightful, but one could wish that the manner of its announcement was also as delightful.

No. 14A is a variant of the last shell. It also is on a Connecticut chest-on-chest. Both this piece and the succeeding have full-column spiraled corner inserts, and they are no doubt made by the same man or by a close imitator, since the finials are very similar. No. 13A still further resembles a butterfly by having antennae grown out at the top; but it is to be observed that the radiates in Nos. 13A and 14A are unique, each keeping its curvature at the center, so that a curious design results, compelling the insertion of a connecting link at the center of both shells. The quaint scroll on the No. 14A is an addition not found on No. 14. (*Page 90.*)

No. 15 shows the shell on a Goddard clock case. The measurement across is 8½ inches. In one of these that the author owns the shell is applied, and in another it is cut from the solid block and fitted on to the long panel. No. 16 shows a Goddard shell on a knee-hole table in the author's possession. The convex shell is always, as in this case, a little simpler in the handling, although in other respects it is in Goddard examples an absolute reverse of the convex shell here shown. The shells on the Goddard secretaries and chests-on-chests are practically identical with this except for size. No. 17 is a naturalistic shell which nevertheless shows some effort at tasteful decoration in addition found on the top front, just over the central drawer of a chest-on-chest. Nos. 18 and 19 are odd conventionalized patterns used as the central top ornaments of the front, under the plinth of Connecticut chests-on-chests and on a southern secretary.(*Page 92.*)

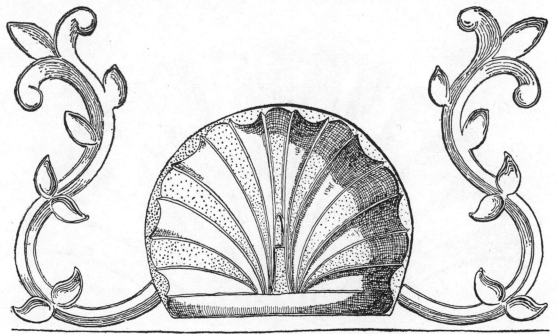

23

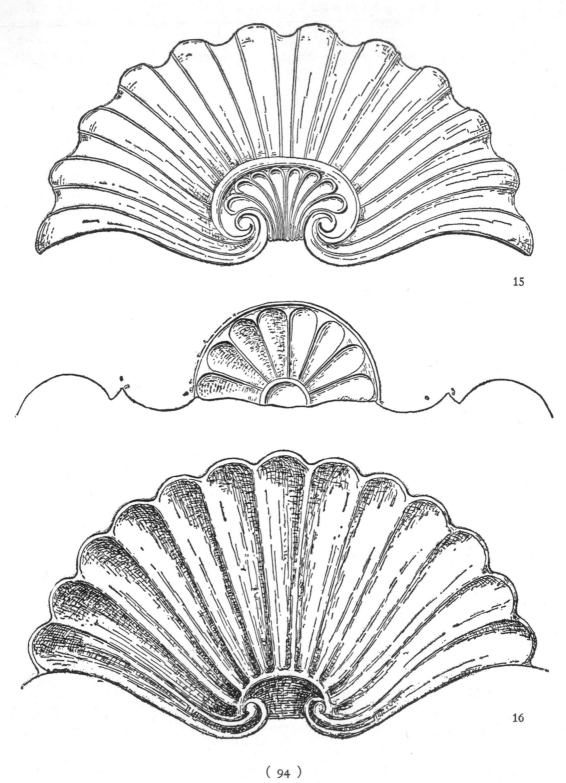

15

16

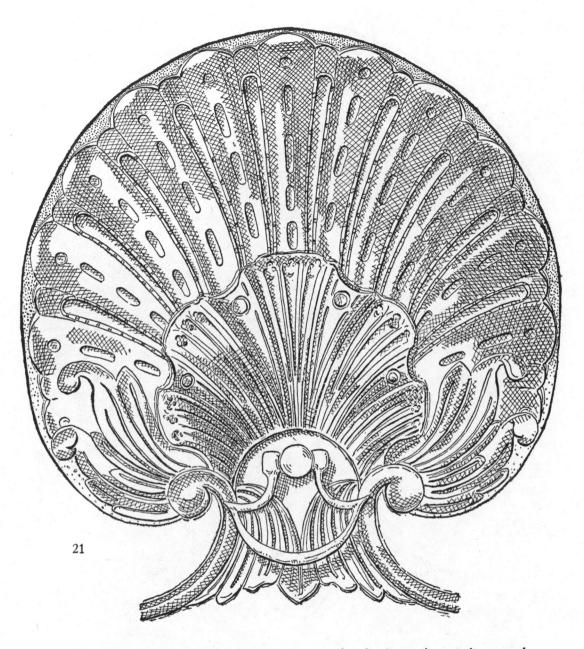

21

The above shell merely shows the cut-out portion for decoration on the central nearly square-faced drawer of a lowboy or highboy base. It is of course surrounded by decorative scrolls which are applied and which appear with sufficient clearness in Volumes I and II. The method here employed of inserting a second smaller shell in the center of the larger one is of course a purely conventional but nevertheless attractive decoration. The designer here even went so far as to add foliage scrolls at the base. The stippling around the outer edges is to avoid the irregular reflection giving an unfinished appearance of the flat surface.

22

The shell decoration above is the incised portion. It is of course surrounded by applied scrolls. This volume shows the complete architectural details of another Philadelphia piece, a lowboy, with still further variations. The fertility of invention by the old designers is amazing when we consider that they almost invariably achieved graceful results. There was a subconscious ruling motive which seemed to restrain the designer's hand from graceless forms, at the same time that he was stimulated to an infinite variety of details. Of course the knob here, while necessary, is an intrusion, whereas on the preceding page a place is left for it.

37

38

The word "southern" in this connection ordinarily means south of New York. No. 20 is a pattern of somewhat unusual design, obviously not of Rhode Island origin, but I think it should be traced to Connecticut.

There is a large class of shells cut into the solid, but in conjunction with applied ornaments, and found on Philadelphia highboys and lowboys and in one instance, as in No. 21 (*Page 95*), on the base of a Pennsylvania secretary of extremely individualistic design. Probably such a piece would be prized by a collector more than the conventional design, but its intrinsic merits are not so great. No. 22 details another composi-

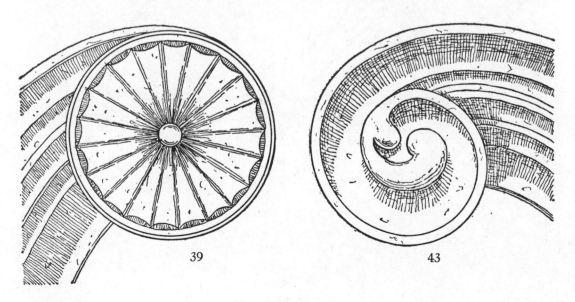

39

43

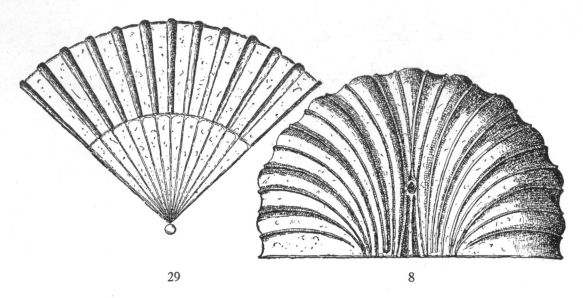

29   8

tion such as is found on the Philadelphia lowboy and highboy base. The designer, of course, did not attempt to copy anything in nature, but tried to make a beautiful design and certainly succeeded.

No. 23 is a design found in this form, or something approaching it, on a number of pieces which we suppose to have been simplified by a country maker from the finest Philadelphia types. They might have been done from memory, or might frankly have been a simpler design. (*Page 93.*)

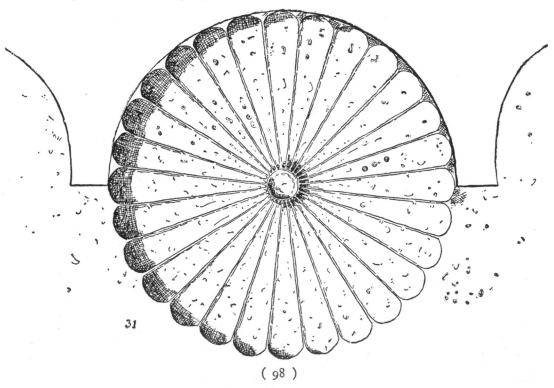

31

34

50

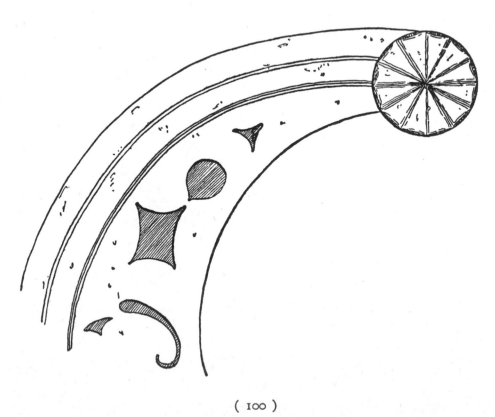

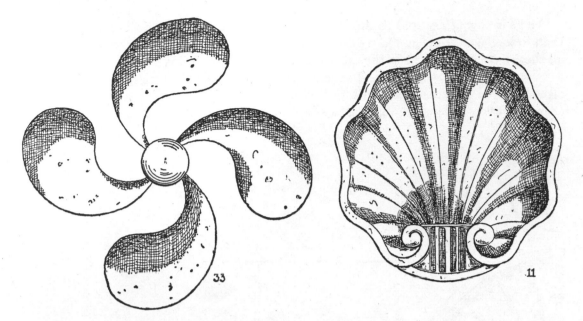

In the center of the seat frame in front and in the base mold of chests of drawers a shell was often carved. A shell on the leg is invariably a part of the leg, but on the frame or on cabinet pieces it may either be applied or cut from the solid, which latter form is at times difficult or impractical.

The shell became a very popular ornament as adapted to the keystone of an arch in cupboards. Probably its earliest architectural use was in large examples carved to cover the entire demi-dome of niches in stone, or cupboards of wood. It should, however, be carefully pointed out that the shell-top cupboard is more often in the form of a fan; its rays supposed to emanate from a central sun which is sometimes gilded, and the rays themselves are gilded or parcel gilt, the space between being done in blue gradually changing in tint from the sun to the zenith. In the simpler forms there is no gilding, and in the simplest there is no painting beyond the plain white. Of course, where the dome is worked into a shell there is no shell in addition as the center of the external arch, as the motives would mix, and the small shell would be cast into insignificance by the large one.

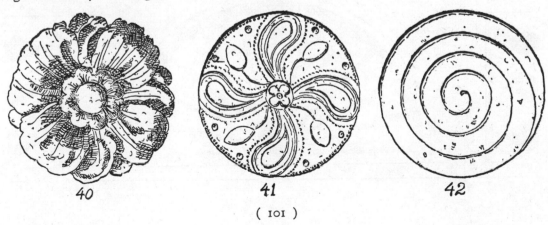

We pass now (*Page 106*) to the setting forth of designs which recall us to fans rather than to shells, although in No. 24 there is a very elaborate transition example. Of course all these examples are cut in the solid wood, that is, they are concaved, or in some cases a great part of the work comes to the surface. No. 25 should strictly be called a fan, although it is common enough in ordinary speech to refer to it as a shell. The best examples even of fans are made in a slight curvature from the plane first down as the

30

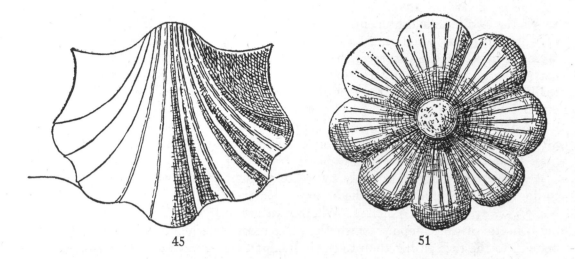

45

51

center is approached and then up and then down again. This is a very much better form of fan than the flat carving. We have in No. 26 an unusual fan form from a pagoda-top highboy. There is an evident mixture of motives here between the fan and the shell. No. 27 (*Page 107*) is a fan from a Connecticut example supposedly of the Chippendale type, but of course a good deal modified. One observes here and in the following designs an increasing number of radiates. This is in accordance with progress from the bold and simple to the intricate in detail, and, while supposed to be an improvement, was not. No. 28 (*Page 88*) is an extreme type in the number of the fan radiates. The drawer pull is seen at the center. No. 29 (*Page 98*) is on what is usually counted as a Queen Anne desk, in the center of the long drawer. It is a pure fan. The inside section represents the plain ivory or bone, and the outside section the same covered with the folding fabric. One doubts if this is as early as the pure shells, but that is to be explained by the continuation of the Queen Anne style in highboys and lowboys through the eighteenth century up to the Revolution. No. 30 (*Page 102*)

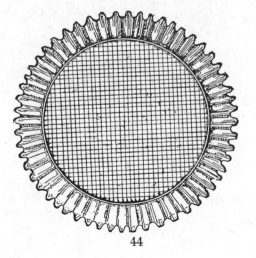

44

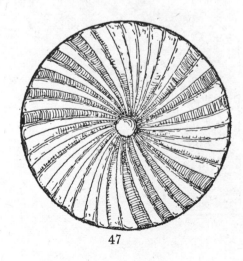

47

shows the two fanlike ornaments on the so-called New Hampshire highboy, a number of which have been found, a semicircular fan being in the center, and the quarter segment being at the corner of the cornice, a duplicate of the visible portion being carried around on the end. In No. 31 we have an approach to the rosette style, but really merely a doubling of the fans already shown. It is found on two or three pieces, either single or doubled on the bases of highboys and lowboys. (*Page 98.*)

Possibly the central ornament on the top of a Hepplewhite secretary No. 32, with a central sunburst design surmounted by an eagle and a pair of floral designs below, may as well be shown here as elsewhere. (*Page 25.*)

A simple odd design, probably by a Connecticut maker who did not wish others to do his thinking for him, is the ornament on the drawer of a highboy and lowboy, No. 33. (*Page 101.*) It is incised. Whether we are to attribute this to one of the pleasing conceits of the Chapins, or whether, like most other good things in the world, it belongs to the race rather than to the individual, we cannot say. The broken arch of a secretary top appears in a quaint design with cutouts on the gooseneck and a rosette terminating it. It would be a little difficult to assign a date, but it would be the latter half of the eighteenth century. (*Page 100 bottom.*)

There is a very large series of rosettes terminating goosenecks on the top scrolls of highboys and secretaries. A somewhat rich example is No. 34. (*Page 99.*) The diameter of this excellent piece is 4⅞ inches, and the thickness is ⅞ inch. The extreme

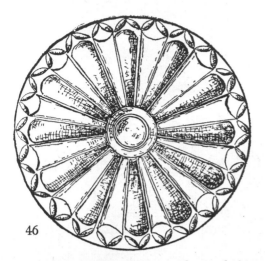

46

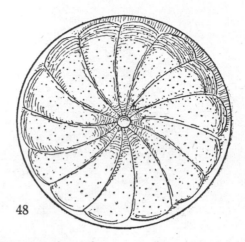

48

vertical cut below the surface of the plane is ½ inch. The center is raised ⅛ inch higher than the rim. This center is stippled. No. 35 (*Page 100*) is a spiraled rosette terminating a molded and dentiled gooseneck. Some are of the opinion that the spiral form simplified from this, used by the Chapins, was derived from the Philadelphia examples. In the original which was owned by the author this gooseneck is cut from a four-inch stick of timber, and the rosette is worked out from the solid, which is a very unusual and careful arrangement. The rich rosettes used on the Philadelphia crestings are exhibited in No. 36 (*Page 100*) with a foliated decoration above the spiraled rosette. This ornament is also found on some of the best Philadelphia clock cases as well as highboys and secretaries. No. 37 (*Page 97*) is a variant of the last design, and it is pleasing from the fact that the upper leaves roll over so markedly. No. 38 shows a similar, but simplified, rosette in which the maker has worked out a kind of tripled spiral. Nos. 39 (*Page 97*), 40, 41, and 42 (*Page 101*) are all used in this same manner, and are all about the size of the No. 34. These spirals are usually attached to a plain surface, and one notable instance comes to mind of a wonderful piece which was left without any rosettes.

No. 43 seen as the terminal of a gooseneck is also highly interesting as being almost identical with the carving on the comb and fan-back Windsors of the Philadelphia type. (*Page 97*.)

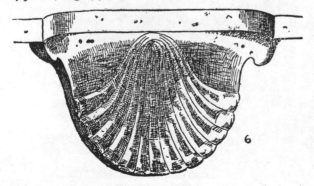

6

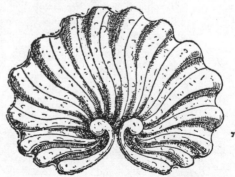

7

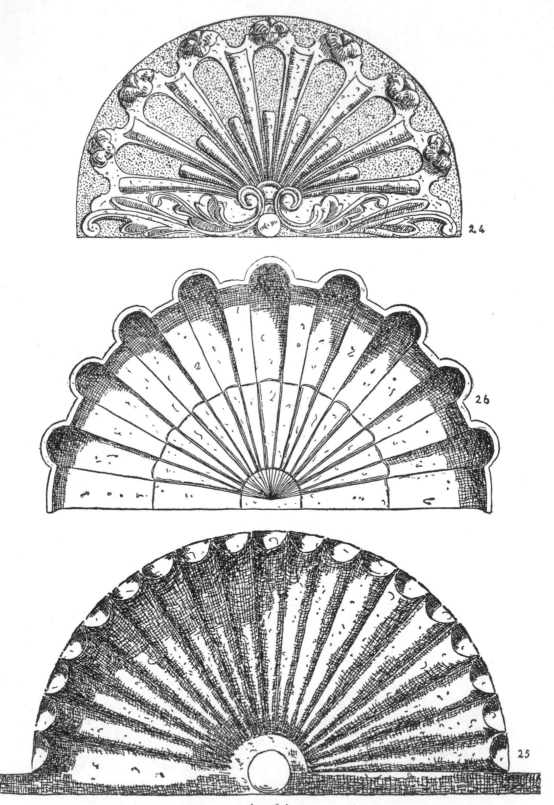

24

26

25

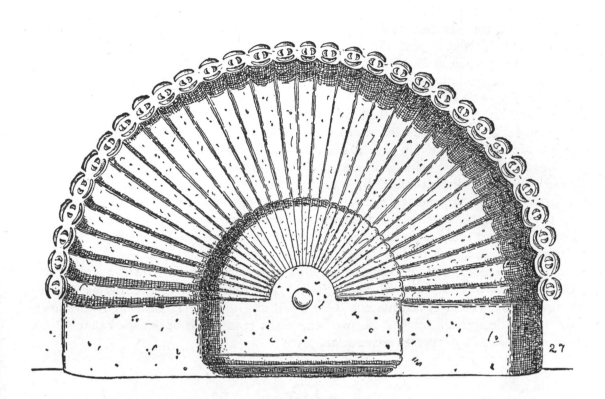

27

(107)

Additional rosettes are the sunflower No. 44, the fan-rayed types, Nos. 45 and 46; and the spirals, Nos. 47 and 48. They are effective. (*Pages 103 and 105.*)

On a chest-on-chest is No. 50, the gooseneck rosette with foliage dependent on center. It is reminiscent of similar foliage, like ring ornaments, on rich Georgian mirrors. (*Page 99.*)

On page 103, top, right, is a shell used to show the base decoration of a skirt (No. 51). On page 94 in the center is an incised shell on the skirt of a highboy believed to have been made by Goddard. On page 104 is a carving found on a Pennsylvania arched top. It does not follow the usual lines and possibly was not done by Philadelphia School, being more naturalistic than most decorations.

At the bottom of page 107 is an amusingly intricate decoration which is neither a fan nor a shell, but has no less than thirty-three rays. It is found on the knee-hole desk now in and probably originating in Connecticut. This shell or fan is on the high-boy base No. 405, FURNITURE TREASURY.

No. 99, page 87, and the tailpiece on this page show extremes of drawing of the scallop which was the original simple form. The designer arranged his carving to decorate his space most adequately. One could extend the representations of known varieties of design still further, but we believe the reader will be satisfied that he has here a very broadly representative selection.

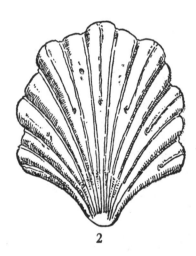

2

CORRECTION AND COMMENT ON ARTICLES SHOWN IN VOLUMES I AND II

The numbers refer to those under the pictures.

4. The combination of scratch carving on the panel with the linear carving on the stiles is unusual, but arises out of a spirit for spontaneous decoration without that careful harmony of thought which would be found in an architectural unit.

6. While the top of this chest is paneled in the style usual in England, very early American examples rarely adhere thus closely to the foreign type. The decoration on the skirt is found in the earliest chests. In fact, among the entire number of chests here shown this is the only oak chest with this ornament. On pine chests a scroll on the base of the front is not so unusual.

8. The splicing of the legs, though well done, shows plainly. Also the best method by a V cut in the old leg. This article and that above it, having a diamond pattern in the panels, have by some been referred to as of English origin. But there is no reason to doubt that American cabinetmakers copied and adapted a great many varieties of English chests, both by memory and from examples now perished.

12. While the band or interesting strap mold on the drawer is occasionally dignified by the name "band of eternity" because it returns on itself and has no end, it is not necessary to suppose that cabinetmakers then or now have consciously carried their theology into their theory of decoration, however pleasant it would be to attribute such lofty or learned motives to the faithful artisan.

25. Date about 1690–1705.

30. The feet seem unusually small. Whether they are original or not the author has not verified. The feet in conventional chests either appear as full-sized prolongations of the stiles, or short, full-sized prolongations, on which ball feet are placed, or large ball feet as large or larger than the stiles.

43. One can plainly discern where a mold ran around the drawer. This corresponded to the panel molds above. In such cases the drawer was usually recessed.

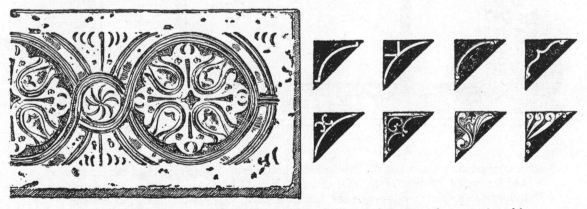

Above is a scroll consisting of large and small loops found on chests and architectural work.

At the right are simple and elaborate open scroll brackets, used in the Chippendale style of a later period with straight-leg tables and chairs.

44. Date about 1670–90.

45. This method of drawer decoration is also seen on some oak cupboards as Nos. 446 and 447, and on two chests on frames, Nos. 210 and 211, encouraging the supposition, also borne out by the style of the ornaments, that all the pieces were made by the same artisan who probably had his shop at Salem or Ipswich.

47. Date about 1670–90.

50. Date about 1690–1705. The same sort of turning is found on court cupboard 466, and on 210, 211, and 212. The spool turning in the beds of that name, otherwise very unworthy and late, is probably a revival from these pieces.

61. Date about 1670–90.

68. The series of "Hadley" chests dating some earlier and some later than our usual reference to about 1690 has now been increased in observed numbers by the Rev. Mr. Luther of Amherst to above one hundred examples, and he has prepared a very careful and minute description of them, which has now been or is about to be published in a volume devoted exclusively to this style of chest.

87. For gauge read gouge, the reference being to the concaved notches cut on the corners. Also the index should be similarly corrected.

88. Owner: H. H. Armstrong, Hartford.

Chippendale glasses of the three-part type are much more rare than the Empire and degraded Empire styles. Of course, a piece like that above is English and indulges in all the rococo ornament that bothers the taste of the purist. Nevertheless, the total effect is rich rather than tawdry, because the carving is delicately done and, being covered with gold leaf, certainly has its merits. At any rate, the rarity of a piece like this is enough to arouse no little interest.

89. So far as now known this carved panel pattern is unique.

It is understood that the very large collection of Mr. George Dudley Seymour of New Haven, many pieces of which are shown in this work, has now been generously donated to the Atheneum. He thus shares in generosity with Mr. J. P. Morgan who also donated a collection.

93. The Fuessenich Collection has now been dispersed in various directions, and no attempt will here be made to trace the present owners of individual articles, many of which have changed.

94. In stamping a decoration a steel punch of large size was filed on the end to show the particular pattern desired. When the stamping was done on oak the design of the pattern was pretty clear, but on pine, owing to the softer surface, there was often no attempt to impress anything more than a plain punch mark.

95. This chest should be ascribed to the gift of George Dudley Seymour. By the words, blocked panel, it is meant that a wide beveled edge raises the panel at the center above the surface of the front, but of course the panels themselves are not, properly speaking, blocked.

97. It was frequent in Pennsylvania to construct chests of walnut rather than oak, and even when, somewhat later, pine became common, the finer chests of Pennsylvania still adhered to walnut. Of late a great many painted chests have come to market.

101. This particular type of foot is much liked. It is called the turnip top. By an optical illusion this and all other turned feet seem in a picture to "toe in."

GENERAL REMARKS ON CHESTS

It is a present habit to speak of all chests as blanket chests. There is no reason for coupling with the chest the name of the contents, which varied, of course, without limit.

Also chests of drawers are now called chests, but to do so is to confuse terms. Also the name Salem chest is given to all sorts of chests of drawers, some made far from Salem, being of various types. The name really connotes nothing.

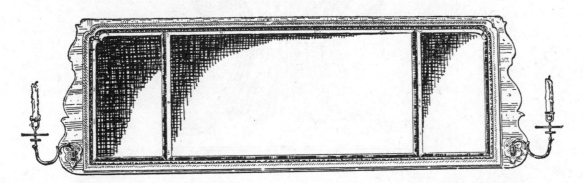

A simple glass in three parts and terminating with bracket sconces. The glass itself seems complete without the projections beyond the main frame. This is one of the rare glasses of the Georgian period that cannot be seriously objected to in the matter of style.

126. This porticoed front with turnings like pillars is, of course, purely for decoration. The portion above the pillars is thus given the effect of a frieze.

131. The carving motive is sometimes called the band of eternity, ending, as it does, on itself and forming an excellent end stop. See also 138.

132. The space where the initials are placed was left purposely for them, and in some cases we find such surfaces not used. The personality attaching to initialed furniture is highly desirable. It is a pity that in the generalizing of the present day this feature of individualism has fallen out of use.

135. Of course the so-called arches are merely short flutings with appropriate terminations. The test of this proper termination is that a ball fitting into the fluting shall roll to the very end and fit the space.

139. This style of carving is cramped in so narrow a space that it does not leave room for the full development seen in 124.

155. This box shows a naïve and not unusual fitting or blending of two carving motives together. Thus the small flutes sometimes form the entire carving, and sometimes are doubled as in 135. The lunettes sometimes fill all the space, as in 162, and more precisely in 157.

202–3. The turned urn knife box which is very handsome is not shown in Furniture Treasury because all the specimens the author has found were reproductions copied from types of English origin. It is usual to find a doubled ogee foot, turning both ways, unless the foot is on a square corner. This is a persistence of style brought over from Queen Anne style. No foot more graceful has ever been devised. It is found on clocks as late as 1820, a good hundred years after its first use. (English, *Page 27*.)

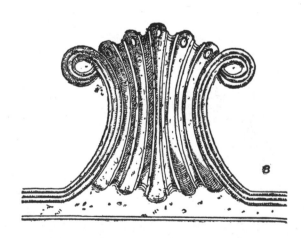

The shell decoration above appears on the top of a bookcase of a period about 1760 or 70. It is flanked by a gooseneck scroll and offers some difficulties in the way of definition. The reeded or sheaf of wheat back of a Chippendale chair is suggestive. As a matter of fact, of course the decoration is purely an imaginary form.

208. A statement made by the author that the square stretchers have a sharp edge, indicating that they originally supported a shelf, should be confined to apply to this piece only. It is by no means true, that all square-edged stretchers carried shelves. Indeed, in the next example, 209, there is a clumsy fitting of the shelf at the corners where there is not room for its thickness without an awkward connection with the rounded corners of the square on the post. The entire shelf may be an addition, if not a replacement of a thinner shelf as suggested in the caption.

212. The spool turning here is the precise reverse of ball turning and is not found, often, perhaps never, on seventeenth-century furniture before its last decade. Compare the peculiar turning on 466.

214. This chest-on-frame and the two following it are doubtless a little later than the style of 208. The construction being in maple points to that conclusion. The turnings suggest those of gate-leg tables and butterfly tables. While some gate legs are referred to a date as early as near the middle of the seventeenth century, the author is becoming increasingly dubious of that date.

CHESTS OF DRAWERS

219. The habit of varying the widths of the drawers arose from the individual taste and need, and also from the love of originality. Here, for instance, we find a middle drawer wider than the bottom drawer.

By an optical delusion a chest with all drawers of equal vertical widths will appear to show narrower drawers approaching the bottom. For this reason the conventional chest of drawers soon showed graduated drawers, increasing in widths toward the base, as the appearance gave a better sense of balance and stability.

The John Goddard above is the grandson of John I. The style of furniture illustrated clearly indicates that fact. The shop, however, was on the Point, as was his grandfather's. This maker is mentioned elsewhere.

On the right is the top of a Hepplewhite mirror with an oval containing fourteen stars. Some undertake to date glasses by the number of stars and the number of balls. They are, therefore, called constitution glasses.

220. It appears by examining a great number of chests of drawers that the size of the foot (ball) decreases as the period becomes later. A very massive ball almost uniformly indicates an early date. Of course the stile leg is earlier still, and scarcely reaches with rare exceptions into the eighteenth century. But it co-existed for a hundred years or more with the ball foot.

227. The small size of the foot influences the attribution of a late date.

228. A humorously large ball to be attached to the small, square stile. In fact, the foot is earlier, strictly, in type, than the stile, which was before this time wider than deep.

247. This contoured, waved, or serpentined front had four modifications. 1. The front here shown, probably the earliest. It terminates with a chamfered corner, usually carved, and has of necessity a very large and, before we become acquainted with it, a clumsy-appearing foot. 2. This type is found in 253, in which the serpentine is reversed, affording the oxbow, with a quarter- or half-column corner. 3. The plain oxbow, something as in 261. 4. The later plain serpentine as in 255. This type ran into the Hepplewhite period and sometimes occurs with the French foot.

256. This type and that immediately adjoining exist in America in great numbers, usually with line inlay or a full decoration with veneer. It is not a rigidly strong foot and is liable to injury. The swell (the term generally used) or bow front was graceful and became very popular.

259. The straight fronts, with, or more often without, the decorative corner quarter column, are numerous, especially in Pennsylvania.

261. An error in printing: the date should be 1770–80. The claw-and-ball foot existed alongside the ogee foot for at least fifty years, but the finest examples of high chests of drawers or desks with bookcase tops have the ogee foot.

265. Date should be 1770–80. One surmise as to the origin of the block front may be as good as another that it arose, as in 262, from a modification of the oxbow front.

21

Scroll at top of individualistic Pennsylvania tall cabinet.

It was found to have more emphasis and variety than a plain curve and gave a handsomely contoured top. We treat the subject at some length under *John Goddard*.

266. Date a misprint for 1770–80.

269. Date a misprint for 1770–80. A block-and-shell chest of drawers with quarter columns, the last possible enrichment, is shown under *John Goddard*, the present volume.

272. Date a misprint for 1770–80. Comparing this example with 275, it appears that the latter has a small drawer under the long drawer. This drawer is a variation and is shown in this volume in a drawing. But from an esthetic standpoint 272 is better because the absence of the small drawer allows the shell on the cupboard door to show to advantage.

273. It is more than probable that this foot is a Connecticut modification of Goddard's superior foot shown in 272. His manner of terminating the block with the little scroll was an inspiration such as geniuses in design experience.

276. This form of foot, while more flamboyant in its supporting side bracket, is an evident endeavor in Connecticut to surpass Goddard of Rhode Island. The effort fails. Without Goddard's foot we might think this very fine, but it lacks the elegance and reserve of the foot in 272. Further, 272 shows the foot well tucked under. It does not project, and must not, beyond a vertical line dropped from the outside of the hip. A knee-hole piece exhibited in a museum showed its spurious character by a neglect of this detail.

281. The Sheraton (also Directoire) chests of drawers modify the plain Hepplewhite corner shown in 279 by using a corner post, turned throughout, as here, or at least in a simplified form, or the part at the base free of the frame. This construction is more

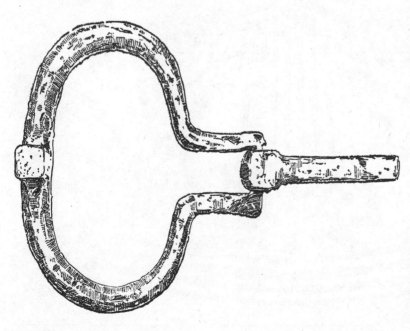

An amusing episode is connected with this rare knocker. I saw two such in an inn in Gloucester, Virginia, and offered as high as a hundred dollars for them, but in vain. This one, fully as good, was thrown at me for a small sum, in New England. This is the knocker concerning which critics said there was no such animal and blamed me for inserting a reproduction of something which did not exist. The small end passes through the door and a mortise hole in the iron latch bar and is clinched. A turn opens; a blow knocks.

elaborate than the Hepplewhite type, as the Sheraton requires a mortised or at least a slotted, post.

282. This rather rare foot one would say should be more common as it is so generally

It is known that the sofa here drawn was bought from Phyfe. For his period the arrangement of the back is effective, the clustered grape scrolls being undoubtedly the ancestors of the later and cruder Victorian central cluster. The lyre detailed below, it has been suggested, is almost identical with that used on clocks of the period, which one collector believes were made by Phyfe!

found in Hepplewhite tables. Also on desks very frequently. It should be noted that the taper on this foot, as well as elsewhere, is all gained on the inside. The effect to the eye appears as a slight outsweep, but a straight edge laid on the outside shows the entire length of the post to be without curve.

283. The shortness of the foot is a defect in taste and also makes cleaning under such a piece impossible without removing it.

CHESTS–ON–CHESTS

Careful observation shows that Goddard never attempted an elegant highboy, but expended his attention, for rich decoration, on high pieces, on the chest-on-chest, and the secretary — that is, the desk with shelf top imposed. We have good evidence that Goddard made highboys — usually with Queen Anne feet, but never in a rich design.

His two recognized nine-shell pieces are 317 and 701. Apart from these his pieces *now known* are probably limited to six shells. Unscrupulous "pickers" are not wanting who allege that they know of other nine-shell pieces. Discovery of such pieces may be made, but at present when we follow up clews the sought-for prize is always in some other town than that we have reached.

298. The type of drawer decoration here shown is attributed, with little hesitation, to the Chapins of Windsor and Hartford, Connecticut, Eliphalet and Aaron, who worked separately. In the author's researches he has traced the finer examples to Eliphalet. That here shown has recently come to light and is one of the finest examples now known to be extant. The work of these makers was usually in cherry.

299. This form of a broken pediment is strangely very unusual, especially in America. English clocks and major examples often use it. Its elegance when, as here, accomplished by fine dentils is apparent, though the finial is a very weak member, so much so as to cause one to wonder whether it is original. Obviously a single finial should be more pretentious than one of three. Here the flame arises without an urn from which it may issue.

309. This piece is in the Garvan Collection, now largely made over to Yale University. It is understood that the University was given practically a free hand in selecting such of the collection as it desired.

In this example the taste displayed in the location of the finials, by perching them on the extreme outside angle of the cornice mold, is questionable, though this practice is observed in some other instances as in 310. Of course, the piece is most satisfactory in all its lines. The rise or ramp of the gooseneck is more rapid than usual, and therefore the central opening is broader than in the usual type, where the flatter curve gives ample room for finials lining with the outside of the body of the piece.

314. This example, now removed, is typical of the so-called North Shore type, a name correct enough if it is understood as including the latitude of Boston and all points north near the Atlantic coast. The features found in these examples are finials of this or similar type (those on 311 have the appearance of added Philadelphia finials), fluted pilasters, blocking square or nearly square at the top and seldom with true shells — perhaps never; a true bonnet top, never having an outside mold on the

curved opening; and perhaps other features. It seems probable that the idea of the blocking was borrowed from Newport (the Goddard school), but not fully adopted in its completion.

318. The method of terminating the blocking is probably never found in Goddard's work, and the contour of the base is particularly characteristic of Connecticut.

323. A type of foot found on Long Island or in Connecticut, where also, perhaps, the chests of drawers with only three drawers originate. At any rate, they are more common in Connecticut. See for the same clumsy foot 707 and 1715.

This example, like some others known, is a puzzle in that the fine shells of the lower section were not used for the central top drawer. The contrast between the base and the decidedly inferior fan at the top is so marked as to warrant the supposition that the upper section was by some other hand. The shape of the scroll top also is not the best. Compare this example with the beautiful Goddard piece 321 on the opposite page. Here, although the blocking is omitted, the shell is like that below it, and the bonnet with its molds is equal to the style and scale found on the balance of the piece. This comparison is one of the most striking and convincing as to the superiority of the Newport type.

324. One feels at greater liberty to make critical estimates of pieces in a museum. In this instance the combination of styles, whereby the base and the upper section contrast rather markedly, is certainly a defect, though the piece is very noteworthy and elegant. It shows the beginning of those unhappy experiments attendant on the coming in of the Empire influence. There is a shift, not only in the shape of the upper section from that below it, but a shift in the decorative elements exhibiting an effort to be original, which failed. Now known that this is not McIntire's.

. (Below on the left is pie-crust tray identical with a pie-crust table in carving. It is about 18 inches in diameter and of course formed of one piece.

To the right is a scroll found applied on a Chapin high chest of drawers which suggests naïvely the idea of a Philadelphia scroll. However, its very simplicity is alluring. It has hitherto been impossible to trace the designs of the Chapins so as to settle the question whether they did these things for themselves or from the indis-

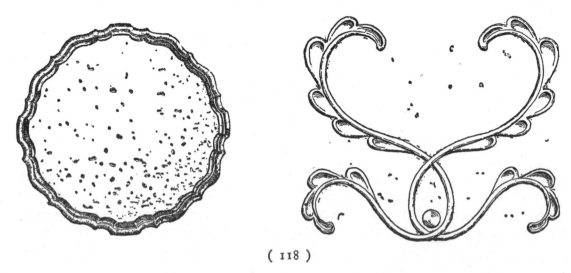

tinct memory of what they had seen. They had, however, the merit of reserve, and never went beyond the limit of good taste.)

337. In all the finer examples William and Mary highboys and lowboys have the thin bent lining about the skirt, projecting here as a cock bead, and hiding the end wood. The absence of this detail throws a piece of this style into the second class.

342. It is now proper to name the location of this piece. It has been removed from the Old Manse at Concord to the better fire protection in the new building of the Concord Antiquarian Society. This piece of furniture was, it is believed, in the Old Manse when the grandfather of Ralph Waldo Emerson looked out of the window at the Battle of the Bridge, as this part of the Concord fight ought to be called.

The construction keeps a continuous vertical line of blocking through both sections. Strict attention to harmony of design, of course, demands a setback on the front equal to that on the sides of the top section. This setback appears on other block-front examples.

360. Philadelphia exhibited in her artisans' work the most elegant form of the high and lowboys. The climax of decoration is found in the carving even of the quarter columns, hitherto merely fluted. Also the finials reach in vase pattern with flowers the highest degree of elaboration.

Owing to the difficulty, without the assistance of a sculptor, of making a satisfactory portrait bust, the practice swung to the safer carving of urns with flames, or to the richer type here.

361. In artistic development there has always come a time when a decorative motive tended toward a too great degree of ornateness. While the base of this piece may be allowed not to transcend the dictates of the highest taste, it is a question whether the bonnet front is not overdone.

364. Three kinds of decoration mark the shapes of the tops of high pieces. There is first the full bonnet form as in 361; second, the top front almost or often identical with 361, but carrying no bonnet; and third, the style in 364 showing a pierced support of the scroll. The omission of the bonnet in 364 would be necessary to show, by abundant light, the details of the piercing. See also 365, where the front is braced by a supporting board run back from the pedestal (now unoccupied) between the goosenecks.

366. This top carries its goosenecks so far apart that the omission or the loss of a large central finial is very marked and greatly mars the beauty of the piece.

369. The top of the cartouche is broken off, and should be restored. The specimen was resigned from the Garvan Collection owing to its near similarity to other examples in the collection. The sharp rise of the gooseneck left a space too scant to place the finials in line above the corner pilasters. Contrast this with the top of 363, which in that particular is superior. The shapes of the goosenecks are better in 363, 365, etc., than in 368, according to most tastes.

The lowboy, precisely matching the highboy, has since been discovered in Pennsylvania and is shown in this volume.

376. Perhaps this is another Chapin piece, but far more probably it is a Connecticut attribution to some other maker. The enrichment of the shell by the application of a second, reversed, secures a fine ornament. A name is on a drawer.

LOWBOYS

415-416. The names of the owners should be reversed.

435. This splendid specimen is in the possession of the Currans, of Philadelphia, though it has been removed from their shop to their private collection. A highboy with the same elements of carving in the top was sold at the highest price reached by the Reifsnyder sale. The base of that highboy was, however, without a suggestion of this style. The claim is made that the top of this piece exists. If so, the reassembled specimen would rank as the best highboy known.

CUPBOARDS

444. Spell Paine, not Payne. The author used a picture of this piece in a court trial, when he was asked if he knew a better American cupboard than 455. This 444 came to knowledge later than 455. It is, we suppose, the handsomest specimen known, of American makers. The question at the trial was on the value of 455 at the time the author bought it. He proved that the price he paid was all it was worth at the time and more than anyone else had offered. The only witness for the plaintiff was an English dealer who had not established a business in America at the time the transaction occurred.

469. Now in the Garvan Collection, Yale University, as is also 472. The author has owned eight court or press cupboards, and has referred collectors to five other available cupboards which they have bought, and has in addition declined to buy any one of six others, his reason being that two were spurious and the others too valuable.

543. Curiously enough this style of cupboard and also 545 have practically disappeared from the market, though they used to be numerous about Philadelphia, at very low prices. The reasons probably are that their small lateral size, also their mahogany (or walnut) material make them highly desirable. They are pure in taste, and have no marks of the country cabinetmaker.

561. The author has never been attracted to pieces of the Hepplewhite and later periods which are marked by huge oval or other shaped inlays. They lack restraint and are in this thought to be somewhat trivial in their ornamentation.

582-86. This room is among the best in America. The house altogether exceeds in decorative merit any other in New England. By a happy chance it was secured for the Historical Society at Marblehead, being knocked down to a friend of the Society for five thousand dollars!

DESKS

629, 630. Compare the bases, particularly the bracket scrolls, with the simpler lines of Goddard pieces in 626-28. The ornate scroll is an almost certain mark of Connecticut as distinct from Rhode Island (Goddard school) origin.

632. The carving on the leg, being confined to the front only, is not complete, or satisfactory, as to style. Indeed, even the rear legs ought to have been carved. It is apparent from the great rarity, possibly uniqueness of this type, that in the heyday of Chippendale taste desk styles kept to the cabinet form with drawers nearly to the floor. Yet 632 is a very beautiful and now much sought type.

651. One wonders whether the open shelves on the top were a part of the original.

They are certainly very convenient, and, the piece being six feet in length, they do not intrude.

One questions the taste of the numerous small drawers, particularly on the ends, where of course if drawers existed, they would collide with the side drawers. This piece has been extensively copied in all sizes, and usually in a cheap construction.

700. This exquisite piece, perhaps unique, is of such great beauty and distinction that it deserved fuller treatment, but it did not come to light in time to dwell upon it. The beautiful shaping of the cabinet and its numerous receptacles is noteworthy, but the rare shape of the whole structure is startlingly attractive. Mr. Brinton has called it a lowboy secretary, and we have no quarrel with him on the name. Compare with 632. This piece has more drawers in the base, hence the name. Yet perhaps high-leg secretary might answer.

701. See also 317. These pieces, both, of course, by Goddard, are fitted with the rare corner boxes, but this specimen has also quarter columns above. It is generally admitted to be the supreme specimen, not only of Goddard's work, but of American taste, and in the judgment of the writer it is not equaled in beauty or merit by any English example. Of course, they had no block-and-shell pieces anyway.

A curious feature of this piece is its severely plain cabinet. It would almost seem that the cabinet was made last, and marked a halt called by the customer on expense. But as it was made for Amos Brown, we must seek, and so far in vain, for another explanation. The insertion of a rest for the falling lid was an ingenious but not commendable device. The piece is formed as if it were part of the drawer front, and by the overlap it was necessary to make so small a section that it was broken off by use.

The author copied this base from data before seeing the piece. He did not copy the interior.

702. The odd and graceless lines decorating the base mold arise partly from the crude blocking out of the negative. The author does not know whether glass was originally in the doors. It is usual to assign this piece and the three following to the North Shore, but we cannot be certain.

708. Five similar pieces are known to the writer, and probably others exist of John Goddard workmanship.

717. The broken top or cartouche in 369 is supposedly properly finished here.

725. Of course the feet are partly lost. The top is later in style than the base, though both may have been together.

726. Here we reach a distinctly Hepplewhite period throughout. It is a decided declension from the Chippendale type, but the effect is graceful. The feet are an unfortunate style, because frail and protruding, but are very commonly found broken.

The style of sustaining the fall front by brass segments is known on earlier pieces. It was a very good change, worthy of general adoption. A single failure to remember to pull out the wooden supports of the earlier style could ruin the front — and usually did.

727. Since with rare exceptions the old dressers were cut down, we suspect that a great many better pieces have shared the same fate. One Philadelphia highboy in particular had the beautifully scrolled top completely destroyed to accommodate it to a low ceiling. The cresting of No. 727 is so unsatisfactory that one wonders

whether it is not an accommodation or an imperfect restoration in its cresting. At any rate, the scroll top is not equal to the quiet dignity of the style below it.

SIDEBOARDS

753. The detail whereby the legs are set at such an angle that they show three sides for decoration adds elegance and daintiness.

758. The handles are hardly proper for this period. A later oval plate handle should have been used in restoration.

771. Note that the legs are rounded in at the top very like a Chippendale chair leg.

777. A considerable number of sideboards, often called hunters' side tables, like this example, are found in the South, particularly in North Carolina. They are frequently in pine throughout, including the legs.

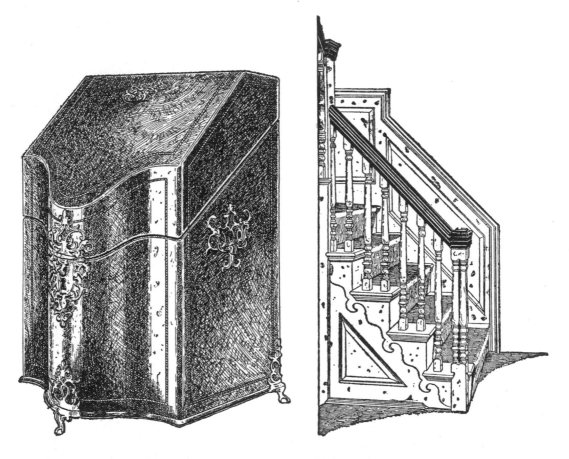

The knife box here shown differs a little from most in that all the trimmings are in sterling silver. The handles, the escutcheon and even the feet, which last are usually delicate ogee brackets of wood. The rich inlay and fine serpentine front of this specimen place it in the highest class of the bevel top boxes. The stair, in front of the great chimney, dates about 1735.

798. Pieces of this sort and the one following were sometimes used in the dining room, the tops being filled with china. Such pieces might supplement or take the place of a sideboard.

Cabriole legs, either disc foot or ball and claw, for china cupboards are found in England. The writer has not come upon an American example, but such probably exist, or did.

TABLES

800–02. There is known to the author only one other long Pilgrim period trestle, that being in the Bolles Collection, Metropolitan Museum. One or two short examples, like 805, have recently been found. The collector should be very careful not to confuse the Shaker type of the early nineteenth century with a true Middle Age trestle and board table.

814. An important discovery has recently been made concerning this table. It has always been entered, in various volumes on furniture, as a drawing table. The author and two well-known connoisseurs recently determined on a more thorough investigation, by which it appeared that the table was always substantially as it is. Some former owner cut slots in the end frames for the insertion of tongued leaves, which, however, had no relation to the original table. The word "drawing" in the description should therefore be withdrawn.

830. A table with a lighter post and thin top is found in large numbers in Connecticut and to some extent elsewhere. It served as a small dining or a kitchen table and dated probably from about 1750 to 1800. It is distinguished from the Pennsylvania table by being lighter and plainer, and from the tavern table by its greater length. The frame was plain, never scalloped or contoured. The turnings were often similar to 845, but the frame was not so deep, and the style sometimes had a middle stretcher.

859. The turning is the same as those so well known in fine gate-leg tables.

893. In some quarters the butterfly table is now called a rudder table, of course from the shape of the leaf bracket. No tables have been more extensively imitated, in old woods, and sold as originals. Their detection sometimes requires more knowledge than a collector possesses.

913. A butterfly table with two brackets on each side has been found.

948. Tables with split gates, of hard pine, come from Spain. See also 953 and 965.

1010. Tables with these features were very probably made in America, but the presumption is always in favor of an English origin.

1108. As to size the text gives a partially wrong impression. Tables to be in the first class as pie crusts should not be less than thirty-three inches in top diameter, but by as much as they exceed that size they increase in importance. One forty inches across recently came on the market.

Smaller pie crusts are very beautiful, but have nothing like the value of the large size.

1542. The statement that Fuller was not married when he came to America has been denied. It is a point easier of determination than most moot points. The cradle, however, is no doubt American.

1775. We express no opinion as to the origin of this chair.

1776. We express no opinion on the origin or merit of this chair.

1787. This chair was in the Martin House, Swansea, Mass., in a collection.

1799. The only missing parts in this chair are the balls on the front posts. The most massive of Brewsters and far better than that at Pilgrim Hall, Plymouth, which gave the name to this class. That chair is much lighter. It has been cut off and various parts are missing. It has been copied with all its defects and offered as an original. A number of these spurious chairs have been found.

1810. With reference to the original types of Carver and Brewster chairs, no doubt there were English examples, now almost unknown, but in the foreign chair the wood is oak. Most Carvers and Brewsters, American, are maple, and occasionally ash, probably the original American wood, very soon abandoned.

1824. The slat-back Pilgrim chairs are comfortable, and no others of the early period are comfortable until we reach the deeply shaped Windsors.

1842. In naming this a courting chair one should not be beguiled into supposing the

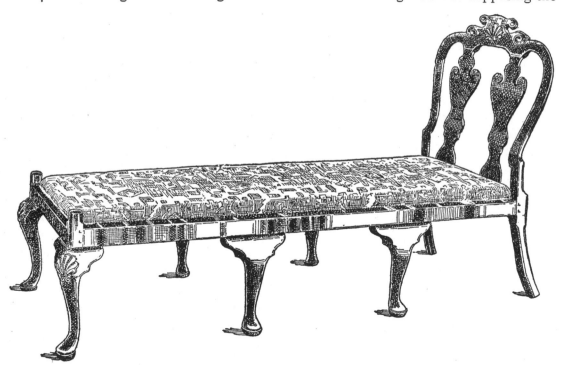

The day bed above in the Queen Anne pattern has the unusual feature of two splats in the head. The grace of the piece is thus enhanced. The width of the head would have required a clumsily wide single splat.

The knee is enriched with a shell, and the curious projection of the corner of the frame at the foot is, of course, to keep the cushion in place, but to our thought it does not increase the grace, but probably does increase the value of the piece. It appeared in *Antiques*. Another example which is probably as good belongs to the Currans of Philadelphia.

type is generally so called or so used. We cannot, of course, state that other types were not so used.

1887. The heaviest and probably earliest and best type of mushroom chair. The mushroom must always be a part of the post, and never doweled on.

1888, 1889. It is pretty well understood now that these chairs are a French type modified in Canada.

1893. In the restoration the feet should have been bulbous, larger than the turning above. So also 1898.

1910. A number of these chairs, mostly without arms, have come to light.

1984. The most desirable type of cane chair has the front posts as here set on a diagonal with the seat. Compare the carving running all about the back panel with the plainer uncarved sides of the panel on the next chair. Also the element above the seat on the front post is plain turned in 1985 instead of in the form of a full Flemish scroll as here. Compare the out-pointing angle of the leg with 2032.

2088. The date is perhaps better stated as Eighteenth Century.

2091. This chair may be French in inspiration or origin.

2103 and 2104. Some little loss is observable in the length of the feet. See the next page.

2111. The style of the back does not argue against a Connecticut origin.

2132. Upholstered backs in the early Georgian style, as here, are exceedingly rare. They are also very rare in the Chippendale time. If found upholstered, backs as a rule occur on sofas rather than chairs.

2135. In terming this leg a Queen Anne type we are using a loose phrase. The Queen Anne style is often referred to all early cabriole furniture up to the Chippendale epoch. The fact is that the type persisted through the early Georgian time. It would be more accurate to use the early Georgian designation, which, however, is not popularly known. The cabriole leg was not only not designed by Chippendale, but was abandoned by him early in his career. In America the cabriole leg with claw foot, associated with a Chippendale back, seems to have persisted in popularity.

2152. This chair has a splat quite the same as one used in Chippendale chairs; and also the same leg. The differentiation between the styles is the rounded seat and the rounded top rail.

2216. The handsomest Chippendale chairs, marking the highest and richest development aside from the Randolph "Sample chairs" are 2216, 2220. This is merely an expression of an opinion. In 2220 the carving on the corner of the seat rail lifts the chair into a higher class than 2216.

2226. Remarkable for the absence of the usual bracket scroll on the leg. The inner line of leg is in one unbroken curve to the rail. A very few other examples are known.

2227. A chair around which sharp disputes have raged. Perhaps the solution is that one or more of the known examples are original, and one or more are copies. The best-known authority considers the applied ornament at center of seat rail a later addition.

2238–39. The shape of the arm of a Chippendale chair is often a puzzle. There is a wide variation. The upholstered chair 2241 is conventional. But in the open-back armchair the shape here which approaches the early Georgian is no doubt earlier and better than that on 2243, which verges toward the Hepplewhite. Many fine models of side chairs in Chippendale style have no known existing corresponding armchair, so that copyists are in danger of error and often produce an incongruous arm.

2259. This chair belongs in the country Chippendale class, which copied the Chippendale ladder back, but no other feature suggesting Chippendale.

2363. The finest-known type of Sheraton upholstered-back chair. The late Louis Myers had a chair, since sold, which he mentioned as the best known. He had not seen this beautiful example. There is a stop flute on the handsome front post, and the scroll is carved. Unfortunately an inset oblong veneer in the square of the post does not show. It is a peculiarity of this type that while it looks light, the concealed back and back rail are very heavy, and the chair is substantial.

A large box as elaborate as the one above and on casters of course indicates it was to be pushed about on the floor very much as the wine wagon was used. One would surmise that this was a rich gift piece or the effort of some hostess to produce on her floor something so striking and rich as to overcome all rivalry. The container is decidedly secondary to the standard on which it rests. The attachment of the foot is not so attractive perhaps as it might be. The Metropolitan Museum lists this English article as a traveling knife box.

THE ART OF COLLECTING

A collector is not a queer animal to be stared at with wonder or ridicule. Almost everybody collects something, however worthless.

What normal and bright boy fails to have a pocket full of his precious things? It is the person who does not collect that is abnormal and dull. The spirit of the collector consists in that divine curiosity which desires to observe and compare and on occasion to cherish whatever comes to the attention of human intelligence.

Thus dictionary makers are word collectors and so are all writers, assembling as they do words with delicate shades of meaning and sometimes to stump their readers with a rare but good word.

From marbles to palaces, collection goes on and always has and always will because it is a necessity to every thoughtful mind. What gardener fails to wish to assemble the different varieties of some favorite flower? Stamps, drawings, books, autographs — there is no end to the objects that have an inevitable appeal.

A good collector possesses a rare degree of intelligence. The brain of an ordinary individual is developed and enriched by collecting. Every man ought to set it before himself as an aim to know at least some one thing in the world better than any other man. This ambition is not unattainable because there are so many objects on which one may set his mind at work. The sum total of the world's learning is vastly increased and becomes in time an imposing and almost unbelievable mass of knowledge through the division of labor by which an individual gives attention to something of which other individuals know little. If we want a watch repaired or a button sewed on or an appendix cut off, we can easily find an expert in these or ten thousand other specialties. The libraries and the museums can gather their stores of knowledge only because there are collectors, of information or of things.

In these days you shall go to an astronomer and he will tell you what elements are in a star so distant that he must use his telescope to find it. Our astonishing stores of information gathered within a generation are all the results of the spirit of the collector. The enrichment of life and the enjoyment of the world are inherent in the collector's occupation.

Wherever a century has been backward or a neighborhood or a man, it is because men have confined themselves to what they know, considering it a sufficient body of information. One may say that the chief characteristic of the rustic is to think slightingly of the knowledge that is not his own. This arises from the false assumption that unusual knowledge is not useful.

It would not be difficult to show that very few facts have been collected and cataloged that were not found sooner or later to fit into the great scheme of life, and some of them least valued have finally been found essential to the victory over disease or the progress of the race in some important particular. The person who is not a collector of some kind is a moron. It is true that collectors are often selfish. In fact, some of them are monumentally selfish, but we notice that selfishness only when the importance of the work that such men are doing at last dawns on us. Selfishness in minor matters is not so observable.

It is said that so many lines of human thought and endeavor have been followed that there is nothing new under the sun. The classic author of that observation was sour. He was intelligent enough to know better. It is a curious paradox that the longer the world stands the more rapidly new knowledge or new things come to light. More information perhaps has been dug out in the past hundred years than in all previous time. At least, if we say two hundred years, we think a good argument could be made for the claim. Yet the most learned man in the world will tell us that we are in the elementary stage of learning about things. He would look with astonishment if we asked him whether his special knowledge was not nearly complete. They tell us of an astronomer, one of the greatest, who at middle age met socially a rich young woman of prominent family and just out of school. She said to the gentleman, "What do you do, sir?" He replied, "I am a student." "What do you study?" "I am a student of astronomy." "Astronomy! Why, I finished that last year!"

The person who knows all about a thing comes near to being a monumental idiot. If he makes such a statement about his knowledge he clearly indicates that he has not scratched the surface of his subject. Had he done so he would have revealed a mine of knowledge underneath.

In the simple subject of interior decoration one is led along until he finds there is not such a thing as "knowing all about it." There is no beginning of the subject that we can reach, and happily there is no ending. An initial inference is that we must have something to decorate. That means architecture. That means a setting. That means the world. In a thing as apparently simple as a chair or a desk, how many designs are there, how many kinds of wood, how many methods of construction, and of finish, how many uses to which the article may be put? How many ramifications in history, how many stimulations in art, what a body of sentiment, what a range of uses is involved!

Anything is good which stimulates us to learn, because suddenly we have thus found the joy of life. Even a novice soon finds that his department in collecting ties him up with all history. I have in mind a poor immigrant who was not allowed under Russian tyranny to learn to read or even to sign his name. Through the handling and appreciation of quaint and beautiful things he came to have a broad knowledge of men and their arts. He was more cultivated than many of his customers who had had every advantage. If we wish to enrich the life of a young person, we have only to drop in his mind one stimulating thought. It is a germ which, taken up and developed, becomes like a great oak burrowing in the ground and aspiring to the sky.

To know any one thing well is to escape an inferiority complex. How often do we see learned and brilliant men asking some humble artisan about an article or a process! The inquirer and the listener respect each other, and so a meeting of minds occurs.

Aside from purely religious inspirations nothing enhances the delight in living like intimate knowledge of some art or science. Only the learned ever know enough to be truly humble, and only the learned have an inexhaustible store of meditative joys, of designs that reach out eager for embodiment, of ideas struggling to the birth. Only ignorant people are bored with life. The more we study, the more zest there is in living. Place a person before a great painting or any work of taste and skill and the reaction of that person will reveal the extent of his development. A neglected truism.

Collecting is a joy because it is a challenge to observe nicety of line, of color, of adaptation. Without the past, no future. Without the past, no foundation. Without the past, a child would come into a very small fraction of the cultivation which he is so readily able to gain.

Of course, not every collector is a good one. Indolence or blindness arrest a development, otherwise every collector might become like Adam in his garden giving names to all things and all aspects of life. A collector is not respectable unless he goes on. If he stands still he becomes a fossil. Everyone can teach him, and every item of knowledge can be made to fit into its proper segment. We cannot help collecting, and we cannot avoid enjoying it, and we cannot escape a mental development by it. To observe is to bind ourselves to civilization.

What is a beginner to do in order to enrich home life which still must be the center of a lasting order? The first thing is to specialize rather narrowly. A broad culture is of course the only foundation for a successful specialist. We are presuming that the broad culture has been acquired. Presumptions cost nothing. Let us suppose then that a collector centers his attention upon the fireplace. Who first built a fire? We cannot learn. We can, however, trace the matter back in one of the most fascinating trails of investigation, and we can see the cartoons on the walls of historic buildings of the first fire maker. We can consider the effect upon society of a hearth. We can infer the progress involved in cooking food rather than taking it raw, and in melting down what in its original state was useless. We can imagine the shapes of the fireplace from its crudest beginning until it became the focus of the Romans and the glory of modern architecture. We can find the beginning of folklore and of the epic at the evening fireside. We can trace ghost stories from the shadows on the whitened wall. We can be present at courtship, at birth, at sage consultations, and at death by the fire. We can find in the fireplace the first means through the escaping smoke of preserving provisions, and so lifting the level of life from the winter hunger of the improvident savage. We can and must take up one by one all those vessels and implements which the fireside caused to develop until the art of the smith and the founder and the carver made society rich and complex. We can at last arrive at the conclusion that the germ of household joys, of art, science, literature and religion started at the fireplace, extending to the fireroom and then to all those stimulating and delightful settings which raised life to its present highest form.

One person of my acquaintance has collected some ten thousand articles of household iron, and has made it the nucleus of a museum which he will leave to his city. There is nothing else just like it and probably no other collection is so steeped in sentiment and suggestion. In a room set forth with such articles what a fine background is supplied for any rational life!

Out of the fireplace came such phrases as "between two fires." The hanging of the crane, the trammel, the great kettle; the rolling in of the huge back log, the mysterious wraith-like emanations from the embers that glow and change and disappear, the sense of plenty, even of opulence, of comfort and cheer, and the victory over the harshness of nature — all these are here and how many thousand more suggestions that grow and spread until life is sweetened and lifted and deepened.

In order to get into the spirit of the thing we shall be obliged to read Whittier's "Snowbound." Then we must follow through literature back to old Prometheus who stole the fire from the gods and was therefore the first civilizer. We must learn something of the manner of working iron and copper. We must note that the handsomest and best stone for a fireplace is the gneiss which is beautiful with its mica bits and which splits smoothly without drilling. We shall investigate and learn that bog oak will never take fire if used for the chimney tree. We may need to acquire knowledge of tiling and the old square shape which was never laid with spaces between.

We must then begin to furnish our fireplace, and if we decide on a lug pole instead of a crane, we shall want long trammel poles and at least four kinds of trammels and as many varieties and lengths of pot hooks. A hanging kettle and a baled flapjack cooker, a swivel teakettle, and a sauce kettle, and probably a great brass kettle will be wanted. Then there is the pair of andirons with hooks for spit rod, and a roasting jack to turn it. We want a long-handled kettle, some cast-iron skillets, a Dutch oven with a helmeted cover to pile the coals on top, a whirling broiler, and a revolving toaster. If we can find them we should get a number of old skewers and a skewer hanger, a large variety of forks, some with heart decoration, of skimmers, flapjack turners, great iron spoons. We need to hang them along the chimney tree. A large pair of tongs and a long iron slice are placed against the jamb hooks. Pipe tongs and a sugar cutter are convenient. A lead melting spoon and a bullet mold will go well with the long musket and the carved powder horn hung high over all. Perhaps we can find that rare thing a pie-plate handler, and certainly we want a fire carrier. A standing spit for a chicken and a tin nursing bottle might be handy. Some Betty lamps and a little charcoal gridiron will help in the equipment. A gophering iron will be required in a good house and a loggerhead, if we are to have burnt sack. Possibly we can find a holder for dipping a rush in the fat.

A heart-shaped waffle iron will add much. A couple of trivets are indispensable, and some low fire dogs would be handy. At any rate, we have now made a beginning and from time to time may add a quaint, twisted fork or the easily found foot warmers.

A few wooden scoops and spoons hung in one corner will please the housewife. Our oven with its arched door is in the rear and requires a sheet iron cover with a handle. There will be various other utensils which are more properly consigned to the shed.

A great fireplace like this, seven to twelve feet in width, and shoulder high, is something for a child to remember always, as it will help to form character and is worth fighting for. By the time the novice collector has completed his setting he will have established a continuity with a thousand generations of his ancestors. The sacredness of fire will mean something to him and he will be fascinated by the story in Barton's Lincoln of how fire had been preserved from the time that it was carried from Virginia in a kettle on the axle, in numerous migrations enkindling new material until it reached Illinois. Every night during migration the fire kettle was taken off and helped to prepare the evening meal until it kindled a blaze in the green logs on the westernmost hearth stone.

The collector will not be satisfied with a modern so-called Cape Cod firelighter which of course could not exist until the kerosene era. He will do his searching at the unfashionable shops and in the remote districts, always giving a little more than is asked by the people who do not know how to value their possessions and declining to buy at all as a rule where they have an exaggerated idea of the worth of common things.

The writer has often made long country journeys, swapping books for old iron, always to the mutual satisfaction of the buyer and seller. His best recent find was a pair of andirons, yoked together by an arched member. The andirons required frequent removal to clear the hearth, and to lift them as one piece (page 222) was a New Hampshire idea. It has been possible without systematic search to find several hundred distinct sorts of articles each in from two to a score of varieties.

When the fireplace garnishing is complete one may then turn to restoring the old latches, hinges, and fixed hardware of an old house, which has always in part at least been replaced by later and poorer examples. By the time this pleasing occupation is finished the collector will have started new lines of thought that will lead him on for years.

As a little touch gives atmosphere, attention to a thing so small as a wall hook is worth while. They were found as turned pegs or sometimes whittled with a hooked end. As articles of wood could be made by the fireside in the long winter evenings, many things from a great bowl to a spoon were whittled or burned out, the only cost being a congenial labor, while the little daughter of the family read aloud a tale of the olden time. The spiles for the sugar sap could be made at such times, the spinning wheel could be mended, and the flax breaker put in order. I had an uncle who made his own apple parer which I have often used. The paring knife was held in the hand and carried across the apple while the fork was revolved by a crank. A bushel an hour was an easy stunt. Of course in the evening the bootjack, the sacred cod style being preferred, was also taken down from the side of the fireplace so that the boots could be greased with mutton tallow heated in a porringer and held over the blaze to dry in.

Thoreau swore by the old fireside whereas moderners swear at it. His way was better.

I have outlined the beginning of a collector's experience but one could begin with various other lines of collecting. They all lead to the same place in the end — a proper appreciation of the handiwork of other generations, a love of honesty, the quest for beauty and solidity. All these fine things blended by historic imagination and illustrated by literature and shared with one's friends broaden life and make it pregnant with meaning so that one is able in the present to summon the past and the future and so live in the eternity of today. By as much as we have the spirit of the ages the moments mean more to us, and we span the gap between the first fire maker and the last home maker.

One may start to collect American pewter or silver or glass or china, or maple or mahogany furniture. With leisure and means all these, of course, gathered at the same time eventuate in an atmosphere which gives mellowness and dignity to life.

Those who do not collect say that collectors are men of one idea and that they are sharp and shrewd. Can you name me any profession or business which is free from being warped into dishonesty and greed? The world being what it is, it is necessary for every buyer to keep his head and pay a just price and no more. I have known some very mean-minded collectors, and I have also known some who were the salt of the earth, the joy of their friends and the comfort of the poor. There is particularly one fallacy which ought to be nailed. It is often assumed, by what right I know not, that the gathering of a collection is of necessity taking means that could otherwise be given to the poor. Just now I know many scores of people to whom I could do no greater kindness than to relieve them of some heirloom for its equivalent in cash that they might ease the pinch of circumstance. Not a few are living today in some degree of comfort because those who could do so have exchanged coin of the realm for some old relic. It certainly seems to me that it is better for the self-respect of the seller to part with something not too highly valued than it is to be the recipient of a dole. It is forgotten that the seller wishes to sell and is happy that he has something which can be turned into a means of living. My experience is that if anyone is bitten it is more likely to be the buyer than the seller. In numerous instances I have known of owners being offered from three to ten times what an article was worth in the market and declining to sell. The prospective buyer was in love with a particular specimen and willing to pay by the nose for it. For some time now one's heart has ached for the stream of beseeching owners who wish to sell at any price, though the would-be buyer has nothing available to spend.

Again, since most worthy articles gravitate toward museums, they are far better so placed than in the hands of the improvident or of persons who cannot provide a safeguard for their goods. In a museum an article is always open for the inspection of the former owner as well as for the general public. The writer was obliged to dispose of his seventeenth-century collection and could have done so to a private individual, but declined to let it go except into fireproof quarters, and into the hands of an institution with a perpetual charter and a mind to preserve and display the articles. At that museum I am welcome to enjoy the collection still going under my name and that of the donor. He enjoys it, and I still enjoy it. The museum and the public enjoy it. We are all happy and are all wise in what we have done. Ten thousand persons see the objects of my love where only one could have seen it in my home, and I certainly cannot enjoy anything alone. This is no merit, but a part of human vanity and pride to display what one has gathered — a spirit which is now overlooked by the public since the articles are in the ownership of the museum.

It is true that where private collectors are able to place their property in a safe location and where, as in England, they occasionally open their doors to the public there are some advantages. But sad to say probably nineteen-twentieths of the good old belongings of our ancestors have been burned up or destroyed. One of our friends has incorporated his own private collection. That is well. It insures it against dispersion and continues it as a family possession. One would say, however, that it is almost an obligation to sell good old things unless one can care for them properly. I have in mind an almost priceless article in a cheap frame house. It is not only subject to fire, but to theft. The owners exercise their legal right to hold it, even though they have been offered at least twice what a dealer would ask for it. Should we not at least safeguard an article hoary with age, beautiful in design, rarely found?

A collector therefore may be any sort of person according to his motives in collecting. A despicable creature, though a man of means, said to me one day, "I want to pick up a rare old banjo clock back in the country, from somebody who has no idea of its value." I did not tell him to go anywhere, but it was unnecessary. He is on the way. How different the spirit of the Hartford gentleman who paid a vast sum to a lady who had sold him an article containing a bunch of papers wherein was a Button Guinnett signature. She knew nothing of that until he came back to her with many thousands of dollars. Such men are the salt who preserve society from decay. While not all are as fortunate as this noble man, many have done what they could.

The collector must in some degree defend himself or he will go to the wall in pocket and in reputation. I was blazened abroad in black headlines in a suit for fraud, but was able to prove that the seller had been overpaid by the standards of the time. It is a cowardly thing to make an unproved charge public where the honor of a decent citizen is involved. Though this happens every day, there is no remedy, since a clean bill from a judge will be noticed by only a small fraction of those who saw the charge.

A collector must needs deal with all sorts of people else he must go out of the world. It is pitiful when those who love their ancestors and their ancestors' belongings must needs part with them, but it is better that the articles should go into the hands of those with proper appreciation of the value than to a speculator. I remember a good woman who wept when a clock went out of her house, but she had deliberately made up her mind that it was better to part with an article than to have her two children quarrel over it. She divided between them the proceeds. She was happier in selling than in keeping. When we say that a person is compelled to sell, that is equivalent to saying that the money means more to him than the goods. Haggling has a bad connotation, but what sensible man would pay more than he believes an article is worth, unless as is often the case he has the buyer's fever and is bound to become an owner? Every collector knows that he does at times pay more than he thinks is proper. That is only saying that he forsakes reason for sentiment, and unless we at times did such things, we should be rather inhuman.

METHOD IN COLLECTING

My friends have done me the honor of saying that I am a successful collector. If so, it may be worth while to outline my method for the benefit of anyone who cares to read it.

1. Depend in the last analysis on your own knowledge of the subject, and buy without reference to fads. If a thing appeals to you, that fact is often enough because you are the person who is to enjoy it.

2. Buy on your first inspection. A good thing may not long lie about. If you wait too long, you will only be buying what everyone else has rejected. That is what the

dealer calls a sticker. I should say that ninety per cent of the most desirable things are taken within a week of the time they get into the hands of a dealer.

3. Pay cash on the spot for what you buy because thus you will be a favored patron.

4. Never come back with a complaint or ask to have an article placed in your house to see how it will look. The dealer will be influenced by knowing that he is dealing with a man who will never come back with a story of a misunderstanding.

5. Pay the price, for if you negotiate too long you will lose the article. Get it or leave it the day you look at it. If it is good, a round sum is better expended on it than a less sum for an article slightly inferior.

6. Have the article taken away while you are at the shop and moved by your own agent or yourself. There can never be any doubt in such a case about substitution.

7. Investigate at once when you learn of an article. Let no grass grow under your feet. Notify your correspondents that you wish the first information.

8. Pay for goods, not for labels or stories.

9. Be influenced by the condition of an article so completely that you are willing to reject it if vital parts are missing.

10. Become known as a good buyer, which means that if an article is worth while, you are in the market for it. Thus you will learn of the best there is going.

11. Buy with reference to complementary articles to complete the furnishing of a room. Some of the greatest collections, in fact all of them, seem to have been made without reference to this important matter. One man spent about a million and had very few good chairs. Any article you purchase has much more value if you place it with another article with which it naturally goes. There is just now a highboy in the hands of one person and a lowboy in the hands of another. These are complementary pieces and will each be worth considerably more if they can be brought together.

12. Buy in the rough, that is, before articles have been repaired or restored. Thus you may buy for a lower price and will be more certain what you are buying.

13. Depend for the most part on finding your articles in the hands of dealers. Their charges are less than a private owner will ask. Furthermore, life is not long enough to visit private dwellings unless you are previously notified by the owners in such dwellings that they have what you desire. The search for antiques has been too thorough and too long continued to give much satisfaction to a beginner in following over gleaned ground. There are not in the seas as good fish as have been caught, or if there is an occasional fine fish, the hope of hooking it is too remote.

14. There is not much luck in collecting. It is a matter of steady purpose and system.

15. One's knowledge of values and varieties grows very rapidly by systematically seeing a great many old pieces for sale. Limited experience leaves one in the dark regarding the merits of an object and the present worth of it. If one is seriously collecting, he should go far and see much. This process does not require very much time because after a little most objects will be familiar, and it is only here and there in a shop that something will be found that differs from what the collector knows already.

16. If you find you have made a mistake by overpaying, be philosophical and forget it. If an article which you have bought proves to be spurious, break it up and be rid

of it at once without passing it along to make trouble for others. Of course it is well to say to a dealer that he has sold you such and such an article, but never ask for money back. Just tell him that he is "in bad" on your books and will ultimately lose.

17. Do not have your repairs made by the person from whom you buy. Employ an independent repairer who is as near you as possible and whose work you can watch. Substitutions are not rare.

18. Experience indicates that it is useless to advertise for a particular article. If you so advertise you will get a multitude of letters about other articles. I have never yet been able to find a piece by advertising for it, strange as that may seem.

19. Get the article you are considering into a brilliant daylight. Dark holes are no places to buy furniture. It is well enough to take for granted that the brasses are new unless indubitable evidence to the contrary is forthcoming in the brasses themselves. Dealers often apply new brasses or knobs even when they are afraid to go any farther.

20. Remember that plants are now common of foreign furniture in remote inland towns as well as in large cities.

THE DECORATING PROFESSION

Practically this profession amounts in most cases to buying for a client. That is to say the decorator visits the shops and advises the buyer what to obtain. If the shop will not give a good commission, its furniture will not be recommended. As a consequence any article on which a price has been set that is no more than it is worth is not recommended. The legitimacy of this practice is not challenged, but the results are deplorable. Applying our attention for the moment to new articles, either alleged copies or alleged new designs, it is the practice of one of the largest department stores to give the decorator a commission of twenty-five per cent. In this case the buyer pays no more than would be paid by dealing without the intervention of the decorator and has the advantage real or imaginary of expert advice. But if, as often happens, these special reproductions are in the hands of someone who does not set a price high enough to permit a good commission, the buyer is a sufferer because his attention is not called to such goods, and in that case he is worse off with a decorator than without.

Broadly speaking, commercial articles are never correct in line or construction and should be wholly ignored by decorators and by their clients. There is a small class of decorators who have their own stock in trade, and who are of all grades of competence and character, just like other people in fact. As a rule furniture is secondary with them and rugs, draperies and wall paper are primary. There is no competent authority to pass on the competence of the decorator as, however, is the practice in the learned profession. Anybody can pose as a decorator without a license or an examination. The buyer must guess since he can hardly judge as to the ability of the person into whose hands he falls. In practice this business is nearly all done on the basis of friendship. A buyer knows some decorator and is perhaps intimate with her, for she is recruited from out the ranks of some social set. Of course business in general, even bond selling, is done in the same way, which may account for the present depression.

It is a rule, perhaps without exception, that the larger the commission the more inferior are the goods dealt in. Upholstery particularly is a snare. The only way to be certain what goes into it is by seeing the goods as the work is done. One may buy an entire wing chair at the large shops, the upholstery of which under the surface costs less than a single pound of high-class hair. The labor and materials exclusive of the final cover on a good wing chair cannot possibly be furnished except by a sum between forty and fifty dollars. As the entire chairs are offered for twenty odd dollars the inference is plain.

An article like the wing chair ought to be seen in the frame. It should be ironed like a ship. Any worthy frame requires more labor than a finished poor article is sold for. The danger of pressing for lower prices is responsible for continuous degradation of quality.

If the decorator does not understand cabinetmaking, how will she know whether a mortise or a dowel is used in the frame?

In the article of beds a modern attachment of the posts to the rails is cheap in all senses but saves a few dollars. In secretaries a delusion is successful from the matter of size. A miniature secretary can of course be sold for a small sum. Nearly all the old examples were of a stately size, and a generous width is still found convenient for the user.

Style is not always expensive but in cases where it is expensive it must go. Notice the jig-saw scrolls on the tops of commercial hall clocks. They resemble the false fronts of a prairie city saloon. The makers could use a straight top, but they always prefer the shoddy imitation of a scroll.

Names play a large role in furniture sales. A designer as he calls himself selects a name to go with his design. One Windsor chair maker named a specimen of his product after Priscilla. No law was broken, but the unthinking might not know that the first Windsor chair dates about a hundred and twenty years after Priscilla was born. Something similar may be said of a Winthrop desk, a name given to every conceivable form. So also somebody took the works out of a melodeon, a Victorian article, and arranged it for a desk. He called it a spinet desk, ignoring the fact that spinets were about a hundred and sixty years before the time of his melodeon. Is there any possible reason for calling a melodeon a spinet? Why should anyone imagine that such an article is either an antique or the copy of one? There is nothing whatever in style, age or design to recommend such a mongrel article. One is reminded of the mother of Carlyle who defined her infant much as the baby Lincoln was defined as "lang, and spraggly, and ill put together."

The main line of defense against bad taste is to follow some manual showing furniture of the eighteenth century. Anything in that period was in good taste, and anything offered that resembles it closely is safe so far as the outline is concerned, whatever may be said of the putting together. Nor is there any defense for the unfortunate buyer who seeks to know whether the article in question is really mahogany. He may test indeed some inside portion like the upper frame of the table leg, and if he finds the wood is soft, he will know it is bad. It is probably baywood or gum wood.

One serious difficulty of a decorator is that the client has a desire as a rule for the latest period of antique design, and when shown eighteenth-century or late seventeenth-century patterns greets them with a shake of the head. In other words, the buyer himself does not encourage the best patterns.

Passing now to the matter of buying antiques such articles are ordinarily sold directly with small commissions or with none. Consequently most buyers go alone when they seek antiques, and however much they might need advice they will find it very difficult to get any that is valuable, but even so if they are continually looking and continually comparing with good manuals on the subject they may avoid wrong forms. As to avoiding spurious articles that is as may be. It is, however, to be admitted that many dealers in antiques reproduce excellent copies which they sell at moderate figures since the work is done at odd times when nothing else presses. If a buyer today is thinking more of style than of age he will find in many an antique dealer's shop far more reliable designs than in the great shops, but the buyer must learn by experience which he is often willing to pay handsomely for, whether his purchases are old or new. There is no golden rule for ascertaining this fact. Some persons early acquire a flair for the subject and some never will. A great majority are hoaxed occasionally.

Since the great demand of the flush times is over it appears that there is still a quantity of good articles on the market. This is partly owing to the forced sales of which there have been so many of late, and of which the dealers have taken advantage. We have called attention to the repeated sales of the same article owing to the death or insolvency or removal of the private owner, or the passing of the article from one dealer to another. The English sources of near antiques are practically inexhaustible, and there is no reason to suppose that they will not continue to be availed of in America partly by Americans buying abroad and partly by the importations of dealers.

We cannot ignore the main point that the decorator is in business for a living. It would be too much to ask that a person highly cultivated in the matter of styles and construction should take up decorating and follow it purely for the best interests of the public. Persons in business are sometimes altruists, but they do not enter business originally for that reason. Altruists do not know how to make money, and if they had much money, they would not go into business. Practically nineteen-twentieths of the active dealers must borrow money or do a small business, and sometimes both. Competition is certainly sharp in this vocation as in any other. It seems to be only the twentieth man who makes good. The dealers are not to be envied. The best of them have an uphill fight, and the others one finds it difficult to feel sorry about. For a generation not one article in a hundred has been sold for more than its worth estimated in a period of enough years to bridge depressions. A larger proportion of antique articles has been sold under price rather than over price. The consumer has the best end of the bargain, especially if his enjoyment and use of his purchases is taken into account. His dwelling is or may be dignified, beautiful, distinguished and filled with the sentiment of the early day. A generation hence every man will be considered fortunate who possesses a fair number of specimens that represent the days of long ago. In this connection I have often wondered why more owners do not have pictured and cataloged for a private illustrated manuscript volume their old possessions. Such a book would be a joy to themselves and a source of rich information for the generations to come. At the same time such a volume stored in a deposit vault and with an annually amended valuation for insurance would be of a positive large financial value in case of a fire. Insurance adjusters are skeptics when told that this and that lost piece was worth one or two thousand dollars. The signatures of one or two fair-minded men who may by good hap be found should be added to such a summary. The pictures also if clear and good would form a basis of appraisal for settlement, especially if they had been signed by competent judges as being original specimens. We may warn owners, however, that such a book is a fearful snare. Inspection of it reveals the gaps in the collection even more strikingly than it shows the important objects of the collection. So unless an owner wishes to be led into temptation he will please pass by and overlook the suggestion just made. Nevertheless, a process of making typed and pictured records is highly educational. One often learns when attempting to put down the facts how slight is his knowledge of style, structure, and merit. He is obliged to be more precise than in a casual conversation and the consequence is a sharpening of definition and a more real and just appreciation of one's belongings.

One inevitable result of such a process will be to force a critical examination of the articles left us by Aunt Huldah or bought in from grandmother's estate. In this year of grace the reckoning would throw us back into a period whose specimens we cannot long tolerate if we have practiced eyes. The result must be a weeding out and a consignment to the attic of these dear heirlooms. To that attic we may go occasionally and weep. There is reason to weep, because when the dear departed left these things they threw their heirs into an awkward predicament. But after the weeping fit is over one may go down stairs to rejoice in the improved taste indicated by the articles with which he has surrounded himself. Here, then, is the hope of the future that one by one those specimens which show bad lines or bad structure may be consigned to the limbo still existing around most dwellings.

But it will be asked "are we never to be allowed peace by the stylist and the antiquarian? Will you never let us alone?" No. Why should one be let alone in an ill-fitting garment or an ill-fitting environment? If life is a process as we have been informed, there is many a semi-old piece of furniture which should take to its heels and be supplanted by something that the children will not be ashamed of. If one's affections are entwined around an airtight stove, the thing to do is to transfer the tendrils to something less scorching. At least let us get back to the old fire frame if we do not proceed the whole length to the ancient fireplace. The remedy for a low love is a high one. It certainly ought to be as easy to love a good thing as a bad one, though experience shows that this presumably good hypothesis is not true.

HOPE FOR THE SMALL COLLECTOR

The minds of broad critics have finally settled down to this dictum: that simple specimens of antique furniture often have as much grace and charm as the richer woods and elaborate designs. What is still better, the collector's wife will be glad to perceive that the collection of such simple furniture has a vogue and provides a background of good taste and pleasing repose. Unhappily some have learned this fact too well and as late as 1930 buyers were found to pay outrageous prices for simple pieces still numerous as to which there was no reason in the law of supply and demand for the figures obtained. But within a year it has been possible to obtain good maple high-boys at a price at least as low as equally good reproductions. This rule, while it does not hold of all types, will be found applicable to a sufficient number so that a small sum expended wisely will go far. In a series of years by taking advantage of the ebb and flow of fads and buying articles when they are not in fashion, one may obtain an excellent collection for a few thousand dollars.

When the well-educated and earnest family seeks persistently those styles which have approved themselves either under the names of great masters or as types which go deeper than any single personality and are bedded in the sound convictions of the race we may certainly anticipate a healthful toning up of the American home which is at present about the dreariest background imaginable for a normal human spirit. Revolutionary fervor may be expected to show itself in enough courage to banish the horribles and bring back the antiques, or if that is not feasible, to bring back their forms.

STANDARDIZATION

What we lack particularly in our personalities and in our homes is a deep-cut character. The trend toward standardization has ruined a good many men and a good many residences. The old world with its severing dialects, mountain ranges and small national limits, has emphasized character. We have lost as well as gained by the even diffusion of the same kind of knowledge or error. A washed-out personality and a trivial commonplace interior are fostered by the trend of American civilization. It is really laughable to observe the scared and even horrified look on the face of the average buyer when shown something distinctive and out of the ordinary run. She wants something like her neighbor's and her neighbor again wants something like the next neighbor. The vicious chain of gregarious taste is established. When people are all alike they can never be very attractive nor can their surroundings be so. Happily there is here and there an individual who is ready to entertain ideas, who dwells on the merits of life and its constituents rather than on the dull low levels of sameness. At the present rate of progress or lack of it, it will be a great many years before our dwellings indicate thoughtful discernment. There is room for pioneering in every fair village and in every residence ward of our cities. In spite of our humdrum quality of mind we perhaps have more capacity of independent thinking than is usual in an old civilization. Gradually not a few are learning that the question to ask is not what is Mrs. Grundy doing, but what would be a worthy thing to do.

The preparation of everything beforehand to swallow "as is" without inspection or rumination reminds me of a friend who comes down to breakfast and, referring to the numerous prepared cereals, asks his wife, "Well, what kind of gape-and-swallow have we for breakfast this morning?" We are getting to be like the little fat birds in the nest, heavier than their mothers, who at the first sound of the fluttering wing, open their mouths so wide that to one looking down into the nest there seems to be nothing but mouth, which of course is just the intention. The state feeds the town, town the individual, and the state looks to the nation. Instead of leveling up, we are leveling down. In the effort to feed everybody alike, to clothe them alike, to govern them alike, the inevitable tendency is to make them think alike, which means that they need not think at all. It is overlooked that there must be a source of money and of ideas. That source is at last the individual. We have swung so far from individuality that, like all those people who have all things in common, nobody has much. There is a multitude of persons who shun like the plague being any different or thinking any differently from their neighbors. As that which the average man does and thinks is only an average level of accomplishment the result is that distinction is taken out of life and society becomes flat and stale. A cartoon recently appeared showing a gentleman waiting at the door of a beauty parlor for his wife to come out. A procession of women was issuing from the door, and each was the spit and image of the other, so that the poor husband looked on distracted and unable to distinguish his spouse. It was an excellent commentary on modernity. The word standard is eagerly connected with many kinds of furniture. If it is standard, it is wrong.

But the puzzled public will say, what sort of person are you to be taking such a position? Are you not in the same breath telling us that we should follow a recognized style in furniture? That question uncovers that difference between the past and the present. If Chippendale ever made any two patterns alike, they have never come to light, and the same is to be said of all the old stylists in furniture. There being no machines, there was no tendency to follow the same details. A general outline of resemblance was all those old makers cared for. In the chair splat I have myself cataloged some five hundred designs, but have seen several times as many more. It is true that one period ran to one kind of wood, but a customer thought himself declassed by buying something just like his neighbor's. The designer honored him and he insisted on being honored by some special variation from a type in his furnishings. Life gets its interest by such a variation. There is no uniformity in nature. Not even two blades of grass are alike. One will hear the careless say of the Chinese, they all look alike. That is a proof of superficial observation. There is in nature and art a holding to one central line of development, but the ramifications from that line are always different. Of thirty-six hundred snowflakes photographed each was a pure geometric pattern perfect in symmetry and each very beautiful, and the presumption is that if the investigator had not grown tired he could have gone on indefinitely photographing an almost infinite variety. Meanwhile no one would mistake a snowflake for anything else. One is equally cold with another, and all are formed from the same substance. There is harmony without sameness and no one can say that he ever saw a snowflake not in good taste. I recognize that these statements seem to contradict what I have said elsewhere on the lack of good new design and the necessity of going back to the old. Yet the contradiction is apparent, not real. The norm remains constant, the development varies. I do not deny the possibility of good new design. I only state that it has not yet appeared. That is to say, it is safer to take as a basis a fixed outline and to derive our varieties through reasonable adaptation and decoration. But to expect a machine to do this or to ask the public to accept something angular and abnormal and graceless is too much. One could respect a designer who really designed. At present one looks with wonder at his lines as if his nerves were troubled by a nervous jerk, producing nameless forms. Even sameness is better than ugliness.

To say in brief what merit there is in collecting: it is the chief means of preservation. Without the collector there would be indiscriminating waste. There would be forgetfulness of whatever good work had been done in the world. Progress, in other words, is impossible without preservation of the past. If there is no preservation every individual would be born into an empty world. Amnesia is much talked of lately, and we are wondering whether it is more common than formerly. Suppose a person suffers from this affliction, he is like one who has lost all the past. A work of fiction describes such a man who began anew to learn to read and to multiply. This is a handicap which the race would suffer unless it preserved what it had done. It is appalling when we look on the other side of the subject how much has been lost. A famous lecturer in a former generation used to speak on the lost arts. Nearly all the architecture has perished. What painting have we produced by the supreme genius of the Greeks? In our conceited catalog of our present knowledge we overlook the knowledge that has been. There were whole nations that have left not a vestige of literature and there are those who suppose that it was not considered worth while by them to make records. Whatever the cause, humanity was impoverished. It is a terrible indictment to a race to leave nothing behind it but dust. The past is the springboard to the present and the only hope of the future, therefore. Probably not one ten-thousandth part of the world's best creations have been preserved.

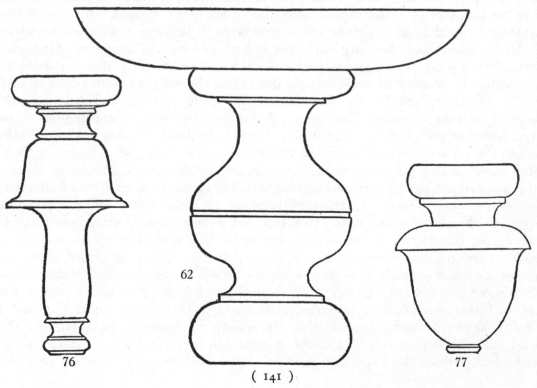

62

76

77

WHERE AND WHAT TO COLLECT

For a long time now the supply of very desirable American antique furniture has been decreasing. The buyer may reflect that it will never increase. As time goes on and material a hundred years old comes under the classification of an antique, it is to be remembered that there was a rapid falling off in style from 1800 to 1830 when the bottom was reached. As a consequence, while old furniture can be found, it will not be good. Even now throughout the West the market is fed largely from the inexhaustible sources of degraded Empire and the styleless styles of 1830–50. Material that will not sell in the East is put off on persons who, from their location, have not the opportunity to study styles unless they read manuals. Good antiques are a fixed quantity. It is absolutely impossible to increase their number except by the now rare event of objects coming into the market which were never available before. Of course in the aggregate a good many such things do come into the market, but in relation to the furniture that is already known their proportion is almost negligible. Antiques are not a commodity like potatoes that can be increased on demand. The consequence is that when the demand is good the temptation is too strong on a certain class of purveyors to produce an article made of old wood. In this production America cannot compete with England or the Continent because over there they have great quantities of old material to work over and apt artisans who can afford to work, or at least who must work for a small wage. Their products are therefore imported and for a long time by collusion or carelessness a good supply has been brought into the country without paying duty as "over one hundred years old." Just now a notorious American dealer has been caught by the government with an underpriced inventory of importations. There is here and there a dealer who advertises as handling American antiques only. But the number of shops actually restricting themselves to this policy is very small. Most of them frankly advertise English antiques or specialize in English, Spanish, or French articles. They do so especially where the goods are English on the argument that such furniture was imported in the old times. It was, indeed, brought into the South in quantities, but the North almost exclusively supplied its own market. The South has long since been denuded of almost everything that could be purchased, so that southern dealers not uncommonly make a virtue of necessity and advertise that they import. The great markets of the North also must be fed. All this would be very well but for two objections. The first is that there is a strong sense among people who do not inherit their antiques that they would like at least to possess something made by eighteenth-century Americans. They have the highly developed passion of patriotism which extends to what the fathers owned as well as to what they were. Thus there is a powerful temptation to regard an antique as American provided it has the least resemblance to American workmanship. There is a considerable class of English antiques which approaches nearly enough to American peculiarities. The detection of its origin, therefore, becomes more difficult. After a large experience of seeing such articles the origin is in most cases plainly discernible. There is always a small number of objects the origin of which is most difficult to ascertain. Since the American article is worth from two to twenty times as much as the foreign, the owner will allege domestic origin and so have the articles entered in catalogs if possible.

The principal objection, however, to foreign articles is not that they are foreign, but that they are not old. Sets of chairs are particularly exploited made in such a way that few can detect the fraud.

It is to be remembered that in all parts of Europe the good thing must run the gauntlet of native buyers. There is still much wealth abroad and a numerous class of cultivated collectors. They are not likely to let us into the market at fair prices since another profit must be added to articles brought to this country.

There has also been an embargo placed by some countries, such as Sweden, upon allowing the fine products of their ancestors to leave the country. In France also and Italy, while there are past masters at the production of what looks old, a government permit is necessary for the export of almost every good early article.

It has been estimated in my hearing by very careful and experienced men that beginning in the south of Europe not one per cent of the things imported as old are so. As one goes north, though the proportion rises in England to perhaps five per cent, it is still too small to appeal to a person of good judgment. That is, the man who keeps his head will not buy unless he is the one in a hundred thousand who really knows. A New England museum was notoriously done by a dealer who removed from Europe to America. When his fraud was discovered he was obliged to take back the goods, but the only manner in which he could avoid condemnation was the plea of ignorance, which he seems to have made good, though I could never be persuaded that he was as big a fool as he made himself out.

If these things occur and the gauntlet is run in such public instances, what hope has the ordinary private buyer of escaping unscathed? This traffic goes forward because credulity or conceit of knowledge permits it. Novices can scarcely believe how successfully the old can be imitated, but the conclusion of the whole matter is that it is much safer to buy at home and from those who have established an unblemished reputation for a long series of years or from private owners who have inherited and whose character is known and who must dispose of their belongings.

A very important phrase in the previous sentence is "who have inherited." Any number of collections of recent acquisition are dispersed. On the death of their owners they are thrown on the market, and the word "collection" seems to have an hypnotic influence. It is forgotten that the collector got his collection like every other buyer, and perhaps more spurious or otherwise undesirable furniture is acquired from collections than from dealers. The good and bad are unloaded together, and the modicum of good "sweetens" the bad. It is a subtle temptation to call a lot of furniture a collection. The objects are perhaps a dealer's stock. When a large dealer died his goods were sold as his collection, and it is probable that that name realized a large sum. During his life he had removed to his home a number of his more important pieces, and any man who insisted on getting into his home was penalized about a hundred per cent. It is reasoned that a collector will carefully pass upon articles that he buys. That seldom happens. How many instances have you known of collectors calling in a wise friend and bidding him ruthlessly throw out every doubtful specimen? I know one such. This cleaning process should give satisfaction to a collector. He does not clean house. Why, is one of the mysteries. Perhaps he thinks he knows his collection is all good. Perhaps he knows it is not. In either case it remains as it is and is at last sold as a collection.

Of course, careful collectors quietly dispose now and then of articles they no longer believe in, but this is dangerous. Such an article may get into the hands of a dealer as "part of Mr. ——'s celebrated collection." The collector does not wish this to happen. So sometimes he puts the offensive specimen in a barn chamber, and it does not see the light again until he is dead and his executor, knowing nothing of the circumstances, imagines it was a treasure hidden away as a prize sometime to be repaired. Of course, the only safe proceeding with a spurious piece is to destroy it. How often is that done? Another way is to give it to a poor relation!

There are a few articles which a collector will be debarred from possessing if he confines himself to native goods. One of these is a large bookcase, though even these are said to have been made in Baltimore. Nearly everything else may be had here but not in a form as rich as the alleged foreign product.

Treating now of the period of the articles collected, the buyer will learn that the eager demand for seventeenth-century styles has ceased and the quest has shifted to mahogany. There is no reason why the pendulum should not swing again. The oak and maple of the seventeenth century exist in very small quantities. The most any buyer not a millionaire can hope for is to furnish one room in oak cabinetwork and maple chairs of a corresponding period. Such purchases are still highly desirable at almost any price, and the prices are not now prohibitive.

Next in order is the early Dutch, that is, William and Mary style. This class, though larger than the oak class, is quite limited in quantity, but it can never cease to be desirable. It is walnut.

The early Georgian style, following hard upon the late Dutch or Queen Anne and scarcely distinguishable from it, is attractive in outline, stylistically almost above criticism and, if the walnut is in good condition, altogether desirable to possess.

The Chippendale type exists in large quantities so that one might almost furnish a house with it. The beds of this period which always have a square base if not a claw are difficult to find and in the earlier periods practically nonexistent.

Coming to the Hepplewhite time, the shield- or heart-back chair is very appealing in its beauty, but the cabinet furniture of corresponding date does not class with Chippendale styles.

Sheraton designs are almost always light and graceful, but except as beds they seem not to be very much more available than the Hepplewhite. Sheraton blends into the Adam and the early Empire style in a fashion such that no one can and no one need discriminate precisely between them. The early Empire, now popularly, but with no warrant, usually called Phyfe, exists in good quantities though very few seem to care for the chairs except in an extremely limited rich design, and in that I think the public taste is correct. In fact, in the matter of style as one goes back there is a better taste manifested continuously till we enter fully into the early Georgian and the Queen

Anne. Sheraton, however, influenced by the classic designs, got rid of the rococo of the Chippendale time.

Of later furniture the less said the better. The revival of French and Gothic styles in the Victorian era produced a vast quantity of unworthy material. Such furniture, however, is largely the stock in trade of the purely commercial or small dealer as he finds it to be easily obtainable and salable. It serves as a pot boiler.

The collector should avoid giving much attention to labels. They are an insidious snare and take the eye away from the furniture itself. The material, however, is worth being noted, not so much in itself as because it may indicate the date. I could never submit to the dictum that the wood used is more important than the style. The form is before the material.

To the wholly inexperienced it may be necessary to say what is ordinarily taken for granted, that the name of a style like Chippendale never means his own manufacture, but only a design executed in his spirit, and the same is true of all other makers, including Phyfe. This last, however, is a name thought to be connected with his manufacture when it should be classed as a style. In the long list of makers there are only two or three of any account earlier than 1720, so far as their direct connection can be established with articles of furniture. Queen Anne's time does not supply us with prominent American makers whose work we can be certain of. There are probably eight or ten, more or less, pieces in America made by Chippendale himself, including the chairs called the Randolph samples.

The collector should pay not much attention to statements about dates. Possibly no one can establish the date within fifteen or twenty years. In the case of the earliest beds one cannot tell within a hundred years. In Queen Anne cabinet furniture there is a leeway of fifty years at least. More and more we are finding that furniture was made out of its period. It takes a good man, so good that he is not to be found, without great expense and delay, to distinguish between the 1850 Chippendale and the Chippendale that was made in its proper period.

Also there is a Chippendale that is not worth having at any price, because at times that designer proceeded to finical extremes or made designs which were not approved by the consensus of good taste. It is the wide comparison of hundreds of specimens that establishes the standard of beauty and taste.

Values cannot be correctly judged at auctions. There is a wealthy buyer, perhaps, who is quite determined to obtain a certain article. His agent may have orders to buy it without reference to price. It is only in the long run that a valuation can be established and that only in a general way. A steamship rises and falls but keeps on a general level. Hence fancy or enthusiasm or stubbornness or a lack of buyers may make a variation in the price obtained. This variation may range from a low level to several times that amount. It is for this reason that the valuation of antiques for collections or in estates is always vexing and never satisfactory to all concerned.

LABELS

A dealer was recently approached by a man who said he had a Simon Willard clock label for sale. The dealer asked the price. "How many do you want?" was the answer. The dealer did not want any.

But is it possible, one will say, that label imitations are frequent and difficult of detection? The answer is that they are profitable and are easy to do. Is there anything that is easy and profitable that lacks persons to undertake it? An entire newspaper was imitated and sold well. Not only so, but it was done several times over.

Old account books and any early books with blank pages are bought to obtain the old paper on which the spurious label is to be printed. The old type is now available, that is, their style is, which is quite precisely like the old. Line engravings may also be made from clean old labels. It is easy to yellow paper and fray its edges.

Old newspapers containing advertisements of cabinetmakers are sought. The advertisement as torn out may often serve as a label.

A certain dealer, who has now gone to his reward, did a great business in this line.

Fiction is one of the necessities of life, and ever since the days of Job and Ruth wonderful stories have been told. This is all quite honorable. Authors are properly praised and even receive academic prizes.

The cabinetmaker's art is also very respectable and the gathering of fine old specimens of that art. The fun begins, however, or the fury, when the furniture man enters the realm of fiction. Somehow the things don't mix, or, if they do, they mix other people. Fiction is very pleasant, but we should take it straight, and pay a couple of dollars a volume instead of a couple of thousand, or even much more, as has been done when literature is supplied as labels.

A labeled clock is perhaps worth twice as much if the salesman can persuade the buyer that the literature has reference to the timepiece.

Perhaps more money is paid for stories than for furniture. A lady wrote me recently: "I want a piece, Dr. Nutting, that has a story." Why not employ a novelist? Mr. Hergesheimer writes excellent stories about furniture. One, concerning the court cupboard, hinged on the absence of one of the doors. He found this piece in the hands of a dealer before I saw it. The old fellow who dickered over it was represented as keen beyond any comparison. He did not, however, observe that the cupboard lacked a drawer also! I supplied that drawer and this wonderful old piece now appears in No. 452 FURNITURE TREASURY. A dealer whom I knew never had a specimen in his shop of which he could not say, "Thereby hangs a tale." The tale was as gossamer thin as that of a comet. He is dead now. I don't know where he has gone, but his tales go with him. They were wrong stories. A dealer once said to me, "We don't buy stories." No, but he sold them. He trotted them out religiously, or rather, irreligiously. With a vivid imagination, unhampered by realities, why should he buy stories when he could make them up with a finish better than old patina?

In the Holy Land there is a story with every locality. People are very indignant when they ask a dragonman a question and he can not answer it. As the ages go on every generation adds a little and in time the hazy legend becomes a clear-cut history. Voltaire's famous saying, "A history is a lie agreed to," is particularly applicable to furniture. However, as great musicians play a tune with variations, so the masters of the art of dealing may be detected if you get them to tell you again about a piece of furniture. A few elaborations and asides vary so markedly from the first form of the tale that in time a marvelous romance could be concocted.

The only basis of purchase should be the merit of the specimen.

Only those things will bear the test of time that are honest in construction and rational in outline. Eastlake is now sunk. It has gone the way of the spool bed and the whatnot. That, however, was the best name ever given to a human construction. They could not think of a name and wisely gave up trying.

A firm recently put out a new specimen alleged to be made on the lines of an antique which I recommended. By comparing the cut of the "copy" with the original, it appeared that there were ten visible features of the original lacking in the new specimen, and how many invisible evasions one can never know, but when one can see so much wrong, one suspects what can't be seen is worse. The firm was careful not to quote the volume or the page of the original specimen. When legal measures were taken, they paid a round sum for their "inadvertence." Yet this firm was composed of men of old American ancestry and supposedly high ethical training. Why, then, should we pitch upon some poor alien immigrant and load the sins of Americans upon him? How clearly does the merit of the old lines appear when it becomes profitable to allege that we are copying them? Cast all your devices to chaos, but let me surround myself with what faithful, wise hands have made, with the resultant forms of elegance and taste and sweetness, which have been handed down to us by the genius of other ages. I see, as in a vision, a community arising which uses wittingly the rich materials of the world we live in, until excellence is no longer a rarity, but good homes, fit abodes for human dignity, shall be as abundant as pure water, clean air, and the universal glories of sunsets, free to all who wish to look. Sordidness and ugliness are unnecessary. They are even expensive and, in the end, fatal to the fabric of society, and roll the race backward. Exquisiteness of line, how much it adds to the joy of life! We have not too much unalloyed pleasure. Our poor humanity in the general run is so very little advanced. The oriole builds a far daintier house than the man. These things need not be. Idle men, if only inspired to put their wits together, combining the various trades and arts, may form fit abodes for themselves. We have scarcely begun to make our surroundings worthy of humanity on whose face should be stamped splendid memories and more splendid visions.

For more than thirty years I have sought diligently everywhere, all the time, for the remaining embodiments which hold beauty and harmony, and lift life into one continuous quest for excellencies that still swarm in the world. Let us see in stone and clay their potentialities, and live and act toward a rational development, until every American is housed in substantial and attractive quarters. It is not too much to ask or hope. In fact, we dare not hope anything less if America is not to fail and fall away pitifully from what we believe is her finer fairer destiny.

When we look at the raw materials in pigments, and marbles, and granites, and woods, we can readily see almost in our grasp historic and prophetic delineations directly on the interior walls of our homes. If they can be on the walls of a few, they can be on the walls of the many. For good things spread in any healthful society. It is the worst statement possible that good architecture or decoration must be rare. The test of sanity and a mark of character are that these things should impart themselves and multiply themselves.

For the American woman the masters of decoration, in happy genius of creation, have wrought and have left examples capable of enriching, sweetening, and beautifying life. It is for her to interest herself in this past, to multiply it in the present, to endorse and make secure what eager workers have produced, so that the American home may be a shrine and cling with its charms to the young life that now runs away from it and its tasteless vulgarities. Is it too much to hope for a passion of creative beauty and a love of durable realities? We are a people among whom fashions spread rapidly. If the fashion could spread of surrounding ourselves with what is worthy of humanity, we should be dissatisfied until we have made something and made it just as fine as it can be.

Almost all the delight in life arises from conforming external things to ideas. Every real artisan loves the quality of what he does more than the money he gets for it. His pay is mostly in a lasting satisfaction that he has produced something good for all time.

It is important for every educated person to go beyond the mere jargon of antiques. It is important to compare the approved forms of excellence with the shapes of the things which are presented for approval in the shops. It is important to investigate with utmost care the character and antecedents of those who present objects for our approval. Otherwise we may mar our homes and make them weak and ridiculous, and a few years may see their contents falling to pieces, and our descendants will apologize for us, by saying, "They meant well, but they did not know."

Ethics have a larger place in furniture than in painting, because a painting is open to all. Its merits are on its surface. But the quality of furniture consists at least as much in what is out of sight as in what is on the surface.

A western woman, and not very far west, built a house at an expense of a quarter of a million dollars. She pestered me for two weeks, when we were fellow guests at a summer hotel, to look at the pictures of the furniture with which, as she supposed, she had decorated her dwelling. I suspected what was coming, and begged off as long as I could. Finally she cornered me with her pictures. They were all exhibits of the Van Buren period, stuff which she had picked up in the commonest wayside shops of New England, stuff thrown out as too clumsy to be kept in decent homes. I sighed. She insisted on a judgment. As the lady was of a notable family, distinguished for force and capacity, I said, "Madam, you are a large-minded woman. You can bear the truth. The best that you can do with this furniture is to throw it out."

"Why," said she, "I paid $35 for that bureau!"

"Well," said I, "is a bureau costing $35 worthy to go into your pretentious house? Even if it were, I must tell you that, as a beginner, I obtained some of this stuff, but I paid $5 for my bureaus and sold them for $2.50."

What did this lady do? Had she wanted advice or admiration? Did she pay for what was worth a great deal to her? Not she. She retained everything, practically as it was, for a series of years, and finally gave an order to a western decorator to do over her house interiors and refurnish it. Her commission was executed. The last state is worse than the first.

One can state, as a general rule, that collectors do not want to know.

In collecting they depend upon what they call their taste. How this taste was developed does not appear, but it is often avowedly based on the intuitions. Like the president of a great national society who furnished her state room with ante-Civil War horrors, people say they get things because they like them. In that word "like" is the gist of the matter. It is not an intelligent liking unless it is based on some study and a wide observation. She should have an inkling of classical outlines and at least a smattering of history. Lacking these, what does a liking amount to? A mere whim, a vague report, an ambition to be in the swim.

What does the lore and the patient skill of the past count with such superficial treatment? The art and artisanship of great minds for thousands of years are embodied in their relics which have come down to us. The flowering of genius and its happiest inspirations should be the more carefully considered, since most of them have perished, and unless we cherish them, they will speedily all be gone.

Consider the art of the Flemings, the Spanish, the Florentines, the master minds of old France and old England. What a sum of beauty in design represents the achievements of the Greek and the Oriental! Without hesitation I say that any person who sets up a new standard of taste without carefully studying the standards of the past is like the nineteenth-century mechanic who started with his jig-saw and his lathe to show those old fellows something.

Is the slapping of a lot of color on a chest or a face the last word in art? If the conceit of the persons who mean to purchase could be deflated, and such persons would modestly seek for harmony, restraint, and merit, the battle would be nearly won. "Early American" would then connote something, so that it would not be mistaken for the American Indian.

The most stinging commentary upon present conditions is the modernistic painting and the new art furniture. I am glad they have the grace to name it "new" and not to try to make our ancestors responsible for it, like the commercial reproducers. There was a theory once that a picture should tell its story. It is now, however, a picture puzzle. A number of illustrations have lately appeared in magazines dedicated to beauty which no one could say with confidence were the representations of anything in heaven, earth, or sea. In fact, the artist himself puts his tongue in his cheek, well knowing that if he can execute something that cannot be named, it will be sought for.

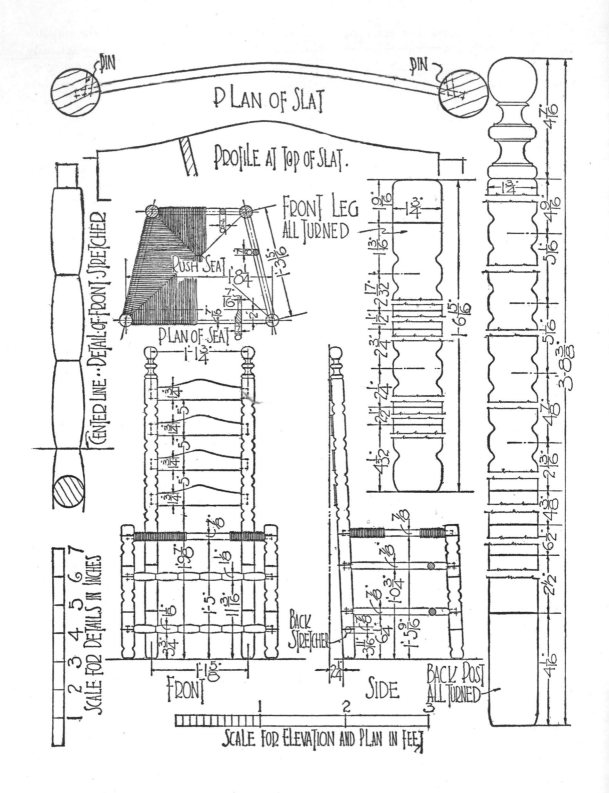

PLAN OF SLAT

PROFILE AT TOP OF SLAT.

FRONT LEG
ALL TURNED

RUSH SEAT

PLAN OF SEAT

CENTER LINE ·· DETAIL OF FRONT STRETCHER

SCALE FOR DETAILS IN INCHES
1 2 3 4 5 6 7

FRONT

BACK
STRETCHER

SIDE

BACK POST
ALL TURNED

SCALE FOR ELEVATION AND PLAN IN FEET
1 2 3

(150)

CHAIR DETAILS

An attractive, turned, "four back" maple chair (*Page 150*) of a date about 1710–20. The measured detail is complete, but I point out that the sausage turning in front is nearly always liked for its quaintness.

It appears also that in having a slight backward rake of 2¼ inches it becomes more comfortable than the very light vertical backs which were so common about 1750–80. There is no need of pinning this chair at the seat where the rush holds it securely; pins at the bottom stretcher and the top slat are sufficient.

For style the slats should be kept thin, and they should be bent, not sawed, and preferably from green lumber to be dried in the form. Dry lumber, even when wet for steaming, will not hold its shape so surely as lumber bent before it is dried. A chair of this sort is not too heavy, yet its 1¾-inch post is sufficient to give it dignity and solidity. The slight rounding of the back leg at the floor is a good style mark, and also it prevents the slivering of a leg kept full to the floor, and has a less bald effect.

One sees that the seat rungs are flattened in front; that is, they are not turned. Thus they are provided with a greater stiffness to prevent the spring so often seen in rush seat rungs. But the side and back rungs, being shorter, do not require this stiffening.

The size of the seat is far more generous than in the usual chair of this style. Seats were often made very meager in these old rushed chairs.

Many old chairs worn off at the bottom are copied in the same reduced condition and are neither so comfortable nor so good in appearance. The front ball should not be reduced more than appears here.

The finish on these chairs as found is often black paint, which of course is well enough, since it will go with any color of furniture in the same room. But where we find a natural maple or slightly stained finish the effect is, as a rule, more pleasing. Further, many finishers of old and modern chairs do not know how to use black paint without having it become sticky in humid weather with disastrous results.

Occasionally these chairs are found in red paint and rarely in green, but giving them a mahogany stain is poor taste, which the public is rapidly outgrowing.

The use of this chair is various. It serves for dining room, living room, or chamber. Probably for this reason it is popular. A chair that will be presentable and useful anywhere is a good sort.

The wood may be maple, birch, or beech — no other. It is never proper in walnut, and softer woods like poplar are not strong enough. There is no difference in merit between maple and birch. Birch takes a prettier finish, particularly if it is wished to enrich the color somewhat from the honey shade.

There is another, but more pretentious chair than this of precisely the same style and period. It has five slats, each wider than the other, ascending; is 50 inches high, posts 2¼ inches in diameter, a big Queen Anne stretcher in front and sausage turnings at sides.

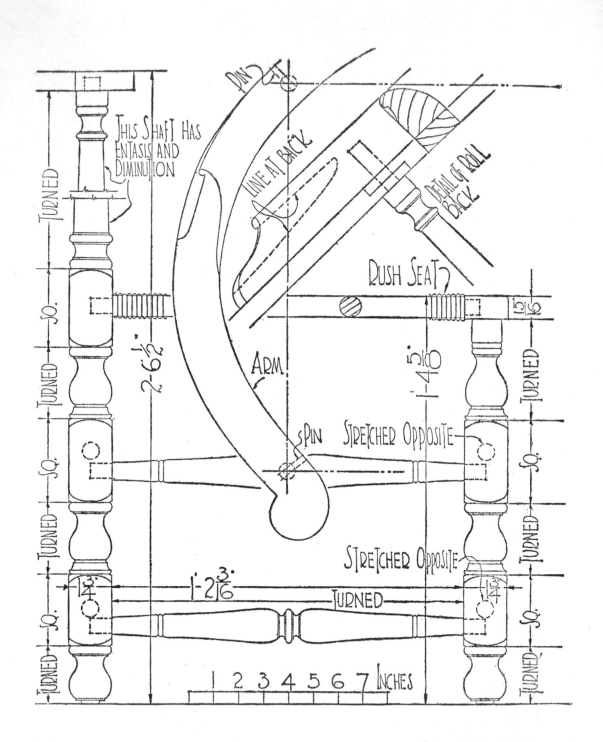

This Shaft Has Entasis and Diminution

Turned

Turned

Turned

Turned

Turned

Turned

Sq.

Sq.

Sq.

Sq.

$2'-6\frac{1}{2}''$

Pin

Line at Back

Detail of Roll Back

Rush Seat

Arm

Pin

Stretcher Opposite

Stretcher Opposite

$1'-4\frac{5}{8}''$

$1'-4\frac{3}{8}''$

$1'-4\frac{3}{8}''$

$1'-2\frac{3}{16}''$

Turned

$\frac{15}{16}''$

Turned

Turned

Turned

Turned

Turned

Sq.

Sq.

Sq.

1 2 3 4 5 6 7 Inches

It is also found as an arm, but with two Queen Anne stretchers, 21 inches between shoulders, and 2⅛ inches large diameter.

The measured drawing (*Page 152*) of a turned maple corner chair shows a simple adaptable pattern, of a design probably as early as 1700–20. The feature of pleasing quaintness is the staggering of the stretchers to prevent too much wood being cut from one point, an excellent precaution which at a later date was abandoned. Another feature of interest is the manner in which the thickened portion of the back is made. The "roll over" secured by a deep cut in the back of the arm runs out after a little. This chair is rather light and fairly comfortable. It is approved by many as an occasional chair. As shown "domes of silence," a big name for a little thing, are inserted in the feet. Chairs so made will move with utmost ease.

This chair can be used for a desk, or for a customer at a desk, or in a living room or a den.

I have made a rough computation of the varieties of styles in chairs which have come to my attention in museums, private dwellings, and shops. The number extends to several thousand. One thousand, about, are in FURNITURE TREASURY. It is obvious that in the old days every maker sought for individuality. At least some detail was different, not only in every set of chairs, but in every piece of cabinet furniture. Thus the maker was able to offer his customer something distinctive, and could at the same time stamp his handiwork with his own peculiar taste, marking the piece as his own. It was not necessary for him to sign it to recognize it. In this way his mind was always being stimulated to produce an agreeable and tasteful article. So far as this spirit is absent from his handiwork so far it becomes tame, shows the want of thought and feeling. The passion has gone and only a formula remains.

It is admitted that sometimes the artisan was mistaken. Chippendale made many mistakes. Hepplewhite a few, Sheraton still less. Some of the other makers, like Shearer (inventor of the sideboard), Ince, and others, seem to have made more misses than hits in the matter of taste. American designers have had their predecessors in error. But the difference between the past and present lies chiefly in this: there was at that time a strong undercurrent of good taste, even more evident in architecture. Men thought about such things with sole reference to one matter only: the merit and appearance of the finished work. They were not proceeding as today on confined lines to do what manufacturers can best do in quantity production. They had been captured by the sense of beautiful appropriateness. Since they worked wholly by hand, any form that occurred to them as desirable was adopted. In the earlier time still, before Chippendale, the name of the designer is lost in his work. But he wrought not less effectively than in the later time.

The author has fussed over designs perhaps as much as the next man. In only one instance has he ever ventured an adaptation, and then he feels that he made a mistake. He still thinks the adaptation was a good one, but he still maintains that there were old pieces which had satisfactory lines so that the adaptation was unnecessary. Today the flat-top desk is shouldering out the old slant top. In a way this is well, because such a desk can be approached from either side and serve anywhere in a room for a table. But even here there are plenty of old English desks of this sort, though the American type is practically wanting.

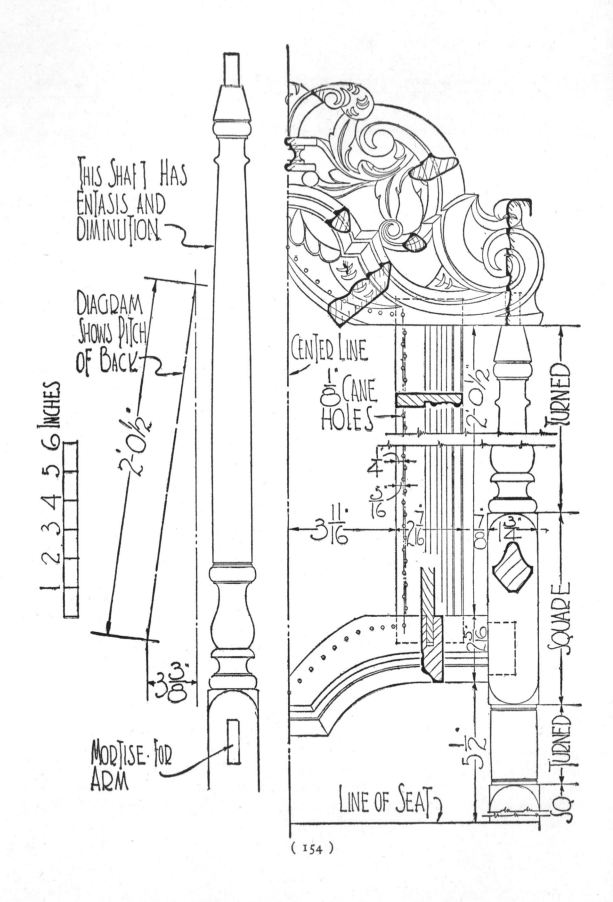

THIS SHAFT HAS ENTASIS AND DIMINUTION

DIAGRAM SHOWS PITCH OF BACK

1 2 3 4 5 6 INCHES

2'-0½"

3⅜"

MORTISE· FOR ARM

CENTER LINE

⅛" CANE HOLES

2'-0½"

4¾"

3/16"

3 11/16"

2 7/16"

7/8"

1¼"

2 5/16"

TURNED

SQUARE

TURNED

SQ.

5½"

LINE OF SEAT

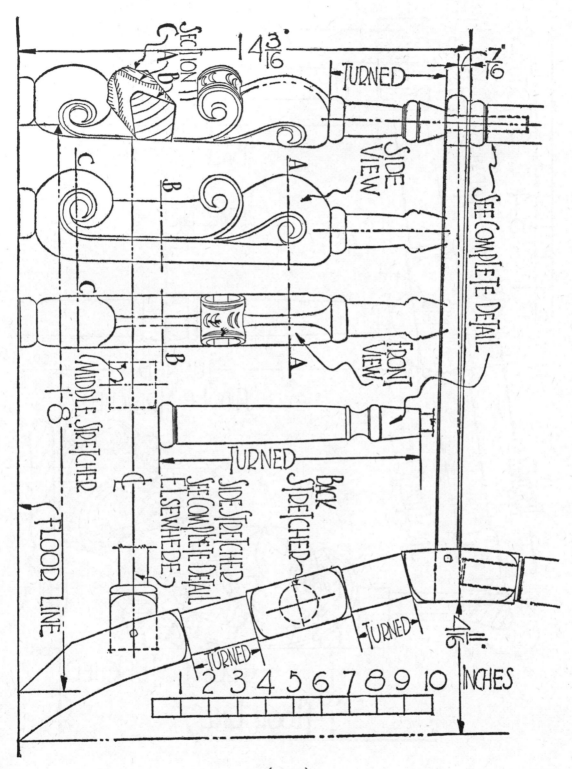

SECTION C D

SECTION A B

14 3/16"

TURNED

7"/16

SIDE VIEW

SEE COMPLETE DETAIL

C

B

A

FRONT VIEW

C

B

A

MIDDLE STRETCHER
1'-8"

TURNED

BACK STRETCHER

SIDE STRETCHER
SEE COMPLETE DETAIL
ELSEWHERE

FLOOR LINE

TURNED

4"/16

TURNED

1 2 3 4 5 6 7 8 9 10 INCHES

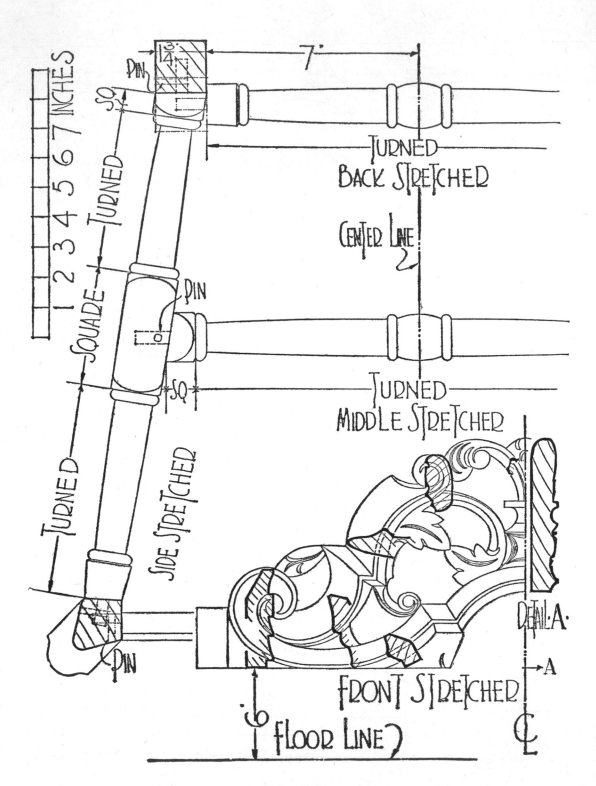

7"

TURNED
BACK STRETCHER

CENTER LINE

TURNED

SQUARE

TURNED

PIN

SQ

PIN

3"
1/4"

TURNED
MIDDLE STRETCHER

INCHES
7 6 5 4 3 2 1

TURNED

SIDE STRETCHER

PIN

FRONT STRETCHER

DETAIL·A·

A

C L

6"
FLOOR LINE

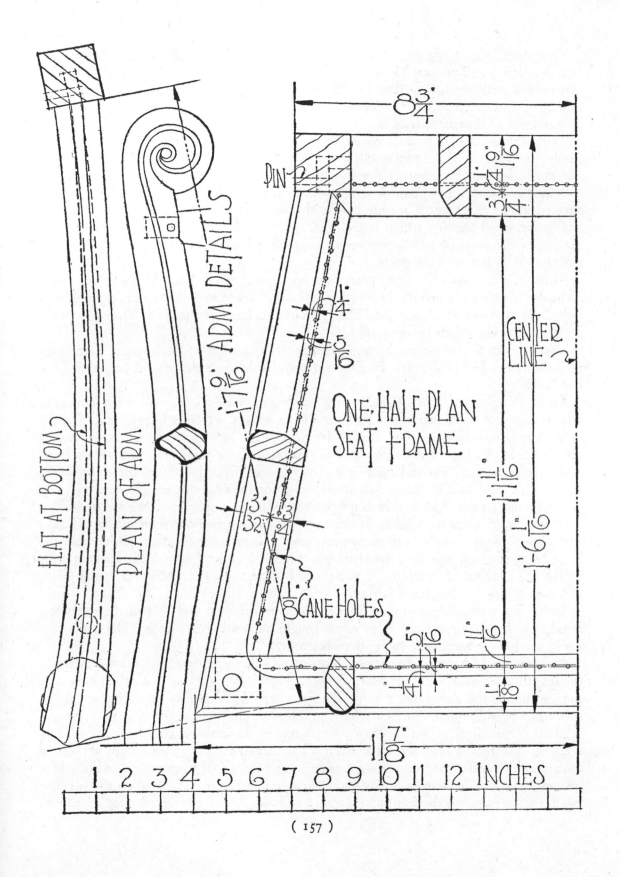

FLAT AT BOTTOM

PLAN OF ARM

ARM DETAILS

$1'-7\frac{9}{16}$

PIN

$8\frac{3}{4}'$

$\frac{9}{16}$

$3'-4''$

$\frac{1}{4}$

$\frac{5}{16}$

ONE-HALF PLAN
SEAT FRAME

CENTER
LINE

$1'-1\frac{1}{16}$

$1'-6\frac{1}{16}$

$\frac{3}{32}$ $\frac{3}{4}$

$\frac{1}{8}$ CANE HOLES

$\frac{5}{16}$

$\frac{11}{16}$

$\frac{1}{8}''$

$11\frac{7}{8}'$

1 2 3 4 5 6 7 8 9 10 11 12 INCHES

This chair (*Pages 154–157*) has been reproduced for the Williamsburg restoration. It is No. 1985, FURNITURE TREASURY. I am happy to present no less than four pages of working drawings of it. The intricacies, while numerous, have, I think, all been noted. A monumental labor is required to get details of such an article, and extends to hundreds of measurements.

The merit of the chair is its remarkable height which produces a stately effect indeed. The pattern of the two scrolls in the top rail and below the seat is also not without much delicacy and grace. Negatively, however, the leg and arm support are not so handsome as the full Flemish scroll, which might have been repeated, instead of a turning above the seat. The side panels also are plain reeded members without the handsome scroll carving which is the final touch of decoration on such chairs. The placing of the cresting wholly above the posts is handsomer but weaker than setting the crest rails between the posts.

In the original chair the front posts rake backward, which I consider a defect. Also a chair of this sort is inevitably weak. Obviously, made as a side chair, it would not have held together at all, but would have broken its back at the seat. That was saved by the stiffening which the arm affords.

The wood of this chair, in the original, appears like maple. Such chairs were made in walnut, beech, and maple. In England the maple examples would probably have been lacking.

An amusing puzzle arose regarding the turning of the back leg. To have done it in one piece would have required a swing of fifteen inches, which is impractical. On the other hand, no evidence that the old leg was made in two parts appears. It was decided that the leg must be doweled as shown, but the joint was so good as to be completely hidden. The old turning had flat places here and there, the stock being too small. This chair affords a rich opportunity for the study of the old methods, and one is bound to say that in this example everything was sacrificed to appearances.

One of the devices resorted to in the very fine caning (which never in the old days had a border strip) was to bore every other cane hole on a strong slant. Otherwise, the holes being so close together, the strip would have ripped off as we tear apart stamps on the line of their perforations. The top and bottom back rails, however, being thick, did not require the staggered boring.

There is a flattening in the original in the curvature on one side of the main top scroll, which of course arose from a too rough calculation of space. The arms also vary, one having more side swing than the other.

An arm should have, in fine styles, most of its side curvature on its last quarter of the length, that near the front post. Some fine arms swing much more than this, and then go under the name ram's horn. There is very little entasis even on the longest turnings. Such emphatic arms are hard to find, but they are surpassing for style.

Another peculiarity in this chair, which makes its construction irregular and is certainly a defect is that the back stretcher is turned for its whole length without a square at the ends like the other stretcher. Another proof that every maker was a law unto himself. It is to be noted that the caning on the seat is bored on the bevel of the flattened rung, on the front and sides. An obvious device to prepare for a cushion.

The unrivaled wainscot, the inauguration chair, in Connecticut, of the younger Governor Winthrop. Recently came to light. The seat is very high, about 22 inches, planned for impressive dignity. Oak.

Unique maple corner chair. The arm is one piece three feet wide. The back with nine spindles and four purely decorative finials above is excellent. Date 1694, Rhode Island.

Front post 19¼ inches, total height 41¼ inches. Seat outside 19½ inches square; post 1⅞ inches diameter.

The cresting of a baluster-back chair (side) with tenon ends for entering the posts. The width between shoulders is 12 inches, the height 6¾ inches. Material maple, though walnut is found.

An Upholstered Sheraton   An Unusual Writing Chair

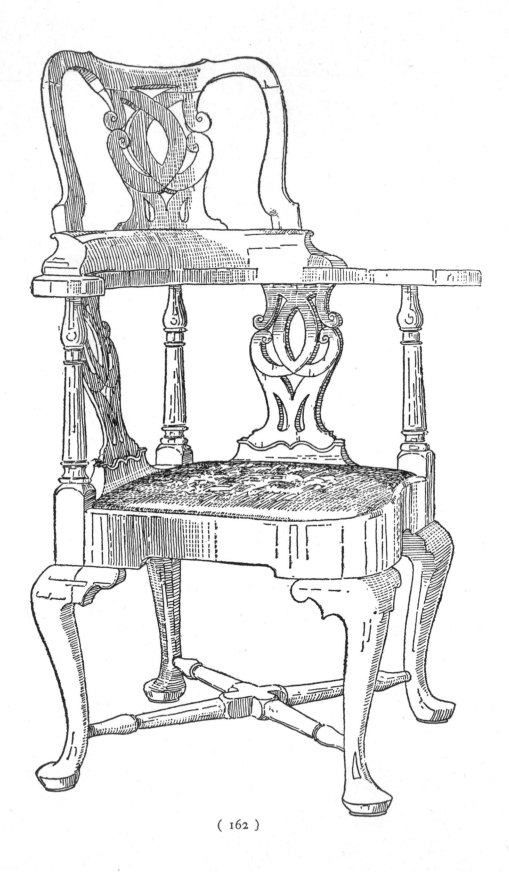

A remarkably consistent chair of uniform merit without a trace of mixture of style is that on p. 162.

Some chairs richer as to the feet have been found, as all claw feet. But this chair, taken through and through, is Queen Anne. I give no scale plan but the following data: Wood, walnut. Untouched. Date about 1735, so that though we say Queen Anne, we mean early Georgian!

Height, 43½; height to top of heavy roll on back, 31½; height to top of front arm, 29¼; height of seat, 15⅞. Square of stretcher, 1⅜. Toe of foot vertically below perpendicular on outside of knee.

Outside width of arm, 29½.

Lower splats, ⅜ thick. Width at top, 4¾; at middle, 6¼; at base, 6.

Diagonal to outside of posts, 26. Diagonal to outside of knees, 28½.

Diagonal inside legs (stretcher shoulder), 21¾.

Back rail (upper) over all, 18½.

Slip seat from front curve to back corner, 21⅝.

Slip seat cross diagonal, 22½.

Upper splat, $^{15}/_{16}$ thick, 7½ wide at top, 7⅞ wide at middle, 8¼ wide at bottom. Leg bracket, 2⅛ wide.

Knee, without bracket, 3 square (size of stock).

Small part of arm, 2½ x 1¼.

Scroll, widest, on front arm, 4; and 3¼ front end to narrowing.

Imposed rail splice, 2½ wide, $2^{11}/_{16}$ high.

Outside width of imposed (spliced) rail, 25¼.

Back seat rails, 2 x 3½ x 14⅜ to shoulder. Posts, 2 square.

Front rail, 2 x 3¼.

There is a raised cupid's bow scroll where the splats enter the plinth of the seat.

The harmony of the imposed back with the splats is perfect. The curve of the seat rail on each side is well shown.

The splats all show interlacing, by slight carving. The section of the heavy splice rail has an initial roll-over, running out to the surface.

When these chairs are simpler they are found with only the front corner foot shaped, the others being straight turned with button feet (see chapter on Feet).

A peculiarity of these chairs is that even in the rich type the arm is usually a plain flat scroll, as here, without the spiral roll-over of the later fashion as found in Chippendale.

Of course, the leg is turned as one stick, and the lower cabriole section is shaped afterwards, but there is a place where this curve coincides with the turning so that the turner can shape it as a guide. Of course, these chairs never had casters.

I have seen only one other corner chair which equals this in merit. The corner chair, often going under the name buffet, was not popular after the Chippendale time. If it existed, I have not seen it. It was probably designed to be set in the corner of a room to occupy the position in which a buffet would otherwise have been.

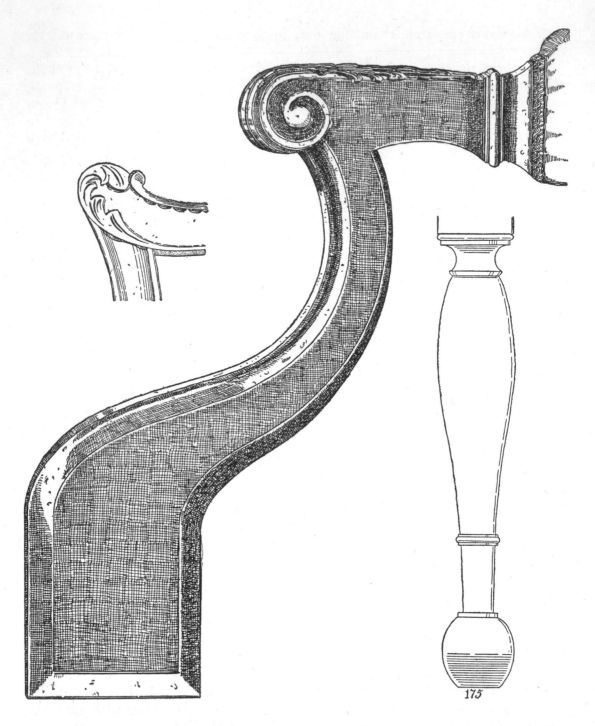

175

A good Chippendale arm carved on the top, and upholstered back of the wrist. The lower section is attached to the seat by screws from the inside, or by dovetailing. Above, a Chippendale ear; below, the leg of a simple Sheraton chest of drawers, described under Feet.

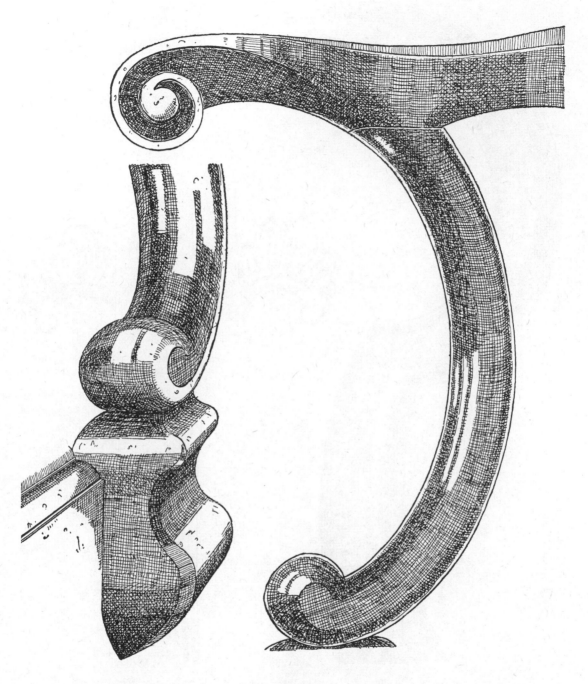

The side and front view of a Chippendale arm, with bracket support dove-tailed part way into the seat. The joint of an arm and support is shown. The seat rail has a quarter round mold, marked on the seat.

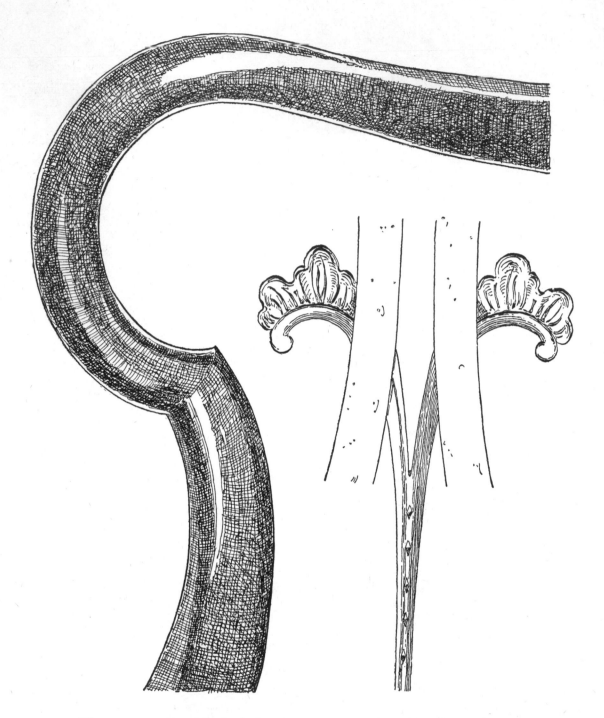

The contour, seen sidewise, of a Queen Anne arm, but more properly speaking, early Georgian. See Chairs, Furniture Treasury. The splat detail of a Chippendale chair should be reversed.

A charming old kitchen in the Essex Institute, shows a barrel cradle, two tin ovens, a New England "five-back" chair, and a spinning Jenny (flax wheel). It is seen that the walls are done in so-called paneled sheathing. That is, boards with molded matching are run from floor to beam or girt. This sort of wall finish came before true, rectangular paneling in America, and was always the preferred finish on simple rooms. It was common to find this finish on the inside walls only, as it was not important on such walls to ward off cold. The boards were thus a single-thickness partition. On finer houses, as here, the sheathing might be continued on the outside, either over plaster or over a filling of brick or clay.

The chimney being here in the corner, the summer beam encounters the chimney at one side of the center. The outside girt corresponds to the summer beam, but is always smaller because sustained by the wall. Heavy muntins in the square sash. This period should be 1770 or later because of the side oven. This sash probably came in, however, about 1720.

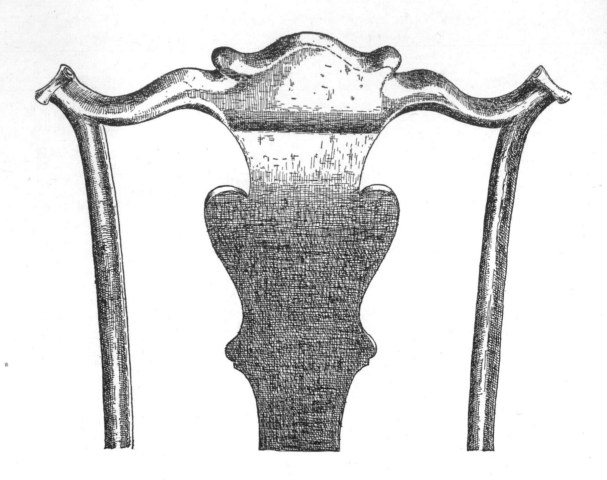

The chair back above is the reverse of that on page 99. The hollowed scroll of the ear is especially good.

An interest attaches to the manner in which Chippendale chairs get their strength. Though they look light and frail, they are not so. The top rails are heavy, but are wittingly rounded off to overcome that effect. The splat is only 7⁄16 thick and beveled. The top rail is 1 1⁄8 thick and hollows slightly so as to require 1 3⁄8 stock. At the center it is 4 inches wide, and rolls back gently to half that width, but this roll gradually lessens till at 5 inches from the center it is not observable. The back is rounded from the top and bottom as well shown in the drawing. The outside width of the ear is 1 3⁄4. At the narrowest point the back rail is 1 1⁄4. The posts are 1 1⁄4 x 1 1⁄4. The legs of this chair are claw-and-ball with acanthus decoration, and there is a shell decoration at the center of the seat rail (*No. 51, Page 103*). The posts are fluted.

The splat of this chair would in some designations throw the date back to early Georgian, but it is occasionally found, as here, with a Chippendale seat 22 front, 16 1⁄2 back with a very slight rounding. The whole height is 40 1⁄4, the width 21 1⁄4 (outside top rail). This rail is carved to show a very slight rise as it crosses the post to form a corner scroll.

The beautiful Hepplewhite chair shown on pages 170–171 is the armchair of No. 2322 in FURNITURE TREASURY. It is unusual in that the shield back draws in markedly above the arm instead of attaining its greatest width, as most such chairs do, at the top of the post. The post is, of course, as always in these chairs, in one piece, the connection with the lower member of the heart outline, also in one piece, being shown. If a piece of wood can be selected with a curved grain for this bottom member, in which the central decoration, part of the same piece, is cut, it strengthens the chair. One mortise takes in the three reeds of the back which are left, in construction, with a web of solid wood which, really dropped into a slot in the segment, forms the tenon. At the top the splat enters the top rail by three tenons, one at center, one at each side. Thus the entire splat is one piece and not so difficult of construction as would seem.

In all Hepplewhites the side rail of the seat should curve as shown, allowing a right-angled joining with the front rail.

The side chair of this style is an inch narrower and an inch shallower on the seat and, of course therefore, on the back, and requires a special drawing scaled down from this.

The cross stretcher should, of course, always be blind dovetailed and driven in from the underside.

Care must be taken that the outside stretchers are flush with the posts as in all early cabinetwork.

The expert carving really makes the chair, which should not be attempted unless an expert is available.

The serious constructional difficulty is the arm which requires dainty handling. There is room for only a small mortise where the arm post enters the arm. The back post must not be weakened by anything larger than a three-sixteenths stove bolt run into the arm diagonally and secured by a blind nut below, as an old bed bolt, and the head must be covered on the post by wood whose grain runs up and down.

The dainty carved star (*Page 174*) at the end of the arm and the nice contour of the arm add much to the grace of the chair. But the arms and their attachments are about a third of the cost of the chair. We show a sketch of the entire chair, page 171.

In the daintiest of these chairs is a very slight hollowing of the back, not more than an eighth of an inch.

This is called the three-feather chair with drapery. A five-feather pattern, also very handsome, exists, varying in some other particulars. It is shown on the following page. The draftsman has not shown the mortise joints, which should be like the chair just described; the diagonal lines shown are mere surface junctures of the carving. The aperture from which the drapery issues is difficult to show, but the semblance of a conical petal really appears. The swelled, properly serpentined, front is the best design, though these chairs are found also with flat fronts, but never with plain single curve. It is a double flattened cyma (ogee).

These chairs are found both with slip seat and upholstered frame. Tastes vary. If upholstered, the goods must be carried to the underside of the rail and tacked there, whether or not ornamental tacking appears as in No. 2343, FURNITURE TREASURY, on the outside.

The mold of the back frame is dainty. There is a very small cock bead on each side and a double ogee between, rising at the center to the height of the cock bead.

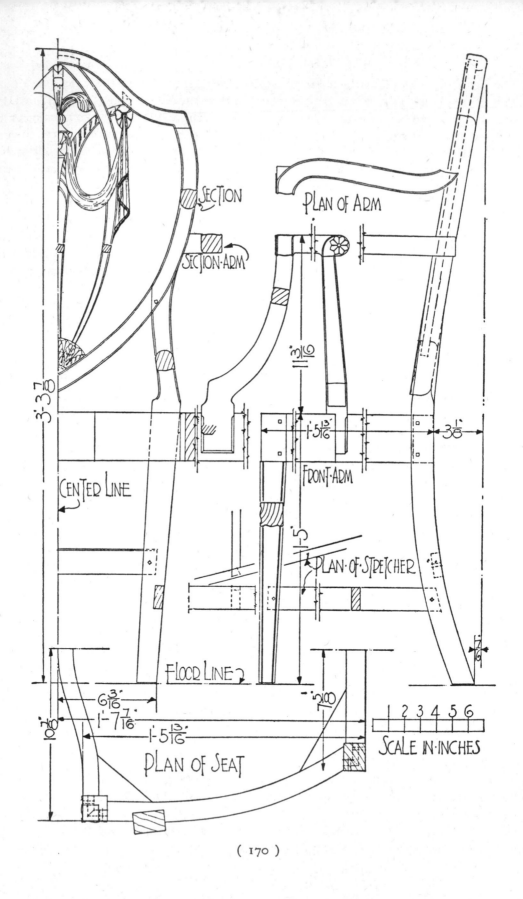

SECTION

SECTION·ARM

PLAN OF ARM

CENTER LINE

FRONT·ARM

PLAN·OF·STRETCHER

FLOOR LINE

PLAN OF SEAT

$3'\cdot3\frac{3}{8}''$

$11'\cdot3\frac{3}{16}''$

$1'\cdot5\frac{13}{16}''$

$3\frac{1}{8}''$

$1'\cdot5''$

$\frac{7}{8}''$

$6\frac{3}{16}''$

$1'\cdot7\frac{7}{16}''$

$1'\cdot5\frac{13}{16}''$

$10\frac{1}{2}''$

5.00

1 2 3 4 5 6

SCALE IN·INCHES

The upper left chair on page 174 is an Austrian design, somewhat suggesting the German eagle, and forming a shield below the heads. Whether some American maker copied the foreign chair, or the chairs found here were imported, I have not been informed.

The chair at the upper right was obtained by me for a friend, from Halifax, where it was believed to be spoil from the ship which was taken from the immortal Lawrence, when he sat in this chair and cried, "Don't give up the ship." I have never seen another chair of just this form, and its use at sea suggests not a little ingenuity and grace and compactness. The seat slats are jointed at the center so that the chair folds. The grace of the curved sides and the sheer simplicity of the design are fascinating.

On page 175, is a Sheraton outline of chair No. 2391, FURNITURE TREASURY, with the three feathers carved at the top and drapery underneath.

Of course, the back rail is in one piece, mortised and set down upon tenons projecting from the back post. It is shown here to take the trend toward fan decoration appearing here in the spandrels and so much used in mantel decoration and about fan windows at the close of the eighteenth and the beginning of the nineteenth centuries.

On page 176 top, left, is a chair belonging to the author, of the transition Hepplewhite period, in which the splat enters the seat as in the Chippendale style. This chair, therefore, should not be called either Hepplewhite or Chippendale; probably we might designate it as of the Federal period. It has an attractive urn and good rosettes terminating the outside reeds. Of course, the splat is all made in one piece, and the decorative folds below the V base of the urn are the ties connecting the reeds for strength.

On the right is the exquisite pattern of a Hepplewhite. The daintiness of the carving and the ingenious devices by which the parts are tied together with cross members are meritorious features. The bases of these chairs vary very little. The back posts converge always toward the bottom.

At the bottom of page 176, left, is the oval back found more frequently on English Hepplewhite chairs and is not as handsome a pattern as the shield back. The reeds or splats, whatever we may term them, do not seem to blend happily with the oval. The back looks more like a gridiron and does not suggest the harmonious grace of design that we love to associate with the Hepplewhite back.

On the right of this chair appears another design of a transition between the Chippendale and the Hepplewhite, unusual in outline, there being three broad feathers with drapery below terminating in a fringe.

It is obvious that these splats of Hepplewhite and Sheraton chairs are susceptible of almost any variation of conventional outline. The Sheraton cabinet pieces are, all in all, perhaps superior to the Hepplewhite, being in a strictly classical design. But in chairs the Sheraton back is not so popular in America as the Hepplewhite. In the Sheraton design a plain vertical reeded back with three, four, or five reeds, permits the construction of an inexpensive chair which is yet in good taste, although it has no special attractiveness.

It is also true that the good Sheraton chair is rare, that is, in an elaborate design. It is the lightest chair made of mahogany.

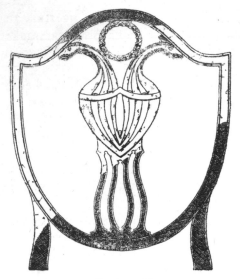

Austrian Design (Page 173)

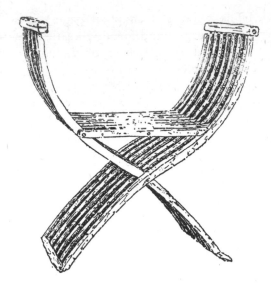

Lawrence's Chair (Page 173)

Below, left, is the detail of the post and arm connection of the measured plan, page 170.

Below, right, is the only Windsor rocking-chair I have seen.

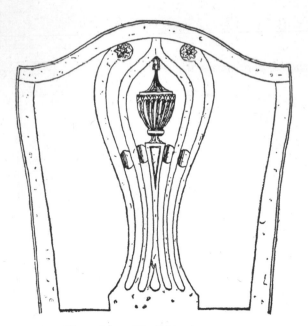

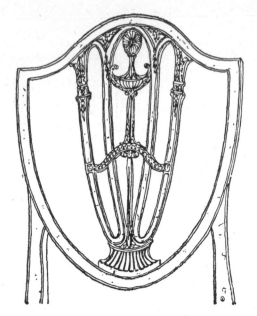

Transition Chair Back   Rarely Beautiful Hepplewhite

Below, left, the oval Hepplewhite back more common in England.

Below, right, transition back of a pattern found in the South. Three feathers rather heavy in outline.

These chairs often lack a good outward sweep of the back leg.

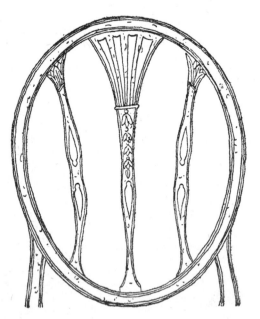

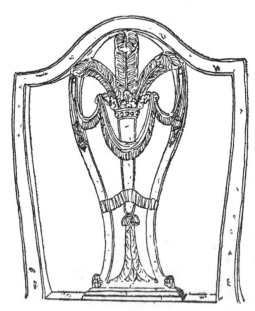

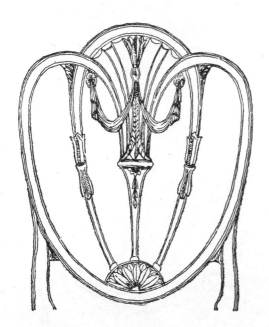 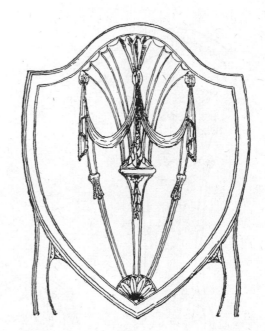

The chair back on the left consists of intersecting curves following a motive found in a good many Hepplewhite chairs, but in the writer's opinion no better than the pure shield-back shape. It is a good instance of the fact that intricacy of treatment does not always secure greater beauty of result. For the best effect in many designs there should be certain main emphatic outlines.

The swag or drapery issuing from the petals of a flower is a motive repeated in a considerable number of Hepplewhite and Sheraton chair backs, and is seen on both the chairs on this page. The decorative element on the external reeds is also found in many Hepplewhite backs. In this and the other chair here a wood bracket is established between the post and the oval member of the frame. This is not frequently found in the Hepplewhite chairs, and while it doubtless adds strength, it does not give the clean line of the sharp angle of connection more usually found. The carving on this chair is dainty and elegant.

The chair on the right has very much the same central splat as the other chair, and undoubtedly the design of the one was carried over to the other. Both of the chairs are sufficiently rare to be desirable. For the base see FURNITURE TREASURY, No. 2347. My own feeling is that the pointed base of the back is rather more effective than the rounded base because it provides a marked line of departure, and emphasizes the design; but opinions differ.

The failure to serpentine the front of the Hepplewhite design loses an element of taste which is difficult to obtain and adds much to the appearance. The hollowed seat now and then found in these chairs occurs, also the straight front. The former adds a line of grace, but we think the serpentine front is the better decoration.

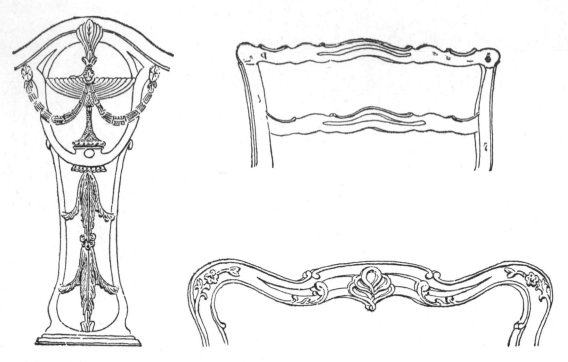

The left-hand figure above is the splat of a chair found in the South, the urn and drapery of which are the same as the well-known Goddard chair of which about thirty exist that are known, but whether made by John or his son Thomas has not been fully established. In this example, however, we have a variation consisting of one three-feather design following another, both reversed. This design resembles a good deal the corn-husk decoration, but feathers are clearly indicated in the carving.

On the upper right is what we may call a waved-back Chippendale also found in the South. A pleasing and unusual design. Each slat is pierced.

Below, right, is the well-known honeysuckle pattern often going by the Greek name anthemion. A considerable number of these chairs is known, and they are also found in England, but whether they are all English does not yet appear. The design is fine and intricate. The Greeks used it a great deal on their friezes, and it was adopted also for separate individual decoration. The decorative motive on the ears is unusual, and in general this back is distinctive and perhaps the handsomest pattern found of the popular ladder backs, which are, at least at present, fancied more than the splat-back Chippendales.

It is observed that the Chippendale backs fall into two very marked classes, one emphasizing the ear as the prominent decorative feature, and the other seeming to ignore it as much as possible, as in this instance, and carrying the connection between the back and the top splat around in a uniform curve with the same lines as the two elements which it joins. Personally I like the marked emphatic ear the better of the two, occurring in conjunction with the splat. In the matter of construction probably the splat is the stronger of the two; at least it has come through the usage of the years in better condition.

(179)

A good, consistently carried-out Flemish scroll, running around the back panel is a feature of the chair on page 179. These backs are always rather narrow, or at least appear so in comparison with the height. The top rail rests solidly between the posts and is, therefore, the preferred type. But no device was ever found of old, or in the present day, to prevent a chair of this kind from working loose between the back and the seat. (The entire chair appears in FURNITURE TREASURY, No. 2021.)

On page 181 the crests of two more Flemish backs are shown. Both are set by mortise between the posts. Of course, these chairs are all caned and may be named as Carolean in date, meaning always Charles II.

On page 181 is still another variant of these stately chairs, which, of course, appear at their best, as they were designed to be used, against the wall. Hence the name, side chairs. Further, these chairs are among the most uncomfortable objects ever devised by man for his own use and behoof. The answer is that they were mostly constructed for decorative purposes. When made as armchairs with cushions they became tolerable. But a good cane seat is more unpleasant than a board.

Of course, the cane was regarded as a step forward toward luxury. The rush seat was apparently avoided in this type as not elegant. There was an effort to arrive at a chair humanly useful and at the same time beautiful. It was at last reached, to a moderate degree, in the rush-seated chair of the more decorative kind. Perfect comfort, however, did not come until the time of the American deeply shaped Windsor. The English Windsor of usual form is uncomfortable as can be, for the shallow elm seat cannot be shaped, and the back lacks the accommodating American lines.

The difference between the feet, some resting their scrolls directly on the floor, and others having shoes or balls under the front feet, is variously explained. Some suppose, plausibly, that one pattern was used for different heights. Whoever had an ancient high table might desire chairs high enough so that the sitter could place his feet on the table stretcher. Therefore, chairs could be made with or without shoes as ordered, for be it remembered, all furniture was made to order, a fact which accounts for the infinite variety, since two individuals seldom agreed perfectly in taste.

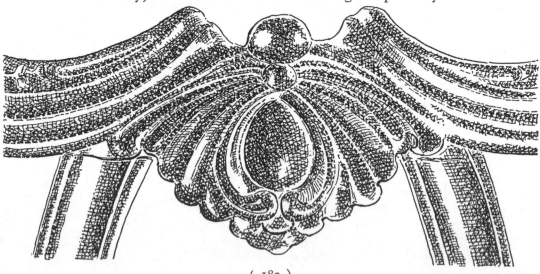

The above paneling arrangement from the Metropolitan Museum is a gorgeous, fully developed example of its period — from 1730 to 1760. The heavy bolection mold about the magnificently tiled fireplace is the strongest note of period. But in this very style, made without a mantel, we have a curious but not uncommon inharmonious note. That is, the pilasters running down between the panels over the fireplace have no bases. They hang in air. They are an incomplete adaptation. This lack is annoying. They need bases just as much as the long pilasters, extending to the floor. The break in the cornice to carry the capitals to the ceiling is effective and commendable. But in the case of the short pilasters this enlarged effect of the capital still further emphasizes the lack of the base. The fluting of the pilasters is the most beautiful part of the detail. There are properly wide boards on the floor, though the cracks that must open between them are catchalls. The only other solution is a wood-blocked floor, or tile.

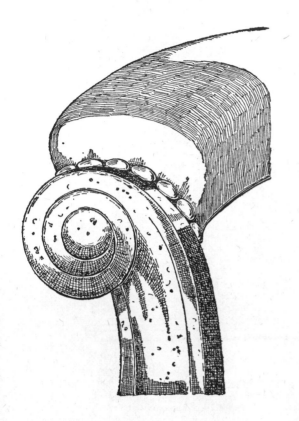 

At the left is the spiral termination of a Chippendale arm support, which some would perhaps call Georgian though probably not. Upholstery which stops before the end of the arm is reached is very much more durable. There is another style appearing on page 164 in which the upholstery is kept still farther away from the end of the arm. An arm which is upholstered at the very point will become shabby and very soiled in a very short time, and that style of upholstery is to be utterly avoided, either in the purchase of antiques or of new furniture. It is amazing to what lengths a whim will go by providing dainty silk or other fabrics to cover the ends of arms. Who of us has not been in hotels of standing and reputation which nevertheless had in their public and private rooms chairs open to this serious objection? It would be necessary to do over the arms every week in order to keep the guests' rooms dainty. This consideration, it would seem, would weigh with every hotel proprietor.

The chair on the right is an ancient peculiar specimen in southeastern Connecticut. in which the heart motive is employed repeatedly in the reeded balusters. The slight mushrooming of the arm and the style of turning would indicate a date about 1700. Individual chairs of this sort always have a fascination.

It was a habit too frequent in Connecticut to use a splint seat like this instead of the rush seat. Our English ancestors came mostly from those parts of England where there were many lowlands in which the rushes throve, and they seemed familiar from the first with the use of rushes for the seats as found in the Carver chair.

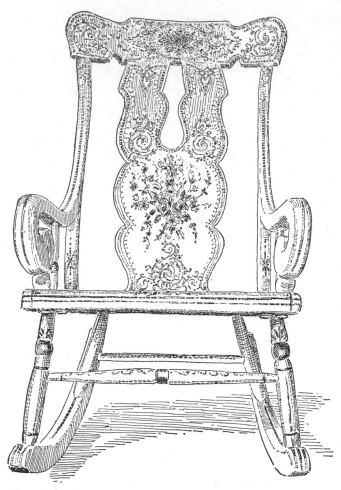

I show above as a matter of curious interest a Pennsylvania rocker corresponding in date with the Boston rocker. About the only element of grace in construction is the shape of the arm, which indeed may indicate that this chair goes back to 1830. The matter of greatest interest about the chair, however, is the extremely elaborate decoration. The ground work is cream color and the scrolls are in gold. The flower decoration, which is very beautifully done, is in rose colors not at all loud, but full of harmony and grace.

Pennsylvania presents a very great variety of individualistic types of furniture, varying from the most elegant to the simplest. It has the distinction of possessing practically the only American oak chairs. It also has probably the only wainscot chairs in walnut found in America.

As peculiar to the location are the numerous built-in cupboards, so constructed because with the solid stone walls of many early houses there was a tendency to build in wood cupboards rather than to make partitions for closets.

There is some degree of rivalry and prejudice between New England and Delaware valley types of furniture.

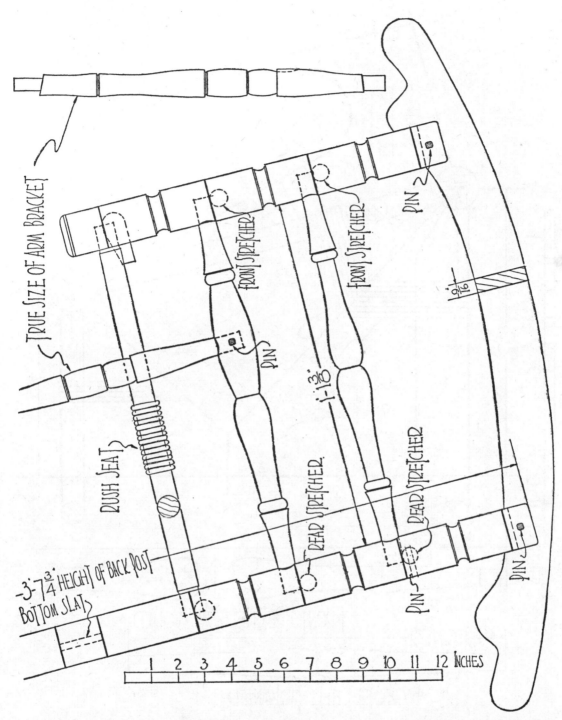

TRUE SIZE OF ARM BRACKET

FRONT STRETCHER

FRONT STRETCHER

PIN

PIN

PIN

$1-\frac{3}{16}$"

$\frac{9}{16}$"

RUSH SEAT

REAR STRETCHER

REAR STRETCHER

PIN

PIN

$-3-7\frac{3}{4}$" HEIGHT OF BACK POST

BOTTOM SLAT

1 2 3 4 5 6 7 8 9 10 11 12 INCHES

On this and the two pages which follow appear the measured drawings for that rare thing, an early rocking-chair, dating probably in the first quarter of the eighteenth century. The indication of date is, of course, in the style of the turning and the extreme shortness and contoured type of the rocker itself. The rocker sits on a strong backward slant and is very comfortable, being an almost perfect lady's chair. The original in my home is a favorite. The arm is a feature common in Connecticut but found elsewhere in New England called the short arm with the double support, the base of the

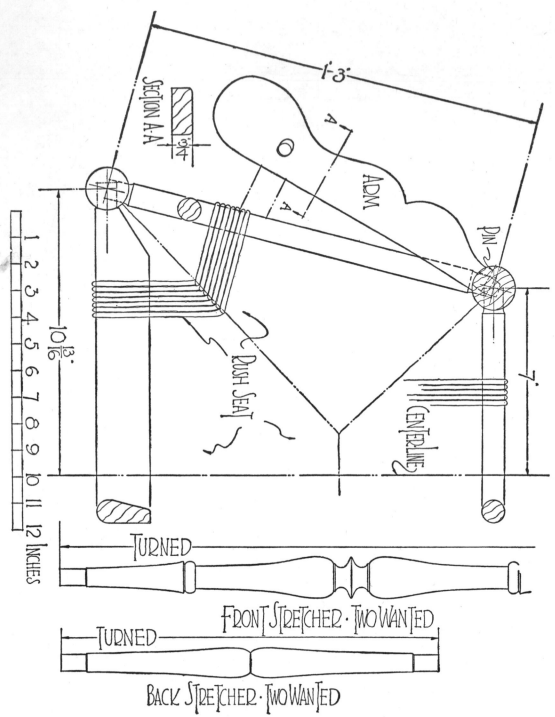

SECTION A·A $\frac{3''}{4}$

1'·3'

A A

ADM

PIN

10 $\frac{13}{16}$''

1 2 3 4 5 6 7 8 9 10 11 12 INCHES

RUSH SEAT

CENTER LINE

7''

TURNED

FRONT STRETCHER · TWO WANTED

TURNED

BACK STRETCHER · TWO WANTED

sustaining spindle running into the upper rung and bearing against the rush of the seat. This rush must be put on before the arm is in place. The inside of the support is hollowed away about a third of the diameter to fit against the rush, but even so, the pitch of this sustaining post slants outward so as to give a broad effect and plenty of room for a generous-sized person. The agreeable shaping of the five-slat back completes a chair moderately light.

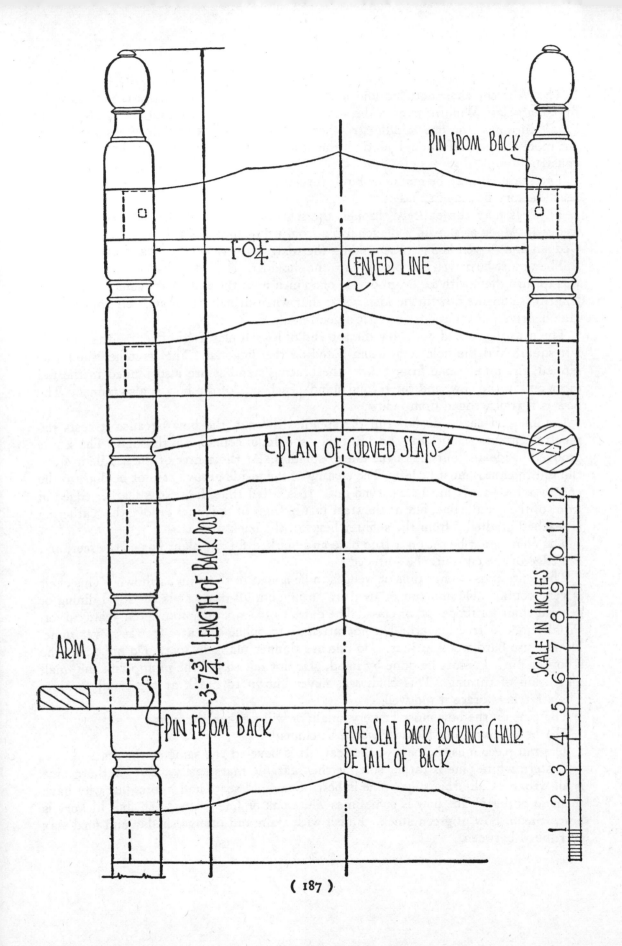

PIN FROM BACK

1'-0¼"

CENTER LINE

PLAN OF CURVED SLATS

PIN FROM BACK

LENGTH OF BACK POST

3'-7¾"

ARM

SCALE IN INCHES

1 2 3 4 5 6 7 8 9 10 11 12

FIVE SLAT BACK ROCKING CHAIR
DETAIL OF BACK

The Windsor chair detailed and measured on the following pages is probably the first high-class Windsor ever to be so shown. The perfect contours of the vase, the "fat" turnings, the fine middle stretcher with fillets, thick and deeply shaped seat, cut more than a half through, and all the other features are in the best-known form of construction.

The material may be maple or birch turning, knotless *one*-piece pine or whitewood seat, hickory bow and spindles.

The legs may run entirely through the seat, in which case they should be foxtail wedged. Made as shown, a diagonal pin from below may hold them; or they may be wedged and driven home, thus sending the wedge into the end of leg, flush.

They must be driven completely into the shoulder. An old and good way of making was to turn them with a glue groove ¾ of an inch from the end, or they may be grooved lengthwise on the dowel, the idea being that when driven home and left smooth, the glue is driven out and does not get a good hold.

The drafting should not show the top end of leg cut slanting; of course the ends are left square and the hole also, being bored on the diagonal. The stretcher should be pinned, the middle one from below; the bracing spindles are also pinned in the tail piece and in the bow, and the second spindle each side of the bow is also pinned. The bow is foxtail wedged from below.

Commercial chairs do not run the spindles through the bow because it costs too much to cut and smooth the end. But they should, of course, run through. The seat is grooved inside and outside of the line of spindles. At the center of the saddle in front the full thickness must be left. The cutting of the inside groove cannot be done to the end by a router. It must be carved out. It is noted that the seat is feather edged in front of the spindle line, but at the start just in front of the inner groove the feathering is reached gradually from the slighter bevel of the back of seat.

The chair must be set on a true base and marked for the slant cut of the feet, and the edge of the cut must be softened.

There are thus twenty pins or wedges to be added to the plan as shown. This chair is very comfortable and can be used by an invalid, all day. It is the ideal dining or general chair for its period or class. The date is 1760–90, but oftener ten years earlier. Pitfalls in construction are: Do not attempt to splice a seat. It was never done. Do not use hard wood in seat. Do not use thinner plank in seat. Do not scant the scooping out. It must be done by hand. Do not fail to get the plump and the small dimension of turning. This chair was never known to break at the small turning. The stretchers brace it too well.

The pins on the bow must be very small, or will weaken the bow.

The bow looks frail. Heavier would be clumsy.

The tail piece must be part of the seat. It is beveled the same as the seat.

Eastern white pine is rather soft for this seat. It mars easily. But southern pine is all wrong. California sugar pine is best. Some old seats had knots, but why have them to bother? The bow is sometimes white oak or fine-grained ash, but hickory is best. Steam bow of green stock. Finish with stain and orange shellac and final wax all rubbed between.

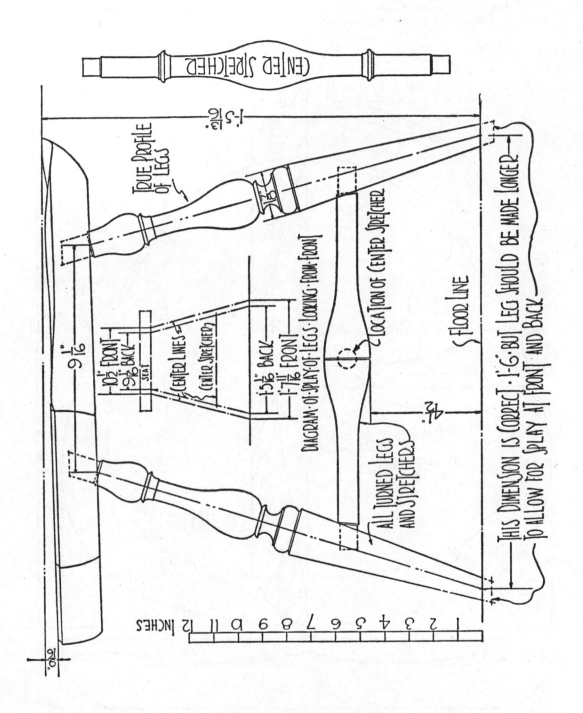

CENTER STRETCHER

TRUE PROFILE OF LEGS

1'-5 13/16"

9 1/16"

10 1/2" FRONT
9 1/2" BACK
SEAT

CENTER LINES
(CENTER STRETCHER)

1'-5 1/2" BACK
1'-7 1/16" FRONT

DIAGRAM OF SPLAY OF LEGS LOOKING FROM FRONT

LOCATION OF CENTER STRETCHER

FLOOR LINE

4 1/2"

ALL TURNED LEGS AND STRETCHERS

THIS DIMENSION IS CORRECT · 1'-6 · BUT LEG SHOULD BE MADE LONGER TO ALLOW FOR SPLAY AT FRONT AND BACK

5/16"

1 2 3 4 5 6 7 8 9 10 11 12 INCHES

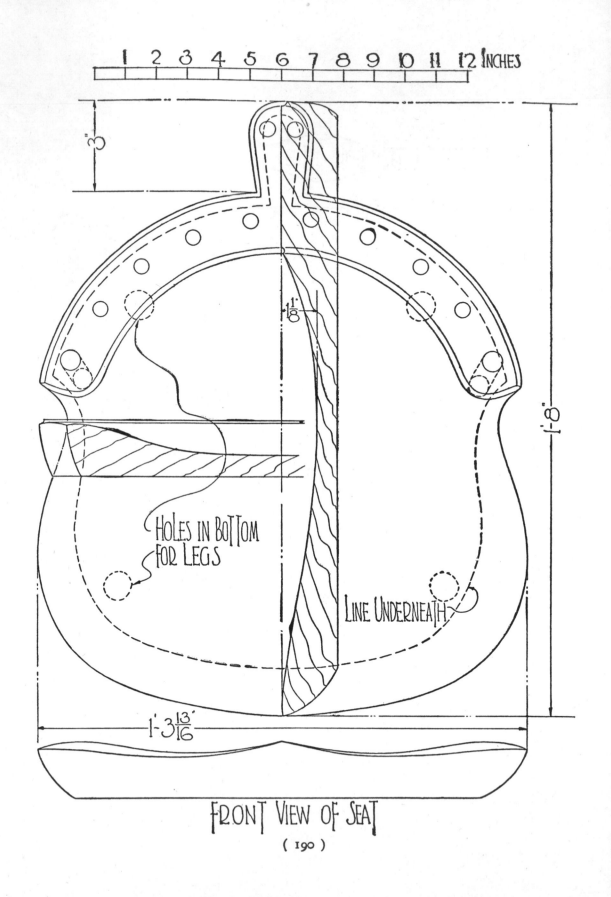

1 2 3 4 5 6 7 8 9 10 11 12 Inches

3"

1⅛"

HOLES IN BOTTOM FOR LEGS

LINE UNDERNEATH

1'-8"

1'-3 13/16"

FRONT VIEW OF SEAT

(190)

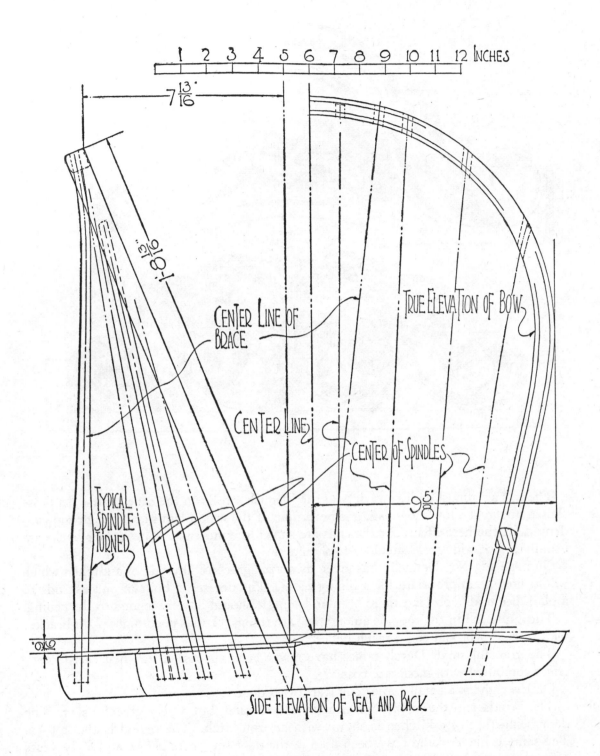

1 2 3 4 5 6 7 8 9 10 11 12 Inches

$7\frac{13}{16}$

$1\cdot8\frac{3}{16}$

Center Line of Brace

True Elevation of Bow

Center Line

Center of Spindles

$9\frac{5}{8}$

Typical Spindle Turned

Side Elevation of Seat and Back

There is an almost endless variety of the Flemish scrolls on the cane chairs. In those shown above the lower one is a good example of the true Flemish, although too condensed for the best effect. At the ends are shown the mortises. These chair backs are usually a foot wide from shoulder to shoulder.

On page 223 Mr. Donnelly has given us a very graceful drawing of a kitchen which would now be appropriate for a dining room. The dresser is built in and extends to a plain beam above. Had there been no beam, it should have extended to the ceiling.

The cupboard in the room is among the rare things. It has good high, plain bracket feet, so that a broom could reach under.

The graceful small Dutch tables have never been surpassed for their satisfactory effect combined with moderate cost.

On the right is a small corner cupboard with doors.

The Windsor in the foreground is of an odd turning, but a very graceful seat. The door being that of a kitchen is shown with an iron latch. The period is about 1750. The same L hinge would have been used in the door ten years before and forty years after this date, but the doors of the front room would have had brass box locks.

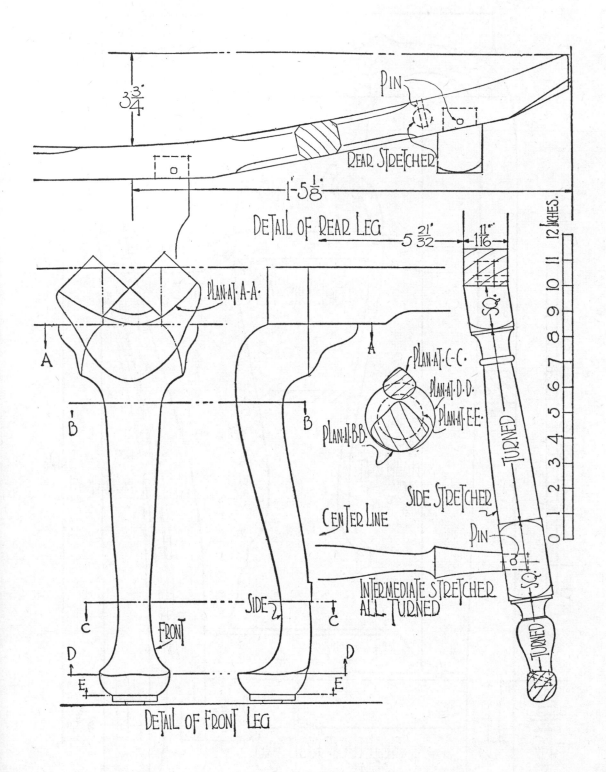

$3\frac{3}{4}$"

PIN

REAR STRETCHER

$1'-5\frac{1}{8}$"

DETAIL OF REAR LEG

$5\frac{21}{32}$"

$1\frac{11}{16}$"

12 INCHES.

11
10
9
8
7
6
5
4
3
2
1
0

PLAN·AT·A·A·

A

B

PLAN·AT·C·C·

PLAN·AT·D·D·

PLAN·AT·E·E·

PLAN·AT·B·B·

A

B

SQ.

TURNED

SIDE STRETCHER

CENTER LINE

PIN

SQ.

INTERMEDIATE STRETCHER
ALL TURNED

SIDE

FRONT

C

D

E

C

D

E

TURNED

DETAIL OF FRONT LEG

(193)

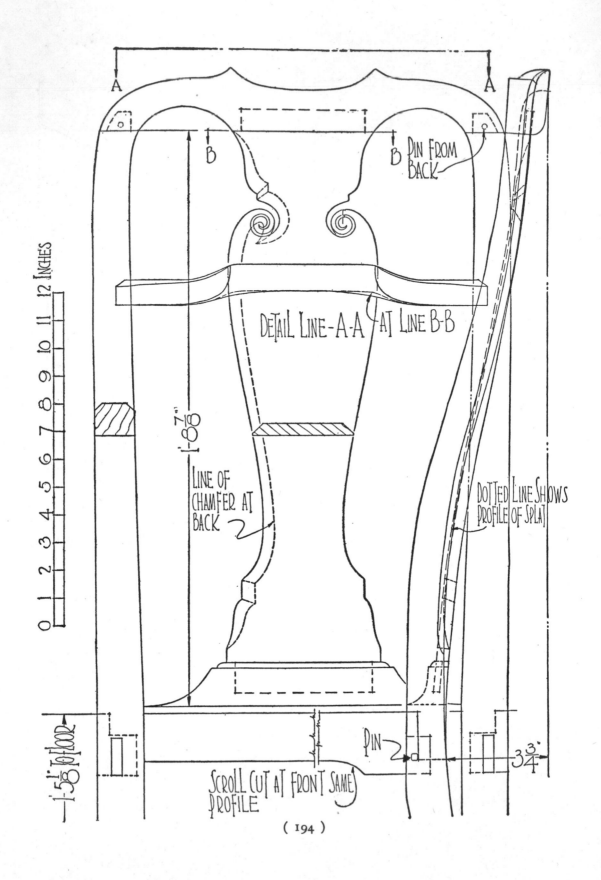

A A

B B PIN FROM BACK

DETAIL LINE - A-A AT LINE B-B

DOTTED LINE SHOWS PROFILE OF SPLAT

LINE OF CHAMFER AT BACK

12 INCHES 11 10 9 8 7 6 5 4 3 2 1 0

1'-8⅞"

PIN

1'-5⅛" TO FLOOR

3¾"

SCROLL CUT AT FRONT SAME PROFILE

(194)

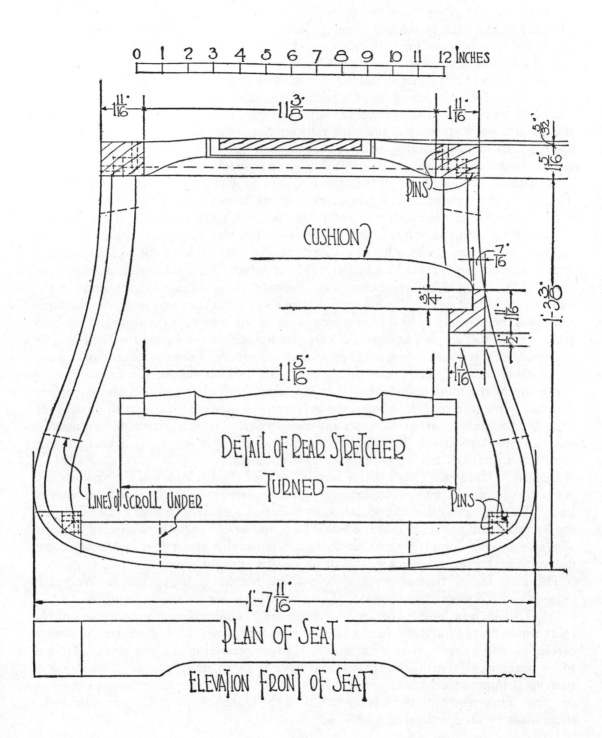

0 1 2 3 4 5 6 7 8 9 10 11 12 Inches

$1\frac{11}{16}$" $11\frac{3}{8}$" $1\frac{11}{16}$" $\frac{5}{32}$" $1\frac{5}{16}$"

PINS

CUSHION

$1\frac{7}{16}$"

$\frac{3}{4}$"

$1\frac{11}{16}$"

$1'\text{-}3\frac{3}{8}$"

$\frac{1}{2}$"

$1\frac{7}{16}$"

$11\frac{5}{16}$"

DETAIL OF REAR STRETCHER

TURNED

LINES OF SCROLL UNDER

PINS

$1'\text{-}7\frac{11}{16}$"

PLAN OF SEAT

ELEVATION FRONT OF SEAT

On the five pages following are plans for a Dutch chair of the period preceding the cabriole leg. Thus we have the Spanish foot and a splat which enters a low cross member in the back instead of running into the seat. Undoubtedly this device was employed to give room for the rush seat, which could not otherwise be used.

The fiddle back splat is a prominent feature of these chairs always. It is, however, narrower than is employed in the rich cabriole-leg chair. The saddle back rail with a heavy scroll roll proceeding from a whorl is another feature always found in good chairs of the period. Chairs are made without this carving, but they do not belong in the same class; furthermore, the back rails are always molded.

These chairs are generally, as here, shown with a somewhat small front post, and in good construction, as here, the side of this leg or post follows the bevel of the seat and is not square. In cheap chairs it is found square as it is much easier to construct so. The arm of these chairs is, as a rule, marked by one heavy twist, as here, but there is a wide divergence in the manner of ending the arm with the roll-over. This chair has not much curvature, nor has it much enlargement of the arm at the roll-over.

Many of the fine chairs otherwise strictly of this pattern have the ram's-horn arm, with a very strong outward and downward curvature and a somewhat enlarged section. That arm is, therefore, shown as an alternate. It is difficult to draw and connect as it curves in two ways. The inner scrolls are wider than the outer ones. In the finest examples there seems to be a lateral narrowing of the arm as it runs toward the back post. In some examples, however, it keeps its full width. It enters the back post by vertically long tenons. The strong spoon-back curvature of the uprights or back posts is a feature of the Queen Anne time. Undoubtedly it is supposed to represent the curvature of the human spine, but it is the spine in an alert position and not in the position of modern repose. That is to say, it sweeps forward on the small of the back and fits a person who sits quite intent and wide awake. The splat, it would be observed, has the same curvature. It must be strong to attain this shape. It is also strongly beveled on the back to give an impression of thinness.

Regarding the feet. They also are beveled so that the back part of the Spanish foot is narrower than the front of it, conforming to the narrowing of the seat from front to back. The neglect of this important point will spoil a chair. All four of the seat rails are flattened and not turned, as the seat is large and would not otherwise keep its form. The side chair is found in great numbers and is usually about two inches narrower, not varying, however, otherwise except by the omission of the arm.

The material of these chairs may be walnut, maple, birch, or beech. Walnut is regarded as the more elegant wood. There is little choice between the others.

It is curious how long it required for designers of chairs to arrive at the use of the splat which arose directly from the back of the seat frame. If we consider the matter carefully, it will appear that the reason lies in the material of the seat itself. If it was to be covered with rush, the splat would have been an interference. A good job of rushing is impossible with any interruption of the seat by anything beyond the four corners. Thus wherever there is a splat as of the Queen Anne or Chippendale styles there must be an upholstered seat.

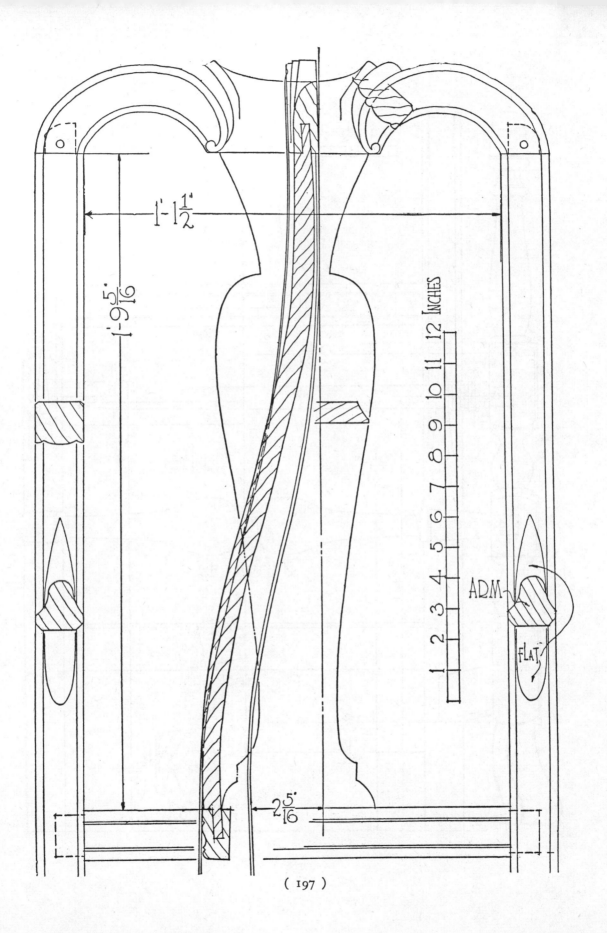

1'-1$\frac{1}{2}$"

1'-9$\frac{5}{16}$"

2$\frac{5}{16}$"

ADM

FLAT

1 2 3 4 5 6 7 8 9 10 11 12 INCHES

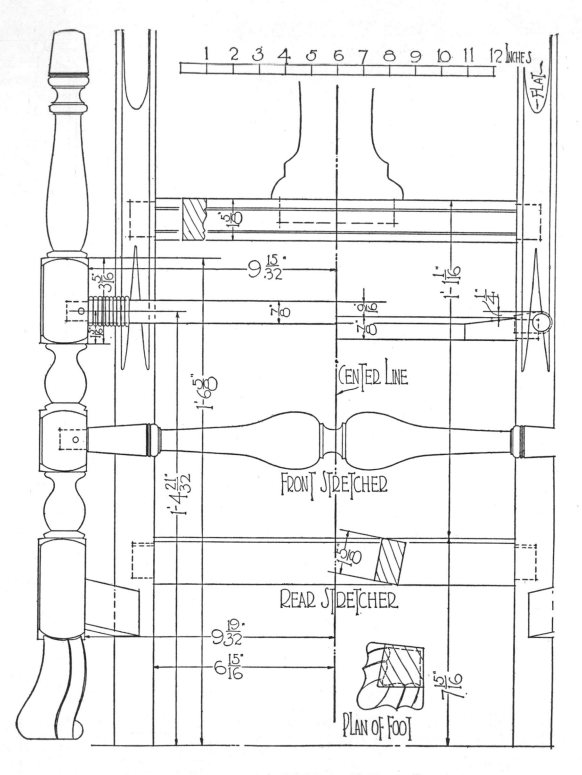

1 2 3 4 5 6 7 8 9 10 11 12 Inches

FLAT

CENTER LINE

FRONT STRETCHER

REAR STRETCHER

PLAN OF FOOT

(198)

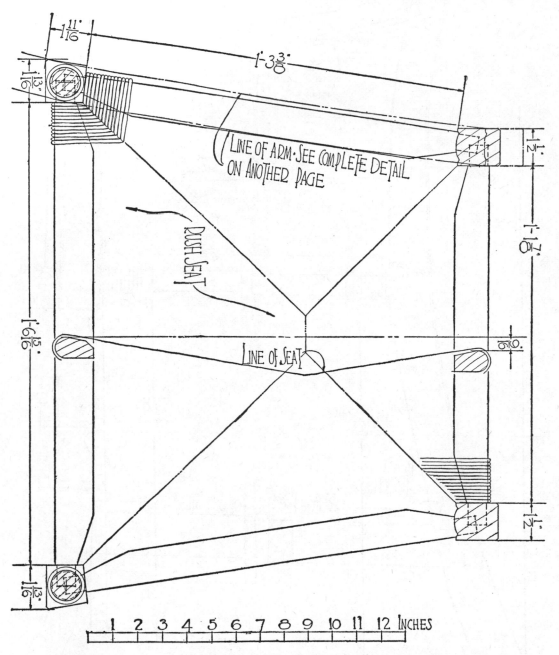

$1'-\frac{11}{16}$

$1'-3\frac{3}{8}''$

$1''-\frac{3}{16}$

LINE OF ARM · SEE COMPLETE DETAIL ON ANOTHER PAGE

$1'-\frac{1}{2}''$

RUSH SEAT

$1'-7\frac{1}{8}''$

$\frac{9}{16}''$

LINE OF SEAT

$1'-6\frac{15}{16}''$

$1''-\frac{3}{16}$

$1'-\frac{1}{2}''$

1 2 3 4 5 6 7 8 9 10 11 12 INCHES

Above is the seat frame for the detail shown on the two foregoing pages. It will be seen, as in all fine work, all the outside members of the seat frame are broadened. The front rung often falls a half of the diameter below those at the side.

(199)

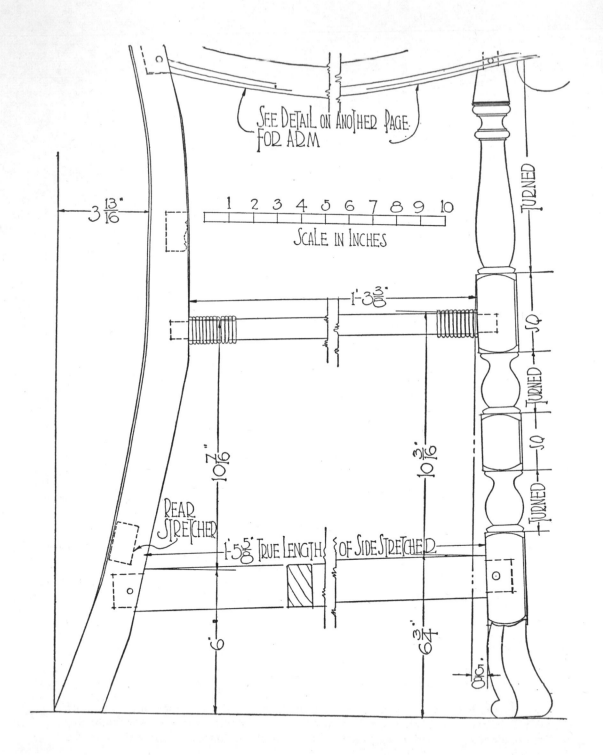

SEE DETAIL ON ANOTHER PAGE:
FOR ARM

$3\frac{13}{16}$"

| 1 | 2 | 3 | 4 | 5 | 6 | 7 | 8 | 9 | 10 |

SCALE IN INCHES

$1'-3\frac{3}{8}$"

TURNED

SQ

TURNED

SQ

TURNED

$10\frac{7}{16}$"

$10\frac{3}{16}$"

REAR STRETCHER

$1'-5\frac{5}{8}$" TRUE LENGTH OF SIDE STRETCHER

$6\frac{3}{4}$"

6"

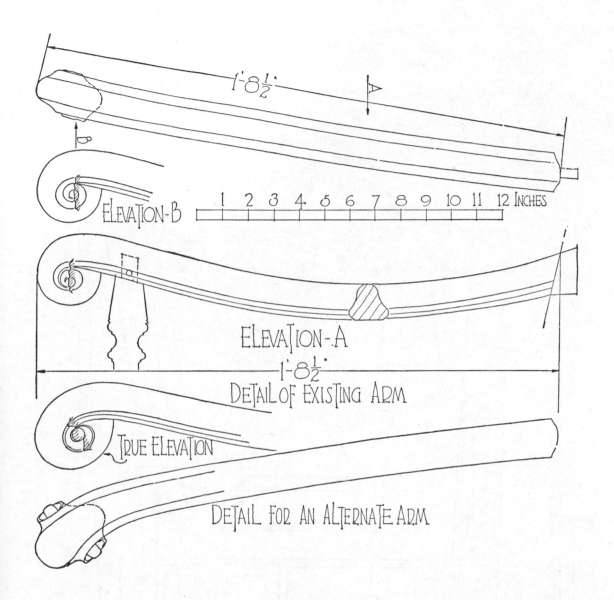

ELEVATION-B

1 2 3 4 5 6 7 8 9 10 11 12 INCHES

ELEVATION-A

1'-8½"

DETAIL OF EXISTING ARM

TRUE ELEVATION

DETAIL FOR AN ALTERNATE ARM

The arm as found for the chair, the plans of which occupy the pages immediately before this, is shown in the three drawings at the top of this page. Another arm, however, of the ram's-horn type is often found on the chair which is otherwise just like this. In order to give the cabinetmaker the benefit of that design we have shown it above in the two lower details.

We should say also that in many of these chairs the arm narrows a little as it approaches the back post, perhaps a quarter of its width, on a long taper, for the whole length. However, some of the best chairs are made as appears above.

GREATEST RELIEF OF CARVING $\frac{3}{32}$

OPEN

GREATEST RELIEF OF CARVING $\frac{1}{16}$

OPEN

OPEN

OPEN

OPEN

SHOWS CURVE LINE A

A

$\frac{1}{2}$

$1'\text{-}5\frac{3}{8}''$

$3\frac{3}{16}''$

$1'\text{-}4\frac{3}{16}''$

$1'\text{-}3\frac{1}{16}''$

$1\frac{1}{2}''$

$1'\text{-}9\frac{11}{16}''$

PLAN OF SEAT

$1'\text{-}3\frac{3}{16}''$

CORNER BRACE.

$1'\text{-}5\frac{1}{16}''$ TO FLOOR

$1'\text{-}3\frac{11}{16}''$

16
15
14
13
12
11
10
9
8
7
6
5
4
3
2
1

SCALE IN INCHES

On page 202 is a very rich New York City design of a chair by William Ashe. As it is about the only outstanding Chippendale which we can definitely ascribe to New York, it is proper that it should receive more attention on that account.

The emphatic feature in it is the richly carved and handsomely designed splat with a tassel, the base of which is raised a little above the lace pattern which crosses below it in order to separate it in feeling. This lace pattern is the most intricate carving. It has a wave something like a linen fold. It is probably fair to call it a lace pattern rather than a linen fold, unless we are to presume that it represents a border worked on the linen fold. The graceful acanthus leaf on the side of the central vase supplies a satisfactory completion of the motive. A heart-shaped pierced opening below flanked by beveled scrolls makes up the rest of the splat. At the top, however, there is shell work, pure rococo ornament, of course, on the enlargement of the splat where it joins the top rail. The ear of this chair is most satisfactory.

Unfortunately the feet on the two chairs available to me are not quite equal to the back. They are of the claw-and-ball pattern, and carry the engrailing on the front frame and, of course, the acanthus leaf on the knee. The defect seems to be in the foot, which is a trifle too high for perfect form.

On pages 204 and 205 are two rooms, the former most delightful and taken from the Metropolitan Museum restoration. It is a pity that with a looking-glass and a lowboy as rich as this the authorities did not think it was worth while to install a better bed-stead or, at least to put a spread on the bed to hide the roping. The chair back on the left is of the pure cupid's-bow pattern, of the turned Dutch type. The chair on the right shows what we have called a country Dutch style, a somewhat crude top rail. The ceiling is done in a much more elaborate way than was usual; in fact, it is better than any other I happen to have seen being divided off by intersecting rails and stiles into great panels.

The bed belongs to what is usually termed a hired man's pattern.

In the other picture on page 205 is the setting of 1690 and earlier. That is, the chairs are somewhat earlier. On the rug on the left is the only good baby Carver chair that I happen to know. On the left is a side Carver chair of more than usual merit. The fire irons are of the gooseneck or, more properly, goosehead pattern.

The obtaining of good rooms for this volume has been the most difficult part of the work. It is very seldom that all of the elements combine harmoniously. Some of these were taken from my own assembly before they were dismantled and sent to a museum, and the others are from various private houses and museums.

The fireplace above is from the Jaffrey house, Portsmouth, New Hampshire. Features to be emphasized are the red brick tiling forming the hearth up to the fireplace line, and that these are always laid close together. Next the heavy torus mold about the fireplace. Then the tall, impressive stop-fluted pilasters with their broken cornice capitals. It is my belief that the mantel was not originally installed, but was subsequently put in place. It appears that there is no structural provision for the mantel, and this scheme of imposing a mantel where none was originally has been found in other Portsmouth houses. When the fashion changed calling for a mantel, and fashion and convenience pulled in the same direction, we may easily judge what the result would be.

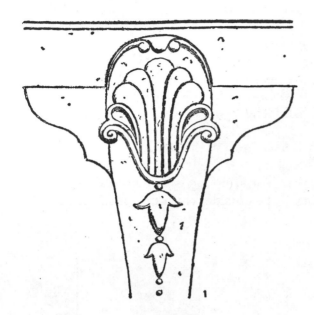
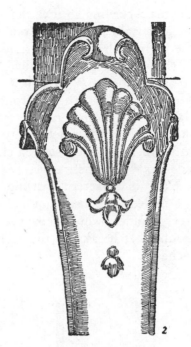

Although the number of motives in furniture carving is almost unlimited, there were certain styles which appealed more strongly to the taste than others, so that we have an odd situation illustrating the tendency of the average man to fall into a rut and stay there. As a consequence, several motives of very great beauty were neglected for a narrow range of the types which became standardized and conventional. With all the world to choose from the fingers will count the often repeated designs.

The main body of furniture carving produced from 1720 to 1780 consists of the shell, the acanthus leaf, the C scroll, and the husk (corn flower), which last is confined to Hepplewhite and styles contemporary with it. The fretted motives of later Chippendale are unusual in America.

The styles of feet are treated under a chapter by themselves, and another chapter treats of shells.

We show grouped here a number of chair knees or complete legs.

Nos. 1 and 2 show the entire carving motive on early Georgian, ordinarily called Queen Anne, knees.

The mass of fine carving was found in variations of the acanthus leaf, a motive probably never surpassed and even insurpassable in its perfect adaptation for a chair knee, or hip (interchangeable names).

Nos. 4 and 5 are two views of one leg. No. 5 is seen on the diagonal. The bracket portion, or that part extending beyond the square of the top, is always glued to the main leg. A great stick of timber would otherwise be required. The skill of the designer showed itself particularly in his manner of tying the carving on the bracket to the main carving so that the whole would be felt to be a unity. The No. 4 shows the leg at a right angle, from one side, although it should be carefully noted that neither the leg nor the upper section is ever exactly square. The carving follows the frame of the seat, of course, which is generally of the proportion of 21 across the front to 16 across the back, though these ratios given here in inches vary as much as an inch. But always the corner in front is an acute angle. The purer Chippendale styles have either sharp corners on the frame, or are very slightly rounded. A strong round, as shown on 1 and 2, belongs to the early Georgian and Queen Anne. The foot going with No. 4 is a fully shaped claw-and-ball. The measurement on No. 4 in width outside is $5\frac{13}{16}$ inches.

No. 3 is a pattern showing framing connections at the seat. The central spandrel is stippled, as is usual and proper. The effort to make it smooth, where it cannot be freely sanded, would show the tool marks. The stippling is a device to overcome that trouble. It breaks up the surface lights. The outside width on this diagonal is $5\frac{3}{16}$ inches.

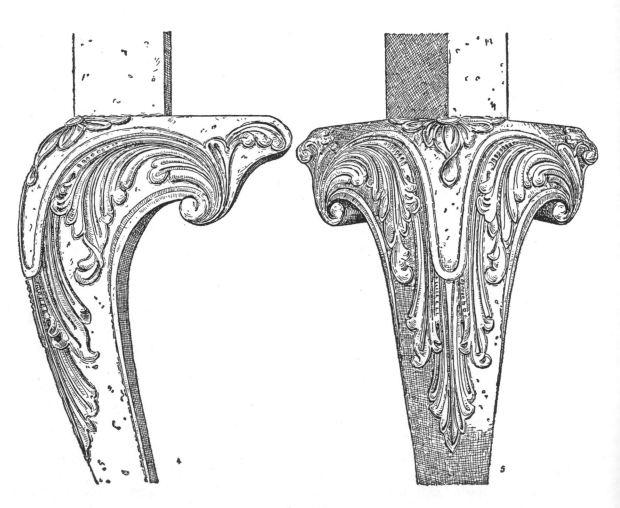

The only five-ladder-back Chippendale that has happened to come to my attention. Found in the South, but whether domestic or foreign does not appear. It is of rare grace and lightness. The arm in this style has departed from the heavier, more impressive scroll of the Georgian and Chippendale. It indicates a date after, say 1760, and usually after 1770. The same arm also appears on Hepplewhite chairs.

The attachment of these arms to the back post was never satisfactory. The main strain must be borne by the rigid seat attachment. The repair of the back attachment can best be made with the smallest size of stove bolt with a blind plugged nut below and a thin plugged piece behind. A large bolt makes worse the defect one is remedying.

The important carved knee of course has its brackets attached in a continued line from the line on the frame.

All Chippendale ladder backs so far as I have observed have straight legs. The style came into popularity but not into general use owing to the cost, probably. Sometimes elegant Chippendale chairs had perfectly plain legs, or legs with one bead on the corner. It would appear that the greater part of the straight-leg chairs had the upholstery running over the frame, but some have the slip seat. Where the upholstery runs over the frame, the upper part of a molded leg must be smoothed to take the upholstery. That is, the molding must be cut away to a flat surface. The straight leg on slip seats never finishes off very satisfactorily at the top. It seems inconclusive.

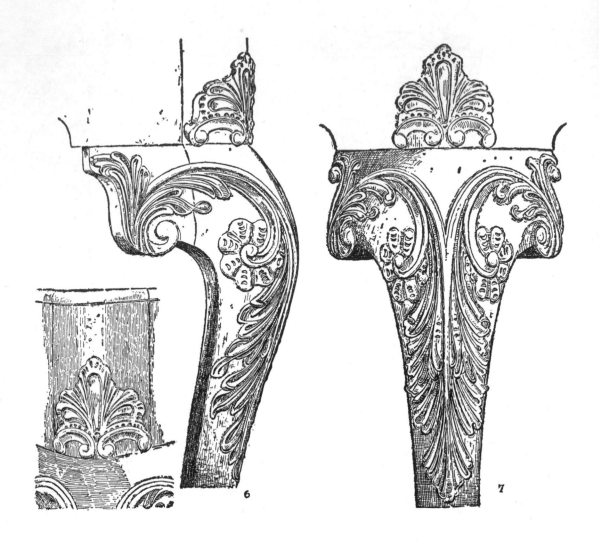

6 7

No. 6 is a leg rounded on the frame corner and carrying a rococo carving on that corner. If it tied in with an extension running down onto the hip, a richer and more valuable specimen would have been produced. This drawing shows the line of connection between the bracket and the leg. It requires from 3 to 4 inches in the square of the stock to carve these legs, and allow for the curvature, though 3 are usually enough. The length of the leg to the frame is 13 ½ inches; to the top 17 ¼ inches, a good and usual height of Chippendale chair seat. A wide frame adds much to strength, especially if there are no stretchers (underframe). It is a question whether stretchers help much where the frame depth (up and down) is 3 inches or nearly 3. A stretcher weakens a leg by the cutting of the mortise about as much as it stiffens the leg. No. 7 shows the diagonal of No. 6. The space above the carving on No. 7 was open enough to admit of sanding; hence it is not stippled.

No. 8 illustrates a much simpler leg, the carving of the knee being quickly done, and gives the foot also.

No. 9 is a rich stool leg with a lion or dog foot, more usual in the early Georgian than in the Chippendale time. It exhibits the additional motive of a rope molding, called more generally, in an elaborate form, an engrailing, about the bottom on the seat frame. There is also carried up a scroll onto the frame corner itself, greatly enhancing the beauty of the style. A variation is seen in No. 10. (*Page 213*.)

No. 11 goes back to a naturalistic leg, with cloven foot and a marked angle joint.

Chippendale's later method, the straight leg, used by him quite generally after about 1751, is detailed in No. 12. This work should never be found applied. The leg holds its full size throughout, not tapering until Hepplewhite designs came in. (*Page 214*.)

Nos. 13 and 14 depart from the usual by showing an oak leaf with pendant acorn. The foot has a contracted oak leaf on the French scroll, based on a shoe. (*Page 212*.)

No. 15 is a fully carved style, in which the designer has delighted in giving us variations from the usual. (*Page 213*.)

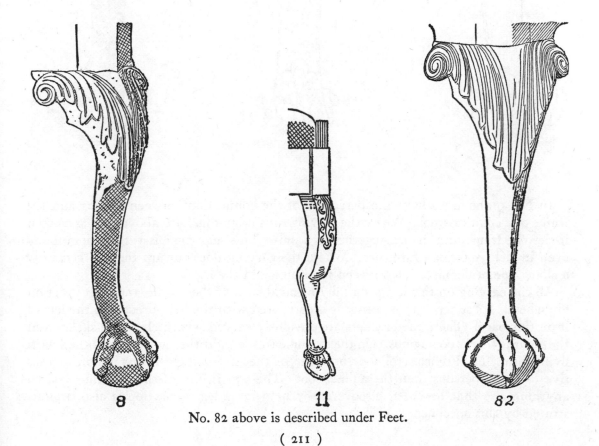

8   11   82

No. 82 above is described under Feet.

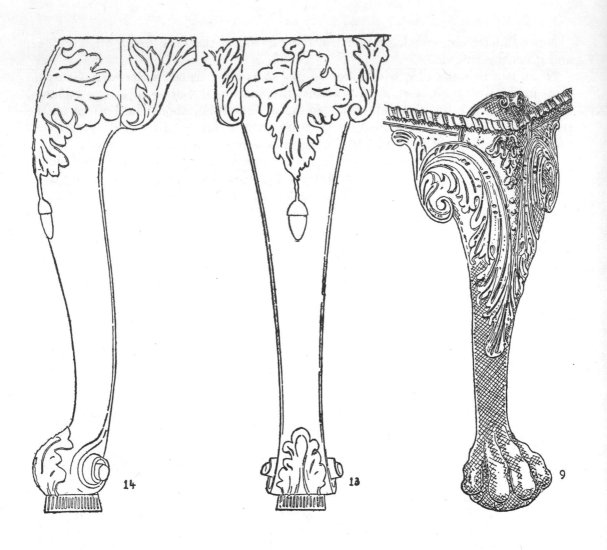

In No. 9 above we have the best form of the connection between the leg and the frame of a chair or stool. Where the carving runs up in this form above the leg mortise it ties the frame and the leg together as a unit. This high type is very seldom found even in rich American furniture. Where the carving does run up there is generally a sharp line of demarcation between the frame and the leg.

All the carving on this leg is skilfully blended so that there is no apparent junction anywhere. Its superiority is seen if it is compared with the legs directly to the left of it on this page. There the brackets are obviously carved separately. The skeleton of the chair is there too obvious. On the example to the right the skeleton is clothed with living form. The French scroll foot, however, on the left-hand specimens is more attractive to many persons than the animal foot. The superiority of the acanthus leaf to anything else that has been discovered by man for a leg decoration is also demonstrated by this specimen.

The intricacy of pattern No. 15 would perhaps not be fully appreciated at a distance. Partly for this reason and partly because of the labor involved, patterns are seldom so complicated as this. Of course, the sudden stopping of the carving with the leg, leaving the frame plain above it, is emphatic and in accordance with the principle that decoration should not cover every part. Here, as often, there is a raised rim or bead at the border of the leg carving which of course runs out to a plain surface just below its bottom termination. It has never been possible to learn who originated this style. It came before Chippendale in the early Georgian period, and ceased about 1760.

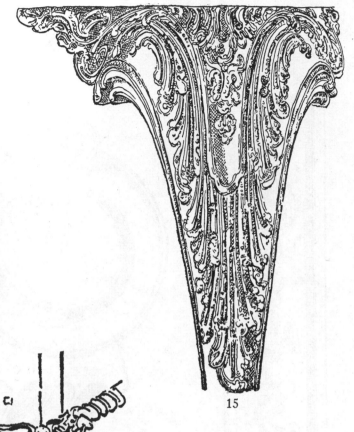

15

10

The superiority of the carving on the previous page to that shown here is obvious. The somewhat bolder design here is effective. We have here the very rare motive of a single sweeping line running up from the leg to the frame without any marked bracket effect, achieved by separate scrolls as in No. 15 above and No. 9 on the previous page. The sudden change to the straight leg induced by the publication of Chippendale's designs was a misfortune. The Chinese fret is more conventional than this foliage.

12

The leg of a Chippendale type of mixed carving motive in the "Chinese taste."
The splat is found in many Chippendales, as shown or slightly modified. Of
course unshaded parts are cut out.

16

17

Passing now to a table leg of remarkable rarity, Nos. 16 and 17 show a masque on the front leg of a small three-cornered table whose origin has not been settled. It was in Cambridge, Massachusetts, about 1800. The other legs are straight with button feet. The table has the conformation of a fine corner chair frame carried up to table height, and was doubtless suggested by the corner chair of the early Georgian period. The table is walnut, and shown under tables.

It was rarely that Chippendale dining-table legs were carved, they being so generally out of sight except the claw-and-ball feet. The card tables, however, when in curved form repeat with little variation the acanthus and other motives found on chair legs. The same is true of the Queen Anne and Chippendale sideboards, so much finer than the later Shearer sideboard with drawers.

The legs of the lowboys and highboys, Philadelphia pattern, appear in general outline in Vol. I of this work. They vary little from chair legs, which, being more numerous, exhibit more gradations of style. The condensed legs of chests-on-chests are found under feet.

A chair back photographed by the author in the South, but very similar to a chair at Bramshill, England, illustrated in *Antiques*, September, 1931. The slight difference seems to be in favor of this chair, which on the top rail ends with a handsome scroll at the ear, whereas the Bramshill specimen is slightly inconclusive at this point. The stop-fluted posts, scarcely found in New England, are usual (though without the stop) on the best Philadelphia and Baltimore specimens.

A feature to compare with Gillingham chairs is the opening with opposed Cs in the splat. The shape of the outline of the beveled carving in the lower part of the splat is a striking reminder of the kidney dial on American shelf clocks.

It will be seen that the ear scroll does not follow the end of the top rail, but that a leaf is added outside the scroll. This is a curious but not unpleasing device. The splat is so reinforced as to form a strong chair. At the base of the splat there is an enrichment.

On two pages following are found a side Queen Anne chair of much beauty and rarity. It has several peculiar features found in the early types, among which is the seat shape, a very heavy square construction on the inside, conforming only on the outside. These heavy sections were supplied in accordance with the Queen Anne time. Another marked feature is the manner of attachment of the front leg, the top of it being formed as a dowel and passing through the seat frame, and so pinning in a solid manner the mortise. The leg, however, would even so have lacked solidity had it not been sustained by its brackets. It is observable that the leg has not vertical sections where it meets the bracket (see sketch following) but flares downward, thus reminding us of an early time.

The heavy retaining mold for the slip seat being worked on a curve all the way required hand shaping.

Another special feature is the repetition of the decorative motives. On the top back rail and the knees we have the same shell, but above it is expanded and below contracted to harmonize with the space.

Again there is a semblance but not a repetition of the scrolls. Above they are Flemish (S) scrolls. Below they are unilateral, both terminating in whorls on the same side.

The acanthus scroll on the splat begins in a whorl much the same, but develops into foliage.

The contour of the back viewed sidewise has a double curve, as well as when viewed in front.

The grooving between the three toes runs high on the leg and ends as abruptly as a flute.

A single corn flower is provided as a pendant for the leg shell.

Back legs have the usual contour followed in Philadelphia chairs both of the Queen Anne and the Chippendale time, a circle flattened fore and aft, before it passes into a square section at the frame. The comparison between this "bell" seat and the angular Chippendale seat is very marked. Also the strong effect of height here as compared with the broader, lower Chippendale back.

We may use this walnut chair as a type showing a very strong change from the King Charles shape which immediately preceded it. This chair was quite foreign to English tables when William became King. Though the trees were now supplying merchantable walnut from the plantings encouraged by Queen Elizabeth, the styles must be imported. The wood itself was a tree still earlier brought to Europe from Persia and spreading at length through Italy, Spain, and France. Little did the people of that day surmise that what they were expensively nourishing was in an excellent variety being burned as a nuisance on the rich plains of the New World, from the seaboard westward, until five or six generations from the Dutch dynasty that burning would extend to the champaign country of the Illinois, and that we should be imitating their handsome decorations in the virile young city of the Delaware, in the generation directly after them.

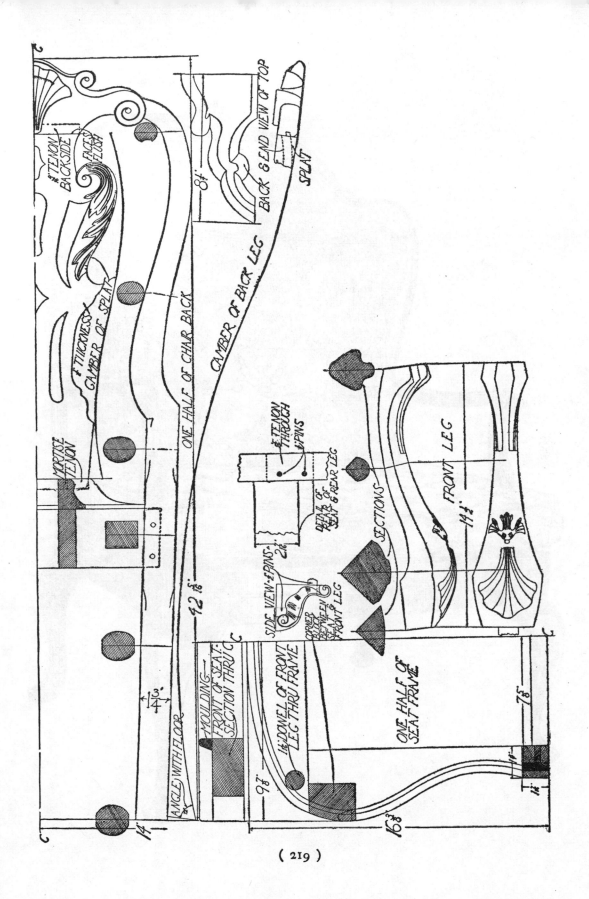

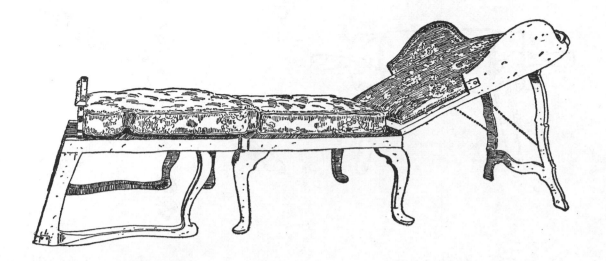

On this and the preceding page are shown the closed and the open form of one of the most remarkable Queen Anne chairs known. It is in the Black house, a public exhibit of a dwelling founded by one of the proprietors of a large section of Maine, at Ellsworth.

The furniture in the dwelling consists of the early types, followed by whatever else the family desired to acquire well into the nineteenth century, and thus is a record of various periods, as a house would be furnished by a well-to-do gentleman.

Of course, the chair is in walnut and the ingenious manner in which it is formed into a couch is sufficiently explained by the admirable drawings. This type of wing chair in which the wing stops at the arm rail is rare, and only one other at present occurs to me. While I have heard a rumor of another chair similar to this one, opening out to form a couch, I have not been able to verify its existence.

The people in old times knew how to accommodate their furniture to their needs as well as we do. They had not only chairs which were transformable, but their beds also, usually called press beds, because they folded inside two long cupboard doors, were the ancestors of the modern spring traps and contraptions.

The slides which they had to pull out on their sideboards, chests of drawers, etc., as sorting or packing shelves were also most convenient.

They found it quite necessary to economize room, owing to the size of their families and sometimes owing to their modest-sized houses. This is undoubtedly the cause of the taking down and removal of the trestle table after every meal. While perhaps the present instance of transformable furniture is early, the custom became rife under Sheraton who devised any number of unfolding chairs as library steps, or stands in the interior of which were packed away a number of conveniences from a looking-glass to a patch box. This chair has width, dignity, and grace. The central top decoration should not be mistaken for the later Victorian carving.

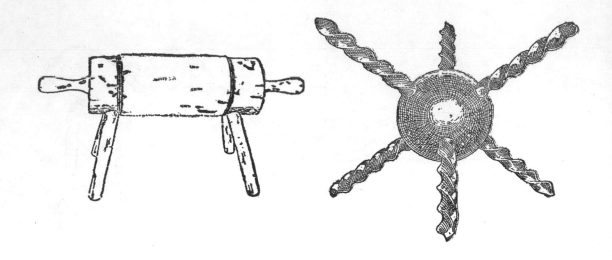

Most of the animals familiar to us appear on this and the finial pages. The rolling-pin affair on legs is a pig. It was banded with a strip of carpet and was used by resting one's stretched-out heels in front of a fire, something so good we wonder it wasn't frequently found. On the right the spider-like piece in mahogany with twisted legs is a cat, so named because it always lands on its feet. A rare, elegant specimen is known, the use of which is to sustain as on three fingers a decorative bowl or salad dish. The turned mahogany ball is 4 inches in diameter and the legs are 5 inches long, with a diameter of ¾ inch. Below is a decorated horse used in the Middle Ages for a trestle board. On the right is a dog, the name given to a small andiron, though in this rare instance coupled up as twins, a New Hampshire find. On the finial pages are a cock, an owl, an eagle, and other bipeds.

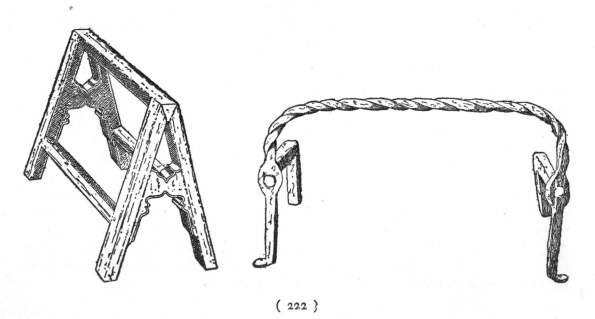

For description of room above see page 192.

On page 228 is the exquisite coffered window shutter found in the South, as in Annapolis. Every other coffered panel is different. To decorate a room even in this portion which is left as a plain panel indicates a fine taste in desiring the whole dwelling to be in keeping. It is seen that the window frame sweeps down with a ramp.

An extremely rich dado and a heavy projected baseboard, giving room for a fine molding above it completes the decoration. The lady is seated in the simple Martha Washington chair. It belongs to the late Chippendale time, the leg not being tapered.

FURNITURE REPAIR OR RESTORATION

So much furniture has been ruined by injudicious repair that a few principles will be stated. If these principles are followed strictly, they will save many regrets and grievous financial losses.

1. Repairs should always be made with old wood from other furniture.

2. Nothing whatever should be cut away from the old furniture to make "a good job." A half inch uselessly cut off might destroy half the value.

3. Splices should always be made on a diagonal or by a V cut, never by a square addition with dowels only.

4. The color of the wood as well as the kind should match the old.

5. Surface repairs should be done, as in veneer, with irregularly shaped pieces, not rectangular sections.

6. It is generally better to splice the feet, if worn off, to give more dignity to the piece even when that splicing is not absolutely necessary. An old piece will otherwise perhaps have a squat appearance that, not being intended by the maker, spoils the effectiveness of the design. The writer pieced an oak cupboard which had lost its feet entirely. The buyer declared he would have given much more for it had it been untouched. But he, while honest, was mistaken. He had passed by the piece, now dignified and impressive, when it was without the feet! Hence, major repairs, even on rough seventeenth-century furniture, must be made.

7. Minor repairs on such furniture ought to be omitted if possible, otherwise a new effect is given which spoils the furniture. The same principle applies to the finish. Such pieces when new were not polished and dainty. That was not the purpose. Had daintiness been sought, the ax marks on the backs and interiors of oak would have been smoothed off. Irregularities should be left, as handmade furniture always showed irregularities when new.

8. Dainty furniture, especially that of the mahogany period, will bear, and even demands, more complete restoration. Furniture of this sort often depends much on surfaces which, therefore, require more treatment than oak.

9. Much fine carving has been partly obscured by many coats of finish. How much the appearance of old sharp carving should be restored at the expense of removing great quantities of gummy material may be left to the matter of taste. Even the removal of finish may hurt the edges of the carving.

10. Of course, all broken or missing parts should be restored and a careful examination of similar old pieces made beforehand, as of finials, to prevent the use of incongruous restorations. Less study is made of finials than of any other parts of the cabinet trade, but the very large number of examples in this volume should prevent even an amateur from going astray.

11. Brasses can be had made to order to match the old. Clumsy brasses easily ruin a restoration.

12. The modern method of leaving brasses dull or tarnished is not the best treatment.

If brasses were polished in the old days, why should they not be so now? If it is desired, brasses may be lacquered and will then retain their finish indefinitely. By all means, cheap brasses are to be avoided. All Chippendale brasses were hand tooled with a bevel, and not cut square on the edges.

Many old pieces are found with big wooden knobs, put on by way of repair before the matter had been studied out as it is now. All such should, of course, be removed when seen to be wrong as compared with good old examples.

13. The restoration of old but clouded looking-glasses is a matter of taste. The old glasses can be resilvered to improve them very much, but they cannot be made good. There are collectors who would never allow new glasses to be installed, even when the old are somewhat broken.

14. Hardware is a matter bearing much study. These volumes are fuller than any other on this subject. The rooms which are the backgrounds of good old furniture should not be furbished up by modern type hardware.

15. The interiors of drawers ought never to be in mahogany in old pieces, nor in oak unless the examples are English.

16. A very highly important matter is to intrust restorations to men of character. The finest piece ever brought from Europe was copied there to order, that the copy might replace the old. But the copyist slyly made another copy which by accident was discovered. Instances are by no means rare of copies new throughout being substituted for the old. The temptation of a poor man, perhaps without ethical training, to do things of this sort is very strong, as the financial advantage to him may be great. Many minor and often all repairs may be made at an owner's residence. Very rare pieces ought never to be allowed to go out of a house. In this connection the author feels that the shifting about for exhibition purposes of rare examples is always a mistake. If people wish their belongings to be seen, or persons of taste wish to see them, arrangements can often be made for visitation. Otherwise the museums should suffice.

17. All the restorations of every nature, including the matter of the refinishing, if any, should be gone over personally between the owner and the workman beforehand, if possible with a third party present and a written order for specific work to be given the workman with the understanding that he will be held responsible for doing more or differently than agreed upon. This is as much for the protection of an honest repairer as for the protection of the owner. For repairs often — almost always — exceed in extent and cost what is at first estimated. Thus the owner may avoid embarrassing disappointments. A conversation with the restorer brings out facts about the furniture that were hitherto unnoted.

18. The removal of old furniture should be carefully superintended. Responsible handlers by truck are now available. Fine pieces are often spoiled by crating, even with the best of care. Truckers may be had who will take goods uncrated.

19. The author could never see the wisdom of leaving in place very dilapidated upholstery merely because it is old. If patchable or possible of being made presentable, well. But rich furniture in a worn-out condition of seat and back is agreeable neither for use nor decoration. A sagged seat has a depressing appearance, often seen below the frame, at a distance.

20. It is often a puzzle to know what to do, if anything, to an important example. The writer once showed the picture of a remarkable specimen to several of our keen and experienced collectors without getting any definite advice. To be sure, this was an exceptional case as a certain part was missing, and no one felt sure what to do. Go slowly is the most important advice about restoration.

21. Last of all, why restore an old piece lacking great value or merit, if major repairs are necessary? Beginners may greatly overestimate the worth of a broken-up piece. If the repairs extend to a quarter of the entire construction, they become questionable as to desirability. It sometimes requires as much knowledge and judgment to restore as the maker himself possessed.

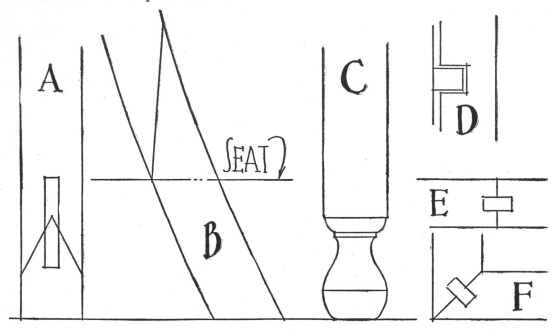

In the diagram A nothing whatever has been cut from the length of the old leg. A diagonal cut has been made in it, and the job is both strong and escapes much attention. A dowel may or may not be added. Sometimes it is not needed. By splicing in this way the old wood in front extends as far as before. The legs of wing chairs are often made when new as in diagram B, the lower part being mahogany or walnut, the upper part hard wood, or even pine. This splice can be pinned, screwed or nailed, because it is all out of sight when the chair is upholstered. It never requires a dowel. In diagram C properly made of wood like the old the old splice will never be seen, but it must be doweled unless one makes a splice like diagram A and cuts the edges all down to agree with the turning. But if the foot must be cut off much to reach a V cut, it is better, on the turning, to refuse to do this and let the splice appear.

The toes of Spanish feet can be replaced and recarved in position.

In corner miters or on thick work a spline should be inserted to make a good joint. As this is wholly out of sight and should have been used when the piece was new, there is no objection to this sort of repair. Diagrams E and F. The heel of a miter may still fit when the outside ends have shrunk. The remedy is not easy. A fine wedge may be fitted in, but it is one of the fussiest jobs imaginable.

Old planes may not be available for patching molding. Molds must then be laboriously worked out with combinations of planes or even chisels. We have treated of flattening warps.

Some of the earliest joints were not glued. The purist may wish to repair without glue. But he may need to repin. The bores on mortise and tenon should not exactly coincide, but be very slightly offset to make the pin draw the joint tight. There is a whole literature on this point.

The insertion of a shim may be necessary in wide cracks. It must be thick enough to rise above the surface, and be reduced after it is put in place.

Bits of carving are easily replaced without being noticed. But splicing requires a good mechanic who will leave a perfect joint. The replacing of drawer runs was anticipated by the best makers like Goddard. He attached a shoe, on the bottoms of drawers when the piece was new, making the shoe broad and flat and covering the joint of the side and bottom, so that it would wear long, and could at length be replaced without any cutting whatever. This remark applies to drawers running on their bottoms. The side runs slotted as D went out earlier. The carrying strips were often slotted at their ends into the corners of the frames and were of oak to bear wear. Also the drawer sides were of oak for the same reason, though the bottoms and backs were pine or possibly spruce. Even so, repairs are by this time required on these seventeenth-century pieces. New side runs may be needed, and the running groove may also need to be filled to its former size. As these repairs do not show, a good job is all that is needed, since it is not to be disguised.

In restoring old lining molds it will be found with some surprise that these are often soft wood on an oak panel, provided they are to be painted. The wood may be poplar, whitewood, pine, or cedar. The large applied outside molds are always oak on oak carcasses.

The drops are often maple because strength requires it. The bosses may be soft or hard wood, as all these parts are always black, which is best obtained by applying nigrosine with a very small quantity of white shellac to hold it. Orange shellac applied with black will in time show up as a deep olive color, and old applied work often appears with that tint. There is no objection, perhaps, to this color, only the repairer should know beforehand what to expect. Nigrosine is better than paint because it has no body and looks old and does not stick.

In applying bosses or other pieces the old maker often depended wholly on glue, which cannot stand the test of the years under modern conditions. It is better to attach these repairs with fine brads, puttying over the heads in addition to using the glue.

The large molds were pinned on with white oak pins, or frankly nailed. In case of pins, none was round. If driven into pine, they still appear square. If into hard oak, the corners are knocked down practically to a circle, so that at first the novice supposes they were turned. To turn them would be unpardonable on repairs. Further, the glue would not stick well on a turned pin. If nails are used, they must be hand wrought.

Wooden knobs on an oak or early eighteenth-century maple piece are small, except

in the Pennsylvania patterns. These knobs should dowel through the face they enter, and project inside and be pinned crosswise with oak. They will never stay in place well by any other method, and this method is often found on old work.

The sizes and descriptions of these knobs are found in the other volumes.

Brasses which in the earliest forms began to come in about 1690 should always be restored as they were if any old ones are left. The cost of copying is not prohibitive, and is now done by at least two good firms, who require only a sample. These brasses are never put on with screws. The 'scutcheons are attached with brass brads; the others are held by the bail posts. On the inside a screw attachment must never be used, but either the clinched wires or the post with irregular or rounded nut. Brasses may be had polished or dull.

Returning to repairs on wood, irregularly shaped mends should be used.

Some museums several years ago set up the theory that all replacements should show as new wood, in the same spirit in which necessary repairs with unfinished stone were made at Athens on the Erechtheum. But in going through the museums I do not find this principle applied, nor do I believe any reason exists for its application that is not overborne by reasons to the contrary. It is, however, fair and perhaps ethically necessary that photographs should be supplied, in plain view, showing the specimen before repairs were made. The unsightliness of white splotches of repair on an old specimen hinder the beholder from getting a proper effect of the old work set in its surroundings.

One beautiful piece comes to my mind which required between two and three hundred bits set in. Had these all been left white, the specimen would have appeared as struck with the plague. They were so well fitted and colored that in some cases the owner himself, though an old collector, could not outline them by his eye.

I think this is the proper manner of restoring an antique of the elegant period, just as in patching a hole in a good old painting. If it plainly shows, it may as well not be done, which decision is sometimes made by collectors.

I like the signs of age on maple, pine, and oak furniture. It is no small part of its attraction. The character marks on a strong old face, if removed, would not leave us the same man.

Particularly we should stand sturdily against the modern craze for color which is ruining much today as ninety years ago, when some fine mahogany was painted over. By what rule of art or taste must all furniture in a house, or even in a room, be of one color? In the human face the eyes do not resemble the skin. Uniformity is a sad and almost universal twentieth-century curse.

Therefore, why try to make fine maple and oak all look alike, or, as so many used to do, stain maple like mahogany because "they are to go together"? As well abolish the sexes and make humanity all one complexion. Is there anything disgraceful about a piece of oak? One would infer so to hear the chatter of the superficial. "Why, it looks like golden oak!" Some old oak did, though duller.

Some years ago a great order of reproduced furniture was rejected because it had pine drawer bottoms. That would not occur now.

The restoration of feet when they are all gone is not so difficult as would appear.

The style of the furniture governs the feet very closely. Yet serious mistakes are made by neglect of this matter. Feet are put on agreeing with the style in vogue at the time of the repair. The proportions of a Spanish foot may easily be made wrong, as I know from endeavoring to restore it. An eighth of an inch too much gave a clumsy effect. The commonest error in foot restoration is to copy an old foot which has worn too much. The only safety is in noting what the whole foot was, as in the chapter on feet in this book.

Looking-glasses are found attached to chests of drawers not having glasses originally. That error can only be shown by a careful examination of periods. A serious decadence had set in when glasses were attached. We find only two such in FURNITURE TREAS-URY (Nos. 288 and 289), and while they are pretty, the date assigned is 1820–30, and the same glasses unattached are better. No large glasses ever occur on antique furniture. The glasses were placed on the wall, or on an unattached base.

It is often found that the ends of high or low veneered chests of drawers were plain. They were so originally on simple examples, and, of course, veneer should never be applied.

The lining mold to cover the end wood on the skirt of William and Mary highboys and lowboys is so thin that it is bent on dry.

The foot on this style below the scrolled stretcher is generally a reproduction for style of the turning just above the stretcher, except for size. This final foot is about a quarter diameter larger. This foot is always doweled into and best entirely through the stretcher, entering the leg above. Originally the dowel was turned on the upper leg and ran through into the foot.

Steps found on the tops of highboys for display were unattached and of simple construction.

The Queen Anne leg of a highboy, if broken, is often renewed for its whole length. This seems unnecessary. A long, slanting splice should give sufficient strength, and thus the integrity of the original is less interfered with. I would rather not use an old highboy at all if the leg is entirely new, because that is half the piece in importance.

Some of the richest finials on highboys or chests-on-chests can never be successfully restored for lack of sure knowledge of what they were, or for lack of a fine original to copy.

The restoration of a claw-and-ball foot is the most difficult matter unless others of the feet remain to copy. The usual error is in lifting the foot too high. The turn at the ankle is quick and low. Success without a model is impossible.

The drops on highboy and lowboy skirts are often missing and often left so. Their proper shape is not difficult to ascertain, and their lack mars the specimen. In the matter of cupboards, errors are often made by setting into a corner a cupboard designed to be built in. If built in, a cupboard should have a cornice identical with that of the room, and this mold must lie against the ceiling. Detached cupboards should always be lower than the ceiling, and they are then treated without reference to the woodwork around the room. The concaves of old cupboards, unless, as once in my experience, they are paneled, usually open in cracks. There is no sovereign remedy. But the domes are, or ought to be, built up of sections of soft pine planks glued and nailed one on another, and showing as rough steps on the rear. Rare cases of segments set in and covered with ribs are found, but these are not the best examples. The best should be carved into radiates across the grain. Cheap specimens only are plastered as plain demi-domes.

In desks and secretaries the fall front must be cleated. Made otherwise, it is sure to warp. A plain cleat is sometimes found on fine work, but the handsomest job miters the cleat in at the upper side, leaving it square on the lower. The cleat is wide to hold the strong warping tendency.

The restoration of the roll front of tambour desks uses a heavy canvas base on which the ribs or reeds are glued.

Sideboard doors are never steamed to bend, if of scrolled shape, but are built up of strips and then veneered.

Brackets on chairs, tables, etc., should be mortised in on one side at least.

The cleat on pine table tops is always and always will be a puzzling matter to deal with. If omitted, the top warps, unless heavier than the old style is found. If a cleat is attached again where it is missing, the top will come and go with the weather and, with the best work, will not always stand. If the overhang on the sides is slight, the top may stand; but fastening it down all over may result in checking unless many coats of finish are first applied on *both* sides, a thing the old makers seem not to have thought out. The sliding dovetailed cleat, not fastened, found on Pennsylvania table tops, avoided these difficulties, and I once found it on a Goddard knee-hole table. I think it was original. Table tops are the commonest and worst source of trouble on old furniture. If they have not warped, they have checked. I have described the cure of old warps. I may say straightening by damp or flame is useless because not permanent. Fine saw cuts are the only remedy. Checks can be filled with a material called wood cement, commercially obtainable. It should be mixed with the stain that will match the surface to be repaired. It is a real boon to repairers. If cracks are wide, however, a small section must be cut out and a strip inserted — a matter requiring much care in matching.

The repair of pie-crust table tops is perhaps the nicest job in the range of cabinet-work. Of course, a pie-crust top that has checked has lost the greater part of its value, whether repaired or not. The edge is easy to patch, but a warp cannot be cured by saw cuts without revealing them when the top is tipped. Patient filling with fine shims precisely matching may succeed.

There is no way of repairing the breaking away of a foot dovetailed into the post or shaft of a tea table, except by gluing. The iron triangular flat brace underneath must be trusted to hold the repair. Such articles cannot bear abuse, and a perfect table can be spoiled by much weight above.

Chair repair is a trade in itself. The commonest breaks in old chairs are the slats. They are bent and must be restored with new bendings, unless the curvature is very slight, in which case the slat may be sawed. The patching of a slat with a piece from the upper part of an old slat is to be advised rather than inserting a new one.

Broken balusters are easily replaced or mended. A fine splat, however, which one does not wish to sacrifice may perhaps be restored by thinning the back and gluing on a shim to bridge the break.

Chair-seat frames of the mahogany period should when new have had inside corner braces, and most of them did, so that they stand well even today, being a triumph of the cabinetmaker's art in that, though they look frail, they are strong. But in case a leg is loose, brackets should be inserted, and this may be done with screws. The repair of a Chippendale chair requires more skill than to make a new one, apart from the matter of design.

The insertion of new splats should not be done without attending to the bevel cut away in the back around all openings and the outside of the splat, to give it an effect of lightness. Arm attachment is elsewhere treated.

REPRODUCTIONS

This subject is large enough to demand admission here, and it is foggy enough to require breezy statement. A great lady turned up her nose at reproductions. What was she? Another edition of her noble father. Reproductions are respectable or not according as their makers are.

Anyone who objects to reproductions is asking for something worse. Either a reproduction or a new design. Give me the reproduction every time, if it is real.

People forget that the world requires much more furniture than our fathers left us. If there was once enough, it is mostly broken, worn out, lost. There must needs be reproductions or degradations. If the dollar is the first consideration in reproductions, they will be bad. Some of the abuses that arise are:

1. The aping of large, rich old pieces by small pieces. As Cram has pointed out, the pernicious thing in architecture is reducing the scale of a cathedral to a village church instead of copying a good village church. A pretentiously styled piece of furniture that is meager in outline and slurs in decoration is responsible for making a desk and calling it after a pilgrim.

The original was stately and satisfactory in line, mass, and structure. The copy is a travesty. The reproduction of simple furniture very faithfully made is productive of charming results. The public are ready to recognize this and look for plain maple well put together rather than sham mahogany ill put together. That is, some of the public are of this wise sort. More will be when they learn they have been imposed upon.

New furniture in great quantities is necessary. Shall we hide away the desirable originals and avoid copying them? Must I restrict myself to the unworthy because the worthy is too sacred? The question would be absurd on its face did not we meet it often.

But why not modern styles? Because there are none. Nobody can describe a modern style. The next time you hear the phrase ask what the speaker means. He probably thinks he means something, but he does not. There is no modern style carrying the name of a period or a designer. There is no modern style to which one can refer and be understood. Nobody will know what he is talking about, the speaker least of all.

2. Another abuse is infidelity to the original. This is the rule, not the exception. So much for the construction, plus the lie. Product, the price of the furniture. There is no faithful reproduction of a Windsor chair sold in the large shops because the

seat of the old is incompatible with cheapness. The new seats are made in several pieces and are thin. Beds cannot be cheap if they are copies. The demand for first-class reproductions is small in the large shops because people are getting too well informed to seek such furniture except at the shops of a specialist.

A well-known magazine which depends on dealers for its advertising recently stated that dowel furniture was proper in the Hepplewhite and Sheraton styles. Of course, such a statement is completely misleading. It may have been made in ignorance and not with intent to deceive. In any case, the publication lost caste. We read about furniture for information and are entitled to get it, after we have paid for it.

If a reproduction is not so good as the original, or at least does not attempt to be, it becomes a spurious article. An alleged copy may be as misleading as a counterfeit sold as old.

The chief sinners are the big dealers and manufacturers. They will tell you they are giving the public what they want. So are the sellers of smuggled opium. So are panders. It is blandly assumed that to supply a demand is legitimate business. A large firm of reproducers recently advertised a desk, whose veneer was, they said, very good. The original was not veneered. "To put it over" is success. The serpent "put it over" in the garden. The demagog "puts it over," if he can.

Those who put it over will eventually be put under. This world is favorable for deceivers. But it is more favorable to truth tellers. The universe is designed for straight people. Crooks thrive only where there are many straight people to cheat.

There will be no great shops producing very worthy furniture until the public demand it. That day has not come, but it will. Education in quality will help. The revival of taste will help. The decency inherent in humanity will help.

3. Frequently wrong things are chosen for reproduction. Frequently the work is poorly done, with poor material. Frequently no good furniture is owned to copy by the producer. I have enjoyed reproduction because I love the good lines, but the last thing to be made by the process is money. If by lavishing a small fortune on the process, I have done anything I ought to be sorry for, I am glad of it. The hand of all commercial people is against the best work because it cannot be sold at a price commensurate with the cost.

What can be more pleasing than to observe the forms brought forth by old masters of structure and to try to follow their seductive and ingenious drawings? In this way the best knowledge also is derived more rapidly. One thinks he knows all about an old piece, but if he turns his back on it and submits to questioning, he soon finds that his knowledge omits the essential from style and misses its charm and merit.

This book shows the working plans of many worthy original designs. There has hitherto been a meager source of such plans or they were scattered and expensive. I have taken no liberties with the originals, most of which I possess or did possess. The local cabinetmaker will here find, probably, enough to satisfy any reasonable desire for patterns. The hope is that such plans may raise the grade of reproductions in America. My other books have gone to cabinetmakers in great numbers. There are hundreds of the earlier volumes in Grand Rapids alone. But a vicious consequence has been an effort to reproduce from pictures. Pictures can give but one aspect of an original. How a chair arm looks or a back or an inside, and a thousand other things are merely imagined.

It is necessary to view a specimen from all points. I once found a large manufacturer copying my copies from pictures. I said to him, "You cannot be restrained by law from making anything you choose from my specimens because I have no copyright on these old designs, but the least you can do is to obtain examples of the specimens themselves. Then the arms on your chairs will not look so much like a snake with a stomach ache." He saw the point.

Another and a very large manufacturer copied pictures from one of my volumes and called the result reproductions. It did not pay him. These books have been a storehouse for copyists.

A keen draftsman familiar with old lines can often produce something by this method that is pretty good. But at no more expense he could be just right, and of course real enthusiasts wish to be right, and good business men should see that to be right pays. I have known manufacturers to buy my reproductions through dealers and have them transported away from their shops and then back again. Such transparent subterfuges are childish. They always come to light. I found in Seattle thirty pieces directly copied from mine; the shop being owned by the greatest store in the world. The goods had been made by a prominent manufacturer.

Except for the so-called lacquer finish and the high price the reproductions were good.

In Hartford one day I saw in a shop window some familiar forms. Going in and meeting a clerk I was told these thirteen specimens were all exact copies from Metropolitan Museum originals. I said: "If you had ever been at the Atheneum, your own museum, a long stone's throw from here, you would have seen the originals in my collection." The gentleman, for he was truly such, was chagrined, for he had been telling me in good faith what he had been told about the furniture. The point the public does not know is that the shops do not want the maker's name on furniture "as they don't care to advertise the make of merchandise they may not always stock." I have often been offered orders if I would leave my name off the pieces.

These are facts the public is entitled to know, but never will know if the dealers can prevent it. This also the public will learn soon: Fine reproductions are not sold in the shops at low prices.

In the sales places they cannot afford to carry goods that are hand turned. The sharp cusp just below the bowl on a Windsor chair leg cannot be secured on a machine lathe; neither can a proper shaping of the seat, more than an inch cut away from the center. Neither can a mortise-and-tenon construction be offered without doubling the price, nor true dovetailing, nor handmade hardware, beveled at the edges, nor the repeated rubbings required for good work. Any well-finished piece must be gone over with coats or rubbings from twelve to sixteen times. The cost is greater (about a third of the whole) than the entire cost of the making of a cheap piece. These are things not learned except by long experience, and that means they are seldom learned at all.

It is easier for me to say these things because, owing to age and literary demands, I am drawing my reproduction work to a close, and trade motives cannot fairly be attributed to me.

THE AGING OF FURNITURE

Almost every day people say, "Can't you age this furniture for me?"

"Certainly," I reply.

"Then please do so."

"Certainly not," I answer. "When you own this furniture you can do what you will with it. But why should I mar new work?"

"Well it is more attractive if it looks old; it agrees with antiques I possess."

One of the finest men I know, whom I trust perfectly, spent a long time aging a new piece to go with his own collection. He could not afford an old piece of the style in question, as, being exceedingly rare, the price was high. I have no quarrel with him, but I do not agree that what he did was in good taste. The piece was for his own permanent ownership. There was no purpose to deceive anybody. But I believe he would not have asked someone else to do the aging.

What would some of the old makers have thought had they been asked to age furniture? That their customers were suffering from brain trouble. If furniture is fine style and color, it speaks sufficiently of the olden time without fictitious aids.

Some years ago the tendency was the opposite one of making fine specimens of the antique look new. The closer we keep to realities the better our taste. The marks of age, unless they are breaks, ought not to be removed.

The burying of wood, the sunning of it, or allowing it to be rained on and a multitude of devices in finishing are freely employed, legitimately I believe, on repairs of the old, but never otherwise. Especially is the practice of using old wood to be deprecated. If collectors wish to be self-deluded, well, but to "fix" a collection to display as antiques, no.

HARD WORDS

This book uses some severe language. Two courses were open to me. I could write smoothly, not touching the evils that are rampant, and please many readers. That is the usual proceeding. It is said to be not "wise" to slash and strike. It is to invite repercussions. But I have chosen to tell the truth as I see it, and if in this and other books the result is strange copy, the people are deserving of getting the truth once in a while. Nearly all language on these subjects has been mild, flat, stale, not because the writers lacked force, but because they have hesitated to use it. For the life of me I cannot perceive any advantage to the reader in glossing over the facts. Unless there be diagnosis there can be no cure. I have deliberately pointed out what I would have paid liberally to be told as a beginner. No malice is held against anybody. I would not indicate particular persons, for the law of compensation will work without anything I could do. But if I repressed all the indignation I feel, the results might be disastrous. Two long articles of mine on Antique Humbugs in the *Saturday Evening Post* acted as a safety valve, but too much pressure has risen in the two years since. I deliberately believe there should be heroic measures taken against humbugs. The great quantity of humbugs is not spurious old furniture, but the wider showing of new furniture said to be as good as the old, or copied from it or made like it, when neither the kind of the wood, the construction, the finish, nor even the style itself is a fair representation.

BEDS

We think of early bedsteads as high, heavy, and broad. But beds like these were always uncommon and found only in the houses of pretentious people. Common people did not have bedsteads, they merely had beds. The straw, or in America often the corn-husk tick, was placed on the floor.

When a bedstead existed in simple homes it was a plain frame with two sides and one post, the frame being in the corner of a room and fastened to the wall, and being without design. It was merely a couple of joists to make a support for a tick.

When the well-to-do began to have bedsteads they were sometimes in the Holland style, built into recesses like stateroom berths on ships. Again they folded into presses and behind closed doors. When built with four posts the event was important enough to originate the term four-poster, a puzzling phrase unless one remembers the simpler arrangements already mentioned.

Even when four-posters became more common the low-posted bed with nothing much above the frame was in common use for all except the master and mistress. Hence the term "hired man's bed" which, of course, had four posts, and the trundle bed for the children.

A four-poster had come to mean four *high* posts. The only object of the height was, of course, to support the hangings and canopy top. In later times the half-high bed with curved canopy, or with none at all, came in as a slow change from the more pretentious bed, used with hangings for privacy and to ward off cold. In the earliest times the mattress or straw bed was often laid on a chest, a table, or a settle growing out of a chest.

Maple for simple beds supplanted the English oak in America, and the bedstead might be plain turned or square tapered or roughly octagoned above the frame.

Though I show upwards of fifty bedsteads in Volumes I and II, I have had a large number drawn in addition for this article.

It is obvious that none of them can be referred certainly to a date earlier than Chippendale, though the simplest might easily be much earlier.

Furniture as connected with a bed never meant furniture in our sense, but referred to the fabrics, valances, hangings, and testers which surrounded the bedstead, the feathers (above the straw), and the often beautiful coverlets. These were usually of far greater importance than the bedstead which was often completely hidden by them.

When bedsteads were carved in the earliest period, they were paneled in repetition of the designs used on chests; but these have completely disappeared, proving that they could never have been very numerous.

The best things in the house, as to value, were the best bed and its furniture, and court cupboard. But the value of a few shillings given in inventories of most bedsteads indicates that these frames served merely as firm outlines to drape the materials.

Some bedsteads still exist in the collections of about 1820 which are huge affairs, reminiscent of the period a hundred and fifty years earlier. But such beds are counted encumbrances now. They are somewhat coarse and clumsy in design.

One cannot always distinguish in the old lists how the valuations are to be divided between the bedstead and its belongings.

Couches and day beds were then, as now, often made up as night sleeping quarters. The horror of the Davenport, however, never existed in the olden time. I did find recently, in Maine, a folding sofa very like, when folded, a simplified Sheraton sofa. It opened with two extra jointed legs and must have dated about 1800. I fled precipitately. Could I have overcome my repugnance, I might now be possessed of what, so far as I know, was a unique construction. It unfolded on hinges to double the closed size.

The bedsteads shown in Chippendale's book of designs are not very attractive to our taste, especially the Gothic and Chinese carving.

The better frames were made with knobs set or inset in the rails, and the commoner beds were made with bored rails, for the bed cords.

A foot rail did not come in until good styles went out.

An occasional bed is found as in the sleigh style with the decoration all on one side. Such a bed might have occupied an alcove, or have been simply a wall bed, that is, touching the wall on the back rather than on the head.

I have recently acquired a bed of curious construction, which I show. It is difficult to date. The heavy canopy frame consists of side pieces which enter the sides of the posts by great dovetails, and there are two high rails at the foot. While I found it in Eastern Massachusetts, I do not venture to suggest its origin. It is of about two-thirds size, 81 inches long, 43 inches wide, and 79 inches high. The wood is perhaps birch. It is, therefore, probably American. (See following page.)

One cannot say that single beds did not exist, but pairs of single beds are unknown to me. Persons who wanted plenty of room in bed had their bedsteads made five feet wide, thus gaining most of the advantages of twin beds without the large space and expense they involve.

The headboard of the richest beds was usually simple, because the draped goods at the head came down close to the bedding.

There were several methods of preparing the foundation for the tick. On very low beds two or three ticks might be placed on the floor itself, affording a sufficient elevation. I have heard of a bed, though I have never seen it, with a plain board foundation set in the frame. The ordinary bed was corded, but heavy canvas (sail cloth) was often laced in on good beds and couches. Then there was an arrangement whereby the foot rail turned like a drum or windlass and, held by a ratchet, tightened the canvas.

In some very early built-in beds paneled doors shut in the space under the rails which was used for storing extra bedding.

The canopy top was originally solid wood panels, soon abandoned for cloth. The netted canopy, if used, overlaid the cloth.

The earliest beds were not supposed to be moved, and, of course, had no casters. The post had an architectural base resting on the floor. To lift it in the air by casters gives a deplorable effect. Casters belong on the lighter turned posts, and, of course, the casters are now discarded for metal discs.

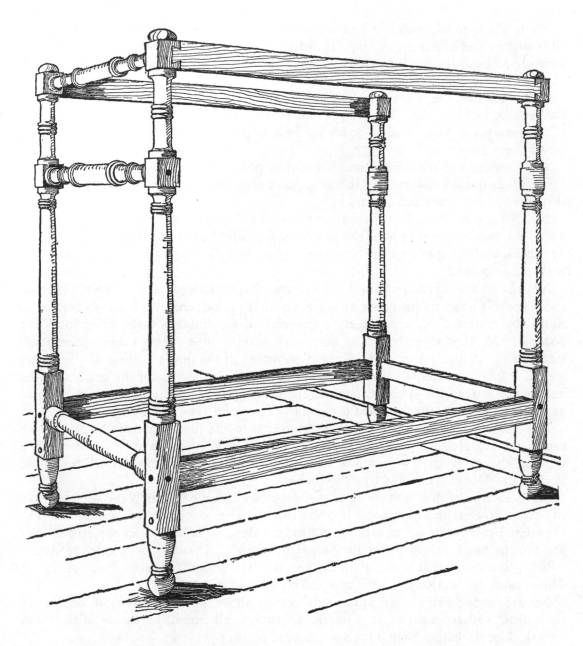

An odd bed of a period probably near 1790. Some have wondered if it were not an ox-shoeing frame, as they point to the rolling rail, with holes at foot for tightening the canvas base. But to be patient with those who sit in the seat of the scornful I point out that the ox is raised by a side windlass. It is a bed; but it could have had no goods running down from the head against the wall. If one were to guess, it might be said the design and the two-thirds size were gotten up by a crusty old bachelor, as a sort of fortified retreat from attack.

While the kind of wood in a bed followed the style of the other pieces of furniture, a mahogany bed of American origin is rather rare. Maple and cherry and birch, being very abundant, were made to suffice. Hence these materials often occurred in the same room with mahogany chairs and cabinet furniture.

One notes that the heavy maple beds had high rails. There was abundant room for the trundle bed beneath. The Chippendale style kept the rails low.

The heavy low posts of 1820–50 are justly unpopular. They have nothing to recommend them.

The mortise-and-tenon connection between posts and rails was good and secure. It avoided squeaks and racks. It was a great drop in style when the Victorian, and then the rickety brass beds, came in.

Bed No. 1 consists of four mahogany posts all alike and deeply fluted, so that a ball will roll down into the ends of the flute and fit. The height to the top of the urn is 67 inches, and the diameter of the post is 2½ inches. An unpretentious Chippendale, with plain square.

No. 2 is an approved design which I was once happy enough to find in the Chippendale type. It has a molded base as always in that period, and this base is never to be ruined by casters. The attachment of the mitered molding is a time-eating job. The posts should stand directly on the floor with nothing intervening except some small metal discs. A nice touch in the turning is cutting of the upper corners of the square with a dainty ogee shape. It is seen that the fluting on the base of the urn is spiraled and at the tops of the spiral returns on the urn. Above, there are clustered columns at whose base is another spiraled ornament. The finial is of the highest quality.

No. 3 is a later bed, probably slipping over into the first years of the nineteenth century, with reeding instead of fluting. These beds often exist without the top section, appearing with a post headed by the turban-like decoration just below the long swell. Dimensions: 3½ by 87½ inches.

No. 4 shows the design favored in the Hepplewhite time in which the square below the rail is tapered and terminates in a spade foot. The post is reeded, not fluted. The chamfered corners of the square are sometimes done on a lathe and sometimes they are done by hand, in which case they are flat chamfers. Dimensions: 2⅞ by 75 inches.

No. 5 is shown with a caster, indicating the late period. It is reeded, not fluted. The carving decoration is on the urn and consists of two loops.

No. 6 is octagoned on the square and reeded above with a finial more decorative than usual and terminating in a flame. Of course, all turned bases are of Sheraton period. Hardly earlier than 1795 and running to 1815.

No. 7 shows a light Sheraton field bed post, the only decoration in the turning being a series of rings or beaded forms on the urn. A bed like this should have an oval canopy frame, whereas a high one should have a flat frame.

No. 8 is a Hepplewhite shape which has cut into the square, on the two sides, showing a molded panel, a feature which entails the work of a carver and enriches the post a good deal.

No. 9 is a Sheraton design with a large brass socket above the caster.

No. 10 is a Hepplewhite design in which is a reeded urn shape instead of a taper top.

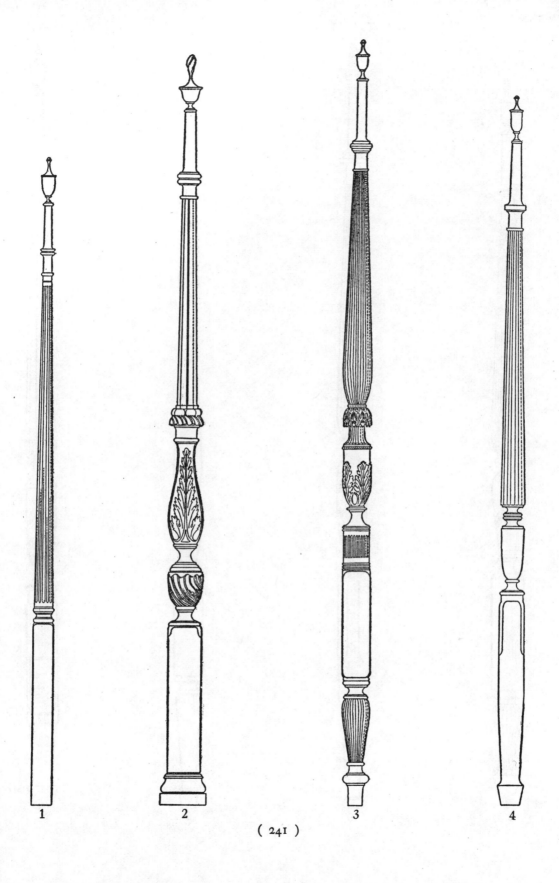

1   2   3   4

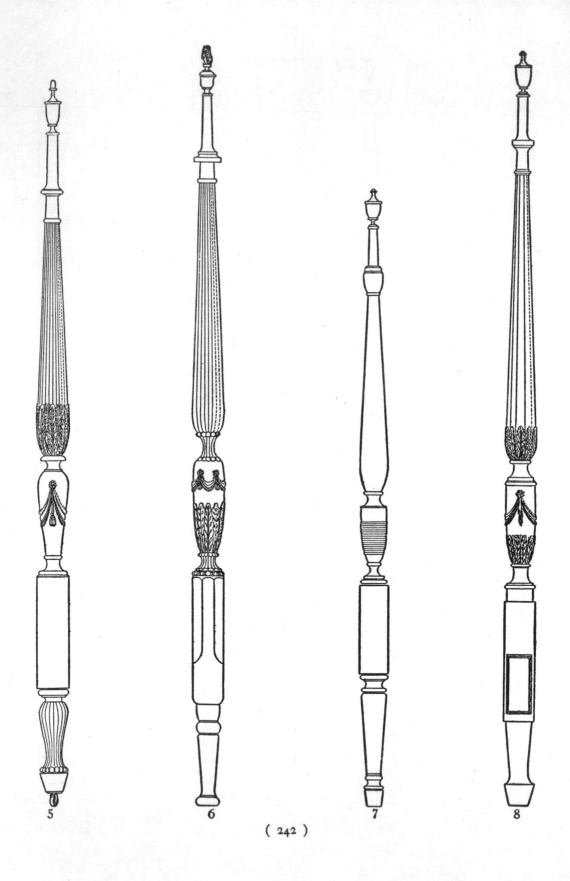

5   6   7   8

(242)

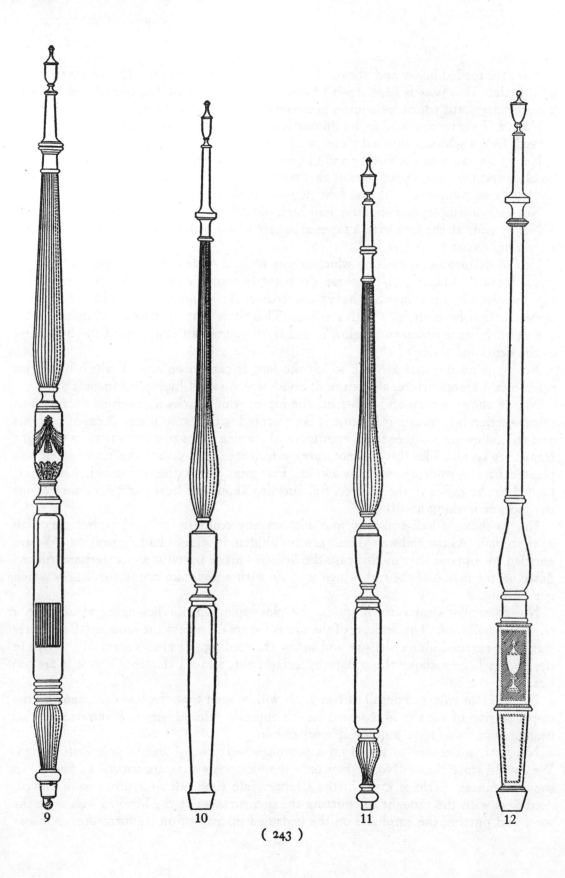

9   10   11   12

No. 11 is reeded below and above. In turning, the corners of the square are rounded off a little. This post is kept down to about 66 inches, including the urn proper and finial, underneath which, of course, goes the arched canopy if used.

No. 12 is very emphatic in its decoration of the lower post where a raised urn is carved, below which a tapered panel is cut out to a point near the foot.

No. 13 has an unusual fluting and untapered plinth-like base of the urn. It should be observed that the upper part of this post does not draw in daintily, but is a little too heavy as compared with the next number at that point.

No. 14 is a simple, but effective half-high pattern.

No. 15 ends at the foot with a tapered square without the spade, an unusual design. It is a light post for a tent bed.

No. 16 delineates something which ought to be avoided in the upper part of the post. Its lack of taper was, of course, deliberately chosen as a style for the spiral carving, but the effect is somewhat heavy and coarse. It would have been better had this upper section been slighter with reeding. This ornament overdoes and helps to kill the more delicate ornaments below it and is, of course, an evidence of the beginning of the degraded styles of 1830.

No. 17 is an unusual form in which the foot is carved on a post which otherwise resembles a Hepplewhite, a mixture of styles which is not highly commendable.

No. 18 shows a claw-and-ball foot, the hip of which lacks a generous sweep. The upper section is interesting because it is decorated with a stop flute. A canopy of this and the following number is an architectural cornice more pretentious than the light frame. A cornice like this did not carry a fish-net canopy, but the tester itself was pleated from a rosette center, as a rule. Hangings about the bed could then be attached to the inside of the cornice, full curtains about the head, and a valance about the foot, or nothing at all.

No. 19 shows a ball-and-claw foot without any contour for the hip, but very rich as to its rail. As the rail was almost always hidden, it seldom had decoration. We are entitled to suppose that in this case the bed was made up with a counterpane tucked down on the inside of the rail, which is made with a swastika ornament, below which is a nulling.

No. 20 shows a mixture of styles, the pineapple top not belonging at all with a claw-and-ball foot. The necking of the urn is too small, unless the same small diameter was to be reached above the urn and below the reeding. It shows want of thought in design. It begins above the square by being light, and all elements above it are too heavy for the base.

No. 21 is an enlarged detail of No. 2. It will be seen that the leaf ornament on the upper section of the urn is repeated on the opposite side. There is a variation in this usage. Some beds have a quadruple ornament.

No. 22 is a decoration found on a southern bed post of the Hepplewhite design. We should state that in No. 21 it is only the foot posts that are carved as found. In some instances, perhaps even in the Chippendale time, all four posts were carved, doubtless with the thought of omitting the bed curtains at the head as well as at the foot, and putting the emphasis on the bedstead instead of on its furniture, as it was

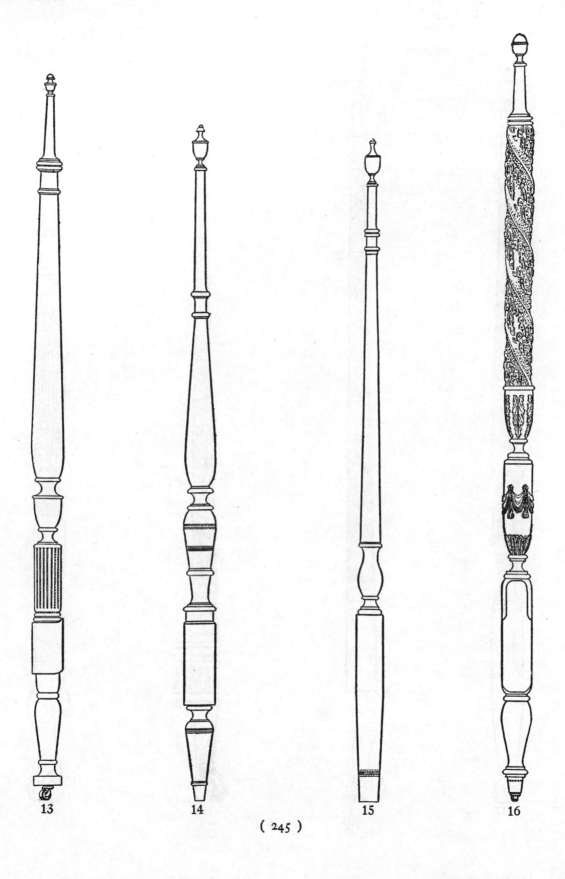

13   14   15   16

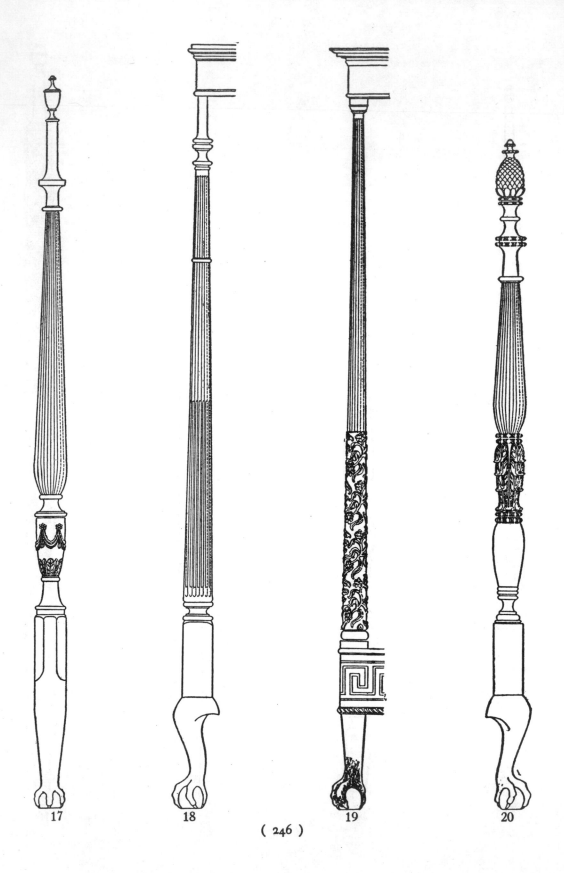

21

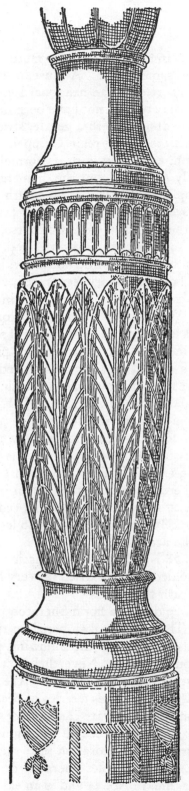

22

called. In a bed of this sort more decoration would have been given to the headboard for the same reason. A museum shows a headboard very ornately carved for a bed of this sort, but the headboard is a modern substitution for the original headboard which may or may not have been decorated. The very finest beds known have a plain, thin headboard, with a gentle, straight slope from the center to the sides.

No. 23 is a very plain Chippendale bed post, and no one can say that it lacks distinction, especially with its formal cornice. The entasis on these beds is sometimes entirely neglected, but the diameter one-third of the distance from the rail turning to the top should be about an eighth of an inch outside a straight line.

No. 24 shows a good deal of taste with the spiral foliage, undoubtedly suggested from the vine on a tree. Of course, the true capitals on these posts are at the enlargement some inches below the top. What purpose was behind this design which is almost universal, we do not know, but it breaks up the long post, and the upper section could be, if necessary, separated, although that is bad construction.

All commercial beds are made in two sections, doweled just above the square of the post. We consider this wholly wrong, especially as the buyer is not informed that his post is in two parts. The object of such construction is, of course, to avoid the frequent warp in a post if it is made in one piece. If, as sometimes happens, the post is made in three sections, that can be supplied at a very much smaller sum, because it entails no danger to warrant it against warping, and the short pieces for turning are always available about a shop.

No. 25 is a fluted Chippendale post richly banded between the parts.

No. 26 carries the carving down on the frame, though in this and most instances only two sides of the post on the square section are carved. The clustered-column Gothic effect of this post tied in two places is a more appropriate use of the Gothic and therefore more popular than in the Chippendale chairs.

No. 27 shows a more pronounced curve on the ends of the acanthus leaves. A very elaborately carved post with no less than eight bands of decoration besides the spiral and the acanthus.

No. 28 is only a slight variation from a post already shown. It is peculiar in that the molded base is carried up very high. The upper section has clustered columns and a rich urn terminal.

No. 29 details a florid Sheraton pattern where the reeding is extended nearly to the foot. There is a sunken panel on the square.

Beds of this and the following pattern are very many times as numerous as the previous patterns. Nevertheless, the square bases are architecturally better, and we believe the decoration to be of the higher quality.

No. 30 emphasizes a series of beads, has a straight taper reeded foot, a reeded upper section, and elaborate carving between.

No. 31 is an agreeable injection here of a Hepplewhite pattern with square base. It carries more decoration near the top than is commonly found.

No. 32 is a simpler Sheraton design. It will be noted that the reeding terminates earlier than in No. 34 and is an easier pattern. The reeds at both ends show as raised work, whereas in No. 34 they are terminated against a turning, an earlier and better and more laborious style.

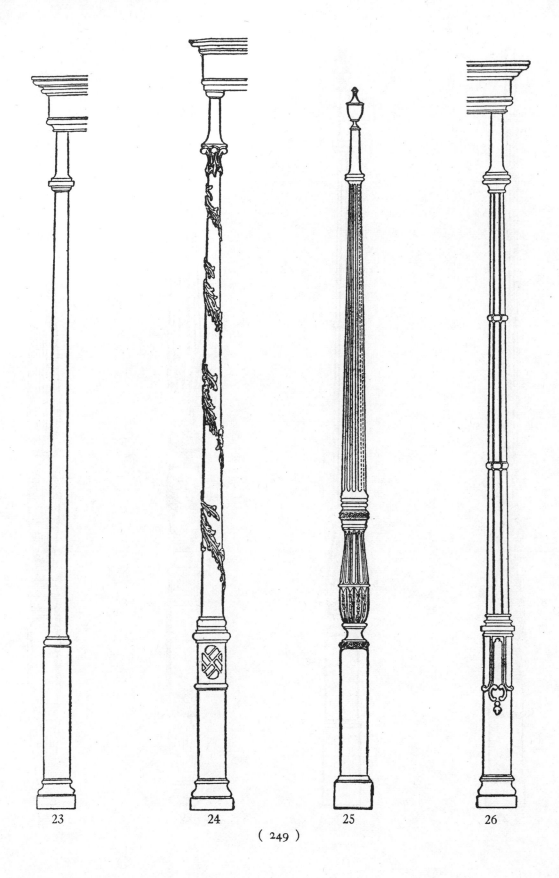

23   24   25   26

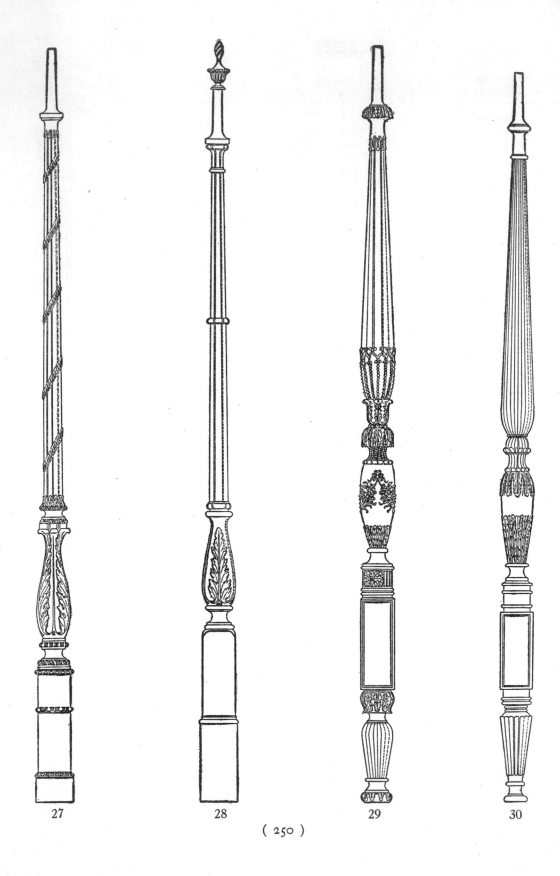

27   28   29   30

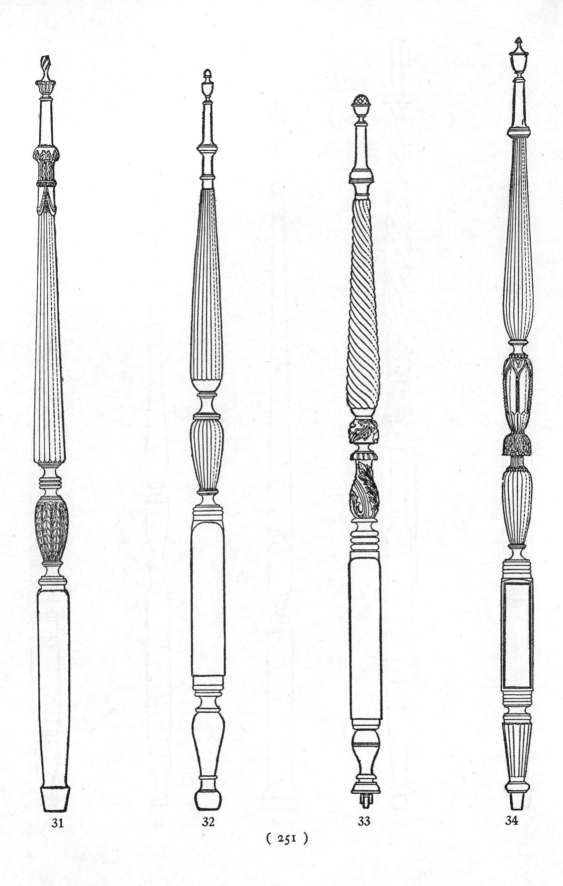

31   32   33   34

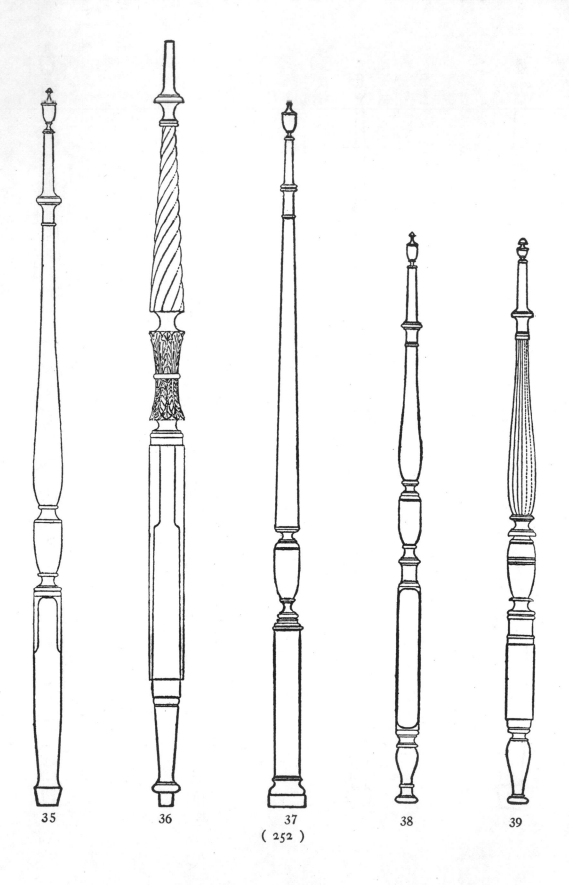

35   36   37   38   39

In No. 33 we are entering on the late Empire design with a heavier spiral reeding. There is a slight attempt at the pineapple form on the crowning urn. It is probable that this bed was used without a canopy, or at least to be so used if desired.

No. 34 also shows a late Empire influence as always when a somewhat turban-like form found in the lower urn is used. The square is paneled.

No. 35 is a simple Hepplewhite without decoration on the upper section, but of excellent design.

No. 36 represents a late Empire pattern not desirable from the standpoint of design. The demarcation between the rail height and the upper section is too high to have any meaning.

No. 37 is a simple Hepplewhite design. The neck of the vase looks somewhat larger than the stem, although perhaps it is an optical illusion. The stem of the vase should never be smaller than the smaller elements above on the post.

No. 38 is a half-high field or tent bed dating about 1790.

No. 39 probably dates from about 1800 and is a trifle heavy for its height. It is, of course, reeded, not fluted.

Completing in these three volumes about a hundred styles of bed posts, we are, of course, omitting many more, but the variations not shown are either unimportant, or they are types too late for serious consideration. Besides the chapter on beds in Volume I beginning No. 1447, there are also details under Nos. 4793–97.

An X-frame bed I do not show because it has no element of style, but was in common use for children or servants or as an emergency addition to the sleeping accommodations in households from the earliest periods down to my own youth, when I slept on such a bed. It was the most compact and convenient affair imaginable, weighing little and far more comfortable than a hammock. It was built precisely like an elongated camp chair, shutting up, of course, from the sides rather than the ends. To a small board were fastened a couple of spindles which projected from the board sufficiently to enter holes bored in the rails at the head of the bed and to hold the pillow from falling. It was a complete construction, and if placed in an open chamber close under the eaves where one could reach up and feel the roof boards, and hear the patter of the rain on the shingles, it was fit for a king or a poet, or both.

In No. 1983, FURNITURE TREASURY, is the oddest contraption I have ever seen. It comprises all the parts of a bed, side rails, posts, legs, and even a canopy frame.

There is a return in these days to the high poster with a netted canopy, omitting the lining. A bed so arranged is altogether the most attractive article of furniture in a dwelling, if we except a grandfather's clock. It may be said that the canopy and tester are of no possible use. If they add charm to a room and a sense of the substantial old time, that is no small advantage.

On page 184 I have sketched a hired man's bed post with a popular urn top. It is 29 inches high and 2⅜ inches in diameter. Sometimes all the posts were alike and sometimes the headpost was a little higher. The material was almost always maple, but sometimes birch. I have never seen an old mahogany bed like this.

On page 254 is a cupboard of most unusual quality resembling a good deal F. T. No. 474. So far is this true that it is probable they were both made by the same person at, or near, Middletown, Connecticut, whence came this specimen. I have noted one English example resembling this. There are two long doors, the space below which is a well. The mold above and below the doors has no return at the end, and thus resembles the usual chest of oak. Some fascinating peculiarities of this piece are: there are only eight main panels in front, and each of them is divided into a double panel, in the center of which is set a large piece, apparently cherry, of diamond shape. At each corner of the diamond is inset a dark inlay about the size of a small lead pencil. The tops and the bottoms of all the false panels have a gouge mold. There are thus on this front sixteen large, sixty-four small inlays, and at each corner of every false panel there is a stamped decoration — sixty-four in all!

Thirty years ago no dwelling having any pretension at all to being furnished with old pieces was considered complete without a spinning wheel. The large wheel, however, for wool spinning was a clumsy affair, in no respect decorative. It was not even rare. Wise collectors soon perceived that it was totally unfit for a living room. The spinning Jenny was more graceful, but even so, the principle holds that the furniture of a dwelling, old or new, as well as all the appurtenances, should be usable. The spinning Jenny was too common to have a value and too obvious as a mere object of decoration. The same remark holds even more true of yarn reels, which were almost always crude, and are at any rate ungainly in appearance. These things are always best gathered in a spinning attic.

Below is a delightful spinning wheel arranged so that the operator could sit and work the treadle at the right. The spindle was on the toggle joint at the right, and as the wheels revolved the joints opened and closed, effecting the same result as, in the ordinary spinning wheel, is gained by stepping back and forth. Thus a cripple or an aged person might have operated the contrivance. Origin probably western New York.

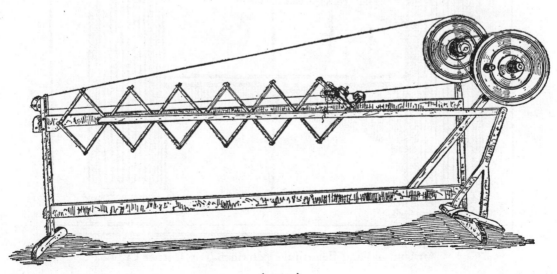

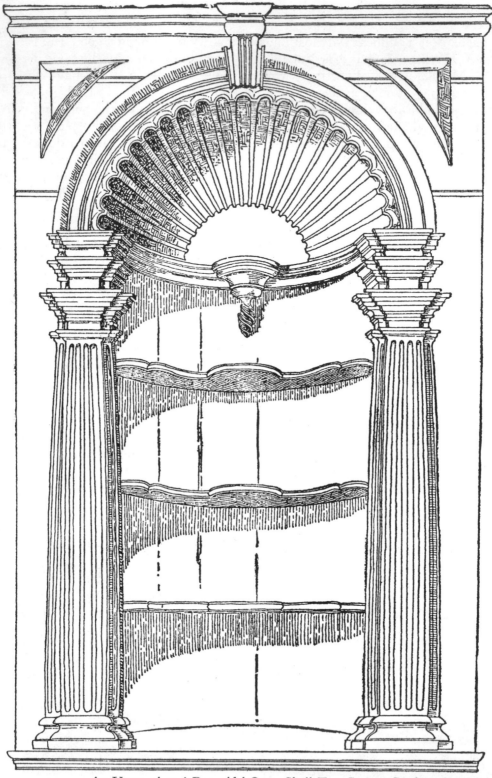

An Unusual and Beautiful Open Shell-Top Corner Cupboard

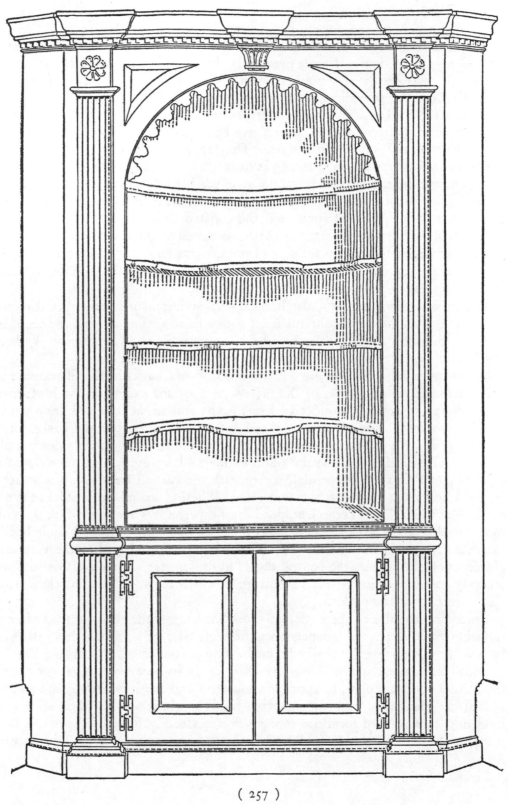

On the foregoing pages are two very interesting cupboards, both open. The peculiarity about that on page 256 is that it is the only rich cupboard that has ever come to my attention without doors. I have previously mentioned that exquisite shell cupboards have their pilasters entirely masked, even when their doors are open. The conclusion must be that the prevailing style when paneling was installed called for an entire closing of the wall space. This delightful cupboard, however, has the completion of an architectural charm, and it particularly has the most amusingly elaborate capitals on its pilasters that one could imagine. They are really doubled or trebled. The very marked entasis there is also so strong as to excite a smile at the naïve effort to do something extraordinarily fine. The sunburst effect below the radiates is the best to be found. The notched edge gives an appearance of strong effulgence of light.

A feature which always connected the construction of these cupboards with the ancient conception of resting the earth on an elephant's back is the semicircular bracket arranged to hold up the sun. I presume we should be allowed to believe that the sun arose beyond the semicircle, and that that event could only be well set forth in this manner.

The cupboard on page 257, also built-in and having a cornice mold continuous with the ceiling, is simpler and contents itself with a mere scallop around the arch, but has over the pilasters that favorite rosette so common in the Connecticut Valley. The break of the cornice to form a capital is good, as are the dentils.

On the page following we have four details of sofa backs in the Sheraton tradition and attributed to the work, or the orders, at least for execution, of McIntire. The upper design represents thunderbolts tied up by ribbon, as it is well known that they could be so held. The other designs speak for themselves, but the basket of fruit is charming, and the device of placing the fruits in the festoons at the sides is a pleasing change. These sofas run about 82 and 84 inches long overall. I have noted it as a curious fact that the Chippendale settee with the carved back is not so much cared for by collectors as are these Sheraton sofas. Whether we are to consider that a failure in taste by the collectors or in Chippendale, it is perhaps wiser not to say. It is obvious that the shortened back of these sofas makes an elegant Sheraton chair back. The extreme rarity of such chairs we may explain by supposing that the emphasis was placed upon the sofa as the central object of ornament; so much is this so that there scarcely comes to mind a set of furniture in which backs as good as these appear in all the setting of the parlor.

Regarding the use of the eagle, an effort has been made to show that after the establishment of American independence the eagle became a natural decorative motive. It was, however, used extensively on looking-glasses in the Georgian day. These various connections and analogies are quite likely to be overdone. A good artist felt free, like a good moralist, to appropriate beauty and truth wherever and whenever it appeared. Hence we find some carving motives which run through all periods. A tendency, however, of furniture construction is steadily from the heavy to the light, reaching in 1820 an almost spiderweb delicacy of outline, as in the late Sheraton, or Adam.

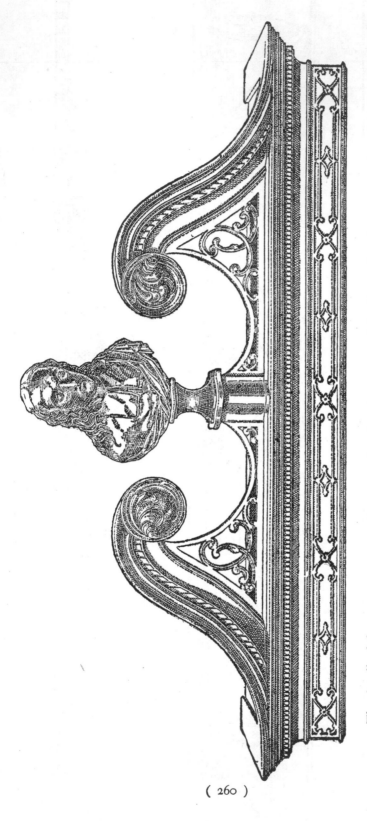

The detail of the separate cap cornice or cresting found on an exquisite Pennsylvania secretary, though it is to be admitted that the decoration is confined practically exclusively to the part above. That the bust is John Milton appears through comparison with a portrait in the New York Public Library. The gooseneck is in one piece with the spiraled and foliated rosette. That is, the rosette is not attached. The stick of mahogany required was four inches square. The sustaining fretwork is properly carved on its face. Altogether a most dignified and elegant bookcase top.

CORRELATION OF FURNITURE WITH ARCHITECTURE

Attention was recently called to the erection of a library in the Tudor period. The furniture was all designed for this library so that it would harmonize with the edifice; at least, that was the avowed purpose. It was a proper purpose, but let us see how the execution came about.

Tables with great bulbous legs were provided. They were handsome and suitable. Then other things of the same period were provided. All very well. But when it came to the question of what should be done about the chairs for the use of the patrons of the library, the architects were at a stand, as Bunyan would say. General condemnation would follow the provision of wainscot chairs for such a purpose, as their use, the seat being a perfectly flat oak board, would be as near torture as modern laws permit. No one would use the library who could help it. The furniture would discourage learning. Was there any way out of the dilemma? Cushions might have been provided for wainscot chairs, but sanitary reasons were against them. Besides, a room of solid nature should not require renewals. To be sure, leather cushions would have been sanitary and durable. Or chairs made with the X frame, and seen only abroad, might have been specified. They were logical because the seat could have been done in plain leather stretched across, and with leather backs, with no objection from the sanitary point of view. Also, such chairs would not have been expensive. But the period so rigidly adhered to up to this point was now utterly forsaken, and Windsor chairs were provided! Of course, they were an anachronism of the worst kind, because about a hundred and fifty years off from the style surrounding them. But behold how it was decided to bridge this gap! Make them of oak! As if the material had a thing to do with the style! In the final settlement, which of course was not a solution of the problem, an impossible Windsor goes into company with things that knew it not, and this was done in the name of adherence to type!

Of course, the best solution would have been oak tables, etc., with maple turned chairs, both of the earliest American period, and not much later than the edifice.

Similarly, the furniture of old dwellings belonging to a city or state is in every instance done without a definite plan. The Jumel mansion visited by a gentleman who wrote me his impressions is renamed by him the jumble mansion! It would seem as if these old houses were used as omnium gatherums, opening wide doors to whatever anybody chose to give or buy. In this home the Hitchcock chair is much in evidence! Shades of our forefathers! Another object of inlaid oak is present without any style at all, but recent.

By what moral right is the prestige of the great State of New York placed behind this catchall? Why, if it is worth keeping, is it not worth decent treatment? One would not mind so much, but this is the rule rather than the exception in historical houses. One of them had the base of a highboy given by the curator himself as a lowboy! Of course it was like a good man cut in two. What are the two parts of a good man worth? There are many people who know better, but I am bound to say that I know of no instance in which a person who understands old furniture has been given authority to reject. As a consequence we have insurance paid on, and watchmen to guard, many objects which belong in the most ordinary dwellings, and which at auction would not fetch enough to pay the expenses of the auctioneers.

PITFALLS FOR THE COLLECTOR

It often costs something to pit our knowledge against that of the other man, but the gambling impulse is strong, and he who risks his money should determine beforehand to be a good loser.

The dealer is a necessity, good or bad. He can often buy to better advantage than the consumer. It is observable in great auctions and elsewhere that the identity of the ultimate customer is kept out of sight. This is especially true if he is a rich man. The dealer known to be such is known also to require a proper profit. Hence whoever is buying much should not get a bad name with dealers. These gentlemen may not be thin skinned, but they are not invulnerable, and here, and especially abroad, they may hunt in packs when they wish to run down their prey. The story is told of a woman buying for a great American shop who went abroad to purchase. The word was passed along by wire, and the entire European front was arranged ahead of her, so that she was properly done. For be it noted, it is not buying a bad piece, but paying too much for a good piece that may floor the buyer.

Dealers of good taste but small capital are often very helpful in getting for a customer furniture they do not own but know about. Knowledge of location is often the principal capital of a dealer. A private buyer on an errand to buy a marvelous piece was trailed for twenty miles by a dealer who wanted to know where it was. He has never learned. The piece is in this volume, still for sale, at last accounts. Square men who spend much time hunting antiques do sometimes come on important things, but collectors' luck is generally bad luck, because men who stop at nothing have been over the ground. If they cannot buy, they arrange it so that no one else can.

Let me first say a kind word for dealers. They are often men who drifted into the business. They may claim no deep knowledge of style or genuineness. They may depend more on the source of their goods than the style to determine worth. Hence dealers may offer in good faith articles which are not "right" or are later in date than they suppose. This remark does not necessarily apply to small dealers only. One of the largest dealers in New York notoriously knew nothing of furniture twenty years ago, though he has learned much since. But he throve more in a state of ignorance than in a state of knowledge.

Many large dealers, if business is brisk, may scarcely have glanced at a miscellaneous lot which they have purchased. They may rely on the pieces they have examined, or on the family from whom they buy, or on some other dealer. Dealers sometimes make mistakes as well as customers.

It is true one has a right to assume that the dealer knows his business. That is not to say that he is dishonest if he attempts to sell something for what it is not. He must be given the benefit of the doubt. There are degrees of knowledge, and no man knows it all. The subject is large. One man may know furniture, another china, another glass, though as to the last, I doubt how much. If a dealer has not made a trip abroad and studied foreign furniture, he is hardly competent to say, in every case, whether an article is foreign or not. A streak of honesty runs through seller, dealer, and consumer just as also a streak of dishonesty, as the fat and the lean in bacon. Sometimes the ethics would be ludicrous if not tragic, as in the case of a man whom I employed as an agent and who, after being instructed, looked up at me in an appealing way and said, "Sometimes we have to lie a little."

Dealing does not make a man a rogue, it only brings out the roguery in him, as litmus paper reveals alkali or acid. One would say that dealers in furniture are no better, no worse than dealers in apples or horses. "Let the buyer beware" is an ancient proverb still applicable, whether a woman wants a piece of decoration for her home or to buy a prince for a husband. It is much the same thing — the decorative value is the main thing. As between the old furniture and the old family the odds are on the furniture.

People have no more right to be indignant because they are beaten in a trade on furniture than when the same thing happens on real estate. The seller of one is as likely to be honest as the seller of the other.

One thing, however, is important. It is never safe for a customer to presume that he knows more than a dealer.

The formula "consult an expert" leads to the same consequences as consulting an expert regarding other investments. We are getting shy of experts.

How can we be certain that anyone is an expert? Reputation? If we are able to pick out an expert, we may be able to pick out our furniture without him. Experts lose their reputations as advisers these days. Men who are pure students of antique furniture perhaps do not exist. They are either collectors or dealers. In either case if a given specimen is a "good buy," the expert may want it. I am continually consulted, often without being shown a photograph. I have, therefore, a printed slip to answer such inquiries and decline to act. It makes clear that an ordinary photograph, usually poor, cannot disclose the details. If it could, the whole piece may be spurious. It is the bottoms, backs, and interiors that must be examined; but sometimes I am favored with a photograph, thumb-nail size.

The methods of construction must sometimes be examined. A piece for twenty years supposed genuine, came apart recently and disclosed a dowel where there should have been a mortise.

Turnings, if old, are no longer round, as wood shrinks one way more than another.

The cutting of new moldings, if by machine, is more precise than handwork.

There is now really little incentive to imitate age in furniture, as the makers seldom obtain, except on a booming market, more than they could get for new work. A chest-on-frame was sold for sixty dollars. It was so good an imitation that it must have been made at a loss. It was the merchant, not the maker, who profited.

The musty smell of an old piece will of course carry over to a new piece made of old wood. Good repairs cannot always be detected.

Photography is the prime assistant of investigation. The surface of a repair in a large photograph will show a difference from the surrounding wood.

In FURNITURE TREASURY, No. 514, the repair under the door is startlingly evident, whereas it is not noticed when we look at the cupboard itself.

The age of wood is no guarantee of genuineness. No good counterfeiter uses new wood. The finish may sometimes deceive anybody.

Furniture found with a reputable old family and known by that family to have been owned by their ancestors has the best warrant of age. Furniture is planted with designing families, but the designs are on the public, not on paper. Most sales are made on the basis that the furniture in question came from a certain family. The consumer seldom gets to the family. Its members are dead or "moved away."

Practically, in almost every case, the furniture is sold by a dealer whose success is in making his customer believe him. Some of the largest dealers do not themselves know what they are selling, and the less they know the better they succeed.

To pass on the merits of furniture is an invidious task, which no wise man cares to undertake, least of all for his friends. If he says the specimen is bad, he gets a black eye from the dealer. If he says it is good, that may raise the price, or he may be wrong and mislead the buyer — a humiliating experience, as unenviable as that of a bank president who recommends bonds that prove bunk. And if the expert will say nothing, both the dealer and the buyer are disgusted with him. The only thing the "friend" expert can do is to leave the country and not leave his address. If he lives where he is known, the balance of his life is made miserable. He is often "quoted" regarding specimens he never saw. In ten years, however good his intentions, he is made out a rogue or a fool or unobliging, and perhaps all three. People will not believe that he does not know about a given specimen. But all these stumbling blocks are capped by an inquiry about the value of a specimen. Nobody knows. Values fluctuate, sometimes rapidly. Oil paintings on a second or third auction sale go down like a stick or up like a rocket. Furniture fluctuates like bonds, no more, perhaps less, but enough to distract anybody.

One of the worst pitfalls for a collector is discovered in buying sets, as of chairs. For often a partial set is added to an order to get a large price for a complete set. A copy was sold at a recent auction and brought thousands of dollars. The original a moment before that brought somewhat more, it is true. The buyer is skilfully led to examine the old chairs as samples of the set, and is inveigled then into taking the entire set. In this case the chairs were sold separately to avoid criticism, or trouble.

The author has a wonderful Chippendale settee. It is composed of the backs of three chairs of a set which had each lost one or both front legs. As a settee of course it required only three front legs instead of six. Hence it was necessary to carve only a new middle leg.

In the buying of clocks the works are sometimes missing, ruined, or inferior. A certain maker naïvely informed me he was making a dozen old sets of works. He charged several dollars extra for each clock to "age" the works. A buyer, after finding a case to be old, might naturally presume the works always belong with it. Not very rarely old works exist without cases. An old case and old works may be put together, thus multiplying the value. Happily there are clock experts who can pass authoritatively on the works.

Old or new English chairs are often passed off as American. If they are old, no great harm has been done the buyer.

Valuation prophets are like religious prophets. They are not all or always inspired. The solidest property is the most difficult to predict about, that is, if truth is the aim.

One counsel, however, I do not hesitate to give: Never buy anything that is fashionable at the moment. Its price is always high. The fashions in antiques change almost as rapidly as gown styles. By buying what everybody is seeking a collection will be accumulated at values above a reasonable future inventory. That which no one wishes to buy now, buy, if it is old, because it will "come back!" When it does, the articles high today may be low. Then buy them. Whatever success I have had in collecting arises from following my own ideas of the style that should be good permanently. The earliest furniture, that of the Pilgrim period, has dropped more than that of later periods. But being so very old and comparatively rare, it has all the elements of good future values.

Very dilapidated furniture can never be of great value. In every purchase all the elements of value must be reckoned — age, rarity, condition, stylistic merit, origin. If a single one of these elements is forgotten, the buyer may overpay. In the matter of origin the native piece is always the better. Therefore, in auction catalogs sometimes and at dealers' often an American origin is claimed without warrant. The name of a supposedly responsible and impartial sponsor is a broken reed to lean on. Care is always taken, as in the sale of bonds, to throw the responsibility all on the buyer. If a small part of the furniture claimed as American is such, then our ancestors must all have been cabinetmakers, except such few as Washington and Franklin and Hancock. They are needed to refer to as having owned the furniture. If all the Winthrop desks came from Governor Winthrop, his house was larger than the thirty-six-hundred room hotel recently built in Chicago. American furniture should bring no better price for having the name of a former owner connected with it. In fact, the tying of it with a name is suspicious, because that allusion (and illusion) may take away one's mind from the fact that the furniture has no merit. If it is fine in itself, it needs no name. If it is bad, a name makes it worse. We wonder that any dead sage could have owned it. We lose respect for his capacity. The foreign article is worth less than the native because it lacks sentimental and patriotic connections. There are also at least two other reasons: such furniture does not fit into the American scene. It looks bizarre or out of place. The other reason, and the main one, is that the profession of making "antiques" has been followed longer and with more good old materials abroad than at home. Only of late have there been masters of the guild here. Abroad the American has for generations been the prey of furniture and picture sharks. Not that one need to cross the ocean to be done brown!

The writer once bought in Venice an oil painting. The price of it had dropped daily, until it reached a point where it connected with my pocketbook. It was to be delivered to me in America, carriage and duty paid. It came after the great war had opened, but before Italy entered the fray. The painting had my own signature on the back, where I had shrewdly (?) placed it to avoid a substitution. But it was not the painting I had bought. That had been done on a canvas covering the picture sent me. Probably the seller has lost count of the times he has sold the good picture and then transferred it to cover an inferior one of the same subject. The only thing to do is laugh at one's own folly. Others also always see the joke. It became a perennial means of entertainment at our house.

Abroad and at home a buyer should carry his purchase away with him. I did so with some trouble with a large piece planted in Springfield, which while old and sold as American was Swedish and worth about a tenth of the sum paid for it. The seller cheerfully helped to stow it in the tonneau of my car. I was afraid someone would see it. I am still afraid.

Consult an expert. But don't pay him. He will get it out of you without your knowing it, and painless extraction is popular. It being an expert's business to know, you are very properly indignant with him if he says he doesn't know. Hence he does not say it. Why make enemies? But expertizing is a business undertaken by few wise men, continued by few honest men, and abandoned by all who wish to retain their friends.

Modern breakfast foods being ready to eat without chewing, the only consideration is the size of the stomach, and even that will increase by steady stretching. Many dwellings are crowded with antiques to the point of saturation. A mere man moving about among them feels belittled and endangered. Side by side the decent articles are rubbed against by the indecent. If the worthy could talk, they would ask to be relieved of their company. The best thing for American homes would be to back against them second-hand furniture vans. The modern articles won't bring much, but remember that whatever the dealer pays saves the owner from paying to have it taken away.

It is within the limits of measured statement to say that nearly all modern, and all questionable antique furniture should be junked. Do not be hard on the makers: The modern maker has failed; the faker is in the hands of God. We leave him there. Doubtless he has a soul. But the patina hides it. We do not consign him anywhere. Profanity is always a waste of energy.

A great good could come from persuading the householder how shabbily done his "reproductions" are, and how they depart from any style that has approved itself to the ages.

It often happens that a room has enough good furniture left in it after the bad is sent away. Crowding loses distinction, and one poor piece pulls a whole room down to its level.

While it is true that truth is hard to get at, the rating of what is commended in a large work like this may at least fix good style in mind. Very little good known American design exists outside the typical examples in these volumes.

The worst faker is not the maker or the dealer in fakes. He is the person who has spurious furniture in his house and allows his friends to think it genuine. I do not now recall a large dealer — though there may be many — who has not a shop where *he makes to order* furniture "to look old." I was once called upon by the architects of a great bank which it was desired to furnish in battered, new furniture. The architects were merely carrying out the behests of the owners, but I am bound to say they did not seem ashamed to do so. Would one feel that everything was right in a bank filled with furniture frauds? Of course the bank people never thought of that. They persevered in their quest and had no trouble at all in getting old wood made into chairs which rocked without rockers. Everything was of the same sort, tarred with the same brush. Further, it fooled the public, whether that was the intention or not. I am often asked, "Don't you think the blank bank wonderful?" I do. And more wonderful the workings of minds that are not content with style, but must have it sick with the rickets. Did people go to Sheraton and Hepplewhite and Adam and say "make my furniture look old"? They would have been chased out of the shops, or committed to asylums.

Such furniture is not made so well as new; it is cheap, if shaky, and is dear at any price. It does not fool the buyer, because he asks for it. Who is fooled?

So the astonishing fact is that Mrs. Grundy or Grubby wants spurious antiques because real ones are too expensive, and for good furniture she has no appreciation.

The basal fact is that when the public is straight as a string, and possessed of a trained taste, the dealers in old and new furniture will be like them. Like bootleg liquor, its purchase damns the buyer, who knows better than the dealer what morals are.

The worm goes into wood by boring a small hole. If wormy wood is used, the surfacing of it uncovers worm channels, and the effect is often an open half boring, of which the worm is incapable or even man with his tools. Some woods, as walnut, are very inviting to worms. But worm-eaten wood is weak; it will often fall apart of itself, and slight pressure breaks it. It cannot be used to deceive even a novice.

The collector should reason that if an object is very rare, it is on that account more likely to be imitated with intent to deceive. The better an object is, the more suspicious. It may be too good to be true. Very much wear on a stretcher is probably more wear than an original ever showed. A gate leg of oak which I saw on Fifth Avenue had stretcher and top well rounded down in places. The table is so rare that I stared and said, "Is that old?"

"Well, not very," replied the clerk who was a friend. In dealing in this table, if the buyer asked no questions, no information was given. If he asked, he was told the truth. The sellers would not tell a lie, they would only act one. But they would say, "You are harsh. That is the way buyers want their furniture." Being a large house, they should know.

Of course, an American buyer should understand that American gate legs are not oak — possibly they never are. They may be walnut, and either English or American, but if of maple, they are American. The under body, if not turned, is likely to be southern, if not English; the unturned are not so attractive as turned legs, and stretchers also turned. The style referred to as gate-leg turning is best (FURNITURE TREASURY 935 for southern origin; 936 for northern origin, or, still better, 949). I would not say that the lack of turning (as in FURNITURE TREASURY 959) is never found in the North, but that the strong presumption is against it.

It may be taken for granted that two gates on a side, hinged at the center, are English. I have seen but one such in America, and think it imported. It is now in the Albany Historical Society, and it belonged to Sir William Johnson who kept close touch with England. It is the best gate leg in this country. It is peculiar in having a small, rounded guide attached at the leaf ends at the joint.

If table leaves are not at all warped, they are suspicious. Yet some fine specimens have not warped. If ancient specimens show the full pear foot, that is suspicious. The old table was dragged about on a sanded floor. A part of the ball, or a pear, if in that form, is worn off. If the table is a little one, the feet are less worn. Fine old tables have often had new feet attached. As that is done at a V angle of the turning, the fact is not obvious without special examination.

New tops on old tables are common. A pine top on a walnut frame is a replacement. The tops split or warp badly. Hence the replacement, which may be a hundred years old or more.

The edges of good-sized tops are never worked, if original, with the thumb-nail mold. They are either square edged or slightly rounded. The joint is (1) matched, (2) rule jointed, or (3) has occasional tongues and tenons (English generally). The rule joint is found at least as early as 1770, but gate legs began to go out soon after that.

Of course, a fine old table frame is worth preserving, but its value should certainly not be more than half that of a like table with the original top. A very sharp edge on an ancient table top is suspicious, but it is very easy to soften the edge on a new top. The drawer is the best indication of age.

The hinges in the oldest specimens are the butterfly type; next in time is an early type which has not the butterfly flare. Most old tables show one or more broken hinges or replacements.

The square-edge joint of the leaf is an almost sure sign of a replaced top. The old tables were not made with that plain joint. At least, I never saw one, though I have seen many plain joints claimed to be original. These replacements were either pine, always wrong, or replacements with proper wood.

One would say that at least half of the good old pieces have experienced some repairs. Only a very old hand at buying will pay as much for a defective piece as for one that has been restored a little. Thus a drawer is sometimes wanting. Examination may be made of an original drawer. A certain new piece of mine after a railroad wreck was in such a condition that a darky said: "They's a bureau down there, boss, that we'll have to bring up in a dustpan." An old bureau in that condition was, after release from a furniture hospital, sold well. Some of this old furniture has, as the deacon said in the prayer meeting, passed through scenes and unseens.

The grapevine telegraph is yet in good condition, so that as soon as a collector starts to buy well, every dealer knows it. As between buyer and seller, each wishing to do as well as he can, there is often an amusing tug of war. As a buying trip of two friends ended, one said, referring to a bout with a dealer, "I held his garments while he stoned Stephen." A judge, referring to a negotiation, said, "While this — I won't call it haggling — was going on." Well, he could as well have called it haggling. One notes that over antiques it is a haggle, over real estate a negotiation, though more may be involved in the former than in the latter case. A gentleman may pay what is asked or he may decline to do so. To prove he is a gentleman he need not pay more than a thing is worth. The one-price scheme for antiques has not become established, and the conditions are such that it never will. Surgeons are said to make a discount to the poor. Dealers in antique furniture charge what they think the traffic will bear, but a rich man is often charged more than a poor one. One dealer, of excellent taste in buying, would be all enthusiasm at first over a new purchase and ask a correspondingly high price. If the piece lagged in the market, his enthusiasm oozed out, and the price fell. One reason for a high initial price on a special or rare piece is that it is not known what it will bring. The market is felt out. Dealers often have preferred customers. Until these have seen the specimen and their options are allowed to lapse, the price holds up.

There is another class of dealers who angle for an offer. Only a very unsophisticated customer will make an offer. But by hook or by crook some offer is at last secured, in which event the price is at once set above the offer, on the theory that nobody would possibly offer as much as a thing was worth.

In spite of these two ways of arriving at an agreement on price, I return to my earlier statement and practice, that it is better to buy on the first inspection or never. If a dealer learns that is your practice, he is afraid to lose you and will be reasonable before he will see you depart. A quick turn is for his advantage. It is thought in the trade a bad thing to have many persons see an article and let it alone. If you are known as a quick cash buyer, you will learn first of a good thing when it comes into the market.

Nevertheless, if you learn — and judicious inquiry among dealers brings out valuable information — that an article has waited until it has become a wallflower, do not pass it by on that account. There may be good reasons apart from the merit of a piece of furniture why it has not sold. Buyers may not have had use for it just then, or they may have followed the old bad practice of hanging off, thinking to buy for less. I could never perceive that a specimen was worth less because many had seen it. A certain article had lain around for a long time till one day a keen buyer took it. At once another buyer who had seen it repeatedly offered to double the sale price. He was basing his action on the other's judgment.

Again there are two classes of dealers, arising from the fact that one is adventitious and another intends to remain in business. The adventitious dealer has, maybe, found something remarkable. He lives in a small town in a quiet way. One big sale is a life-time matter with him. He will live for years on it. He is overborne by these reasons and does not weigh heavily the matter of keeping a good customer. A regular dealer, however, may do much to cultivate good will in a buyer so that future business may develop.

It is too much to attempt to comprehend the seller's motives in all cases. Sometimes he is rich today and poor tomorrow. A dealer had a boy in college who wanted money quickly. The loyal father, who was very fat, chased a customer in an automobile, dropping his price at every other step until the customer in pity stopped and bought, though he did not want the article. I have often thought the dealer may then have aggravated the heart disease from which he died. He did not tell what moved him. He was a Spartan. It was an accident years after that revealed the fact. There are hearts and tragedies among the dealers. Neither wisdom nor character is all on one side.

It is astonishing even now how many quaint or beautiful or interesting articles may be bought at prices not beyond moderate capacity. The same or nearly the same quality may be offered in one shop at half what is asked for it in another. Some goods sell well in one place, some in another. The South and West are no places to buy pillar and scroll clocks, because these coming from New England are rare South, and it is hard for dealers to understand why Easterners pass lightly over some of the goods offered.

So Phyfe is higher in New York than elsewhere because that market is large, and the maker is their peculiar, cherished possession, having lived there.

Iron articles, however, since I once went through Pennsylvania taking all in sight, are higher there in their most important home than elsewhere. They are still telling about "that man from New England who writes books and who came and bought everything," and they are still looking in vain, but hopefully, for his successor.

There is much hidden romance and not a little revelation of fine traits to be discovered in a buying trip. Given a fairly lined pocketbook, a congenial companion, decent weather, and love for antiques, a journey of some weeks by motor is a continual delight. The buyer must have a mellow heart, be prepared to admire everything, exchange information, take his occasional dose of medicine with a grin, and pick up a wide and fascinating fund of experience as well as some articles for his home collection. Suppose he does get the hot end of the poker once in a great while. The annoyance will wear off, and the amusement remain. My worst experiences of being done leave no rankling. I certainly do not want to "get" anybody. One could count on one hand everybody who has done very well in selling antiques. They are welcome to all they get, which is little enough. The buyer also is at times known to be no saint, and some of them can be desperately mean. After thirty years' experience I am not prepared to say that men in one profession are any better or worse than men in another. Some dealers I remember with great pleasure, men of fine, discriminating taste, satisfied with fair profits, and confident that, if they conduct their business with steady decency, they have an occupation as interesting and honorable as any other.

Several precautions a buyer should take.

1. Beware of foreign or fictitious stuff in an out-of-the-way place, planted there to give the impression of local origin.

2. Learn something of your trader before you reach him. There will be plenty to warn against him if that is necessary.

3. It is often easy to discover if there is a small factory in some rear building.

4. You can buy several articles to better advantage than one article.

5. Most dealers have a flair for certain classes of articles. They are specialists in one thing or another. A good book man or dealer in quaint paintings may be found in the most unlikely neighborhood.

6. A gentleman buyer will give every dealer the credit of being a gentleman until he proves himself otherwise. Not seldom is the dealer better read, better mannered than his customer.

7. There is a considerable class of women who almost by compulsion are dealers. Their knowledge may be narrow, but deep in some particulars, and their character for veracity is often high. They are not always governed by the market, but sometimes by personal liking for particular objects.

8. If dealers have not something you want, they may be able to take you where you

can get it. In that case never boggle over commissions, because these are seldom unreasonable.

9. Dealers often lack expert packing knowledge. Therefore, take away small articles and arrange with a local carpenter for the sure crating of large pieces. A marred specimen is a serious loss.

10. Invite coöperation rather than repel it. Admire freely. A poker face is not necessary. Owners are more afraid of admiration than commendation, because they think you won't buy what you openly admire.

11. Look at the backs, the bottoms, the insides of all objects whether you want them or not. Any objection on the part of the buyer is enough to warn you.

12. Cut nails in furniture mean too late a date. New brasses always raise a question. New finish means goods should be offered very low indeed. It was, you may infer, not attractive before repair.

13. Buy all looking-glasses as foreign, whether they are or not. I mean, one cannot tell their origin. The dealer himself does not know, even if he bought them from a house where they have been a hundred years.

14. Ignore all labels, but reckon the original maker's name on a clock face as a good part of the value, sometimes the main part.

15. Care less for surface than construction and establish the nature of the construction if possible. Finish is skin deep, like beauty, and useless without substantial qualities inherent.

16. Ask carefully if any repairs have been made. If the dealer is square, it is worth while. If otherwise, and he misrepresents, he knows himself wrong and liable, if not to suit, to something worse — a bad reputation.

17. Never buy an article that is low in price unless it has style and intrinsic worth. It is easy to fill an entire house with antiques that are scarce worth transportation. There are too many articles really "over a hundred years old" to give them any value merely on that account.

18. Do not fix your mind on one kind of wood in collecting. Be appreciative of all kinds, because every kind of wood has been wrought into excellent shapes sometime.

If a room has maple and mahogany both of the same period, you will neither be arrested nor even lose caste by assembling such furniture.

19. Think less of what your neighbors will say than of what your heirs will say. Nine-tenths of the fun in collecting is to surround yourself with permanent belongings of taste and merit and to let them continue in the family. You will find that your neighbors generally will admire most what is least admirable. It takes some people a generation to learn to be intelligently appreciative. If you are buying for your neighbor, it is best to let him pay, or not to begin. I had a neighbor who never crossed our bounds to see what others came a thousand miles to see. He was a good man and knew birds. He thinks me a good deal of a fool, but is always very polite. Even among savage races they are careful not to offend a maniac, who, as such, is under the special protection of the gods.

20. Avoid merely pretty things. If a thing is not useful, it is not in the best sense ornamental. Bizarre shapes do not promote an early American home atmosphere.

The agreement of one piece of furniture with another provides a neglected charm.

21. The walls of American homes are most neglected. People weary themselves to find what they can best put on the walls, when, if they collected properly, they would want nothing, except in early houses wainscot, besides looking-glasses, maps, old prints, wall cupboards, paintings. The plain wall is altogether best if one has collected wisely. Any figured wall then is either hidden, or obtrusive and inharmonious. A figured wall is the worst possible background. Let the decorator who wishes to paper it for you put on perfectly plain paper and buy something else, to comfort him, to place on the paper.

Practically every well-lighted room has a good deal of the space taken up by windows or doors, and a fireplace, for there ought to be a fireplace in every room. If it is not there, it is easily purchasable. It adds more to the attraction of a room than all the wallpaper, however good. Then there are required at least some important wall pieces in every room, either a secretary or a chest-on-chest, or both. After abundant looking-glasses are added there will scarcely be room for many old pictures and prints and cabinets.

The foundation of modern picture paper, therefore, is never desirable, unless one has an empty house. Let not the decorator be put out. There is plenty to provide for the wall. Shrewd decorators will soon learn that they can sell their customers nothing after figure paper, in the fear of covering it up.

CASE WORK

The development of the chest has not in recent years brought much new knowledge except as patterns varying slightly from those known come to light.

One conclusion to which we may probably come is that some very early oak chests were built in America with paneled tops in the usual English style, and such a chest is drawn above. It obviously dates in the fore part of the seventeenth century and has the rare but excellent strapwork called the band of eternity on the top rail. The five stiles consist of a series of medallions. The panels divided into diamond sections by the X design are simple foliations which could hardly be called fleur-de-lis. This chest has been many years in Ohio, the origin not now traceable.

The literature of chests has been much enriched by the researches of Luther into the Hadley chest design. He has tallied over one hundred of these chests, whereas a few years ago only one was known. The early volumes of this work show a sufficient general range of them.

Constructive details are simple, but somewhat rigidly followed. In the oak examples there is a wide tenon and a deep mortise usually with two pins, as here. The panel backs are often left as they come from the hewing axe, but some are slightly smoothed with a plane, especially on the bevel edge. If the panels fit tightly, they will crack as the second one has in the example above.

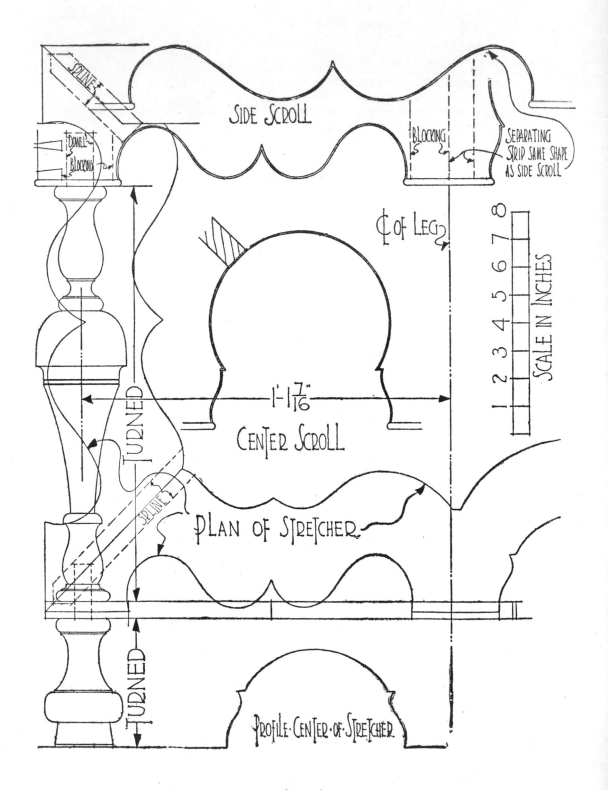

SIDE SCROLL

SPLINE

DOWEL BLOCKING

BLOCKING

SEPARATING STRIP SAME SHAPE AS SIDE SCROLL

℄ OF LEG

1'-1$\frac{7}{16}$"

CENTER SCROLL

TURNED

SPLINE

PLAN OF STRETCHER

TURNED

PROFILE · CENTER · OF · STRETCHER

SCALE IN INCHES

1 2 3 4 5 6 7 8

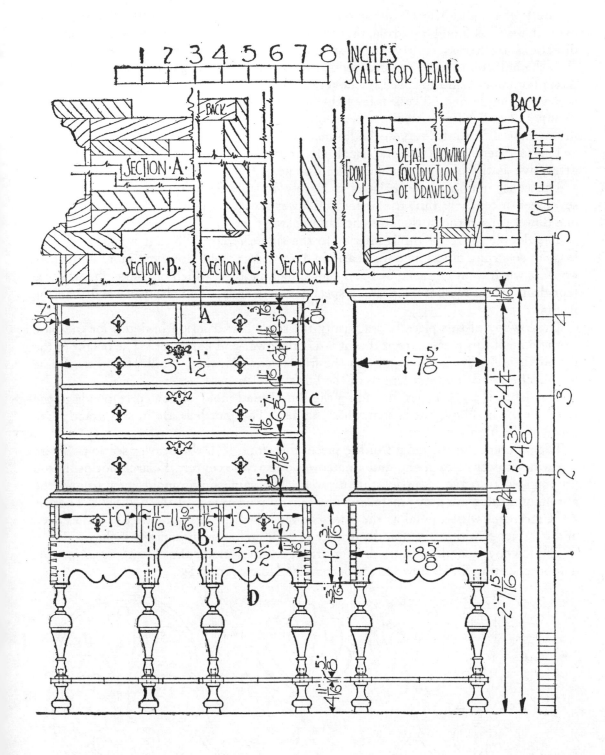

SCALE FOR DETAILS
1 2 3 4 5 6 7 8 INCHES

SECTION·A·

BACK

SECTION·B· SECTION·C· SECTION·D·

DETAIL SHOWING
CONSTRUCTION
OF DRAWERS

FRONT

BACK

SCALE IN FEET

The William and Mary highboy on the two pages preceding is in butternut. However, the type is found, as a rule, in walnut with or without a burl veneer. No specific directions are necessary beyond what appears on the plan. We may, however, say that the half-round mold applied about the drawers was designed for the double purpose of ornament and to cover the dovetailed joints of the blades below. The cornice is a very simple one. The scroll of the skirt while conventional has a good deal of "snap and go" because of the shortness of the members. The specimen is very rare in having only two drawers in the frame.

The feet here shown are the usual cup or bowl turning, which I do not think as attractive as the trumpet turning seen in some of the drawings in my other volumes.

The construction of these bases is largely by dowel, following the spirit of the seventeenth century; thus the upper and lower sections of the leg are separated, but one dowel runs through the stretcher and answers for the foot and leg.

The double mold we think inferior to the single mold. While it is more delicate, it is not so strong in feeling nor so early in date. That mold, however, more frequently appears when we find the early hand-tooled bail handles, which of course follow these tear-drop handles in date. In many specimens the ends are of cheaper wood than the fronts.

The lowboy of this piece is practically the same construction in detail for the base as the base of this piece, except that it is a little lower and narrower. The height of the lowboy is 30 inches. The length on the frame is 31½ inches, the depth on the frame is 18 inches, and the total length of the lid is 35½ inches.

The depth is 19¾ inches, including the thumb-nail mold, which corresponds to the mold on the highboy, but is somewhat thinner. The four legs are in size exactly like those of the highboy.

The difference in the height of the piece, therefore, is in the drawer section. There is a wide drawer at each end and a narrower one at the center, the arch not being too pronounced to leave room for this drawer. The same lining mold runs around the apron, and there are drops instead of the central pair of legs of the highboy. There is an X stretcher with a finial at the intersection. The side drawers are 6⅜ inches deep and 9¼ inches wide. The middle drawer is 3³⁄₁₆ inches deep and 9⅜ inches wide.

The lowboy resembles in its drawer arrangement FURNITURE TREASURY, No. 395. The intersecting finial, however, is better; see No. 60, page 85.

The chest-on-chest was the most serviceable, stately, and economical construction as it provided a vast quantity of storage space.

The example on page 277 has been in vain sought by collectors, but is in a family which has inherited it from an Ipswich cabinetmaker. An amusing instance of the fact that it was never sold is seen in the absence of the rosettes at the crests of the goosenecks. It never had these, the maker of course always intending to supply them, as he would have been obliged to do had he sold it.

The specimen follows several features common to the North Shore cabinetmakers. One of these is the fluted pilaster, flanking the upper section. Another is the finials which are usual to or peculiar to northern New England. A rare feature is the contouring of the top side drawers to follow the lines of the arch of the bonnet. Another merit of the piece is that the drawer ends are shaped to fit against the bulge at the kettle base and not carried down in a straight line as in the less desirable examples.

The foot correctly illustrates the principle that in this ogee form its base should not extend beyond the vertical line from the hip. In fact, in this case they are somewhat tucked under. Spurious pieces not infrequently overlook this feature and produce a foot which extends out beyond the vertical line mentioned and is neither in good taste nor in accordance with any fine early example. The scroll of the foot bracket is intermediate between the Newport type and the more flamboyant design often seen in Connecticut.

As in all fine examples so here the pilaster capital breaks and returns on the top mold and very much adds to the effectiveness of the piece. A miniature shell ornaments the center of the base mold and a conventional fan with scalloped edges the middle top drawer. The entire design is as nearly perfect as may be. No small feature is the completeness of the great battery of brasses, no less than eighteen with bails and eight escutcheons. A careful attention to the hand filing and beveling of these old handles in such a manner that they seem to melt into the background is a highly important feature overlooked in some ambitious reproductions.

The wood is mahogany. It was convenient to import it in shore towns.

In the construction of all pieces with drawers above one another the blade or division between the drawers is either half or full dovetailed into the upright end. Thus any liability to spread is overcome.

In some of the finest specimens this is sometimes a blind dovetail. That is, it stops perhaps a half inch short from the edge, so that it does not appear. Another method in many chests of drawers is to use a covering strip with a mold. This strip is sometimes not more than a quarter or an eighth of an inch thick. It would not be practicable in this specimen, but many styles require it.

The cleat running back from the blade is sometimes dovetailed and sometimes nailed on. In the latter case there is more liability of splitting the wood, as the cleat prevents the drawing of the end together in shrinking without obstruction.

Names have too much influence in furniture; a highboy, for instance, is sought for more than a chest-on-chest merely because the uninitiated have heard the word highboy a very great deal in connection with popular talk about antiques.

The dainty secretary on page 279, in cherry, is a Chapin piece, supposedly Eliphalet. One of the most pleasing features to the modern taste is the modest dimensions of the piece, the writing table being no higher than that of a modern table, and the entire piece is scaled down so that it corresponds with the ceilings of the simpler colonial homes. It is built in three sections, the frame at the base separating. The feet are particularly quaint. It is observed that, although this piece is in a native wood, both the lower and upper parts have quarter columns. The fret sustaining the gooseneck does not show as it should, it being carved to indicate a lattice. The molding of the doors is very attractive. Perhaps the most remarkable feature is the amazingly fine finials. They are detailed on page 65. Where Chapin got his idea for these we cannot know, but they are altogether delightful. The central one is a little larger than the others and has a rounded plinth to rest upon. The scroll of the gooseneck ends in the usual Chapin spiral. The carcase width is 40 inches on the lower section. The width of the upper section is 37⅞ inches. The depth of the base is 20 inches. The distance from floor to the bottom of the retaining mold above the slant top 40½ inches. The feet are 6¾ inches high. It is 8¼ inches from the floor to the base of the mold on the bottom frame. The retaining mold for the upper section ¾ inch each way. That for the base is ⅝ inch wide and ½ inch deep and is worked on the frame. The upper section is 36⅛ inches to the top of the mold on the outside end of the gooseneck. The gooseneck is 9⅞ inches wide from the crest down to the top of the mold on which the lattice rests. The quarter columns have a space cut out below for them 1¼ inches square and above 1⅛ inches square. The writing table height is 29 inches. From the top of the slant lid to the back including the mold is 12 inches. The upper carcase itself is only 10⅞ inches deep. The height inside the cabinet from the writing table to the lid is 11⅛. The width of the central door in the cabinet outside the frame is 8 inches.

This specimen is in the house for which it was made about 1735 in Connecticut, near Windsor. All the hardware is original.

The writer would almost prefer this secretary to any other known in cherry. It has more good elements and more attractive features and less to which an objection could be raised than any other which he knows.

On the page opposite is a cherry specimen belonging to the author. In some respects it differs from any known to me. It has a crude Spanish foot which, so far as I have seen, is unique. The chamfered corners are secured by attaching a thin strip which is beveled not at 45 degrees, but about half as much, and fluted. The demi-dome in the base mold and the bottom drawer is made with inlaid rays. The flower pattern cut in the top drawer is of course below the surface. The star above it is inlaid. The cresting is a true bonnet. The finial was missing and has been supplied by me. It apparently had no side finials. The gooseneck turns upward at the outer end quite markedly in pergoda fashion, and is very amusing in its effect. The brasses are not all original. The piece is not massive in size, but generous.

The block front above, while attributed to Rhode Island with probable reasons, varies quite a little from Goddard's usual patterns. It is rare in that it has the block and the contour of the lid and the knee hole, but without shells, more in the fashion found from Boston north. The blocks, however, are flat on the face, and that design agrees with Newport. There is a slide above the top drawer which makes the piece practical as "a bureau table," as Goddard called such pieces. It is evidently made for a practical person who felt that he could not get both knees into the knee hole far enough to use the table for writing. Pulling out the slides, therefore, not only gives knee room, but adds to the available surface. The door is simple with the Queen Anne top design. Goddard's pieces with knee holes ordinarily had four feet in front.

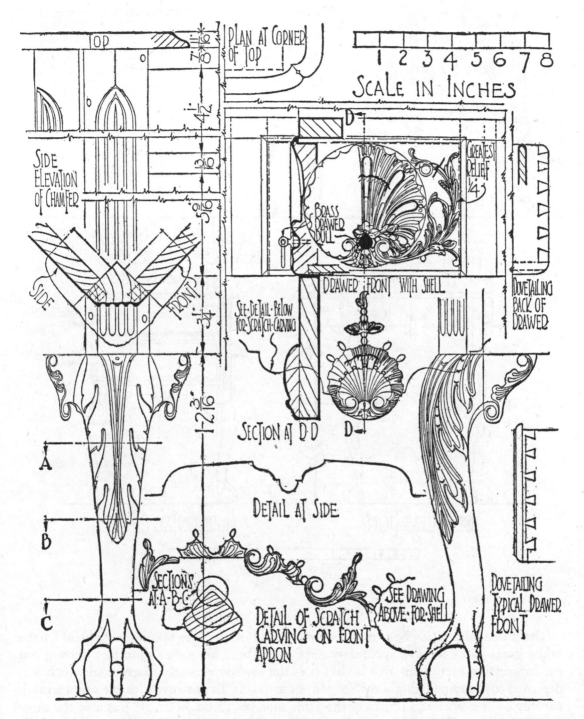

SCALE IN INCHES
1 2 3 4 5 6 7 8

PLAN AT CORNER OF TOP

SIDE ELEVATION OF CHAMFER

SIDE   FRONT

GREATEST RELIEF 1/4

BRASS DRAWER PULL

DRAWER FRONT WITH SHELL

DOVETAILING BACK OF DRAWER

SEE DETAIL BELOW FOR SCRATCH CARVING

SECTION AT D·D   D

DETAIL AT SIDE

A

B

SECTIONS AT·A·B·C

C

DETAIL OF SCRATCH CARVING ON FRONT APRON

SEE DRAWING ABOVE FOR SHELL

DOVETAILING TYPICAL DRAWER FRONT

Details of Lowboy on Page 284

(283)

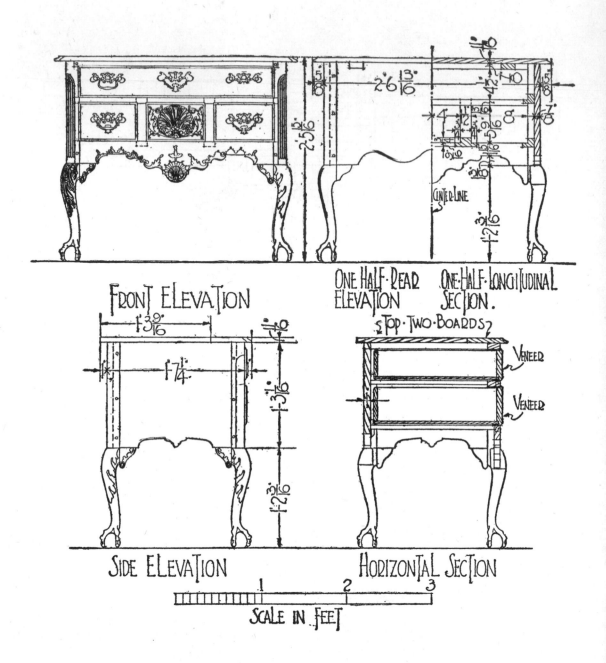

FRONT ELEVATION ONE·HALF·REAR ELEVATION ONE·HALF·LONGITUDINAL SECTION.

SIDE ELEVATION HORIZONTAL SECTION

SCALE IN FEET

The Philadelphia lowboy drawn above is one of the fine specimens which I have taken great pains to have accurately detailed. There are richer examples known, but the interesting fact about this is that it is the lowboy recently discovered which was designed to accompany highboy No. 369, FURNITURE TREASURY, with the same scratch carving on the skirt and precisely the same motives throughout. It has also the same fluted chamfer. The maker veneered in figured walnut the face of this specimen. It has the same somewhat high foot as the highboy.

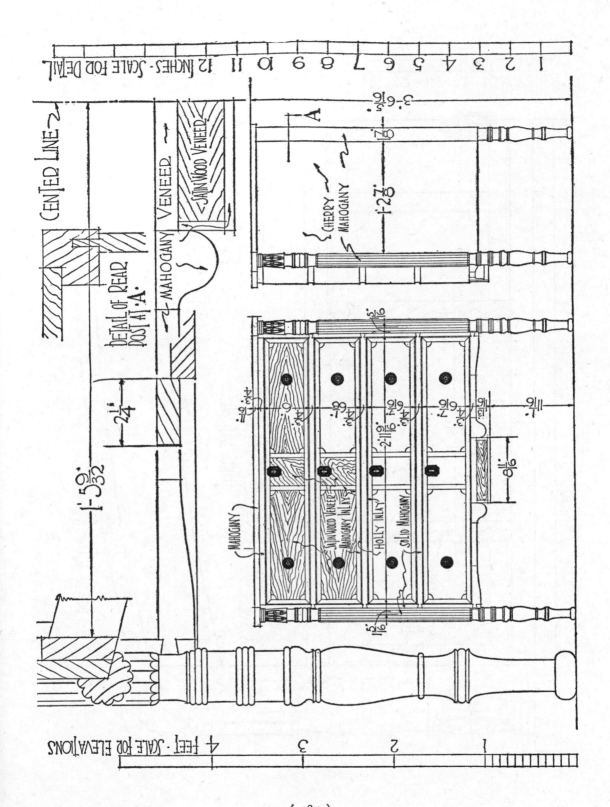

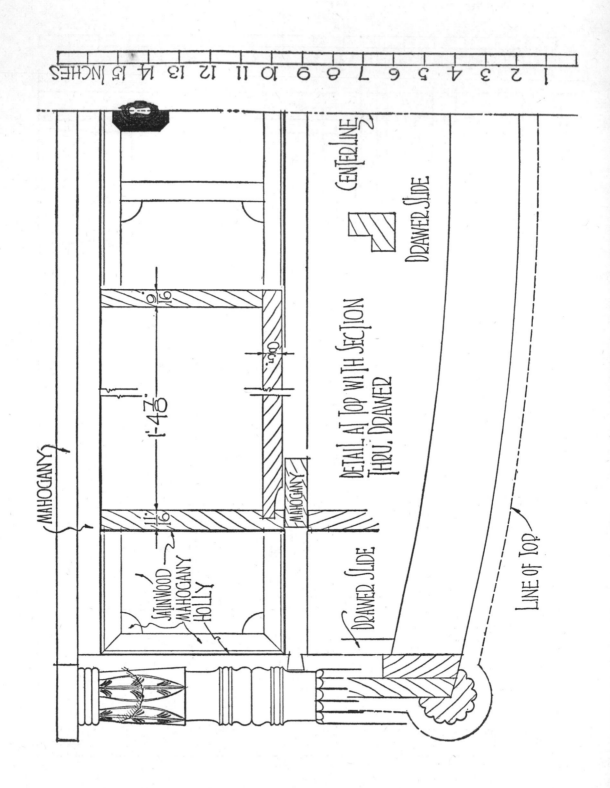

1 2 3 4 5 6 7 8 9 10 11 12 13 14 15 INCHES

MAHOGANY

CENTER LINE

DRAWER SLIDE

$\frac{9}{16}$"

$1'-4\frac{3}{8}$"

$\frac{11}{16}$"

SATINWOOD
MAHOGANY
HOLLY

MAHOGANY

DETAIL AT TOP WITH SECTION
THRU. DRAWER

DRAWER SLIDE

LINE OF TOP

On the second page back and the preceding page are drawings of a satinwood-front Sheraton bowed chest of drawers with reeded posts and carved capitals, and all the original hardware, dainty little brass knobs. The front is mahogany veneered, and the ends are cherry. The piece is the most perfect old specimen possible. The drawers are graduated. The drawing on the opposite page shows a further detail, including the top.

While a piece of this kind does not attain to the dignity and magnificence of the Queen Anne and Chippendale period, it does not fail at all in beauty and stateliness.

On the two pages following are detailed the complete construction drawings for a tambour desk. This type has been much sought for of late years. It has the advantage of compactness and moderate size.

It is clearly seen that the bevel of the leg is as always on the inside and that externally the leg is in a vertical line with the frame. The little central door is nicely outlined with an inlay and the pigeonholes are scrolled at the top with drawers below. Pictures of pieces like this appear in FURNITURE TREASURY, No. 654, somewhat simpler, there being found the kind of peg leg, tapered from both sides, but near the floor only, and not in as good style. No. 662 in the same book is more in the type of the drawing. These pieces also appeared with a bookcase section above, as in No. 729, FURNITURE TREASURY, although that is peculiar in having tambour doors below also, instead of drawers.

There are those who suppose the Windsor writing chair was the earliest. By no means. This chair with its extraordinary high comb is, of course, a pure Windsor back on a pure turned corner chair. The happy device of applying the arm on a chair of this sort results in a wide space for the sitter. (*Page 161.*)

The assignment of a date is not easy. Suppose we make a rough estimate of 1700–1725.

The seat, of course, was originally rush. Writing men — some of them — must stop to think. The tall owner of this chair could have rested his head while he worked it. The turnings, of course, prevent our classing the chair any earlier than the Queen Anne age.

A leather upholstered Sheraton type armchair is unlooked for. In the instance before us we have what the Martha Washington is not — a comfortable chair. This chair is deeper and broader in the seat than usual, and the back is hollowed. It is the most pleasing chair for ordinary use that has been seen, in this style. (*Page 161.*)

The doubling of the arm supports suggests the Sheraton sofas. But even here the designer improved on his model by separating the posts for additional strength. All the lines are neat and trig. There is something very demure and yet smart about a simple Sheraton. Not an ounce, not a line is wasted, but grace and trimness are secured that are at once high art and beauty. It is a constant wonder to me that such a chair should be rare, but I have never before seen its counterpart.

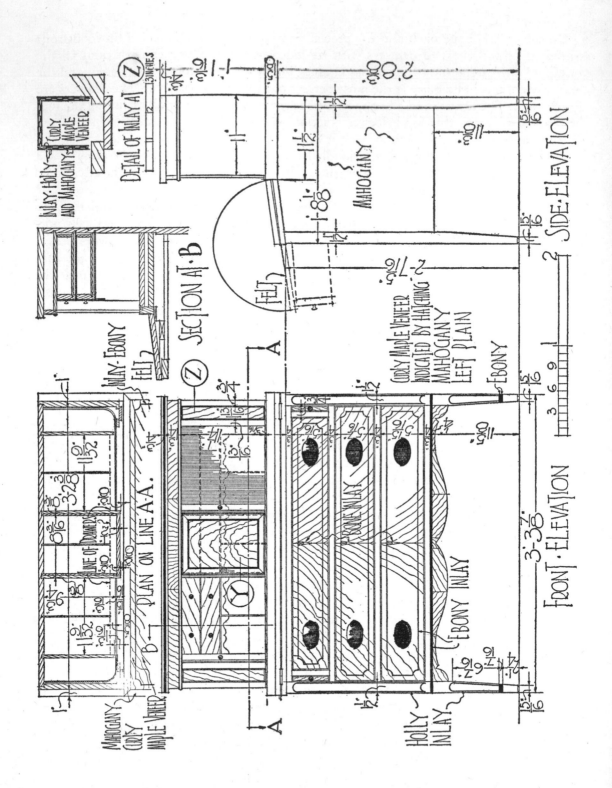

DETAIL OF INLAY AT Z
3 INCHES
Inlay·Holly· and Mahogany· Curly Maple Veneer

SECTION AT·B Z

Inlay·Ebony Felt

Mahogany Curly Maple Veneer

SIDE·ELEVATION

Mahogany

Felt

Curly Maple Veneer indicated by hatching Mahogany left plain

Ebony

Bone Inlay

Ebony Inlay

Holly Inlay

FRONT·ELEVATION

PLAN ON LINE A·A·

(288)

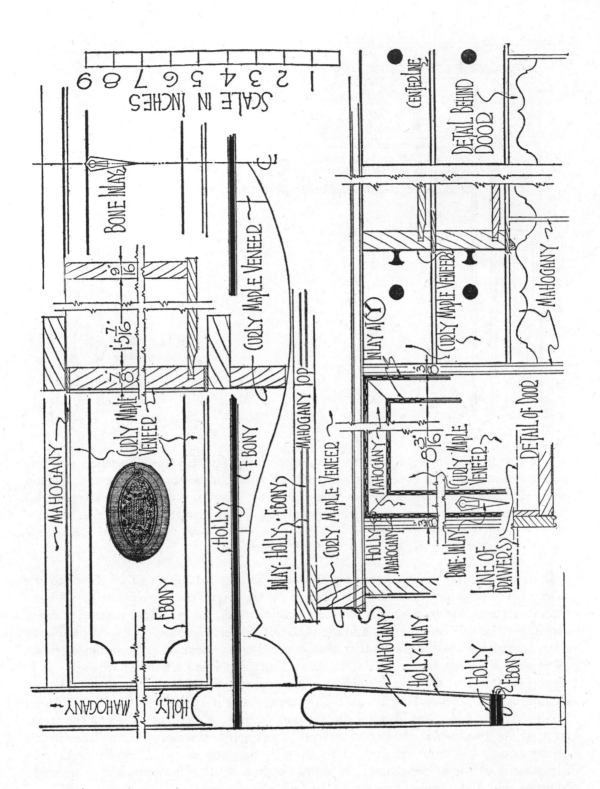

SCALE IN INCHES

1 2 3 4 5 6 7 8 9

BONE INLAY

MAHOGANY

CURLY MAPLE VENEER

$\frac{9}{16}$

$1 \cdot 5\frac{7}{16}$

$\frac{7}{8}$

CURLY MAPLE VENEER

EBONY

HOLLY

EBONY

MAHOGANY TOP

CURLY MAPLE VENEER

INLAY-HOLLY-EBONY

CURLY MAPLE VENEER

MAHOGANY
HOLLY-INLAY

HOLLY
MAHOGANY

BONE-INLAY

HOLLY
EBONY

MAHOGANY

CENTERLINE

DETAIL BEHIND DOOR

CURLY MAPLE VENEER

INLAY AT Y

$\frac{3}{8}$

MAHOGANY

$8\frac{3}{16}$

CURLY MAPLE VENEER

$\frac{3}{8}$

LINE OF DRAWERS

DETAIL OF DOOR

(289)

The mantel above belongs to the Sheraton time approaching 1800 when the fans were popular, and the inverted columns smaller at the bottom. These mantels are much easier to find than the earlier type, but as the taste of the public is satisfied with them, we sometimes weary of trying to point out the superiority of the earlier style.

It has not been thought necessary to add anything further in this volume to the vast mass of wrought iron shown in Volume II. It is true that in recent years I have discovered and acquired some interesting specimens as, for instance, a question-mark hinge, and various other forms and utensils, not hitherto known. I should like, however, to express the judgment that the proper development of antiquarian interests as regards dwelling houses is due to come along the line of house hardware. It is regrettable that so few, if any, dwellings are properly fitted in this respect. The old examples are known and are available in themselves or in copies. So far as I have seen this work applied, it has been on simple rooms almost altogether, whereas the treatment of the dwellings in the period up to 1770 as regards the more elegant front rooms of the houses has been ignored, or fitted with commercial types wholly lacking in suggestions of the ancient time. It is my purpose to fit a few rooms appropriately in order that I may call attention to the finer effect produced by such fittings.

The brackets in use partly for ornament and partly for strength at the corner intersections between table frames and legs and chair frames and legs may be mortised into both sides, but must be mortised into one side at least.

They consist of many geometrical or free-hand scrolls. A few of them were shown on page 109, but we show above and on the pages following sixteen more. One of the most attractive is the top left member. None of these shows the projecting tenon which, of course, should always be left on the lower left side, and at the top on the right if possible. It will appear that the better examples are carved in a grooved form, and that the simpler and less expensive sorts are simply cut-outs.

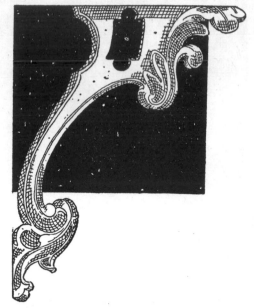

Of course the strongest are those which leave most wood at the joint, but it is a question whether any of these brackets derives its merit largely from its strength-giving qualities. For the most part they are very decorative indeed, and they often double or treble the value of the table.

TABLES

In Volume II I showed a good many shafts for tea tables and light stands, but on the three pages next following I show nine others. The first example on the next page is rather attractive for a small table, but the second one is somewhat coarse and heavy in its upper members. The third is an oddity. On the page next following the first and the second lack grace for the reason that the neck of the vase is too large for the bowl. This arises from using a stick of too small dimensions. In the first example on that page the maker was probably afraid to draw in the neck very much more lest he weaken his table. He could not, on the other hand, enlarge the bowl without having a piece of bigger section to work on. The second example is somewhat better, and the third gets over these difficulties by breaking up the lines more without a very large post. On the following and last page of these shafts the first one shows a twisted carving, but the second is more pretentious, carrying besides a twisting a fluting above. In this case the twisted bowl is too small for effectiveness. The last example is simple and good.

The highest type of these shafts is found in pie-crust tables, examples of which appear in the earlier volumes.

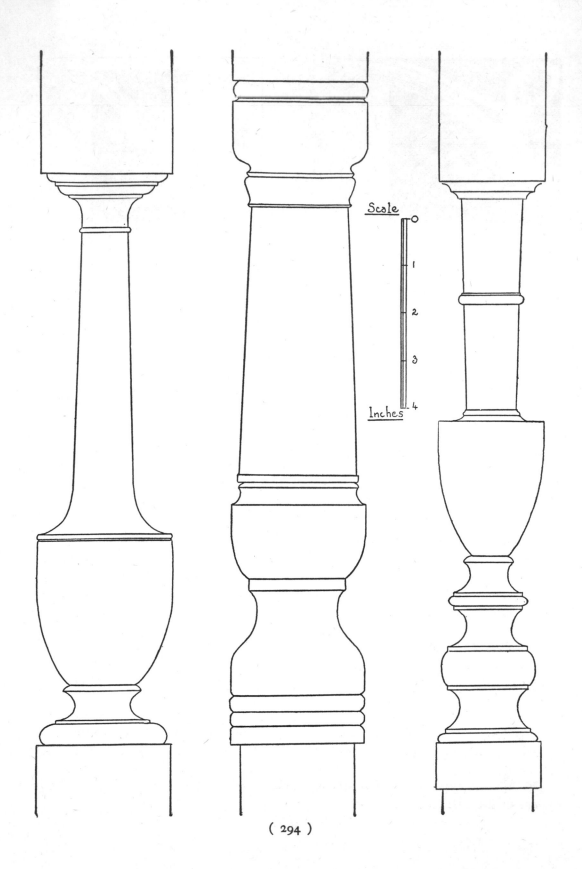

Scale

1

2

3

Inches 4

(294)

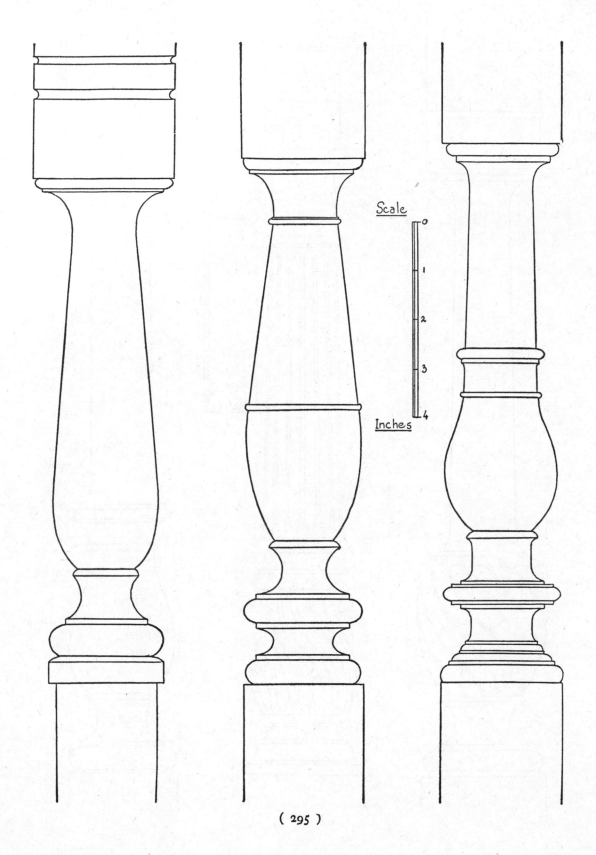

Scale

0
1
2
3
4

Inches

(295)

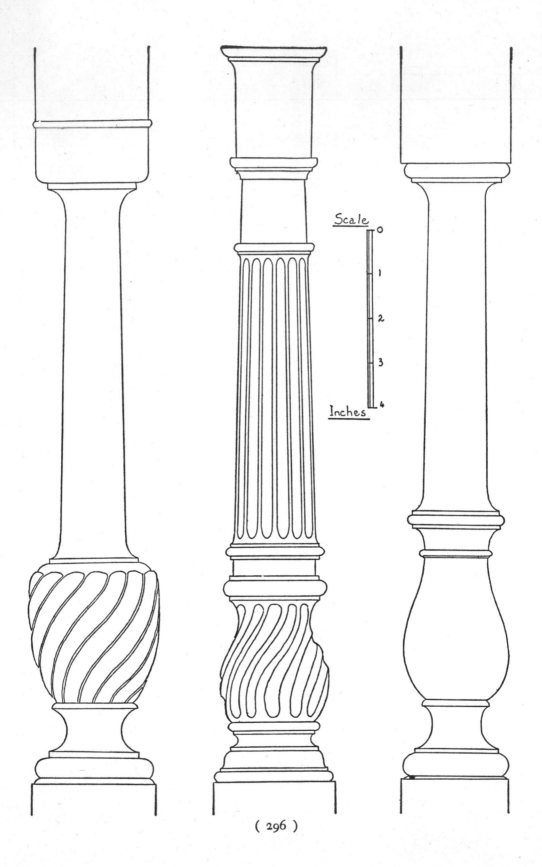

Scale

0

1

2

3

4

Inches

(296)

There are shown under chair details two drawings of the front leg above. This is one of the rarest and most important tables found in this country. It has a stone top and an ogee frame. The origin is not settled, but it is perhaps fair to call it American, as it is known to have been in this country at least four generations. It is walnut.

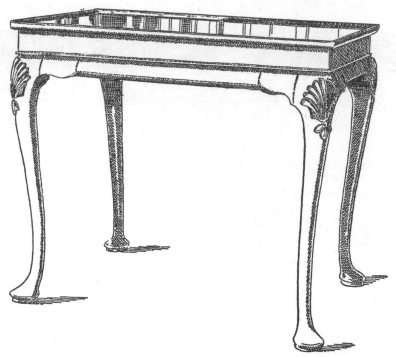

A rectangular-top tea table with a raised edge. A pure Queen Anne foot and a shell quite like that seen on chairs.

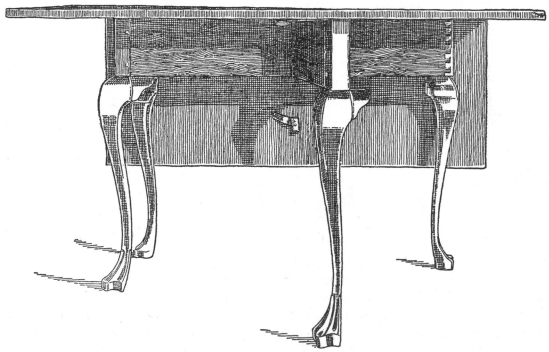

This southern table is a rarity in that it has grooved three-toed or drake feet which give it a great deal of distinction.

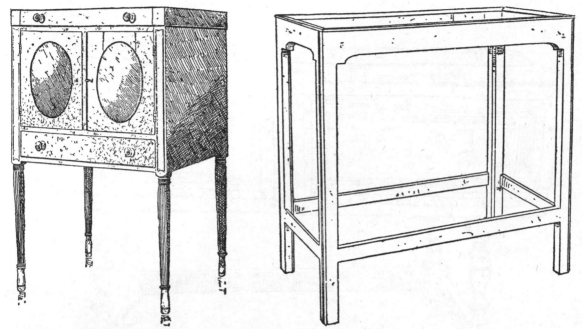

The Sheraton stand on the left has a lifting top with many contrivances for a lady's convenience.

The table frame on the right is very simple with a slight raised edge and bracket corners. It is obviously for a metal fern tray.

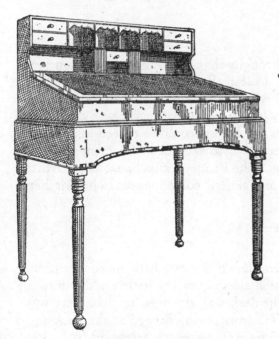

A Sheraton desk.
For description see next page.

A tavern table with scallops.
It is odd for its short drawer.

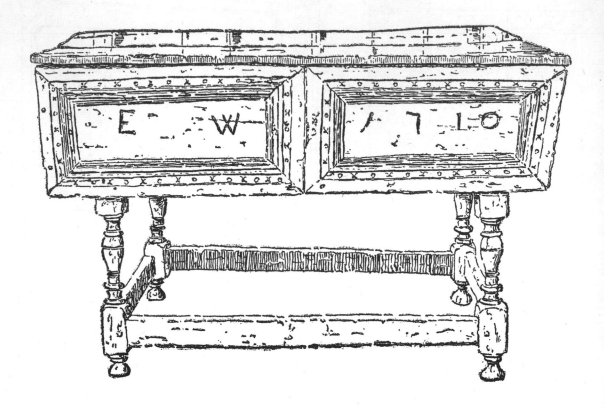

Above is the most distinctive of the mixing troughs that has come to my attention. It is all in oak and crudely initialed and dated. Practically all of the examples of these troughs found are of Delaware Valley origin, whether because the people there ate more than the New Englanders or because they baked less often, or because they were more ingenious. A batch of dough mixed in this fine trough could be placed at a proper position near the fireplace and turned, if necessary, to facilitate the raising of the dough — a very laudable ambition in these days. The Pennsylvania housewife delights in her occupation, or did, and had more ample and artistic conveniences in her kitchen than any other early American.

On the preceding page the Sheraton desk there shown merits a little more attention. At the center there is a miniature tambour which closes over the little middle drawer and is shown open. The arch of the front of the desk was arranged so that there was plenty of knee room. The slant table is not a fall front, being hinged at the back and lifting to give access to the space below. The author was so much attracted by it that he could not resist it. There is a narrow line of inlay on the frontal arch.

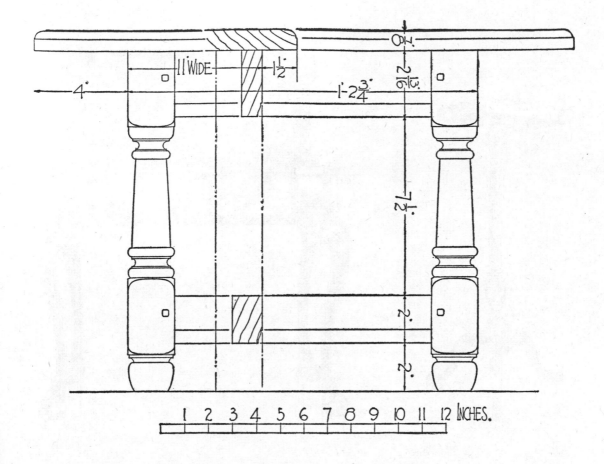

The stool above is drawn from one found in Connecticut near Guilford and of the same pattern of turning as the Thomas Robinson wainscot chair. It is very early, probably not later than about 1640.

There is a curious departure in this stool from the usual habit of a light overhang. A long overhang on a stool is liable to make the stool tipsy, and if the person who sits on it is so, an overturn is probable.

This is the only instance I know of a stool and chair being of the same turning. The presumption is that the stool is one of several to go with the wainscot chair. If this surmise is correct, as seems very probable, owing to the similarity also of the frame and its mold with the chair frame, the case would illustrate the habit of having one chair for the head of the house and stools for the other members of the family. Both chair and stool being in the Atheneum at Hartford, the curious may investigate for themselves whether my surmise is correct. The chair is low, corresponding with the stool. It is an odd fact which I have verified by a great number of instances that a stool of this height, about 15 inches, is preferred today to a chair-high stool.

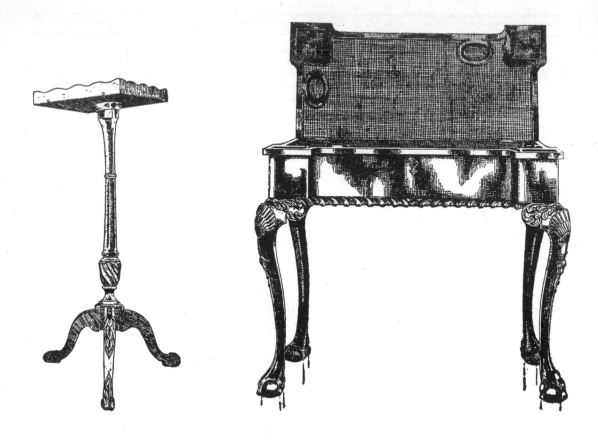

The stand above on the left has a tray top with a waved edge. I saw it at the famous Toddsbury place in tidewater Virginia. It is prettily spiraled on the shaft, and has a kind of French scroll foot. The small of the shaft is also fluted. It is a fascinating piece.

The gaming table on the right is most elaborate, combining as it does a shell decoration on the knee with a foliage pattern, and a nulling on the under side of the frame. The top is prettily contoured, as is shown by the lifted half, and there are four pockets and squares for four candles. Altogether it is rich enough and handsome enough to stand alone.

There is no end in variations of small tables, so that if there were a good house on every corner of a city block, no two persons need have repeated patterns. This rich gaming table is in the South. Baltimore is the home of much good furniture, being second only to Philadelphia in that respect.

The remarkable piece on the left is in the Black mansion at Ellsworth, Maine, a relic of the very early time. It differs from the usual chest-on-frame in being longer and higher and having two drawers instead of one. In fact, it is unique and of the very highest importance for the first period of American furniture, being made with a single arch, indicating a date before 1700. Undoubtedly it is the oldest piece in the house. It is the same dwelling where the unique walnut couch chair elsewhere illustrated is located.

The table on the right is the original from which a design for a coffee table has been drawn.

On the following page is the complete drawing of a walnut tray-top stand of the Queen Anne time. Of course the top is turned with the raised dish rim or tray edge, all terms being used. It should be observed that the legs are dovetailed into the post. In the old construction, of course, the screws would have been hand made.

Little tables of this sort are most convenient not only for tea, but as light stands or bedside tables for books, the modern American being noted for reading in bed, which we can do much more conveniently than the fathers. While this table is walnut, pieces of the same style are also found in mahogany because the simple pad foot or snake foot was simpler to make than the ball and claw. In this instance there is a kind of shoe to protect its edge.

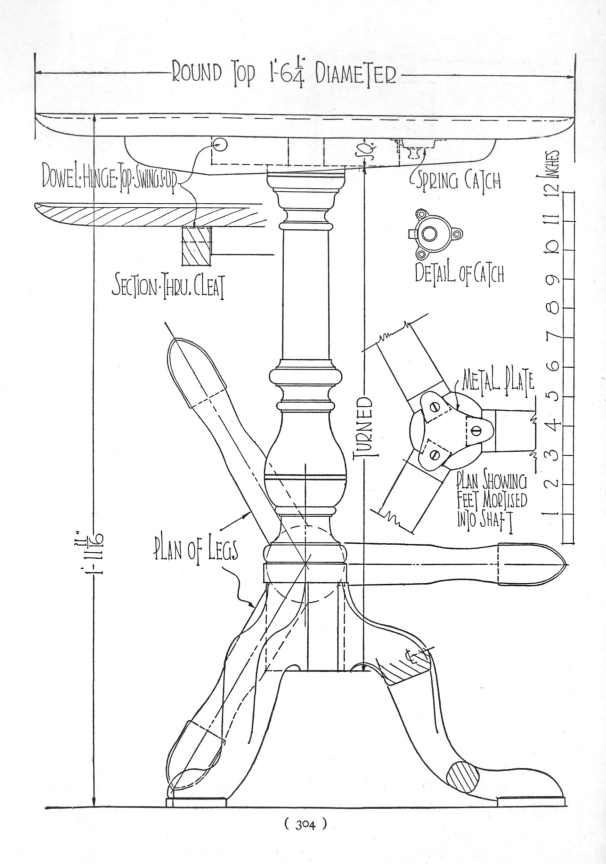

ROUND TOP 1'-6¼" DIAMETER

DOWEL·HINGE·TOP·SWINGS·UP

SECTION·THRU·CLEAT

PLAN OF LEGS

SPRING CATCH

DETAIL OF CATCH

TURNED

METAL PLATE

PLAN SHOWING
FEET MORTISED
INTO SHAFT

12 INCHES 11 10 9 8 7 6 5 4 3 2 1

1'-11 1/16"

LACQUER

The Chinese are the originators of lacquer, and they were working possibly a thousand years before Christ. Japan took up the work and excelled her masters.

The first work had no relief. It was many centuries before the raised work came in, but the improvement was well worth while. About 1700 the art reached its climax of skill.

The process has never been carried on as successfully in Europe as in Japan, partly because the lac is derived from an oriental tree, Rhus vernicifera, which requires to be used soon after its extraction.

It was necessary for the Europeans to resort to varnishes or gums in alcohol.

Furniture was, therefore, sometimes sent to the Orient to be lacquered there. Possibly also orientals were brought to Europe to do the work. Lacquer became as popular as some modern fads and has lately experienced a revival. But what we call lacquer on modern furniture is not. It is a curious fact that the ordinary and cheap finish of commercial furniture is now called lacquer, a scientifically compounded transparent finish, which helps the cheap maker by cutting out many expensive hand processes. These "lacquers" must be used over fillers, and they eliminate metal from their composition.

For the purpose of this work we ignore the use of this sort of finish, as it can never rival hand-rubbed shellacs, oils, and waxes. It leaves an effect like varnish, and appears as a shell covering the wood.

These commercial varnishes resist water, and have their legitimate use on low-priced modern furniture. They are available in the market with directions for applying.

Passing to oriental lacquer, the first consideration is that an article to be lacquered is so completely sealed, hidden, encysted, and mummified that the kind of wood employed, if it can be freed from warping, swelling, etc., is of no consequence. It is merely a foundation. The beauty of a piece of furniture is sought merely by the surface treatment. Pine was in general use.

Secondly, dainty variations of surface such as fine carving or molding are against the genius of lacquer which obliterates all such lines. Hence even the richest lacquered pieces must be without the important lines and surfaces having to do with English or American furniture. Structurally lacquered pieces are, therefore, likely to be bald, without fine cornices. They can never attain a domestic appearance. That is to say, lacquer is not a finish to be applied indiscriminately to various kinds of articles and periods of style, but is properly restricted to use on specimens built as foundations for it. If these are to be in harmony with the lacquer itself, they ought to follow oriental shapes to be in the best taste. At this point most of the errors have been made in the use of lacquer. The oriental surface has been applied to an occidental shape, and both are deprived in the process of their due effect.

When we go as far as to desire lacquer, so special in its origin and in the subjects delineated by it, we ought to go to the full extent of adopting the oriental shape also.

The thickness of the built-up lacquer is so considerable it should wholly supplant anything beyond broad effects as a foundation.

The next consideration is that even oriental lacquered pieces differ as heaven and earth in quality. The sap of the tree from which the lacquer is drawn may be the cheap sedimentary portion of the finer part which rises above it, in the settling process. Then there is the further variation of result arising from the degree of slowness and patience in the applications of the coats, and in the difference in the workmen, varying from the dull hack to the genius. For the high-class lacquerer was an artist of the first order, obtaining effects of enthralling beauty, and employing to obtain them a sensitively developed imagination and a technical skill which together achieved results of almost miraculous merit, so that princes eagerly sought his productions, and he ranked among the most honored men of his age.

When, therefore, we buy a lacquered piece we may be getting anything from a daub intended for the cheap bargain hunter to some rare old work such that no European and no American could hope to rival, even if we had the materials to work with. In the matter of art we are still babes as compared with oriental masters.

The colors are obtained by mixing those numerous ingredients known to be best for any special purpose, as the tradition has been handed down for many generations.

The initial difficulty is not ended when the piece to be treated is completed. Every joint must be filled and paper covered. Any check will, of course, come through to the surface and ruin the work. Process after process of polishing follows before the first lacquer coat. It must be a most fascinating occupation, which few Americans, however, would have the ambition to follow, especially as the work must be done in a very damp place in a dim light. Many coats are applied on the best work, and mother of pearl, gold, and everything to enhance the beauty of the work are among the ingredients. It is obvious that no work can be done here that will ever at all approach true lacquer. The time, the vast labor, the conditions are all against success.

Hence the best we can do is perhaps to obtain an old clock or highboy made in Europe, or possibly and rarely in Boston, or still more happily acquire some specimen brought by eighteenth-century skippers from China itself.

Lacquer in its heyday became an elegant accomplishment for ladies, who were taught the French methods as part of the required education of society girls.

It is not to be supposed, of course, that the goods supplied commercially nowadays as lacquer are truly such. Wherever there is a strong demand there will be some kind of attempt to meet it. Commercial imitations of oriental lacquer are short-cut methods without the use of the proper materials. It would be far better to give up these attempts, partly because they must be unsatisfactory to the buyer after a time, and partly because people who are able to pay for real lacquer can import it from the Orient at a price far less than similar work could be supplied in this country. The writer certainly is not interested in fostering poor imitations. He does not, of course, believe that his feeble protest will affect the multitude who would rather be fashionable than be right.

VENEER

Veneer in the old days was sawed by hand and hence was thicker than any modern veneer. The term "veneer" is applied to the process by which the entire face of a piece of furniture is covered.

The term "inlay" refers to the smaller, narrowed veneer set into the solid wood or as a minor part of the veneer over an entire surface. The early English inlays were on oak. A piece in my possession has sections, set in three-eighths of an inch, and deep-set narrow inlays were general when used in the oak period.

Modern veneers are sometimes as thin as one hundred twenty to the inch and obviously must be applied on perfect surfaces, as they do not admit of much rubbing down.

Various woods are stained or burned to obtain the colors of rarer woods. The supplying of veneer and inlay is a profession. Built-up or laminated woods are really thick veneers glued together, the grain alternating in direction. The result is very satisfactory for some sorts of work like broad surfaces on furniture or wide panels of wall work. Thus surfaces of a stable nature several feet wide may be made without a joint, and the process permits handsome results.

We are concerned here with the old types, principally.

In the mahogany era it was not rare to veneer mahogany itself to secure handsomer surfaces. Thus the whole thickness of the wood was honest mahogany, but the surface was handsomer than the under part. Mahogany shrinks and warps little when of fine quality.

Looking-glasses were quite generally veneered, because their frames would stand better than the solid wood. The first veneered looking-glasses were heavy frames of walnut on pine, very generally cross banded. The wide convex William and Mary glasses and the Queen Anne, narrower, which followed, were veneered and sometimes also inlaid.

The later, and lighter, looking-glasses of the Chippendale time were veneered, especially those which featured fretwork. Lines of inlay began to appear in the Chippendale period and continued through the Hepplewhite time. Ovals of inlay, featuring butterflies or other designs, were common in the upper and lower ends of looking-glasses. All these are now copied as the assembled design is sold by specialists as repairs for old glasses. Veneered frames often rolled at the top, by warp, and some have supposed them made so. An error.

Also it is possible to match the most intricate banded old veneers, consisting of very minute pieces.

The application of old veneer by glue was followed by a weighting of the work with cauls and heavy clamping until it was dry and then reducing the surface by light planing, scraping, or sanding.

Rare woods were brought from all parts of the world to use in combination for designs. A favorite and beautiful pattern for drawer fronts was the plume or feather grain, formed by bringing two pieces opened out from the same board and therefore matching exactly.

Veneering reached its height about 1800, being much in vogue fifteen years either side of this date and on late Empire work to 1845. The inevitable consequence of veneer was that less and less attention was paid to forms and more and more to surfaces. Thus there was a decline of good design as veneer took the place of carving, and straight legs succeeded the cabriole. For a time it was the practice to carve turned surfaces and veneer flat surfaces on the same piece of furniture, but the use of carving decreased, until in the late Empire time (second Empire 1830 and onwards) there was a period of crude carving which supplanted veneer. Under the chapter on Woods the principal sorts used for veneer are indicated.

The practice of veneer was followed in the most ancient times in Egypt, and later by the Romans.

The material was not confined to wood, but tortoise shell was often used, and even ivory and precious stones. The French work of inlay in brass became fashionable, as buhl.

The impression of the man on the street that veneer means cheap work is mistaken. In a good form nothing is more expensive than veneer. There are some handsome cross-grains and burls which cannot be used in any other manner than in veneer, owing to their brittle or gnarly nature, or their tendency to warp.

Veneers are still obtainable in the saw-cut form, up to a sixteenth of an inch thick. They are necessary in the repair of old work.

Small pieces of veneer are sometimes pressed into place with a hot iron. Forms with sand bases on one side are used for curved work. Segments or irregular forms must be cut for clamping and pressing irregular surfaces.

Glue should be bleached with permanganate of potash if used on thin, light-colored veneers, or it may penetrate the grain and ruin the effect by darkening the color.

For marquetry, parquetry, buhl, and intarsia see glossary. The methods of inlay and veneer as practised today have wholly superseded the old methods; the line inlay, for instance, is provided for by an electric cutter or router moved by hand. It is accurate and rapid.

The old wood was prepared for by a toothed plane to roughen the surface so as to make a safe glue joint, and the narrower inlays were prepared for by pricking the background for the same purpose.

An inlay is beveled slightly, being left wider on top so as to fit better when pressed home.

Blister on old veneer where the glue no longer holds can sometimes be cured by slitting the veneer, pressing in glue, and then ironing down the surface. But sometimes patches must be fitted; in which case irregular lines should be cut out on the old along the edges of old veneer where the color changes.

Old veneer may be removed entirely by wetting and heating alternately. All the old glue must be removed by sponging, and then the surface must be toothed.

The herringbone border of veneer is the commonest and most effective pattern, principally used around a plain walnut veneer on highboys, lowboys, etc., of the

William and Mary and Queen Anne patterns. It consists of bands of veneer cut on a diagonal and meeting at an angle. Its width varies greatly, but when very narrow it is not effective. The same name, herringbone, is applied to brick work so laid. The grain is made to show a miter on every corner by reversing it and showing the joint in the middle of the drawer or surface.

Fine complicated inlays are often supplied or prepared glued, on paper, in order that they can be laid all at once. Veneers are hammered down, working from the center outward to expel air and avoid blisters. It was learned in making airplane propellers that the surfaces of glued work should not be brought together while the glue is hot, otherwise air bubbles form by contraction of glue. It is left till only warm, but still very tacky, when it holds best.

The patent modern casein is a form of glue which resists water and is supplanting true glue in general. But old-fashioned cabinetmakers do not like it, and its light color bothers wherever a line of it shows. So that patching especially is done with the old glue.

Since veneer presses are required for large work, such work is no longer attempted except in shops specially equipped.

Veneers and inlays afford a good field for display, the varieties of design being endless. Good fingers plus a good head are required for successful work, and only adepts should attempt anything on old work.

Modern work, when good mahogany surfaces are wanted, must almost always appear in veneer, as San Domingo mahogany is confined to the special cabinetmaker's order shop exclusively.

About 1790–1810 the world went veneer mad. The great ovals on bookcases and chests of drawers are too obvious. The form was neglected for the surface. Clearly, veneer cannot be used well on carved surfaces. Therefore the inference was, omit the carving! But a finely shaped and carved cabriole leg is an aristocrat beside a veneered tapered leg. It is also more durable.

It is probable that the expense of solid mahogany induced the resort to veneer.

The keyholes were sometimes veneered with attractive 'scutcheon patterns. But the diced or checkered veneers bordering the edges of desk falls or outlining cabinet doors were carried to the utmost extent of variety and were seldom omitted from a piece of any pretensions in the Sheraton period.

Of course, effects with woods from afar were made possible, quite different from the more somber or massive styles of the previous generation — the solid mahogany period.

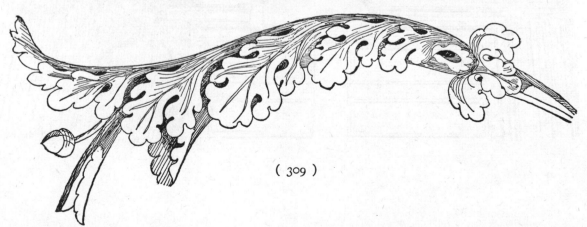

On the page preceding this is an excellent room in the new Concord Antiquarian Society, most of the furniture being of the Queen Anne time. On the page following this is the dining room in the same house with a very excellent setting of a gate-leg table and banister backs which very nearly match the table in type, an unusual feature. The panelwork is attractive, especially the arrangement of the recessed fireplace. On this page is a small room in the same house with a writing chair and a Windsor table. The irregular panelwork is a good illustration of the old method. The walls were filled with panels to close the space, and often without any particular reference to harmonizing the panels, that is, matching one with another in size. The lantern hanging in this room often goes by the name Paul Revere, but of course without reason. This house with its furniture is now among the best.

FINISH

The name comprises everything done to furniture after the woodwork is completed.

The theory that very early furniture was never finished will not pass. It is true that occasionally simple furniture, or even chests of more or less importance, may have been left unfinished, because it was perhaps made on the premises by the joiner who built the house where the furniture was placed. But we have no evidence that this neglect of finish was otherwise than rare.

Surprisingly, in these days when a finish that will display the wood is so general, we learn that paint was very early in use and that it no doubt played a large part in the first period of American furniture. Not only so, but polychrome work was general, particularly on cabinet furniture. Paint is at once the lowest cost finish and the most striking. The first generations in America desired color in their furniture, as they had not too much in their lives. Woods were not at first thought of as beautiful in themselves. It was red and black that appealed chiefly to the first fathers. Probably a great part of the chairs for a hundred years were painted black. The earliest chests were black always on the applied turnings, and often red on their panels, or the lining molds of the panels. The baseboards of the rooms, or, in the absence of baseboards, the plaster near the floor was often black. It was not apparently general practice to oil oak that was not to be painted. The old oak is often too light for wood that has been oiled for generations. Nevertheless, oiling was of course more or less in use since its chief cost was labor. But waxing seems to have been very common. Beeswax from wild or tame honey was chiefly used. The cane sugar we have so cheaply was little known and was expensive. Among the ancients honey constituted most of the "sweetening." It was a staple everywhere, and we have recently discovered that it is free from those ingredients which have made this, above all, a diabetic generation. With much honey, there was much beeswax, and from the earliest times it was in general use to seal furniture, that is, to shield it from the influence of moisture. The first thing the bees did in their conventional conical straw hives, still the symbol of frugality, was to seal the interior with wax.

Old furniture should never be completely refinished if it is possible to avoid it. All the old feeling is lost in refinishing, so that good judges sometimes feel they would almost as soon have a high-class reproduction as an old piece which has been cleaned down to the wood.

While tastes differ, they have markedly changed within forty years. Once it was considered desirable to go to the bottom of all the old finish to make the piece "look nice." That result can, of course, be obtained, but the writer feels that a serious loss is thereby incurred.

Suppose certain crackling of the old finish does show? It only contributes to the mellow feeling of antiquity. Why does one wish to buy an old piece that looks new?

The first consideration regarding old furniture is whether the finish is in such condition that it can be made to answer, or whether it must be cleaned down to the wood and refinished.

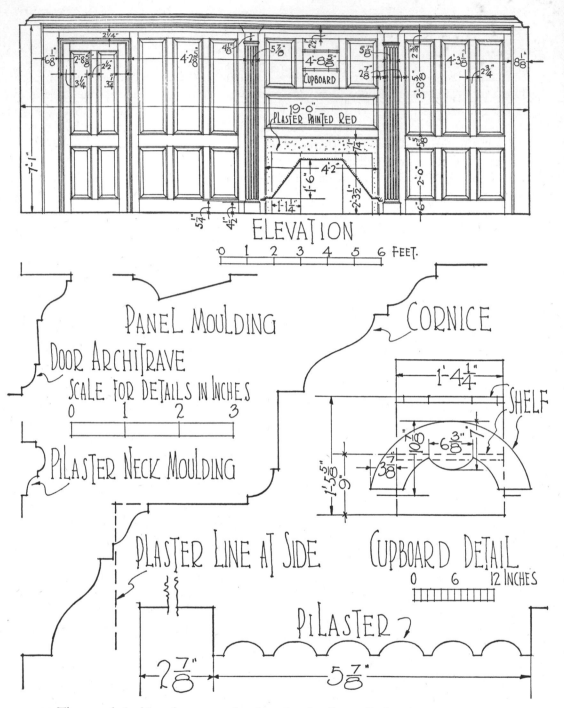

ELEVATION

0 1 2 3 4 5 6 FEET.

PANEL MOULDING

CORNICE

DOOR ARCHITRAVE

SCALE FOR DETAILS IN INCHES

0 1 2 3

SHELF

PILASTER NECK MOULDING

PLASTER LINE AT SIDE

CUPBOARD DETAIL

0 6 12 INCHES

PILASTER

The paneled side of a room showing the fireplace. It is of especial interest owing to the quaint little cupboard over the fireplace, of which a detail is shown. The date is the earlier half of the eighteenth century.

(314)

If to be cleaned down, the only proper material is "varnish" remover. This is a patent chemical product sold under various names and consisting of the remover proper mixed with a material like parafine so that when it is applied it can be left for a few minutes, say fifteen, before drying and rubbing off. Otherwise it will not have time to cut the old finish. It may require a second application. No old furniture should be sanded. Especially on the carving nothing harsh should be used, but only a soft brush, otherwise the fine edges of the carving will be ruined.

A cheap and objectionable method is the use of lye (potash). It eats and roughens the wood, giving it a fuzzy surface, which must be sanded so that one may almost as well have new furniture. The removers do not raise the grain. Furthermore, the potash will darken the grain. It is altogether too harsh.

Sometimes, after cleaning off, little needs to be done. The wood being old, the grain remains more or less stopped with filler, if the wood is oak or mahogany.

But the surface may then be treated as seems best suited to the effect desired. Oil may be used if there is no objection to darkening somewhat. If oil is used, two or three days or more may intervene between the coats. So long as free oil remains on the surface it is too soon to apply a second coat. But old wood that has been neglected is hungry for oil. Of course, the primary object of oiling was preservation. But it was found that by repeated oiling with rubbings between, a beautiful surface was at length obtained.

Table tops to be used for food should always be oiled. The process is long, but there is no objection to the use of the table after two or three coats are applied, the continued process of oiling to be continued in the intervals when the table is not in use. This may go on, in fact must, for years, but the task is not difficult. The top is quickly rubbed over occasionally with not much more time employed than in washing.

The only other method of finishing a table top to protect its appearance is by spar varnish. This gives a finish too glossy, or, as the old-timers used to say, too "slick." It rather kills the old feeling.

There are those who are using refectory table tops without any finish whatever. They simply scrub them. This may answer for a somewhat rude tavern style. But unfinished wood will absorb all sorts of oily substances when a bit of food touches it. No daintiness is possible with such table tops.

A furniture polish will often work wonders on an old piece, but better yet, merely oiling is sometimes sufficient.

Some polishes cut the old finish too much or give an undesirable gloss. Beeswax dissolved in turpentine and rubbed on with a piece of flannel is a good final treatment, and often the only treatment required. A little undissolved wax indicates that the turpentine is a saturated solution.

It is not considered proper by the present writer to affect age for a new piece by disguising the newness with a finish designed to accomplish that purpose. I do not deny that many persons with the highest moral standards may so finish new furniture, because they wish it to combine harmoniously with old furniture. Personally I would not do it.

There is a method of laying on a finish that will crackle in a short time and give the effect of age. I feel that this is approaching, for myself, too near the aging of the wood, or battering it. But if an owner does these things for his own furniture, a private collection, of course that puts the matter in a different category.

No doubt varnish was used on furniture, in some instances, in old times, but more often in France than England or America. The commoner method was an oil finish which is also beautiful after many rubbings and long years.

The greenish or pale bronze patina I once obtained without an effort by using old automobile oil. This greenish tint will also appear if orange shellac is used on the black ornaments of furniture. It is avoided by the use of white shellac.

All the paint shops supply stains of all colors. Old furniture does not require stain. But if new pieces are added, they must be harmonized with the old.

Only water stain should be used with maple. Strange to say, it penetrates more than the oil stain. Experiment shows that whatever the finish on maple, if the base of it is an oil stain, the finish will chip off if struck a smart blow, and show new wood color. With water stain the furniture may be dented, even, but the color will remain.

Maple does not require a filler, or, more precisely speaking, its grain is so close that a filler does no good.

The crackle of age on or beneath the patina, and the age itself help to give pieces, once well finished, a fine surface texture. It requires so much labor to give a new surface a rich old feeling, that the thing is not often attempted, since endless rubbing was the method. In good old households furniture was rubbed down with oil or wax at least once in six months for two hundred years. The interval between the processes is important, though a much shorter interval is better.

But when men speak of "nasty modern varnish" and claim that varnish never was used, how do they account for the fact that lacquer reached a wonderful state of perfection hundreds of years since, that shellac has been obtained for ages, that oil was known before history, and that beeswax was a recognized finish in Egypt and Mesopotamia?

Sometimes in sport I tell friends in a hushed voice that I will give them the secret of a wonderful furniture polish. Procure a large-mouthed pickled bottle, break into it a quantity of beeswax, and add turpentine enough to cover. A small cloth once moistened in this will go over the largest piece of furniture. And the method is probably as old as the cave man, and certainly as good today as anything else. The bees invented a weatherproof material. The soft effect produced by its use as described, after the turpentine evaporates, leaving a gossamer veil of wax, is good enough for the most exacting.

But we have no reason to suppose that, barring the use of old lacquer, a fine trade, there are any secrets, ancient or modern, about the finish of furniture. Even paint itself is as old as civilization.

METHODS

In restoring old surfaces the utmost care should be used in coloring any material that is to fill gaps. Sawdust of the same wood as that to be matched is mixed with glue, the color matched in the mixing. This is better than putty, which should be avoided mostly or entirely. Screw heads should never be puttied. Their surface is large enough to require plugs of wood in which the direction of the grain is also given attention.

Old finishers have until lately mixed their own ingredients, and to do so is still necessary on old work, to secure a perfect match. There are those amateurs who delight in dabbling in finishes, and applying them. Those "long winter evenings" of which we used to hear may not be available now to a class as large as was once the case, but there are still many persons who by habit or age or preference or necessity are at home evenings, if for no other reason than that they have homes which have been beautified and made interesting through the efforts of a generation of loving labor and accumulation. The fussy person must be considered and his taste fed. Not a few of us have minds like that. We have acquired them and are neither afraid nor ashamed to think. We consider that minds were made for that purpose, and that the thoughtful person, at a pinch, can contribute something of value or interest when heels are weary and jazz is wearisome.

The aggregate of persons who enjoy doing things with their hands is large. Why should they be scorned? Is it disgraceful to love good things? We have no slaves to cater to our whims, and we must needs cater to them ourselves. It may save us from being gangsters. Who knows?

The lively people do not require to prove their liveliness by going around in circles. Agitation is not always inspiration.

Hence if we wish to amuse the boy — at least some boys — we should have a room that can be quite messy, never cleaned up, and forever barred from housecleaning. That new basement released from dirt by the abolition of coal and ashes is just the place, because it is cool in summer and warm in winter — just the opposite of the attic.

There, then, go the heirlooms or the gatherings of this generation to be patched, polished, and puttered over.

Being now ready to do a little work, we face the fact that shellac is for many reasons most desirable as a finishing medium. The surface having been prepared if necessary by filler and rubbing, the shellac is applied and allowed at least a couple of days in dry air to set well. In emergency work one day will answer. But objection to haste is that a bloom or cloudiness will develop if new coats are applied over imperfectly dry coats.

The furniture must be rubbed down between every shellac coat. Very fine sand paper is good for the earlier coats but should never touch a carved surface, or even an edge, lest the rubbing should reach the bare wood. Some knack is needed to feel how far to go. Careless rubbing undoes all that went before. The purpose is merely to remove all pebbly or bubbly surface.

PATINA PATTER

It is a fad to talk about patina — usually mispronounced. At its best the surface of fine mahogany made in the latter half of the eighteenth century has a slight bronze

(317)

tint. It is rare to find such finish, because it is not much in evidence except on flat surfaces. It is not a proper use of the term to apply it to any original finish, though this application is now common. It is alleged that this bronze, or coppery, surface can be obtained only by great age. If this allegation can be made good, then it should be easy to know whether furniture is old. But why has it been so easy to deceive the American market by English mahogany of a date from 1850 onward? There is no answer except that skilful workmen are able to produce the effect of patina, or that the bronze tint will show in a few years.

It is the feeling of the writer that form is far more important than finish. But if, as often, the old finish is seriously marred, is it not better to refinish, thus securing a beautiful, harmonious surface like the original?

The patter about patina has been much overdone, both by dealers and collectors. If, as dealers are fond of saying, a piece has the original patina, then we must often lose our respect for the old makers. The insistence on patina is too great, for the price's sake. If the finish appears to be beautiful and old, this appearance adds to the value of furniture. But if the patina does not appear, we should disregard the patter about it.

Again, if the shape of an old piece is graceless, without style, or its condition bad, why talk of its patina? Furniture must be worthy in itself before anything is put on it. Gilding a botch, as was common in 1850, did not produce merit where none existed. And if a piece must be taken apart or otherwise repaired, the patina, if any, will be destroyed. Hence patina is valuable only when there is value and solidity and antiquity *below* it, and that is not a condition frequently found.

Too much emphasis cannot be placed on the employment of the highest class shellac that is possible to obtain. Shellac can be bought for almost any price. Cheap shellacs are a nasty mixture which give all sorts of bother and never permit of good permanent results. If shellac is offered at a lower price, it should be declined. The small additional sum paid for good material will save many fold in future.

Also all shellac coats should be applied thin. Cracking and imperfect drying and cloudiness and rough results are the effect of slapping on heavy coats.

The continuation of the shellac coats can be gauged by the patience of the worker. For a fine cabinet piece no less than seven coats should be applied. Flat surfaces need somewhat more finish than small surfaces, because of their liability to warp. Great care should be taken to shellac the inside ends of highboys or lowboys or chests of drawers as well as the outside, as this may save them. Of course, the inside coats do not require any rubbing. Since this is so, about one unrubbed coat is equal to two or three rubbed coats as a prevention of moisture. The insides of drawers are sometimes given one coat of shellac for cleanliness' sake, so that they may be wiped out more easily. One may or may not rub this inside coat down. The under side of the top should also be shellacked generously. As to the back, it does not make so much difference.

All table tops, and particularly the leaves, must be generously shellacked on the under side. A neglect to do this will undoubtedly ruin the table top. This rule holds good whether the upper side of the table is oiled or shellacked.

All finish, of course, should be applied without having the brasses in position.

The number of coats on chairs depends somewhat upon the appearance desired and the nature of the chair. Maple chairs need one or two coats less than mahogany and walnut. A finish liked by some is a close approach to the bare wood in quaint maple chairs such as is secured by one or two coats of shellac, but these coats, together with all others wherever the surface is in sight, must be carefully rubbed by hand. Turned work is difficult to rub nicely, as every part must be carefully touched, and there is greater danger of removing too much of the finish.

For sanding one should be careful that the paper is fine enough. But at least the last coat and the one before it should not be sanded. The next to the last coat may be rubbed with mineral wool, and the last coat should be with wax or with oil and rottenstone. Wax is liable to give too much gloss, and that finish should be chosen which produces the surface desired. Mahogany will bear a little more gloss because it is more elegant than maple finish.

In all these processes any carving at all must be treated differently from the rest of the wood. Carving, cutting as it does across the grain, tends to show darker than the rest of the furniture. To some that is no objection. If, however, it is desired to keep it lighter, the stain to be applied to it should be thinned to a half or a quarter of the strength applied on the smooth surfaces. It is usual to give one very thin coat of shellac to the carving which is done immediately after the filler is applied, but the surplus filler must be rubbed off and the subsequent rubbings must be done with a very soft brush. The carving is then given a couple of coats of oil. It will probably look a little darker than the rest of the wood anyway. Carving which has the appearance of carrying finish is greatly injured in appearance and in delicacy. Nearly all old furniture has the carving half obliterated by continuous coats of oil, varnish, or shellac.

The habit is sometimes followed of making pieces in part of mahogany and in part of curly maple. In that case it is desired to obtain a contrast, and the curly maple is not stained at all but has an initial coat of white shellac to prevent the stain of the mahogany running into it. If it is desired to add a trifle of color to the curly maple, it may be done in orange shellac.

Above all things, finish should not be hurried. The longer within reason the time between the coats, the better the work will stand.

There is a wide variety in taste as regards the depth of tone in finish. Some like light, some dark mahogany. The later mahogany, such as Sheraton and Hepplewhite, usually carried a finish rather lighter than the old mahogany. The best Chippendale finish is agreed upon as a brown mahogany. The later finishes are paler. Some also prefer a reddish tint in their mahogany, and others dislike it.

Some old mahogany kept in very light rooms has faded if not bleached. Dark mahogany will grow lighter in a light place. Mahogany without any stain at all, as indeed maple or any other wood, will darken in a light place. It is thought probable that a good deal of the light maple was never stained, but has acquired its tint in time. I have tested this matter, being curious to see results. I have a very beautiful curly maple secretary made new. It was finished with white shellac only with a final wax coat. Now at the end of nine years it has a very rich, strong honey color, having

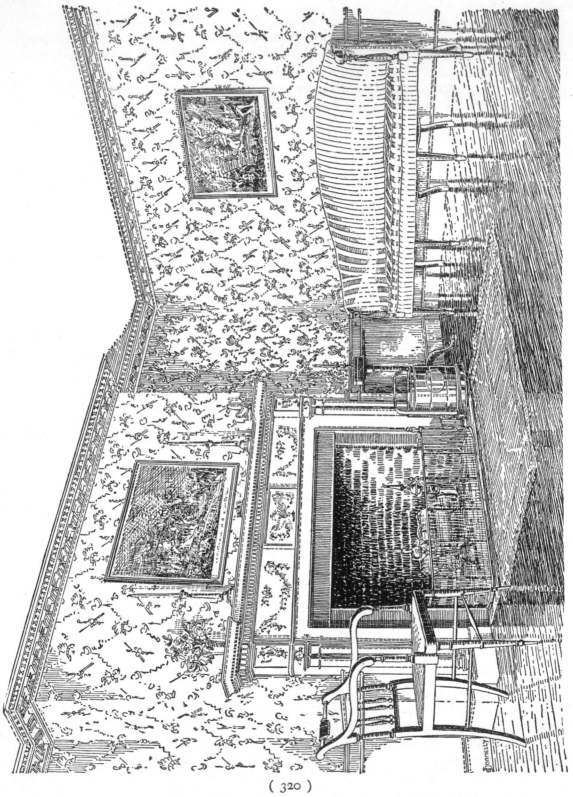

darkened a good many shades. Most persons are not satisfied to wait for nature to do the work. I therefore give below a formula for various stains.

Taste usually calls for stained maple, and the honey color is thought too light by many. Of course, the term is indefinite. There is dark honey and light honey. Very fine new honey has very little color sometimes, so little as to be rather insipid. A richer tone is thought to be more attractive. Sometimes enough stain is required to produce something approaching brown.

Amber is settled upon probably by the greater number of persons as the ideal color for maple. It is somewhat darker than honey color, the variance being in the shade rather than in a change of color. The desirable shade would seem to require a little warmth.

It is desired, of course, where as often a piece of furniture is of more than one kind of wood to give the two kinds the same color, and that is not an easy thing. In a Windsor chair, for instance, the seat, which is, or ought to be, of soft wood, will, if finished with the same material as the maple, or hickory, have a somewhat warmer tint. Whoever likes to experiment with such things may secure the results he desires. The darker the color the more ease is there in blending different woods. The difficulty with a commercial Windsor seat which is made of several pieces is that it must be stained very strongly in order to obliterate the junctions. That objection is alone enough to throw out a commercial Windsor. Of course, the bottoms of Windsor chairs should be shellacked, or even painted to minimize the action of the weather.

Pine may be treated with an oil stain, because there is sufficient porosity in the wood to permit the oil to enter. But the effect should be tested beforehand, or too dark a color will result.

In general, close-grained hard woods like birch and maple are not filled, because to attempt it is useless.

Mahogany, though a hard wood, nevertheless has flecks in the grain, so that it requires filling as well as hard oak.

Some years ago an oak finish was used commercially called golden oak. The objection, however, was not so much to the color as to the garish surface which was not properly rubbed down.

It is difficult for the layman to remember that the finish takes as much time as the construction in many cases. That is why no commercial furniture can ever be well finished. It must be treated with a modern lacquer that does not require rubbing and is too like a varnish.

Returning to the color of mahogany, it should be understood that the brown mahoganies are almost universal on the finest furniture, meaning the Goddard and Chippendale patterns. If they are not brown now, they were once. Pale mahogany lacks quality, richness, and the impression that it is complete. Sometimes pale mahogany, or even that of a darker tint, is difficult even by a person with some knowledge to distinguish from walnut. In fact, it is possible to finish walnut and mahogany so that they will look practically alike.

It must also be noted that there is a difference in the original color of the wood. In a single log of maple there is light and dark. White maple is felt to be the only proper material for furniture. It is the hard sugar, or rock, or upland maple. The soft maple which grows in lower latitudes and on lower ground, and is otherwise called swamp maple, is darker in color and is not proper for high-class furniture. The mixture of these or of light and dark maple of the same sort of wood inevitably shows in furniture and the avoidance of it is a great expense, because it means endless handlings and selections. Even with much care it is sometimes impossible to get all the original wood of a maple construction of the same color. There will be a slight mottling or a trace of curl, or an irregular grain or even a difference in the plain, straight-grain surfaces. These differences should be frankly accepted and no effort made to overcome them, because they give individuality.

Mahogany also sometimes has very light sections, and if all that part is to be thrown away, possibly a very rich wide plank would require to be sacrificed. Undoubtedly it has been partly on this account that furniture is stained. Of course, a buyer should understand that most of the commercial mahogany is gumwood or baywood or some cheap form of mahogany that is of less cost than good maple. Climbers are apt to seek after mahogany because they think it an aristocratic wood, and, like the woman who has a plush coat called Hudson fur, they get an imitation mahogany. Furniture classifies people, and this kind declasses them. I deprecate very strongly the running after any particular wood, even maple, as is done so much today. People seem to become set like cement in their favor of some one sort of wood, as if it were preferable to any other. They do not know, for instance, that no good Windsor can have a particle of mahogany in it, or even mahogany color, and that no maple or birch should ever be finished mahogany color. Particularly it is the unpardonable sin to paint mahogany or walnut. In this connection I am reminded of one of the finest dwellings in Virginia, several of the rooms of which are solidly paneled to the ceiling. The owner recently told me that he had discovered all this paneling to be walnut. He has always supposed it to be pine, because it was painted white. He is proceeding to clean off all this paint. At the time when the house was built, the only cost of walnut was in cutting it. It stood as a forest all about the site. People were offended with it because it was common, whereas it is several times over the most valuable timber growing in this country for fine furniture.

The finish formula below for French walnut supplies a finer tint than the ordinary so-called black walnut, but really red walnut. This black walnut color so-called was the color used for ten or fifteen years before and after the Civil War in the degraded Empire furniture, and the Victorian which was an imitation of the French styles of a previous century. There are, however, certain fashions in furniture which require walnut, and incidentally they happen to be the finer, if not the finest, styles among those called elegant, that is to say, the Queen Anne and the early Georgian.

Cherry, the popular native substitute for mahogany, often appears in the same room with it. Indeed, it is not uncommon in making a set of chairs to make the armchair of mahogany and the side chairs of cherry. The finish of cherry, however, cannot be made to look like mahogany without a rather violent departure from its natural color, which I feel to be a mistake. Happily, most of the old cherry does not vary in shade much from the amber maple. It has a little hint of red in it, however.

The dark oak so common in England is scarcely ever found in early American oak furniture, and it is not only too somber for cabinet pieces, but is an unnatural color for oak. The depth of tone in ancient pieces was largely caused by the creosoting process which it acquired from the smokiness of the room abroad.

Other woods used in furniture to no small extent are whitewood (tulip) and butternut. We do not consider hickory, which is confined for the most part to turned spindles occurring together with maple and pine.

Whitewood tends to a greenish shade. If this is objected to, orange shellac should never be used with it. Yet that greenish tint is not objectionable to persons of good taste. If, however, it is desired to avoid it on account of other furniture of different woods in the same room, it will be found rather difficult.

THE FINISHING ROOM

There are three things to be secured in a finishing room, namely, light, heat, and freedom from dust.

Working by artificial light is very unsatisfactory. The work should be done near a battery of windows where a brilliant light will not only help the workman to get his color, but will assist him in the application of it so that he can do an even job.

In the matter of heat, convenience is a main consideration. For work to progress with a fair degree of rapidity a room should be kept warm. Sometimes, however, conditions are such that the storage space required is too large to be heated economically. Of course, there must be some heat. If furniture in process stored in a cold room is allowed to freeze, the results are bad. But if only a slight degree of heat is available, the time between coats must be extended until the work is thoroughly hard. It must be tested to learn this.

Freedom from dust is not always possible and, unless varnish is used, which we do not advise in any case, fair results are possible even with some dust, because the rubbing down helps to overcome the difficulty. Still, every precaution should be taken to secure as great freedom from dust as possible.

SEASONS IN FINISHING

In summer when there is no artificial heat, especially during dog days, the humidity delays the drying more than one might suppose. It requires three to ten times as long in a humid time as when the air is dry. Any application of a coat when the surface is not thoroughly dry will bother in two ways. It will give a greater gloss which cannot be easily overcome even by rubbing, and it will cause a rising of moisture under the top coat and a cloudy effect. There is no way to cure this except to clean the finish down to the bare wood, and begin again.

Too sudden drying may crackle the surface. The main trouble in finishing is haste.

SPRAYED FINISH

This book is not designed to any considerable extent to serve for commercial finishers. The cheapest furniture is dipped. The expense is about a cent apiece besides the little material, and of course this method is never to be used.

The spraying of the earlier coats, or at least the first coat, is not seriously objectionable. Fine effects, however, cannot be secured without hand application for the most part. The rubbing, of course, must always be done by hand unless there are large, smooth surfaces, in which cases special methods may be applied in large shops, which do not concern us here.

DANGER OF FIRE

All materials used in rubbing should be kept separate on lines and given full access to the air. The piling of old finish cloths together is very liable to cause spontaneous combustion. One should follow the practice of burning all used cloths regularly.

AVOIDANCE OF WHITEWASH

A whitewashed room, particularly a whitewashed ceiling, will cause all manner of trouble by the dropping of specks into the finish or onto the partly finished pieces of furniture.

SYSTEM

Guesswork is an approved method of spoiling finish. If the formulas are not first tested and found satisfactory, great expense may be entailed. Even small shops have a series of thin samples finished after a particular formula and labeled. Any experimental work, of course, should be done on bits of wood until a satisfactory color or effect is secured.

HINTS FOR THE FINISHING ROOM

Sanding of wood must always be done with the grain. A sanding block is used over which the sandpaper is glued or fastened. The beginner will say that it is an absurdity to raise the grain that comes beautifully polished from the cabinetmaker with water stain. There seems, however, at least with maple and birch, to be no other way. It is well to moisten the back of the sandpaper with a sponge so that it will not tend to break.

Material that comes to the finish room from a machine sander will sometimes show a wavy, imperfect line after the finish is applied. Three drum sanders, if properly used, will overcome this effect. Otherwise hand-sanding must be resorted to. It is probably useless to try to lighten by extra sanding the end grain of wood which always takes darker. It is better to allow a difference of color in the surface.

Finishing is too complicated for an amateur who has not a great deal of patience and time. Many finishers who have worked twenty years at the business really do not know the causes of the effects. The materials are handed to them mixed and the work is subdivided. Good finishers are even more rare than good cabinetmakers. The matter of manipulation, as speed and smoothness in applying oil stains, is something that can be properly achieved only through long practice.

THE PHILOSOPHY OF WATER STAIN

It is at first a puzzle that the water stain should have a greater penetrating effect than an oil stain. This is partly because most stains dissolve better in water than in oil. At any rate, they will carry the stain farther into the wood, especially on hard woods. Oil itself will go completely through an inch board, but it seems to leave the stain on the way. Furthermore, the water stain seems to apply more evenly than the oil. The microscopic particles of the oil are larger than the same particles of water. Water stain also is available in almost every color. Strangely enough also the water stain fades less than the oil stain. Happily with pine it is possible to use an oil stain that saves the roughing of the grain.

Staining and the application of the finishes have to do with deep chemical problems. They are too abstruse for the layman. In fact, only long research brings out the methods. Even now improved methods are constantly coming to light.

One of the practical matters is that the soft woods, as the seat of a Windsor, will absorb more stain and absorb it faster than the maple, hence a darker stain must be used on the maple to get the same color as on the soft wood.

For the same reason it is sometimes necessary to apply a second coat of stain to all, or some parts of the piece of furniture. In that case the work should be sanded between the coats.

The application of the stain is usually done with a cold liquid and a rubberset brush, with long strokes. Soft, open-grained woods will allow a stiffer brush than the hard woods. Harsh alkaline stains are better applied with sponges or wood fiber brushes, otherwise the brushes will be spoiled.

The fuming of wood has certain advantages, but cannot be followed in little shops which make only the highest class of furniture. In fact, the grey colors which have for some years been popular are never found in old furniture. Somebody sometime noticed a grey pine or oak surface and thought it very nice. He did not stop to learn that it is never found on the interiors of houses, but is purely the effect of weathering.

It is found that warm wood will take stain more readily. All the materials for finishing ought to be kept in a warm room because some of them tend to thicken when cold and even to settle and solidify in part.

For the same reason, if certain materials are mixed hot, they may form a sediment when cold. Good stains or other finishes, if too much is carried in solution and they are applied warm, may leave a whitish surface after application, because when the temperature is lowered a portion of the constituents solidifies.

The use of a spirit stain is not advised, partly because it should be done in a subdued light and the furniture should be kept in such a light. It is not so satisfactory, anyway, owing to this changing tendency even after it is finished.

One reason for the difference in effect of stains is that woods, particularly oak, have tannic acid naturally embedded in them. The application of a stain with tannic acid, therefore, brings out a darker effect where there is much of it in the wood.

Whitewood has little tannic acid. Sulphate of iron, therefore, will not chemically unite as in oak to give as good a stain. Thus we are faced with the problem of knowing what is in a particular wood to know what reaction it will give to a particular stain. Those who care to go into this thing find it treated in technical works.

The object in staining is not to cover the grain, but to bring it out. We do not wish to make the wood over into another kind. The best stain and subsequent finish

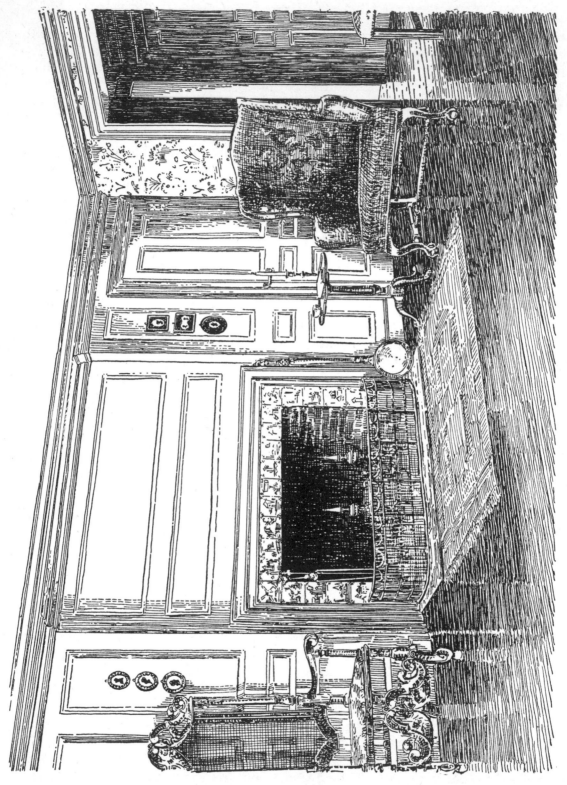

A Parlor with a Cane and a Dutch Wing Chair

are those which give the liveliest effect. For this purpose the stain must be wholly soluble. If any is left on the surface, it is simply wasted and worse, because it must be cleaned off. The stain should remain clear when it is very cold. In that case there will be no insoluble material left on the surface. If the stain is not transparent, of course, one may as well use a paint.

In the finishing of walnut one must be ruled somewhat by the original color of the wood. Walnuts vary as much as any other woods. Sometimes it is desired to bleach walnut, which is done with chlorinated lime, which can be purchased and diluted with water.

Permanganate of potash is also used.

Some formulas follow:

POLISH

Ivory soap	2 bars
Hot water	1 gal.
Parafine oil	1 gal.
Turpentine	1 gal.
Oil of cedar	8 oz.
Ammonia	4 oz.
Alcohol	4 oz.
Rottenstone	

STAIN FOR INLAY MAHOGANY

Bichromate potash	2 oz.
Water	2 qts.

Inlay often comes stained. The above stain rather harsh.

BROWN MAHOGANY

We advise either experiments with commercial stains or the mixing of powder sold for brown mahogany.

WALNUT

A wash coat of shellac, thin, sanded; filled with No. 600 Merrimac solution; shellac; sand; shellac; sand; shellac; sand; shellac; mineral wool; parafine oil, and pumice stone.

For French walnut use white shellac.

For ordinary walnut use orange shellac.

WALNUT STAIN

The same given for Oil Stain on Pine.

OLD MAHOGANY

Mahogany brown	2 oz.
Mahogany red	1 oz.
Potassium bichromate	½ oz.
Water	1 gal.

The result is dark.

OIL STAIN ON PINE, AMBER

Raw Italian Sienna	3 lbs.
Burnt turkey umber	2 lbs.
Turpentine	2 gals.
Boiled oil	1 qt.
Japan drier	1 pt.

AMBER WATER STAIN

Sienna, more or less than 3 oz.	
Nigrosine	¼ oz.
Water	2½ gals.

OAK STAIN

Cabot's conservo	one half
Turpentine	one half

FINISH FOR CARVING

Use first a filler for mahogany or oak, but not for maple. Next a coat of thin shellac, then a coat of oil to stand two days, followed by a soft brush, and another coat of oil to stand for a longer time, and finally a soft brush.

BLACK

One part nigrosine powder to ten parts of water. Then apply very small quantity of thin white shellac. Sand and repeat once.

CHERRY

Reduce the walnut stain to one-quarter the strength given, or use a thin red mahogany stain.

OLD OAK

Bichromate of potash	. . . .	2 dr.
Naphthol yellow	. . . . . .	1 dr.
Water	. . . .	1 gal.

This first coat must be followed as below.

SECOND COAT DARK OAK

Bichromate of potash	. . . .	1 dr.
Sap brown or walnut crystals	.	4 dr.
Jet black nigrosine	. . . . .	4 dr.
Naphthalene black	. . . . .	½ dr.
Water	. . . .	4 gals.

The first coat to be applied freely, then sanded and followed by the second. Then shellac and rub until a satisfactory surface is obtained.

FRENCH WALNUT STAIN

Use the stain for regular walnut, but reduce it.

LIGHT BROWN MAHOGANY

Bichromate of potash	. . . .	⅛ oz.
Mahogany brown	. . . . . .	2 oz.
Mahogany red	. . . .	½ oz.
Walnut crystals	. . . . . .	1 dr.
Water	. . . .	5 qts.

Apply this and follow with a light sanding, then shellac, half white and half orange several coats. Then, of course, as always, rub to a dull finish with oil or wax.

CURING A BLOOM CAUSED BY STRONG LIGHT

This difficulty may be helped by rubbing lightly with crude oil on a soft cloth.

TO TAKE OUT WHITE MARKS

A wax finish will show white marks from water or heat. The spots should be rubbed lightly with alcohol on a soft rag followed by a little linseed or sweet oil.

REMEDYING DENTS, ETC.

Stick or gum shellac heated on a spirit lamp and dropped into the depression should then be smoothed out with a shoe knife, or wet the dent if the wood is clean of finish and evaporate the water with a heated knife until the fibers of the dent are raised.

FILLERS

Ordinarily it is best to buy a commercial filler which is usually applied across the grain. Of course, the wood must be thoroughly dusted beforehand. Also the surplus filler must be carefully rubbed away to leave a clean surface.

There are two kinds of fillers, paste and liquid. In the case of the liquid the buyer is paying a lot for the liquid which simply dissolves for the most part the paste filler. The old-fashioned fillers were not very good, and even before they were used, repeated coats of oil answered instead.

On open-grained woods as mahogany and oak, paste fillers are better because they have more body, and on the hardest grains like maple and birch no filler at all is required.

Filler may be thinned by turpentine if a good base like silex is used. If brown effects are desired, the fillers are colored with Vandyke brown. Ordinarily, however, most of the color is secured by the wood itself and the orange shellac.

The Finish of Curly Maple

Curly maple is beautifully finished by the application of white shellac and nothing else. In process of time it will darken, but if the consumer does not feel that he has sufficient color, the ordinary maple amber stain may be used.

Coloring Fillers

The following colors mixed will give the results as shown: Red and black give brown. White and brown give chestnut. Red and yellow give orange. White, yellow, and Venetian red give cream. Red, blue, and black give olive. Yellow, white, and a little Venetian red give buff.

The following tables are in general use:

Decoction of logwood with: *Gives:*

Strong hydrochloric acid	Reddish yellow
Dilute hydrochloric acid	Reddish orange
Pure and diluted nitric acid	Red
Pure and diluted sulphuric acid	Black
Sulphide of hydrogen	Yellow brown
Ferric nitrate	Black
Potassium chromate	Black
Stannous chloride	Violet
Tannin	Yellow red
Sal ammoniac	Yellow
Verdigris	Dark brown
Potash	Dark red
Potassium permanganate	Light brown
Potassium iodide	Reddish yellow
Cupric chloride	Reddish violet to dark brown
Chrome yellow	Dark violet
Soda	Violet
Alum	Dark red brown
Carbonate of potash	Yellow brown
Magnesium sulphate	Brown
Cupric nitrate	Violet
Aqua ammonia	Dark violet
Potassium sulphocyanide	Red
Zinc chloride	Red brown

Decoction of fustic extract treated with: *Gives:*

Concentrated hydrochloric acid	Red
Dilute hydrochloric acid	Yellow brown
Concentrated nitric acid	Reddish yellow
Dilute nitric acid	Brown
Concentrated sulphuric acid	Dark purple

Decoction of fustic extract treated with: *(continued)*   *Gives:*

Dilute sulphuric acid . . . . Brown red
Aqua ammonia . . . . Dark yellow
Ammonium sulphydrate . . . . Dark yellow
Tannin . . . . Yellow
Potash . . . . Yellow
Stannous chloride . . . . Yellow
Cupric chloride . . . . Yellow
Tartaric acid . . . . Yellow
Alum . . . . Yellow
Pyrogallic acid . . . . Yellow
Cupric sulphate . . . . Orange
Sugar of lead . . . . Yellow
Potassium permanganate . . . . Brownish yellow

Decoction of Brazil-wood treated with: *Gives:*

Strong nitric acid . . . . Dark purple
Dilute nitric acid . . . . Pale red
Strong sulphuric acid . . . . Red
Dilute sulphuric acid . . . . Red
Strong hydrochloric acid . . . . Dark red
Dilute hydrochloric acid . . . . Light red
Aqua ammonia . . . . Dark red
Ammonium sulphydrate . . . . Dark red
Sulphide of hydrogen . . . . Light red
Sulphate of iron . . . . Dark violet
Tannin . . . . No change
Stannous chloride . . . . Light red
Cupric chloride . . . . Dark red

Decoction of Brazil-wood treated with: *Gives:*

Sal ammoniac . . . . Reddish yellow
Sugar of lead . . . . Yellowish red
Potash . . . . Dark crimson
Tartaric acid . . . . Reddish yellow

Decoction of madder treated with: *Gives:*

Dilute hydrochloric, nitric or sulphuric acid . . . . Pale yellow
Sugar of lead . . . . Reddish violet
Soda . . . . Red
Tartaric acid . . . . Pale yellow
Tannin . . . . Pale yellow
Potash . . . . Light red
Sal ammoniac . . . . Pale yellow
Aqua ammonia . . . . Reddish yellow

Decoction of madder treated with: (*continued*) Gives:
Alum . . . . Faint red
Stannous chloride . . . . Light red

Decoction of French berries with: Gives:
Dilute hydrochloric acid . . . . Rose color
Dilute nitric acid . . . . No change
Dilute sulphuric acid . . . . Yellow
Potash . . . . Yellow
Stannous chloride . . . . Dark yellow
Tartaric acid . . . . Discoloration
Sugar of lead . . . . Dark yellow
Ammonium sulphydrate . . . . Faint yellow
Potassium bichromate . . . . Brown yellow
Ferric nitrate . . . . Dark olive green
Potassium iodide . . . . Yellow
Cupric sulphate . . . . Greenish yellow

Decoction of tumeric treated with: Gives:
Hydrochloric, nitric or sulphuric acid . . . . Yellow
Sulphate of iron . . . . Greenish yellow
Ferric nitrate . . . . Yellow or dark yellow
Sugar of lead . . . . Yellow
Alum . . . . Yellow
Potash . . . . Red yellow
Stannous chloride . . . . Yellow
Sodium . . . . Yellow

THE MANIPULATIONS OF FINISH

Even if all directions are followed, the finish may turn out very badly if the manipulations are not proper. It is here that practice is required, although an outline may be suggested.

In the application of stain or of shellac long, steady, sweeping strokes are required. The stain will not go on evenly if the brush touches one part twice and another part once. The stain must look even. The shellac, if there is a lap at the ends of the stroke, will change the color if it is orange. The rapid application of finish and the slow rubbing are combinations to remember.

In rubbing down, the test of proper dryness is that the material that comes away should form a powder. If there is the slightest tendency to daub, the finish is not dry enough to rub. For this reason, when we say delay one, two, or more days between coats, we merely mean that the humidity regulates the time of drying, and that however long is required to get a perfectly dry surface, that waiting period must be allowed.

CUTTING OAK BY THIS METHOD
WILL GIVE THE FINER FIGURE

SLAB GRAIN WILL WARP
BADLY.

DIAGRAM SHOWING MANNER OF CUTTING OAK

If the wood itself has stood about in August until it has absorbed moisture, or if it was not dry enough to begin with, it will show as a cloudy surface in time, and there is no remedy except to clear all the finish off and get the wood into proper condition. If a piece stands around for some months, but not in the humid season, it will probably dry out enough. Cabinetmakers can tell, if they are experienced, when they work the material whether it is in proper condition. Sawdust and borings, if pressed together in the hand, will hold together like a ball, but if dry, they cannot be made to adhere. The shavings that come from a planer are brittle if dry, but if not, they can be pulled out in long curls and will hold together. I have seen old cabinetmakers lay their hands on a board and say that it wasn't dry enough merely from the reaction.

On the other hand, wood with less, we will say, than five per cent moisture is too brittle for carving and is carved at much greater expense than wood with two or three per cent more moisture. Very dry material in a cabinet piece will swell if it is not immediately finished and finished with many coats. The atmospheric conditions sometimes forbid the process going forward fast enough to keep the moisture away from the wood. It is better, therefore, that the wood should have the moisture in it while it is being worked.

There is always some degree of moisture in the air in a normal climate, and dry wood means wood containing the amount of moisture in the air on a bright, clear day. Thus the old makers, by keeping boards on an open loft, got the wood accustomed to the climate.

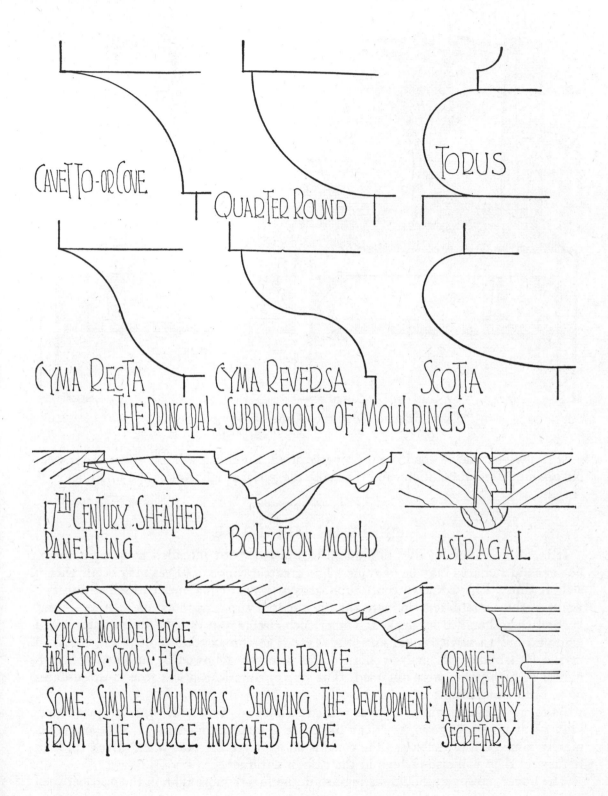

Cavetto-or Cove.

Quarter Round

Torus

Cyma Recta   Cyma Reversa   Scotia

The Principal Subdivisions of Mouldings

17th Century Sheathed Panelling   Bolection Mould   Astragal

Typical Moulded Edge. Table Tops·Stools·Etc.   Architrave   Cornice Molding from a Mahogany Secretary

Some Simple Mouldings Showing The Development From The Source Indicated Above

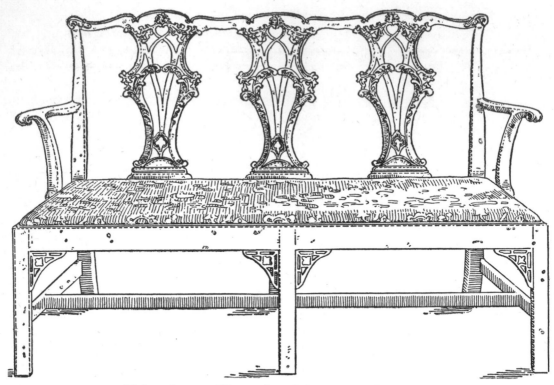

Taken from an Illustration Called a Georgian Settee

It is obvious that if wood is not properly dried, the finish will not adhere to it well. No amount of manipulation can ever make the surface right unless the wood below it is right.

PRICES OF FURNITURE

It is nothing short of silly to name prices in any book intended to be permanent, but general remarks may be of value. The greatest range of prices may occur within a short time. I have known court cupboards of almost equal merit to sell within two years of the same date, one more than a hundred times as much as another — and both of them handled by dealers. Under such circumstances only an impostor could give and only a novice could ask for prices. The climax to date of prices occurred at the Reifsnyder sale in New York. This sale was followed by another at which almost as high prices were obtained. The tide of American prices rose to those dates and ebbed from them.

As to the question whether prices will come back, it is obvious that antiques represent a feature too large in American life to be ignored permanently. Since money is merely a medium of exchange, the conclusion is inevitable that when prices are high in general they will also be high in the case of antiques.

The buyer, however, should distinguish in the future more than in the past between

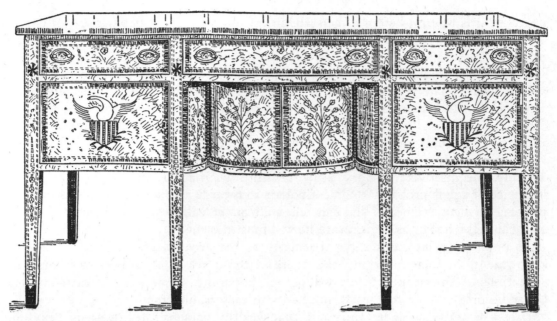

Taken from an Advertisement as an Example of Ornate Work

ordinary and extraordinary antiques. Ordinary antiques go up sympathetically just as cheap common stocks rise when good stocks rise, though the stocks and the furniture of the lower class may have no intrinsic merit. It is worth while to consider that as manuals on furniture multiply and as knowledge increases in America on the subject of antiques, the buyers will become unwilling to spend good money for inferior antiques. The prices on good articles should, therefore, advance more rapidly, relatively, than the prices on goods without merit. This may not be an immediate result, but it will be the tendency in the long run. Fifty years ago there were almost no sources of knowledge regarding American antiques. Since that time so many volumes have been issued on the subject that, if we suppose the public libraries mostly purchase those volumes, there must be hundreds of thousands of Americans who have given more or less attention to them. The author's own books, though mostly large, have gone out to the number of about twenty-five thousand. People do not buy such books merely to place in their libraries. They consult them carefully. As most such works point out the merits and demerits of furniture, the tendency would be to seek the more desirable and to seek less than formerly the inferior examples. Of course, there is a great host of persons who never see a book on antiques and yet buy more or less what they suppose to be antiques merely to keep in fashion. But that has always been true. The few lead, and the few who are informed will for the most part fix the prices.

Sales have indicated that the well-warranted suspicions against most foreign furniture have carried the auction prices on such specimens to a low point. There is already a pronounced revival in the demand for good antiques. Merit does not fluctuate with dollars. A great literary classic is just as good when the author must almost give it away, as it is when it becomes the standard of the world in its department of writing. The real collector will see as much beauty in one of his specimens whatever its market price.

It is vain to predict what style of antiques will take the lead in prices, because tastes switch about. The determination of one wealthy man to obtain a large collection of some class of furniture may cause that class to advance out of all proportion to some other class. That has happened in the past. It is reasonable to presume that as America grows old, furniture made and used by the first generations will enhance in value because more and more its known examples tend to reach their ultimate number. That is, the discovery of very early furniture will become increasingly rare. The influence of age is probably the most potent as regards prices. Prediction is based on pretense or inexperience. Who can tell what buyer will begin to collect largely and who can tell what class of furniture he will most desire?

As population increases and particularly as the great western cities increase the endowments of their museums, the desire of those museums to possess informative collections of American furniture will become apparent. Some western museums have lately become competitors in the market with eastern buyers.

It can be stated with certainty also that wealthy persons as far west as Texas and even Puget Sound are looking about, and when they come with newly filled pocketbooks and a new edge on their appetites, they will be like roaring lions seeking what they may devour. The eastern dealers have of late found that it was a long time between meals. Those who have survived will probably live through anything. With a chastened experience and a hunger born of enforced abstinence, it is easy to believe that collecting will reach proportions limited only by the available antiques, and unhappily not limited even so.

THE UPLIFTING INFLUENCE OF COLLECTING

The broad question of what concerns civilization touches also the matter of collection. If an American citizen has one or two paintings by recognized masters, two or three pieces of furniture of the best period, and a few good books, first editions, and books which are in themselves worthy to be read, aside from their rarity, such a citizen has established himself so far as reaching out toward an ideal civilization. He has some of the products of genius, of imagination, and of skilful execution. His residence has a standard set within it by which the present is to be compared. Such possessions necessarily challenge everything in his home, and everything which he proposes to bring into it. The same spirit, presuming it to be a desire for beauty and excellence, compels him to compare his best with his worst. Such possessions as are highly worthy are felt to be not at home with commonplace or shoddy articles. Any growing man under such conditions would seem to be obliged by the spirit that is in him to cast out the tares because they are a greater annoyance when side by side with the wheat. It is true that many men, even after they have acquired good things, seem to fail in growth. They are old too soon, and their minds crystalize.

It is an old truism that there must be something in a man or he cannot respond to that which is external. As there are certain woods which do not take a good finish, there are minds that lack the stimulus of whatever gland leads us to love beauty.

The exquisite table above was in the Jacob Paxson Temple Collection. It is in the Queen Anne tradition. It would better serve as a dressing table than a lowboy, as there is better knee room. The decoration is in very excellent taste, and it would be hard to match it in America. The three-toed foot in particular carries a fine leaf decoration which is extremely rare. The bracket scrolls are also carved in unusual manner for a table. The carving also on the edge of the top is most unusual. All together, the piece has a richness and completion which place it almost in a class alone.

On pages 455–456 are shown two looking-glasses. The first is called a love-bird glass, from the doves cut out as scrolls on the sides of the cresting. There are two cut-out gold-leaved and carved ornaments. The glass is of that medium size so generally desired, it being 39 inches overall.

The other glass is a Chippendale or late Queen Anne. The raised button in the center of the bottom is attached, and beside the cut-out at the top there is an applied piece which blends with the bird carving.

GLOSSARY

The large classifications that would otherwise be in this glossary are found in separate chapters. See the chapters on Furniture Feet, Furniture Finials, Shells and Rosettes.

We include in this chapter only the names not particularly treated in full elsewhere. The author had the honor to revise and add to twelve hundred terms relating to furniture and hardware for a new edition of an unabridged dictionary, but it seems convenient to include most of those terms here.

Uniform terms are not established to refer to all shapes and styles. There is a variation of names for the same article in many instances. An effort is made to use the name which seems best adapted for general use, but cross references will be included.

Under the principal classifications as above, for instance, Feet, will be found a great number of drawings. The same is true of the chapters on Finials, Shells, Rosettes, etc. Some items regarding books on furniture are included.

Abacus. The top member of a capital with the architrave.

Acanthus. The most-used ornament on Chippendale chair carving. The conventionalized leaf of the *acanthus spinosa*. In furniture it is sometimes much degraded. In architecture used on cornices and capitals.

Acorn. A turned ornament resembling an acorn and commonly found on low bed posts and as a finial on chairs.

Acroterium. Classically the ornament on the corners of Greek temples, but applied to similar top corner ornaments, on walnut and mahogany furniture. *See* Finials.

Adam, The brothers. Men distinguished by much taste, talent, and ability who were both architects and furniture designers in a classical mode, and were contemporary with late Chippendale and the entire Hepplewhite and much of the Sheraton periods. Their work is marked by grace and lightness. It blends with the Sheraton so as often not to be easily distinguished from it, but when so distinguished it shows more pure architectural lines than the Sheraton.

Almery. A variant spelling of Aumbry.

Almoner's cupboard. A livery cupboard.

Annulets. Bands or fillets running around the lower portion of the Doric capital.

Anthemion. A floral or foliated form in a radiating cluster always flat. The Greek name for the honeysuckle ornament. In England, however, it is referred to as the camomile, a totally different ornament.

Antique furniture. Confined by general agreement to furniture earlier than 1830. After that date the degradation or the formlessness of style rendered furniture objectionable.

Appliqué. Said of figures or composition or carved work applied and not cut from the solid. An applied carving.

Apron. Usually synonymous with skirt, the frame with a scrolled edge running about a table, lowboy, etc.

Arabesque. Designs borrowed from the Saracenic architecture.

Archimedean. A term referring to the screw for raising water, invented by Archimedes. Applied to the spiral form of table legs, etc.

Architrave. The lowest member of a cornice. Sometimes applied to a molding or mold about a door or window.

Armoire. The French name for a wardrobe or press cupboard. Sometimes loosely used for a court cupboard.

Arris. The sharp edge or salient angle formed by the meeting of two surfaces, whether plain or curved, especially to edges in moldings.

Arrow spindle. Said of a flattened spindle with an approximate arrow shape at one end on late light Sheraton chairs.

Aster carving. Another name for the sunflower carving, usually three flowers on the central panel of some Connecticut chests.

Astragal. A small half-round or convex bead.

Attribution. A much abused term. A painting or a fine piece of furniture resembles that of a master and is attributed in catalogs or elsewhere to that master, sometimes with a strong degree of probability that it was made by him. Sometimes, however, it is at once recognized by students as having no proper reference whatever to that master. Thus furniture is attributed to Goddard which lacks his well-known stylemarks.

Aumbry. An opening for a cupboard in a wall. Otherwise spelled aumrie.

Back stools. An early name given to chairs.

Bag table. A small square work stand with two drawers usually, the lower drawer carrying a bag.

Bail. The brass handle, falling, as found on Chippendale and later hardware.

Balk. A squared timber. A term passing out of use. Mahogany is sent abroad in this form, but is brought to America in the log.

Ball and claw. *See* Claw and Ball.

Ball-and-ring turning. A turning consisting of a ball and a narrow section alternating. Seventeenth century.

Ball foot. A foot usually large, mostly employed in seventeenth-century furniture. Called in England a bun foot.

Baluster. A turning occurring in various forms used as support for a stair rail, and split in two and used vertically side by side for baluster-back chairs. The side post of these chairs should be a double of the split baluster.

Bamboo turned. The style of a somewhat late Windsor chair imitative of bamboo. Bamboo was also used by Chippendale, but was not turned to any extent, but rather wrought somewhat more naturalistically, in his Chinese types.

Bandbox. A box of wood, papered, or of cardboard papered, usually like the room of the guest where it was used.

Banding. A narrow line of veneer running round the fronts of drawers.

Banister. A variant for baluster.

Banquette. An upholstered bench. French use only.

Barefaced. A name applied to a tenon which has a shoulder on one side only.

Barley sugar turning. Applied to a deeply cut, closely spiraled twist as of a table leg.

Baroque. Equivalent to rococo.

Barrel arch. A straight, simple arch as of a tent-bed canopy.

Barrel chair. A chair resembling in shape a half barrel cut vertically. Sometimes called a grandfather's chair.

Base mold. The main heavy mold at the base of any piece of cabinet furniture. The lack of it indicates a plain or inferior style, or a late style.

Basil. The measurement of the angle of a plain iron grinding, or of a chisel.

Basin stand. An English term for a washstand.

Bassinet. A wicker basket for a child. It is a question whether it was used in America in the old days. It is applied by extension to a child's crib.

Battersea enamel. Found on fine large knobs as those for draperies, and sometimes as the plates of large ring pulls.

Bayberry. The wax obtained from the bayberry for candles in the colonial time. There were laws for the preservation of the bushes from too early gathering. Candles were sometimes dipped, of course repeatedly, to build them up to a proper size, and later the molds came in.

Bead. A half-round mold usually small. Its use is very ancient. An astragal, which see.

Bead and butt. The style of finishing flush panels. A bead separates the stile from the sides of the panel. Often used of the blade or slip between drawers.

Bead and flush. A bead set in flush about a panel.

Bead and reel. *See* Pencil and pearl.

Bearing rail. A rail set in a table or cabinetwork to carry the drawer.

Beaufatt. A spelling found for buffet.

Bed bolt. The covered bolt and sunken nut used in all old-fashioned connections between the bed post and the rail.

Bed mold. That which is under a corona mold of a cornice.

Bedside table. A toilet table with a shelf and often a protected top. A bidet.

Beech. A wood more common in England than America where maple usually, but not always, supplants it.

Bellows. Used to blow coals to a flame and made of wood or leather or metal. Sometimes very decorative.

Bell seat. The rounded seat of the Queen Anne period.

Bench. Strictly I think it is more proper to confine the use of this word to a seat without a back, but in common speech, especially in England, it is applied to a settee or settle.

Bench end. Used of the upright on a settle or bench.

Bergère. A French term for a chair with a round back, upholstered usually.

Betty lamp. A small pear-shaped lamp usually of iron or tin with a wick in the small end.

Bevel. The forty-five-degree cut on many corners of cabinet furniture. A chamfer. Sometimes the bevel varies from forty-five degrees.

Bevel block. A name applied to the slanting mold which raises the front of the panel as on the drawer of a desk or court cupboard.

(340)

Bezel. The circular frame, usually brass, used on banjo and other clocks.

Bibelot. A knickknack. A name used in catalogs and elsewhere to give an impression of importance to a knickknack or a gewgaw.

Bidet. A bedroom stand for toilet use.

Bilboa or Bilbao. A looking-glass with marble or marble and mahogany frame and filigree top. Named from the usual port of origin.

Bird-cage clock. An English brass clock for a shelf or table, like a lantern clock.

Bird's beak. Said of a rounded V cut on the corner as of a lowboy top. Otherwise clover-leaf.

Bird's-beak lock. A lock with a hooked end of the bolt as used on quadrant desk covers or drops.

Blanket chest. Any chest used for the storage of blankets. There is no reason for naming any chest a blanket chest, since any chest could obviously be used for any object. It is as reasonable to call all chests dower or dowry chests, as some do.

Block. The peculiar swell on American cabinet furniture sometimes segmental, but more often simply raised with rounded edges. The segment is not thought to be so good. The square block is often surmounted with a shell as in Goddard furniture. *See* FURNITURE TREASURY, and John Goddard, this volume.

Blunt-arrow turning. Characteristic of the foot in the earliest Philadelphia Windsor chairs.

Board chest, or other furniture. Furniture made with six boards and without a frame.

Bobbin turned. The bulged enlargement on Windsor stretchers.

Bodying in. *See* Filling.

Bolection mold. A large mold sometimes covering the edges of framed panel. It is applied outside the body of the piece and was especially used about fireplaces and indicates a date of the Chippendale period or earlier. *See* index.

Bombé. A swelled or convex surface. *See* Kettle base.

Bonnet top. A scrolled gooseneck or swanneck top as of a high chest of drawers, which is carried back the full width of the top. Same as hood.

Bookcase. Rare in America as a separate construction. Most large cases have been imported. Very common placed above desks to form a bookcase desk, or a secretary, a name coming to be used for a desk with a bookcase top.

Bootjack. The name given to the inverted V cut on the end board of a chest or chest of drawers, as well as to bootjack, made in this manner or otherwise.

Boss. A round or oval ornament common on seventeenth-century chests of drawers and chests and cupboards. An egg. Usually shaped like a symmetrical half egg, but sometimes a half ball. Small bosses around the central one are called satellites. Usually painted black. Applied in conjunction with drops or half spindles. Also called turtle backs.

Bottle turning. The bulbous shape, generally cup or bowl turning used on the legs of William and Mary pieces. See patterns No. 4772 and following, FURNITURE TREASURY.

Boule. *See* Buhl.

Bow back. Descriptive of the bow or hoop running about the back of a Windsor chair and receiving at the top the spindles.

Box stretcher. A stretcher not turned, but with rectangular section sometimes with an enlarged or molded top.

Bracket. The supporting member between the leg and the seat of a chair, or the leg and frame of a table or cabinet furniture. It is indicative of the date from its shape. Pierced brackets are of the Chippendale time, or usually. Very long and narrow brackets of oak are of the seventeenth century. Also, a wall bracket, as for a banjo clock.

Bracket clock. An English name for a table or shelf clock. A wall clock.

Bracket cornice. A cornice supported by brackets or modillions introduced from the early French period.

Branch grain. A term difficult to distinguish between feather grain or plume.

Bread trough. A large, oblong, flaring trough on turned legs common in the Delaware Valley.

Break. The marked projection of any kind of cornice or mold on a carcase.

Breakfast table. A modern term being applied to small dining tables or any table of small size used for a refection.

Break front. The front of a cabinet piece advanced in a portion by a mitered break. The term is not properly used of a serpentine.

Brewster chair. A very few have been found. Like the Carver chair except that it has spindles under the arm and below the seat.

Bridal chest. Same as dowry chest or hope chest.

Bridle. An open tenon. *See* illustration, Mortise and tenon.

Broken arch. Applied to a gooseneck or swanneck decoration, referring to the fact that the two scrolls do not meet.

Buffet. In America usually applied to a corner cupboard or corner chair. Also now often applied to a side cupboard or sideboard.

Buhl. A decorative inlay, of brass or shell, or ivory or silver. Made fashionable by Boule, a French designer.

Bulbous. A heavy turning associated with English refectory tables. Said to be of Dutch origin. Of a watermelon shape. Sixteenth and seventeenth centuries.

Bull's-eye. Glass with a bulbous center. The defective portion left after blowing, and used in outside doors and over them to transmit light, but not vision.

Bun foot. English name for ball foot. See chapter on Feet.

Bureau. Properly a writing desk. A French term. Colloquially used in America for a chest of drawers.

Bureau table. The name given by Goddard to his knee-hole table.

Burjier chairs. A term used by Hepplewhite to designate armchairs connected by a stool. A duchesse.

Burl. Or Burr. A diseased tumor-shaped growth on many trees such as walnut, ash, maple. It probably results from a wound or sting of the bark. Burls are sometimes very large. The grain is snarled in an irregular way as if the sense of direction was lost. The consequence is a material that will not split and hence was very much used for the shaping of bowls whose decorative value is great. Used also for veneer very generally, anciently and now.

The spelling or the form burr is frequent and the usage of spelling and definition is vague. Crotch or root or knotty grain sometimes has this word applied to it, but inaccurately. Our word burly applied to a man gives a good impression of the significance in wood. Burls take a beautiful polish and are highly decorative. Collections of burl bowls and other utensils are made.

Burr. *See* Burl.

Butterfly table. A table the bracket of which swinging to support the leaf is supposed to resemble a butterfly wing. Lately called a rudder table also. Date about 1700–25. Generally maple, often curly, and usually small. An occasional table. See FURNITURE TREASURY No. 892 and following.

Butt hinge. A hinge the two parts of which fold together and are connected by pins in the modern square-edge form, but used since about 1800 on tables, cupboards, etc.

Butt joint. End grains of wood coming together with square edges.

Byzantine. Furniture with oriental suggestions, but specifically a three-cornered chair supposed to have been brought first to Scandinavia and thence to England.

Cabinet. Strictly used for a carcase having doors and drawers or divisions behind them. Formerly a term applied to a room, hence the phrase cabinet minister. Cabinet is distinguished from a chest, the latter having no drawers at the top, and from a cupboard in which the matter of drawers is secondary, and from a chest of drawers which has no doors. *See* chapter listing American cabinetmakers.

Cable. Same as rope mold.

Cabochon. Originally a stone of convex form, not faceted, also the style itself.

Cabriole leg. Literally goat shaped, but very few legs have that shape. Mostly they begin at the frame with a convex knee or hip and continue as a flattened letter S to the foot, which is usually a disc or club foot, sometimes hoof. The leg is the most marked design of the Queen Anne period, though it continued through the early Georgian and early Chippendale, and in simple furniture nearly to the end of the eighteenth century. Sometimes called bandy leg especially when short. There is no strict usage. The leg becomes smaller at the ankle and may or may not be carved. See chapter on Feet and chapter on Chairs.

Cacqueteuse chair. A wainscot chair with narrow back and curved arms of French derivation. The other name is chaise de femme. None is known of American origin, but a few were English.

Camber. A hollowed surface or arch.

Camel back, or camel hump. Applied to the back rail of a Hepplewhite or transition chair.

Camp bed. A cross-legged bedstead with a canvas across the top, made to shut up as scissors. Very common in simple homes up to this generation, but very old in its first use.

Camp chair. A folding frame chair similar to a camp bed, which, while common today, was also in use hundreds of years ago. As an X-stretcher chair, often not made to fold, in a rich form in the sixteenth and seventeenth centuries.

Canapé. A sofa. Never used in English.

Candle board. The small sliding shelf below a table top principally used in Sheraton's time, but similar to the candle slides in Chippendale desks.

Candle box. A box of wood or tin affixed to the wall in which candles were kept.

Candle mold. The early sort was of pewter, the late sort of tin usually in a battery of a dozen or so.

Candle stand. A small light table, either tripod or with four legs, for a candle. French torchère.

Cane chair. A chair of the Charles II period, usually carved.

Cannelated. An alternate description for fluted.

Canopy. The frame or the hood thereon over a bedstead, whether simple or ornate. A tester. Frequently used also of the more pretentious decorative rooflike projections over doors, etc.

Canted corner. Same as a beveled or chamfered corner. Often found on chests of drawers and so forth.

Canteen. A cutlery case.

Canterbury. An English term for a music rack with pockets for sheet music.

Canvas. Used for bed and day-bed tick support.

Capital. The enlarged head of a column, whether carved or otherwise, used in all orders of architecture.

Carcase, or carcass. The main part or body of a piece of cabinet furniture without reference to its doors, projections, or accessories.

Card table. A small table, frequently oval with a swing leg, used for gaming. There is an infinite variety of styles and shapes, continuing through all periods of furniture. All woods and all surfaces. Such tables have been found with five, and even six and seven legs.

Carolean. A designation of furniture from the time of Charles II. Usually cane.

Carpet. The name usually given not to a floor carpet, but to the covers spread on tables, etc. However, floor carpets more usually as rugs came in more or less by the middle of the eighteenth century.

Cartel clock. A hanging clock often of bronze.

Cartouche. A rococo carved decoration in various forms, but usually flat with open-work and often a kidney-bean-shaped center used as the central decoration on high cabinets of the Chippendale time. See finials for illustration. Derived from a Francis I ornament like an unrolled scroll.

Carved. The old term was cut, said of furniture, tool cut, with decoration. It does not apply to turning.

Carver chair. A chair with three vertical and three horizontal turned sections in the back. Variants occur with four and two verticals. Named for a chair owned by Governor Carver of Plymouth. It was first ash, then maple. I found one English side chair of this sort, in oak.

Caryatide. A Greek female figure carved as a support for a mantel or any architectural form.

Casement. A hinged window usually swinging out.

Casement stay. The rod often decoratively formed and punctured or held by a thumb nut to keep a casement window open as desired.

Cassette. A casket or cash box.

Cassone. A decorative box or chest, usually Italian.

Cast. Term used in England for a twist in timber. In America the long warp.

Caster. (*a*) The brass roller used on late furniture. (*b*) A silver or other metal pepper or salt box.

Cathedral shape. Applied to the pointed arch of the glass openings of the late eighteenth and early nineteenth-century bookcases, the arches on the backs of some Sheraton chairs, and the shaping of the board ends at the floor of some simple chests of drawers.

Caul. The form of wood or zinc used heated to press by clamps over a newly veneered surface.

Cavetto. A concave mold, the curve of which is usually a quarter circle much less produced than a scotia.

Cellaret. The deep drawer or bottle drawer in a sideboard. Also a term used for a case of bottles or a wine cooler.

Centered. Said of an ornament in the center of the main element.

Chair table. One with a hinged top which can be thrown up as a chair back.

Chambers, Sir William. An English architect who designed furniture with Gothic and Louis XIV and Louis XVI ornament.

Chamfer. The flat cutting away or beveling of a corner. Sometimes called canting.

Chandelier. Originally for candles, whence the name, and of tin, iron, bronze, glass, or other material, depending from a ceiling rather than attached to a wall.

Chasing. The incised patterns on metal, generally applied to brasses so decorated.

Check. The common term for crack or split in lumber. Abroad used of a rebate.

Chequer. Inset differently colored squares used as a decoration.

Chest. Strictly a receptacle with a lid, and generally a small till at one end. It may have no drawer, or one, two, and rarely three drawers. A very ancient word. Compare cyst. Also colloquial chist. Traveling chest becomes a box in England and a trunk in America. The earliest form of furniture. Old specimens were in oak, or on the Continent, also walnut.

Chesterfield. An overstuffed couch. Called in England stuffed over. A wretched contrivance in which the cabinetwork is hidden and therefore usually inferior.

Chest of drawers. A piece of cabinet furniture consisting wholly of drawers, which grew up from the chest, by the insertion at its bottom, first of one drawer, then of two, and finally the giving up of the lifting top. Vulgarly called a bureau.

Chest-on-chest. A chest of drawers on which another slightly smaller is superimposed. A high chest of drawers, though specifically that term should apply only where the drawers are made in one section, and distinguished from a highboy in having the lower set of drawers near to the floor with short feet, usually bracket feet.

Cheval. A looking-glass which swings between supports and generally large and resting on the floor. Rare in American furniture.

Chiffonier. A high, narrow chest of drawers, late eighteenth century, French period. Used in modern times for a similar commercial American piece.

Chinese Chippendale. (*a*) A bamboo design employed by Chippendale, now rather discredited. (*b*) Used of the fret on chair legs or the applied fret on stretchers or elsewhere in furniture.

"Chinese" taste. A phrase used by Chippendale to describe many of the frets or the pagoda-like effects which he used.

Chintz. Used as a hanging about rooms and beds, etc.

Chippendale, Thomas. A very great name in English furniture and the style derived from his now rare work on cabinetmaking. His style first using the Queen Anne leg finally departed from it to the straight leg, usually fretted. He adopted the ribbon back, though many simpler designs were shown. His style dominated in England from the late 1740s to about 1780. His father was a cabinetmaker in the provinces, and the son established what became a large shop in London. The particulars of his life are meager, but my FURNITURE TREASURY shows 169 of his chair styles besides many tables, beds, etc., as in this volume. He did some work for the Adam brothers who brought back the classical style from their Italian studies. His style was supplanted by Hepplewhite.

Cinquefoil. A foliation with five points, cusps, or foils of Gothic origin seen chiefly in Gothic windows and early old furniture. *See* Quatrefoil.

Clamp. The method and the article used in holding portions of cabinetwork together in the process of manufacture. Clamps are in various forms, sizes, and of wood or iron.

Clash. An English term for the figure in oak, otherwise felt or silver grain.

Classical. Applied strictly first to Greek, next to Roman styles. But loosely used also of Egyptian and oriental styles. Its use in furniture came in markedly under the Adam brothers, and in a delicate or dainty form under Sheraton. A revulsion from the rococo.

Claw and ball. A foot form supposed to be derived from the Chinese, and first found as a bird's claw grasping an egg or ball. Used in the Queen Anne slightly, and generally in the Georgian and the early Chippendale style. When long and narrow it was called a rat's claw and ball. See chapter on Feet, for illustrations in large numbers.

Cleat. A small section or batten used on the ends of table tops or attached beneath them, or for general purposes to strengthen or hold together or prevent the warp of boards.

Cleft. Split or riven. A distinction from sawed. The earliest form of preparing wood for turning purposes.

Clock glasses. Are traced to different makers according to their style, but since they are very much counterfeited, as, for instance, the word patent painted on a new glass to counterfeit the Simon Willard style, they should be verified with the greatest care. Few amateurs can detect a good imitation.

Club foot. A stubby form lacking the grace of the disc foot found on Queen Anne furniture. *See* Foot.

Clustered columns. A carving detail derived from the Gothic and consisting of three or more columns really made as one, but apparently clustered. When very numerous, as if small and tied together in bundles like reeds, the effect is called reeding. Clustered columns were common in good bedposts and in Gothic Chippendale chair or table legs.

Cock bead. A half-round bead projecting slightly a sixteenth of an inch or less about drawers in the eighteenth century. *See* Sunk bead, Quirk bead, etc.

Cocked-hat box. A triangular box for a cocked hat sometimes imposed on drawers for stocks. Pine.

Coffer. A chest, originally an Italian chest.

Coffered ceiling. So called from the great depth of the panels which on that account resemble a coffer.

Colonnette. The small columns used in furniture, as those each side of the hood of a clock.

Comb back. The secondary or higher back on an armchair, named from its resemblance to an old-fashioned high comb. See FURNITURE TREASURY under Windsors.

Commode. A term frequently applied to a chest of drawers, but more properly for a toilet chamber piece.

Communion table. The finest specimens of the refectory or standing table types have been found in early American churches.

Composite. The last great order of architecture, combining the Corinthian and Ionic.

Composition, or Compo. Material consisting of whiting, glue, and rosin, cast to represent carving. It indicates the decline of artisanship, although it was introduced by the brothers Adam. Sometimes called stucco, used on furniture and mantel and wall work. It is modernly available at very low prices and is much used on commercial furniture.

Concave. A hollowed surface as of the end of a Hepplewhite sideboard, or the seat of a Windsor chair.

Concentric. Said of circles that intersect one another.

Confidant, confidante. An English term for a tête-à-tête.

Conform. Same as contour.

Connecticut chest. Incorrectly because loosely applied to the sunflower chest, often also to any oak chest, but with no other reason but that Connecticut is rich in such things.

Console. A much abused term in these days. Properly it was a large bracket, supporting a shelf or table. In the shops almost any wall table is called a console. A loose and objectionable term because it does not mean anything in present usage. French derivation.

Constitution. Used of an architectural looking-glass whose head often has a series of balls in the decoration. Also the term applies to the time of a looking-glass made about the period of the Constitution, 1791 or after.

Contour. The shaping, scrolling, or profile of a piece of furniture or a mold.

Convex. An outward curve as of the end of a Sheraton sideboard or a round Empire glass designed to include an entire room.

Convolute. In the form of a scroll.

Coopered joints. The beveled fitting together of sections to form curves as in circular work or sideboard doors.

Copeland. Published a book of English designs in 1746.

Coquille. A shell in the phrase "Rocaille et coquille" (rock and shell) for the baroque school of elaborate forms in a mixture of combinations, coming from Italy and France and adopted by Chippendale. If kept simple, the style is not bad, but it proceeded to extravagance.

Core. The interior of furniture such as the backing of a pillar.

Corinthian order. A style of Greek architecture with a very complicated capital.

Corner block. The inset blocks, square or triangular, used to reinforce chair or other frames.

Corner chair. A chair in which the back is set on so that the front leg is in the center. Found in Queen Anne and Chippendale time. A buffet or round-about chair.

Cornice. The upper member of an entablature, but in common parlance the group of molds which constitute the capping of any large cabinetwork. Used also of the mold about a room.

Cornish. The old spelling of cornice.

Corona. The large, flat projection in the classical cornice mold, called also drip mold. That is, it is intended to shed rain and prevent it soaking under the soffit, by undercutting the projection.

Couch. Loosely used of a sofa, but specifically narrowed in American usage to a day bed, or lounge.

Counter-boule. A brass groundwork with tortoise-shell inlay.

Counterpane. A coverlet for a bed, originally woven in squares or figures.

Countersink. A conical depression mostly used to receive a screw head, but sometimes in furniture to retain strength but increase grace, as in the bored roll-over of a chair arm.

Court cupboard. An English term of obscure origin. A form used in the sixteenth and seventeenth centuries as an oak sideboard, and the most important piece of American oak furniture. If all closed, it was called in America a press cupboard. If open below, a court cupboard merely. The upper cupboard was often cut back with bevels on the side.

Courting chair. A settle, settee, or sofa built for two persons.

Cove. The shape of a large hollow mold on a cornice. Also used of a niche.

Coved cupboard. One whose top is swept forward like a hood, usually in pine.

Coverlet. A bedspread or counterpane.

Cradle. FURNITURE TREASURY, No. 1564 and following.

Credence. A large oak side table of Gothic origin and often of ecclesiastical use. A retable. A snobbish name for a court cupboard.

Crescent stretcher. A bowed or segmental stretcher on a Windsor chair from which radiating stretchers go to the back leg.

Cresting. A decoration on a top chair rail or the top of a piece of high cabinet furniture.

Cromwellian. Furniture of Cromwell's time, usually somewhat simpler than the

Carolean, but fairly included in the Jacobean period. A Jacobean piece, quite simple. It is frequently called Cromwellian without any surety.

Cross-stitch. A kind of needlework in which the stitches are diagonal and in pairs, the thread of one stitch crossing that of the other, forming a square.

Cross stretcher. Intersecting X stretcher in William and Mary lowboy and some chairs of various periods.

Crotched. Describing the rich grain occurring at the intersection of a branch with a main stem of a tree. The root also at its initial departure may show the same grain.

Crown. A carved motive on chairs, Charles II. Also found painted on cabinet furniture.

Crow's nest. The arrangement of two square boards with four corner colonnettes devised so that a pie-crust or tray-top table could both tip and turn.

C scroll. A carved scroll resembling a C, often found on Queen Anne and Chippendale furniture. Fancifully thought to be used by Chippendale as his initial.

Cupboard-cloth. The cloth of linen or richer materials used as a cover on the lid of a court cupboard and hanging down at the ends.

Cupboard cushion. A cushion placed on a court cupboard to receive silver or other decorative ornaments. Made of various materials.

Cuff, or wrister. A carving, sometimes a molding above a Spanish foot on highboys and lowboys.

Cupid's bow. The doubled ogee curve as in a conventional Chippendale chairback top rail.

Curled figure. A term distinct from curly. A feather-grain cut at intersections of boughs, and largely used for veneer.

Curly wood. As of maple, birch, walnut, etc. A distinctive grain, which, when most emphatic, is called zebra. A handsome material for bedposts or paneling. Rarely found running through the tree, but when so found, of rare importance. To be distinguished from mottled or figured and also from bird's eye.

Curtain knob. Large brass or battersea knobs for draping curtains.

Curtain piece. A span rail when elevated.

Cushion. Used very generally in the ancient times with wainscot chairs or settees. Made of leather or any other material and stuffed with any one of many substances. Also used on open cupboards to rest silver upon.

Cusp. A point or knob, projecting and sometimes carved in Gothic arches. Used also as a pointed projection in the turning as below the bowl of a vase.

Cylinder front. A quadrant fall front of a desk, as distinct from the tambour. The cylinder being built solid or with coopered joints.

Cyma recta. An ogee mold. From the Greek name for wave. Double, it forms the cupid's bow.

Cyma reversa. A reversed cyma recta.

Dado. The paneled or wooden lower portion of a wall. Distinguished from wainscot, which is supposed to run to the ceiling.

Dais. At one end of an ancient hall the raised portion of a floor on which the master and his friends sat to dine. The tables for the retainers were on the main lower floor.

Day bed, chaise longue, or couch. A construction with a head at the end in all periods of furniture. FURNITURE TREASURY No. 1586 and following.

Day-bed back. A Delaware Valley chair with a molded arched back resembling those found in day beds.

Deal. An English term for pine or soft wood. In the term deals it refers to boards of a recognized size.

Demi-dome. A half dome. The shaping of a niche or shell-top cupboard or a plastered cupboard.

Dentil. A toothlike ornament said to be derived from the short projecting ceiling timbers in Greek temples. The spacing between these square projections is the same as the dentil or less. Common on cornices, of the good periods.

Diamond. Referring to the lozenge shape or the carving upon it in the oak and Adam periods.

Diamond glazing. Casements of the seventeenth century ordinarily had diamond-shaped glass in lead. This form or a variation was often used in the glass doors of bookcases.

Diaper. A repeated pattern consisting of inlays of any material whatever or low relief carving. Usually of diamond or square shapes. Originating perhaps with French furniture of Louis XVI time.

Dice. A decoration of a small square as checkers.

Directoire. This brief period is usually included in early Empire. It covers the period of the French political directory from the opening of the Revolution to the crowning of Napoleon in 1804.

Disc foot. A flattened, rounded foot. Queen Anne period. See chapter on Feet.

Dish top. *See* Rim top.

Document drawer. The name applied to the narrow vertical drawers usually one on each side of the central division of a desk cabinet. Their faces were often finely ornamented by pilasters or other decorations.

Dog tooth. (*a*) A conical repeated ornament as a decoration of a molding. Originating in early English work and also found on eighteenth-century mantels and even later. (*b*) A zigzag Gothic carving adapted and used on oak chests.

Dolphin. Naturalistic or conventionalized and used as a French foot. Also a brass decoration on the spandrels of clocks.

Dome bed. A bed with an arched canopy or tester or a true dome. Used only on beds of the Chippendale or earlier period.

Door-stops. Weights sometimes of wood, wedge shape, but oftener castings of iron to hold a door open.

Doric. The earliest order of Greek architecture. Marked by heaviness, simplicity, severity, and majesty, and having little carving.

Double arch mold. Two contiguous quarter-round molds. A decoration around drawers of the Queen Anne period. The single arch was earlier. A doubled astragal.

Double chair. A narrow settle or a love seat supposedly large enough for two persons. Otherwise a courting chair.

Double chest of drawers. Another name for a chest-on-chest.

Dowel. A plain, straight turning usually small. Dowel construction is like that of a Windsor chair put together without mortise or tenon, or surfaces fixed together by short dowels. An objectionable mode where the mortise and tenon could be used.

Dower chest, more properly dowry. A hope chest. The term dower chest is not strictly correct, if it is supposed to refer to the dowager or widowed mother of a head of a house. A chest used to store the plenishing of a prospective bride. A true hope chest often had the initials of the owner carved upon it.

Dovetail. The method of joining by cut-outs in wedge form. It can only be done well by hand. In the earliest use there was one great dovetail at the end of a drawer found on seventeenth-century American furniture; later the dovetails were increased until about 1800 they became very numerous. Used also of a butterfly-shaped inset tie between two boards as a repair on an original table top on the under side.

Dragon foot. A style of late Empire use found on tables and sofas.

Drake foot. *See* Three-toed foot.

Drapery. Besides the ordinary use it also refers to the swag or festoon carving or inlay on bedposts or other furniture.

Draw bore. The method of connecting a mortise and tenon so as to draw it together, and retain it as a tight joint. The boring in the tenon is slightly nearer the shoulder than is the boring through the mortise. The pin will break or refuse to drive if the line of the two borings is very much different. Old pins are often found broken and therefore, of course, not adding any strength. If the wood did not shrink, there would be no need of the draw bore.

Drawing-room chairs. Dainty, carved, light chairs often with medallions of the Sheraton and Adam periods.

Drawing table. A heavy refectory table built with a double top, the under part in two sections which pull out to form an extension. Seventeenth century.

Dresser. An open cupboard set on the shelf of a broad closed cupboard, and called together a dresser. In America made of pine in New England, and pine, walnut, or whitewood in Pennsylvania. The modern use of the word dresser for a chest of drawers is misleading and confusing.

Dressing mirror, or glass. A small glass on standards, or a shaft for use as a dressing glass; when used by gentlemen called a shaving glass.

Dressing table. The true name for a lowboy. Also applied to side tables with one drawer.

Drip mold. *See* Corona.

Drop. A turned ornament either complete or split in seventeenth-century cupboards and chests and table skirts. Also an inlaid husk ornament of the late eighteenth century.

Drop leaf. Any table with a leaf. In England a leaf is called a flap and a leaf table a flap table.

Drum-top. A cylindrical table whose top is supported by a frame usually a plain, flat band so that the whole table top might resemble a drum. Period about 1810.

Duchesse. An upholstered armchair with a stool of the same style which together form a couch.

Duck-bill. Said of the pointed union of the back rail and post on a late Windsor chair.

Duck feet. A term loosely used for Dutch feet, but by some restricted to a three-toed or web foot. Confused with Dutch foot.

Dumb-waiter. Usually a tripod stand with two or three revolving shelves, sometimes very decorative. A lazy Susan.

Dust board. The division separating drawers. It is usually omitted, but it is good as a dust preventive and also to hinder meddling.

Dutch. A style of furniture including William and Mary and Queen Anne, and covering the entire walnut period, the time between 1690 and 1745, about. But thus defined it includes the early Georgian period which is strictly after 1714.

Ears. The name applied to ends of the Chippendale style chair crestings. Examples shown through this work.

Ébéniste. A French name for cabinetmaker.

Ebonized. Wood treated to imitate ebony. This was usual in American furniture.

Ebonoise. The imitation of ebony.

Echinus. A Greek mold with egg-and-dart decoration.

Edgeroll. A molded detail of Gothic origin, like a staff bead.

Edging. The insetting of a solid edge as of a table top, when the face is to be veneered.

Egg and dart. A Greek decoration sometimes on a fillet but usually on a half-round mold, supposed to symbolize life and death.

Egg and tongue. A mold which suggests these terms. Used in the Georgian period.

Eggs. Same as bosses or turtle backs.

Elizabethan. A designation which scarcely applies to any furniture in America. Very little remains of the Elizabethan age, and that little is nearly all retained in England. It is based on the Renaissance style and precedes the Jacobean.

Ellipse. An oval most often seen on late eighteenth-century inlays, and in the shape of the windows over doors of the same period.

Embrasure. The window or other recess in a house with thick walls, the location of a window seat.

Embroidery frame. Sometimes an elaborate frame with rolling supports, and sometimes a small, round swivel frame, each more or less decorative.

Empire. The French style brought in by the savants whom Napoleon sent to Egypt during his occupancy of it. It revived the Egyptian and also the Greek and Roman classic forms with animal feet, and long, curved tripod legs. It was preceded or more properly began with the Directoire forms. The English in adopting it made some modifications and American artisans like Phyfe added decoration peculiar to them.

Empire, Late. A term applied to the second empire, French furniture of 1830 and later. In America this represents the style which is popularly and misleadingly called colonial in New York. Of course it is not in any respect colonial and means nothing. The style is shown in heavy rolled shapes and is clumsy and extreme. The cabinetwork is good. It is almost always veneered, but some chair work is in the solid. It does not come under the definition of antique in the mind of the collector, but nevertheless represents the major part of the trade goods in antiques, especially in the South and West. New Orleans and French America in general imported a great deal in this period. Very little of this style is shown in this volume on account of the date and the lack of merit, but it is familiar enough to everybody. The later Phyfe furniture was also made in this style and is a very wide departure from the Sheraton and early Empire influence of his first work.

Enamel. A finish prepared for by a whiting and glue size which is then covered with transparent French polish. Enamel is used also in the form of china or porcelain finish for drapery and other knobs of about 1800.

Endive. A decorative carved motive which somewhat resembles the acanthus leaf and is not always clearly distinguished from it. It originated in France under Louis XIV, and was adopted by the Chippendale school.

Engraving. The relief produced by cutting fine lines on veneers, afterwards rubbed with black composition. A marquetry term.

Entablature. The entire element in an architectural sense above the columns. It is composed of the frieze and the cornice, and, commonly speaking, the word cornice covers it all.

Entasis. The Greek designation for the slight swell in a column. The object of it is to overcome the optical illusion of hollowness which is always given if the column is in a straight line, that is, tapering without fullness. The enlargement in Greek columns is only three-eighths of an inch on each side in case of the Parthenon. That is to say, it is roughly about one part in six hundred. When this is reduced to a short architectural column, the point is too fine to be imitated. Some of the best old makers ignored the entasis, but they lost something. The enlargement in practice must be two or three times as much as that in the Greek columns in order to be observable. There is a lean or weak effect without the entasis; with it we have a fuller and richer appearance. The entasis reaches its climax about one-third of the distance between the base and the capital of the column.

Escritoire. Same as 'scrutoire.

Escutcheon. The name applied in furniture to the decoration, usually of brass, in a shield or similar shape used about a keyhole. Sometimes it is formed by insetting bone, pearl, ivory, or veneer, and then is called an inlaid escutcheon. On the Chippendale styles the 'scutcheon is of the same size as the plates behind the bails. It goes under the name of the willow pattern, perhaps because some of the styles show an interlacing of design.

Etegère. A series of shelves sustained by columns. What is this but a what-not? It has a good ancestry, but has run out.

Extrados. The outside line of an arch.

Façade. The front of a piece of cabinet furniture, being the same term as applied to an edifice.

Facing. The covering of wood for economy's sake used on a cheaper base. It amounts to a heavy veneer.

Faldstool. A folding seat like a camp stool.

Fall front. Same as slant front.

Fan back. A Windsor chair with flaring spindles and curved top rail. A side chair. See FURNITURE TREASURY.

Fascia. A broad fillet. *See* Molding, illustration.

Faun. A fantastic legendary goat-man decoration, used instead of a caryatide in the Adam period.

Fauteuil. A kind of French carved armchair.

Favas. The detail like the cells of a honeycomb, used in Louis XVI decoration.

Feathered. Otherwise plume. Describing the grain as of mahogany or satinwood, which resembles a feather.

Feather edge. The thinning of a board as in paneling to a fine edge.

Federal. Applying to that period of American furniture from 1776, when independence was declared, to 1791, when the Constitution was adopted. It covers broadly the entire Hepplewhite period, but touches late Chippendale in the earlier years. The name is somewhat arbitrary and not distinctive. As it includes, however, all the transition furniture between Chippendale and Hepplewhite, it is convenient.

Feet. See page 30.

Felt grain. The same as clash.

Fender. A screen usually of fretted or pierced brass with rounded corners, and a foot or more high for the fireplace. Sometimes of iron with an iron network and a brass top.

Festoon. A decoration like a wreath in the form of loops. Sometimes called swag.

Fiddle back. Applied to the marking of a violin back in sycamore or maple when in the solid wood or when as veneer in furniture.

Fiddle back. The second meaning refers to the splat in a Queen Anne chair.

Fielded. Said of a panel which is made up of smaller panels.

Filigree. Wire work in gold or silver. In furniture it is a term used of the looking-glass frame decoration of the Hepplewhite time, and on Bilboa glasses.

Fillet. A ledge for sustaining shelves, also a band used as a connection member of moldings. Used also of a ring or other decorative enlargements on turnings as on the middle stretcher of a Windsor chair and the highest decoration on a bedpost.

Filling. The material and the process used in filling the open grains or pores of wood. It is the first process. Always used with oak, mahogany, and often walnut and some other woods. Not used with birch or beech or close-grained woods.

Finger joint. The toggle joint or finger-like connection on table brackets or wide hinges.

Finial. Decorative termination of chair posts or cabinet furniture. See chapter on Finials, page 60.

Fire irons. The shovel and tongs but not till a late period the poker. Used at the fireplace. In good sets they matched the andirons.

Fish-tail back. The carving on the top rail of a banister-back chair which is supposed to resemble a fish tail. *See* Stag horn.

Fitment. A term in more general use in England for an article or for paneling or for built-in woodwork on the walls.

Five back. A chair with five slats in the back. If arched of Delaware Valley origin.

Flame. The designation of a carving rising from the vase, whether spiraled or naturalistic, to imitate a flame.

Flap. Used of a leaf in England. Incorrectly used for the term bracket which supports the leaf.

Flare. Used of the fan spread of back spindles on a Windsor chair, or of the divergence from the central point of the reeds in the back of a chair.

Flat carving. The simple late carving distinguished from the round.

Flat-top highboy. A Queen Anne highboy made before the days of the scroll top.

Flax breaker. A heavy, rough, slotted horse with a scissors-like bar for crushing flax stems.

Flemish scroll. Fully developed as two scrolls meeting as a right angle as a chair leg or back decoration. FURNITURE TREASURY No. 1984.

Fleur-de-lis. A painted or carved motive on chests or chests of drawers, and in many ecclesiastical forms, probably because it suggests a cross.

Flush. Even or equal surfaces which adjoin, and make one surface.

Fluting. A series of grooves which must be as deep as a semicircle, used on pilasters, friezes, legs, or columns. The space between the flutes is important. The richer the effect the smaller the space. Widely spaced flutes are worse than none, and shallow flutes common in commercial furniture are weak. They must end by a quick turn into which a ball will roll.

Fly rail. The swinging bracket of a leaf table. The name easily shows how the butterfly name arose for table.

Foil. The point at the intersection of circular parts as trefoil, etc.

Folding gate leg. A folding table with an extremely narrow top.

Fold-over. Applied to a writing table as on Sheraton desks, which folds over when closed to a position nearly horizontal.

Foliated. The general term applied to any leaf ornament.

Four back. A chair with four horizontal slats in the back.

Four-gate table. A gate-leg table with two gates on each side, usually swinging from the end, but in the best pattern and the handsomer swinging from the center. FURNITURE TREASURY No. 935 and following.

Four post. A name applied to a high post bed. It arose from the fact that beds originally were fastened in the corners and had only one post. Of course, all beds have four posts, but the name is now restricted to high posts.

Framed. Said of any furniture which has a frame as distinct from a piece which is merely made of boards nailed together.

Francis I (François Premier). Style of French furniture in which cartouche carving is a marked feature.

French foot. (*a*) A foot scrolled or spiraled as a dolphin or modification of a dolphin form. (*b*) A slightly swept-out foot in Hepplewhite style. It must be a continuation of the outside of a piece of furniture in a direct line, and never set out as a bracket.

French leg. The peculiar type of leg adopted from the eighteenth-century French style in Victorian furniture and counted a mark of degradation. Not the same as French foot, which see.

Fret, or fretwork. The cutting out of geometrical details which are either applied or carved on cornices or chair legs or otherwise. A prominent feature of Chippendale style.

Friesian, or Friesland. The name given to a scratch carving often in a wheel form found on pine Bible boxes and chests and on tulip-wood spoon racks, or leppel borties.

Frieze. The section under a cornice; that portion between the architrave mold and the cornice mold.

Fruit wood. A designation of furniture usually of the walnut period in pear, apple, or walnut.

Gadroon. A variant of godroon.

Gallery. A miniature fence or hedge or pierced fret, or miniature balusters mounted by a rail. Used as a guard on tea tables. Sometimes also of metal.

Gaming table. A card table or a table used for any game.

Garland. A floral decoration like a festoon, but not necessarily draped.

Garniture. A word variously applied, but used of a set of mantel furniture as a clock and urns. Also of requisites or appointments.

Gate-leg table. In all forms FURNITURE TREASURY No. 935 and following. A gate leg has two uprights and two horizontals. That is, there is a stretcher which swings with the leg. To be distinguished from a swing-leg table of the Queen Anne period.

Geometric pattern. (*a*) Fret designs, as used by Chippendale. (*b*) The arrangements of molds on some chests. (*c*) The sash arrangements on many Sheraton bookcases.

Georgian furniture, early. A term designating the style from the death of Queen Anne, 1714, to the supplanting of the style by Chippendale, 1745 or thereabout. The term Georgian should strictly be early Georgian so as not to confuse it with the Georges of the latter part of the century. The style is sometimes difficult to distinguish from the Queen Anne. The mirrors have heavier frames and often much gilding. But carved legs are often spoken of when of the cabriole shape and carved, indifferently, as early Georgian or Queen Anne. The style is rich and usually in good taste except as in its later developments it adopted rococo detail. Many good judges consider that Queen Anne is the best style in furniture and that the early Georgian is next in choice.

Gesso. Plaster-of-Paris work gilded, and used frequently on looking-glasses. An Italian decoration. Also applied now to similar wood carving, like the gilded beading next the glass on a mirror frame.

Gilding. Always done on old work with gold leaf, and in repairs gold leaf must be used.

Girondole. Specifically a circular looking-glass, convex. Generally the frame has a candle bracket. The name is used also when no glass is present. It was common in the eighteenth century, but the mirror appeared during the close of that century.

Godroon. Otherwise called nulling. A very early decoration which extended into Chippendale style. Small, short flutes, generally sloped, and inverted, as a portion of a base or cornice mold.

Gondola, French gondole. A chair, the back of which is supposed to resemble a gondola of the mid-eighteenth century.

Gooseneck. A name of the shape of the irregular half arch used in the decoration of highboys, chests-on-chests, and secretaries. Between the two arms there is generally a plinth or pedestal for an urn. Same as swanneck or broken arch.

Gothic. That style in furniture derived from the Gothic architecture. First found in cathedrals as appropriate with the stone decoration. It is designated by the centuries. It was chiefly adapted and adopted by Chippendale and not always happily. There is also a revival in the Victorian period, of which the less said the better.

Gouge carving. Used on the corners of simple pieces in the form of a half-round gouge cut from about 1680 to 1720.

Gouty stool. One arranged to adjust by ratchet so that the top is at any angle.

Graduated. Said of drawers as of a chest of drawers, becoming successively narrower from the bottom to the top.

Grandfather's clock. Synonymous with hall or tall clock. Long clock is a frequent English designation. The shape of the case was developed when the long pendulum was invented, to protect that pendulum.

Grandmother's clock. A miniature tall clock.

Greek cross. The cross the arms of which are of equal length. Found in panelwork on chests.

Griffin. A grotesque decoration of a monster consisting of a lion body with eagle head and wings. Applied on Adam and Sheraton furniture as adapted from the French and Italian.

Groin. The rib at the intersection of vaulted surfaces.

Grotesque. A conventional and sometimes humorous figure, including masques carved on Georgian and later furniture.

Ground. The core or base on which veneer is attached.

Guard. A fender for a fireplace.

Gueridon. A round candle stand.

Guilloche. Interlacing curved carved lines made up of circular forms. Banded decoration in one or more lines. Used on furniture of all periods up to the Hepplewhite.

Hadley chest. One carved all over the front with tulip design. So-called merely because the first was found at Hadley, Massachusetts.

Hair cloth. Often used in the latter part of the eighteenth century and generally in the nineteenth. It is sometimes colored or figured.

Half column. An engaged column corresponding to a pilaster. Sometimes used on serpentine chests of drawers fluted or plain, and attached to the chamfered corner.

Hall. Originally the great hall, the room with the vast fireplace with a dais at one end for the quality. From this room opened the other apartments. The modern use of the hall as the space between side rooms and carrying a stair came in during the eighteenth century.

Hall chairs. Chairs with carved backs more or less grotesque, so named by Manwaring.

Hall clock. Synonymous with grandfather's and tall.

Harlequin. A Sheraton table rising automatically at the center and comprising various fittings for toilet or other use.

Harpsichord. Musical instrument in which the strings are picked by crow quill.

Hassock. Not properly furniture. A stuffed footstool without wood.

Hatching. Trellis-like lines crisscrossing.

Haunch. That part of a tenon which projects.

Hayden. "Chats on Old Furniture," and "Chats on Cottage and Farm House Furniture." Good small volumes, English. 1905 and after.

Heart and crown. A name given to the baluster-back chair which has a cresting supposed to resemble these names.

Heart back. The design of a Hepplewhite chair back. It is confounded with and probably indistinguishable from the term shield back.

Heart pattern. Frequently found in ironwork, in oak applied ornaments, chair backs, etc.

Hepplewhite. A style developed under George III by the designer of this name. The first light and elegant style and particularly marked by shield-back chairs. Beginning in the late Chippendale period during our Revolution, it lasted until Sheraton in the 1790s shouldered it out. Hepplewhite's outsweeping French foot is graceful, but undesirable. He used both carving and inlay. A. Hepplewhite & Co. "Cabinet-Maker and Upholsterer's Guide," 1788. 2nd Ed. 1789.

Herringbone. *See under* Inlay. A veneered band or stripe consisting of grain meeting obliquely.

Highboy. A high chest of drawers with long legs. *See* Tall boy.

High chest of drawers. Where there are more than five drawers, a chest of drawers is often called a high chest, distinguished from a chest-on-chest because the latter is built in two parts. Distinguished from a highboy which has long legs.

High relief. *See* Relief.

Hinges. Fully shown FURNITURE TREASURY No. 4502 and following.

Hitchcock chair. A chair dating about 1835 turned with flat elements in the back and a rush seat and usually stenciled.

Hogarth chairs. Applied to a Queen Anne chair back with a side ramp.

Honeysuckle. *See* Anthemion.

Hood. *See* Bonnet top.

Hoop back. The same as bow back applied to a Windsor chair.

Hope chest. *See* Dower and dowry chest.

Horseshoe back. The peculiar form of the bow, sweeping outward a little at the bottom, found in the best bamboo turned Windsors.

Housing. The grooving of one piece of wood into another. If this is not carried out to the edge of the slotted piece, it is called stop housing.

H stretcher. Three stretchers coming together in the form of an H, as used in Windsor chairs, etc.

Husk. A drop ornament, usually the corn flower, sometimes carved, sometimes inlaid. Late eighteenth century.

Husk. Applied to the corn husk as used for the stuffing of bed ticks or the braiding of rugs.

Hutch. A form of chest which opens in front by doors. Also any swing-top table which has a box or cubby underneath the top.

Imbricated. A carving resembling fish scales, used on chests, etc.

Impost. The support of the spring of an arch.

Ince & Mayhew. Published the "Universal System of Household Furniture" in 1762. Some designs good.

Incised. Applied to those carved ornaments which are cut below the main surface, as in shells on lowboys and highboys. Also in the term incised ornament, incisions which were filled with colored material.

Incurvate. The swept-in arm on some types of Sheraton settees or chairs. Applied also in various other connections to any surface curving inward.

Initialed furniture. Frequent on chests and uniformly found on Hadley chests. Carved on a central panel.

Inkwell. Though usually of metal, one is known of wood with a block front.

Inlay. See chapter on subject. A decorative process in which lines, strings, or any decoration are cut into a solid surface, whether or not surrounded by a general veneer.

Intrados. The inner or under side of an arch.

Ionic. The order of Greek architecture following in time after the Doric.

Italian furniture. While Italy is the source of much of the best early furniture designs, it is not a present source. The export of articles of great merit is forbidden. Nearly all the imports from Italy are of new furniture, whatever the buyers may think.

Ivory black. A black substance for staining made from burned bones or ivory.

Jacobean. The style immediately following Elizabethan, beginning 1603 with the reign of James I. In the Renaissance type. The term is usually carried in a general way up to 1690, but strictly it stops with the incoming of Cromwell, 1653, when the subdivision Cromwellian comes in before the Charles II period. This style is carved and turned.

Jamb. The side of an opening as of a fireplace or door.

Jamb hook. The hooks, usually brass, screwed to the jamb of the fireplace as rests for the fire irons.

Japanning. The same as Lacquer, which see.

Jardinière. A box or jar, or construction primarily designed to take flowers. Sometimes a carved decoration. A vase for flowers.

Jewel box. A small box usually veneered and often inlaid.

Joined furniture. Mortise-and-tenon furniture. Hence the name joiner for a cabinetmaker. The only method of good construction except in turned chairs.

Joiner, or joyner. The first term used to designate a good woodworker who made a joint by mortise and tenon. Before the terms cabinetmaker and carpenter.

Joint stool. A mortised and tenoned stool, turned or turned and carved. From Tudor times through the Jacobean.

Jones, William. Published designs of looking-glasses and tables in 1739.

Kas. A Knickbocker or Delaware Valley wardrobe of large size. Furniture Treasury No. 480 and following.

Kauffmann, Angelica. 1741–1807. A celebrated painter of furniture in the Hepplewhite and Sheraton and Adam design. Of course much is attributed to her that she is not responsible for.

Kerf. A saw cut. If curved, it indicates a circular saw and therefore not old work.

Kettle base. A shape used on some early desks and chests of drawers, shaped like a pot-bellied kettle. Otherwise called bombé. In the best specimens the drawers follow the same shape. In poorer specimens the drawer ends are cut back in a vertical line.

Keying. The splining of mitered joints. Keys were also used in old mortise work of some forms.

Keyplate. The same as 'scutcheon.

Keystone. In furniture the centerpiece at the top of an arch.

Kidney. Used of a table imitative of the kidney in shape, like the kidney bean, used by Sheraton. Also used of a shelf-clock opening which is not kidney shaped at all, but is rounded at the top, drawn in at the center, and spreading wedge shape at the bottom.

Kneading table. *See* Bread trough.

Knee. A swelled or convex upper part of cabriole leg, often called the hip.

Knee hole. A name of a table or desk built with an opening at the center between drawers.

Knobs. Of brass or glass or wood. The last style in hardware in the somewhat debased examples of the early nineteenth century. But small wooden knobs were used on seventeenth-century oak and early maple table drawers. Large knobs are peculiar to the Delaware Valley if old.

Knopped. The old spelling for knob. The swelling or vase on a shaft serving as the finial as on an andiron.

Knotted pine. By immense advertising now made popular for paneling or even furniture among those willing to be led astray. Never found in good old work, unless painted. The knot is rough or surrounded by rough surface. It was not known as an old decoration.

Knuckle joint. Term often applied to the carving on the outside end of an arm of the Chippendale or Windsor chair.

Labels. For chapter on this subject see Labels.

Lacquer. The process otherwise called japanning and in France vernis Martin process. See chapter.

Ladder back. Term applied to the successive horizontal slats of any chair. It was used in the Pilgrim period and the late Chippendale.

Laminate. The building up of wood in layers, indicated by three ply, five ply, etc.

Lancashire chair. An English chair from that county.

Lancet. A pointed Gothic arch.

Landscape panel. One in which the grain runs the long way of the panel.

Lantern. Used of a protection for a light with from three sides up to eight, and sometimes circular, and whether carried in the hand or hung up, from the simplest forms to the most elaborate; with horn or glass.

Lantern clock. A shelf clock suggesting a form of a lantern and usually of brass.

L'art nouveau. Applied to French and other furniture with naturalistic legs taken from the juncture of tree limbs. A modern style often loosely used and without standard form. It is largely discredited.

Lattice. The crisscrossing of carved cut-out work usually showing a cross-over. Used under the support of goosenecks and later cabinet crestings. Also of a similar effect in the backs of Sheraton chairs. Sometimes also an inlaid effect.

Laureling. The use of a laurel motive in carving. Frequently found on chests.

Lazy Susan. *See* Dumb-waiter.

Leather. Used plain or as Spanish leather (embossed figures) and in many colors on furniture from the earliest times through the Chippendale era. He was fond of red leather. Stamped was another name for Spanish leather and was prepared in England, also.

Lectern. A reading desk for church purposes of wood, metal, or stone.

Leppel Bortie. The Pennsylvania German name for a spoon rack.

Library table. One larger than a tavern table, but without leaves and not so long as a refectory table, and of a decorative character. Occasionally used of a large drop-leaf table in the Empire style.

Lid. The top of a chest or the hinged front of a desk, and extended to include the top of a chest of drawers.

Linear carving. A shallow carving with flat relief, such as is usually found on American chests. It was later than carving in the round.

Line inlay. *See* Stringing.

Linen fold carving. A sixteenth-century type common on panels and defined by its name. Derived from the earlier Gothic panel decoration.

Linen press. A cupboard with shelves for linen and sometimes with drawers.

Lip mold. The front of a drawer extended usually only on the top and ends by a rabbet and a thumb-nail mold to cover the drawer joint as a dust stop. On the bottom the drawer is molded, but often does not lap. A style general in the Queen Anne period and extended into the Chippendale.

Listel. *See* Fillet.

Livery cupboard. Short for delivery. An English cupboard of oak, often with open spindle work in part for ventilation. The chatelaine distributed rations to the household for the day from this cupboard, and it was also used as an almoner's cupboard.

Lock, Matthias. 1752. Book of designs derived from the Brothers Adam.

Lockwood, Luke Vincent. 1913, and other editions, two volumes. $30.

Long clock. The same as grandfather's, tall, or hall clock.

Loose seat. *See* Slip seat.

Loo table. An oval table used in the game of loo.

Loper. The slides which support the fall front or slant top of a desk.

Lotus carving. A detail resembling that flower.

Louis Quatorze. Distinguished by elaborate carving and gilding and inlay as in buhl work. The beginning of rococo. 1643–1715.

Louis Quinze. Distinguished by straight line and plain surface and often replaced by irregular curved line, especially in furniture. Rich upholstery. Rococo. 1715–74.

Louis Seize. Straight lines, light and simple construction, and pastoral motives in ornament. 1774–93.

Louis Treize. Square and angular furniture with an appearance of podginess. Often with a horizontal division above the center. 1610–43.

Lounge. A name for a late couch.

Low relief. *See* Relief.

Lozenge. Diamond shaped. The name given to panels of the oak or later periods. Also applied to overlays, or the shape of glass in windows or bookcase doors.

Lunette. A semicircular space, as a window. Often applied to a carving motive on oak chests. It really means a little moon.

Lyon, Irving Whithall, M.D., 1891. The important original American work. Small and with few pictures, but scientific and accurate. A rare book, selling for $120 more or less. A reprint recently issued by his family.

Lyre back. A chair or sofa back or table leg decoration used in late Sheraton and early Empire time.

Made-up pieces. A term used to designate furniture made from parts of originals, to which modern additions may or may not have been made.

Mahogany period. Rare examples before 1745. Fairly established 1750, and continuing through all good periods after.

Mantel. The shelf over a fireplace or the entire mantel-work including the pilasters at the sides and often including the over-mantel of panelwork running to the ceiling.

Manwaring, R. "The Cabinet and Chair Maker's Real Friend and Companion," in 1765, and "The Chair Maker's Guild," in 1766.

Maple period. There is no such thing. Maple was used for turnings from the Pilgrim period and for turnings and flat surfaces preferably, and generally narrow, to 1800 or later. Maple was common as the substitute for mahogany and walnut on simple furniture. For broad surfaces pine was used at the same time on the same piece of furniture.

Marquetry. A kind of inlaid work. *See* Veneering.

Mascaron. A large mask or grotesque face. Sometimes carved in oak or mahogany.

Mask, masque. A carved or metal effigy. When in wood often appearing on rich carved work as a portrait or fanciful figure or a grotesque. Compare mascaron.

Master's chair. Said of a very high or tall chair used for carving or for the master of an English livery company.

Medallion. In furniture a plaque of wood or metal sometimes with carved figures.

Medial or middle stretcher. The stretcher connecting the centers of other stretchers forming an H. To abandon this for all outside stretchers in Windsor chairs is to pass to a late or kitchen type.

Melon foot. Ball foot carved to resemble a melon. See chapter on Feet.

Mermaid clock. So-called from the shape and painting of the wooden back board on which a wall clock was placed.

Miniature. Furniture made for children or as samples, or a miniature grandfather's clock which is called a grandmother's clock.

Miserere seats. The carved choir seats in churches so shallow as to be very uncomfortable.

Miter or mitre. The intersection at the corner of a rail and stile or of a mold.

Modillion. Carved brackets variously shaped, which should strictly be placed vertically under a cornice, but which is also found running horizontally the long way.

Module. A unit of measure in the proportions of a design, specifically the tenth of a semi-diameter of a classical column.

Mold, molding, mould, moulding. A contoured band used to decorate panels or surfaces. Illustrations, see index. There are nine so-called classic molds.

Mortise. A cut-out section usually rectangular to receive a projection called a tenon.

Mosaic. Small cubes of wood or stone used as decoration.

Mother-of-pearl. A shell inlay mostly from oyster shells. Used in japanning, etc.

Motive, motif. The ruling stylistic feature or detail of the same in drawing or carving or design.

Mounts. Applied to the brass or metal used for the feet or decoration of furniture. Also ormolu.

Muntin. The divisions between panes of glass or the openings of multiple doors or frames. Properly vertical, though the entire sash is sometimes referred to as muntin.

Mushroom chair. So named from the bulbous top of the arms.

Name chests. Those having the full name carved or painted, as on some Hadley chests and many decorated Pennsylvania chests.

Necking. The narrow band of mold at the top of a shaft.

Needle-point. The name of a style of handwork decorative upholstery, also the end of a needle itself used to attach light moldings.

Neo-Greek. In architecture and furniture applied to the classical revival of the late eighteenth century, and in architecture to the "lightning splitter" cottages of 1830 and thereabouts.

Nested tables. Small light tables each reduced from the next larger, which slide under one another. Not used in the early period.

Newel. The post supporting a stair rail.

Niche. A semicircular recess for a bust or fountain.

Nonesuch chests. Chests showing in inlay Nonesuch Palace built by Henry VIII. No American examples.

Norfolk Sheraton, or Suffolk Sheraton. An application of the Sheraton back to English Windsor chairs.

Norman tooth carving. A carving resembling a molar, square, found on some chests. To be distinguished from Norman serration.

Notch carving. *See* Gouge carving.

Nutting, Wallace. See books by the same author, flyleaf of this volume. The collection of Wallace Nutting is at the Atheneum, Hartford. Smaller collection of mahogany, not published, at his residence, Framingham.

Oak period. The arbitrary date 1690 is fixed as the end of the period.

Oblong. Rectangular, but longer one way than another.

Occasional table. Any small table to be used as occasion calls.

Ogee. *See* Cyma recta. A broken ogee is interrupted in its curve by a fillet.

Ogival. In the shape of an ogee or cyma curve.

One-piece back. Applied to a Windsor chair with a continuous bow and arm.

Onion foot. A flattened ball foot. See chapter on Feet.

Oriel. A projected window segmental or semi-octagon, usually supported by corbels. A Gothic feature.

Ormolu. Brass and zinc composition resembling gold used for furniture mounts. Sometimes engraved in gilt.

Ottoman. A stool or seat with or without a frame, but covered with upholstery.

Out-scrolled. Describing the outward sweep of any furniture curve.

Outset. Said of turned legs which are more than one-half disengaged.

Out-splayed. Slanting or curving outward. Same as splayed used of a table leg.

Overdoor. The decorative form of the woodwork above a door. Usually made by a break of the cornice.

Overlap top. The top or lid of a cabinet piece which projects beyond the frame.

Over-mantel. The panelwork more or less decorative between the mantel and the ceiling.

Overstuffed. Furniture in which all the emphasis is on the upholstery which covers every part of the piece.

Ovolo. A mold. *See* Molds.

Oxbow front. The reverse of serpentine. A complete hollow with a complete swell on each side and a half of the central section repeated on each end as on a chest of drawers. The line followed by the erroneously so-called Winthrop desk, which, however, has the top drawer or breast drawer sloped inward at the top.

Oystering, or oyster-shell veneering. Formed by the diagonal cutting of a small section of wood so as to show grain suggesting the oyster. It is trimmed to fit other pieces and set in solidly as a veneer. A somewhat different meaning is the effect of splitting and opening an oval grained board for matching doors.

Pad foot. Same as disc foot in Queen Anne furniture.

Painted furniture. Chests and chests of drawers of the late seventeenth century with decorative painting. Also later painting.

Palladian. In the style of Palladio, the Italian architect who adapted Greek forms to the arch and supplied the foundation of the style developed from him by Christopher Wren and Inigo Jones.

Palmated. A narrow carving often used on the stiles of chests imitative of the palm branch.

Panel. A board set into a mortised frame often with a feathered edge. The sunken panel is below the surface. The flush panel is flush with the surface of the rails and stiles, though there may be a mold that is sunken, and the raised panel which rises above the surface of the rails and stiles. The earliest style is the sunken panel which may or may not have a lining mold at the sides. The flush panel is most usual. The raised panel was mostly on early work, and sometimes a mold runs around the raised part. True paneling was used abroad earlier than here. Our earliest paneled rooms were about 1700, but paneled walls are not, as a rule, earlier than 1730. All cabinet furniture, practically, of the seventeenth century was paneled on the ends and often the drawer fronts. It is really the only satisfactory method of building deep cabinet furniture. The Chippendale era introduced broad, flat surfaces without paneling; the consequence was that they cracked open, or are doing so now under modern heating conditions.

Papier-maché. Used for decoration before the middle of the eighteenth century and later.

Parcel-gilt. The name applied to decoration which was in part covered with gold leaf.

Parchment panel. Same as linen fold.

Parchment scroll. Or panel. A rolled effect given by a spiral carving on the edge of a surface, as a linen fold or a Chippendale chair back, particularly in America the Gillingham type.

Parlor. Literally the talking place. So named because it was the monk's refectory and they were allowed to talk at meals if ever. The earliest parlor, therefore, was the dining room. When a separate dining room was provided the parlor got its name as the "best room." The dining room was first designated as the dining parlor.

Parquetry. The decoration of a floor by inlay as mosaic. *See* Veneering.

Paterae. Elliptic or circular carved or inlaid ornaments.

Patina. The peculiar copper-color tinge acquired on old finish, said to be impossible to duplicate. This statement is challenged. Patina is also often used to indicate in the phrase "the old patina" the original finish. Patina is a term which rises from the surface acquired on old bronze.

Pear drop. An elongated pear shape same as tear drop, said of brass drop William and Mary handles.

Pear foot. The turning so shaped common on tavern and many other tables at the foot. See chapter on Feet.

Peasant carving. Same as linear carving. Shallow carving and flat surface between.

Pedestal. A low, solid stand. Also the portion beneath an architectural column. Also a table built in pedestal form.

Pediment. The pointed cresting over a cabinet piece or a door or an edifice. The name is also applied to a curved cresting, but not so generally.

Peg. Name given to a leg or foot with a rapid or conical taper.

Pellet. The plugs used to conceal screw heads.

Pembroke table. A small table usually about three feet square with drop leaves held up by brackets. Made in all good periods often with a contoured top. The connection with the Countess of Pembroke who is said to have ordered a table of this sort, may be fanciful.

Pencil and pearl. These names designate the appearance of the small decorative mold turned and set about panels or otherwise. The number of beads between the pencils varies.

Pendant. Any ornament depending from a part of furniture.

Pendulum. The short pendulum was used on many shelf clocks. The invention of the long pendulum, some say in the 1680s, originated the need for the long case or grandfather's clock to protect the pendulum. The pendulum on a hall clock is of a length to swing in one second. The shorter the pendulum the quicker the beat.

Period furniture. That which can be distinctly referred to a style of a certain date.

Petit point. Tent stitch. A short slanted stitch used in worsted or embroidery worked in straight lines from left to right. The favorite rich decoration as for Queen Anne or Chippendale chair seats.

Pewter. Not treated in this work, but in general use to eighteen hundred and in some cases later.

Philadelphia chair. Applied to Queen Anne and Chippendale chairs having the side rail mortised through the back post and wedged, though this style has been seen in New England.

Phoenix. The designation of a bird used on early Chippendale and early Georgian looking-glasses. As this bird is somewhat different from any in existence, we think the name a good one.

Phyfe, Duncan. A New York City maker who came from Scotland and became a large manufacturer beginning in the Sheraton tradition and adopting successively the early Empire and finally falling away into the late Empire. For nearly a half century his work in various styles was found. His name dominates in New York, but there are many other makers in the same styles.

Pianoforte. As an antique found in the Empire outswept-leg style, and also with Sheraton and Hepplewhite legs. The smaller the leg the better. That is, there is a coarse, heavy leg which is late and verges toward the square piano.

Picture papers. Some were hand painted and imported from China, others were made in printed design before 1750. They were, of course, a substitute for paneling. A flock paper made of ground-up felt is on a room in the Webb house, Wethersfield, where it was when Washington used it.

Pie-crust table. Illustrations in FURNITURE TREASURY, Vol. I. A round table of any size with a carved and scalloped edge raised above a depressed center. The standard large size should be 33 inches across or more. Good examples tip and turn and have a carved shaft, carved knees, and very wide claw-and-ball feet. To be distinguished from a plain turned, or molded raised edge, which is called a dish or tray top.

Pierced. A term designating an open fret or scroll as in ladder-back chairs, or the decoration of a high cabinet top.

Pier glass. A looking-glass between windows or in a narrow space.

Pier table. A table built usually to go with a pier glass, from the back of which the glass rises, but is not attached to the table, but to the wall.

Pigeonholes. The compartments as in a desk cabinet or top.

Pilaster. A rectangular or half-round column affixed to a wall or carcase. If rectangular, it is about a fourth of the size of a square and is designed to correspond with any pillar or complete pedestal.

Pilgrim chest of drawers. A small chest of drawers of oak or maple and usually with the drawer, and built on a frame.

Pilgrim furniture. The American name for furniture of the century 1620–1720. Practically synonymous with Jacobean up to the eighteenth century.

Pillar and claw. Tables, as pie crusts, with a central shaft and claw feet.

Pin. All furniture of the best periods was pinned at the mortise. The strong pins are of white oak. Sometimes they are inserted from the inside and do not show on the surface, but in many locations they unavoidably appeared, and their absence means poor or late furniture.

Pine period. There is no such thing. Pine was used for flat surfaces from 1690 to 1830. It was very seldom used for the legs of furniture and should never have been. It goes with maple frames and is never in an elegant form. Pine wall paneling was used from the first.

Pin grain. A fine and unobtrusive quartering in oak.

Pipe box. A box open at the top with one or two long compartments for church-warden pipes. There was usually a drawer below for the tobacco. See boxes, FURNITURE TREASURY.

Pipe tongs. Miniature tongs usually decorative for picking up a coal to light a pipe.

Pivot. Used of a swing leg as on a card table, distinguished from a gate leg which has a stretcher connection also.

Planted. Said of a mold affixed to the carcase.

Plaque. *See* Medallion. Also used of porcelains.

Plaquette. A patera.

Plinth. The base usually plain for a column or an ornament.

Plugging. Inserting wood into brick walls for attaching paneling, etc.

Plume grain. *See* Feathered.

Pockets. The recesses bored out to afford entrance for the heads of screws as table tops of period 1800.

Pole-screen. A screen standing on a pole for a fireplace.

Pollard. The grain caused by successive lopping off of branches to secure figured veneer.

Polychrome. Ironwork in several colors; or inlay which gives an effect of several colors. Also used of any piece of furniture which has more than one color of paint or decoration.

Pond lily. Carving found on an American Bible box.

Porringer corner. A protruding, strongly rounded corner as of small table top. The semicircular part ends with an angular cut.

Poudreuse. A powder stand.

Pounce. A powder in color used by cutters of marquetry to mark out design.

Powder stand. A rich form of a wash stand used for powdering the hair. Chippendale manner.

Press. A wardrobe or a cupboard into which a bed is turned. Also a smaller cupboard for linen.

Press bed. A bed with four or six legs in jointed frame arranged to fold within a closet, the doors of which could then be closed. The ancestor of the folding bed.

Prince of Wales feathers. A style using a three-feather carving in honor of the Prince of Wales in the Hepplewhite time, followed also by Sheraton.

Profile. The contour or shaped outline of a piece of furniture.

Prospect. The name applied to pictures delineating landscapes, cities, or private places, where we should simply say painting, engraving, etc.

Provenance. The region in which a piece of furniture is found; the habitat or home of a particular class of furniture.

Punch decoration. The outlining of lunettes or other figures by punch marks or other figures frequently found on pine chests.

Quadrant. Brass segmental support for the fall fronts of desks, etc. It is occasionally found in the latter part of the eighteenth century, and is a better fitting than rests of wood which pulled out, as it avoided lapses of memory which might break a fall front completely off at the hinges.

Quadrate cross. Cross members from sides of a square found on some chests.

Quarter column. A piece, inserted usually, made by quartering a turning and used on the corners of cabinet pieces either plain, fluted, or carved in foliage. Much used in the fine period with mahogany.

Quartered lumber, as oak. It is prepared by quartering the log and sawing the balance of it directly from the center to the bark, or parallel to the rays. All early clapboards were cut with a froe from the center of a four-foot log and hence were quartered.

Quatrefoil. A Gothic decoration of four sections with foil points. *See* Cinquefoil and trefoil.

Queen Anne. A style of furniture prevailing from about 1703 to long after the death of Queen Anne. It was supplanted between 1740 and 1760 by Chippendale's style.

Queen Anne panel. One having an arched top with short horizontal lines below the arch running to the edge of the panel.

Quilled. Stop fluted. The filling part way of a flute with a round rod of brass or a carved reeding changing to fluting.

Quirk bead. A small half-round or fillet next to a sunken fillet.

Quirk mold. A sunken groove and even sometimes a fillet at the side of a bead.

Rabbet. A joint formed by cutting away an open mortise for drawer ends, used even in the seventeenth century for side-run drawers, along with the type which had one great dovetail.

Radiates. Carved or inlaid rays, as of a shell.

Rafraîchissoir. A cooler.

Rake. A term used of a leg or other part of furniture that is neither horizontal nor vertical. Otherwise called splayed or slanted.

Ramp. A name applied to the quick curve ending in an angle of some American and Queen Anne chair posts. The quick curve of a stair rail before it enters the landing post. Chairs with such posts also called Hogarth chairs.

Rays. Applied to the grain of wood as shown in cross section. Also to the carved or inlaid lines from a sun ornament.

Rebate. A right-angle channel on the edge of a board or other section of wood cut for framing.

Recess. A niche or any alcove.

Reeded panel. A cane chair the back panel of which has side members which are reeded.

Reeding. A decorative form usually on shafts or posts, such as would be shown by tying a bundle of reeds together.

Reel turned. In the term ball-and-reel turning for ball and ring.

Refectory. A seventeenth-century standing table of oak for dining. Long and narrow. Occasionally in walnut if continental.

Regence Period. 1715–23. The period of the rule of Philip, the Duke of Orleans.

Regency Period. 1811–20. The period of the rule of George, Prince of Wales, afterward George IV.

Relief, low. Carving with slight elevation above the ground. High relief: Carving usually more or less cut under, and with varying degrees of depth. The old terms are baso and alto.

Renaissance. The period remarkable for the recovery of the lost arts and the origination of new ones in the fifteenth century.

Replica. Properly a copy made in the same period as the original and by the maker of the original. A reproduction is not a replica, but a replica is a reproduction.

Reredos. An altar piece for the back of an altar.

Restored. Properly restricted to furniture where the major parts and especially the important stylistic portions are original. It is not proper to make a complete chair from one leg and name the result a restoration. Much so-called restoration of this sort is done by completing chair sets.

Return. The working of a mold or other surface to repeat the main element at the end of a strip back to the carcase.

Rhode Island type. A Chippendale chair so designated in a catalog with an interlaced splat and a cupid's-bow crest, and voluted arms with knuckled terminals, and grooved or fluted tapered front legs. The designation is unsatisfactory.

Ribband or ribbon back. The shaping of the splat of a Chippendale chair so as to resemble a ribbon.

Ribbed foot. A Queen Anne foot with three or four toes. The space between is carried up as a flute some distance on the leg.

Ribbon inlay or carving. Work so shaped. Eighteenth century.

Rim top. Synonymous with tray top or raised edge. A turned edge about a tripod table. More rarely the same edge on a rectangular tea table, otherwise called a dish top. To be distinguished from pie-crust edge which is carved.

Ring handles. Brass rings backed by round brass plates used on early Empire furniture. A descension from the oval type.

Rocaille. Rococo ornament.

Rocker. Rocking-chairs become common after 1800; before that they were rare and only two or three are known before 1750, and never in elegant form.

Rococo. The style of ornament under Louis XIV and Louis XV and adopted by

Chippendale with shell or rock forms or dripping water, or too often without any recognized resemblance to anything.

Roe. A figured veneer, spotty like a fish roe.

Roll top. A tambour desk with a segmental cover.

Rope mold. A carving representing a rope, eighteenth century. Same as cable decoration.

Rosace. A circular ornamental member, enclosing usually a rosette.

Rosettes, in furniture. See page 87.

Roundabout chair. A corner chair. A buffet chair. Sometimes used of a round-back chair whose legs are set in the ordinary fashion.

Roundel. A background for ornamentation, in circular form.

Rudder table. Same as butterfly table.

Rule joint. A joint on a table leaf, such as is used on folding carpenters' rules. It is next after the groove joint, in date. Examples of the rule joint are known as early as 1770. It has been universally used since it became established, as when the leaf is down it leaves no open space between the leaf and the top.

Runic knot. An interlaced ornament found in the early northern European nations.

Runout. Before the days of miters the running to a point of molding.

Rush holder. Spring nippers of iron on an iron base to hold a rush light.

Rush seat. A chair seat built of rushes or reeds or flags indifferently so named. These must be cut, of course, in a certain phase of the moon or it is unlucky to use them. They are cut in June and carefully cured, otherwise they would decay. They make a seat which, properly manipulated, is very durable and picturesque, and is the usual material for turned chairs. The splint seat of split hickory is not so good and probably not so early.

Saddle. The central highest point from which a down curve proceeds, as on a Windsor chair seat. Also used of the entire seat and of a hollow chair's top rail.

St. Andrew's cross. A cross in the shape of the letter X. Found on chest panels. This was also the very popular shape of the rich early seventeenth-century chair supports in England.

Salient angle. An outside angle projecting beyond the main surface, as in fortifications.

Salt, below the. The salt was kept in a vessel of some pretension to beauty or decoration. The common people or persons without note sat below it, the guests or the quality sat above it.

Saltire. The X-stretcher arrangement, made in the form of an arch or ogee.

Sampler. Cross-stitch or other stitch usually on linen done by children as exhibits of their educational progress and religious training. Most of them are nineteenth century, but a few are earlier, and very quaint or fine ones are much sought for.

San Domingo. See Woods in Furniture. The finest quality of heavy mahogany.

Sausage turning. A turning for chair rungs, resembling a string of sausages.

Savery, William. See List of American Furniture Makers.

Sawbuck table. A table with plain or scrolled X frame of oak or maple or walnut.

They were held in place by a truss passing through the center of the intersection. Found in their finest form in the Delaware Valley.

Scale carving. *See* Imbricated.

Scallop. The carving of a shell resembling that of the same name, worn by returning palmer from the crusades. *See* Shells.

Sconce. A bracket for a wall light.

Scotia mold. *See* Molds.

Scratch carving. The simplest sort done with a V tool.

Screen. Usually to shield the face from the fire, and in the earlier types a frame covered with fabric and arranged to raise or lower on a pole. Measured drawing in this volume. Also a jointed covered frame in two or more parts, common in Japan.

Scriptoire. A writing desk.

Scroll decoration. A curved detail, as the Flemish scroll.

'Scrutoire. The old name for a writing desk or bureau, derived from the French style.

'Scutcheon. *See* Escutcheon.

Secretary, or secretaire. A fall-front desk.

Secret drawer. Very common in most old desks, but easily found in a few moments' investigation. Erroneously thought to be important.

Serpentine. On a sideboard or a chest of drawers a curve with one full swell and two full concaves and two half swells coming to a point at the corners. When reversed it is called an oxbow. Also used in a more general sense of a waved surface.

Serrated. A Normal zigzag termination of dentils, or an independent zigzag carving. Frequently found on oak chests.

Serving table. A side table for serving in a dining room.

Settee. An open seat for two or more persons with a wooden or cane back, and arms. Opposed to sofa which is upholstered in the back. In many old works on furniture the term is loosely used applied to a sofa or settle or any long seat with a back.

Settle. A form of a settee all of wood, with solid wood ends and a back sometimes hooded. Usually of oak in England and sometimes in Pennsylvania, where it is also found in walnut. The simple form is usually in pine. It was built solidly to the floor in the back to stop a draught toward the fireplace. The seat was often hinged, and a box was built below it.

Sewing table. Same as work table.

Shaped. The same as contoured or conformed, referring to a serpentine or a curved figure on furniture tops or frames of chairs.

Shaving stand. A small dressing glass.

Shearer, Thomas. An English maker to whom the invention of the sideboard, usually accounted as of Hepplewhite design, is ascribed. Cabinet Maker's London Book of Prices, 1788.

Sheathing. The ceiling or the sides of a room in wood with or without bead or other mold at the joint of the board. Where the sheathing runs vertically with a feather edge mold it is called feather-edge paneling, though there is no true panel. The inserted beveled board was cut thinner, as a rule.

Sheep's-head clock. A wall clock so-called from the shape of the wooden back on which the brass case was affixed.

Sheffield plate. Rolled silver plate on copper in use from about 1760 on. Often very beautiful and fashionable as a substitute for silver.

Shell top. A term applied to a demi-dome cupboard carved or ribbed as a shell.

Sheraton. A marvelous inventive genius whose work was more in designing than building. He devised light, straight-leg furniture of every sort and published a book of designs. The principal feature of his chair back is the use of horizontal and vertical members. The legs may be turned and reeded or taper square. Each of the designers of the period borrowed from every other, and designs identical in style are found under two names. Sheraton was a man of cultivation and of unrivaled deftness as a draftsman. He was influenced by the revival of the classical designs such as the Adam brothers rendered popular. His style was supplanted by the Directoire and the early Empire at the close of the eighteenth century. The Cabinet-Maker and Upholsterer's Drawing Book, 1791 to 1794; The Cabinet Dictionary 1803. The Cabinet-Maker and Upholsterer's Encyclopaedia, 1804 to 1807. Sheraton's work was so like much of the French that it was called Louis Seize à l'Anglaise. The collector will, of course, understand that all furniture design is eclectic. A part or the whole of many English designs was taken from Flemish, French, Italian, or other furniture. If the classical motives were banished, little would be left.

Shield back. The name of the outline of a Hepplewhite chair back. Some distinguish the chairs with the point below and angles above as shields, while those rounded below are called hearts. The distinction can hardly be made good.

Shim. A thin piece or slip of wood driven into a crack or used to strengthen a weak or broken splat which is first reduced in thickness so that the shim can be applied as a splice without changing the shape of the splat.

Shoe. A small turning often found below a scrolled chair foot or a long member, like a skid set edgewise and with a scrolled end as a base of some chests of drawers. Used also of a long boxed base on a chair or table.

Show wood. Applied to an upholstered piece with some exposed woodwork. The wood showing on a piece which is nearly covered with upholstery, as the exposed wood on the end of an arm, the balance of which is upholstered.

Shuttle pattern. A shape formed by the intersection of lunettes, one of which is reversed.

Sideboard table. The Shearer sideboard has monopolized the name, so that we add the word table to the term sideboard which in Queen Anne and Chippendale time preceded the conventional sideboard. The early table had no drawer.

Side chair. A chair without an arm. Probably the name arose from the fact that such chairs were arranged about the sides of a room.

Single arch mold. A half round carried about drawers of highboys, chests of drawers, etc., in the William and Mary period. An astragal.

Single gate table. A gate leg with one gate on one side, with one leaf. A tuckaway table.

Six back. A chair with six slats in the back. With this large number they are usually of Delaware Valley origin. The slats are arched. One such chair has been found with seven backs and cabriole legs.

Six-legged highboy. Used to designate the William and Mary style. One lowboy also is known with six legs, and one highboy of the type is known with four legs.

Skirt. The same as apron.

Slant front. The slanting lid or cover of a cabinet or desk or secretary. It must be cleated to be good.

Slat back. Any chair with horizontal slats, otherwise a ladder back.

Sleepy Hollow. A name given with a loose designation to any round-back, deep, upholstered chair.

Slides, or sliders. Also called lopers. Vertical slides at the ends of a top drawer of a desk which draw out and support the writing table.

Slip. The grooved strip on which a drawer bottom runs.

Slipper foot. A descriptive name for the elongated Queen Anne foot, practically the same as snake foot.

Slip seat. A frame seat slipped or dropped into an open chair frame and removable. Called also loose seat.

Slot screws. Screws fixed in metal slots permitting the wood to come and go.

Snake foot. A flattened pointed foot, a variation of the Queen Anne foot. See chapter on Feet.

Socle. A plinth or base to a cabinet piece.

Sofa. An upholstered settee. Furniture Treasury No. 1586 and following.

Sofa table. A table usually English with leaves at the ends in Sheraton design.

Soffit. The under side of an arch or any decorative member.

Spade pattern. A carving on some chests suggesting the shape of a spade.

Spade toe. See chapter on Feet.

Spandrel. The space curved on one side and with the other two sides straight between an arch and a corner.

Spanish foot. A ribbed foot curling under. See chapter on Feet.

Spherule. A little sphere. Such are used in repeats on cornices.

Spindle. Any small turned piece, as of a Windsor chair.

Spinet. A musical instrument antedating a piano. Smaller than a harpsichord with one string of brass or steel wire to each note.

Spinning Jenny. A flax wheel. Always small and to be distinguished from the spinning wheel which was for wool, and large.

Spinning wheel. The large wheel for spinning woolen yarn.

Spiral. A turning worked by hand in a spiral form of chair, or table legs.

Splat. The upright central back piece in a chair. Usually Queen Anne. Called banisters only when there are several and narrower.

Splay. A bevel or rake or straddle, as of a chair leg or court cupboard side.

Spline. A thin section set into deep grooves to join boards or planks. The spline should be of diagonal grain, otherwise it will have no strength. It is the only proper method of connecting heavy tops in furniture. If stopped short of an end to conceal it, it is called a blind spline. It is also used to set in diagonally across mitered corners of bracket feet, to make them a solid unit. To connect boards less than an inch thick by a spline may result in the curling of the surfaces. In that case a shallow matching with dowels is safer.

Splint seat. A seat made of thin, flat strips of hickory or other wood to take the place of the rush seat, but less comfortable and less durable and less ancient. It was probably introduced where rushes were not common.

Split gate. Said of a table the gate of which is a half of one of the legs. Usually of hard pine and often of Spanish origin.

Split handles. Brass drops like split turnings used on Queen Anne period furniture. The halved tear-drop handle.

Spool turning. The reverse of ball turning. Late seventeenth century. To be distinguished from the machine-turned spool beds of the nineteenth century.

Spoon back. Applied to the shape of a Queen Anne chair back, which is supposed to fit the human back and supposed to be of the shape of a spoon handle.

Spoon rack. A rack usually carved and with slotted rails for receiving spoons and often with a box below for knives. Frequent in the Delaware Valley.

Squab. A loose cushion.

Staff bead. Same as return bead with a quirk on each side.

Stag horn. A scroll on the top rail of a banister-back chair roughly resembling a stag horn. *See* Fish tail.

Stamped decoration. Struck into the wood from a punch filed to a geometric figure.

Stamped or stampt. An old term for printed, as referring to wall paper, calicos, etc.

Standard. The supports holding up a toilet glass frame; also used as the shaft of a table.

Standing table. A table with a frame as distinguished from the earlier trestle and removable board.

Starfish carving. Found on a Bible box.

Steaming. A method of treating wood to prepare it for bending in a form.

Steeple top. Said of andirons or other furniture with a spire-like finial.

Stenciled. A style of decoration on the Hitchcock chair at the beginning of the machine period.

Steps. (*a*) Receding shelves for china, as on a highboy. (*b*) Movable steps for ascending a high bed. (*c*) Library steps, often in conjunction with a folding Sheraton chair.

Stile. The vertical member of a panel frame or any vertical construction of a single piece. The lock stile meant that side of a door which carried the lock. Used in conjunction with rail which is mortised into it and is horizontal.

Stippling. Impressing a plane surface with dots to break up the reflections on the backgrounds of carving.

Stone-top table. A side table with a marble top which is, however, never so designated. Queen Anne and Chippendale time. Used as a sideboard or hall table. To be distinguished from the Victorian marble-top furniture.

Stone-top tea table. A slate set in the center surrounded by a wide band of inlay.

Tops regarded as foreign, possibly Swiss. Much prized in America. Furniture Treasury No. 1041 and following.

Stools, use of. Before 1700 chairs were rare and often only the head of the house had one, the rest of the family sitting on stools. They were often high enough so that the feet, to avoid chilblains, could be rested on the table stretcher.

Strapwork. A carved detail resembling a strap and often interlaced, as a large guilloche.

Stretcher. The lower connecting and bracing member of a table or chair to stiffen the legs. When turned, called a rung.

Stringing. A narrow band of inlay running about a drawer or a square leg. Same as line inlay.

Stub tenon. A short tenon.

Stucco. *See also* Compo. Made of glue whiting, etc., for pressed decorations.

Stuck mold. A mold worked on the solid and not applied.

Stud. A knob as found for the cording of an old bed.

Stuff over. *See* Overstuff.

Stump foot. A short, awkward foot of country-made Dutch chairs.

Style. The distinctive form of furniture as derived from the period, as Chippendale.

Summer-house chairs. Rustic or scrolled frames and back which might be in iron.

Sunburst. The complete circular carving of rays from a center. *See* Sunrise.

Sunflower. A decorative carving on some Connecticut chests, called also an aster.

Sunk bead. A half-round mold sunk below the surface, not common, nor usually as good as a cock bead.

Sunrise carving. A semicircular fanlike carving representing the sun one-half above the horizon. Sometimes also in the form of inlay. Either may be on a flat or demi-dome surface.

Surbase. The group of moldings in architecture at the top of a pedestal. In furniture the part between the cornice and plinth.

Swag. Suspended or draped ornament or festoon.

Swanneck. Synonymous with gooseneck.

Swedish. A type of furniture somewhat resembling our Pilgrim period, except that it is quite generally painted. It has been imported into America and an effort made to pass it off as Pilgrim furniture. Hence it has fallen into evil repute. The designs, however, are often meritorious and picturesque. Sweden has now put a ban on the export of fine examples.

Sweep. Used for long, sweeping curve.

Swell front. Goddard uses the word swell to indicate one of his block fronts. We apply it more generally to a rounded drawer or segment, or to a chest of drawers built with one convex curve.

Swept whorl. Said of a top rail of a Chippendale from the peculiar knuckle-like ear.

Swing leg. A pivoted leg ordinarily attached to the frame by a finger joint as of a card table.

Tabernacle. A small cupboard, decorative, used for precious articles or possibly jewelry, and doubtless named from the elaborate constructions of metal or stone in cathedrals.

Table clock. The same as shelf clock. A short clock actuated by a spring.

Tabouret. A stool.

Tall boy. The English term for highboy.

Tall clock. Same as grandfather's or hall.

Tambour. A rolling slide made by gluing light half rounds or slats to canvas or linen.

Taper. A term applied to legs diminishing regularly toward the foot as Hepplewhite or Windsor.

Tapestry. Perhaps always imported. In a rich house used for wall hangings.

Taproom table. Same as tavern table.

Tassel. Said of a silk tassel or of the carved semblance of the same, as on a Chippendale chair.

Tavern table. Otherwise called a taproom or an inn table. An occasional table, small, which derived its name from the fact that in the old days, as yet in England, a patron of an inn was served where he happened to sit by bringing up a small table for his drink or refection. A small, four-leg table without a leaf.

Tea caddy. A box usually veneered or inlaid or otherwise decorated. Of course, they were also found in metal.

Teaster. A variant spelling of tester.

Tea table. Usually a tripod table often with a rim or pie-crust top, circular for the fashionable service of tea, which went out of date just before the Revolution. *See* pie-crust and rim and dish and tray. Sometimes rectangular.

Tear drop. A brass drop handle for drawers of the William and Mary and Queen Anne periods.

Template. A pattern of wood or metal.

Tenon. A reduced section with a square shoulder made to fit into a mortise.

Term. An architectural column or stand. Originating as a boundary post, often topped by a statue. The term is square and usually vase shaped. Much affected by Chippendale.

Tern feet. On three-legged work of Louis XV and the Chippendale style.

Tester. The goods, cloth, or netted covering, synonymous with canopy for a bed.

Tête-à-tête. A sofa for two formed with an S-shaped back, so that the occupants sit on opposite sides.

Thicknessing. The increasing of the thickness of a top by attaching mold under its projection.

Thistle. Found painted on some American furniture of about 1700 with the English royal elements of the fleur-de-lis and the crown.

Three back. A chair with three horizontal slats in the back.

Three-chair back. Any long seat made with three backs connecting.

Three-drawer chest. A chest with three drawers, but with an upper section with lifting lid like true chest. Very rare.

Three feathers. A carved decoration in honor of the regent whose arms bore this device in the Hepplewhite time. Sometimes it was varied by a five-feather design.

Some have tried to persuade us that this was an American revulsion from royalty.

Three-part glass. A type of looking-glass common in the Empire time and growing more rare with earlier styles. Used on a mantel. It is always long horizontally.

Three-toed foot. The drake foot. A Queen Anne modification of the disc foot.

Thumb-nail mold. *See* Mold.

Thunderbolts. A name given to a bundle of reeds diverging on Sheraton sofa decoration.

Thurming. A so-called square turning.

Tiger stripe. Same as zebra stripe, a round-and-round stripe as in curly maple.

Tilt top. Said of a table with hinged top.

Timepiece. The name given by Simon Willard to a shelf clock, usually called a banjo, especially when placed on a bracket. It does not strike, hence the name.

Tip and turn. Said of a tea table made so that the top tips and turns.

Toilet table. Resembling a card table, but without the double top. Same as dressing table.

Torchère. The French term for a candle stand usually ornate.

Tortoise shell. Used in japanning or in buhl work.

Torus mold. A large, regularly rounded, convex mold. Small mold of the sort is called an astragal.

Tracery. Fretwork, either cut from the solid or overlaid, also such work in wood or metal in Sheraton doors with silk backing.

Trafalgar type. A late Empire chair with rope-mold top rail and a carved slat.

Trammel. An adjustable pot hook for a fireplace. Also an instrument for marking ellipses.

Transitional. Descriptive of any chair which has elements of two contiguous periods, as Queen Anne and Chippendale, or Chippendale and Hepplewhite. A mixed design.

Tray top. *See* Rim top.

Treillage. Trellis work made with laths.

Trencher. The flat vessel, large or small, wood, pewter, or silver, used by individuals at table, or a large receptacle for the roast. Individual trenchers hollowed from both sides were sometimes used, and reversed for the second course.

Trenching. Same as grooving.

Trestle and board. The earliest known form of a table supported either on a horse or a T trestle. The top is removable. Only two of seventeenth century are known of American origin.

Trestle-end gate leg. FURNITURE TREASURY No. 942.

Triangular chair. The earliest form known. It's doubtful if any are American.

Triglyph. Three vertical V-shaped applied decorations, about one diameter apart or less and chamfered at the top and bottom to agree with the vertical angle. Applied on the frieze or drawer of oak cabinet pieces. A copy of the Greek decoration.

Tripod. Referring to three-legged tables splaying from a central shaft, pedestal, or standard, found in nearly all styles.

Triptych. A carved or painted three-part piece the sides folding over the center.

Trivet. A three-legged openwork frame of iron, often with a handle, to place over coals to hold a vessel as a porringer.

Troichilus. A complex hollow curve.

Trumeau. A pier or pier glass.

Trumpet turning. A William and Mary leg design distinguished from the cup turning or bowl turning which has a trumpet surmounted by an inverted bowl. See drawings FURNITURE TREASURY Nos. 4772–76.

Trundle bed. A child's bed, low, on trucks, made to be pushed in the daytime under a large bed.

Truss. In furniture the bar to stiffen a table frame and running between the supporting ends.

Tuckaway table. A small, oval, single gate leg the top of which hinges when shut to a vertical position. FURNITURE TREASURY No. 941.

Tudor rose. A carved rose conventionalized.

Tulip. The conventionalized carving of a tulip. Used on the side panels of sunflower chests, on painted chests, and in Pennsylvania hardware. An ancient and widely diffused decoration.

Turkey work. The designs like oriental rugs in texture specifically made and imported in sizes adapted for the upholstery of the seats and backs of chairs.

Turning. Lathe-worked portions of furniture. Usually applied to decorative turning. A plain, straight turning is called a dowel.

Turnip foot. See chapter on Feet.

Turtle backs. The same as bosses.

Tuscan. A variety of the Doric order of architecture.

Two back. A chair with two broad slats in the back. Very few are known, and they are probably of the seventeenth century.

Two-chair back. Any seat made with a back of two chairs connecting.

Undercut. A French mold also called sloper nose which is undercut; also carving that is cut in high relief and cut away sufficiently on the back to give an effect of standing almost free and with portions actually separate from the back. High relief carving.

Underframing. The same as stretchers. That is, that part of a frame below the main frame which is surmounted by a top, as a table.

Underslung. Said of a drawer upheld by side rungs, but having no rail beneath it.

Unicorn. Found painted on some Pennsylvania chests of about 1800.

Uprights. The back legs of a chair.

Urn top. Said of andirons made with an urn finial, or of beds, or of chairs, so turned.

Valance. A border of hanging material or any material on a bed rail.

Varangian. A three-cornered chair supposed to have been introduced into England from Scandinavia and to have been brought from Byzantium. Possibly one may be American. It is a very uncomfortable turned chair with a wooden seat.

Vase end. A pattern largely used on trestle tables. A half section of a vase pattern is the usual design of a Welsh dresser.

Vaulting. Same as arching.

Vauxall. Applied to heavy plate glass of the old style.

V brace. Applied to the brace-back Windsor which has two raked spindles in the tailpiece.

Veneer. See chapter on same.

Venetian sun blinds. Used before the Revolution and painted.

Vernis Martin. A French lacquer of the eighteenth century.

Vignette. A running ornament of fine leaves and tendrils of the Gothic period.

Vitruvian scroll. A classical form.

Voider. A butler's tray.

Volute. The spiral scroll capping Ionic and other columns. Found also on the ears of Windsor chairs and some goosenecks.

Wagon seat. A double seat of the Windsor type usually, or with slat back, used in New York and Pennsylvania in market wagons and removable for use in a dwelling.

Wag-on-the-wall. A clock attached to the wall and without a long case to protect the pendulum. Probably of Dutch origin.

Wainscot. Properly wagon oak. That is, quartered oak fit to use in panel oak, since the early wains were made of that material. Now applied to the wall finish higher than a dado, which is properly of quartered oak, but is applied to paneling of other woods.

Wainscot chair. A chair with a solid back. There are very few of American origin.

Waist. The central smaller section of a tall clock.

Walnut period. The same as Dutch, including William and Mary and Queen Anne, 1690–1745 or thereabouts. Continuing more or less in America to 1760.

Wardrobe. A cabinet piece with doors full length or part length with drawers below, for hanging or storing garments. Rare in America, if of American workmanship.

Warming pan. A brass, shallow, covered pan for coal to move about between the sheets. The earliest had an iron, the latest a wooden handle.

Warp. The curl of planks or boards. The curl is always away from the center. That is, the center is the lowest point near the heart of the tree.

Wash hand stand. The English name for a washstand. The inference is amusing.

Washington, Martha, chair. A Sheraton armchair with upholstered back. The term is sometimes applied to a lower back chair of Chippendale type, but probably improperly.

Washington, Martha, looking-glass. A Georgian looking-glass. It derived its name from the fact that one of these was found in the Washington family furniture.

Washington, Martha, table. A work table with drawers and chamfered corners. Sheraton time.

Water bench. A low bench with cupboards below and a shelf above, often with a row of drawers. Used as the family wash bench in the Delaware Valley.

Water gilt. Gold-leaf gilding on brass mounts.

Water leaf. An elongated laurel found on late eighteenth-century furniture.

Wave mold. A late, undulating line of molding.

Web foot. A specialized Queen Anne foot, cut with three or four toes with a connection between somewhat resembling a web foot.

Wedgwood plaques. Used sometimes inset in Sheraton furniture.

Welsh dresser. A dresser always in oak, originating in Wales, and improperly applied to any American dresser, which is never of that material and never has the end board contour of the Welsh dresser.

Wheat ear. A carving attached to wires of filigree mirrors. Also used on Hepplewhite chairs, usually in clusters of three or five on the top rail.

Wheel back. A decoration on some English Hepplewhite and transition chairs and Windsor chairs. Very uncommon if in America.

Wheel chair. A chair with a circular seat distinguished from the wheel back.

Wig stand. Same as powder stand.

William and Mary. Designation of furniture from about 1690 to 1703. Walnut with six-legged chests of drawers and chairs with high backs.

Willow pattern. The scrolled brass plate of various shapes used on Chippendale furniture and sometimes pierced, whence possibly the name was derived. The edge must always be carefully beveled and filed by hand. Otherwise it is a cheap stamped modern affair. The attachment must always be either by wires clinched on the inside of the drawers or by brass with irregular nuts within.

Window seat. A long bench without back but with ends to place in a window recess.

Windsor chair. A stick-leg chair. Any furniture the seat of which is solid wood and receives the legs by a boring. The backs are formed of spindles running into a bow or a bent top rail. The English type has a hard-wood seat, often elm, which is thin and therefore not deeply shaped, and uncomfortable. The back is often attractive, but the arms never. The legs lack grace. The American chair with a thick, deeply shaped and therefore comfortable seat of one piece had its legs set in farther from the corners and achieved a greater grace in the turning, and the rake of the leg. A work by the author on this chair is out of print, but FURNITURE TREASURY shows more illustrations of the Windsor than that book, beginning with No. 2507. This volume shows the only veritable Windsor rocker I have ever seen. Of course, it is late, made after the good Windsor style. The Windsor chair is the only chair which is both comfortable and cool, its closest rival being the rush-seated chair.

Windsor table. There is no reference to the town Windsor, Connecticut, in this name. A table whose legs run in as dowels to the top, and whose turnings resemble somewhat Windsor chair legs.

Wine cooler. A lead-lined box ofter veneered or carved for wine cooling.

Wine wagon. A receptacle for wine bottles which was rolled about the table. Otherwise called a traveling wine holder.

Wing chair. A chair with upholstered sides to protect from the wind, popular in the Queen Anne and Chippendale time.

Woods in furniture. See chapter on same.

Work box. A veneered rectangular box sometimes on a stand for ladies' use.

Work table. A small table or stand in early form with four legs, later with three, and drawers designed for a housewife's work table.

Wormholes. Applications recommended to arrest the eating of worms is the injection or fuming with gasoline or burning sulphur. Of course the finish will be injured.

Wrister. *See* Cuff.

Writing table. Applied to a table with a flat top, and usually with drawers. Also applied to the slant top and the section back of it on a writing desk when turned down.

Wrought iron. The usual material for all shaped utensils about a fireplace and for applied hardware on an edifice. Its best development in America was in Pennsylvania. Cast iron, however, has been used for about five hundred years, but for heavier articles.

X stretcher. Same as cross stretcher.

Yoke. The hollowed shape as on a chair back usually called a saddle.

Yorkshire furniture. English furniture from that county.

Zebra stripe. The marked circular stripe on a curly maple leg or post.

Zigzag carving. A toothed Norman decoration on arches or chests.

THE PERIODS

Date	American	Foreign		Remarks
—1603		Tudor		
1558–1603		Elizabethan		Very heavy, little exists
1603–1649	1620 Pilgrim oak cabinets	Jacobean (Stuart)	Louis XIV 1643–1715	Turned, carved
1649–1660	Maple chairs	Cromwellian		Turned, somewhat simple
1660–1689	Oak, maple, and walnut	Carolean		Cane seat, carved frame
1689–1702	Walnut and maple	William and Mary	Early Dutch	Bold turnings
1702–1714	Walnut and maple	Queen Anne	Late Dutch	Cabriole leg
1714–1740	Walnut and maple	Early Georgian	Louis XV 1715–1774	Queen Anne cabriole leg
1740–1754	Walnut, early mahogany, and maple	Early Chippendale		Queen Anne leg, carved
1754–1785	Mahogany, cherry, and maple	Late Chippendale	Louis XVI 1774–1789	Straight leg, fretted
1776–1791	Federal	Hepplewhite and late Chippendale		
1780–1800	Mahogany	Adam		Classical, overlaps others
1780–1795	All mahogany from this time	Hepplewhite	French foot	Shield and heart
1795–1810	Jeffersonian, 1801–09	Sheraton		Straight leg, classical
1792–1810	Constitutional, Madison, 1809–17	Directoire		Egyptian sources. Long curves
1810–1820	Constitutional, Monroe to 1825	Early Empire		Long curves, somewhat coarse
1820–1835	Jackson, 1829–37	Late Empire		Coarse, clumsy
1837–	Van Buren, 1837–41	Victorian	Imitations of Louis XV	and pseudo Gothic

UPHOLSTERY

Little help can be given on a subject so technical where work is out of sight, but that little we attempt to give.

Regarding beds, the box spring which seems the best thing for a good bed begins with a wooden frame the sides of which are cut like an L so that the frame will sink beneath the bed frame in part and for about half of its depth project over the bed rail flush with the outside. The same process of construction should be followed with the foot and the head. This makes necessary a frame built with cut-out corners. The section which sinks below the bed rails is, therefore, rectangular, but the section which goes over them has corners notched to match the particular post of the bedstead to which the box spring is to be fitted. About an eighth of an inch all round is left for ease in installation of the lower projection, and a quarter of an inch is left on the notched corner each way so that the sheet may be drawn in between the posts and the spring. The box is made about a sixteenth of an inch smaller than the outside of the rails, top, bottom, and sides, so that after the goods are applied it will not project over the rail. The box must be made of soft wood, otherwise it would be too heavy to handle. It consists of solid sides, but of slats set flush into the bottom to go under every row of springs which are placed as near together as feasible. The springs on the outside over the rails are only half as deep. The springs require a strip of ticking or some such material between them and the wood to which they are attached, so that they will make no noise. The top of the spring, after all springs are tied properly, is covered with burlap, then with a layer of cotton batting, and then six pounds or more of hair very carefully picked out and distributed evenly. The amount depends upon the size of the spring. The ticking is then applied over every part, including the sides, ends, and bottom, to keep out dust. We are thus particular because this construction makes a perfect bed as to appearance and comfort and style. The old method of sinking a square-edged spring between the rails and sustaining it with irons has been abandoned. The objection to it is that it leaves a hard edge where the rails are and not only narrows the bed, but in process of time has a bad appearance, as the use of the bed may leave the edges higher than the center. A box spring like this is installed from the foot, which has no rail. The projecting rabbet at the head is put in place first, and then the foot will drop into place. The total depth of the spring should be about nine inches.

Some modern mattresses are made with an inner spring. The method, however, of using all hair supplies a fine job and directions are confined to that only. The quantity of hair depends upon the size, but ranges from thirty-two pounds for a medium-hard single mattress to fifty or more pounds for a wide bed. There is a difference in tastes, some people liking a very hard mattress. The only manner in which a customer is sure of his material is to watch the process, unless he is dealing with a party of the utmost reliability. The writer was supplied with inferior materials by a man who had gained his confidence.

The very highest class of materials is superfine white curled hair. It is better than customers order as a rule. The next best and the usual material for a good bed is the best quality of black drawings. Beds made up in this manner are not cheap, but will last a long time and are cool. The objection to cotton or various patent or widely advertised fillers is that they are heating, and tend to pack together.

The material of the tick should be, of course, the best, and the plain blue stripe is substantial, but some prefer a fanciful figured ticking. The manipulation of the hair to secure an even surface and the proper stitching of an edge to hold form are matters requiring probity and skill. A second stitching, called the imperial edge, to hold the edge from bulging, is often used. A mattress of this sort well filled and properly tied, placed above the spring which has been described is the foundation of a perfect bed proper to go with the good old design of a bedstead.

Of course, in the old days such beds were unknown. There was a feather bed on top of a husk bed which in turn was on top of a corded foundation or a laced canvas.

The upholstery of chairs and sofas, like that of beds, covers a multitude of sins, as it is usually done. The chairs of the best periods, Queen Anne, Chippendale, Hepplewhite, and Sheraton, having usually an open and enriched back, require only a seat for upholstery. The slip seat is made with a play of about an eighth of an inch to allow the material to go around it. The slip frame is halved at the corners and should be a solid job, often projecting at the back with cut corners, or slips under the base of the splat.

The upholstery of old chairs was distinctly uncomfortable and was not meant to be anything else, since the side chair was used merely for meals or brief occupancy. Webbing is tacked across the under side of the slip frame, and the best hair is then evenly distributed and covered with the material selected over a cotton foundation to hold the hair in place. The material should go around the sides of the frame and tack on the bottom, which is then covered with plain goods.

If the slip seat is not used, the webbing strips in the old days were attached near the upper edge of the seat frame and so had little depth. The material should completely cover the frame and be tacked on the under side. Most modern jobs on antique chairs are ruined by cresting the seat too much and hiding the back of the splat near the bottom. Old chairs were so upholstered that the seat did not rise much.

If it is desired to make a more comfortable chair, that object should be secured not by putting in more material at the top, but by attaching the webbing at the bottom of the seat frame so that springs may be introduced as on a box spring, or so that a deep layer of hair may be used. This method of using springs is very much followed in the case of wing chairs or any other easy chairs.

It will, of course, be noted that the richest chairs are made with a slip seat. This is essential in order to leave visible a frame with a handsome outline or carving. It is also the most sanitary and the least expensive upholstery, since a slip seat may easily be removed for renewal or cleansing without removing the chair with it. It is always an unwise proceeding to allow any good piece of furniture to leave the house. Most of the damage to old furniture comes about by such removal.

In case upholstery is used on the arms or the back, there was very little hair in the old days used on the wings, and that, of course, all on the inside. None at all was used under the goods which ran over the arm, but the entire back of a wing chair must be covered. The expense is sometimes large with fine goods, and the device is followed of using plain goods for the back in some cases. The fitting of the goods about the arm of a stylish wing chair is very difficult, as it is necessary to avoid cutting the material, and only an expert can accomplish this object properly.

Cushions are amongst the oldest objects of upholstery, being almost as old as civilization. They may be of all hair of any selected grade, or of half hair and half down. Down is the breast feathers of the goose, and the best quality is sold for several dollars a pound.

It is entirely proper to use a cushion with a rush seat or a wooden seat, or with any easy chair, and of course on squab stools.

A great number of fine old carved chairs has been ruined and fine finials have been cut from the tops of turned chairs to upholster them.

As to the materials for the final cover of upholstery, the choice is extremely wide, and almost anything is allowable except that plush should be avoided like the plague. Much misapprehension exists regarding very early chairs, people presuming that the upholstery was simple. On the contrary, the oldest chairs that we know were covered with the richest upholsteries. The splendid examples of oak and walnut in the sixteenth century were upholstered with the most exquisite material procurable, such as magnificent velvets and cloth of gold.

It was the simpler chairs like the rushed seat examples of 1620 to 1720 that were fitted with buff leather cushions. Such cushions, however, are inviting for their substantial and comfortable qualities. Leather was also used on the seats for rich chairs more or less in the Queen Anne and Chippendale periods. A red leather for dining chairs is particulary appropriate, or for dens or halls or even reception rooms. Leathers of various colors to suit the scheme of a room are also employed and are available in various grades, even richly stamped leathers in the Spanish style for chairs of that type or approaching it.

It is not necessary to enter upon the matter of upholstering settees or sofas or stools, as the methods are the same as followed with chairs. It is well for convenience to divide the cushions of a sofa.

No suggestions are given regarding overstuffed furniture called in England stuffed over, for the reason that it is abominable. The inside of the chair may be made as comfortable as possible and in good taste. But who uses the outside of a chair? Of course, the fashion of overstuffing arose from the appeal it makes to manufacturers to cover up cheap construction.

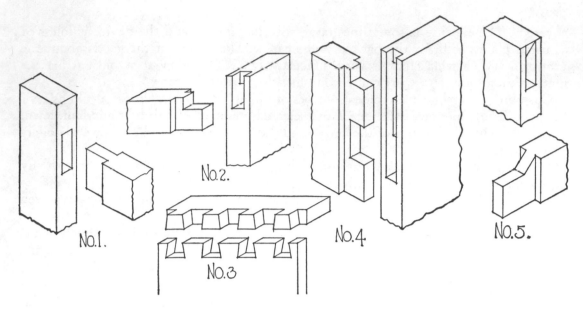

MORTISES AND JOINTS

In the illustrations above No. 1 represents the most usual method of plain mortising. It is the joint used for the stretchers of tables and chair legs of the earliest types. It perhaps should go without saying that the fitting should be very carefully done, so as to go together with some friction. The same mortise may be used for the main frame of the table below the top, unless the frame is narrow, in which case it would be necessary to make an open cut like No. 2.

No. 4 represents the usual method if the members are wide, and shows a doubling of the tenon. There is no advantage of cutting away between the two tenons. It is as simple to leave the tenon as one. The No. 5 is called a foxtail wedge, made so that a wedge can be driven in on the under side and glued.

Of course, in the No. 4 the same method would be used if the mortise was closed at the top, and in modern cabinetmaking the tenons would be cut back, as a rule, to the main shoulder. In fact, all these little quirks and variations which were so common in the old work were often of slight advantage, if any.

In the case of the joining of a turned piece it is always good practice to leave the end of the turning square, so as to join it just the same as one would if there were no turning.

No. 3 represents the method of dovetailing used from about 1740 onward. A shop that employs several men often deputes all the dovetailing to one man, who does nothing else day in and day out. Good cabinetmaking is manifest in perfect dovetailing more than anywhere else, except in the mortise joint.

For the insertion of shelves it is usual to cut a plain shallow rabbet the width of the end of the shelf and to drive the shelf in from the back, but to stop the groove about half an inch from the front so as to secure a blind joint.

The most difficult joint and one which was used by Goddard is a dovetail on a miter called a secret dovetail. Instead of the plain miter dovetail, sections rise on the slope of the miter. The object is to connect the square of a post, as a highboy, with the frame in a more secure manner than could be done with a plain miter. Goddard then sometimes faced the legs of his Queen Anne highboys with a heavy horizontal veneer so that the face of the whole piece showed grain running one way.

The plain keying, like a dovetail except for the right-angled cap, is not used in the good old work, but is the common method in machine box joints. It is practically the same joint as the finger joint of the swinging bracket on a Pembroke or a straight-leg mahogany dining table. The ends of the keys are rounded on the outside, and the pin, running through all, makes a hinge.

The plain butt joint I scarcely remember to have seen on early furniture, although tables are frequently met with having this plain joint on the leaves, and the owners allege that they are original. We find the occasional very short mortise and tenon, perhaps three, running across the length of the leaf, as often in English work. It is the same joint as is used for the insertion of separate leaves. We also find the shallow groove joint like a matching, except that it is shorter in the tenon; and we find the rule joint, which is the latest and most difficult to make and the most finished job.

The blades or slips or divisions between the drawers of a chest of drawers should be and usually are dovetailed to prevent the spreading and may or may not be blind dovetailed. If the frame is to be covered by a mold, the dovetailing is not blind because it is hidden by the applied mold. This dovetail is often single, that is, it is flared on one side and right angled on the other as the strain is not great.

In the Hepplewhite and Sheraton time it was usual to groove the leg the whole length to receive the end panels which were rabbeted for that purpose, but the groove must be deep enough to permit of pinning.

The backs are usually put on by rabbeting the back posts and sinking the back flush with the post. The old wood preferred for this purpose was chestnut, perhaps because it came in very wide boards or because it was light and easy to work or because it was cheap, or for all of these reasons.

The best construction which carries the divisions solidly all the way back between the drawers is most unusual, probably because it added to the weight, but it was the only method of keeping one drawer's contents wholly separated. Otherwise the pulling out of one drawer would reveal the contents of the drawer below it. Dust also could easily intrude. It would seem that economy of materials and labor were considered in the old day just as they are now.

The attaching of the top on a chest of drawers from the Sheraton time forward was by the use of screws driven in from below, but in the earlier time the usual method was by glue blocks in the mahogany period.

The attaching of the lock required sometimes a very long lock bolt, especially on the Chippendale 'scutcheon, since the keyhole on the willow pattern could not be placed near the upper edge of the drawer front. The locks were always attached by open mortise from the back, the modern mortise lock not being known. In fact, the hardware is a means of determining the age and authenticity of a piece to which it is attached.

Probably the earliest method of attaching the bail to the handle as in the Dutch period was by a flattened wire which was clinched on the inside. It is very easy to see if this clinching has ever been disturbed. A little later when the post was used with its nut, it becomes more difficult to determine the age because it is easy to cut modern nuts in an irregular pattern as was done in the old day. However, an examination of the screw-thread will show whether it is handmade or not. The hand thread was never so fine, that is, never had so many threads to the inch as the machine thread, and it was always slightly irregular. Elsewhere Goddard's method of attaching a shoe to the drawer bottom is described.

The investigation of old pieces can thus be sometimes traced to a particular maker by his peculiar methods which he followed in all his work. There was no uniform system such as we have at present. Individual makers also often showed a partiality for certain moldings. This method of identification can go too far and reach wrong conclusions owing to the paucity of data.

This is particularly true of feet. The same maker, as Goddard, might use on a Queen Anne leg a large round disc foot or an elongated foot with a rounded point, very aptly called a slipper foot, or a more pointed foot coming to an angle at the top and going by the unhappy name snake foot. A large piece of furniture, Goddard found, would bear a widely swept foot of larger dimensions.

It is not possible, except in a work devoted exclusively to cabinetmaking, to indicate more than a small part of the various practices governing cabinetmaking.

COLLECTORS' YARNS

There should be more human interest in volumes describing collectors' experiences than in almost any other kind of literature, because in the course of collecting character marks are brought out with cameo distinctness. I have often thought that a collection of tales of this sort ought to be made. We have room here for a few such.

The outstanding instance of a collector's experience is probably that of Mr. William G. Goodwin, of Hartford, whose fine spirit has been mentioned by Mr. Erving in a paper of his. Mr. Goodwin purchased some old books and papers for which he has great fondness. On a careful examination of his acquisition he discovered a letter bearing the signature of Button Gwinnett. The value of this letter was so great that he determined to sell it. On taking the proceeds to the seller of the documents to him he probably seemed like a divine Providence. To have handed to her a check for a great many thousand dollars for something she did not know she had ever possessed may stand as a unique example in the experience of collectors. In addition to the miraculous surprise was the still more rare nobility of turning over the entire proceeds to the original owner. Thus it happens that the most obscure of the signers of the Declaration of Independence is the one who, from that very fact, left least autographs, which are listed at a higher figure than those of any other American.

The Romance of a Table

So many have asked me to give the full story of the famous trestle and board shown as No. 800 in FURNITURE TREASURY that I am determined to do so. I was calling on Mr. Elmer Richardson at Rockville, Millis, Massachusetts. He is a relation of mine and, strangely enough, is also an intimate friend. He said that since I was interested in early furniture he wanted to tell me of a table that was sold in his neighborhood at an auction some years previously. It consisted of a pine board only twenty-five inches wide and some eleven feet long, and laid upon two T trestles with a truss rod connecting them. The old affair had been stored away in the attic of the Richardson tavern because, in one of his numerous progresses, the hearty and many-mealed General Washington had eaten from this board. The table had not been preserved for its antiquity or beauty. It had no beauty, and the owners knew nothing and cared less for its antiquity.

It was, however, as developed, the only Pilgrim trestle and board known except that from the Bolles Collection in the Metropolitan. My friend Richardson said, "I think I have a picture of that table." He produced it. I have never fainted away, and it seemed that this was a bad time to begin. I was informed that two fools bid as high as fifteen dollars for this table, not only because Washington sat at it, but because Millis was set off from Medway, and people from the two sections were in rivalry. The farmers, battered rather than embattled by this time, looked with astonishment while the table was knocked down. It was always knocked down after meals in the old fashion. It seemed the buyer had removed to the West and had lost his wife, to please whom he had made the purchase. I had at that time a commercial traveler in Illinois. My telephone call to him nearly ruined me, but I instructed him to leave everything, go to the state and owner with whom the table was, to take an express wagon with him, and not to leave the house until he had purchased the table. He was a very honorable man and wished to save me from my follies. He wired back that he had found the owner and the table and that he could make a better one for three dollars. He had, however, gone as high as seventy-five dollars. I wired him back that he had not followed instructions. It is the only difference that has arisen between us in a generation. He went back and advanced his offer a hundred dollars more and was then told that the owner would take up the matter with me personally, which he did. He explained that a board as wide as that was very remarkable and that such a table must be worth five hundred dollars. I wrote him that I had many boards wider than that and, while I knew I was a fool, I disliked very much being taken for a consummate fool; that if he wished to send the table cash on delivery for half the sum that he named, I would take it. In a few days the table arrived. I was ashamed to admit how much I had paid, because at that time the price was proof in the opinion of our beloved Mr. Erving that I was a plunger.

Nevertheless, the table proved to be the most important in my collection. When during the great war it was a matter of absolute necessity for me to dispose of this collection, a dealer sold it to a collector for a handsome sum. Mr. Goodwin later requested me to buy it for the Atheneum. Had I been buying for myself, I should soon have owned it. I thought, however, that the multiplied price would bear reduction, and while I was negotiating for it, the wealthiest American family purchased it. Mr. Goodwin was too gentle to eat me alive, but the drop which I experienced in his estimation was like a tumble from an airplane. It is presumed that the article reposes with the family mentioned. To the uninitiated the incident is a most apt example that rarity and age rather than association give value. The value of the table from the Washington association was fifteen dollars. From the age and rarity of the piece it was several hundred times that sum.

Moral: Never buy furniture from the names connected with it. I repeatedly tried to impress that matter in this volume and elsewhere, but apparently I am whistling against the wind. Buy furniture from its rarity, quaintness, intrinsic merit, condition, beauty, or style. More than half of the value, as a rule, lies in the first qualification. It may be well to add that the kind of wood of which this table was made had no bearing on its value. The trestle happened to be maple or birch, and the top a thin and narrow piece of pine with one end cut off. It had, however, the spirit of the Middle Ages, was probably made before 1650, was the distinct and only type known during the Middle Ages and back to the year one.

The Story of a Chair

As the most important seventeenth-century chair known in this country is No. 1799, Furniture Treasury, its story will be told. I was making a picture only three miles from my town of Framingham of a road beautifully overhung by elms. An elderly gentleman, I presume now dead, came out from a dwelling by the side of the road and said that he had a chair which he thought I would be interested to see, as he knew I cared for such things. I examined the chair which was then in the precise condition in which it appears in the picture. It was apparent at once that it was a far better chair in condition and in style than the chair preserved at Pilgrim Hall, Plymouth, which had belonged to Elder Brewster of the "Mayflower," and had the reputation of having come over in that vessel so deeply freighted with freedom, and, were all legends true, also freighted with enough other things to have sent her to the bottom before she left the English Channel. The Pilgrim Hall Brewster is, however, apparently of ash and in all likelihood was made by John Alden on a springboard lathe from roughly octagoned sticks cut in the forests of Plymouth. It is in very bad condition, being so worn off at the bottom that rungs and many of its spindles are missing. Further, it is made on a lighter pattern than the Tufts-Brewster chair on which I had stumbled. These Pilgrim chairs have a value in proportion to the size of the posts, and their condition. The Tufts chair was intact except for the absence of the balls on the front posts. Furthermore, the diameter of the posts was the largest I had ever seen on a Pilgrim chair, and they had the peculiarity often seen in such chairs of being largest at the top. Mr. John Tufts stated that he did not wish to sell the chair, in fact, he had been offered fifty dollars for it, but was showing it to me as a matter of curious interest. It will be seen that it has a double row of spindles in the back, rows under the arms, rows at the side beneath the seat, and a double row in front beneath the seat. The posts had a large diameter of two and a half inches. The seat was always of wood set in a rabbet in the turnings of the seat frame. Mr. Tufts stated that it had been in his family for eight generations of record, and that all parts were original.

After a trip abroad I was notified by Mr. Tufts that, as I liked the chair, he had taken pains to ask his heir about it, and that the heir did not care for it. Mr. Tufts, therefore, sold it to me with the understanding that I would always keep it. I paid what I suppose at the time was a full price. Later, when obliged to sell my collection in the war, I notified the buyer that I reserved the chair. He took the collection to his place of business, and I went after him to get the chair. "What," said he, "you wanted to retain it?" "You knew perfectly well," I replied, "that I stipulated to retain it." "I am so sorry," said he, "but I have sold the chair." My contract of sale was written, but I had omitted to write in the reservation of the chair as I was under the impression I was dealing with a man who was accustomed to make good on verbal agreements. I wrote to the buyer of the chair and offered twenty-five hundred dollars for it. Although she was a person of character, it proved that she had no tenderness, as she did not reply to my letter, although I had very carefully explained the circumstances and while I could make no demands, I wished to make my word good with Mr. Tufts. There was nothing to be done. A suit against the dealer would have availed nothing.

Chairs of this type are so few that they scarcely form a class. It is a matter of the keenest regret to me that the outcome is what it is. Of course, I could not afford the chair. It is a millionaire acquisition. But for the sake of my agreement I intended to own it no matter what the cost.

How easy is dogmatism, regarding furniture, overthrown! Dr. Lyon in his wonderful pioneer work carefully pointed out that he had made inquiries from all available sources in England and could not learn that the Carver and Brewster type existed there. In fact, years after that book was published it was necessary for English writers on furniture to send to America for pictures of this type. During a picture pilgrimage in England I had made a determination not to enter a furniture shop. For three days steady in a Taunton hotel we were shut in by continuous rain, and had hot-water bottles in our bed on the fourth of July. In desperation I finally entered a charming half-timbered gabled house where early furniture was sold. At the very door the first object on which my eyes rested was a Carver chair! I bought a lot of old iron and then asked the dealer where he got that chair. "I picked it up yesterday," said he, "near here." Asked if he had ever seen one before, he replied, "No." It was rarely good in its turnings, but of course of oak. As he placed almost no value upon it, I told him to include it with my old iron. On reaching America I notified a dealer of very high integrity that he should see me immediately, which he did. On entering my premises his eye rested on this chair. "Where," said he, "did you get that?" I grinned like a Cheshire cat, and said that he knew where I had been all summer and that I had just returned. Also that I did not wish to deal in antique furniture, but that if he wanted the chair, he should take it and that quickly. He at once gave me a good sum and took it to his place. Shortly afterwards a dealer from the great metropolis called on him and said, "Bring out your stuff you have hidden away, and that of course is really the best find you have made lately." The dealer went to his basement and brought up the Carver chair. At once the buyer shouted, "It is sold! I did not ask the price." He would not leave it in the shop an hour, but took it with him with the parting remark, "The joy of it is, it is so distinctively American!" No doubt he did well with his purchase, but another tradition has been blown sky high. (Trammels, by the way, with good saw teeth were eighteen pence in England then, but ten dollars in America, and they were for sale abroad in lots of fifty.)

And only yesterday I learned of an alleged English block front, a thing which the English dealers admit does not exist in our particular American fashion. As to this I do not believe the piece has the block, or if so, I do not believe it is English.

A Pine Court Cupboard

These articles are far more rare than the oak cupboards, though of course with less value. For a year I had offered up and down Boston's Charles Street a thousand dollars to anyone who would supply me a pine court cupboard. At length on the North Shore I learned of one for sale for one-eighth of that sum. It appeared, on sending for it, that it had been sold the previous day to a dealer on Charles Street. I went to him at once and asked the price. He informed me that he had decided to make a collection and would not sell it. That was the one occasion when my angry passions arose against a dealer. I said, "Mr. ——, I have really kept you going since you started in business here. Unless you name a price on that cupboard I will never buy another thing from you." He answered, "I wouldn't sell that piece for less than five hundred dollars." I handed him a check for that amount and said, "I now own this cupboard. You have tried to hold me up. You have stated that you did not dream I would give five hundred dollars for it. I want to tell you that if you had not been asleep, you would have asked a thousand dollars, because that is what I have publicly offered for a long time." This man is now dead. Heart disease probably! He was notoriously the hardest man to deal with in Boston, but my relations with him were always most harmonious.

The Pine Carved Chest

Seeing one day on the same street a carved pine chest, I asked the price, and was told twenty-five dollars. It seems that the admittedly first authority as a dealer had sold the chest the previous day for fifteen dollars to the dealer in whose shop I found it. The next morning, as the owner of the chest, I was called on the 'phone by the dealer who had sold it to me. He said, "I know you never sell anything separately from your collection. But there is a pine chest here that you bought yesterday and have not yet taken away, so that I thought perhaps you would sell it, as there is a customer here who wants it very much." "Certainly," said I, "I will sell it." "How much?" "Five hundred and twenty-five dollars." Ahem, from the other end of the telephone. "I think you misunderstood me. I mean the chest you bought yesterday for twenty-five dollars." "No," said I, "I understand." "But," he replied, "you don't imagine I would pay that price?" "No," said I, "I do not." There the conversation ended.

A year from that time when the collection was sold it was entered in the inventory at that price, and brought it, and this particular dealer bought it.

A Brewster Settee

Hitherto these stories have related to good purchases. Lest the reader should imagine vain things, I will now proceed to relate an instance of the opposite character. In Hartford I was told by a person on whose judgment I relied, a cabinetmaker, that he had heard of a Brewster settee in Springfield, which was for sale for five hundred dollars. Now such a thing had never been heard of, and, as I had been some time out of touch with events and not buying, the information set me all agog. Proceeding at once to the dealer's in the outskirts of Springfield, I found the specimen, which in material and workmanship and age seemed a veritable Brewster settee. Inquiring the price, I was surprised to hear some thousands named. Being very persistent, I finally made the purchase at seventeen hundred and fifty dollars, and with a good deal of difficulty squeezed the specimen into my tonneau. I soon learned that I had purchased one of the excellent Swedish pieces. It had been planted where I found it very much as a mine is salted. My almost uniform success in purchases up to this time had blinded me to certain dangers. I banked on the fact that the piece was old and the style was fine, both of which statements still hold. Nevertheless, these Swedish goods have been so much exploited as American before the unwary that now no one will look at them. I have repeatedly tried to dispose of this marvel at ten per cent of what I paid for it. But there are no bidders, and I seriously believe that very few persons would remove it as a gift. The seller, by the way, assisted me with a good deal of courtesy, not to say enthusiasm, in loading it on my car. The incident has given me many a good laugh. I never even took the trouble to express my opinion to the dealer. A person who cannot take his medicine merits contempt. (*Page 533.*)

I do presume, however, that if that settee was in Sweden today, the government by its new ruling would not permit its export. That being so, maybe the settee will "come back." That will be when stocks quoted at one and a half sell at a hundred!

Of course it is vision which counts in buying. Only the vision needs to be hindsight. In the buying of antiques one's position is almost precisely the same as in the buying of stocks. On the upward market most buys are good. On the downward market, what is good?

An esteemed friend in a neighboring town many years ago called me up to know if I would be interested in some side Carver chairs. In those days the police were not so careful about speed. I arrived at the dealer's and paid the asking price, eight dollars each. We were both satisfied. It was not long before two cyphers could fairly have been added to that figure, and on the right side, too.

BLOCK FRONTS

Block fronts, especially those with shells, have become so important that one great house is supposed to have turned out at least a hundred "originals." I have several shops in mind where such things are on sale, and I have an owner in mind who has two or three originals on which he expects a larger price than such things were worth in the roaring 29s. I think he will get his price, if he does not age too fast. I was notified of such a piece which I was not to be permitted to buy unless the person who had bargained for it released it. Of course that increased my eagerness. But on a very careful examination, it appeared that the fronts were all new, one of the best pieces of work imaginable. Again, an inquirer for Chippendale chairs thought that good reproductions were too high. He therefore bought English reproductions which looked old and were not so well made, and which cost somewhat more. The triumph of the faker is at present almost universal. People who began with good reproductions have now gone on to "original," which they say they can obtain at very low figures. People do not ask for the furniture to be old, they only ask for it to look old. Everywhere good things are turned down, and the spurious is chosen. It would be a fair judgment to say that not more than one buyer in ten thousand discriminates. Obviously, the dealer does not bother with that lone ten-thousandth man. Why should he? He is in "business." Only yesterday a buyer in the midst of a city where good things are numerous informed me that he was not keen on antiques, but since he could buy them cheaper than reproductions, why shouldn't he? He wanted some furniture anyway. Once such things would have nettled me, but a broader view and the mellowing of time teaches one to be philosophical.

COLLECTING TABLES

The far-shining example of the rise in values is the case of the wonderful communion table, No. 811, FURNITURE TREASURY. The story is an epic or, at least, a comedy. I wandered into a shop in Exeter and saw this table. The dealer had found it at old Salisbury, the last town in Massachusetts going north by the shore. It was the communion table of the first church built about 1650. The dealer had bought a load of stuff, all his vehicle would carry, for eight dollars. He counted this table at about two dollars. Obviously it was the best thing of the sort. As it stood in the church, we will say on a dais, the band of carving would be visible to the congregation. It has no carving on the other side. At that time such things were not highly appreciated. When I learned that the price was six hundred dollars, I went away a little provoked because I felt the dealer was trying to do me. A proper price seemed to be three hundred dollars, and afterwards when the table was sold I so expressed myself to the dealer. "Why didn't you say so," said he. He held the table for some time and lost courage. Finally, a keen city dealer proposed that he pay a hundred and twenty-five dollars for a half interest, and if he could sell it, the Exeter dealer would then get half of the price. It was a very pretty scheme. After a while, so the Exeter man says, the dealer sold the table for six hundred dollars. He then informed his country correspondent that they never could sell that table, and he could have his share back for the sum paid, or the city dealer would buy out the other half and end the matter. The country dealer was always hard up and he accepted his one hundred twenty-five dollars. Whereupon the city dealer turned over the table to his customer. It was purchased by a lady who after awhile determined it was too massive for her house. She therefore turned it in to the city dealer for other furniture. Going into his shop one day I was astonished to find this table which I was told I could have for four hundred dollars. The presumption is that in the exchange the dealer had benefited and could therefore make this price. Being very poor at the time, I hesitated, but finally took the table. Next morning I was importuned over the 'phone to accept a hundred dollars for my bargain and allow the table to be turned over to a man who was, according to the dealer, standing on one foot in the intensity of his interest to obtain the specimen. I had never sold a thing like this, but poverty is a strong persuader. I was afterwards told that the new purchaser was paying a bonus of two hundred and fifty dollars and not one hundred, as I had been informed. This gentleman afterwards went abroad to live and sold his entire collection to a great New York shop. There I found this table for sale at three thousand dollars. It was sold to a collector. Before its previous sale the buyer had wanted the two planks of the top jointed a little better where they met. Someone called the attention of the new purchaser to this insignificant repair, and in no time he turned the table back to the New York shop under the plea that he had been done. There again I found the table, but could not pay the price. I was informed that after six months the remaining items of the collection would be reduced in price, and if that table was amongst them, I could buy it. The matter passed out of my mind, but I happened into the shop the very morning that the manager of the department came forward with the reduced schedule. I bought the table for sixteen hundred dollars. In a lecture at an historical society I told this story, and the gentleman who had turned the table back as not "right" was present. He went out after the lecture without speaking with me. The New York dealer had had the entire story from me and had told him what had been done with the table, but he did not seem persuaded until he heard the lecture, when it was too late. When my collection went to the Atheneum this was properly counted the supreme specimen of an American table. It is shown as found except for the oak brackets. The mortise hole for them appeared and the location of the old nail near the small end which secured the bracket to the frame. It was, therefore, possible to make up these brackets with precision. There was scarcely any variation between the shapes of these refectory table brackets, as an examination of Volume I shows. There is another table in existence of American origin with carving on the frame, but the legs had been cut off. This is the only table, therefore, with the carving, found in America, and with the apparently full length of the legs. I have heard that it is insured for fifteen thousand dollars; but however that may be, it will probably stand for long, if not forever, as the great exemplar of American tables, an aristocrat as compared with the trestle and board whose story we have told. The dimensions, which are generous and massive, are given with the picture.

A peculiar instance of lack of appreciation is connected with table No. 828, FURNITURE TREASURY. When old Sudbury was settled, I think from Wayland, the new church organization took the old communion table, leaving the communion set for the old church. That generation passed away, and nobody cared for this piece, dating from 1655. It was given away to a butcher, who cut meat on it. A lady of the church, who had intelligence and feeling, saw this proceeding and asked to be given the table again for the church. It was placed in the lower rooms and used as a serving table at church suppers. My feeling was that if the church did not care enough for it to install it in its place of honor, it had better go to a museum. By this time, however, some appreciative church members desired to retain it. I proposed to them to accept a fund of one thousand dollars, the interest to be used in support of public worship, and engaged that the table should go to a museum if it left my hands. It now reposes in the Atheneum, which now, therefore, has the two communion tables which for age and sentiment and merit must always place this museum in the front rank as the repository of the best "standing tables," as tables with a frame were called in distinction from the trestle and board which was taken down daily.

Of course both these tables are American white oak frames.

While talking of tables, some amusement may be derived from the court cupboard table, No. 1011, Furniture Treasury. This amazing specimen has the same construction as a splayed court cupboard, and the posts above the shelf are precisely like, in shape, those found on court cupboards. The same may be said of the drops and the framing below the shelf. I came upon this table in a South Shore shop. It appeared that a bride had found it in her husband's attic, and the story goes that she was going to be rid of the curious old thing for ten dollars. Some cautious friend warned her that it might be valuable. Whereupon it was placed on sale, as I have indicated, at thirty-five hundred dollars. In buying I have followed the practice of determining the limit of price beyond which I would never go. It may be a foolish practice, but still there are limits even to the acts of an enthusiast, if he retains a grain of common sense. I offered three thousand dollars, but the table was sold to a wealthy collector for the larger price. It is altogether the best thing of the kind found in this country, and of course should go with a court cupboard. A much dilapidated specimen was later found. It is observable that this table has a small gate leg at the back so that it could be used for a breakfast table, a coffee table, or a gaming table.

Afterwards I visited the Washington shrine in England, at Sulgrave Manor. I was endeavoring to get a picture of the Manor for my collection. The gentleman in charge, seeing me, came rushing out at a cricketer's pace across the broad lawn to inform me that picture making was prohibited. I asked why, and learned that it was because the management feared if the public made pictures they could not sell as many postal card pictures. As I had journeyed a hundred miles for the express purpose of getting this picture my impression was unpleasant. I agreed to buy any number of the pictures, but the refusal held. Paying the fee, we went through the house and the gentleman in charge expatiated at length over the great state bed in the great state chamber. As we were leaving I said to him, "You have an odd table by the side of that great bed. That is more important than everything else you have in the house altogether, but you did not mention that." "Oh," said he, "I remember now the London museum people *did* tell us that that was extremely rare." It appeared from his remarks that there was no other known in England. It was almost an exact duplicate of the court cupboard table above described! (By the way, I had already secured my picture when I was estopped.)

The English are keen organizers. They formed the Sulgrave association to purchase the Manor and present it to Americans. They then collected, so the report goes, nineteen-twentieths of the purchase and restoration price from Americans! But, do not try to make pictures there and do not fail to ignore the clumsy bed, and to pay careful attention to the wonderful court cupboard table.

Talking of tables again, my ancient friend Dr. Albert VanderVeer, one of the ablest and noblest men I ever knew, who went on in his nineties to the next world, was showing me about the rooms of the Albany Historical Society. We paused at the great four-gate table, which opens from the center like a star. I read a legend upon it that it was loaned by a certain lady. I took out my notebook to make a record of her address. The doctor looked, jumped in the air, gesticulated, and remarked with much emphasis, "Don't you dare to try to buy that table" and repeated himself. I grinned. In a few days the table was the property of the Society. (*Page 534.*) In a good number of instances where I have seen fine articles on loan, or found wonderful old houses for sale, I have made well advertised inquiries as to the address of the owners, and in many instances the local people have scurried about and secured the ownership. I count this among my best efforts for the preservation of our worthy relics. The same thing occurred in relation to the famous McIntire Pierce house at Salem. I got a price on it one morning and then watched to see what would happen. Within three or four days the Essex Institute owned it. A little pressure judiciously applied is sometimes a very excellent thing.

The Story of a Cradle

Whoever visits Pilgrim Hall, Plymouth, will see a great painting of the lading of the "Mayflower." Prominently in the foreground is a sailor, or a stevedore with his leg over the ship's rail tugging aboard an oak cradle. The artist was shown this cradle and informed that it was brought over by Dr. Samuel Fuller of the "Mayflower" passenger list. The conceit of painting it was an excellent one and adds a fine human element to the picture. But the cradle did not come in the "Mayflower." It is made of American white oak, with oak panels in the ends and pine panels in the sides. It has been repeatedly pictured and reported as being in Pilgrim Hall, but a lady, now old, if an American woman ever can be old, who was rocked in it, tells me that it never was in Pilgrim Hall, but always privately owned. There is in Pilgrim Hall the Dutch wicker cradle in which very likely Peregrine White was rocked in the "Mayflower," though the voyage was of such a tempestuous character that any additional rocking would seem to have been unnecessary. Nevertheless, little Peregrine found it a refuge in Provincetown harbor. There is another cradle in Pilgrim Hall which is built of pine with applied strips to simulate panels. This is entered in a very ambitious work on furniture as an oak cradle. The writer of that work, should he examine the cradle, would be very much chagrined to find it of soft wood. Probably he illustrated it and described it from a picture only. That cradle, in a glass case, is reputed to have been owned by the other Fuller on the "Mayflower." If the English before 1620 were making pine cradles, it is interesting to know it.

But the famous Samuel Fuller cradle (No. 1564, Furniture Treasury) came down in the Fuller family and passed into the Cushman family who intermarried with the Fullers, and in the Cushman family I found it through the courtesy of my friend Mr. Stephen Alden, another "Mayflower" descendant. Every generation has been taken in childhood, in the Fuller or Cushman line, to be rocked ceremoniously at least once in this cradle. It was given to the young man of the owner's family by his mother, and in his charge I found it. He stated very positively that he did not care enough for the association to keep the cradle if he got his price for it, but that whoever bought it must pay well. I had taken with me five hundred dollars, hoping it would be enough to buy the cradle, but the young man asked only two hundred and fifty, so that it seemed useless to mention the other sum. The cradle as found had lost its rockers and I believe one spindle. I restored that spindle and, getting an oak beam, exposed, from the Marsh house in Wethersfield, built in the early seventeen hundreds, I made these rockers, leaving the undressed surface of the beam on the outside. The object is by many regarded as the most interesting and the most dearly cherished of my collection at the Atheneum. I hope successive generations will still bring their babes to it. I had placed this cradle in my own dwelling house, but somehow it was not a joy to the partner of my joys, and she seemed to take still less interest in it when a caller one day remarked that it was big enough to rock a bull calf. Under the circumstances it seemed diplomatic to place it in the museum collection. This cradle, properly studied, is like the bone of an extinct animal. Half of the history of cabinetmaking can be derived from delving into its construction. Its obvious similarity to an oak chest, its charming spindled hood, ending with split spindles against the post, its knobs at the foot for rocking the child, its shadow chest molds, its notched and scratch-carved pine top, its use of the wide pine panel, and the oak panel for a narrow space, and a hundred other items properly allocated in one's mind, supply a picture of materials and craftsmanship and the shaping of loving hands, probably those of John Alden or Kenelm Winslow, all matching the spirit which hovers within, reminiscent of the sturdy battlers who have been hidden in its depths till they emerged from this enormous chrysalis to take their part in the making of America.

I was also able to obtain the cradle No. 1567, FURNITURE TREASURY, for the Rhode Island School of Design. It is more decorative than, but hardly as stately as, the Samuel Fuller cradle.

Some violent protests were stirred up when I stated in my previous volume that Samuel Fuller was not married when he came over and that he would have shown great faith, even for a Pilgrim, to bring this cradle under the circumstances. Letters came in to me alleging that he was very much married before and after coming to America. Sometimes I mean to get a year off and look further into his history, but as my informant placed the cradle in Pilgrim Hall when it was in my possession, I feel that I must verify the marriage record. Anyhow, a cradle is a symbol of faith and love, something constructed to protect and honor our small humanity. I feel that in its fine, new, fireproof headquarters it is worthily located. Of course, the people of Plymouth could have had the cradle as a permanent possession.

After I had purchased this cradle a business shock compelled the dispersal of the collection. I sold it for fifteen hundred dollars. The dealer resold it at a good advance. But after awhile I could not sleep well owing to the loss of that cradle. I finally repurchased it at just ten times what I paid for it in the first instance. A weathy collector, sitting cross-legged beside it, said to me, "Let me have that cradle. I would rather look at it than St. Paul's cathedral." But I had made up my mind that it must go to a museum.

Thus the mystery of the number of antiques in the market is in part solved. The carved communion table was in eleven ownerships inside of three years. The cradle was in six ownerships in two years. A rare folding gate-leg table was in five ownerships within three days. I know of one dealer who has owned a famous piece four times and in every case he has sold it for less than he paid and then rebought it for less than he sold it. Meantime it has been owned by others.

Cradles seem to interest only real collectors. The ordinary hooded, cherry or mahogany cradle goes begging. Sometimes it is used as a wood box. I anticipate that it will be the receptacle of a beer cask under "this freedom." In fact, it is used and abused, but I have not seen a baby in one of these delightful constructions in fifty years. It is now denied that rocking addles the brain, but as most of us were born since the disuse of the cradle, we cannot attribute to that article of furniture our condition of intelligence or the lack thereof. There must be something else. If we could only learn what it is! Some say it is because we take too many baths, and the gleaming teeth and exuberant health of those who keep their coal in the bathtub seem to bear out the theory. Certainly the condition of the American mind cannot be attributed to too much study of the antique. Thinking is very hard on the brain. There is only one thing worse for it and that is not to think.

There are a procession of people who do not know that when they are in the presence of good things their reactions indicate their caliber. The other day I was studying the most remarkable of our fireplaces in its construction and in its furnishings. It was of stone with special features of strength and age and rarity and picturesqueness. It had within it and around it more than a hundred and fifty articles, mostly curious, some unique, many ingenious, all teeming with human interest, that had been used for hundreds of years in old American homes. A gentleman stood with me admiring it while his wife sat impatiently in the car. Finally she came in and with one side to the fireplace, she gave him a look which said much and withdrew. She was in the presence of so much that she did not know! Worse, she did not care. Such a person may not be wholly dead, but certainly is dead in the upper story. One is reminded of the trail to Cripple Creek over which thousands have passed for many years, until finally a man slipped and grabbed a gnarly shrub which came away with his hand. Beneath the root was the richest gold deposit, from which a good fraction of a billion dollars has been taken out. The reason people are bored with this world is that they do not get acquainted with it. The world is opaque like a wooden Indian to those without eyes. The world is an alabaster statue. We can see through it if we just look. Thoreau was a poor Concord boy, but he saw what had been there for others to see from the remotest generations. A paradise is not hunted, it is observed.

One of the best American chests was found in a poorhouse. It took about six generations to find a man who could see it. We may wait long for the appreciation of good, but it will be highly appreciated sometime. What is the rubbish of the dull soul is the pearl of the discerning. The old mummies are rather repulsive, but they were all notable men in their day, else they would not have been embalmed. One of the recognized and desirable artist's pigments is composed of ground-up mummies. When we are looking at some magnificent canvas scintillating in the sunlight, or magnificent in the glow of the russet and gold in the west, we may be indebted to this splendor because we are looking on mummy pigment, and the old dead things live again with a finer light, a nobler meaning, a grander reach than any of these materials experienced or produced in the old days.

To the blind eye an antique is a dead thing. I have seen men of wealth and of alleged intelligence emphasize the fact that they would not give a nickel for a carload of such things. They are very anxious to make this announcement because they wish to make their intelligence manifest. And they succeed; we see it, such as it is!

Everything lives when it is touched with life, and imagination, and love, and understanding. Everything is interesting when we have learned enough about it. Everything is vital, if we are. The universe has no black holes as soon as a shining intelligence looks at it. There will be no glory in the present unless it is shaped from the abundant latent materials of the past. We cannot name a thing that is not waiting for the touch of a human hand, for the inventive genius of a teeming mind, for a clarified and purposeful imagination. There is not a particle of waste material anywhere, ever, and never will be. The waste of one generation is the substantial erection into harmonious lines of the next generation. The earth is a cradle for the generations to come.

Temporary Exhibits of Antiques

Before the recession of business there was a series of exhibits in antiques arranged in the great eastern cities. We will say that in New York City this and that dealer would send to this exhibit some of the articles he had for sale, not omitting those which had grown antique in their possession, because they had kept them so long and involuntarily. There was another class of dealers who could not see their interest in such an exhibit, and were not represented.

If one took a few hours to go about to the best shops, he could see ten times as much as at an exhibit. The same thing perhaps might be said of a world's fair. The investigation of a great manufacturing enterprise is more informing than a miniature reproduction of it. To be sure, those who cannot or will not travel find their advantage in something that is brought to their own city. But between the permanent museums and the numerous general and special shops there is more interest and instruction than in any temporary gathering together of objects to exhibit. If we attend these exhibits, we do so in part because we may meet there persons we are desirous of seeing. It is, however, almost never true in the nature of things that the best articles can be or will be allowed to be transported from their proper location for such temporary exhibits. Neither precious nor massive objects are good travelers. With our multiplied means of locomotion in these days, it is better that we should go where the articles are. The Boston Museum of Fine Arts has recently added to its previous attractions the Tyler Collection, and in the quiet and orderly retreat furnished by a museum is the ideal atmosphere for observation and study. The same may be said for the gatherings of the past in many of our cities. But it may require an age of development before the ordinary mind seeks after the museum.

Years ago I had an experience in New York which would have been laughable had it not been tragic. I wished to visit the Metropolitan Museum, and I had forgotten what street in the eighties was the most convenient bus station to reach it. I was in a hotel with more than a thousand rooms, and I inquired at the information counter. No information. I asked at the clerk's desk. No information. I asked the porter, and the bellboys, and the cashier. No information. Some of them had never heard of it, none of them had ever been to it, none of them cared to know about it. The most intelligent thought it was up Central Park way. Yet this magnificent gathering of a value of about a hundred million dollars, from every part of the earth, and from all periods of history, ancient and modern, and of all kinds of the productions of men, their masterpieces of taste, skill, imagination, all this with efficient and cultivated guides to show one about amongst the splendors of painting and sculpture and artisanship, and all about ten minutes away, excited no more ripple of interest, nay, half as much as a drop of rain. Museums are doing a great deal in the way of offering their facilities to the public. They tell us at the end of the year how many thousands have visited them. One is bound to say, however, that in all one's experience a crowd at a museum has never been encountered. Here is free education requiring only a pleasant use of the eyes. It is almost like an excess of light, blinding the dull vision. We think still more methods will be devised for luring the public to our museums, but the work is not yet successful. Not one goes within a museum where there should be a thousand. It would be unbelievable if not verified that millions in the City of New York itself neither visit its museums nor know where they are. Yet this museum is in the greatest city in the world, and probably the greatest city that ever existed, and into which multitudes of thousands of persons pour daily from afar in addition to its own teeming millions. Of the visitors most have been before, and some many times before.

One rather wearies of the boasts about modern popular education. It really does not exist yet, except sporadically and superficially. It may be that social students can tell us whether the careless mind is capable of culture, and what the outlook is. We know that it is always the remnant that is saved, either artistically or spiritually, but why need it be so? Emphasis has been laid on the facilities for travel, but it is a grave question whether the minds of men are broadening, or at least sufficiently to prove the fact. Every man goes to his own place. There are aggregations of men that move about from the cradle to the grave in their chosen narrow circles and are unhappy elsewhere. A young man on the east side of New York paid a visit to Boston. After two or three days, although he was among friends, a new scene and better air, he hastened back to the place of his upbringing, crawled into his swarming hive and is happy. He says he will never go again. The case is not isolated. Men are interested in narrow ranges of thought and activity. It was an ironic commentary that the senators of the United States had not sufficient aptitude to learn the use of the dial telephone. A living idea especially if it stands for beauty, or honor, or order, knocks in vain for entrance to the politician's head. It is said that there is a toad which is developing wings. It is thought that in a couple of billion years more it may learn to fly. There may be hope for the professional politician, but not this one that is alive now, nor for his son nor his son's son. But why wait for the toad? Why wait for the inevitable impulsion of forced growth to make something out of us when we have hands and eyes and a literature of dazzling magnificence?

The Western mind is alert in certain directions only. But it is a proverb from Shakespeare on that the average boy does not wish to learn. Japanese and Chinese children are not of this sort. One of our alert Americans in the Philippines has developed a scheme of charts by which he teaches the Moros the alphabet in a single day and teaches them to read in a week. In the year of grace nineteen thirty-three there are many places where it is against the law to teach a child in an American school before he is six years old. The whole trend of modern civilization in our Western world is to keep the youth back. We might almost as well place them in dark rooms or carry them in pouches as the kangaroo carries its progeny.

To be sure, we have movies. But take the gun and the bad girl out of the movies and what have you left? Possibly two per cent. Here is the greatest agency on earth, potentially, for uplift, which means or should mean teaching something of real interest that will brighten and enrich life. They pay a man seventy-five thousand dollars a year to make the movies decent. They seem to have dragged him down and drowned him so far as any virile and successful direction is concerned.

With this vast agency found in every village, what pictures of glory and beauty, what visions of the permanent and the desirable aspects of life could be shown! The whole world has it here in its grasp, this means of becoming magnificent in manhood and womanhood within a generation. There is no more stinging indictment possible against things as they are than the unlimited stores available from the ages and the infinitesimal application of them to the going generation. Moralists are often fond of saying that our youth are the finest youth that ever were. If so, they are getting the worst treatment that any generation ever got. They have been brought into the world to be kicked into hell, and the administration of society is doing the kicking.

What is the use to say that a young man or a young woman is normal and admirable and dependable, when the things that really matter, the beauty of the home, the orderliness of life, the treasures of thought, the edifice of a noble society are unknown, untaught, unloved, unsought by teacher and pupil?

Pick out the first ten young people you meet on the street and ask them these questions:

1. Name ten great facts in the world's history.

2. Name ten statements of great ideas.

3. Select the materials and the contents of a dignified home such as will be favorable for founding new families.

What will be the result of this experiment? Try it. Some of us have tried it a good many times and have not confined ourselves to the youth alone. We have taken people who have not only graduated from high school, but from college, like the American who thought he had done the Louvre thoroughly in an hour and a half. The abysmal poverty of ideas, the bottomless profundity of the emptiness of anything really worth while is so quickly apparent that we may drop our quest, too suddenly and too terribly answered.

HOW THE OLD CABINETMAKERS WORKED

Their rooms were never well heated in winter. They did their gluing close to the fireplace. Under such conditions they could not produce as good work as the same skill would produce with controlled temperatures.

They had no drying room. All their lumber was first air dried and then dried under a shed, and finally stored on the open beams above the shop. By this method their boards required some five years' seasoning, and their planks twice as long. A section as large as a bedpost might need fifteen years to put it in perfect condition. Even so, a good many of the posts show bad checks. In the lumbering operations they were careful to cut the timber when there was least sap in it, which was an assistance in drying.

Their material never became brittle from overdrying, but the fact that their table leaves warped so much is an evidence that they did not wait long enough for the drying process, or that they failed in the finishing process.

It is a great mistake to infer that because a piece of cabinetwork was built hundreds of years ago it was, therefore, very well built. Poor work is done in every age of the world, and most of the poor work perished. Where it remains to us there are numerous warps and checks in much of it. We get an exaggerated idea of the quality of their work from the fact that only the best of it has withstood the test of the years. But very little old furniture is anywhere near perfect. If the defects in it are the marks of legitimate use, they are rather prized than deplored. But lumber is an uncertain quantity, a material each piece of which has its peculiar character. Thus it was found that certain sorts of lumber were good for certain kinds of furniture or parts of a single piece of furniture.

Imitation is as old as life. It is a mark even of the animal creation. It has always been a practice to give a table leg the semblance of some object in nature and to treat one wood so that it looks like another. Our ancestors were not above this imitation, in which, of course, no more deceit was intended than in a painting, where the artist does his faithful best to imitate a tree or a sky. We, therefore, need to distinguish between imitation and counterfeiting. Forgery with wood is as real and as criminal, rightly considered, as when done with a pen. The motive is one consideration; the strength and character of the work are another consideration. The customer is taken into the confidence of the cabinetmaker and knows precisely, or should know, what he is obtaining.

The old cabinetmakers worked out most of their own tools. They made their own plane blocks, handles, clamps, etc. One is amazed to find in modern English works the details of toolmaking by hand, for the English are in some particulars as conservative as the Chinese. In the days when a hand plane, even, is made of metal, modern directions for making a plane of wood are nothing if not absurd. There is no possible tool which can be made by hand as accurately as by modern machine method. There are American shops where gauges are made in routine order to one twenty-thousandth part of an inch. Of course such work by hand is impossible.

It is still true, however, that the eye is the truest gauge, and in the matter of shape and style the machine shows its lack of intelligence. The most accurate measurements ever made by man are by the reflection of light through a lens, the last touches of whose shape are given by hand. The thoughtful cabinetmaker of the present day will, therefore, make a nice choice between methods; he will choose machine tools where their work is superior, and he will adhere rigidly to hand tools where he finds them superior. He knows he cannot cut a good dovetail by machine. He knows that accurate fitting, as of mortises, is best done by hand. He knows that no planer and no sander can produce work as perfect as hand scraping. Reflection of the light will quickly and amazingly reveal this fact. If a table top is placed, after being finished, where proper reflections may be obtained, the slightest unevenness is shown. It may not be possible to measure it, or feel it with the hand, but the light shows it, and mars it seriously as a piece of finished work.

The old cabinetmaker, even when his work was not perfect, but was as perfect as he could make it, created something which was full of humanity. We see the combination of thought and dexterity all over his completed work. He sometimes used wooden pins where nails or screws would have been better, because he could make the pins. He could not possibly attach an arm to the back post of a chair as securely as we do. There were weak spots on hand work, just as there are in machine work.

It is a curious commentary on every human production that it inevitably reveals character. Either when the work is new or when it is old it writes a history of its nature, hence the more handiwork in it the more eloquent it is. We may even love it for its imperfections if we see in those imperfections an eager effort to reach an ideal. It is what the man is trying to do rather than what he does that excites our sympathy and admiration.

The old cabinetmaker was not self-conceited like the modern carpenter. He knew that great artists and artisans had gathered up the supreme examples of human handiwork and had added to them their own fervent adaptive genius and had produced lines which had a history of beauty and strength. The carpenter and the cabinetmaker owned exquisite copperplate books which exhibited the highest skill ever achieved in design and execution. Nearly all the great cabinetmakers issued books which enshrined the best product of their imagination coupled with their dexterity. In fact, many of the greatest books were by designers who handed their thought on to others to be executed. It is an amusing tribute to the genius of the past that nearly all the best works by architects or cabinetmakers begin by a full exposition of the five classical styles in architecture. They recognized and there was a norm, a superb basis of design, which exhibited the matured skill and taste of the ages. In this they showed their superiority to the less thoughtful modern worker, who, blinded by his own conceit, presumes that it is easy to surpass the achievements of the ages. The very core of the idea of collecting is to preserve and exhibit the climax of human achievement. Without a vision of the past the future is chaotic. Today the greatest need of cabinetmakers is to recognize that they are not beginners, but builders along a magnificent tradition, and that they are simply adding stones to an ideal temple. The sacredness of materials is as much overlooked as the sacredness of human nature. A clarified and inspired worker drilled to the last degree of human accomplishment as the athlete is trained for his supreme test, such a worker, taking up materials prepared for him through the evolution of countless ages, would only achieve his object of putting his thought and skill and aspiration into wood and stone, by understanding that his material is to be reverently used and turned out in terms of hope and love and pride, rather than in terms of dollars.

The old cabinetmaker was superior in that he knew his sources better than the factory worker. There is proof positive that he had the designs which were supreme. A perfect line with him was his religion. He had no more business to depart from it than the earth has to wander away from its orbit. The unity of thought and feeling and skill with materials is something that multitudes have not yet become conscious of as a basal reality. Raw materials unfortunately cannot speak, especially to the dullard who does not understand the language of creation. But everything that we find as raw material in this world is, if we could know it, really in the attitude of prayer, to be taken up and shaped by some good man into harmonious uses and stimulating beauties. Consider how the elements have waited to be recognized and to have their secrets revealed. Consider how we are just learning many of the latent properties inherent in material, which have been longing for discerning spirits to recognize them.

There is, properly speaking, a scheme by which every chemical element and every growing thing is to find its place where it will give harmony, and a connective sympathy between itself and other parts of creation. It is only the man who believes this who really enjoys his work and sees that it fits into a universal plan.

Considered on this broad basis, every man is ennobled when he reaches out his hand to help in the process of making a finished and splendid world. An honest man is he who tries to fit into the harmony of law. An honest skilful man driven by the subtlety of life and imagination, really does fit into the law of development. Whatever he leaves behind him is an expression of power going out from his finger tips like an electric current, a power harnessed and stored and ready to flow into materials to give them the impress of thought. This power has been growing since ages before the cave man. It has now reached possibilities under instruction and the pride of carrying on, such that its achievements already excite our admiration and satisfy our artistic and moral feeling. I believe that the spirit of the ancient cabinetmaker, the spirit of the temple builder, the spirit of the artist, is still latent in men and not so far beneath the surface but that it may be summoned forth and burst into a finer flower of achievement. There is noticeable in history a curious ebb and flow, but in the ages there is a march of humanity. If we did not believe that we were to do better work, almost infinitely better, life would be dull indeed. Thus properly considered, what has been done is interesting only as an indication of the stirring imaginations that have already mastered men. If they were not prophetic, they would be pathetic. Who cares for an old piece of wood, into whatsoever shape it has been wrought, unless it is the impress of human progress, and the challenge to better it?

METHODS OF TURNING

Professor John J. Coss of Columbia University found abroad the old prints reproduced on this and the following page and presented me with them, knowing my interest in old methods of turning. The illustration above shows the old springboard to which a cord is attached then run around the stick to be turned and connected with a treadle. This is the simplest and the oldest method. Of course, it would reverse the direction every time the foot was lifted, and the turner could use his tools only when his foot was going down. This archaic and stupid method was used in England up to a very recent date in the turning of Windsor chair legs. No doubt the lathe, which could be made and set up in a day, was the sort used by John Alden in turning the first furniture at Plymouth.

The illustration on the next page is supposed to indicate the design of the last word in modern turning. It is arranged with an ordinary crank treadle and would revolve continuously, but of course at a very low rate of speed.

I have somewhere called attention to the bow-string lathe as used today in Egypt. The operator uses an ordinary bow, like an Indian's. The string is wrapped around

the end of his stick to be turned. One hand pushes this bow back and forth and the operator cuts on the return stroke. Reduced as he is to one hand, he supplements his digits by holding a tool in his toes. The wonder is that the treadle used by potters, and presumably hundreds of years old, was not adapted for turning.

Modern lathes have a motor connected directly, without belts; their usual high speed is 3600 r.p.m. A good motor is arranged with four speeds. The object is this: a piece of very large diameter of course revolves faster at its periphery than a small piece. The high speed would be too great. The motor can be immediately shifted to a lower speed. Also the best motors are arranged to reverse and have a head extending to the left, on which a very large disc can be clasped or attached. This method is used in the hollowing out of a dish-top or pie-crust table or a great bowl, and the speed is only 250 r.p.m. The ordinary rapid speed would cause the wood to fly off on a tangent, as the movement at the outside of a 33-inch turning even at the lowest speed is very rapid. It is as good as a play to watch an apt turner. When he roughly takes his piece down to a round he attacks it with a huge concave chisel and the fragments fly like hail. I have a picture of my turner with his hair filled with chips.

Modern turnery is nearly all purely mechanical, the hand-held tool being abandoned and cutters by various devices are brought against the stick to be turned. But there can be no character in such turning. Several thousand pieces a day can be turned out in a machine lathe. In handwork I once had a wonderfully rapid expert who could turn out fifty exquisitely modeled chair legs in a day, but the average worker can produce only about thirty-five.

The frequent use of calipers and comparison with the pattern are essential, though there are men whose eyes are so accurate that they scarcely need the calipers, if they are repeating the same turning. A stick with a half dozen, more or less, inserted, short, sharp spurs, at the important points of the turning, is first pressed against the prepared dowel. This marker outlines at once the work to be done and with accuracy and speed. The usual fault in turning is the neglect of sharpness as in the case of cusps and fillets. Also a vase curve is too often flattened, and snap and brilliancy are lost. Of course, no two hand turnings are exactly alike, nor need they be. An approximation is all that can be hoped for, and it is fully as satisfactory as the highest degree of precision.

The work is sanded on the lathe, and in some cases stain and shellac are applied to small articles so as to finish them completely, as, for instance, sand shakers. The wood is hot, and holding a saturated cloth against it quickly accomplishes handsome results.

The lathe back rest is required for long turnings. This rest is reputed to have been invented about 1795. Before that it was impossible to turn small long pieces like the spindles of a Windsor chair, which were, therefore, before that time, if delicate, whittled out by hand. Even a heavy stick like a bedpost will vibrate or buckle away from the tool and requires the back rest, which consists of two small wheels near together braced against the turning piece from the rear.

The turner of Windsor or other maple chairs supplied scratch marks as guides for the location of the stretchers, because he could do it with great rapidity with a spur gauge above mentioned.

For dainty small turnings, as a miniature patch box with a stem as small as a quill and a cover a sixteenth of an inch thick, the turner must exercise the daintiest skill. Turners were obliged in the old times to submit such delicate specimens of their work to show what they could do before being admitted to the guild.

All proper reproductions must, of course, be hand turned for the most part. One accustomed to these things can tell thirty feet away whether a chair is hand turned or not. I have before remarked that an old turning is no longer round, owing to shrinkage.

FURNITURE IN THEATRE AND FICTION

There is needed a setting for theatrical scenes and for the illustration of fiction. For this purpose those who paint the pictures or set the scenes require at least a rudimentary knowledge of furniture which they sometimes fail to acquire.

A notable college professor of history set forth a scene of Columbus before Ferdinand and Isabella, in which a Buchanan period office chair was occupied by the secretary of the monarch, and this historical (?) pageant was paraded through the streets of

Plymouth as the best that America could do, by and with the advice of a neighboring university. Of course such things only render representations ridiculous and must bring a blush to any serious student.

In theatres, when some old-time play is produced, as of the age of Goldsmith, the stock article that used to be pushed out on the stage was a Victorian sofa. That seemed to the producers to satisfy all historical and artistic requirements. They called it the "atmosphere." A play to transport one to the time when it was written derives remarkable advantage from a correct setting. Otherwise the genius of the actor must be transcendent to drag the public back, in spite of itself, to the time of the play. It is a handicap to which an actor ought not to be subjected. Whatever his success without a setting, he will have a far more striking success if helped by being placed himself in the surroundings of the time of the play. Costume is important, but the background is a still more emphatic note. These anachronisms are like the remarks of a caretaker in one of my old houses. She wished to be dramatic and was explaining the magnificent linden trees in front of a house of 1760. "The family brought over the little trees from England in tomato cans."

The illustrators of novels are some of them obviously being careful to make their interiors correspond with the date of the tales they are depicting. I have detected in their work several chairs and tables copied from my books — unique but proper setting, which added much to the interest and reality of the novel. Some of the interiors in this volume have a charm far greater than any one piece of furniture. If they are not all credited, it may be safe to attribute them to the excellent Concord Antiquarian Society.

In this connection the modern accessories necessary in any room deserve attention because all of them can easily be disguised or made invisible. New dwellings may have radiators covered in and hidden under the windows. If they are otherwise already placed, a screen made like the front of a livery cupboard may even make their presence an attraction, which is saying much for a radiator.

The fireplaces should never be furnished with a gas log, one of the most meretricious devices possible. If a fire is wanted, it should be real. If a fire is not within means, at least some real wood ought to be placed on the andirons. The modern filigreed fire set should be banished and only a shovel and tongs leaned one on each jamb, against the proper hook. By all means let the copper fire lighter be banished, for which Cape Cod has been made unjustly responsible.

The lighting fixtures should never show an electric light, though for convenience the lights should be present. Ground glass, either in a lantern or a globe, ought always to intervene between the light and the eye. The bulbs made up to imitate a candle or a flame are objectionable as they create no illusion. The frosted glass does all necessary in actually screening the source of the light.

To be sure, there are those who will use nothing but real candles. They are only for the wealthy with numerous servants. The fixtures themselves are often too elaborate and of foreign form. There are plenty of good old American forms. Sconces which cannot otherwise screen lights should be fitted with small, straight, frosted chimneys. The problem is simple with lanterns except for the "parlor," now a living room, and the dining room. In simple, very early houses lanterns are proper even in such rooms, but in no fine furniture period, that is, anything of the William and Mary time or later, except in crude kitchens and halls. If movable lights are required, they may be fitted on early iron stands and screened with the small ground-glass chimneys. I deprecate the introduction of fitted glass lamps, in colors, into any old rooms. These adaptations of the kerosene lamp are tawdry and wholly out of period. Glass lamps of the whale-oil time shaped much like candlesticks may be tolerated in a room of about 1800. Nearly all otherwise good settings are marred by wrong lighting fixtures because unless an owner is very particular and gives wise attention to the matter, the fixture people will tell him it is not practical to match his setting, or will supply a wrong setting and persuade him it is good enough.

Some of us cannot afford to be right, if our houses are not fitted properly. But when the work is newly installed there is no excuse for lack of harmony. But how often do we find it?

Windows also may have the old forms, though no attention to this matter is necessary until we get back to 1790. Earlier the muntins must be heavy. By 1750 the sash must be small; by 1700 they should be casements, leaded, and supplied with proper early fasteners.

Beams show up to 1750 about, but in fine rooms they are cased and the summer beam is paneled in fine rooms. No black beam, or obvious hand hewing should ever show.

Here in Framingham the town hall, a nineteenth-century building, has been done over with a black rough-hewn beam showing, with white on the balance of the room. No such beam is possible. The marks of the hewing were carefully obliterated on beams left in sight, and they were made with chamfers. But they never showed at all in the period of the room, nor for seventy years before. The construction is only found in very early English buildings.

In America it is not uncommon in "restoring" an old house to uncover the beams, whatever the period. They had begun to case and hide these beams two hundred years ago — in fact, just about 1730.

Note how in the Wentworth-Gardner house, 1760, Portsmouth, the ceilings are plain plaster, and in the earlier Royall House, Medford, the beams are cased!

I have in "Connecticut Beautiful," a volume out of print, but available in many libraries, given extensive attention to old houses. Many volumes wholly given to this subject, by various authors, can be consulted, as also sporadic attention in my other books of the States Beautiful series, none of which are available, except Virginia, outside of libraries.

THE RIGHT THINGS TOGETHER

A gentleman in search of a country place finally made his bargain in a good old home room simply but effectively furnished. As he handed over his check to bind the bargain he said, "I don't mind telling you now that you could not have dragged me out of this room with wild horses." I was the seller. The room had cost to furnish less than two hundred dollars, and it could be done today for the same figure. The buyer knew nothing of old furniture. He felt it.

When I speak of the charm or lure of old furniture in old settings, I am not expounding a theory, but going on the basis of a thirty-year experience. I know it is easily possible to spoil a good room with ten thousand dollars, or to make a bad room good with one hundred dollars. The right things with the right things will do it. The right things with the wrong things spoil it. Ladies with fine taste, in general, can go wrong without experience in furniture combinations. Their social friends, of course, will not tell them they have done the thing wrong. There is nobody who dare tell them, their husbands least of all. But there are plenty to say "wonderful, superb, fetching, delightful," "how did you ever do it?" "Oh, it was easy," is the reply. It is.

But what is the earnest American woman to do? There are millions of them. There is a simple rule by which she cannot possibly go wrong. Let her take a good compendium on furniture (like mine, for instance!) and get for a room every article of a period. If she makes a single exception, she may go wrong. Only really skilled persons can blend adjoining periods. Let her not listen to the siren voice of the dealer who tells her that what he wants to sell goes well together. There is also another comfort in this infallible rule. If the old is not all available, she can get the new with the old and there will be no jarring note. The expert may be able to separate old from new, but he cannot say that the effect lacks charm.

It is impossible to make a room otherwise than successful if this method is adhered to like the laws of the Medes and Persians. The method proposed will be impossible, if carried through the house with the use of the best period alone, without generous expense, because there is always some desirable piece required, but not available without wide and long search. Many duplicates, or near duplicates, will be found, but something will be rare. The way out is found by most collectors in choosing objects of the time that is well represented in the shops, that is, the late periods. This is always a mistake, if any time later than 1820 is chosen. It will not be ten years before the buyer will become dissatisfied with late clumsy furniture. Then with grudging expense and regret all must be done over again. It is far better to select a period in excellent taste and fill in any necessary gaps with proper new articles. Thus a gentleman bought a new court cupboard because he never hoped to find an old one within his means, but secured other objects of the period in old examples.

Though it is impossible to get old beds in twin sets, what is the objection to a very wide old double bed? The old beds were rather cramped for two, being four and a half feet wide. But a head and foot rail five feet long may be supplied. The result is a bed so wide that only very fussy persons could object to it, and the effect of the large bed is finer. It allows of higher posts than single beds, if the period calls for high posts, and it should do so, because thus the canopy can be kept so high as to be consistent with modern ideas of ventilation. Narrow canopied beds of the best periods look top heavy, and their posts make a forest in the bedroom. The only concession is the new head and foot rails, which are out of sight, and the headboard which is, or should be, very simple, and narrow, and also out of sight.

There is a great quantity of flat-topped Queen Anne highboys to be had at low figures. To be sure, the lowboys are less common, but may be had, or a good reproduction. But the idea of using a lowboy as a dressing table is not practical. It cannot be approached, in spite of its alleged knee hole. An old side table, however, is easily come by, and is entirely right as a dressing table (the "vanity table" really did not exist in any good period). If, then, a chest of drawers is added, as may be desired in a large room, all the major pieces are provided. Odd chairs are easy to get, as few bedrooms require more than three chairs, some only two. If one is an arm, a wing, a roundabout, or an easy chair, the other may be a side chair which need not match even in the old time. Looking-glasses are numerous, and as one cannot tell old from new, the job is done! Rugs, pictures, clocks, shelves, desks to taste (good taste!).

Beginners are always stumbling over the question of the dining room. They call for an extension table, and in the modern meaning of the word there was no such thing. Flounder and twist as one will, that is the truth and the whole truth. What then? There are several resources. If the room is to be very old, get a drawing table which is virtually an extension. I am bound to say I never knew anybody to get one except an English fake, but my experience does not cover as I wish it did. The drawing table has not been found here. But a somewhat long and narrow table has been found, with end leaves. It may be in the Atheneum, with the Seymour Collection, (see FURNITURE TREASURY No. 975). Here, with the end leaves down, is an effect like a short trestle table, and there is plenty of room for four persons at the sides, the ends not being available when leaves are down, but put up the leaves and you have a table for ten or twelve persons, and a desirable table. I own that I have never seen another in use. It is one of the mysteries. The next resource would be two short trestles, of course new, used together or separately, side by side or end to end. Then we come on three or four periods all of which provided two- or three-part tables, all available in the old style, except the best, the claw-foot Chippendale, which must be new, an American piece, or an English fake. The two-part straight-leg tables are somewhat common. Rather too many legs, either as Sheraton, Hepplewhite, or Chippendale! Also the same in three parts. The usual resource, however, is a two- or three-part table, on standards with three or four branching legs, of the Empire style, and ordinarily called after Phyfe. Too common and too late and too much lacking in design for the old collector; just right for the novice collector. Then comes the similar table, except for the legs, in the Queen Anne or Chippendale style. So here are six styles of two- or three-part tables, after we leave the Seymour example.

The objection of the collector to the three-part tables is that they cost too much. Such persons should then go back to the earlier times or go to the modern furniture shop. The two-part table, however, is not very expensive, and with the leaf which is inset with it, at will, it makes up in adjustments of three lengths, which should be satisfactory.

CROWDING THE STAIR

Do not do it. One of the finest collectors I know has crowded his stair on both landings. It detracts from the spaciousness so attractive on a stair. (The word spaciousness ought to be coined, for nothing will take its place.) A pinched stair, either by construction or by overfurnishing, is too suggestive of a tenement. Besides, people like to go side by side on stairs, women especially. Then, too, the stair is the most effective place for courting. A certain Connecticut governor's wife became such by proposing on the stair after she had passed the shy youth, a house guest, many times, and finally turned and asked, "What did you say?" Then he said it. You could not do that on a narrow stair. Just one thing will go on the landing if it is spacious — a hall clock. But on the wall, as one goes up, what a place for old prints, alternated with old looking-glasses! They make the hall the most delightful quarter of the house. But the stair should have broad treads, and be in no hurry to arrive at the top. A straight stair has no mystery and no charm, however rich. And a spiraled stair is a trap. Begin the stair well back in the hall; make its bottom step broad and inviting. Give resting places for old people. Also for young people. Down south many fine houses hid the stair, as Jefferson's and the Harland house. The stair is the most evident, the most used, the most beautifully adapted for decoration, and the most hospitable part of the house. Who that has once seen his shining-eyed sweetheart coming down the stair to him at the foot can ever forget it? See the mother carry up in her arms the sleeping babe, and see her rest and kiss it on both landings.

See the grandfather make his feeble way alone with the help of the baluster rail after he has carried his wife out for the last time! See the trooping youth at their wedding gathering that thronged up and down these eloquent steps! See the roguish youngster sliding down the rail when he thinks nobody is looking! See the girl of five or six, the most beautiful creation of God, run down laughing with arms wide to greet you! Ah! the stair.

There is almost too much of dear humanity about it — the steps that use it or did use it. The best stair I knew was at grandmother's little house under the hill, near a brook. If you can believe it, this stair started up — from where do you suppose? The spacious pantry! Who ever heard of such a beginning? Still, it was handy to take a cooky as one went along to bed, and besides the smell of the cooky there was the old pine odor on the sheathed unpainted stair, and above the quick slope of the roof, just right for a small boy, but requiring humility of elders.

And beyond the landing were barrels and boxes of good and queer things, and storage space for chests and spinning stuff, and in the other gable a little room with one window that looked out on the sweet corn garden — the best in town. There was an hour-glass table and a generous bed — none of your single affairs. A little lonely, to be sure, for a five-year-old, but grandmother slept just below in the kitchen bedroom, and if imagination became too active, one could thump on the floor or even call out.

The rafters showed, but between them was pasted the current literature of grandmother's childhood. It was my introduction to romance. If I could hear the rustle of bird feet on the roof, in the morning, if I could catch the rippling song of the brook and be put to sleep by it as then, if I could hear grandfather's call to the flapjacks already announcing themselves through the floor crevices! Toilets were brief. Item, one pair of trousers — and nothing more. The pump was in the kitchen. Happy? Grandmother's eye was the most eloquent of love that I have ever seen, except that of John McAuslan. When she looked at you she gave you benediction in her smile and wrapped you round with her glance.

All the furniture I remember, in addition, is the broad dresser shelf in the pantry; a table always closed and pushed to the wall after meals; and a wall clock, which of all clocks that ever were had the loudest tick, especially as it approached eight, bed time, when its tempo solemnly increased, and its hands swept like hurrying fate, and its voice was a diapason.

Furniture gets its importance through the events connected with it. I remember a certain large chair — but, let us speak of something else. There are little chairs for children, in the number of the imponderable values. No price can be set on them with their flattened front posts, rubbed down by playing horse on the sanded floor. They are in the class with the silver spoon showing tooth marks and the toys sent home from the Civil War to their children by fathers who could never come. There are sacred chapters on furniture, in volumes never seen by the public, but of utmost preciousness. Perhaps Chippendale is innocent of their design, but their outlines are sufficiently appealing, for their seats are just as high as our hearts.

ADVERTISING AND SILHOUETTE WORK

It is often amusing and effective, in illustration, to accent the salient lines of furniture, to compel people to see them, just as cartoonists exaggerate the features of a face. Donnelly has done this in some of his silhouettes (which, by the way, a down-easter pronounced "salutes," it being his impression, I think, that the name was given them as Christmas greeting cards).

The lines of much old furniture are easily caricatured in illustration so as to add humor or tone to the work. An extraordinarily high-combed Windsor, a table with legs extremely spindly or overbulbous, an overdone looking-glass frame, impart a snap and flavor to a drawing, and relieve the possible tedium of the text.

If the illustrator takes care to introduce odd forms of old things in his pictures, he will catch the eye he is paid to catch. There is a wide field, only partially cultivated, for these effects. A smart figure requires a smart setting, and if this can be supplied, even when it is not nominated in the bond, it is so much to the good with the public, that god whom it is sought to placate.

A figure without a background may be good, but still better if sketched in a telling setting. The singer asks accompaniment. It would often happen that a sketch submitted by an artist for illustration, and rejected, would gain acceptance by an unusually good placing, for even if the advertiser does not understand these things, he may feel their charm.

Examples of the overemphasis on curves, the fining of lines more than in the
original, and the bringing out in a brilliant way the stylistic features in articles
of furniture. (*Donnelly*.)

The revival of the use of the powder puff affords room for the exaggeration of
lines in a William and Mary side table. It compels people to see the features of
the leg turning which they might otherwise overlook.

(415)

FOREIGN WORK

My steadfast adherence, in description and illustration, to American examples is not owing to lack of appreciation of the wonderful antiques of Europe. But American work and specimens in America have never been fully set forth. Pictures have been particularly weak. I do not feel that America has contributed very much to design beyond the magnificent exception by Goddard and his school. But we do not get the best foreign work over here. The foreign museums were old before we had any. They have been gathering for centuries what we are only in this very generation gathering. So slightly has American work been looked upon by men educated abroad to head American museums that it may fairly be said no museum heads before the past ten years have given more than a contemptuous attention to American work. Mr. Kimball of the Philadelphia museum and Messrs. Cornelius and Halsey at the Metropolitan, with the sympathetic coöperation of Mr. Kent, are really the pioneers in their attention to American furniture in museums themselves.

The serious consideration and publication, first by Lyon and then by Lockwood, of furniture examples found here and mostly made here were landmarks of progress. Unhappily, those works were put forth without full illustration and mostly before the discovery of half the present available material. Nearly all work aside from this has consisted of tales about families, in which I have been induced to indulge briefly in this volume. What is really important, the knowledge of lines, and the showing of full examples of the whole and of details, has been slurred over.

But of course, the mere cursory viewing of European examples shows us at once the source and the inspiration of most American work. We have never gotten out in America magnificent works in color, such as are found abroad and which works, of course, are hardly available to the ordinary collector. There is a good reason why we never can issue such works. The examples do not exist here. Sometimes a portion of them, such as are in private hands, may be obtained for America. But the representative articles are in the foreign museums. Color seems important only in the case of rich inlays, marqueterie, and buhl work. There is little of this here. The exquisite lines of good Newport, Philadelphia, and Hartford work are well brought out without color.

However, there is nothing like a study of American furniture to fit one to see the merits of foreign furniture. Until recently Americans going abroad thought no more, unless they were specialists, of visiting furniture collections than of a visit to the moon.

All that has changed. With the study, often enthusiastic and sometimes intensive, of American furniture has arisen a yearning to see the earliest examples reposing abroad, so that now many Americans derive the keenest enjoyment of a European visit from the inspection of the available objects. And more Americans would do well to follow their examples before they fill their minds and empty their pockets, tempted by the alleged but still alluring foreign trade items.

WOODS IN FURNITURE

A distinction must be made between the best woods, intrinsically, for use in furniture, and the woods actually used. Oak was used in carved work in the Middle Ages and the Renaissance, and even locally as late as the latter part of the eighteenth century, owing to persistence of type as in provincial England. But it lacked the properties requisite for delicate cutting.

Even the supreme carver, Grinling Gibbons, lived before the mahogany age. Some of his best work is in pine, a material very inferior. Pine had, however, the advantage of cutting rapidly. Commercial considerations have governed every age of artisanship, and after looking over the whole field, ancient and modern, it appears that our "commercial" age is not more so than other ages. There are persons today who desire the best materials and workmanship and are willing to pay for them. There have been such people in every age, but they have always been in the minority.

Gibbons found that pear wood was very suitable for fine carving. Its use required more labor than a softer wood, but the results were superior in delicacy.

The best wood for furniture depends also on the kind of furniture. For undercutting and small ornaments a semi-soft close-grained wood like the tulip, otherwise called whitewood, is better, because less brittle than finer woods. This wood is excellent for elaborate mirror frames, as also is basswood.

Another consideration is the style. It would not be appropriate to use mahogany for work of a style before mahogany came in or after it went out, a rule often transgressed. The strength of oak is so great that it is indicated even now as the proper wood for massive furniture, though its grain is not adapted for the best carving.

Amboyna. East Indian, used chiefly in inlays which are beautifully variegated and of a reddish tint.

Apple. A very hard, close-grained wood, which polishes handsomely. It is found in a considerable number of cabinet pieces of the early Georgian and Chippendale periods in America and is liked by collectors, though not so valuable as mahogany. It is perhaps the most perfect wood for turnings and was long the stock material for tool handles.

It is even superior to maple and birch. Only good judges can distinguish it from birch.

Ash. The usual wood in the very first turned American chairs was shortly abandoned for maple, a much more suitable material. Also used as a bending wood, but see Hickory.

Basswood. The American variety of the linden. It is light and soft, and very much resembles whitewood with which it is used indifferently, and sometimes confused. It answers for carving, but is not a high-class wood for furniture.

Beech. The word "book" comes from the earlier form of the word for beech, because books had covers made of beech. Beech is more common in English than in American furniture. Its early use was in cane or baluster-back chairs, but later it almost monopolized the trade in the turnings of Windsor chairs in England. The grain is close and yet distinguishable by those accustomed to it from maple. It is hard and good in all respects except liability to worm attack.

The beech tree is vital and will spread rapidly if given half a chance. It has been recklessly cut off in America until it is almost rare. Its decorative quality when growing is superior to that of the maple, and its adaptability for furniture is as favorable.

Birch. This wood is as old as language, because the tree is distinguished throughout the north temperate zone. But the canoe birch, or paper birch (Betula papyrifera), is not only the handsomest as it grows, but the best and hardest for furniture. It grows, however, on high lands, or in coldish regions. The wood in large trees is dark, and all birch takes a handsome finish, which, when stained as mahogany, deceives the novice. However, the cells in mahogany are clearly noticeable, on a near view, whereas birch has a very close grain. It is strong like maple and takes a fine finish, but the canoe birch was not, near the coast, and in the colonial period, so readily available for furniture. The common birch growing in clustered form, of a grayish white, is a punky wood of no value for furniture.

Seventeenth-century birch furniture in the age of oak is not rare. It is a popular modern wood and is often used indiscriminately with maple. As a turning wood it is unsurpassed.

Box. A hard, close-grained wood, nearly white. A choice wood for small and dainty turnings like sand shakers, and in request for engraving which requires intricate, small cuts. The wood occurs commercially as small round stocks and is not, therefore, adapted for use except for delicate work. It is one of the heaviest woods, and an aristocrat for which apple wood must often serve as a substitute.

Butternut. A wood belonging to the walnut family, but differing in color and somewhat in texture. Occasional cabinet pieces are found in this wood, which is not always easy to distinguish from light-colored walnut in furniture.

Cherry. Owing to a slightly reddish tinge, a favorite substitute for mahogany, though it has a closer grain and is lighter than good mahogany. A wood largely used by the Chapins (which see) for beautiful rendering in furniture. The cabinet wood is ordinarily the black cherry.

A vogue for this wood in furniture is difficult to understand, as it is only a poor cousin of mahogany, and was of course used in the early days only on account of its cheapness. Its period of use is, therefore, the same as that of mahogany. It had the good fortune, therefore, to be wrought into the better shapes of furniture, which are, if beautiful, of large value, but never equal the value of old mahogany.

Chestnut. A wood in good demand in early days for the backs of cabinet pieces (a favorite with John Goddard) and furniture interiors. A coarse-grained wood not so strong as oak, but closely resembling coarse oak. The old spelling was "chesnut." This glorious tree, nearly annihilated in the North by a mysterious blight, is said to be likely to revive.

Cypress. The American variety is a southern wood, very durable, and, while popular in modern furniture, was not much in use in the early days. Cedar is a close relative of cypress, but its use is more for linings and interiors than otherwise, and it is not recommended.

Ebony. Hard, heavy, durable, and, when black, prized in the Orient for cabinetwork, but confined in America mostly to inlays or veneers. Even so, more available woods are often stained or painted black in imitation of ebony.

Gum. A common inferior commercial wood in the South and used in great quantities in modern furniture in which form it is frequently given a finish like mahogany and passed off for it.

Many other rare woods are used occasionally for inlays or veneers. It is probable, however, that in America two pieces out of three of worthy furniture are in maple, then in frequency, cherry, pine, mahogany, and walnut follow, with oak trailing the list, because it is found only in the earliest types which are now rare.

Hickory. Often called white walnut. To be distinguished from butternut. The hickory grows only in North America.

Hickory is the finest wood known for bending, or for small sections under strain. It was therefore generally used for Windsor chair bent parts and spindles. But large old hickory trees tend to be coarse in the grain, and young hickories were preferred. It was also almost exclusively used for light wagon spokes.

The substitutes for hickory bending stock were white oak and ash. These materials when used for bending should be of fine grain. Woods are like human beings. Every tree is different from every other, even in the same locality. Old trees tend to coarseness. I recall a chair rung of ash which was like a bundle of reeds, and could be plucked apart with the fingers. Oak also is sometimes as coarse as chestnut, and difficult to distinguish from it. Young hickory is altogether better for bending than the best oak or ash.

Holly. A white, fine-grained wood whose principal use was for line inlay or veneer, alternately with other woods.

Maple, hard or rock or sugar.

This wood reigned almost supreme in New England for simple furniture from 1760 to 1820 or thereabouts, and much earlier for turned work.

The swamp or soft maple is neither so strong nor so handsome, but it entered into furniture to some extent, as near the shore and on low lands it was temptingly available.

Rock maple grows on uplands very commonly and is rarer in Pennsylvania and the South. But in southern highlands there are often good maples, as in the Carolinas.

Rock maple is very hard and close grained. Where used for floors the finish of maple wears off in lanes most used. Hence it is very unsuitable for that purpose.

For carving it has cost the writer a great deal. It requires a mallet on the graving tool, and on a certain job a carver wore out completely one of his tools, whose edge would dull in a few minutes.

Curly maple is a difficult wood to work. It will chip in planing and it breaks in bending. The exquisite results left us in curly maple turnings or flat work are beyond praise. The zebra grain shows complete bands of curl.

Curiously the bird's-eye maple is scorned in these days. Perhaps the cause is that it was used much in the early nineteenth century. But the prejudice against it is unwarranted, if the patterns into which it was wrought were good.

Maple frequently has an irregular grain which gives what is technically called figured maple, a handsome effect, admired by some collectors.

The use of maple for the underbody of Windsor chairs was common. Quantities also of chairs in Queen Anne and simple turned types are common. Probably a majority of the highboys and most of the beds were in maple.

It is sought now for simple uses. Of course, it combines with pine properly, because broad surfaces are better in soft woods. Pine has more beauty than maple. It is a mistake to desire pine in furniture legs, as it lacks strength, and seldom were pieces showing style done with pine underbodies.

Mahogany (Swietenia mahagoni). This is the true mahogany, the queen of cabinet woods. It is hard, heavy, strong, durable. It is adapted for cutting into any form which wood ought to take. Little liable to warp or shrink, it answers all reasonable demand that should be made for fine furniture, by which we mean furniture of the more elegant periods. There surrounds it like an aroma the magnificent traditions of the great cabinetmakers. It is connected with the sentiment of old family feeling, since its use occurred in the late Colonial, the Federal, and the Constitutional periods. It was popular and referred to as the standard from 1740 to 1840, and in the revival from 1890 to the present time. The great body of the best American furniture is constructed of it. In this respect its only rival is walnut. But mahogany is comparatively free from the attacks of insects, and permanence and beauty are combined in it more than in any other wood.

Sad to say, good mahogany is now rare and expensive, and, if the present vogue for it continues, it may before many years be no longer available.

This fact is carefully glossed over among modern makers and dealers, and inferior woods which are not true mahoganies and are available in great quantity are substituted.

Of old the principal source of fine logs was San Domingo (Hayti). This is the same true mahogany as is found in the West Indies, more particularly the islands. Cuba is at present the larger source, now that railways are enabling merchants to obtain the wood at a distance from the shores, which has been cut off wherever it was feasible to load it on vessels.

This wood is a dark reddish brown and, in good specimens, straight in the grain. The sap wood is narrow. It has flecks of lime in the pores. When cut near branches it furnishes curly or feathered grains now mostly used for veneers.

What is left in San Domingo runs small. Cuba still produces large logs.

Mahogany, Honduras. This Central American wood is lighter in color and weight. It varies greatly in quality, much of it being pale, soft, spongy, coarse, and fuzzy. The terms in use regarding mahogany are often vague and misleading. Honduras and Mexican mahogany are often called baywood. There is also a Laguni wood sometimes passing for Honduras mahogany.

Mahogany, Mexican. This wood is not so good as the preceding, but may be had in larger logs, and inclines to be shaky and brittle or soft. Better specimens are called Tabasco. Of course, mahoganies, like other woods, bring greater prices in proportion to their width. Of old it was the practice to use large logs for pie-crust tables, all fine specimens being of one piece, even up to thirty-three inches and more.

Mahogany, African. This is not a mahogany, and is very inferior. It must be emphasized that there is great difference in quality in mahogany, as in other woods, even when growing in a single vicinity. Every piece of mahogany must be judged by itself. One can tell it by the weight, with his eyes shut. If it is very heavy, it is very good. Much commercial furniture is the African "mahogany."

Mahogany, Indian. Not a true mahogany and shaky in many instances, but good specimens are useful.

Under Birch attention is called to its use as a substitute for finish in dwellings for mahogany; big mountain birches are often called mahogany birches.

There is also Australian wood, like eucalyptus, which is often passed off in furniture for mahogany. The novice should understand that inferior mahogany is at a lower price in the market than our good native woods and not so good for furniture use. Much of it has a grain that is almost as course and slivery as hemlock and is totally unsuitable. As a rule, it is not real mahogany, but many buyers do not discriminate and are persuaded that when they have an article sold for mahogany, they have a good thing.

Oak. The wood chiefly used in the Gothic period for furniture, especially in England and continued late in the sixteenth and throughout the seventeenth centuries, sharing in popularity with walnut, which finally supplanted it. However, the English provincial cabinetmaker often used oak even on Chippendale styles. Walnut was common on the continent a century before it became so in England.

Oak suggests massive and not specially delicate treatment. It is in England and America seldom found in a fine grain. When carved, therefore, it was best adapted to bold, suggestive lines rather than dainty details.

In America its use was almost entirely confined to seventeenth-century chests and chests of drawers. Maple was found so superior for turning that in chair work it soon took the place of oak, and an American oak chair is extremely rare, being found mostly in the wainscot type.

The English oak (Quercus robur) is counted in England somewhat superior to American white oak (Quercus alba). But the opinion is perhaps based on a prejudice rather than the fact. The best white oak supplies a very excellent material for furniture, as it can be obtained in good lengths free from knots. English oak connotes, historically, the sentiment of solidity and dependableness in the English character and means the more to England as it was the material for those ships which made her the great empire she became. Hence the saying obtained currency that England was surrounded by oaken walls. Nevertheless, long timbers of English oak probably never existed. There is only one length of log in a tree. Oak early became scarce in England, and the great hall of Westminster was supplied with its arches by Irish oak, which was long a source of English builders. At present little oak is supplied commercially for furniture by England.

The color of English oak has long been a question provocative of sharp discussion, and is still little understood.

Oak, white (Quercus alba). This American species is heavy and hard, and was found the best oak for American furniture, and long cuts may be found, two or three or even more to a tree.

Oak, red (Quercus rubra), distinguished by spiked leaves, is somewhat softer and coarser than white oak. It was sometimes used in furniture, but was inferior to white oak.

Oak, live (Quercus virginiana), an evergreen oak, growing in the southern United

States, heavy and hard and much used for ships' knees, but seldom for furniture. Oak furniture in America means, nearly always, seventeenth-century furniture.

English oak and white oak are distinct species. It may be possible by analysis to distinguish between the woods as found in furniture. Practically it is easier to distinguish the stylistic features. The quartering of English and American oak may exhibit practically identical features. If the oak is dark, it is more likely to be English for the reasons above given. Those few persons who can detect the differences in the woods by their grains are not available as experts. This statement means that they are aged or wealthy and do not act as appraisers. But if they are active tradesmen, they may or may not know, so that, between their doubtful knowledge or doubtful veracity, their opinions are of doubtful value.

In a piece of American furniture called oak it is usual to find a hard-pine lid, as in chests and cupboards, and often pine panels in drawers. Oak drawer bottoms in walnut and mahogany furniture are an almost sure mark of foreign origin. But many English pieces have fir or Norway spruce drawer bottoms. Such pieces are easily passed in America as native.

Oak blackens when subjected to water, and the English climate affords water in the air much of the time. Further, the bog oak in Ireland, actually dug out of the muck and sometimes many centuries old, is black, and the name black oak at times is synonymous with bog oak. Chimneys being rare even in the late Gothic era, the oak was blackened also by creosote. To top all this black character given to English oak, the oak showing in half-timbered houses was often painted black and is today. The English claim also that oak darkens with time alone — a questionable statement. Rather, it blackens by the influences, one or other, mentioned above, it has experienced in several hundred years. For weather alone tends to bleach most woods, including oak. Oak kept in a dark place may be darker than that which has felt the influence of the sun near a window. Certain it is that an occasional piece of old, but light, English oak furniture is seen.

Olive. A rare wood in American furniture, but sometimes found in veneers.

Pear. A favorite carving wood, loved by the great masters of the art for smoothness, toughness, and fineness. Seldom used in furniture, but sometimes as well as apple in "fruit wood" furniture, substituting for walnut.

Pine, yellow or hard. This species is now practically non-existent as used in early furniture. A rare tree here and there remains, in the north. It is not the same wood as southern pine.

Yellow pine was found in large trees, and hence chest tops were made from it. It was as hard as oak, and one is puzzled to know why the common white pine was not chosen. The probable conclusion is that the yellow pine was heavy and believed, therefore, to harmonize better with oak.

One investigator came to the conclusion that the wood we call yellow pine was hackmatack (larch), still a common wood. But larch is a light-weight wood, and softer than yellow pine. We do not believe in the investigator's conclusion.

Pine, white or "pumpkin" (Pinus strobus). This wood, confined in early furniture use to the eastern states where alone it occurs in America (except Canada), is soft and light. Occurring in very large trees, it was found convenient for floors, shelving, and any broad surface. It is used in conjunction with maple, this latter for the turnings. It is not seriously given to warping or shrinking. But the very merits which made it popular, its ease of working and its lightness when made up, were objections in fine furniture from liability to mar.

The so-called white pine of California is Pinus lambertiana, a somewhat harder wood, and is now often used instead of white pine, but of course did not enter into early furniture.

The early makers were careful to use clear pine, even in panelwork. The shrewd advertising of lumber men has induced architects to use knotty pine for paneling and even for furniture. After examining a vast number of old houses I have yet to find knotty pine exposed in any good room. It can never be smoothed about the knot.

I am persuaded that it is always in bad taste. If a solitary old example of knotty pine finish, unpainted, could be found, the principle of following the exception rather than the rule is not good.

Poplar. Some mention of this wood is included under tulip wood. There are several varieties, but in America it is an inferior wood, owing to its being soft and light and spongy.

Rosewood. From South America and Ceylon, was a favorite in the nineteenth century, but it was used very little except for veneers in the earlier periods.

Satinwood. A wood related to mahogany found in the East Indies, yellowish, hard, close grained, and durable. Used almost exclusively for veneers. There is also a West Indian satinwood of another species.

Sycamore. Allied to the plane tree, and so named in Scotland. It warps badly, but is strong and hard and with an attractive grain and a glossy surface. It is not an important furniture wood, but enters somewhat into turnery and veneers.

The buttonwood or buttonball is the plane tree but indifferently called sycamore in America. Cut in a certain manner, it produces lacewood.

Teak. An East Indian wood, often used in China for the manufacture of European patterns, as Chippendale. English examples were taken to China and wrought there in teak at a small cost, being used by Europeans in the Orient and sometimes imported into England or America.

Thuya. From North Africa. Supposed to be the Roman citron, used for veneer. Brown in color and having fewer spots in the figure than amboyna.

Tulip (whitewood), commonly called poplar south and west of New York City, but quite distinct from it. Another name is yellow poplar. A commercial wood popular in Pennsylvania and farther south for flat work, like cupboards or dressers, as a substitute for walnut. Sometimes found in Windsor chair seats, as it is light and easy to shape. The grain is fine, and when carved very suitable, since it is spongy rather than brittle and bears being undercut as in looking-glasses. This wood is peculiar to America and is named from its flower resembling a tulip, but also resembling the magnolia.

It has a greenish tinge strongly emphasized by an orange shellac finish to which objection is often made. The wood was not seldom used in New England on simple chests of drawers, and was a favorite wood for the interior ends and back of drawers, alternately or mixed with pine.

Walnut (Juglans regia) is a wood of singular derivation. The first syllable signifies foreign or strange. The word was, therefore, in the mouths of early English people, equivalent to "strange nut." Thus curiously the very word indicates that the wood is not native to England. In the time of Henry VIII and particularly in that of Elizabeth the royal interest was vigorously exerted to induce the planting of the walnut in England and thus to overcome the need of importation, so popular had the wood become. It is a handsome wood, close grained and easily worked, but is so subject to the worm that its introduction is to be deplored. Mahogany is free from this danger.

From 1690 to 1740 walnut was the fashionable material for furniture. It therefore covers, in its early use, the time of Charles II and, in its later use, the early Georgian period and the whole of the intervening Queen Anne period. To be sure, the pad, disc, or Dutch foot was so popular that it continued in that particular in common use long after Chippendale styles came in, but the material became maple or mahogany, the woods lapping over in period.

Walnut is native to northern China and Persia.

It came into the occident by way of Greece and Italy.

French walnut is counted superior to the English of the same species. The Italian is also highly prized.

The question of the use of this walnut is largely academic, as it was in such sharp demand for gunstocks, and owing to the winter 1709 in Europe, the use of mahogany or American walnut was forced on the customer. This event may be fairly considered a blessing in disguise.

But the conservatism of the English prevented them from drawing to any extent on the American walnut supply, once seemingly unlimited.

It was not till the degraded period that Europe began to import our walnut in quantity.

Foreign walnuts were more subject to the worm than our native walnuts.

Many of the richest foreign specimens of furniture have fallen to pieces from being turned into powder by insects.

The burrs or burls (warts and richly figured sections) were and are in keen demand, especially as veneers on highboys, lowboys, and secretaries.

The oystering of small diagonally cut sticks fitted to one another as veneers was a favorite foreign use, seldom if ever found in America.

In America, owing to the great abundance of walnut in Pennsylvania and Virginia, the wood was in very general use even for the simplest forms of furniture and for dwellings, not only during the classical period, but through the eighteenth century. But in New England, though there was native walnut, it was not common, and walnut furniture in that region is confined mostly to the finer styles. Maple, on the other hand, being everywhere abundant, in New England, substituted, along with cherry, for mahogany.

Walnut, black (Juglans nigra), is a wood often used, and found in America, for furniture. This wood is of about equal merit for use with English walnut, but is somewhat darker. It became very unpopular with collectors at one time because it was the material of the degraded dark ages of furniture, 1830 to 1890. But the objection to the wood should not hold; the objection should be to the shapes into which it was tortured.

Walnut, white, see Hickory.

Whitewood, see Tulip.

The manner of preparation of woods for furniture in the old days has only a curious, rather than practical, interest for us, because the old methods are wholly abandoned, except in the case of stock four inches or more in diameter. This is still obtainable only in an air-dried condition.

Whether the practice of painting the ends of green lumber to prevent its drying faster than the balance of the piece was used in the old days I have not been able to ascertain.

Furniture stock was first dried in the open air and then placed under cover without heat, as kilns were unknown. Thus it required some years to dry thoroughly an inch board. Lumber turned into furniture, if in a moist climate or in the humid months of the year, will shrink too much. The modern method of steaming lumber to drive out the sap and then drying it in a kiln, if the process is not hurried, probably produces better results than the old method. Under the chapter on "Finishing" there is a very important observation regarding finishing on both sides of wide sections.

The old method left, perhaps, five per cent by weight of moisture in the lumber, and that was proper enough. Lumber with less than four per cent of moisture is too dry and brittle and is liable to swelling in the humid months. By the old method lumber, of course, could never be drier than the air that surrounded it, but as the content of the air varied with the seasons of the year, the results were not uniform. Very much of the talk about the good old methods in furniture is unwarranted. It is rather the exception than the rule that old table tops are not found warped or cracked or both. This is particularly true of maple. The warping was caused by neglecting to finish both sides alike. The inner or under side is never finished, but it should be. Broad sections fixed in place so that they could not shrink necessarily split. Hence the panel system is better than the broad surfaces of the Chippendale period. The panels could come and go. Style drove out the good old method of paneling. The system used in Pennsylvania, and to some extent in Rhode Island, of inserting a dovetailed cleat on the under side of broad surfaces and not fastening the cleat permitted movement. However, on fine work one end of the dovetail was made blind, and the other one was plugged, and a little space was left.

Lumber that was not dry enough would show a clouding or a bloom through the finish.

The practice of quartering lumber was, of course, to prevent warp rather than to reveal a fine figure. Incidentally, however, the figure in modern times became an important commercial matter. Most slab wood will warp. Planks cut from the center of a log are, of course, in effect quartered. Hence heavy lumber is better to work up, since it is more likely to come from the centers which were generally reserved for heavy stock. The quartering is a cutting from the edge directly towards the center of the log and of course wastes more or less stock. The early clapboards were all riven in this manner like narrow segments, with a froe. Thus, incidentally, they had a wedge shape, and were durable.

Bending woods like Windsor chair stock were bent when absolutely green. Thus they held their form better than woods that were first dried and then wet for bending. Probably woods which had gotten a little too dry were boiled in water to restore their elasticity. The question of seasoned and unseasoned woods in Windsor chairs is taken up elsewhere in this work.

Mahogany logs probably were, as they still are, kept afloat in fresh or preferably salt water. Thus the sap was driven out, and it was easier to season the planks cut from sap-free logs. The claim is made that water-soaked logs are darker in color. Probably this is true to some extent.

Veneers were all cut with a hand saw and therefore were always thicker than modern veneers which can be made to a thickness of a hundred and twenty to the inch. The old veneers could be glued down on the somewhat rough surface left by the saw, or only partially smoothed. Thus they kept their place better. The surface was then planed or sanded down to the proper thickness. It was a tedious, but a satisfactory, job.

Stools have been treated elsewhere, but this rich English specimen, of the Jacobean period, is a fine design.

The right-hand mold shows a clock cornice.

CABINETMAKERS IN AMERICA

Adams, Nehemiah, Salem, Mass.

Afleck, Thomas, Second Street, Philadelphia, Pa. (1768). Furniture maker.

Albine, John, Baltimore, Md. (1796). Cabinetmaker.

Alden, John, Plymouth, Mass. (1612–72). Probably made the Governor Prince court cupboard and others similar, with the Plymouth chests of the same style. It lies between him and Kenelm Winslow, the earliest names of furniture workers in America.

Allen, Benjamin, Braintree, Mass. (1757). Cabinetmaker.

Allen, Joseph, Philadelphia, Pa. (1785). Cabinetmaker.

Allis, Captain John, Hatfield, Mass. (working 1702). "Hadley" chests.

Always, John and James, New York City (1786–1815). Chair makers.

Anderson, Alexander, New York City (1789).

Anderson, John, Annapolis, Md. (1746). Cabinetmaker and carver.

Allison, Michael, New York City (c. 1820). Label on late Empire animal-foot table: "M. Allison's Cabinet and Upholstery Furniture Warehouse, No. 46 & 48 Vesey Street, New York, May 1817." Was contemporary and neighbor of Duncan Phyfe. Made a lyre work table.

Appleton, ——. Secretary of Sheraton period.

Armit, Joseph and Stephen, Philadelphia, Pa. Established at the time of Gostelowe.

Artman, John, Charlestown, Mass. (1803). Cabinetmaker.

Ash, Gilbert, New York City (1756). The maker of one and supposedly of another variety of the Chippendale chair. One of these has tassel and lace drapery in its beautiful splat, another has a back with simpler lines. The former has French scroll feet, very rare in American chairs. The latter has good claw-and-ball feet and acanthus knee carving. The back of one is shown. "Gilbert Ash Wall St. 1756."

Ashe, Thomas, New York City (working 1774–1815). Also his son Thomas, Jr.

Austin, Samuel, Philadelphia, Pa. Established at the time of Gostelowe.

Bacon, Pierpont, Colchester, Conn. (c. 1760). Cabinetmaker.

Badlam, Stephen, Dorchester, Mass. (c. 1800). "Looking-glasses & Cabinet Work" on sign in form of a two-part looking-glass frame. Was Brigadier in Revolutionary War and advisor of Alexander Hamilton.

Barnard, Abner, Northampton, Mass. (c. 1774). Not a cabinetmaker by trade, but made the wedding furniture for his daughter Anna. Worked in cherry. Very fine pieces.

Bass, Elisha, Hanover, Mass. (c. 1800). Maker of a sheraton type sideboard.

Belden, —— 17th C. A partner with Allis, son of Captain John Allis of Hatfield, as joiner.

Biggard, John, Charleston, S. C. (1767-   ). Windsor chairs.

Brinner, John, Broadway (1762). Cabinetmaker. Reproduced Chippendale designs.

Bliss & Pelatiah, Springfield, Mass. (1810). "Cabinet Business."

Brocas, John, Boston, Mass. (1736–37). Cabinetmaker.

Brown, John, at meeting of cabinetmakers in Philadelphia, July 4th, 1788.

Brown, William, Baltimore, Md. (1796).

Brown, William J., Baltimore, Md.? (working 1818).

Burkhart, John, Wheeling, W. Va. (late 17th century?). Chest of drawers.

Burling, Thomas, New York City (working 1790–1800). Bookcase-secretary of inlaid mahogany, broken arch left off top, plain bracket feet. Label: "Thos. Burling, Cabinet and Chair Maker, No. 56 Beckman Street, New York."

Burnham, Benjamin, Hartford, Conn. (1769–   ). Maker of a block-front desk of cherry.

Burrage, Thomas, Charlestown (1788). Cabinetmaker.

Buthe, William (working 1810).

Buss, S. Hitchcock type chair brand. Chairs in Rhode Island.

Cane, David, Philadelphia, Pa. Established at the time of Gostelowe.

Carilile (Carlile?), John, Providence, R. I. (1762–1832).

Cermenati & Bernarda, Salem, Mass. (c. 1810). Label: "Cermenati & Bernada, Gilders and Looking Glass Manufacturers, opposite Albert Grant's Hat Store, Essex Street, Salem."

Cermenati and Monfrino, Boston, Mass. (c. 1800). Label on looking-glass in architectural style, with glass frieze: "Cermenati & Monfrino—No. 2 State Street, Boston."

Challen, William, New York City (c. 1797). Came from London. Introduced the "fancy" chair.

Chapin, Aaron, E. Windsor, Conn. (b. Chicopee, Mass., 1753 or E. Windsor, Conn.) Then Hartford, after c. 1783 (working 1783–1825 or later), (d. 1838). *See also* Eliphalet Chapin. Our remarks on this maker's style are quite appropriate also to Eliphalet Chapin. Sometimes this maker swept inward the inside scroll of his bracket feet instead of outward to conform with the outside, if, indeed, the feet so found are original. A plain latticed fret supported the double arch scroll and is common to the Chapins and frequently occurs on their work. It is thought probable that the Chapins had seen the spiral terminating some scrolls on Philadelphia cabinetwork. Worked mostly in cherry. One piece of Aaron's at least is in mahogany; all others cherry. A labeled sideboard is known. His dentils are generally at right angles to the cresting mold, instead of vertical.

Chapin, Eliphalet, Windsor, Conn. (1770–   ). Worked, perhaps always, with cherry and produced some of the most distinctive, beautiful, and meritorious furniture of New England. A special feature is the spiraled rosettes terminating the broken arch; a plain, poor, and also a uniquely fine finial. Making Chippendale chairs 1781. His brother (?) Aaron's work is often difficult to distinguish from his. The finest specimen now known of this Chapin's work is a carved inlaid secretary-bookcase, now, after having been owned in California, returned to its original home in the dwelling of Mrs. Emma Fuller, Suffield, Connecticut. This maker used ball-and-claw and ogee feet and fluted quarter columns, sometimes brass stopped and decorated in one instance with brass capitals and bases, and in this respect being perhaps unique, since the style is otherwise restricted to clocks.

Chapin, Silas (1793–1828). "Big Flat Tiogo Co. New York." Distant cousin of Aaron Chapin of Hartford.

Claphamson, Samuel, Philadelphia, Pa. Chippendale era. "Late of London."

Cheney, Benjamin, East Hartford. First half of 18th century.

Cheney, Silas E., Litchfield, Conn. (1799–1821). Made fine sideboards.

Claypoole, George, Philadelphia, Pa. Established at the time of Gostelowe.

Clifton, Henry. Was partner with James Gillingham before 1768 in Philadelphia.

Coffin, William, Boston, Mass. (c. 1758). Cabinetmaker.

Coit, Job, Boston, Mass. (1742). Cabinetmaker.

Collins, Daniel, Boston, Mass. (1758). Cabinetmaker.

Connelly, Henry, Philadelphia, Pa. (1770–1826). Excellent maker in the early Empire style, similar to early Phyfe. Shops at 16 Chestnut Street and 44 Spruce Street. Table in Sheraton style, two part, carved on leg and stile.

Cotter, S. Name appears on a chair from Salem, Mass.

Courtnay, Hercules, Philadelphia, Pa. Chippendale era. "Late of London."

Cowperthwaite, John K. (working 1818–25).

Cox, Joseph, Dock Street, New York City. Upholsterer from London.

Coxe, William, Philadelphia, Pa. (1785). Windsor chair maker.

Cresson, Jeremiah, Philadelphia, Pa. Established at the time of Gostelowe.

Culliatt, Adam, Charleston, S. C. (1757–   ).

Davies, John, came on "Increase" to Boston in 1635. Furniture maker.

Davis, John, Boston, Mass. (1736). Cabinetmaker.

del Vecchio, Charles, New York City (c. 1810). Shaving stand, labeled "Charles del Vecchio's Looking Glass and Picture Frame Manufactory, No. 44 Chatham Street, New York."

Dennis, Thomas, Ipswich, Mass. (1703). Cabinetmaker.

Dennis, Thomas, son of Thomas, Ipswich, Mass. (1706). Cabinetmaker.

Disbrowe, Nick, Hartford, Conn. (1612–83). Maker of the so-called Hadley chest. Probably also of applied ornament chests. Name cut on drawer of Hadley chest: "Cutte and joyned by Nich. Disbrowe." Some believe this maker is also responsible for the sunflower and tulip chest. His is the most celebrated of the exceedingly meager list of 17th-century cabinetmakers. Kenelm Winslow of the Plymouth Colony is another. The inscription mentioned has been challenged because it is proved that Disbrowe was illiterate. Of course it might have been cut by someone else, but be correct as to its statements. It is considered strongly probable that the inscription is correct.

Dix, Samuel (1637). Came to Boston with two apprentices, William Storey and Daniel Linsey.

Doggett, John, Roxbury, Mass. (1809). Looking-glasses, carving, cabinetmaking. Did work for the Derbys of Salem.

Eaton and Grey, Boston, Mass. (c. 1820). Label: "Eaton & Grey, Saddlers, Harness, Trunk and Cap Maker, No. 40 Court Street, Boston."

Egerton, Mathew, Brunswick, N. J. (1739–1802). Family in business three generations — furniture known being largely the Hepplewhite type.

Egerton, Mathew, Jr. (–1837). *See* previous name.

Elfe, Thomas, Charleston, S. C. Cabinetmaker.

Elliott, John, Philadelphia, Pa. (c. 1765). "John Elliott at No. 60 South Front Street, between Chestnut and Walnut Streets, Philadelphia. Sells by wholesale and retail, looking glasses. . . ." As Elliott also imported glasses, on which also his name as dealer was probably pasted, one cannot know whether an example is English or American.

Forster, Jacob, Charlestown, Mass. (1781–1838). Serpentine chest of drawers with claw-and-ball feet. Built his shop at corner of Main and Union streets. Furniture of a type belonging to an earlier period. Labeled. A large maker.

Forster & Lawrence (Chas. Forster and Edward Lawrence), Charlestown, Mass. 19th C. Forster was son and successor of Jacob.

Frederick, Charles (working 1815).

Freeman, William, Baltimore, Md. (1810). Cabinetmaker.

Frothingham, Charlestown, Mass. (1760–90). Blocked secretary-bookcases, without external shells. Doors with scrolled panels, square tops, also various oxbow and other pieces. Label in Hepplewhite type sideboard: "Benj'm. Frothingham, Cabinet Maker, Charlestown, N. E." (b. Boston, April 6, 1734) son of Benjamin, also cabinetmaker, with shop near Milk Street. Served in Gridley's Artillery seven years from 1756. Became Major of Artillery in Revolution. Friend of Washington, lived on Walker Street and lost building when British burned Charlestown in 1775. Entertained Washington after war in rebuilt house. A so-called North Shore Chippendale type is found made from Boston northerly, and including Charlestown. When we find a blocked piece with shell in FURNITURE TREASURY No. 704 we surmise it to be of Charlestown or northern origin. The blocking does not run down on the foot in the same fashion as Goddard's work. See explanation under the chapter on Feet.

Fullerton, William, Boston, Mass. (1742). Chair maker.

Gant, Thomas, Philadelphia, Pa. Established at the time of Gostelowe.

Gautier, Andrew (1720–84).

Gaw, J. & G., Pennsylvania. Name on Windsor chairs.

Geffroy, Nickolas, Newport, R. I. (c. 1800). Label on inlaid mahogany looking-glass. "Nickolas Geffroy, Looking-glass manufactory, No 127 Thames Street, Newport, R. I. . . ."

Geib, John, & Son, New York City (c. 1805). Inlaid pianoforte. Also organ builders. Bowery corner North Street. Geib, John, Jr., New York (1815). Pianoforte.

Ghiselin, Reverdy, Baltimore, Md., early 19th C. Chairs by him now in St. John's College, Annapolis.

Gibbons, Thomas, Boston, Mass. (1739). Cabinetmaker. In partnership with Lenier Kenn.

Gillingham, James, Philadelphia, Pa. (c. 1760–75). Maker of fine Chippendale type furniture. One of his types of chairs is well known and very handsome (compare No. 2189 and No. 2224 FURNITURE TREASURY). Gillingham classes with the celebrated Philadelphia makers, Savery, Gostelowe, Randolph. Advertised in 1768 after dissolving partnership with Henry Clifton.

Gillingham, John, Philadelphia, Pa. (1735–91). Uncle of James. Patronized by Franklin.

Goddard, John, I. A sketch of him by Norman M. Isham, a very careful, keen student of Colonial architecture, appeared in a bulletin of the Rhode Island School of Design, April, 1927. An abbreviated sketch by myself, founded largely on Isham and with some new material, was contributed to the American Biographical series.

Job Townsend was at work as a cabinetmaker in Newport at least a year or two before John Goddard was born, January 20, 1723/4.

In 1755 John Goddard had already made exquisite pieces, and he was, therefore, at thirty-one, the leading cabinetmaker of his day.

A side table with stone top in the Queen Anne tradition made by him in 1755 is shown on this page and Goddard's bill for it. This table was unknown to earlier writers, or, if known, not mentioned, as of course it would have been on account of the early date of the receipt.

Recd Newport Septr 27th 1755 of Capt Antony Low Thirty Pounds in full for a Mahogany Table Frame   John Goddard

The great Philadelphia makers who excelled in lowboys, highboys, and chairs followed the English tradition, but Goddard, by the design of the block front with shell, founded a style not only superior to any other American style, but superior to any English examples.

Goddard's furniture has been found to some extent in Virginia and Maryland, to which it could easily be shipped from Newport. Rare examples also exist in the states intervening, between Pennsylvania and Rhode Island, and also in Massachusetts. The great body of his productions has been found in Rhode Island where

Providence March 27 1786
Received of Mr Zebulun Utter one pound
Sixteen shilling L.M. in behalf of Mr
Townsend Godard of Newport for
Two Clock Cases Caleb Wheaton

his finest pieces still remain. The two supreme examples are owned in Providence. He was the cabinetmaker of the Moses Brown family and their connections and also did work for other persons in Providence. John's father was Daniel, a shipwright. He lived in Dartmouth, Massachusetts, where John and two sisters before him were born. As he married Hannah, daughter of Job Townsend in 1746, the presumption is that he worked in Job's shop at that time, in Newport. For the will and inventory following the Newport Historical Society is to be thanked.

The receipts and the early date of one of them, the side table, and the double-shell clocks shown are new material. It is now believed that Goddard went to England

Made by John Goddard 1761 and repaired
by Thomas Goddard his Son 1813
Health Officer of the Town of
Newport appointed by the
Hon Town Council, Member
Nicholas Taylor Esqr & my Son T Topham.

This inscription and the next are in the *Lisle* secretary, Providence.

(432)

during the British occupation of Newport. A great family, some young, and in narrow circumstances were instanced by a friend as disproving the rumor of his going. His shop was on the water, at the Point, Washington Street. As late as 1800 it still belonged to his sons.

The time of his purchase of this location, 1748, may mark the date, nearly, when he went into business for himself. Thus he had seven years from that time to 1755, the date of the first receipt, to establish his independent reputation.

Goddard was using walnut for some of his work as late as 1763. His richest pieces are mahogany.

Copy of Will of John Goddard I

Be It Remembered that I John Goddard of Newport in the County of Newport in the State of Rhode Island, Joiner, being indisposed in body but through divine Aid am favoured with the use of my natural Faculties, think fit this thirtieth day of the Sixth month called June, in the year of our Lord one thousand seven hundred and eighty five, to make this my last will and Testament in manner following for disposing of that temporal Estate wherewith it hath pleased God to bless me, in order to prevent as much as possible any controversies that might arise otherwise concerning the same.

Imprimis, my will is that all my just Debts and funeral charges be well and truly paid in a convenient Time after my decease.

Item, my wish further is that my Dwelling house and lot of Land whereon it stands with the Stable in Newport aforesaid, shall be and remain to and for the use and benefit of my beloved wife during the time she shall remain my widdow and a home for my Children that is now at home with me, and I earnestly recommend to them that they live together in one Family in love and harmony. I also give to my said wife all my stock of Mahogany and other Stuff to be worked up for the support and Benefit of my Said wife and Children which is at home with me.

Item, I give and bequeath to my two sons Stephen and Thomas Goddard all my Tools of every kind which I used to work with in carrying on my business, I also give to my said two Sons Stephen and Thomas the use and benefit of my Shop where I used to work, so long as their Mother shall live in consideration of their working up the Stock of Mahogany for their Mother in such Furniture as will be most profitable and when worked up to be appropriated as aforesaid.

(433)

Item, my will is that my wife and children keep and preserve the Books which I bought of the Widow Fryers of Isaac Pemington's works, as Family Books which I recommend to their reading.

Item, I give and bequeath to my beloved wife and my nine children, viz: Townsend, Job, Henry, Stephen, Thomas, Benjamin, Mary and Rebecceah Goddard and Catherine Weaver all the rest and residue of my estate of every nature or kind whatsoever that is not heretofore given away both real and personal to them, their heirs and assigns forever, to be equally divided between them share and share alike excepting the privilege of my wife in my dwelling house and the use of my Shops to my sons Stephen and Thomas as aforesaid and the account I have against my Daughter Catherine Weaver of household Furniture is to be deducted out of her Share or Part of my Estate. The reason that my son Daniel Goddard is not included with my other Children is that what I have heretofore done for him at divers times may be equal to his share of my Estate which I desire he may be Satisfied and content with.

And Lastly I hereby nominate constitute and appoint my son Townsend Goddard my Executor of this my last will and Testament and I do hereby utterly disallow revoke, and disannull all and every other Will and Wills, Legacies, Bequests and Executors by me at any time heretofore named, willed or bequeathed ratifying and confirming this and no other to be my last Will and Testament.

In witness whereof I have hereunto set my hand and Seal the day and year first above written.

Signed, sealed, published and declared by the above named John Goddard as and for his last will and Testament in the presence of us

THOMAS ROBINSON

JOSEPH WARRIN   JOHN GODDARD

PHILLIP TRAFFAM

Copy of Inventory of Estate of John Goddard I

AN INVENTORY of the personal estate of John Goddard late of Newport, decd., shown by Townsend Goddard, this first day of the eighth Month called August 1785.

In the Shop	5 Benches of Joiners Tools	£18. 0.0
	Stock of Mahogany & other stuff	13.10.0
Stable	3 Tons of Hay £9. 2 Cows £9.	18. 0.0
	2 hogs 24/ 1 old horse 60/ Boat and oars 90/	8.14.0
	2 Iron shovels, 1 hoe, 2 pitchforks (Old)	0. 8.0
	Sundry old casks 6/ Corn 18/ Cart body 18/	2. 2.0
In the Great Room	1 Clock £9. 3 Mahogany Tables £16	15. 0.0
	8 Mahogany Chairs £6 Desk and Book case 70/	9.10.0
	1 looking Glass	1.16.0
Keeping Room.	3 Old Tables 18/ 5 Chairs 15/ Pipe box 1/	1.14.0
	Shaving box, Razor, hone and small glass	0. 8.0
	Desk & paper case old 20/ Bed, Bedstead and bedding old, 60/ Sundry books 60/	7. 0.0
	Tea Table Furniture in Beaufit	0. 6.0
	11 Silver Spoons, 8 Teaspoons, Tea Tongs..	5.10.0
Bedroom	2 Beds, Bedspread & Bedding, Small & old	4. 4.0
	1 Case with Bottles 6/ Wearing apparel	4.16.0
Kitchen	3 old Tables, old meal Chest 12/ 6 old Chairs 12/	1. 4.0
	1 Stand, 1 pr. Bellows, 2 pr. handirons, 2 pr. Tongs & Shovels, 9 Candlesticks and Lamp	1.11.0
	1 Gridiron, 1 Toaster, 3 Trammels, 3 Flat Irons, 1 pr. Steelyards and Candle box	0.12.0
	1 Lanthorn, 1 Jack, Dripping pan, 2 Spitz	1. 0.0
	A horse to dry clothes & Cannister	0. 3.0

Closet	24 Pewter plates, 4 platters, 1 Bason, 3 porringers, 1 Coffee pot	£0.18.0
	14 earthern plates, 3 milk pans, three earthen dishes, 3 bowls, 1 Tunnel, one mug, 1 sauce pan	0. 6.0
	Table Knives & Forks, Warming pan, some old earthen and tin ware	0. 6.0
		£116.18.0

	Brought over	£116.18.0
	Potts, Kittles, frying pan, pails, Bread trough Churn &c. in the sink room	2.10.0
Storeroom	Safe and some old Lumber	0. 5.0
Cellar	Some old Cask	0. 5.0
Great Chamber	1 Bed, Bedspread and Bedding	4.10.0
	2 Tables 30/ Case Drawers 48/ 6 old Chairs 9/	4.07.0
	1 looking Glass	1. 0.0
Store Chamber	Bed, Bedspread & Bedding, old	2. 8.0
Keeping Room Chamber	1 Bed, Bedspread & Bedding 48/ old Case Drawers 30/ 2 old Chairs 4/	4. 2.0
	1 old Chest, 1 old Casc Drawers	0.15.0
	Some old Lumber in the Garret . . . . /	0.16.0
		137.21.0

	Table Cloths & Towels, old	0.12.0
	Sundry Notes of Hand	62. 7.0
		£200.16.0

Thomas Robinson
Edmund Townsend

Shell-and-Block Furniture and John Goddard

An attempt is here made to gather and correlate what has already been set forth regarding this furniture, and to add thereto some previously unknown or untreated examples, together with further deductions, warranted by comparison of all the material. The treatment one should notice refers not to block fronts particularly, but to the block and shell.

The flute, as used by the Greeks, was worked at its top into the form of a demi-dome. It was necessary only to broaden, without greatly deepening, this flute, to give it the form of the concave block as used in furniture in some foreign examples, particularly English.

The Romans used the niche for statuary, or the outlet for a fountain, in the form of the demi-dome. By the time of the Renaissance, if not before, this demi-dome was crested with a shell. This form of construction came into England through the designs of Palladio, and the studies of Inigo Jones, Christopher Wren, and others. The shell-top cupboard design was thus well established by the time of Queen Anne. Its beauty was unquestioned. The only question was the cost of it.

Now the shell-top demi-dome cupboard is so closely like the first known concaves with shells on furniture that it scarcely leaves room for invention. From this cupboard, and from the demi-dome flattened, used on furniture, it was a short step, on the part of the innovators, to the application of the concave block with shell, an early form in which Job Townsend applied it. Of great interest is the fact that on the central ornament of a cabinet he carved a real shell with curved radiates in a form as fine as Goddard after him.

The concave shell and block are thus not only the earliest form, but they antedate by hundreds of years the development of the convex shell. The first concave follows the half-circle shape, or approximates it. Someone, Townsend or another American, either following an English front with three side-by-side concaves or on his own inspiration, adopted the scheme for three such ornaments without shell on a cabinet. Right here we reach a point where the great inspiration occurs. There was, of course, since the early times an oriental and then a Roman external demi-dome. This was the outside of a niche in its conforming outline. That is, the outside was a block or, as Goddard called it, a swell. The inside was simply the reverse. Whether one of the Townsends, Job or John, of the next generation, and probably a nephew, or Goddard thought of combining a triple decoration consisting of a central concave surmounted by a shell flanked on either side by a convex demi-dome similarly surmounted, we shall perhaps never know. Job, father-in-law, and John Goddard, son-in-law, working harmoniously in the same shop at first, no doubt talked over the idea together. But then was born the finest decorative motive in furniture. And then only did the name block and shell become appropriate, for the concave shell alone suggests no block or swell. Indeed, the matter growing up from a convex outline continued to be called a swelled front, and the term was continued later in a common style of house front in New England. The flattening of the block from a segmental form was a happy change largely forced by the necessarily moderate thickness of the furniture front. A true segmental form was not felt necessary in the miniature dimensions of a cabinet. The flat arches and shallow recesses of Renaissance architecture may also have suggested the flattening of the curve.

Thus the Newport school took what in the comparatively clumsy construction of a rare English front was three magnified flutes and, reversing the two outward ones, capped all by shells and secured by contrast an exquisite form of the daintiest taste. Chippendale often made mistakes in design both as regards form and structure. He reveled in providing an infinitude of forms, as if to say, "If you don't like this one, take another." It is not too much to say that John Goddard has not left an embodied mistake. Harmony marks all his main motives and every detail. The device of the inner foot scroll was no mean design. In the six main forms of furniture to which the block and shell was applied, there is no sense of straining after effect, or of incongruous adaptation. The idea was so simple that, as with all such happy achievements, everyone could say, "Why, that's easy. I could have done that." But only Goddard did it. And when he did it, he achieved something purely American. He also crowned and completed the great mahogany age. With all the wealth and beauty of design contributed by England and the continent — so great that many new-rich persons rush abroad to import good and bad, chiefly bad — there is not one shape that can

Goddard was not beyond making somewhat simpler specimens than his three-door bookcase tops. That here shown is of a smaller, more domestic type with a lovely cabinet. The detail on the right gives the stop-fluted quarter column in conjunction with the block and shell. Both these specimens have always been, as now, in Rhode Island — the larger in Providence, the other in Newport.

for a moment stand side by side with the best achievements of Goddard. Nor is anything so distinctive, nor so nearly approaching originality.

Besides being beautiful, this furniture is stately. No other specimens of furniture are so impressive as a block-and-shell high secretary or a chest-on-chest. These are the aristocrats of furniture.

The idea that beauty has no reality, but is wholly a matter of individual taste, requires slight modification. It is more correct to say that whatever forms have received for generations the endorsement of cultivated minds as beautiful are truly such.

One naturally asks, "Why then is this style of furniture so uncommon, and why has it always been uncommon?" There is a sufficient answer: its cost. A secondary, but by no means subordinate answer is that a high degree of skill was required to produce it. Its impression on its age is, however, apparent by the almost innumerable sunrise ornaments on cabinet furniture, a simple and degraded form, of small expense, not

One of Goddard's richest straight-front chests of drawers, with stop-fluted quarter columns.

requiring thick material, and readily passing muster with the uncritical who always form the majority.

Not to be led too far afield, it may be sufficient to say that nearly everyone at all acquainted with the block-and-shell style esteems it highly for its intrinsic beauty. Those who do not like it are always those who are not acquainted with it.

The writer can, however, go so far as to say that where the blocks lack the shells they appear incomplete, and that their attractiveness may fairly be questioned. The suspicion arises that the expense of cutting the shell has often induced buyers to be content without it. Reference, of course, is to those blocks which return, that is, curve down, on the top drawer, as if in preparation for cutting the shell.

The attractiveness of plain blocks alike on every drawer and having the lid or top of the chest of drawers contoured to agree with the block is undeniable. The writer's feeling is strong that all blocks should be of this character unless shells surmount them. There are many lovely plain bracket-footed pieces, made originally at modest expense, of this character.

The block-and-shell construction is usually made with an applied shell. The exceptions quoted by Isham in his monograph on secretaries are only two.

The writer has since tallied two knee-hole pieces, one or two low chests of drawers, three clocks, and one other specimen, all carved from the solid. There are probably several others so constructed. Generally the distinction between the applied and the cut-from-the-solid shells is ignored. But this is a matter of very great importance. Obviously to cut a shell raised above a base which was to be finished in an absolutely smooth, flat surface requires not only much skill, but the utmost painstaking. One slip of the tool will dig a hole in what is intended to be the polished ground from which the block rises. It is for this reason, doubtless, that a device was used in some Newport pieces of carrying the carving down to a slightly concave and roughened surface on the lids of secretaries, or of carving a grooved scroll around the edge of the shell.

The cutting of a block of mahogany into the detached shell form was comparatively simple when it was temporarily fixed for this purpose on a subbase of hard wood. It must be said for the old cabinetmakers that they succeeded admirably in attaching such blocks to plain surfaces. The blocks almost never came loose, and in many cases it is necessary to inspect them sharply at the junction to learn whether or not the blocks are attached. Of course, if a drawer is removed, the junction on a straight line of the two pieces is readily seen on the under side. The ordinary device for the narrow doors of secretaries or clocks was to cut the small block separately and insert it in a panel frame at the top of the long section of the block by a contoured line on the base of the shell block. Some clocks forego the panel and are cut from the solid, so that the entire door is one piece.

It is clear that the economic reasons weighed heavily with cabinetmakers in former times as now. John Goddard, in writing to Moses Brown, said, "There is a sort which is called a Chest on Chest of Drawers & Sweld front which are Costly as well as ornimental." It was the exceptional man in those days as now who had both the taste and the means to order the best styles. Goddard himself made some chairs and other pieces which were quite ordinary and from cherry wood.

The appeal of a shell cut from the solid, that is, not applied, is very strong to anyone who likes permanence and artistry. It was almost questionable taste to apply these shells, just as it was questionable taste to terminate a columnar block with a rounded surface as if prepared for a shell. We should think very slightingly of a piece of sculpture which had the nose cemented on. Nevertheless, the external appearance at least at a slight distance was the same, and most of us think we are very fortunate to obtain specimens with applied shells.

The value of a piece whose shell is not applied will of course be taken into account by the wise buyer, since such a piece should be worth very much more. It is amazing that not a few pieces have changed hands without any investigation by the buyer of this interesting question.

The plain block on the drawers below the shell should invariably be sawed in one piece with the entire drawer front, and it is as a rule found in this manner. A few pieces which are made otherwise should be dismissed from consideration as being

A Connecticut example, shown to be such by the shape of the bracket scrolls.

(440)

tawdry originals or still more tawdry recent imitations. The temptation to apply even the plain block of course arises from the difficulty of obtaining, at a modest price, fine, heavy, and thick mahogany. A small block was, however, sometimes attached on the inside at the center to give room for the lock.

Whether the rounded block or the flattened block was the earlier, the square block is generally used by the Newport school when it is surmounted by a shell. There is, indeed, a variation in different specimens in the curvature of the block as it falls away to its base, but the shell itself for fine style requires a pretty sharp shoulder curve. Influenced probably by analogy, even plain block pieces of a squarish contour are counted more valuable than the rounded block.

Since plain round blocks are found on some Queen Anne pieces the inference has been drawn, and probably with warrant, that the round block is earlier than the square block. If this be true, it is a case in which the later style has a greater artistic and market value. The round block approaches very closely to some of the contoured fronts which are found in England and elsewhere. As every living thing is a growth, it would not be reasonable to suppose that Goddard or anybody else produced the perfect block front and shell all at once.

A sort of convex shell midway between a sunrise pattern and the later shell has absolutely straight radiates. Such are sometimes found on Queen Anne table legs or frame ornaments, and on Queen Anne corner chairs. They appear also on some clocks produced by the Newport school of cabinetmakers. A small, plain scroll terminating in spirals sometimes surrounds the shell. The suspicion arises that this was a device to save a carving on which the tool had slipped, as it afforded an opportunity to take out any slight irregularity at the edge of the shell. However the device arose, it is an added element of beauty and commends itself both practically and esthetically. It has been supposed that when the radiates are numerous they enhance the value of the style, just as people presume that a Windsor chair with a great many spindles is therefore superior. It is true that a very small number of radiates, as five or six, indicates niggardliness of style. The richest known piece, however, of American furniture has only seven full raised radiates on its lower central shell, and the same is true on the central upper door. Obviously the size of the shell should have something to do with the number of radiates. If the shell appears on a three-door bookcase or on a clock with quarter columns, it must of necessity be small. Our conclusion is that while a meager number of radiates detracts from the style, a moderate number is better than more, because minute divisions have not so much character.

A more important matter is the shape of the radiates. The one or two nearly vertical radiates are almost exactly straight. The next one on each side curves slightly. But the third radiate, reckoning from the top, shows a marked curve, which curve should increase on every successive radiate, until the outside or bottom radiate shows as a decisive ogee curve, the inside end of which ends in a quick spiral on a minute round center, which indeed is very like the termination of the scrolled foot on the best Goddard furniture. The height of the shell above the plain surface varies. It is in part governed by the size of the shell, and in part by the feeling for style. A large shell in an example examined by the writer rises an inch and a sixteenth. The thickness of shells of the same size is often very much under this dimension. Such shells lack boldness and, in the writer's opinion, the highest merit. A thickness on a large shell less than seven-eighths of an inch, one would say, is a detraction from merit. But shells otherwise of the best Rhode Island type are sometimes not more than three-quarters of an inch.

The center core or hinge of the shell also varies. In simpler specimens it is sometimes left plain. When decorated as we usually find it, a considerable number of devices was used, better shown by the illustrations.

At the present writing shells are found on the following styles of furniture in conjunction with blocks: chests-on-chests; four-, three-, and two-drawer chests of drawers; knee-hole "bureau tables," as Goddard called them; secretaries with bookcase tops, desks without tops, and tall clocks. The knee-hole pieces were probably designed for boudoir use and could be used either as desks or as dressing tables. In fact, the bureau table was the New England answer to the Philadelphia lowboy. It served the same purpose and is certainly not inferior in beauty. In the estimation of many it is the daintiest piece of furniture ever devised. All the knee-hole pieces we have seen with three shells were of the Goddard type. There are also highboy bases with pure single central Goddard shells, concave, and one or more lowboys.

There has just now come to light a lowboy from Rhode Island, with the center concave and shell precisely like those on the Newport examples. This lowboy is attributed to Goddard, but possibly belongs to Job Townsend, for it has the Queen Anne foot. But the Queen Anne foot was used for economy to a late period of the eighteenth century. Again we emphasize that the intaglio shell is very ancient and not a block unless accompanied by the raised reverse of itself. But in FURNITURE TREASURY, Figure 412, is an English lowboy with a central arched recess, at the top of which is a shell. On either side is a pillar, showing thus an architectural arch somewhat similar to what is seen on American court cupboards.

We have no highboys or lowboys with both block and shell. The chest-on-chest with these elements we have, as it allows a base mold.

An effort to connect block fronts with highboys and lowboys is not wholly successful. There is, indeed, a wonderful cherry block-front highboy of Queen Anne period as to style, but of a somewhat later period as to date, which is blocked throughout, but it has no shell cresting and lacks a good molded connection of upper and lower sections. Two or three lowboys with block fronts without shells have also come to light, but the writer would rather be excused from commenting upon them. One, however, found in Newport is graceful, the top being contoured, and so of course no shells were required. An inherent difficulty in applying the block front to the highboy and lowboy is that a heavy base mold is a part of the style, and designers naturally felt that a base mold should be somewhere near the floor. If it were to be set high in the air, on long legs, it would lose very much of its appropriateness and beauty. Partly for that reason, perhaps, the favorite foot on the block-front pieces is an ogee bracket rather than a ball and claw, since the bracket foot seems to lend itself best to the heavy base mold and permits of carrying the block idea down to the floor. It is noticeable that the block-and-shell pieces of the richest character have bracket feet.

In fact, an extremely compressed ball-and-claw foot is not graceful, and in any case, used on a block front, it somewhat interfered with the continuity of the block, which on the other hand lends itself admirably to the bracket foot.

It is puzzling to observe that Lockwood in his original work, and even in his supplementary chapters, and Isham in his monograph, pay no attention whatever to the block-and-shell clock. This is the more strange because the exquisite examples of these clocks make a strong bid for supremacy in style and beauty as compared with any other cabinetwork whatever. Furthermore, the author has tallied about fifteen examples of these clocks, and there are those who claim to know other examples. There is also in existence a bill, shown in this chapter, in which Caleb Wheaton, the most noted maker of clock works in Providence in his day, is found selling clock cases for the account of Townsend Goddard, the son and executor of John Goddard. It would appear that members of the Society of Friends sometimes purchased in London clock works by Tomlinson, Monkhouse, and perhaps Wagstaff, the latter being himself a Friend, and closely associated with Philadelphia clocks. The buyers then took the works to John Townsend or John Goddard to be cased. Beautiful examples are also known of these cases containing the works of Caleb Wheaton and other American makers. One of the finest cases, however, in the Garvan Collection at Yale, bears no name of the works, or at least on the dial. In fact, the Metropolitan Museum specimen bearing the name of John Townsend does not of course show the name on the face, but on an interior label. The data prove: that John Goddard and John Townsend both made the clock cases with block and shell.

These are the only clocks of which it can be said that the case is more important than the works. The clocks vary in style from the bonnet head, either with plain arch or with a keystone breaking through, to the more elaborate bonnet with an S scroll or broken arch above the dial arch. The finials bear a striking resemblance to one another in all the specimens the writer has examined. They are a carved, somewhat flattened urn, fluted and with very small and unobtrusive bases, but with good spiral flames. In one example the central flame twists in an opposite way from the side flames.

The block-and-shell section appears both with and without quarter columns at the corners of the waist of the clock. The writer made the remark, in showing in his FURNITURE TREASURY one of these clocks, that Goddard, working consistently, should in the latter part of his career have made a clock in which he repeated the block and shell on the plinth in accordance with the general style used in the chest-on-chest. These books had not been on the market a week before Mrs. Henry W. Drowne of New York City wrote to the author: "We have the clock." Since that time no less than three other such clocks have come to my attention, two of them having astonishingly small twin shells below the main shell on the plinth. While this would seem to be the supreme development of the style, the lower shells do not have the spiral shape, and it is barely possible that they were an earlier style. (*See chapter on clocks*).

The vexed question of origins as regards block-and-shell furniture is not fully settled, and probably never will be. But there are two pretty well defined types, the Newport and the Connecticut.

The Newport type holds to a bracket of a restrained contour, whose chief adornment is the little scroll on the outside of the foot terminating in a button or whorl, or in one instance set off by a wing ornament (Lisle). Another feature absolutely peculiar to Newport, when the specimen has a high top, is the continuation of the mold around the curved crest opening. This greatly adds to the elegance of the effect. The block effect goes uniformly through the base mold.

The Connecticut type, both bracket and ball foot, has a somewhat flamboyant scroll at the sides of the bracket. Sometimes this scroll is fairly attractive, but more often it is quaint rather than handsome, and occasionally almost ugly. The bracket feet in Connecticut average larger than those of Newport. (*Page 46*).

In some Connecticut specimens an effort was made to approximate the lowboy, by using cabriole legs and ball-and-claw feet, as shown in a two-drawer lowboy. The result is not satisfactory. In regular lowboys the leg is of one piece running up through the frame, and hence rigid. In the two or three Connecticut examples, using a cabriole leg much higher than a bracket, the leg should logically run into the frame. But the maker erred by attaching these legs in the style of a bracket. The result was insecure. It was a cabinetmaker's mistake, incurred in attempting to improve on the Newport type, under the erroneous impression that a ball-and-claw foot is better than a bracket foot. Ball-and-claw feet, if short, may be applied bracket-wise successfully, as we find them in oxbow desks or chests of drawers. In the best specimen, Mr. Erving's, the bracket is mortised into the leg to make the latter secure.

The Connecticut type also generally uses a shell with a gentle curvature where it rounds down to its supporting base, and the radiates on the outside shells are sometimes very numerous, as many as twenty-one being found, whereas the Newport type is limited to an extreme of fifteen in those the writer has seen.

In the Newport pieces the central shell is merely the reverse of the side shell, or very nearly. But in the Connecticut pieces the central shells often reduce sharply the number of radiates, as in the Shipman chest-on-chest, where the object seems to have been to obtain contrast rather than likeness between the shells, there being nineteen radiates on the obverse shells, and only eight on the central shell. Indeed, the maker introduced two striking variations. On the central shell he has imitated a butterfly. On the outside shell he has made the radiates on both sides alike, so that he found it necessary to carve a central vertical radiate of unique outline, disappearing where the side radiates touch at their most outward sweeps. The result is not very successful, but is delightful nevertheless, as an essay in originality.

In the specimens known to me the triple door in the upper section is found exclusively in Newport types. Goddard alone seems to have envisioned this strikingly beautiful detail, which carries the eye through one single architectural motive from top to bottom. This triple motive is found on Connecticut chests-on-chests, but not, so far, on secretaries. And even on the chests the style fades off on the base mold.

The straight bracket foot is perhaps not found with the block and shell in Newport specimens. But the straight bracket with contoured lid is found there. The ball and claw are more usual outside of Rhode Island.

In the cabinets of the block-and-shell specimens the writer has seen curved radiate shells in several specimens, but usually their outlines approximate the simpler, straight sunrise pattern.

There is a variation in Newport itself in the drawer edges. Both the lip drawer and the cock-bead edge are found, but nowhere was a plain flush drawer used. The cock bead is on the frame, not on the drawer.

The blocked panels — usually two, but in the supreme instance three — above the doors in the secretaries seem to be peculiar to the Newport type. Inside shells on rich North Shore secretaries are found, but not in Newport.

The finials of the Newport style in all specimens examined are fluted urns with spiral flames. They are most delicate and beautiful, conforming to the size of the pieces they decorate, and are superior to any others. One Rhode Island piece now has Philadelphia highboy finials, but they are wrong restorations, as nothing of the kind appears in New England elsewhere. These Newport finials are alone sufficient to identify a specimen. They are not found elsewhere.

The evidence is strong that the Connecticut block-and-shell specimens were inspired from Rhode Island, owing to the less successful method, in Connecticut, of carrying the block through the base mold. In one specimen it is not so poorly done; in another the block confuses the motives of the scrolls, as our illustrations show.

The North Shore (possibly extending into southern New Hampshire) and the Massachusetts Bay specimens show plain blocks without shells; or if an attempt at a shell appears, it is central, at top or bottom, and concaved, and not crowning a block. That is, the triple motive, central concave, side convex shells, seem not to be found except in Rhode Island and Connecticut, and the supreme type (No. 317, FURNITURE TREASURY) in Rhode Island only. A knee hole with a sunrise carving of thirty-three rays is found in Connecticut. But the side blocks are not carved.

Conclusions Regarding John Goddard

1. A great part of his work followed the Queen Anne traditions. Various tables, lowboys, highboys, etc., known to have been made by him, or uniformly credited to him by tradition, have the cabriole leg and Dutch foot.

2. Since in his time boys began as apprentices very early, and since his imperfect education indicates he must have been taken out of school early, he was undoubtedly making furniture or parts of it in his father's or father-in-law's shop by 1737 when he was fourteen years old.

3. He was in business for himself with some reputation, making furniture for out-of-town patrons by 1755 when thirty-two years old, and the furniture was Queen Anne in design.

4. The style of bracket foot employed by him in the 1760's was a holdover from the Queen Anne time.

5. The custom of fixing hard-and-fast dates, for styles, once more appears, in his work, to be lacking in accuracy.

6. The first clock-case hoods traced to the Newport school and continuing at least to 1769, show the round head of the Queen Anne time. Goddard was the outstanding

representative of this school, the others being Job Townsend, his father-in-law, and John Townsend, who was either his cousin or, at least, a man of his own generation.

7. The work found in Connecticut with the block and shell, and often attributed to him, lacks the reserve, the style, and the grace of the work known to be Goddard's.

8. The Connecticut block-and-shell pieces were made in Connecticut by a man or men who tried to improve on Goddard's work, but fell short of it. The principal failure is seen in a more exuberant and extensive foot bracket, and the contrast often found between the central shell and the outside shells and the lack of the mold on the double reverse arches on the top.

9. The phrase "the Newport school" should properly be restricted to John Goddard's generation ending in 1785. His son and successor, Thomas Goddard, accepted the new European types and the influence of Hepplewhite. He made some furniture following the early models, but departed from it later. Hence the "Newport school" is a term losing significance if carried beyond John Goddard.

10. Mahogany being a finer medium and susceptible of more elegance and securing greater permanence in carving, owing to its density, than cherry, we find the richer pieces all in heavy mahogany. That cherry was used by John Goddard in simple pieces is allowed to be true. But a block-and-shell piece in cherry is almost certain to be of outside manufacture.

11. The dynasty of the Goddards, if we include the father-in-law Job Townsend, lasted through four generations, but the fourth-generation John Goddard II should be distinguished from his grandfather to avoid confusion of his furniture label, a copy of which we show, from the original Goddard ownership. It is not known nor even supposed that John Goddard I had a label. The bill here shown dating 1755 is now for the first time brought to light and is the earliest document known, connected with furniture, to be signed by John Goddard.

12. Goddard had only "5 benches" of joiner's tools. Hence he never could have done a large business. Himself, his too sons working with him, and two journeymen would have filled his shop.

The numerous pieces traced to the Newport school indicate we must know today a great part of his richer creations.

13. A clock at £9 "in the great room" must have been a fine article. While the relative values of money are seldom easy of close estimate, we see by the inventory that the clock was worth as much as two cows, or as much as fifteen hogs, or as much as twelve mahogany chairs. It is likely, therefore, that the clock was one of his now justly celebrated shell-and block examples.

14. It was still the practice at the time of the will to cook with a jack and spit, and to eat on pewter or earthenware or even wooden trenchers in families of some standing.

15. The term "cabinetmaker" was not yet so established, but that the will begins "John Goddard, Joiner."

16. There is at first a puzzle in the price obtained for two clock cases at £1-16s, a few months after a clock in the inventory was appraised at £9. The clock cases supposed to be referred to would now be worth, to make, about $300 each, and as antiques $5000 each with works. This is a good advance from about $4. Yet it is no more than

the advance on Corot's paintings. The explanation may in part be found in an effort to settle the estate, for quick cash. Hay at $15 a ton was as much as it is now. Cows were worth $45 as against perhaps double that price now.

But foods have not advanced proportionately with labor. In 1800 a dollar was the daily wage of a cabinetmaker, and if he preferred his pay in wheat, he got one bushel. Today (*Spring, 1933*) a cabinetmaker can buy thirty-six bushels for a day's labor. Obviously the money mentioned in the receipt we show was a partial or final payment.

17. As to John Townsend of John Goddard's generation, he was working in Newport in 1764, 1767, 1769. If he worked in Middletown, Connecticut, there is no record to show when. His wife died in Newport, 1802. All data, except a "card" said to have been found in a chest-on-chest, places John Townsend in Newport.

18. Townsend Goddard was probably the eldest son, because first named in the will and also named as executor.

19. Only two sons were cabinetmakers, Stephen and Thomas.

These two had previously worked with their father in the same shop and continued some time in the same place after their father's death.

20. Catherine Weaver, the only married daughter, had furniture supplied by her father and not paid for. (Some of this furniture is now known.)

21. The Connecticut block-and-shell fronts, therefore, cannot be traced, at present, to the Townsends. It seems that they were made by persons who got only part of the Goddard idea.

New London, Middletown, and Hartford are the most probable places of their manufacture. The Townsends seem rather to have dwelt, in an earlier generation, in southeastern Massachusetts. But the Massachusetts Bay and North Shore schools of cabinetmakers seem not to have produced fine block-and-shell examples. Their work rather excels in the elaboration of their desk cabinets.

22. Variants of the block fronts without shells are found outside the United States. The great range of mahogany drawers in the Cathedral at Havana suggests a block front, and the blocking extends through the bracket foot, as Mr. William B. Goodwin of Hartford discovered. This piece of furniture may antedate John Goddard of Newport and be nearer the time of his father-in-law, Job Townsend. It has been suggested by Goodwin that Townsend may have visited the West Indies to buy mahogany. A scrutoire in a German work, while not blocked, approximates the form.

23. Fronts variously referred to as contoured, shaped, or scrolled are often found in English pieces, especially in the cabinets of desks, usually called scrutoires. But none of these forms here known, at least, or known in England by the writers on furniture, are true blocks, which should show the same contour on each side of the raised portion, and none has shells above.

———————

Goddard, John, grandson of John I. Son of Stephen, also cabinetmaker, lived on northeast corner of Bridge and Second street, Newport, R. I. (b. 1789, d. 1843). His label is shown in this volume.

Goddard, Stephen, 4th son of John I. Worked with his father and inherited the business with his brother Thomas. (d. 1804.)

Goddard, Thomas, 5th son of John Goddard I. (1765–1858). Worked with his father and, inheriting the shop with his brother Stephen, carried on the business for many years. Produced some work in his father's style, but mostly followed the age by shifting to the Hepplewhite and Sheraton types. A number of excellent pieces by him are known. He was a respected citizen of Newport.

Goddard & Engs. Cabinetmakers from Newport, had chairs for sale on a Brown dock in Providence in 1782. Some say they had a shop and others that they had merely a show room.

Goodwin, Ansel, Northampton, Mass. (c. 1790–1800). Label on Windsor chair: "Made by Ansel Goodwin, Northampton, Mass."

Gostelowe, Jonathan, Philadelphia, Pa. (1744–1806). Made exquisite Chippendale types especially rich in carving, among them chests-on-chests, clock cases, etc. Classes with James, Savery, and Randolph. A label in a serpentine chest of drawers with chamfered and fluted corners reads in part: "Jonothan Gostelowe, Cabinet and Chair-Maker, At his shop in Church Alley, about midway between Second and Third-Streets." He later had a shop at 66 Market Street. The distinction he makes between cabinet and chair maker is important as showing the customs of the time. He was a man of considerable importance, being a major in the Revolutionary army and engaged in the production of ordnance. His father, George Gostelowe, is thought by Brazer who has worked up his records to have immigrated from Sweden. He married a niece of Edward Duffield the clock maker. The inference is that some of the exquisite clock cases containing that maker's works were by Gostelowe. He was a man of property acquired and inherited. His prominence in his trade was indicated by his being chairman of a guild of cabinetmakers. Various articles of a wide range were sold when he retired, and his heirs had other goods. An appraisal of Gostelowe in comparison with other Philadelphia makers seems to place him ahead of Savery and probably all others in the large list of Philadelphia cabinetmakers, except perhaps Randolph.

Grinnell, Peter, Providence, R. I. (c. 1820). Label (in part): "Looking-glass & Picture-frame Manufactory, Providence. . . . Peter Grinnell & Son, Main Street, nearly opposite the Providence Bank."

Gruez, John, New York City (also from Paris). Successor to Lannuier. Listed in directory 1821.

Hall, Peter, Charleston, S. C. (1761–68).

Hays, Solomon, Beaver and Broad streets, New York City (1754).

Hitchcock, Lambert, Hitchcockville, Conn. (working 1818–43). Made the famous Hitchcock chair, the front legs in good examples being slightly curved and the back stenciled and in rare instances carved; ground work usually painted black.

Holden, Asa, 32 Broad Street, New York City (1812). Advertised ball-and-spindle-back fancy chairs.

Holman, Levi, chair maker, in 1814, residing in district No. 5 (Salisbury, Vt.). Above found in Week's History of Salisbury (Vermont).

Holmes & Roberts, Colebrook, Conn. (1838–40). Made wood-bottom chairs. Sold out to Hitchcock in 1840.

Hope, Thomas, Charleston, S. C. (b. England 1757), (m. 1793, d. 1820). Was an architect. Made a cupboard for a Knoxville, Tenn., house.

Hopkins, Gerrard, Philadelphia, Pa. (1767–   ). Desks, bookcases, chairs, etc. Served apprenticeship with Robert Moore.

How & Roulain, Charleston, S. C. (before 1765).

Howard, Timothy, Lynn, Mass. (1764). Cabinetmaker.

Howell, William, Boston, Mass. (1717). Cabinetmaker.

Hubon, Henry (working 1820).

Huey, J., Washington County, Pa. (1808). Hepplewhite chest of drawers, marked.

Hunt, Francis, Boston, Mass. (1753). Joiner.

Hutchinson, John, Charlestown, Mass. (1803). Cabinetmaker.

Jenkins, John, Boston, Mass. (1747). Joiner.

Jenney, Samuel (1633–   ).

Johns, Isaac, Baltimore, Md. (1796). Cabinetmaker.

Johnson, Edmund, Salem, Mass. (1793–   ).

Johnson, Jonathan (before 1700).

Jones, Joseph, Philadelphia, Pa. Established at the time of Gostelowe.

Jones, Thomas, from London, went to work as apprentice to Gostelowe in 1773 for a four-year period.

Kenn, Lenier, Boston, Mass. (1739). Cabinetmaker. Partner to Thomas Gibbons.

Kent, William. Looking-glasses with carved scrolls, terminating with free foliage pendant, and with eagle crest.

Kidder & Carter, Charlestown, Mass. (c. 1810). Label, in part, "Kidder & Carter, Manufacture and Sell Looking Glasses and Tinfoil, Wholesale and Retail at Their Store, Main Street, Charlestown."

Kneeland & Adams, Hartford, Conn. (c. 1793). Looking-glasses. "Cabinet and Chair makers. Best warranted clocks and time pieces, elegant looking glasses."

Lanning, John (c. 1778). Chair maker in Salem, New Jersey.

Lannuier, Charles Honoré, French-American cabinetmaker, New York City (1805–19). Carried on somewhat extensive business. Much work attributed to Phyfe was probably by him.

Lawton, Robert (working 1794).

Legaré, Thomas, Charleston, S. C. (1739–   ). Joiner and coffin maker.

Legaré, Solomon, Jr., Charleston, S. C. (1754–   ). Distinguished family.

Lehman, Benjamin, Germantown and Philadelphia, Pa. (1786). Cabinet and chair work. Name on price list.

Lemon, William, Newbury Street, Boston, Mass. Carver. Made work for Derby House, Salem, formerly attributed to McIntire. Also upholsterer and gilder and cabinetmaker.

Lincoln, Thomas (1778–1851).

Lloyd, William, Springfield, Mass. (1779–1845). Made chest of drawers, sideboard, and card tables. Advertisement: "Sideboards, clock cases, desks, bookcases, bureaus and card tables, Springfield, July 6 1802." Also had label "William Lloyd."

Lothrop, E., Boston, Mass. (c. 1810). Gilder, whose label is on architectural looking-glass. "E. Lothrop, Gilder, No. 28 Court Street . . . Near Concert Hall, Opposite the New Stone Store, Boston."

Macbride, Wm., New York City. Windsor chairs.

McDonald, William, Boston, Mass. (1796). Cabinetmaker.

McIntire, Samuel, Salem, Mass. (1757–1815). Very celebrated architect of many fine dwellings still standing in Salem. Designer and maker of much furniture in the Sheraton tradition. It is now known, however, that part of the furniture formerly attributed to him was made in Philadelphia, or carved in Boston. It is not likely that he made all of the richer examples that go by his name. He was the most notable architect of the old school in New England except Bulfinch. Of course the Chippendale style furniture attributed to him was seldom of his construction.

McIntire, Samuel Field, son of Samuel, Salem, Mass. In business there as carver in 1815.

Magrath, Richard, Charleston, S. C. (1770–   ).

Marks, S. H., Canaan, N. Y. Name stamped on Hitchcock type chair.

Mason, Roger, Boston, Mass. (1635–   ).

Mattocks, Samuel, Boston, Mass. (1728–29). Chair maker.

Messenger, Henry, Boston, Mass. (d. 1681). Chair maker.

Meyers, John, Philadelphia, Pa. (1785). Cabinetmaker.

Mills & Deming, New York City (1793–98). Maker of a very rich sideboard for Governor Oliver Walcott. "374 Queen St. [later Pearl], Hartford, Conn. . . . all kinds of cabinet furniture and chairs. . . ."

Moon, Robert, Front Street, Philadelphia, Pa. (1768). Furniture maker.

Moore, Robert, Philadelphia, Pa. (1760–   ). Was also in business in Baltimore.

Mott, William, 51 Broadway. Advertised chairs similar to William Palmer, also white and green and gold.

Nelson & Gates, Burlington, Vt. Makers and dealers in chairs (1840–   ).

Noyes, Samuel S., East Sudbury, Mass. (c. 1810). Label on bow-front chest of drawers: "House Furniture, of the most fashionable kind, made, sold, and exchanged by Samuel S. Noyes, cabinet maker, East Sudbury, near the Causeway."

O'Neal, Patrick, Philadelphia, Pa. Established at the time of Gostelowe.

Packrow, John, Charleston, S. C. (1762–   ).

Palmer, William, 2 Nassau Street, New York City (1802), (working 1818). Advertised black and gold "fancy" chairs with cane and rush seats.

Parker, Thomas M., Providence, R. I. (c. 1820–30). Chairs like Hitchcock's with label: "Manufactured by Thomas M. Parker, Green Street, Providence, R. I. . . ."

Phelps, Timothy, father and son, Hartford, Conn. Prominent cabinetmakers. Early 18th C., and son continuing to near its close.

Phippen, Samuel, Salem, Mass. (d. 1798). Well-known manufacturer.

Phyfe, Duncan, Fulton Street, New York City (1768–1847). Born in Scotland. Made some Sheraton types but chiefly known for Directoire and early Empire examples. Wrought very daintily and with much distinction in his earlier period. Followed the declining styles and in later years produced clumsy degraded Empire. Being the most celebrated New York maker, which scarcely has any other great name, he is very highly thought of in that vicinity, and properly so, but his productions should be appraised by their style and date, the later being worthless, and some of the earlier being as good as any produced of their kind. The earlier examples cannot be distinguished from the best Sheraton styles. There is a book regarding him by *Cornelius*, Metropolitan Museum. Like the English makers, his type does not mean his own manufacture.

Pitman, Mark, Salem, Mass. (1779–1829). Labeled secretary.

Poor, Samuel (before 1700).

Pratt, Phineas, working in Weymouth, Mass. (1622).

Proctor, Cardan, New York City (before Revolution). Tall clock, claw-and-ball feet in front, bracket feet behind. Double-arch chamfered corners below, quarter columns above.

Prouty, Amariah T., Glens Falls, N. Y. Was born at Langdon, N. H., sometime after 1801. Bureau bearing mark, "Amariah T. Prouty, Glens Falls, N. Y." No record of his being a cabinetmaker.

Randolph, Benjamin, Philadelphia, Pa. (c. 1762–92). If Randolph made the marvelous chairs (FURNITURE TREASURY Nos. 2160–61, 2162, 2064, etc.) he was not only the greatest American cabinetmaker and carver, but no one else except Goddard nearly approached him. But see discussion under those names and numbers. The pieces are in all probability Chippendale's own work, imported by Randolph as patterns. Yet this maker stands as high as any, and is certainly not surpassed by Savery. His shop was at the Sign of the Golden Eagle in Chestnut Street between 3d and 4th. "Make all sorts of Cabinet and Chair work likewise Carving, Gilding, etc. Performed in the Chinese and modern tastes." From a very elaborate advertising card of 1770. Imitated from Chippendale. This maker had a larger shop than Savery and was obviously ambitious of very fine work.

Rank, Johannes, Jonestown, Pa. (1763–1828). Chest painter.

Rank, Peter, Jonestown, Pa. (1790–1800). Chest painter. Also a Peter, Jr.

Rawson, Joseph & Son (working 1790–1800).

Renshaw, Thomas, Baltimore, Md. (1814–15). Painted settee.

Richard & Dike, Montague, Mass. (1854–   ). Made stenciled furniture.

Richmond, —— (working 1763).

Rivington, James, New York City (between 1760–70). Reproduced Chippendale designs.

Roberts, Samuel, Robertsville, Conn. (1805–40). Near Colebrook township. Inherited chair mill from his father who made chairs the latter part of the eighteenth century. These chairs were similar to Hitchcock types but were made long before his date. In fact, Holmes and Roberts who did business as a partnership from 1838–40 sold their entire plant to Lambert Hitchcock and Arba Alford. Sold out to The Union Chair Co. in 1849. The latter made Boston rockers, also.

Rosett & Mulford, Elizabethtown, N. J. Label in tall clock advertising other "fashionable" furniture.

Sass, Jacob, Charleston, S. C. (1783–   ).

Savery, William, Philadelphia, Pa. (1721–87). This celebrated maker has had attributed to him many pieces made by other Philadelphia makers. It is more discriminating to term certain highboys Philadelphia pieces until or unless we shall be able to assign the work more definitely. The highboys and lowboys of the finest type, seen in Vol. I of this work, are all of that character. New England produced no work of this sort, the chests-on-chests of Goddard being of the block-and-shell sort. The Philadelphia highboy and lowboy in some examples exhibit the greatest degree of elaboration and ornateness found in American furniture. Savery's shop was small, and it is impossible that he created everything glibly attributed to him. But others undoubtedly produced as fine work, especially in chairs. Trade was brisk; much furniture went to inland towns and by sea cargo to more remote points. Philadelphia had the reputation, the shops and the trade for years and for long distances. A label of his created his vogue. Died in his 67th year. Besides pieces directly traced, he is also known to have made two maple chairs, a mahogany arm chair, and a serpentine chest of drawers. Most of this furniture is simple.

Selzer, Christian, Jonestown, Pa. (1771–96). Chest painter.

Selzer, Johannes (John Selzer, son of Christian), Jonestown, Pa. (1763–1845). Chest painter.

Seymour, John, Boston, Mass. (c. 1790–1810). A considerable number of tasteful pieces of cabinetwork have this maker's label. Among them are secretary-bookcases with reeded Sheraton type legs, and banded inlay; also tambour desks with drapery inlay. Light-blue paint was often used in the interiors. Label in fine tambour: "John Seymour & Son, Cabinet Makers. . . ."

Shaw, John, Annapolis, Md. (1770–85). Table, serving, attributed to him.

Sherburne, Thomas, Boston, Mass. (1765). Cabinetmaker. Had a shop in Back Street.

Simonson, John, Baltimore, Md. (1810).

Sinclair, William, Flowertown, Pa. (working 1803). Label states this boldly. Secretary and other furniture.

Skillin Brothers, John and Simeon, North End, Boston, Mass. (1793–98). Carvers. John (d. 1800.) "Eminent carver." They did crest of chest-on-chest in Garvan Collection, Yale University, formerly attributed to McIntire. Also did capitals for the State House. (Spelled Skellin, Skillins and Skillings.)

Smith, Ebenezer, Beverly, Mass. (1805). A candle stand, tilt top, mahogany, with bill. ". . . To Ebenezer Smith, Dr., July 20, 1805. . . ."

Smith, Eliakim, Hadley, Mass. (1735–75). Chest maker.

Snoden, David, Boston, Mass. (1747). Chair maker.

Snowden, Jedidiah, Philadelphia, Pa. Established at the time of Gostelowe.

Snowhill, Andrew, Spottswood, N. J. (1809). Name in desk.

Spencer, Jarrard, son of Thomas, Hartford, Conn.? Latter half of 18th century. Chair maker. There was also a Jarrard, Jr., and an Obadiah, and others of the name.

Spencer, Thomas, Hartford, Conn. (1639–87). Supposed to be a turner.

Stapleford, Thomas, Boston, Mass. (1681). Chair maker.

Stitcher & Clemmens, Baltimore, Md. (1804). "Cabinet and Chair makers" (label).

Stokes, James, Philadelphia, Pa. (1800–10). Architectural looking-glass with label: "James Stokes . . . Looking glasses, etc. . . . corner of Market and Front Streets, Philadelphia."

Stone, Ebenezer, Boston, Mass. (1787). Windsor chair maker.

Storer and Taylor, New York City. Name on Hepplewhite chairs said to be English in which case this name would signify a dealer.

Storey, William (1637–   ).

Sweeney, Richard, Boston, Mass. (1796). Chair maker.

Taylor, N., name occurs on Windsor settee and case of grandfather clock.

Thomas, Mahlon, Mount Holly, probably New Jersey (1797). Name on bottom of chest of drawers.

Titcomb, Edward, Newbury, Mass. (c. 1690–1710). Four pieces are known, one painted, perhaps on tulip wood, one oak (FURNITURE TREASURY, 327) and one of maple of almost the same pattern. One of these bears this maker's name. They have the Flemish scroll leg, rather clumsy, and show three legs in front.

Todd, James, Portland, Me. (c. 1820). Architectural (tabernacle) looking-glasses.

Toppan, Abner, Newburyport, Mass. (1764–1836). A bill dating 1795 for a mahogany swell-front desk (a serpentine). This is an interesting hold-over in style from a period at least twenty years earlier. Also an odd sideboard.

Townsend, Christopher, Newport, R. I. Early 18th C. Brother and co-worker with Job.

Townsend, Job, Newport, R. I. (b. 1699, d. 1765). Had a cabinet shop in Newport with his brother Christopher. Worked in the Queen Anne tradition. Some believe he originated the use of the block and shell, but no such examples of raised block and shell by him are known, and the probable just conclusion is that John Goddard who married his daughter Hannah developed and perfected that unique and exquisite design. At work in Newport 1725. Father-in-law of John Goddard I.

Townsend, John, son of Christopher, Newport, R. I. (working 1760–70). Cousin of John Goddard, and nephew of Job Townsend. Made block fronts and other furniture. Fine workman. Label: "Made by John Townsend, Newport" in secretary-bookcase, card table and clock. The honor of designing the raised block-and-shell front is thought by some to be shared between Job Townsend, father, John Townsend, nephew, and John Goddard, son-in-law and cousin. Lockwood states a block-front chest-on-chest bears trade label of John Townsend, Middletown, Conn.

Townsend & Axson, Charleston, S. C. (1763–   ). Cabinetmakers.

Tracy, Elisha, son of Nathan, Scotland, Conn. (b. 1744, d. 1809). Possibly Norwich. Chairs of his are found.

Tracy, Nathan, father of Elisha, Norwich, Conn. Did good work.

Tremain, John, New York City (1751). Cabinetmaker.

Trumble, Francis, Philadelphia, Pa. Established at the time of Gostelowe.

Tryon, Isaac, Glastonbury, Conn. (1772). Maker of an unusual highboy with some suggestions of the Chapin type. Name in chalk on a drawer bottom. F. T. 376.

Tuflt, Thomas, Philadelphia, Pa. (bought shop 1780).

Tuttle, James C. (working 1740).

Wadsworth, John (working 1796).

Wallace, Robert, Beaver and New streets, New York City (1753).

Ward, Miles (before 1700).

Ware, Maskell, New Jersey, lived near Roadtown, Cumberland County, b. Dec. 13, 1776, lived to be 79 years old. Learned his trade from John Lanning with whom he lived as a boy. Had seven sons, five of whom made chairs. There is now one great-grandson George Ware, of Roadstown, N. J., still at the trade. His work principally notable for the four- and five-arched slat backs with bulbous feet.

Wayne, Jacob, Philadelphia, Pa. (c. 1795). Son of John.

Wayne, William, Philadelphia, Pa. Married daughter of John Gillingham. Some of his work now known.

Webb & Scott, Providence (working 1790–1800). Cherry secretary-bookcase, with ogee feet and arched top. Inlaid. Label: "Webb & Scott, Cabinet & Chair Makers, Benefit-Street, Providence, Rhode-Island."

Welch, John, b. Boston August 19, 1711. Ship carver by trade. Carved a looking-glass frame.

Wharton & Davies. Introduced a line of "fancy" chairs in 1817 both painted and in curly maple.

Wheeler, Samuel, Boston, Mass. (1748). Chair maker.

Willard & Leonard, 137 No. Sixth St., Philadelphia, Pa. Looking-glasses. Date unknown.

Willard and Nolen, Boston, Mass. (c. 1812). Found on back of architectural looking-glass. The Willard is said to be Aaron Willard, Jr.

Willett, Marinus (1740–1830).

Winslow, Kenelm, Plymouth, Mass. (1599–1672). "Coffin maker" of the Old Colony, a term practically synonymous in that day with joiner. The term "cabinet-maker" was not used. Probably oak furniture made by him still exists.

Woodin, Thomas, Charleston, S. C. (–1772).

Wyman & Carne, Charleston, S. C. (1764–   ). Looking-glasses, chairs, tables, etc.

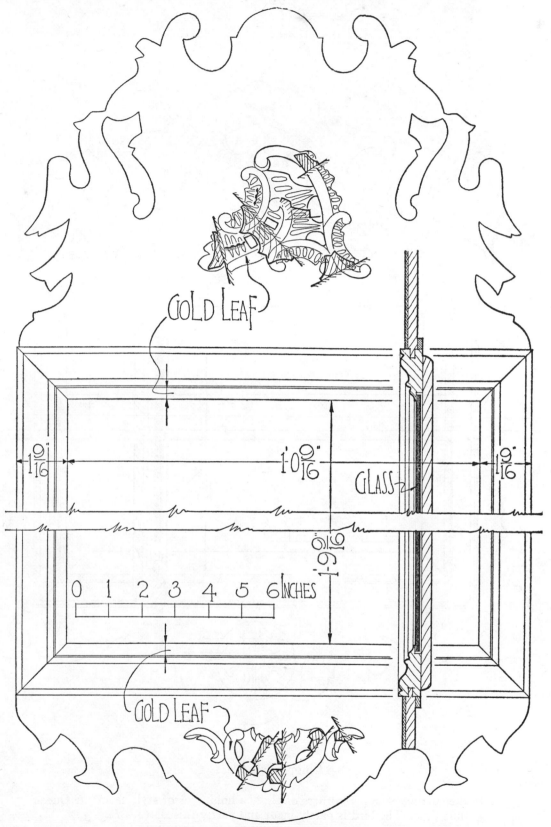

GOLD LEAF

$1\frac{9}{16}$"

$1'0\frac{9}{16}$" GLASS

$\frac{9}{16}$"

$1'9\frac{9}{16}$"

0 1 2 3 4 5 6 INCHES

GOLD LEAF

Queen Anne Love-Bird Glass (*See Page 337*)

(455)

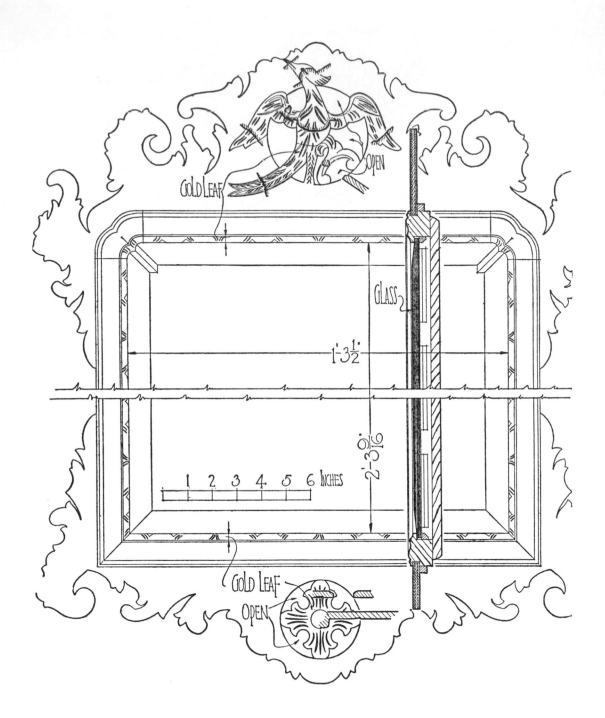

Chippendale Glass

Note the cutting of upper corners of glass, a hold-over of style from the Queen
Anne time. The bird is partly incut and partly raised. (*See Page 337*)

CLOCKS

I am happy to present an unprecedented number of clock hands, various measured clock-case drawings, and some material on odd or rare examples hitherto neglected.

The great number of clocks shown in Volume II, more than in my out-of-press "Clock Book," together with the material here, supplies a source of style and detail which will be a great satisfaction to collectors.

The hands of clocks are the last touch of beauty on good works. The neglect of them mars all other construction and, by contrast with it, is offensive. Their neglect arises from the necessity, now and in the old days, of filing them by hand. There is no decent commercial hand available today if it becomes necessary to repair an old clock. And when a repairer files out a new hand he will, unless he compares periods and individual makers carefully, make a bad job.

Certain distinctive hands belonged with Lemuel Curtis, or certain makers of tall clocks.

The reasons for the hands being in steel was that they were so delicate that no other material was strong enough. Brass hands, when short and heavy, were sometimes used, but bear no comparison for daintiness of design with the steel hands. An occasional cast-brass hand is found, but it is always, of necessity, coarse.

The design was worked on a piece of steel which was sawed out with delicate precision. But the hand was not then completed, by any means. It was filed on a bevel so as to leave the thin edge out, securing the last degree of daintiness, and showing an outline as if sketched by a pen. In order to facilitate the work, soft steel was used, which was afterwards annealed to secure a beautiful blue surface.

Curtis was the designer of the banjo hand, which was formed by a succession of circles diminishing from the center to the outside end, though an English design has been found from which he undoubtedly borrowed.

By borrowing the design of these hands and attaching them to otherwise ordinary banjo clocks, it has been sought to dispose of such clocks as Lemuel Curtis instruments. Practically all other makers of banjo clocks, and their name is legion, including the Willards, employ simple hands, the barbed-arrow type usually.

The date of early English and even American clocks can often be arrived at approximately by the style of the hands. The importance of this indication arises from the peculiar circumstance that great numbers, perhaps the majority of old clocks, bear no maker's name. The early brass English clock works, made by the proud members of the clock maker's company, were careful to sign their clocks. I have, however, a very fine clock, apparently an Elnathan Taber. His cleaner's record is five times repeated on a card fastened inside the door. The case is the highest type used by Simon Willard, who sold his tools and name and designs to Taber, a very high compliment. But the odd fact about this clock is that it has a fine brass face with scrolled brass spandrels, and no name. It is an indication that the customer desired the earlier and finer face. This clock is shown here with measured drawings, it being as good a type of Willard case as I have seen. One of the finest known John Goddard cases has works without a name. This indicates that the works, or at least the dial, were imported and the case made to order to contain them, and that the English maker, not knowing how the works were to be set, did not care to engrave his name on them.

American works were also at times sold without cases to go long distances, and the omission of the name is thus to be accounted for. One of the finest Will Claggett clocks I know, with name on the brass arch, has a common pine case. The record of the owner is that the works were originally placed on a shelf and, later, that his grandfather cased it. He values the clock chiefly owing to the case!

Of course, a case is never necessary and, in the earliest clocks, was not provided. The clock and the case, when both are fine and harmonious, still constitute the most beautiful decoration for an American home.

The writer turns, as years go on, more away from freak clocks, toward those best accomplishments of our distinguished American makers. We have some examples of cases equal to any known abroad, and we have makers who, by their mechanical genius or their capacity, stand high enough to cause us pride and satisfy our patriotism.

The traditions of the English case styles were abandoned after the first generation of American makers, like Bagnall, Will Claggett, and Luscomb, and then followed the fine single or double arch hoods. The pagoda English style is not, after the earliest date, found here.

The drawing of the Goddard case with a shell repeated on the plinth has been done with the proper feet. Hepplewhite feet, with the sweeping French curve, always continued in a straight line with the body of the piece above them, and were not proper when set out on a molded base.

The material of American clocks rather preceded than followed the styles in furniture. That is, clocks were like looking-glasses in this, that they were made of the best woods as dainty affairs, set apart from furniture. Nevertheless, many makers seeking a low-selling value, used cherry instead of mahogany, and sometimes they used very effectively curly maple which, carefully employed on a fine design, achieved much distinction.

There are two sorts of clock enthusiasts, those who think of the case, and those who think of the works. A select small third class gives attention to both. The country is flooded with coarse English cases containing better works, but all sold to the importer at very low figures. Such cases have no place in an American home. The waists are too broad, and these clocks, unless brought in by ancestors, are, of course, without hereditary or patriotic associations.

The feet of old clocks often break when the old weight-cord gives out. The heavy weight, which breaks just as the winding brings it to the highest point, strikes the bottom with such an impact as to smash the dainty ogee feet or the bottom of the case, or both. Hence there are many new feet on old clocks, and they are often wrong in style. The modern brass cord is safer and, even so, should be renewed on the slightest evidence of wear. Seven years is a safe interval.

In collecting it is to be remembered that the date of furniture is our guide to good style. Anything after 1830–35 is best ignored in our purchases. Thus we avoid the machine-made "cathedral" and other shelf clocks. The Eli Terry (or his inheritor, the *early* Seth Thomas style) is about the latest type that is tolerable for design. It is not alone the vast numbers of the later clocks, but their forsaking classical lines that bars them from the attention of the educated collector.

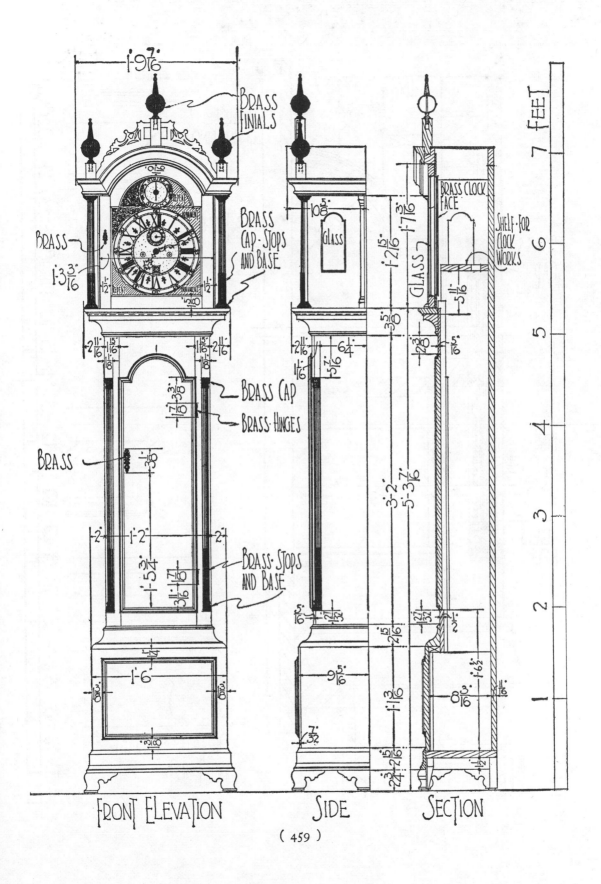

FRONT ELEVATION   SIDE   SECTION

(459)

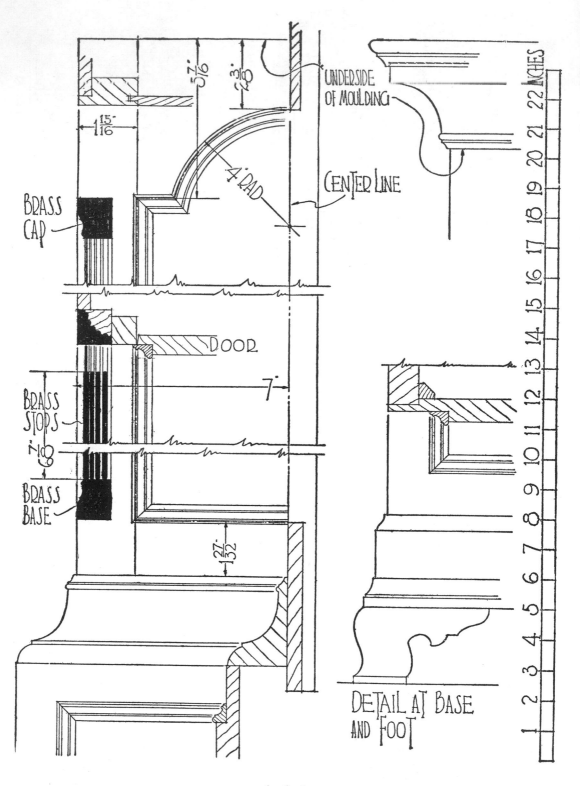

UNDERSIDE
OF MOULDING

CENTER LINE

5-7/16"

2-3/8"

15-1/16"

4" RAD

BRASS
CAP

DOOR

7"

BRASS
STOPS

7-1/8"

BRASS
BASE

27-1/32"

DETAIL AT BASE
AND FOOT

1 2 3 4 5 6 7 8 9 10 11 12 13 14 15 16 17 18 19 20 21 22 INCHES

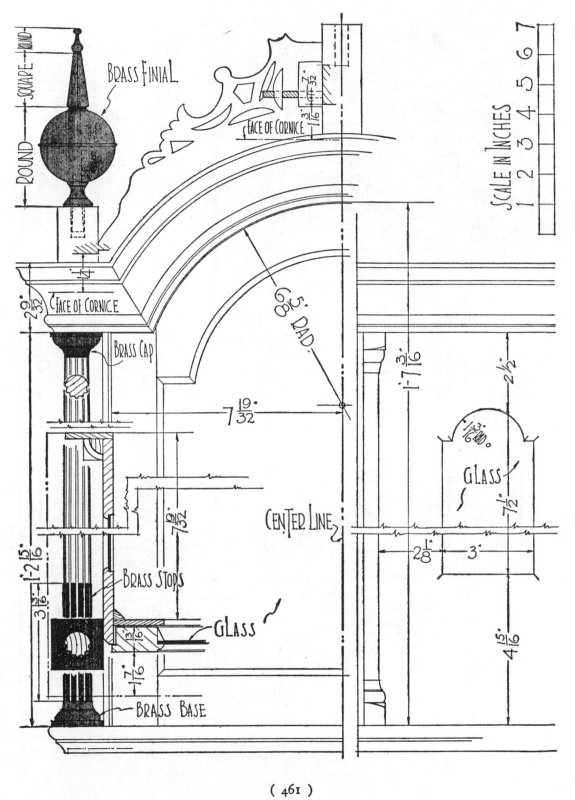

BRASS FINIAL

ROUND — SQUARE — ROUND — ROUND

FACE OF CORNICE

$2\frac{9}{32}$"

FACE OF CORNICE

$\frac{3}{16}$" $\frac{7}{32}$"

6' 8 5' RAD.

$7\frac{19}{32}$"

BRASS CAP

$7\frac{9}{32}$"

$1-2\frac{15}{16}$"

$3\frac{3}{16}$"

BRASS STOPS

GLASS

$\frac{3}{16}$"

$\frac{7}{16}$"

BRASS BASE

CENTER LINE

SCALE IN INCHES
1 2 3 4 5 6 7

$1-7\frac{3}{16}$"

$2\frac{1}{2}$"

$1\frac{3}{16}$ RAD.

GLASS

$7\frac{1}{2}$"

$28\frac{1}{8}$"

3"

$4\frac{15}{16}$"

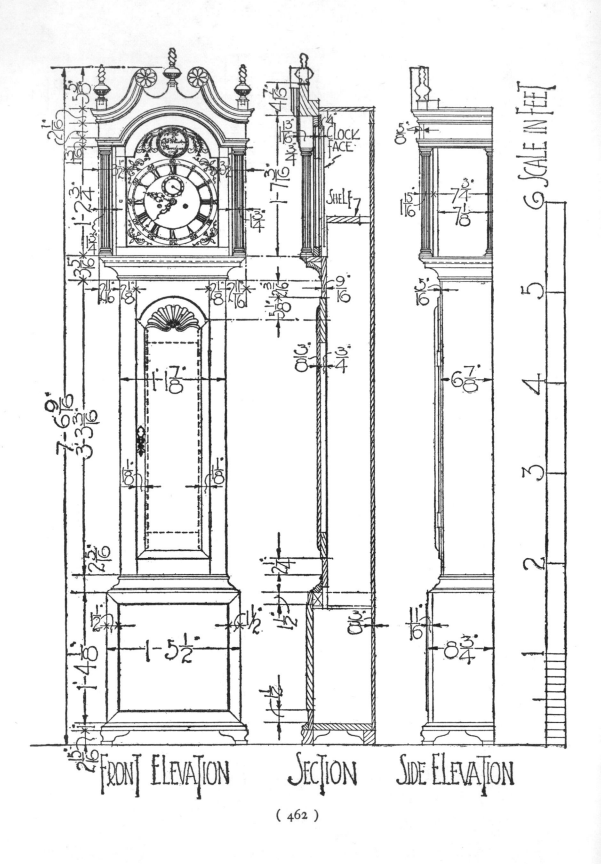

FRONT ELEVATION   SECTION   SIDE ELEVATION

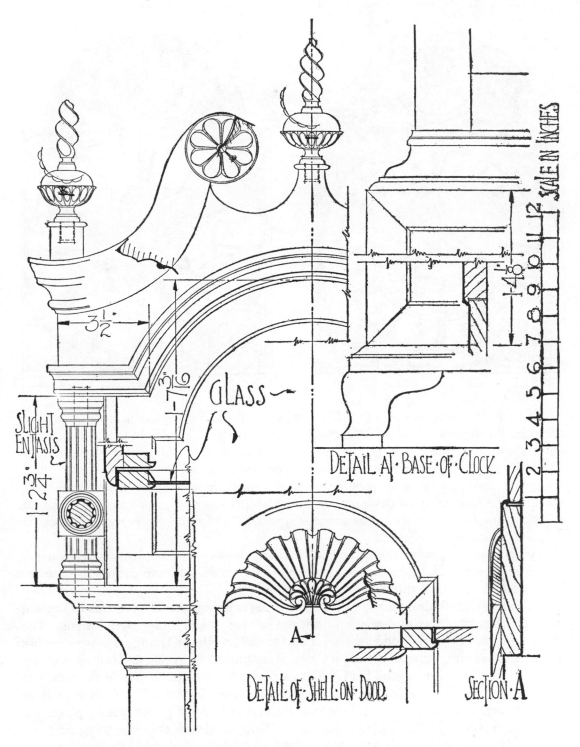

SCALE IN INCHES

$3\frac{1}{2}''$

$-7\frac{3}{16}''$

SLIGHT ENTASIS

$-23\frac{3}{24}''$

GLASS

$-1.4\frac{8}{10}''$

DETAIL AT·BASE·OF·CLOCK

A

DETAIL·OF·SHELL·ON·DOOR.

SECTION·A

Block-and-Shell Clock Detail of Clock on Previous Page

(463)

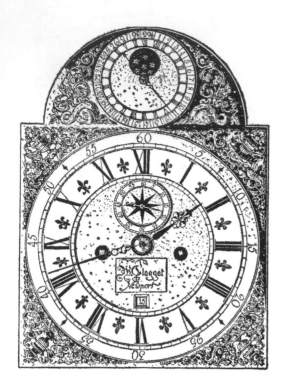 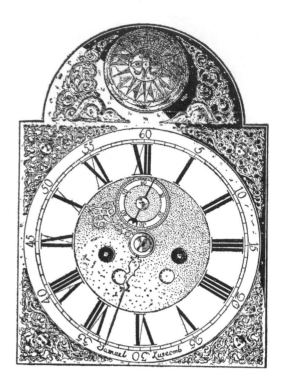

Above appears the face of a Will Clagget in which the name plate is rectangular and attached on the lower half of the face. The other method as seen in the previous volumes shows the name in large characters swept about the upper part of the dial — "Will Claggett." (Spelled by him with one or two t's.)

On the right above is a clock by Samuel Luscomb who dates among the early makers. Both of these clocks have very beautiful brass work, the Luscomb example having a fine feminine face in the spandrels, and both of them the early and excellent dolphin ornaments in the arch.

My purpose in showing these and the following clocks is to complete the full variety shown in Volume II. I have been particular, therefore, to have drawn three more lighthouse clocks, each different from the other.

The two tall clock designs shown on the five pages going before are, so far as known, the only ones available as measured drawings in these highly approved designs. The block-and-shell clock in Goddard's style and found in Rhode Island, was presumably of his manufacture, because it cases a Caleb Wheaton set of works, and our data under Goddard show receipts signed for Goddard's estate by Wheaton. While the face was no doubt originally silvered, the brass has been reached by polishing. The high class of engraving, however, done by Wheaton for clocks and for paper money plates for the State of Rhode Island is in excellent taste. One could wish only one thing different about this clock — the shell was not designed to crown completely the block, as was done in the fine clock door shell on page 94, top.

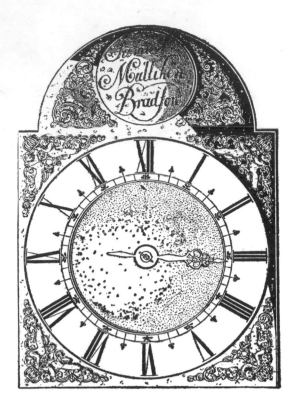

I show a Samuel Mulliken dial, which has but one hand. It is thought from this circumstance that this man, the elder Mulliken and not the Revolutionary Mulliken, was located in Bradford before he went to Newbury and that the clock is a very early date. See his name under Clock Makers, page 516. The octagonal clock shown above on the right is that at the Newport Historical Society.

On the previous page, at the left is shown a clock possessed by the Metropolitan Museum which is of great interest both from the maker's name and from its beauty and rarity. Wall clocks of this sort are extremely rare, and this specimen is the most attractive I have seen. The name is simply Willard, Grafton. As this town in Massachusetts was the first place where the Willards made clocks, it is probably from the hand of Ephraim, or Simon I.

The clock on the right on the previous page is a girandole of the rare and celebrated Lemuel Curtis type in the collection of Mr. Cluett of Williamstown. The large brass knob which opens the lower door is a surprise to collectors. A smaller one like the upper brass decoration on the side brackets would have seemed more fitting, but this is the way they did it. The depending chain should be draped over the eagle's wings. The clock is embellished with a thermometer. I know no finer specimen.

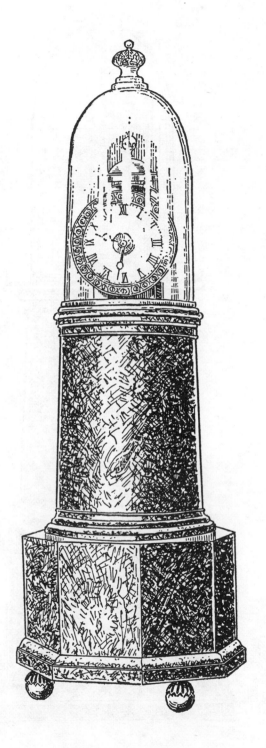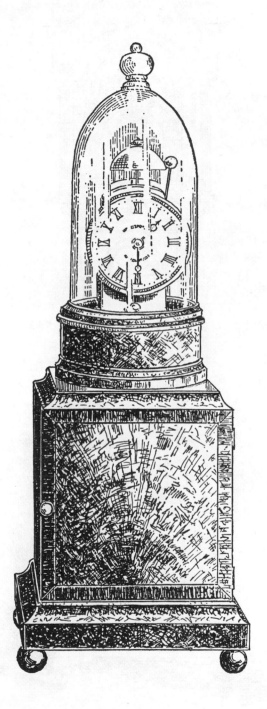

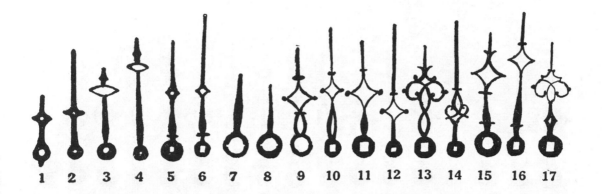

1 2 3 4 5 6 7 8 9 10 11 12 13 14 15 16 17

The clock on the previous page on the left with the shell repeated on the plinth is one of two or three of that type known. They are, of course, the most important clocks in America. None of these clocks has ever been illustrated hitherto in any volume on the subject. The chamfer on the plinth is beautifully closed with a scrolled chamfer stop at the base. The clock has all the features of full development of Goddard cases. The manner, however, of basing the finials is odd and different from anything that is elsewhere known to me. There are, of course, half colonnettes at the back of the hood to match those in front.

The English shelf-clock type is very handsome, compact, and excellent. There are any number imported, new and old. American makers did not take to the design at all. Of course, a pendulum clock is better anyway, and a good one can be made at less cost than the English spring shelf clocks. That fact lies at the basis of Simon Willard's successful attempt to design a shelf clock with a pendulum, that is, the banjo clock without the supporting bracket. This design took the world by storm. But the works were not in their use confined to the banjo type of case. Various other cases proved appropriate and beautiful, from the lighthouse clock to the shelf clock with ogee feet, and even the looking-glass clock. These cases, not of the banjo type, are as much or more sought for than the "timepiece" form (banjo).

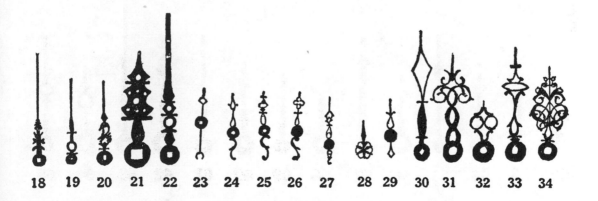

18 19 20 21 22 23 24 25 26 27 28 29 30 31 32 33 34

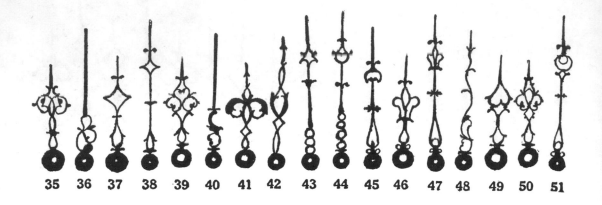

35 36 37 38 39 40 41 42 43 44 45 46 47 48 49 50 51

CLOCK HANDS

Among the clock hands presented are types of many origins. Indeed, clock hands embody the history of design. They are a very curious record of the thoughts of men regarding beauty for perhaps fifty generations.

Where only the hour hand appears, it may be because the date is so early that there was no minute hand employed, the hour being graduated into five-minute intervals and read approximately from one hand. Of course the cruder and heavier hands are the older. In some cases it has not been possible to trace the origin, but without much fear of successful contradiction it may be said that the complete design or the inspiration of it is English or Dutch. For instance, the hands 88 and 89 naturally suggest the origin of the Lemuel Curtis hand, a succession of circles each smaller than the preceding. This is seen in its extreme development in No. 107, though that is the sweep second hand of a Lancaster County clock, Pennsylvania, of the very high grandfather's type.

It is still possible that other Goddard cases may be found. The one of which we show the detail drawing was found in Nantucket, and its mate is supposed to be there. The story is that two identical clocks were made for two brothers. The last one heard of for sale was held at $15,000!

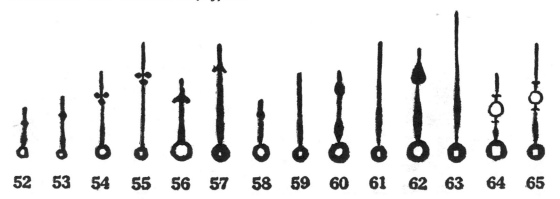

52 53 54 55 56 57 58 59 60 61 62 63 64 65

(470)

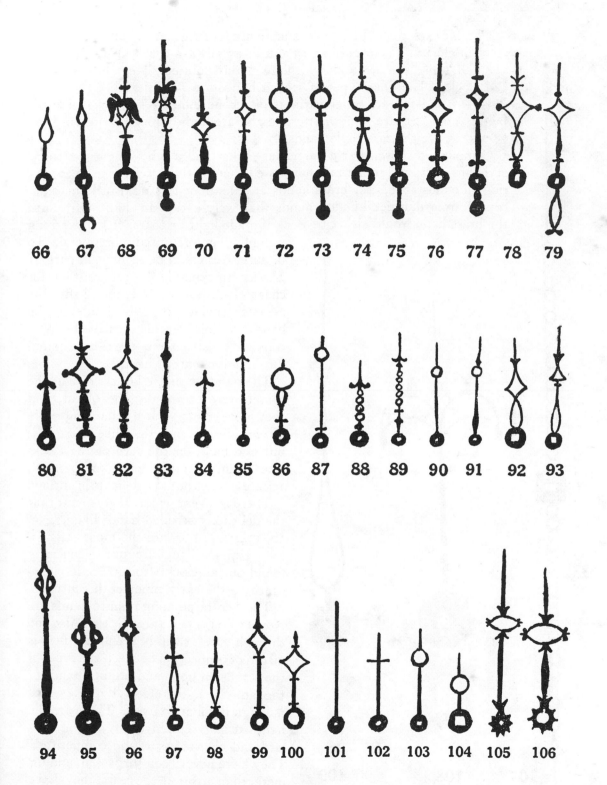

66 67 68 69 70 71 72 73 74 75 76 77 78 79

80 81 82 83 84 85 86 87 88 89 90 91 92 93

94 95 96 97 98 99 100 101 102 103 104 105 106

The simple hands like 70 and 71, 12, 15, and 16 are found generally on banjo clocks or American shelf clocks. The types like 13 and 17 are always the hour hands on tall clocks. The small, short, simple hands which are merely pointers, like 7, 8, are second hands on tall clocks. The finer types of second hands are the miniatures 23 to 27. Nos. 167 and 170 are other variants of second hands. The types like the pairs, 21 and 22, are somewhat crude and are found on early clocks. Nos. 68 and 69 are the rare eagle hands.

Comparison shows that a particular maker had a fancy for a particular style of hands, and sometimes he showed them without reference to the period. For instance, cast brass hands are mentioned as used in Lancashire copied from daintier London hands that were earlier in date. Of course the brass hand would either be weak if made light or coarse if made strong

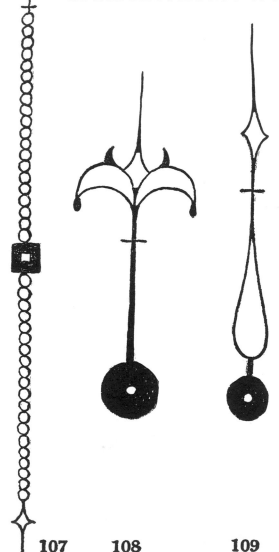

107   **108**   **109**

enough. They required more metal. To be sure, this could be secured in part by greater thickness. As competition for cheap clocks arose it was found that the greatest saving could be made in the hands. A considerable part of the work could be constructed in the time required for filing one pair of hands.

The hands with the largest disc at the center were commonly the oldest, and they were made with a balancing spike of considerable length, since there was but one hand on the face of the clock. The Pennsylvania hands like 107, 108, 109 are among the most delicate in outline.

There is a very general agreement that the delicately scrolled hand, like 37, 39, 50, 134, 135, 136, are the most satisfactory types. They are quite generally found on tall clocks from the mid eighteenth to the early nineteenth centuries.

Their corresponding minute hands are Nos. 113, 115, 144, through 161. Also 196 through 202. It will be seen that there is no direct connection between the types of the scrolls on hour and minute hands of the same clock, therefore. Each develops a design peculiar to itself. These are the hands usually employed by Simon Willard and his successors and competitors. They have never been surpassed, and for more than a hundred years they have

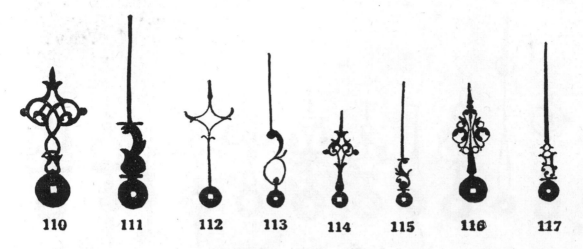

110   111   112   113   114   115   116   117

never been equaled. The present styles of hands, even on very expensive commercial clocks, show a more rapid degeneration than appears on any other class of antiques whatever. There is a very heavy wooden hand, such as one might whittle out, on an electrical clock recently put on the market!

It will be observed that Bagnall and Claggett used somewhat heavier hands and with more metal left in the fret than was found in clocks fifty years later.

Nos. 105 and 106 seem to be peculiar to the Moulton clocks made in Rochester, New Hampshire. There were two Moultons and another maker in that town who all used these hands.

Nos. 101 and 102 are plain crosses. Nos. 116 and 117 are William Claggett. The curious design of No. 121, where the hand is fully balanced, adds no little beauty to the face of a clock.

Nos. 118 and 119 are very dainty and unusual designs whose attraction is the greater owing to their oddity.

The heart design so much beloved in hardware and so often running into an arrow shape by gradations appears in 169, 171, 172, and 173.

We may suppose that the maker of 177, the gridiron pattern, made it simply to be different.

A hand like 212 would be earlier than 136 on account of the heavy web, the term used of the connecting metal that is left after filing out.

The arrow being a very early means of designating direction, some semblance to it was naturally sought for in the hands as appears in 5, 6, 56, 57, 60, 62, 66, 80, 83, 84, 85. It thus appears that hands group into a series of general outlines.

Another favorite element is that which has the ball and spike like 72–75, 86, 87, and others.

The student will see that where two, three, or even sometimes four hands appeared on a clock face they were all made to distinctive patterns, having no necessary agreement, beyond the fact that they were all light or all heavy, but this does not hold true of the arrow hand or the ball and spike, where the hour and minute agree except in size.

(473)

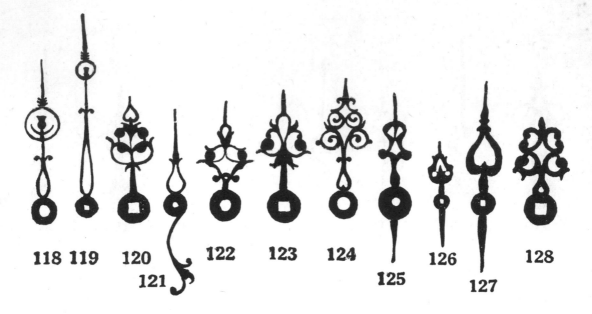

118 119 120 121 122 123 124 125 126 127 128

To sum up the matter of beauty and taste we may say that the designs like 39, 135, and similar hands are on the whole the most satisfactory and most in use of that period in American clocks when fine cases were made. That is, the latter half of the eighteenth century, and that the earlier hands, say the second quarter of the eighteenth century, were more like those mentioned as belonging to Claggett and Bagnall, somewhat like 116, 129, etc. Also, that the minute hands corresponding as No. 48 and its variants, which go with the hour hands just mentioned, are very excellent. Most of the other patterns are either in the class of the curious and the freak or the very simple conventional like 10, 103, etc. All thes are blued steel hands, filed on a bevel. Of course the Lemuel Curtis is the handsomest banjo hand. Beyond we expect nothing better than the simple design like 84 and 85.

A recent inquiry was received regarding a wall clock something like a Dutch wag-on-the-wall, on which the date 1492 appeared. Of course, such a date is always suspicious, very much as if someone had presumed that the credulous would believe the clock came over with Columbus. A great many clocks are dated in this way and with other incredible dates.

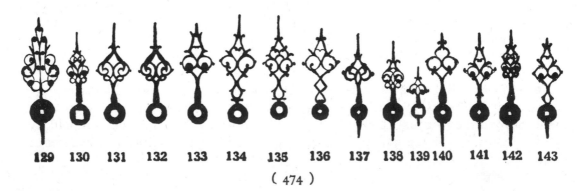

129 130 131 132 133 134 135 136 137 138 139 140 141 142 143

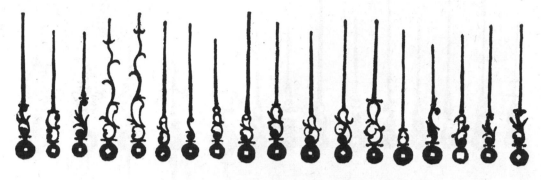

144 145 146 147 148 149 150 151 152 153 154 155 156 157 158 159 160 161

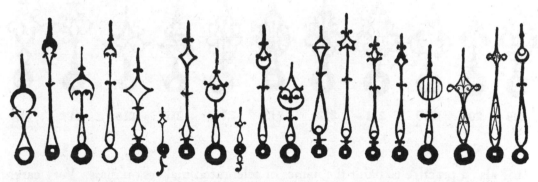

162 163 164 165 166 167 168 169 170 171 172 173 174 175 176 177 178 179 180

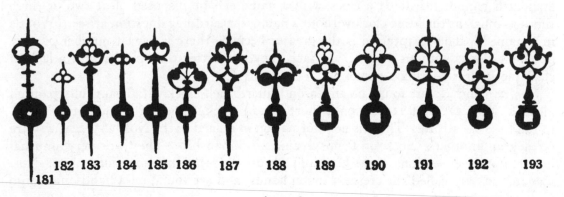

182 183 184 185 186 187 188 189 190 191 192 193
181

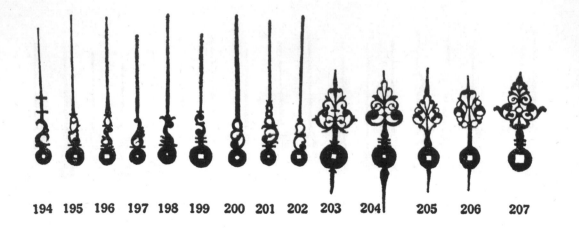

194 195 196 197 198 199 200 201 202 203 204 205 206 207

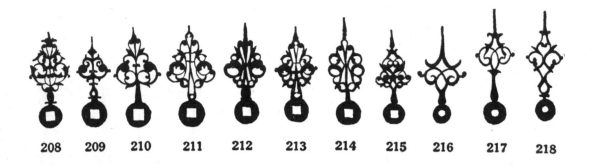

208 209 210 211 212 213 214 215 216 217 218

It is also a practice to paint the names of celebrated makers on dials. Very careful inspection by an experienced person will indicate that the name was not painted at the same time as the dial. Sometimes the maker who uses this name merely means that he has constructed a clock in the style and with the care which marked the original. In that case the maker may frankly say that the clock is his own make.

The painting of a name on an old dial is something which a dealer without moral standards cannot resist. If a clock with a name can be disposed of at two or three times as much as the same clock without a name, the sardonic question arises, "What's in a name?" The temptation is the greater because there is a vast number of very excellent clocks without a name. In fact, they are better than clocks with a lack of their merits but bearing a name.

Nos. 219 and 220 are found on an Aaron Willard shelf clock with beautifully painted glasses. Nos. 221 and 223 are on a short, broad clock, almost a grandmother's size, in the Essex Institute. There is no information in regard to it. Nos. 223, 224, 225 are on a grandmother's clock of Pennsylvania workmanship. They are very unusual hands, the lower sections of the hour and minute repeated interrogation points. Nos. 226 and 227 are called the crescent moon hands, and are found on a handsome banjo

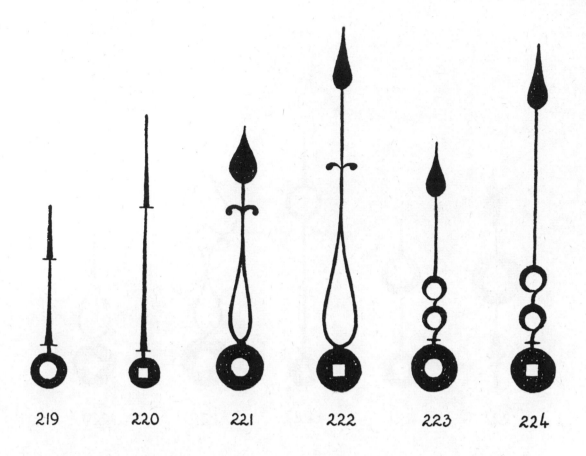

219   220   221   222   223   224

without a name. Nos. 228 and 229 are very delicate hands which, though not complicated, are attractive. They are found on a James Doull tall clock. No. 230 appears
on a Dublin clock dating about 1810. It shows the arrow point so noticeable in 220–
24 and 246–49, but of course is a somewhat late design. Nos. 232, 233, and 234 are
found on a clock built in the Gothic style, but apparently late. Nos. 235 and 236 are
on a looking-glass clock of about 1830. Nos. 237 and 238 are on a grandmother's clock
with a very plain case and the date not given, but apparently of the early nineteenth
century. They are a good pattern. No. 239 is a slight variant, the curvature of the
barbs being in an opposite direction. Nos. 240 and 241 are on a Simon Willard banjo
of a very early type, but whether original hands or not I do not know. Although so
simple, they are attractive. Nos. 242 and 243 are the dissimilar hour and minute
hands of a clock apparently in French design and probably about 1800. Nos. 244 and
245 appear on an Empire clock and apparently are intended to simulate sun's rays,
though with a flattened disc and having pure arrow points. The date is probably about
1830. No. 246 is on a clock of 1675 by Johannes A. Fromanteel, London. It belongs
to the period when only one hand was used, and when the maker was content with a
mere arrow point. Nos. 247 and 248 are on an odd wall clock of foreign origin and
somewhat doubtful antecedents. They are of the pure heart pattern. Nos. 249 and

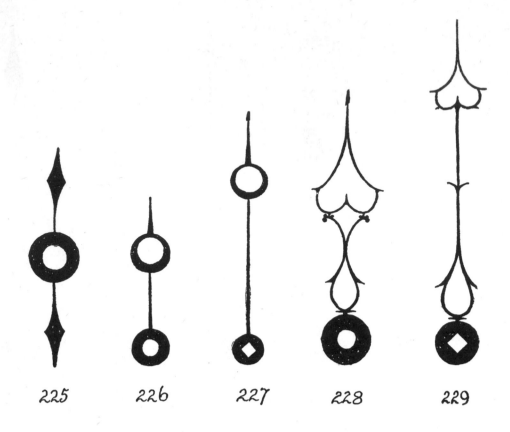

225   226   227   228   229

250 are the simple hands on an English shelf clock. No. 251 is an effective hand on an Italian shelf clock. Although it is so long, it is the hour hand, there being no minute hand.

No. 252 is thought by Britten to be on a sixteenth-century clock. It is about true size. The clock is portable, about 12 inches wide. No. 253 is in Soltykoff, on a castle-shaped clock of about 1560. It is thought to be German.

Nos. 254 and 255 are on a musical clock made by Clay, an early eighteenth-century English maker. It is remarkable as showing hands apparently the basis of those developed later in the century and so much used. They are peculiar for the width of the hour hand and the open S shape of the long hand.

The star-shaped hand No. 256 is on a lyre-shaped Sevres clock, of blue porcelain, of the period of Louis XVI, and now in South Kensington Museum. No. 257 is the single hand on a Bowyer clock, dating 1623. It is a very rich specimen. Nos. 258 and 259 are not traceable to any source.

The celebrated Thomas Tompion built a clock in 1670 on which is found the bold design No. 260. It is a tall clock with an exquisitely engraved dial. The year 1683 is the date of the lantern clock carrying the hand No. 261. An English specimen, the pendulum in front of the dial.

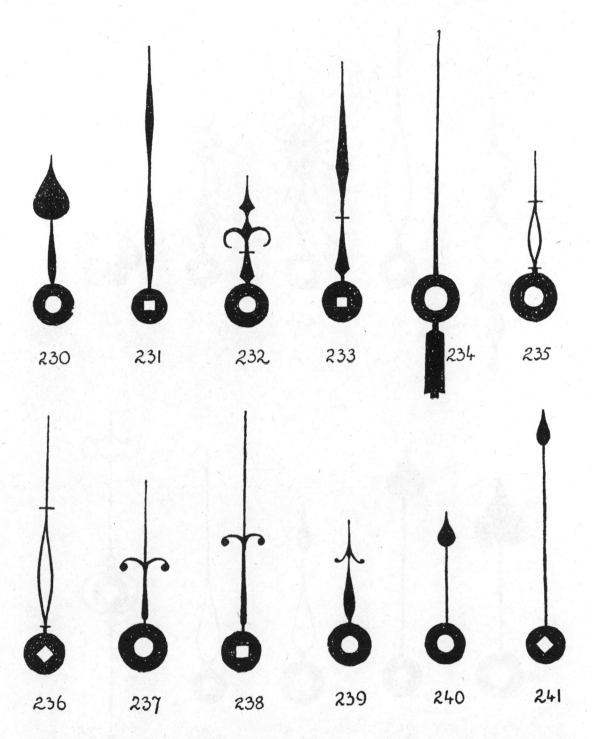

230   231   232   233   234   235

236   237   238   239   240   241

Nos. 262 and 263 are drawings made directly from my John Goddard-Caleb Wheaton tall block-and-shell clock. They should be compared carefully with Nos. 274 and 275, which appear lighter because they are purposely drawn from appearance, the web

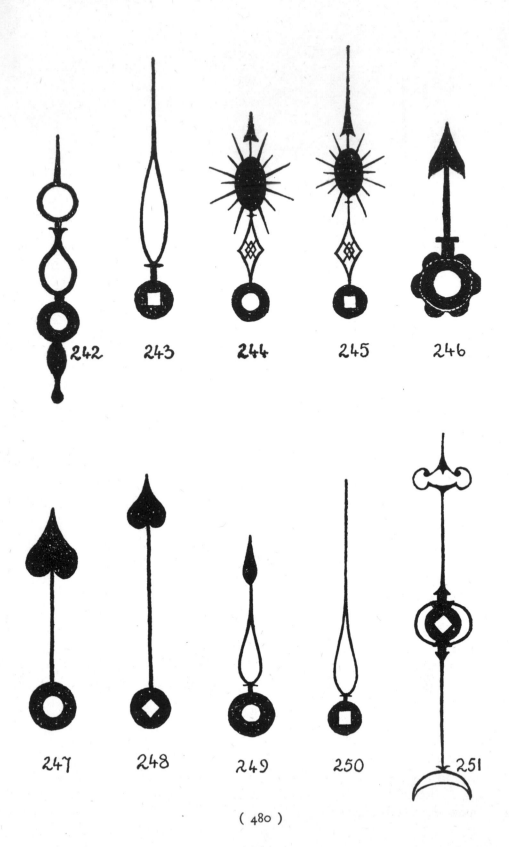

242 243 244 245 246

247 248 249 250 251

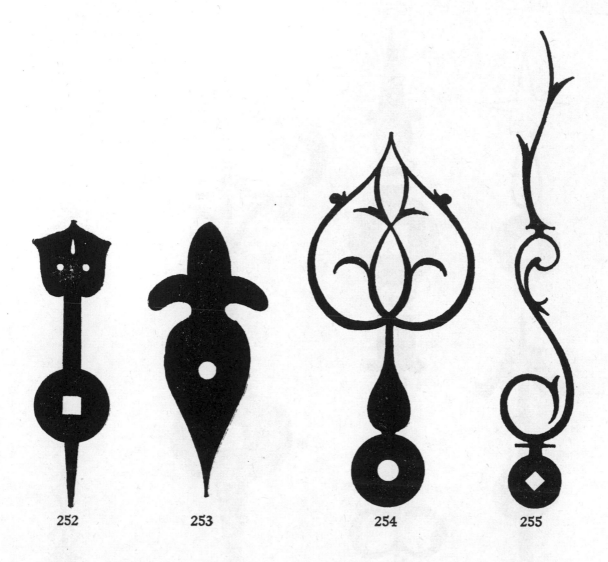

252   253   254   255

being beveled and the drawing made from the upper face of the hands on my Simon Willard tall clock. The hands Nos. 262 and 263 are, on the contrary, drawn the width at the back side. Both of these patterns with minor variation constitute the great bulk of the good American hands after 1750. In fact, they established themselves as a standard New England and Philadelphia hand. They are (Nos. 262 and 263) very exact in size and may serve as models for any maker who has occasion to restore a good Willard or Wheaton type or other fine makes any time before 1825.

Nos. 264 and 265 are another handsome example of Thomas Tompion, London, almost exactly one hundred years before our Declaration of Independence.

J. Lorimer, an English maker, is responsible for the unusual specimens Nos. 266 and 267. The date is 1790. John Smith, an English artisan, about 1695, gives us Nos. 268 and 269, in the latter going into a very intricate broad design. It will be seen that the

256   258

261   257   260   259

minute hands are more often in this and similar scrolls, even when the hour hands vary widely. Nos. 270 and 271 are on a long clock formerly in the Wethersfield Collection, by Richard Comber of Lewes, England. Very fine examples.

Joseph Knibb, an English maker of 1685, gives us the beautiful specimens 272 and 273.

Under Nos. 262 and 263 I took up the Simon Willard hands Nos. 274 and 275.

It is probable that the fairly good hand designs run into the thousands, but we

262   263   264   265

close our sketch with the hunter's hands, probably late, Nos. 276 and 277, of English design. Several other sporting hands are known. The many English works, chiefly the vast stores of Britten, show other curious shapes. It is sufficient to point out, besides the odd designs, the best known types.

Rittenhouse, the highly celebrated Pennsylvania maker, used hands, of course, of English derivation, quite like the Claggett, Bagnall, Harland, Willard types.

The arrow and its derivatives, and the heart, supplied probably ninety-nine per cent of the good designs. The arrow and heart sometimes converge, blend, and interlace so as to puzzle one who attempts to classify them.

266   267   268   269

The collector is again warned not to be too certain of the origin of a clock from its hands. There is no possible method of making sure of their being original unless the clocks are where they ever were, in families of the highest repute. Even then one may not be certain a hand or both hands of a clock have not sometime been broken and

270 271 272 273

replaced. Collateral evidence is required. But the higher the artistic skill shown in the hand, the more likely is it to be original.

A good clock hand is about a sixteenth of an inch in thickness. In sawing them out deftness is required, as the lines must not be infringed upon, but again unless the saw cuts closely to the line, filing will be an increased labor.

In speaking of the thickness, reference is to the hands with delicate weblike contours. The very early hands, especially where only one was used, are often thicker, but even so, three thirty-seconds of an inch is ample, unless the hand is cast.

It appears by reference to the faces that the length of the hour hand should just

274   275   276   277

exceed the inner circle of the face, touching lightly the base of the numerals, while the minute hand reaches completely over the numerals to the outer circle, if any.

The second hand is short, for its little dial, and as a rule quite plain, so that it is shown only exceptionally in this list. But if a sweep second hand is used (compare well-sweep) it is as long practically, as the clock face will accommodate.

About half the hands shown are in the collection of W. F. Hubbard of Hartford.

The glass on old clock faces is always poor. Fine quality of glass is proof of substitution.

The names of the hoods or cases are: the sarcophagus top (F. T. 3319, English or very early American); pagoda top (F. T. 3327), usually English; the single arch top (F. T. 3343); the double arch top, or the arch and broken arch (F. T. 3322); the flat top (F. T. 3297); the fretted arch, a single arch (F. T. 3284); the fretted flat top (F. T. 3299); the closed pediment top, English perhaps always (F. T. 3312); the boxed top (F. T. 3263); the bell top, described by its name; the lyre case (F. T. 3362); the timepiece or banjo (F. T. 3366); the banjo, a timepiece with a bracket (F. T. 3365); the girandole (F. T. 3395); the kidney dial (F. T. 3407); the lighthouse (F. T. 3423); the balloon (F. T. 3443); the grandmother's or miniature tall (F. T. 3447); the pillar and scroll (F. T. 3454); the late Empire (F. T. 3458); the lantern (F. T. 3474); the looking-glass, "banjo" works (F. T. 3475); the cathedral (F. T. 3492); the wag-on-the-wall (F. T. 3500); the chamber, shelf, bracket, table, interchangeable names for short clocks; the wall clock, attached to the wall. Of course, there are many others. Dr. E. A. Locke has a handsome tall clock which winds only once a year, has fifty-pound weights, and a pin-wheel escapement! (F. T. 3287).

Miss Sarah G. Bagnall, a neighbor of mine in Framingham, is the sixth lineal descendant of Benjamin Bagnall I. Herself and her brother Francis A. Bagnall of the State Teachers' College here are the great-great-great-grandchildren of Benjamin I; the daughter of Francis A. is the seventh generation. They with George Bagnall of Buffalo are the only four living Benjamin Bagnall I descendants bearing the name of Bagnall. The name originally was Bagnaulde; one Henri de Bagnaulde went from Normandy to England in 1066 with William the Conqueror. There the name was changed to Bagnald, then to Bagnall, never Bagnell.

Miss Bagnall has been kind enough to furnish me with the following data, which, as Benjamin Bagnall I is our most celebrated early maker, is worthy to be inserted.

A Walter Bagnall settled at Richmond, Maine, traded with the Indians and was killed by them. He was unmarried.

A Bagnall family settled near Plymouth, and at Wellfleet, Massachusetts. Neither of these Bagnalls was connected with the clock maker's family.

Benjamin Bagnall I, a Quaker, was born in England in 1689. Benjamin I came to Massachusetts Bay Colony and settled in Boston 1713, and is uniformly designated as a watchmaker, though the only work we have of him is in the form of clocks. His home and shop were at the corner of Washington and Water Streets, extending down to Devonshire Street, then Pudding Lane.

By his will it appears that he was twice married. In the Genealogy of Charlestown, page 45, it appears that he married Elizabeth Shove, and on page 863 of the same book it appears that her parents were the Rev. Samuel Shove and Dorothy Thompson of Charlestown.

The eldest child of Benjamin I and Elizabeth Shove, was Benjamin, Jr., who was christened at King's Chapel in Boston, March 3, 1715. There is a tradition in the family that he was christened in this church so that if, when he grew up, he did not wish to adopt the Quaker faith, he might possibly get back his father's estate in

England, forfeited when his father became a Quaker and left England for the colonies. Benjamin Jr., however, remained a Quaker and married a Quaker, and became a clock maker like his father, although he is listed as a merchant at the time of his marriage.

That Benjamin I was married a second time is shown by his will where he refers to his wife as Sarah Bagnall. In the Vital Records of Rhode Island, Vol. XII, page 81, we read: "Mrs. Sarah Bagnall, widow of Benjamin Bagnall of Boston, daughter of Abraham Redwood of Newport, died in Cranston, Jan. 7, 1791, aged 88 yrs."

The date of Benjamin Sr.'s death is to be found in the Massachusetts *Gazette*, 1773, and contains the following: "Last Sunday died after a short illness Benjamin Bagnall, watchmaker of this Town, aged 84 yrs., one of the people called Quakers. He came from England to America early in life and has always resided in the Place. He was a good husband and a good Parent; honest and upright in his Dealings; sincere and steadfast in his friendship; liberal to the Poor, and a good citizen; he acquired the Regard and Esteem of all who had the Pleasure of his Acquaintance."

Miss Bagnall also finds in Vol. XIII, p. 147 of Vital Statistics of Rhode Island as recorded by the Friend's Society Records: "Died, — Benjamin Bagnall aged 84 yrs., a member of the Society of Friends, in Boston, July, 1773." This was Benjamin I.

Sarah Bagnall, his second wife, was the daughter of Abraham Redwood, who founded the Redwood library in Newport.

The will of Benjamin Bagnall I, dated May 6, 1772, and probated in Boston, Aug. 20, 1773, reads in part:

"... Know ye, that I, Benjamin Bagnall of Boston, in the County of Suffolk, in the Province of Mass Bay, in New England, Watchmaker being weak of body ... make and ordain this my last Will and Testament ... and as touching such unholy goods and effects wherewith it has pleased God to bless me in this life, I give and dispose of the same in the following manner, To my wife, etc., etc." (From Records, Court House, Boston, Mass.)

The two daughters living at the time of their father's death were Elizabeth and Martha. Elizabeth married John Mifflin of Philadelphia, a rich Quaker merchant. Their son Thomas Mifflin was three times governor of the State of Pennsylvania. When the Revolutionary War broke out he raised a body of troops, Quakers, in Philadelphia, brought them to Boston at his own expense, and delivered them to General Washington, who placed them in the Commissary Department as Quakers did not bear arms. General Washington made this Thomas Mifflin his aide-de-camp. Into this company, being also a Quaker, enlisted Robert Bagnall, son of Benjamin Jr., and so first cousin to Thomas Mifflin. Robert Bagnall was appointed by General Washington as an express, and on horseback carried messages and moneys between General Washington and the Continental army through the war. Being dressed as a Quaker, he was not suspected.

Benjamin Bagnall's second daughter Martha married Abraham Borden of Newport.

After the war Robert went into the "far country," into Ohio, to take up land, but died shortly of a fever, leaving one son Thomas, the grandfather of Sarah G. Bagnall, who furnishes this information.

Robert had married Mary (Molly) Rhodes of Newport, R. I., a Quakeress and lineal descendant of Roger Williams and of Governor Arnold of Rhode Island.

The quaint notice of the marriage of the second generation taken from the New England *Weekly Journal* of Aug. 9, 1737, follows:

"Last Thursday in the Afternoon Mr. Benjamin Bagnall, Jun. eldest son of Mr. Benjamin Bagnall, of this Town, Merchant, married to Mistress Anna Hawden, Daughter of Mr. James Hawden of this Town, Shopkeeper, in the manner of the Quakers. The marriage was solemnized in the Old Brick Church, the Quaker Meeting House not being large enough to contain the vast Concourse of People of all Perswations who came to see the Solemnity. The parents of the married Couple gratefully acknowledge the Favour of having the marriage solemnized in said Meeting House. His Excellency, our Governour and several of the Council and of the Justices, etc. attended the said Marriage, which was carried on with becoming decency. It being a rainy time, His Excellency favoured the Bridegroom and his Bride with his Chariot."

The great popularity and social prominence of this family are witnessed by the above notice. Also the kindly fellow feeling which by that time had been established between members of the different creeds in Boston.

ADDITIONAL NOTES ON SHELLS
See Pages 87–108

There is a class of shells cut as pairs in the shallow half dome of many fine old secretary tops (F. T. Nos. 703 and 705). Perhaps they are clear enough as they appear there. But it is to be pointed out that wherever these shells are used there is not a shell on the exterior of the door. To repeat the shell would be redundant ornament. As the doors of these bookcases would ordinarily be kept closed, the beauty of these shell domes is hidden. These shells are a variation of the single shells used in niches or corner cupboards. Their beauty is unquestionable. Goddard, however, put most of his decoration on the front. I have never been able to determine beyond the shadow of a doubt the provenance of these shells. But they are found in Rhode Island and on the North Shore of Massachusetts and in Connecticut, sometimes with and sometimes without block doors. I feel certain that they are not Goddard's work, because I have not found them to occur with other indubitable marks of his design. They are found in several instances with the claw-and-ball foot and never with the applied molding around the inner reversed arches of the crest.

CLOCK MAKERS OR DEALERS

American, with a very few of the most celebrated English makers

This list includes about 1700 names of American clock makers or dealers. It includes the list published in my "Clock Book."

The terms below, hall, tall, long, and grandfather's are interchangeable.

Also the terms shelf and table are interchangeable.

A wall clock means a clock without a case, or a short-cased clock attached to the wall.

In the many instances where no data is given the reader will understand that any maker listed any earlier than 1800 in all probability made tall clocks. Shelf clocks in England were in use long before this time, but were manufactured here only very rarely.

The date of Simon Willard's patent for a timepiece, 1802, marks the principal date for the departure from the tall to the shelf clock. After that date tall clocks were manufactured in large numbers, but the manufacture dropped off gradually, until by 1835 it had nearly ceased except in very conservative sections like Pennsylvania.

"Timepiece" was a term used by Simon Willard for a clock without a strike. The name "banjo" did not originate with him, and he seldom used the bracket beneath his timepieces.

A

Abbott, Moses, Sutton, N. H. (c. 1820).

Abbott, Samuel, Boston, Mass. (1827–32). Made grandfather, shelf, and banjos.

Adams, Jonas, Rochester, N. Y. (1834).

Adams, Nathan, Boston, Mass. (1796–1825).

Adams, Thomas A., Baltimore, Md. (1804). Watch and clock maker on Market near South.

Adams, William, Boston, Mass. (1823).

Agar, Edw., New York City (1761).

Aiken, David F., Yarmouth. Hall clock with rocking ship.

Aikinson, Peabody, Concord, Mass. (1790). Apprentice of Levi Hutchinson.

Aird, David, Middletown, Conn. (1785). Advertised November, 1785, as watchmaker. This person changed his name. Charles Brewster said to be his correct name.

Allebach, Jacob, Philadelphia, Pa. (1825–40).

Allen, James, Boston, Mass. (1684).

Allen, Jared T., Rochester, N. Y. (1844).

Allen, John, New York City (1798).

Allen, William, Annapolis, Md. (1772). The Maryland *Gazette* for December 10, 1772, announces that William Allen, watch and clock maker from Birmingham, has joined Jacob and Claude.

Allyn, John, Hartford, Conn. (1657).

Allyn, Nathan, Hartford, Conn. (c. 1800). Watchmaker.

Almy, James, New Bedford, Mass. (1836).

Alrichs, Jacob, Wilmington, Del. (1797–1857).

Alrichs, Jacob & Jonas, Wilmington, Del. (1793–97).

Alrichs, Jonas, Wilmington, Del. (1780–93).

Altmore, Marshall, Philadelphia, Pa. (1832).

Amant, Fester (or Peter), Philadelphia, Pa. (1793).

Anderson, David D., Marietta, Ohio (1821–24).

Andrews, F. C., Bristol, Conn.

Andrews, L. & F., Bristol, Conn. (prior to 1840).

Andrews, N. & T., Meriden, Conn. (1832).

Ansonia Brass & Clock Co., Ansonia, Conn. (1855).

Anthony, L. D., Providence, R. I. (1849).

Ash, Lawrence, Baltimore, Md. (1773). An advertisement appeared requesting the return of a lost watch to "Mr. Lawrence Ash, watchmaker in Baltimore."

Ashby, James, Boston, Mass. (1769). "Watchmaker and finisher from London, near the British Coffee House in King street, Boston, Begs leave to Inform the Publick, that he performs the different Branches of that Business in the Best and Completest Manner at the Most Reasonable Rates."

Ashton, Philadelphia, Pa. (1797).

Atheaton, Otis, New York City (1798).

Atkins & Allen, Bristol, Conn. (1820).

Atkins & Downs, Bristol, Conn. (Early 19th C.). Shelf clock, Empire style.

Atkins, Eldridge G., Bristol, Conn. (1830).

Atkins, Ireneus (or Irenus), Bristol, Conn. (1830–60). Made first-rate 30-day brass clock, movement for which was invented by Joseph Ives.

Atkins, Joel, Middletown, Conn. (1777). Clock and watchmaker.

Atkins, Merritt W., Bristol, Conn. (1856).

Atkins, Rollin, Bristol, Conn. (1826).

Atkins & Son, Bristol, Conn. (1870).

Atkinson, James, Boston, Mass. (1745). Advertised in Boston *Gazette*, Jan. 8, 1745, "Watchmaker from London," "makes and sells all sorts of watches and clocks." Aug. 6, 1745, "Removed from Cornhill into King Street, near the Exchange, Boston."

Atkinson, Leroy, Baltimore, Md. (1824–30). Assayer of silver plate. Probably brought up as clock and watchmaker. Grandson of Mrs. Anne Maria Atkinson (q. v.) who had a clock and watch shop at 33 Market Space from 1796 to 1819, who died in 1823, naming Leroy Atkinson as her grandson in her will. She was probably the widow of Matthew Atkinson, who in 1787 announced the removal of Matthew and William Atkinson (q. v.) watch and clock makers, from Gay Street to Market and Holiday Streets, and the mother of William.

Atkinson, Matthew and William, Baltimore, Md. (1787). The Maryland *Gazette* for September 18, 1787, announces the removal of Matthew and William Atkinson, watch and clock makers, from Gay Street to the corner of Market and Holliday. Believed to be father and son, and that William was the father of Leroy Atkinson, assayer of silver plate for Baltimore.

Atkinson, M. & A., Baltimore, Md. (1804).

Atkinson, Wilmer (fl. 1848–). Clocks said to have been made by his wife. First name also spelled Wilton. Date of perhaps only clock known is on the dial of the moon, and the days are numbered by an indicator fixed point.

Attmore, Marshall, Philadelphia, Pa. (1832).

Austin, Isaac Upper Delaware Ward, Pa. (1783). Watchmaker.

Austin, Isaac, Philadelphia, Pa. (1785–1805).

Austin, Orrin, Waterbury, Conn. (1820). Had factory on Beaver Pond Brook in which he made parts of clocks.

Avery, ——, Boston, Mass. (1726). Made the clock which hangs in the Old North Church of Paul Revere fame.

Avery, John, Jr., Preston, Conn. (1732–94). "One of the members of the Avery family who had inventive genius, he was a self-taught silversmith and clock maker."

Avisse, Charles, Baltimore, Md. (1812). Jeweler and watchmaker.

Ayres, Alexander, Lexington, Ky. (between 1790 and 1819).

B

Ba——?, Robert.

Babbitt, H. W., Providence, R. I. (1849).

Babcock & Co., Philadelphia, Pa. (1832).

Babcock, Geo. W., Providence, R. I. (1838–53). Dealer, name found in small clocks by various makers, including Willard banjos and E. Willard hall clocks.

Bach, Valentine, Frederick, Md. (1798). Watch and clock maker.

Bachelder, Ezra, Danvers, Mass. (1793–1840).

Bachman, John, Bachmanville, near Soudersburg (b. 1798). Made cases for Bowman and Baldwin.

Bacon, John, Bristol, Conn. (1830).

Bacon, Samuel, Annapolis, Md. (1752). Watchmaker from London, advertises in the Maryland *Gazette* for May 14, 1752, from Mrs. McLeod's, Annapolis.

Badlam, Stephen, Lower Mills, Dorchester, Mass. (1751–1815). Cabinetmaker of Cummens clock.

Badley, Thomas, Boston, Mass. (1712–20). Associated with Joseph Essex, 1712. Advertised in Boston *Gazette*, March 6/13, 1720/1. "Thomas Badley, late of Boston, watchmaker, his estate was declared insolvent."

Badman, Joseph, Colebrookdale, Pa. (1780).

Badollet, Paul, New York City (1798).

Bagnall, Benjamin, Boston, Mass. (1712–40). Classed with Wm. Claggett of Newport. They are among the earliest makers in America of fine clocks, and their clocks are eagerly sought. *See* Peter Stretch for another name as early. (*See* Page 487.)

Bagnall, Benjamin (son of Benjamin 1st), Boston, Mass. (1770). Had a shop at Cornhill near the Town House. Cornhill in this connection is now a part of Washington Street.

Bagnall, Samuel (son of Benjamin 1st), Boston, Mass. (1740–60). Worked in his father's shop, was an invalid and was left a fund for his support in his father's will. He also had a shop in Boston.

Bailey & Brothers, Utica, N. Y. (1847).

Bailey, John, New Bedford, Mass.

Bailey & Ward, New York City (1832).

Bailey, William, Philadelphia, Pa. (1832–46). In directory 1819–20, Bailey, William, Jr.

Bailey, *see* Bayley.

Baker, Eleazer, Ashford, Conn. (1764–1849). Clock and watchmaker.

Baker, George, Providence, R. I. (1824–49).

Balch, Benjamin (Balch & Son), Salem, Mass. (1837).

Balch, Charles Hodge, Newburyport, Mass. (b. 1787). In 1817 he was appointed superintendent of the town clocks. (A generation later than Daniel.)

Balch, Daniel, Newburyport, Mass. (1760–90). He took care of the town clock, 1781–83, and perhaps longer.

Balch, Daniel (son of Daniel 1st), Newburyport, Mass. (1782–1818).

Balch, Ebenezer (b. Boston, 1723). Hartford 1744, later Wethersfield.

Balch, James (Balch & Son), Salem, Mass. (1837).

Balch, Joseph, Wethersfield, Conn. (1760–1855). Son of Ebenezer. Clock maker and silversmith.

Balch & Lamson (James Balch & Charles Lamson), Salem, Mass. (1842).

Balch, Moses P., Lowell, Mass. (1832).

Balch, Thomas H. (son of Daniel 1st), Newburyport, Mass. (1790–1818).

Baldwin, Anthony, Lancaster, Pa. (1810–30).

Baldwin, Anthony, Wayne (b. Strasburg, Pa., 1783, d. 1867). (fl. Lampeter Square, from 1810).

Baldwin, George (brother of Anthony), Sadsburyville, Pa. (1808–32).

Baldwin, Jabez (brother of Jedediah), Boston, Mass. (1812 and earlier). Apprentice of Thomas Harland. Successor to William Cleveland in Salem; later established the firm of Baldwin & Jones in Boston.

Baldwin, Jedediah (brother of Jabez), Hanover, N. H. (1780). Apprentice of Thomas Harland.

Baldwin, Jedediah, Rochester, N. Y. (1834).

Baldwin & Jones, Boston, Mass. (1812).

Baldwin, S. S., & Son, New York City (1832). "Dealers in Clocks, Watches, Jewelry, Silver Ware, etc."

Banks, Edw. P., Portland, Me. (1834).

Banstein, John, Philadelphia, Pa. (1791).

Barber, James, Philadelphia, Pa. (1846).

Barker, B. B., New York City (1786–1802).

Barker, William, Boston, Mass. (1823).

Barklay, J., Baltimore, Md. (1817–24). Clock and watchmaker and jeweler at 46 Baltimore Street. From 1812 to 1816 he appears as a member of the firm of J. & S. Barklay (q. v.)

Barklay, J. & S., Baltimore, Md. (1812–16). Did business as watchmakers and jewelers at 44 or 46 Baltimore Street.

Barnes & Bacon, Bristol, Conn. (1840).

Barnes & Bailey, Berlin, Conn. (1831).

Barnes, Edward M., Bristol, Conn. (1841–45 or later).

Barnes, Thomas, Bristol, Conn. (b. 1773, d. 1855). E. C. Brewster sold clocks in the South for Thomas Barnes about 1815–17.

Barnes, Timothy, Kirkland (village of Clinton), N. Y.

Barnes, Timothy, Litchfield, Conn. (1749–1825). Made wooden clocks.

Barnhill, Robert, Philadelphia, Pa.

Barns, John, Maryland (1756). "Ran away from the Subscriber, living at West River, in Anne Arundel Co., Md., a servant man, named John Barns, born in London. He is a clock maker by trade and has some of his tools with him. Kensey Johns." Maryland *Gazette*, Sept. 30, 1756.

Barrell, Colborn, Boston (1772). On the Dock near Mr. John Head's. Tall clocks, watches.

Barrow, Samuel, Philadelphia, Pa.

Barrows, James M., Tolland, Conn. (1832). "Manufacturer of Silver Spoons, and Dealer in Watches and Jewelry."

Barry, Standish, Baltimore, Md. (b. 1763, d. 1844) (working 1784–1810). Learned his trade from David Evans. Advertised as watch and clock maker and engraver. Had shops at Market and Gay Streets.

Bartholomew & Barnes, Bristol, Conn.

Bartholomew & Brown, Bristol, Conn. (1822–37?).

Bartholomew, E. & G., Bristol, Conn. (c. 1820).

Bartholomew, Hills & Brown, Forestville, Conn. (1835–   ). Built factory and thus began settlement of this village. Made wooden clocks. This factory, after passing through several intermediate hands, became nucleus of E. N. Welch Mfg. Co.

Barton, Benjamin, Alexandria, Va. (1832).

Bassett, N. B., Albany, N. Y. (1813).

Bateson, John, Boston, Mass. (1720). He died in 1727, and left in his shop an eight-day clock movement valued at £25 10s. and a silver repeating watch valued at £90.

Batterson, James, Boston, Mass. (1707–30). In October, 1707, James Batterson, "lately arrived from London," opened a store in Boston for the sale of watches and clocks: "The Sign of the Clock Dial of the South Side of the Town-House in Boston."

Batterson, John, Annapolis, Md. (1723). Described as a watchmaker, purchased a lot in Annapolis, 1723.

Battles, A. B., Utica, N. Y. (1847).

Baugh, Valentine, Abingdon, Va. (1820–30).

Baur, John N., New York City (1832).

Bayley (or Bailey), Calvin (brother of John and Lebbeus), Hanover, Mass. (1800).

Bayley (or Bailey), John (brother of Calvin and Lebbeus), Hanover, Mass. (1770–1815). "One of the most skillful mechanics of his time." Many of his clocks in Hanover and surrounding towns still keeping good time.

Bayley (or Bailey), John (son of John 1st), Hingham, Mass. (1815–20).

Bayley (or Bailey), Joseph, Hingham, Mass. (1808).

Bayley (or Bailey), Lebbeus (brother of John and Calvin), ——, Me. (c. 1800).

Bayley, Simeon C., Philadelphia, Pa. (1794).

Beach & Byington, Plymouth, Conn. (1849).

Beach & Hubbell, Bristol, Conn. (1869). Largely engaged in manufacturing the movements of brass marine clocks.

Beach, John, Hartford, Conn. (1813). In partnership with his father under the name Miles Beach & Son. Clock makers.

Beach, Miles, Hartford, Conn. (1799). "Silversmith and jeweler. Clocks, watches, swords and hangers, copper kettles."

Beals, J. J., & Son, Boston, Mass. (1849). Dealers in Connecticut clocks.

Beard, Duncan, and C. Weaver, Appoquinemonk, Del. (1755–97). Also Odessa, Delaware. Tall clocks.

Beard, Robert, "Maryland" (1774).

Belk, William, Philadelphia, Pa. (1796).

Belknap, Ebenezer, Boston, Mass. (1823).

Bell, James, New York City (1804).

Bell, John, New York City (1734). Eight-day clocks in Japanese cases.

Bellerose, G. I. H., Three Rivers, Quebec (c. 1790–1807). Tall, inlaid straight-bracket foot, light gooseneck scroll, fluted quarter columns. Moon motion.

Benedict & Burnham Co., Waterbury, Conn. (1850–55). See Waterbury Clock Co. In 1850 they joined Chauncey Jerome in a joint-stock company in New Haven, —— the Jerome Mfg. Co. After a year or two Mr. Burnham and others sold out to the Jeromes.

Benedict, S. W., New York City (1829).

Benjamin, Barzillai, New Haven, Conn. (1823). "Gold and silver watches, Duplex or vertical movements, warranted for one year."

Benjamin, John, Stratford, Conn. (1730–96). Clock maker.

Benny, Jonathan, Easton, Md. (1798). Watch and clock maker.

Bentley, Eli, West Whiteland Township, Chester Co., Pa.

Berry, James, New York City (before 1793).

Bessonet, John P., New York City (1793).

Bevans, William, Norristown, Pa. (1816 and earlier).

Bichaut, James, Boston, Mass. (1729). Boston *Gazette*, July 21/28, 1729. "Lately arrived from London, makes and mends all sorts of watches and clocks."

Biddle, Owen, North Ward, Pa. (1769). Watchmaker.

Biegel, Henry W., Philadelphia, Pa. (1813).

Bigger, Gilbert, Baltimore, Md. (1799). In 1784 went into business for himself. Listed from 1796 to 1816 at 115 Baltimore Street.

Bigger & Clarke, Baltimore, Md. (1783–84). Advertised as "Watch and Clockmakers from Dublin" with a shop on Market Street.

Bill, Joseph R., Middletown, Conn. (1841).

Billings, Joseph, Reading, Pa. (1779).

Billon, Charles, Philadelphia, Pa. (1813).

Billon & Co., Philadelphia, Pa. (1797).

Billow, Charles & Co., Boston, Mass. (1796).

Bingham & Bricerly, Philadelphia, Pa. (1778–99).

Birdsey, E. C., & Co., Meriden, Conn. (1831).

Birge & Fuller, Bristol, Conn. (1830–35).

Birge, Gilbert & Co., Bristol, Conn. (1835). Gothic Clock (spires).

Birge, John, Bristol, Conn. (1830–37). First was wagon builder. Afterwards purchased the patent of the rolling-pinion eight-day brass clocks, bought an old factory and began to manufacture these clocks. Sent peddlers south and west with them. Continued clock business and farming till a few years before his death.

Birge, Mallory & Co., Bristol, Conn. (1830).

Birge, Peck & Co., Bristol, Conn. (1830–56).

Birnie, Lawrence, Philadelphia, Pa. (1774). Watch and clock maker.

Bisbee, J., Brunswick, Me. (1798–1825).

Bishop & Bradley (James Bishop and L. B. Bradley), Plymouth, Conn. (1825–30).

Bissell, David, East Windsor, Conn. (1832). "Watch and Clockmaker and Dentist."

Bixler, Christian, Easton, Pa. (c. 1750).

Bixler, Christian, Easton, Pa. (1785–1830).

Blakeslee, Jeremiah, Plymouth, Conn. (1841–49). With Myles Morse.

Blakeslee, Marvin & Edward, Heathenville (near Plymouth), Conn. (1832).

Blakesley (or Blakeslee), Milo, Plymouth, Conn. About 1824 he was employed by Eli Terry, Jr., and some time afterwards became a partner with Terry.

Blakeslee, Ziba, Newtown, Conn. (1768–1834). Church clock and clocks and watches of all kinds.

Blasdell, David, Amesbury, Mass. (1741).

Blasdell, Isaac, Chester, N. H. (1762–91). Son of David Blasdell of Amesbury. Probably Isaac Blasdell's were the first clocks made in New Hampshire.

Blasdell, Richard (probably son of Isaac), Chester, N. H. (c. 1788).

Blundy, Charles, South Carolina (c. 1750–c. 1760). Makes and mends all kinds of watches and clocks.

Boardman, Chauncey, Bristol, Conn. (1813). Began making clocks about 1813 in North Forestville (village in Bristol). Began to make brass clocks 1838, and continued this until his failure, 1850.

Boardman, Chauncy, Bristol, Conn. (1820–30(?)). Late Empire, not carved.

Boardman & Dunbar, Bristol, Conn. (1811).

Boardman & Wells (Chauncey Boardman and Joseph A. Wells), Bristol, Conn. (1815). Soon after 1820 they built a factory in North Forestville, one of the most important of that time.

Bode, William, Philadelphia, Pa. (1796).

Bodeley, Thomas, Boston (1720). Clock maker.

Boehme, Charles, Baltimore, Md. (b. 1774, d. 1868) (working 1799–1812). Watch and clock maker, also repaired watches and clocks.

Bogardus, Everardus, New York City (1698).

Bois-de-Chesne, John Francis, South Carolina (1772). Clock and watchmaker from London. Has a shop in Tradd Street.

Bond, William, Boston, Mass. (1800–10). Silversmith and chronometer maker. Portland, Me., 1783.

Bonfanti, Joseph, New York City (1823). He advertised for sale German and French clocks.

Bonnaud, ——, Philadelphia, Pa. (1799).

Boss & Peterman, Rochester, N. Y. (1841). "We strive to Excel. Dealers in Watches and Jewelry. Try us before purchasing elsewhere. We feel warranted in saying that all watch and clock work entrusted to our care will be executed better than at any other establishment in this city."

Botsford, S. N., Hamden (Whitneyville), Conn. (1856).

Boughell, Joseph, New York City (1787).

Bower, Hy., Philadelphia, Pa. Grandmother clock.

Bower, Michael, Philadelphia, Pa. (1790–1800).

Bower, William, South Carolina (1772).

Bowman, Joseph, Strasburg, Lancaster Co., Pa. (1799–1892). In business fifty-five years, very actively till 1850.

Bowman, Joseph (father of Joseph), New Holland, Pa.

Bowne, Samuel, New York City (1751). Advertised "Japanned and Walnut cased Clocks."

Brace, Rodney, North Bridgewater (now Brockton), Mass. (1830). Several years since (1800), Rodney Brace came from Torrington, Conn., and commenced the manufacture of small late Empire clocks, with Isaac Packard. They sent them to all parts of the country in wagons, and were among the first to introduce small clocks.

Bradley & Barnes, Boston, Mass. (1856).

Bradley & Hubbard, Meriden, Conn. (1854).

Bradley, Nelson, Plymouth, Conn. (1840).

Bradley, Richard, Hartford, Conn. (1825–39). Watch repairer.

Bradley, Z., & Son, New Haven, Conn. (1840).

Brand, James, Boston, Mass. (1711).

Brand, John, Boston, Mass. (1711). Boston *News-Letter*, Jan. 21/28, 1711/12. "Watchmaker, from London, Maketh and Mendeth all sorts of Clocks and Watches, at very easie Rates, and is to be found at the Sign of the Spring Clock and Watches, near the Draw-Bridge in Anne Street, Boston."

Brandegee, Elishama, Berlin, Conn. (1832). "Manufacturer of Cotton Thread, Clocks of all descriptions, and Dealer in American Goods."

Brandt & Mathey, Philadelphia, Pa. (1799).

Brandt, Brown & Lewis, Philadelphia, Pa. (1795).

Brasher, Abraham, New York City (1757).

Brasier, Amable, Philadelphia, Pa. (1795–1820).

Brastow, Adison & Co., Lowell, Mass. (1832).

Brearley, James, Philadelphia, Pa. (1793–1811).

Breckenridge, J. M., Meriden & New Haven, Conn. (b. 1809, d. 1896).

Breneiser, Samuel, Adamstown, Pa. (1799). Advertised May 21, 1799.

Brenfter, Walter, Canterbury, Conn. (c. 1800?). Brass hall.

Brewer, Isaac, Philadelphia, Pa. (1813).

Brewer, William, Philadelphia, Pa. (1795).

Brewster, Abel, Canterbury, Conn. (1775–1807). Made clocks and timepieces, and repaired watches.

Brewster & Ingraham, Bristol, Conn. (1843–48), (see above). Late shelf spire clock. Very popular. Small value therefore.

Brewster, Elisha, Co., Bristol, Conn. (1833–62) (b. 1791, d. 1880). Traveled in South selling clocks for Thomas Barnes of Bristol. For some time worked in Plainville. In Bristol painted clocks, dials, and glass. In 1833 bought clock factory of Charles Kirk, employing him to conduct it until about 1838. In connection with Shaylor Ives he invented a new spring for clocks and manufactured the first spring clocks made in this country. In 1843 he formed partnership with Elias and Andrew Ingraham, which continued till 1848, when he bought them out; afterward associated with himself William Day and Augustus Norton, later buying them out and carried on the business alone until 1862, when he retired. He had a branch house in London, England, for the sale of his goods, conducted for about four years by Epaphroditus Peck, and twenty years by his son, N. L. Brewster.

Brewster, George G., Portsmouth, N. H. G. G. Brewster, Portsmouth, N. H., impressed on the works.

Brinckerhoff, Dirck, New York City (1756). "At the Sign of the Golden Clock."

Brokaw, Isaac, Bridge Town, N. J. (c. 1750). Garvan Collection.

Bronson, I. W., Buffalo, N. Y. (1825–30).

Brooks, B. F., Utica, N. Y. (1847).

Broughman, George, "Maryland" (1774).

Brown, David, Providence, R. I. (1834–50).

Brown, Gawen, Boston, Mass. (1750–76).

Brown, J. C., Bristol, Conn. (1827–55). In 1835 William Hills, J. C. Brown, Jared Goodrich, Lora Waters, and Chauncey Pomeroy built a factory where the Welch Co. now is (1885). Mr. Brown bought out the rest of the firm, and in 1853 built what is still called the J. C. Brown shop. Upon his failure this passed to Mr. Welch, and from him to the E. N. Welch Mfg. Co.

Brown, John, Lancaster, Pa. (18th C.).

Brown, Joseph R., Providence, R. I. (1849).

Brown & Kirby, New Haven, Conn. (1840).

Brown, Laurent, Rochester, N. Y. (1841).

Brown, Robert, Baltimore, Md. (1829–31). Advertised in 1829 as jeweler and watch and clock maker at 26 North Gay Street, and again in 1831, but in 1833 and thereafter as Robert Brown & Son.

Bryant, Thomas, Rochester, N. Y. (18–).

Buckman, George, Baltimore, Md. (1802). Buckman was a watchmaker at 30 Jones Street.

Buel, Olando, New Preston, Conn., or Staten Island. Tall clock.

Bulkley, Joseph, Fairfield, Conn. (1755–1815). Leading clock maker in Fairfield after the death of John Whitear, Jr.

Bullard, Charles, Boston, Mass. (b. Dedham, Mass., 1794, d. 1871). Was apprentice and successor of the English artist in Roxbury, who painted glass fronts and dials for Simon Willard. In business for himself, Boston 1816–44. Painted for many clock makers, but kept certain designs exclusively for Simon Willard. Worked as late as 1865, after returning to Dedham.

Burdick, M. H., Bristol, Conn. (1849).

Burkelow, Samuel, Philadelphia, Pa. (1791–99).

Burkmar, Thomas, probably in Boston (1776).

Burnap, Daniel, East Windsor and Andover, Conn. (1780–1838). Born 1760 in Coventry (now Andover), Conn. Learned his trade from Thomas Harland of Norwich. In 1776 he was in East Windsor, Conn. Shortly before 1800 he came back to Andover and worked there till 1838. His clocks had tall cases, brass works, and silver dials beautifully engraved, often also moon phases, calendar attachments, and chimes. The workmanship is very fine. He was also a silversmith.

Burnham, Enoch, Paris, Me. (c. 1800). Tall, mahogany inlaid, arched fret, French foot, ship motion.

Burot, Andrew, Baltimore, Md. (1819–27). Appears in 1827 as watch and clock maker, at 97 Bond Street.

Burr, C. A., Rochester, N. Y. (1841). "Wholesale and retail Dealer in Watches, Clocks, Jewelry, etc. Has on sale Gold, Silver, Duplex, Anchor, Independent Sec'ds, Patent Lever, Lepine and Vertical Watches, French, Mantel, Wood, Brass 30 hour and 8 day clocks."

Burr, Ezekiel & William, Providence, R. I. (1792).

Burr, Jonathan, Lexington, Mass. (c. 1835). Shelf clock, wooden movement.

Burrage, John, Annapolis, Md. (1769). In October, 1769, Frances Knapp advertised in the Maryland *Gazette* for a runaway servant John Burrage, a watch and clock maker by trade.

Burritt, Joseph, Ithaca, N. Y. (1831).

Burrowes, Thomas (father of Thomas H.), founder of public school system in Pennsylvania (1784–1839). Strasburg, Pa. (fl. 1787–1810).

Bush, George, Easton, Pa. (1812–37).

Butler, N., Utica, N. Y. (1803).

Byington & Co., L., Bristol, Conn. (1849).

C

Cain, C. W., New York City (1836).

Cairns, John, Providence, R. I. (1784).

Cairns, John, 2nd, Providence, R. I. (1840–53).

Calame, Olivier, Frederick, Md. (1819). Watch and clock maker.

Calendar Clock Co., The, Glastonbury, Conn. (1856).

Camp, Hiram (nephew of Chauncey Jerome), New Haven, Conn. (1829–93). Entered clock-making business of his uncle, at Bristol, 1829. In 1845 went to New Haven. When the Jerome Mfg. Co. failed, it was succeeded by The New Haven Clock Co., and Hiram Camp was its president for about forty years.

Campbell, Charles, Philadelphia, Pa. (1795–99).

Campbell, John, Maryland (1773). Watchmaker.

Campbell, Robert, Baltimore, Md. (b. 1799, d. 1872) (fl. 1819–35). Silversmith and watch and clock maker at 126 Baltimore Street.

Campbell, William, Carlisle, Pa. (1765), Philadelphia, Pa. (1799).

Canby, Charles, Wilmington, Del. (1815–50).

Canfield & Foote, Middletown, Conn. (1795).

Canfield, Samuel, Middletown, Conn. (c. 1796). One of the firm of Canfield & Foote.

Capper, Michael, Philadelphia, Pa. (1799).

Carpenter, Anthony (b. New Holland, Pa., 1790). Began business in New Holland, 1820; d. New Holland, 1868.

Carpenter, Anthony W. (son of Anthony). Succeeded his father and continued in business till 1860.

Carpenter, Joseph, Norwich, Conn. (1747–1804). Clock maker.

Carrell, John and Daniel, Philadelphia, Pa. (1791–93).

Carryl, Patrick, New York (1758). Clock maker.

Carver, Jacob, Philadelphia, Pa. (1785–99).

Cary, James, Jr., Brunswick, Me. (1806–50). Apprentice of Robert Eastman, 1805, and partner, 1806–09. Cary had an apprentice, in 1830, Aaron L. Dennison.

Case & Birge (Erastus and Harvey Case and John Birge), Bristol, Conn. (1830–37).

Case, Dyer, Wadsworth & Co., Augusta, Ga. (1835). Seth Thomas made the cases and movements for them. They merely put the parts together at Augusta, and sold them.

Case, Erastus (brother of Harvey), Bristol, Conn. (1830–37).

Case, Harvey (brother of Erastus), Bristol, Conn. (1830–37).

Case & Robinson, Bristol, Conn. (1856).

Castan, Stephen, & Co., Philadelphia, Pa. (1819).

Cate, Col. Simeon, Sanbornton, N. H. (18–?).

Cater, Stephen, South Carolina (1744). Clock and watchmaker, also repaired all sorts of watches and clocks.

Chadwick, Joseph, Boscawen, N. H. (1810–31).

Chamberlin, Lewis, Elkton, Md. (1824). Watchmaker.

Champlin, John, New London, Conn. (1773). Advertised, "materials for repairing Clocks and Watches."

Chandlee, Benjamin, Baltimore, Md. (1817). Watch and clock maker. Worked alone from 1814 to 1818 at 98 High Street, and from this date until 1823 he was associated with Robert Holloway, as Chandlee & Holloway.

Chandlee & Holloway, Baltimore, Md. (1818–23). Watch and clock maker at 98 High Street.

Chandlee, John, Wilmington, Del. (1795–1810).

Chandler, Abiel, Concord, N. H. (1829–58). Son and successor to Maj. Timothy Chandler. He was also a maker of mathematical instruments. Lyre clock, odd movement.

Chandler, B., Nottingham, Pa. Went there from Philadelphia in 1710. Later moved to Baltimore. Tall clock. Perhaps the same as Chandley or Chanley (q. v.).

Chandler, John, of Suffolk, "Maryland" (1774).

Chandler, Major Timothy, Concord, N. H. (1785–1840). Came on foot from Pomfret, Conn., 1783. Hired a man named Cummings, who was apprentice to Simon Willard, and set up clock making in Concord.

Chanley, Benjamin, East Nottingham, Pa. (1766).

Chapin, Aaron, & Son, Hartford, Conn. (1825–38).

Charter, ——, Pennsylvania (1785). Watch-case maker.

Chase, Timothy, Belfast, Me. (1826–40).

Chaudron, P., Philadelphia, Pa. (1799).

Chaudron, S., & Co., Philadelphia, Pa. (1811).

Cheney, Alcott (son of Elisha), Middletown and Berlin, Conn. (c. 1820–50). He worked with his father until about 1835, then bought his father out and carried on the business for a number of years. While he lived in Berlin, his shops were just over the Middletown line; the Cheney clocks were therefore marked "Middletown."

Cheney, Asahel, Northfield, Mass. (1790). (East Hartford earlier).

Cheney, Benjamin (son of Elisha), Berlin, Conn.

Cheney, Benjamin (brother of Timothy), East Hartford, Conn. (now Manchester) (c. 1745–80). They were among the first clock makers in New England. Their clocks had tall, carved, cherry-wood cases and wooden works. In their shops John Fitch, inventor of the steamboat, was apprentice.

Cheney, Elisha (son of Benjamin), Middletown and Berlin, Conn. (c. 1800–35). First made screws for the pistol factory of his brother-in-law, Simeon North, in Worthington Parish. When North's business was moved to Middletown, Cheney engaged in manufacture of clocks, first tall case clocks, afterwards mantel clocks.

Cheney, Russell (son of Benjamin and brother of Elisha), East Hartford, Conn., and Thetford, Vt. Learned the family trade of clock making and became a skilful workman, but probably did not stay in the business.

Cheney, Timothy (brother of Benjamin), East Hartford (now Manchester), Conn. (c. 1776–95).

Chester, George, New York City (1757).

Child, John, Philadelphia, Pa. (1813–35). Mantel clock similar to English.

Child, True W., Boston, Mass. (1823).

Chollet, John B., Philadelphia, Pa. (1819).

Church, Joseph, Hartford, Conn. (1825–38).

Church, Lorenzo, Hartford, Conn. (1846).

Cito, J. C., Boston, Mass. Lyre clock.

Claggett, Thomas (son(?) of William), Newport, R. I. (1767–77). Ran a fencing school in Providence in 1777.

Claggett, William (probably father of Thomas), Newport, R. I. (1715–49). Classed with Benj. Bagnall. These two were among the earliest makers of fine clocks in America. William was first in Boston and advertised there in the *News Letter* in 1715/16, using then "Junior" after his name.

Clapp, Preserved. "New England." Beautiful dial printed from engraving. Essex Institute, Salem, F. T. 3314.

Clark, Benjamin, Wilmington, Del. (1837–50).

Clark, Benjamin, Philadelphia, Pa. (1790–1819).

Clark, Benjamin & Ellis, Philadelphia, Pa. (1813).

Clark, Daniel, Waterbury, Conn. (1814–20). Zenas Cook, Daniel Clark, and William Porter owned a clock factory in Waterbury in 1814.

Clark, Edward, Philadelphia, Pa. (1797).

Clark, Ellis, Philadelphia, Pa. (1811–45).

Clark, Ephraim, Philadelphia, Pa. (1780–1810).

Clark, Herman, Plymouth Hollow (now Thomaston), Conn. (1807).

Clark, Jesse, W. & C., Philadelphia, Pa. (1811).

Clark, Joseph, Danbury, Conn. (1800).

Clark, Joseph, New York City (1768). Danbury (1732).

Clark, Robert, South Carolina (1785). Clock maker.

Clark, Sylvester, Salem Bridge (now Naugatuck), Conn. (1830).

Clark, Thomas, Boston, Mass. (1764). Boston *Gazette*, Nov. 5, 1764. "Clock and Watch-Maker from London, Shop the South Side of the Court-House."

Clarke, Ambrose, Baltimore, Md. (1757–1810) (fl. 1783–c. 1790). In 1783 "Bigger & Clarke, watch and clock makers from Dublin," were located on Market Street. The following year Clarke is working alone as a watch and clock maker and jeweler. His last advertisement as a watchmaker is dated 1787.

Clarke, Charles, Philadelphia, Pa. (1806–11).

Clarke, George G., Providence, R. I. (1824).

Clarke, Gilbert & Co., Winsted, Conn. (1842).

Clarke, John, New York City (1770–90).

Clarke, John, Philadelphia, Pa. (1799).

Clarke, Lucius, Winsted, Conn. (1841). In 1841 he purchased business left after death of Riley Whiting, and associated with himself William L. Gilbert — Clarke, Gilbert & Co.

Claton, C., Philadelphia, Pa.

Claude, Abraham, Annapolis, Md. (1779). Watchmaker.

Claude & French, Annapolis, Md. (1783). In the Maryland *Gazette* for October 9, 1783, Abraham Claude formed a partnership for conducting a watch and clock-making business with a man named French. This may have been James Ormsby French who in 1771 was in business in Baltimore.

Claudon, John-George, South Carolina (1773). Watchmaker from London.

Clayton, John, Charles Town, S. C. (1743). "Watch Maker from London, who cleans, mends and repairs, both Clocks and Watches, either plain or repeating."

Clements, Moses, New York City (1749).

Cleveland, Benjamin Norton, Newark, N. J. (b. 1767, d. 1837).

Cleveland, William, Salem, Mass. (1780). Apprentice of Thomas Harland. Was ship owner, watchmaker, and merchant.

Cleveland, William (nephew of William), Worthington, Mass., Salem, Mass., and Norwich, Conn. Resided first at Norwich, Conn., where he learned the trade of silversmith, watch and clock maker from Thomas Harland. Soon after marriage (1793) he set up in business at Worthington, Mass. He removed to Salem, Mass., where he remained in business a few years, thence went to New York. Returned to Norwich, 1812, and died there 1837. He was grandfather of President Grover Cleveland.

Cleveland, William, New London and Norwich, Conn. (1770–1837). Entered partnership with John Proctor Trott, under the firm name of Trott & Cleveland. Advertised as clock and watchmakers, goldsmiths and jewelers.

Coe, Russell, Meriden, Conn. (1856).

Coggeshall, G., Bristol, R. I. (c. 1800?). Tall.

Cohen & Levy, Baltimore, Md. (1819). This firm of watchmakers is listed at 11 Market Street in 1819.

Cole, James C., Rochester, N. H. (1812–). Served apprenticeship with Edward S. Moulton, and established the same business (1812), adding that of watchmaker and jeweler. Square top with fret, tall clock.

Cole, Shubael (son of James C. Cole), Great Falls (now Somersworth), N. H. (18–?).

Collins, Elijah, Boston, Mass. (1727). Watchmaker.

Collins, James, Goffstown, N. H. (c. 1830?). Mirror clock.

Colvin, Walter, Trenton, N. J. (1785). Clock and watchmaker.

Conant, Elias, Bridgewater, Mass. (1776–1812).

Conant, Elias, Lynn, Mass. (1812–15).

Conant, W. S., New York City (c. 1820).

Conrad, O., Philadelphia, Pa. (1846).

Conway, Thomas A., Baltimore, Md. (1819–24). Conway was a watchmaker at Hawk Street and Marsh Market Space from 1819 to 1824.

Cook, E., Rochester, N. Y. (1824).

Cook, William G., Baltimore, Md. (1817–24). Located as watch and clock maker at 5 Baltimore Street from 1817 to 1824.

Cook, Zenas, Waterbury, Conn. (1811–20). Bought part of clock factory in 1811. Zenas Cook, Daniel Clark, and William Porter were proprietors of clock factory built on Great Brook, Waterbury, in 1814.

Coolidge, Henry J., New Haven, Conn. (1787). Made and sold all sorts of clocks and watches.

Copeland, Robert, Baltimore, Md. (1796). Copeland was a watchmaker at 9 Thames Street, Fell's Point.

Copper, T., Olneyville, R. I. (1849).

Corey, P., Providence, R. I. (1849).

Corliss, James, Weare, N. H. (1800). "It is said he stole the trade by peeking into Emery's windows nights."

Cornell, Walter, Newport, R. I.

Couper, Robert, Philadelphia, Pa. (1774). Sold skeleton watches exported from London.

Cox & Clark, New York City (1832). "Importers and Dealers in Lamps, etc.; also French China and Mantel Clocks, Silver Ware, etc."

Cozens, Josiah B., Philadelphia, Pa. (1819).

Cranch, Richard, Boston and Braintree, Mass. (1771–89). "Before the war carried on business near the Mill-Bridge in Boston." Sold all kinds of watch and clock makers' tools. Said also to have lived at one time in the Ruck house, the oldest perhaps in Salem. He was father of Justice Cranch and brother-in-law of John Adams.

Cranch, William. Astronomer, Boston, Mass.(?)

Crane, Simeon, Canton, Mass. (?)

Crane, William, Canton, Mass. (1780).

Crehore, Charles Crane, Boston, Mass. (b. 1793, d. 1879). Made clock cases for Simon Willard, Jr., and Benjamin F. Willard, also some for Simon Willard, Sr., and many other clock makers.

Critchet, James, Candia, N. H. (c. 1800).

Crocker, Orasmas (?), East Meriden or Bangall, Conn. (c. 1831). Built a factory for making clocks, but the business proved a failure.

Cross, James, Rochester, N. H. (18–?).

Cross, Theodore, Boston, Mass. (1775).

Crow, George, Wilmington, Del. (1740–70).

Crow, John, Wilmington, Del. (1770–98).

Crow, Thomas, Philadelphia, Pa. (1795).

Crow, Thomas, Wilmington, Del. (1770–1824). Clock and Watchmaker. Sold springs for table or musical clocks of any size.

Crow, Thompson, Wilmington, Del.

Crowley, John, Philadelphia, Pa. (1813).

Crown, Henry, "Maryland" (1774). Watch-case maker.

Crowther, William, New York City (1820).

Cummens (or Cummings), William, Roxbury, Mass. (1788–1834). Apprentice of Simon Willard; then engaged in clock-making business. Had a son William, who assisted him. Made excellent clocks, hall, shelf, and time-pieces.

Cumming, John, New York State (1774). Settled in "Oswald-Field in Katts-Kill in the County of Albany and Province of New York."

Cure, Lewis, Brooklyn, N. Y. (1832).

Currier, Edmund, Salem, Mass. (1837).

Curtis & Dunning.

Curtis, Lemuel, Concord, Mass. (1814–18), Burlington, Vt. (1818–57). In 1816 took out a patent on an improvement on the Willard timepiece. Moved to Burlington, Vt., 1818 or 1820, and died there 1857. Curtis modeled his clocks on the Willard timepiece, but used more ornament and more beautiful proportions. One feature of the Curtis clock is the circular pendulum box, called girandole. The most highly valued clocks, with possible exception of S. Willard's lighthouse.

Curtis, Lewis, Farmington, Conn. (b. 1774, d. 1845). "He had a workshop in a little red gambrel-roofed shop, just back of the Farmington Country Club and now used as a caddy house. He was a silversmith and clock maker, his line running more to clocks 'that played tunes and clocks that showed the moon's age.'" Mabel S. Hurlbert, in Hartford *Times*, July 21, 1928. Good picture of the shop in "Farmington, Village of Beautiful Homes" (pub. 1906), p. 11.

Curtis, Solomon, Philadelphia, Pa. (1793).

Curtis, W., Newburyport (1800–20?). Banjo, with bracket.

Cushing, Geo. H., Braintree. Grandmothers. Very fine. Same dial pointer as Durfee.

Custer, Daniel, Reading, Pa. Bonnet top, carved tall clock.

Custer, Jacob D., Norristown, Pa. (b. 1805, d. 1872). He began the manufacture of "grandfather clocks" about 1831. In 1842 he commenced the manufacture of clocks to propel the lights in lighthouses.

D

Daft, Thomas, New York City (1786).

Daft, Thomas, Philadelphia, Pa. (1775). "Watches and Clocks of all sorts, made and carefully repaired, and sold. . . ."

Daggett, T., Providence, R. I. (1849).

Dalziel, John, New York City (1798).

Dana, George, Providence, R. I. (1805). He and Thomas Whitaker bought out Nehemiah Dodge.

Dana, Payton. Providence, R. I. (1849).

Dana, Peyton and Nathaniel, Providence, R. I. (1800).

Danner, Alexander. Made cases for the Shreiners and other Lancaster, Pa., makers.

Darrow, Elijah, Bristol, Conn. (1822–30). In 1824 joined Chauncey and Noble Jerome.

Davidson, Barzillai, Norwich, Conn. (1775). Worker in gold and silver, and offered for sale handsome assortments of jewelry and timekeepers.

Davidson, Barzillai, New Haven, Conn. (1825). Made a clock with wood works for New Haven Meeting House, $260, 1825.

Davidson, Samuel, "Maryland" (1774).

Davis, David P., Roxbury, Mass. (1847–56). In partnership with Edward Howard.

Davis, John, New Holland Patent, Pa. (1802–05).

Davis, John, Philadelphia, Pa.

Davis, Peter, Jaffrey, N. H.

Davis, Samuel, Pittsburgh, Pa. (1815).

Davis, William, Boston, Mass. (1683). He came from England to pursue his trade, and David Edwards became surety for Davis and his family, that they would not become charges upon the town.

Davis & Babbitt, Providence, R. I. (1810).

Dawson, Jonas, Philadelphia, Pa. (1813).

Day, Israel, Baltimore, Md. (1807). Day was a clock and watchmaker at Ann and Alisanna streets, Fell's Point.

De Forest & Co., Salem Bridge, Conn. (1832).

Delaplaine, James K., New York City (1786–1800).

Deloste, Francis, Baltimore, Md. (1817).

Demilt, Thomas, New York City (1798–1818).

Demilt, Thomas, Philadelphia, Pa. (19th C.).

Demilt, Thomas & Benjamin, New York City (1802–18).

Dennison, Aaron L., Roxbury and Waltham, Mass., and Birmingham, England (1850–95). A pioneer of American watchmaking. In 1850 he and Edward Howard started a watch factory at Roxbury. In 1854 they removed to Waltham. When this factory was sold, 1857, Dennison remained as superintendent for a while. After several changes, this developed into the present Waltham Watch Co. Dennison subsequently settled in England, and devised machinery for making watchcases at Birmingham.

Derby, Charles, Salem, Mass. (1846–50).

Derby, John, New York City (1816).

De Riemer & Mead, Ithaca, N. Y. (1831).

De Saules & Co., New York City (1832).

Deverell, John, Boston, Mass. (1789–1803).

Dexter, Joseph W., Providence, R. I. (1824).

De Young, Meichel, Baltimore, Md. (1832).

Diehl, Jacob, Reading, Pa. (1776–1858).

Disturnell, William, New Haven and Middletown, Conn. (1784). "Clock, Watchmaker, and Jeweler."

Dix, Joseph, Philadelphia, Pa. (1769). Watchmaker.

Dobbs, Henry M., New York City (1794–1802).

Dodge, Ezra, New London, Conn. (1766–98). All kinds of clocks.

Dodge, Ezra W., Providence, R. I. (1824).

Dodge, George, Salem, Mass. (1837).

Dodge, Nehemiah, Providence, R. I. (1794–1824). Succeeded Ezra W. Dodge. In 1799 was associated with Mr. Stephen Williams for short time. Later had Gen. Josiah Whitaker as partner. On retirement sold to George Dana and Thomas Whitaker. Also a silversmith.

Dodge, Seril, Providence, R. I. (1788). Apprentice to Thomas Harland.

Doggett, John, Roxbury, Mass. (1802–09). Made clock cases for Willard clocks, and others.

Dominick, Friedrich, Philadelphia, Pa. (1760–80).

Doods, Joseph.

Doolittle, Enos (nephew of Isaac), Hartford, Conn. (1772–1808). Cast bells after 1788.

Doolittle, Isaac, New Haven, Conn. (1743–1800). Also bell founder.

Doolittle, Isaac, Jr. (son of Isaac), New Haven, Conn. (1759–1821).

Doty, John F., Albany, N. Y. (1813).

Douglas, John, New Haven, Conn. (1800–20).

Doull, James, Charlestown, Mass. (c. 1790). Very good hall, and Massachusetts pattern shelf.

Douty, Henry, Philadelphia, Pa.

Dowdney, Burrows, Philadelphia, Pa. (1768). Watch and clock maker.

Dowle, Robert, New York City (1793).

Dowling, G. R. & B., Co., Newark, N. J. (1832).

Downes, Arthur, South Carolina (1768). Watchmaker.

Downs, Anson, Bristol, Conn. (1830).

Downs, Ephraim, Bristol, Conn. (1811–43). Began clock making in Waterbury, Conn., 1811, working for Lemuel Harrison. Later he made at least two horseback trips to Cincinnati, O., making clocks there for Lumas Watson, 1816–21. In 1822 he settled at "Ireland," later Hoadleyville, now Greystone, working at clocks with Seth Thomas, Eli Terry, and his brother-in-law, Silas Hoadley. He began business for himself here, but in 1825 removed to Bristol. The "looking-glass" clock was a favorite. He alone of all the Bristol clock makers neither failed nor made assignment in the "hard times" of 1837. He retired from business 1842–43.

Drown, R. W., Newburyport (1810–20?). Banjo clock.

Droz, Charles A., Philadelphia, Pa. (1813).

Droz, Humbert, Philadelphia, Pa. (1797).

Droz, Humbert A. L., Philadelphia, Pa. (1811).

Droze & Sons, Philadelphia, Pa. (1813).

Drysdale, William, Philadelphia, Pa. (1819–51).

Dubois & Folmar, New York City (1816).

Ducommun, A. L., Philadelphia, Pa. (1797).

Dudley, Benjamin, Newport, R. I. (1840).

Duffield, Edward, Philadelphia, Pa. (1741–47). Lower Dublin, Pa. (1747–1801). A particular friend of Benjamin Franklin. Maker of fine tall clocks, in cases by the best Philadelphia cabinetmakers.

Duffield, Edward, West Whiteland Township, Chester County, Pa.

Dunbar, Butler, Bristol, Conn. (1810–30). About 1810 he was associated with Dr. Titus Merriman, making clocks. Later Springville, Pa.

Dunbar, Jacobs & Warner, Bristol, Conn. (1849).

Dunbar, John, Baltimore, Md. (1796). Dunbar was a watch and mathematical instrument maker.

Dunbar & Merriman, Bristol, Conn. (1810–).

Dunheim, Andrew, New York City (1775).

Dunlap, Archibald, New York City (1802).

Dunning & Crissey, Rochester, N. Y. (1847).

Dunning, J. L. Associated somewhat with Lemuel Curtis.

Dupuy, John, Philadelphia, Pa. (1770).

Dupuy, Odran, Philadelphia, Pa. (1735).

Durgin, F., Andover, N. H.

Dutch, Stephen, Jr., Boston, Mass. (1800–10).

Dutton, David, Mount Vernon, N. H.

Dutton, Reed, Milford, N. H. Dealer. A sticker, "Bought and sold by Reed Dutton."

Dyar, Warren, Lowell, Mass. (1831).

Dyer, Joseph, Concord, Mass. (1815–20). He was a journeyman with Lemuel Curtis, and when the latter moved to Burlington, Vt., Dyer carried on the business alone. Later he went to Middlebury, Vt.

E

Easterley, John, New Holland, Pa. (1825–40).

Eastman, Abel B., Belfast Me. (1806–21). Earliest clock maker in Belfast. Came here in 1806 from Concord, N. H.

Eastman & Cary, Brunswick, Me. (1806–09). About 1809 Eastman sold out to Cary.

Eastman, Robert, Brunswick, Me. (1805–08). James Cary, Jr., was his apprentice. In 1806 Eastman took Cary as partner (Eastman & Cary). About 1809 Eastman sold out to Cary.

Eaton, John H., Boston, Mass. (1823).

Eberman. Notable family of clock makers. Made the town clock still in the loft of the court house, Lancaster. John Eberman, son of John, came to America 1749. Uncertain whether he or his son John made the clocks bearing the name, but certainly the son made many.

Eberman, John (1776–1846) Lancaster, Pa.

Eberman, Joseph, Lancaster, Pa. (1780–1844). Well and favorably known (fl. 1780–1820).

Eby, Christian, Manheim, Pa. First of name in Manheim. Father of Jacob and George.

Eby, George (son of Christian, brother of Jacob). In business with Jacob.

Eby, Jacob, Manheim, Pa. (fl. 1830–60). Made fine clock, and beautiful hands, especially sweep second, and case with eagle inlay.

Edmunds, James, South Carolina (1745). Watch and clock maker.

Edson, Jonah, Bridgewater, Mass. (1815–30).

Edwards, Abraham, Ashby, Mass. (1794–1840). A self-taught clock maker.

Edwards, Nathan, Acton, Mass. Handsome tall clock.

Edwards, Samuel, Gorham, Me. (1808–). Came from Ashby, Mass., about 1808, and for many years carried on manufacture of wooden clocks.

Egerton, Matthew, Jr., New Brunswick, N. J. (1793). Cabinetmaker. Made tall clock case. His label reads: MADE and SOLD by MATTHEW EGERTON, Junior, Joiner and Cabinetmaker, New Brunswick, NEW–JERSEY.

Eliot, William, Baltimore, Md. (1799).

Ellicott, Andrew, Sr., Baltimore, Md. (1778). Clock and mathematical instrument maker.

Ellicott, Joseph, Buckingham, Pa. (?).

Elliot, Hazen, Lowell, Mass. (1832).

Ellsworth, David, Windsor, Conn. (b. 1741, d. 1821).

Elvins, William, Baltimore, Md. (1796–1808). His name appears as watch and clock maker at Fell's Point in 1796, and may have been here previous to this; he continues to be listed until 1808. He was first at 32 Thames Street, and August 19, 1799, announced his removal from 4 Fell Street to 10 Bond Street. He was at 12 Fell Street from 1802–08.

Embree, Effingham, New York City (1785–94).

Emerson, Dudley, Lyme, Conn. (1788).

Emery, Jesse, Weare, N. H. (1800). Made the first clocks here.

Emmett, Edward Tillett, Boston, Mass. (1764). Boston *Gazette*, July 16, 1764, "Clock-Maker —— Has just opened shop on south side of Town-House in King St."

England, James, Baltimore, Md. (1818–30). He appears for several years as a goldsmith, silversmith, and jeweler, and in later years as a jeweler and watchmaker only. He had a shop at 24 Bond Street, Fell's Point, from 1807–19, and from 1818–29 at 22 Bond Street, probably the same shop under another name.

Ent, Johann, Philadelphia, Pa.

Ent, John, New York City (1758). Advertised as follows: "John Ent, Clock and Watch-maker, at the sign of the Dial, has moved to the house of Mr. John Wright, Watch-maker, in Bayard street, where he continues to make and repair in the newest manner, All Sorts of Clocks and Watches, whether repeating, horizontal, or the plain kind. Gentlemen and Ladies that are pleased to honor him with their Employ may depend on the greatest care and Dispatch imaginable."

Ent, John, Philadelphia, Pa. (1769).

Ent, John, Germantown, Pa. (1783).

Erb, John, Conestoga Centre, Pa. (fl. 1830–60).

Essex, Joseph, Boston, Mass. (1712).

Esterlie, New Holland, Pa., (b. 1778) (fl. 1812–30).

Eureka Shop, The, Bristol, Conn. (before 1837). "Built by a great partnership."

Evans, David, Baltimore, Md. (1770–73). "At the Sign of the Arch, Dial and Watch, Gay street." A David Evans was a nephew of David Rittenhouse and a cabinetmaker of a clock case for Rittenhouse.

Evans, John, Charles County, Md. (1754). Watchmaker.

Evans, Thomas, New York City (1766).

Evans, William M., Philadelphia, Pa. (1813–19 or longer).

Everman, Jacob, Lancaster, Pa. (1773–1837).

Eyre, Johann, Philadelphia, Pa.

Eyre, Matthias, Philadelphia, Pa. (1775). Made watch mainsprings.

F

Fahrenbach, Pius, Boston, Mass. (1856).

Fales, G. S., New Bedford, Mass. (1827).

Fales, James, New Bedford, Mass. (1810–20).

Fales, James, Jr., New Bedford, Mass. (1836).

Faris, Hyram, Annapolis, Md. (c. 1790). Designed clock faces.

Faris, William, Annapolis, Md. (b. 1728, d. 1804). Clock and watchmaker, designed mechanism of works for "Month Clock."

Farmer, John, Philadelphia, Pa. Watchmaker. Mentioned in the will of Ann Cox. Book A., No. 216.

Farnum, Henry & Rufus, Boston, Mass. (1780). Apprentice of Thomas Harland.

Farr, John C., Philadelphia, Pa. (1832). "Watches, Jewelry and Silver Ware."

Farrar, C. & D., Lampeter, Pa. Tall clock, fine applied carving under scroll top. Case perhaps by Jonathan Gostelowe.

Faver, Christian, Lampeter, Pa.

Favre, John James, Philadelphia, Pa.

Feasig, Conrad, Reading, Pa. (1781).

Fellows, James K., Lowell, Mass. (1832).

Fellows, Read & Olcott, New York City (1829). "Importers of Fancy Hardware, Watches, Jewelry, Watch Materials, Tools, etc."

Fellows, Storm & Cargill, New York City. (1832). "Watches, Jewelry and Fancy Goods."

Fenlester, Alexander, Baltimore, Md. (1807). Watch and clock maker on North Calvert Street in 1807.

Ferrigo, or Perrigo.

Ferris, Tiba, Wilmington, Del. (1812–50).

Fesig, Conrad, Reading, Pa. (1758–1815).

Fessler, John, Fredericktown, Md. (1782–1820). Used lantern pinion, of early date.

Fessler, John, Jr., Frederick, Md. (c. 1800–20). Watch and clock maker, son of John, Sr. Continued his business.

Feton, J., Philadelphia, Pa. (1828–40).

Field, Peter, New York City (1802). Watch and clock maker.

Field, Peter, Jr., New York City (1802–25).

Fiffe, H.

Filber, John, Lancaster, Pa. (1810–25).

Finley, John, Baltimore, Md. (1754). Clock maker.

Finney, John, Charlestown, Md. (1754). "Makes and Mends Clock and Watches, in the best and cheapest Manner. . . ."

Fish, Isaac, Utica, N. Y. (1846).

Fisher, John, York, Pa. (1779).

Fisk, William, Boston, Mass. (b. 1770 Watertown, d. 1844). Made nearly all Simon Willard's clock cases in 1800–38, also made them for Aaron Willard, and other clock makers. On Boston Neck, in business with his brother Samuel after 1792.

Fite, John, Baltimore, Md. (c. 1783–1818), (fl. 1807–18). Watch and clock maker, having a shop at 227 (or 217) Baltimore Street from 1807–17, and residing at 8 German Street.

Fitz, ——, Portsmouth, N. H. (c. 1769).

Fix, Joseph, Reading, Pa. (1820–40). Also Joseph Fix, Pennsylvania.

Fletcher, Charles, Philadelphia, Pa. (1832). "Imports Watches, Jewelry, Mantel Clocks. . . ."

Fletcher, Thomas, Philadelphia, Pa. (1832). "Manufactory of Jewelry and Silver Ware, and Furnishing Warehouse. Extensive assortment of Watches . . . Mantel Clocks. . . ."

Fling, Daniel, Philadelphia, Pa. (1811).

Flower, Henry, Philadelphia, Pa. (1753). Watchmaker and repairer. Fine cabinet-work.

Floyd, Thomas, Upper-Moor-Fields, S. C. (1768). Made, cleaned, and repaired all sorts of clocks.

Folmar, Andrew, New York City (1810).

Foot, Charles J., Bristol, Conn. (1856).

Foote, William, Middletown and East Haddam, Conn. (1795). In partnership with Samuel Canfield.

Forbes, John, Hartford, Conn. Tall clock, owned by John H. Schmuck, Naugatuck.

Forbes, Wells, Bristol, N. H. (c. 1840).

Ford, George, Lancaster, Pa. (fl. 1811–40). (d. 1842). Tall clocks and nautical and surveyors' instruments.

Ford, George (son of George), continued his father's business.

Ford, Peter, Yorktown, Pa.

Ford, Southerland, Charlestown, S. C. (1741). "Clocks and watches carefully taken care of by the year." Clock maker.

Forestville Manufacturing Co., Bristol (village of Forestville), Conn. (c. 1830).

Forres, Christian, Lampeter, Pa.

Foster, John C., Portland, Me. (1834). "Horography, Watches, Clocks and Timekeepers of all escapements cleaned and adjusted."

Foster, Nathaniel, Newburyport, Mass. (1818–28). In 1818 he opened a store on State Street, where he carried on "the clock and watch making business in all its branches." He had charge of the town clocks from April, 1818, until 1828, and perhaps later.

Fowell, J. & N., Boston, Mass. (1800–10).

Foxcroft, James A., Baltimore, Md. (1822–39). First appears in 1822–23 as watch and clock maker, and in 1829 as a jeweler, watch and clock maker at 37 S. Calvert Street. About 1831 he formed a partnership with Gabriel D. Clark (1813–96) who had learned his trade with Foxcroft, under the name of James A. Foxcroft & Clark, which continued until his death in February, 1839.

Francis, Basil, Baltimore, Md. (1768). Advertised January 7, 1768, as a "Watchmaker from London in Market Street, Baltimore Town, [and that he] makes, sells and repairs all sorts of Watches. . . ."

Francis, Basil, & Alexander Vuille, Baltimore, Md. (1766).

Franciscus, George, Sr., Baltimore, Md. (1776–91). Tools listed in inventory for clock making and jewelry.

Franck, Philip, New Berlin (probably Pa.). Hall clock.

Francony, Jacob Heagey (c. 1790).

Frary, Obadiah, Southampton, Mass. (1745–75). Made some good brass clocks for families, and a few for meeting-houses.

Fraser, Jacob, Philadelphia, Pa. (b. 1801, d. 1877)(fl. Lincoln, 1834–).

Fraser, William (1835–1910). Carried on business of his father William. His grandsons continue business, and own many of the tools of ancient Lancaster Co. makers. Said to be oldest firm of clock makers in continuous business in United States.

Frazer, Robert and Alexander, Lexington, Ky. (1801–03).

Frazier, Samuel, Baltimore, Md. (1822–24). Watch and clock maker on Ross Street in 1822, and on Queen Anne Street in 1824.

French, James Ormsby, Baltimore, Md. (1771). Watchmaker.

French, Lemuel, Boston, Mass. (1790). Inlaid tall clock.

Friend, Engell, New York City (1825). "Clock maker and brass founder."

Friend, George, New York City (1820). "Clock maker and brass founder."

Fromanteel, Ahasueres, London (1630–60). There was a second Ahasueres working about 1675. Made clock with verge escapement and oak case veneered with ebony and hour hand with silver, also fine bracket clock. This celebrated family of eight or more makers were among the earliest and best in London.

Front, Daniel, Reading, Mass. (1770?). Made fine ball-and-claw scroll-top Chippendale style shelf clock. Was at Reading, Pa.?

Frost, Jonathan, Reading, Mass. (1856).

Frost & Mumford, Providence, R. I. (1810).

Frost, Oliver, Providence, R. I. (1800).

Fry, Jacob, Woodstock (Conn.?). Handsome tall clock, with double arch top, ending in brass rosettes. Painted face with moon motion and calendar. Owned by Guy Beardsley, Hartford.

Fyler, Orasmus R., Burke, Vt.? (c. 1830).

G

Gaillard, Peter, Reading, Pa. (Adv. June 19, 1798).

Gaines, John, Portsmouth, N. H. (1800).

Galbraith, Patrick, Philadelphia, Pa. (1795–1811).

Gallome, C., Baltimore, Md. (1819). Watchmaker at 19 Bond Street.

Galpin, Moses, Bethlehem, Conn. (before 1821). Not a maker, but a peddler, though he put his name on clocks he bought from others. Chauncey Jerome, with five or six others, trusted Galpin with a large quantity of clocks, and he took them to Louisiana to sell in fall of 1821. In the course of the winter he was taken sick and died there. One of his peddlers came home without one dollar. Chauncey Jerome lost $740.

Galt, Peter, Baltimore, Md. (1777–1830) (fl. c. 1800–25). Watch and clock maker.

Galt, Samuel, Williamsburg, Pa. (1751).

Galt, Stirling (brother of Peter), Baltimore, Md. (1802). Watchmaker.

Gardiner, B., New York City (1832). "Furnishing Warehouse, Manufacturer of Silver Ware, and Importer of Lamps . . . Clocks. . . ."

Gardiner, John B., Ansonia, Conn. (1857).

Garrett, Benjamin, Goshen, N. Y. (1820).

Garrett, Philip, Philadelphia, Pa. (1819).

Garrett & Sons, P., Philadelphia, Pa. (1832). "Importers of Watches. . . . Manufacturers of Jewelry, Silver Spoons, Spectacles, etc."

Gates, Zacheus, Charlestown, Mass. (1831). Also Harvard, Mass.

Gaw, William P., Philadelphia, Pa. (1819).

Gaylord, Homer, Norfolk, Conn. (until 1812). Homer Gaylord made clocks on his father's farm in Norfolk until 1812, when a freshet tore away the dam, after which he moved to Homer, N. Y.

Geddes, Charles, Boston, Mass. (1773).

Geddy, James, Williamsburg, Md. (1774). Watchmaker.

Gegye, Rene, South Carolina (1740). Clock and watchmaker and mender.

Gehring, John G., Baltimore, Md. (1827–31). Jeweler and watchmaker at 76 Ensor Street.

Gelston, George S., New York City (1832). "Manufacturer and Importer of Fine Jewelry, Watches and Fancy Goods. Orders left with Hugh Gelston, Baltimore, punctually attended to."

Gelston, Hugh, Baltimore, Md. (1832). "Importer of Watches, Jewelry, etc."

Gemmil, John, Carlisle, Pa. (?). Hall, walnut broken arch top, with rosettes. Bracket feet. Brass dial? Spandrels.

Gerding & Simeon, New York City (1832). "Importers of . . . Mantelpiece Clocks. . . ."

Gerrish, Oliver, Portland, Me. (1834). "Clocks, watches and jewelry repaired."

Gibbons, Thomas, Philadelphia, Pa. (1751). Watchmaker from London. "Makes and mends all sorts of clocks and watches."

Gilbert, Jordan & Smith, New York City (1832). "Dealers in Combs, Cutlery, Jewelry, Silver Spoons, Spectacles, Thimbles, Needles, and a Variety of Fancy Goods."

Gilbert Manufacturing Co., The, Winsted, Conn. (Incorporated 1866–71 to date). After re-organization in 1871, called The Wm. L. Gilbert Clock Company. Still doing business.

Gilbert, William L., Winsted, Conn. (1823–66). In 1841 or '42 he joined Lucius Clarke, the firm name being Clarke, Gilbert & Co. Later it became W. L. Gilbert. Still doing business.

Gill, Caleb, Hingham, Mass. (1785).

Gill, Leavitt, Hingham, Mass. (1785).

Giraud, Victor, New York City (1847).

Glingeman, Jacob, Reading, Pa. (1784).

Glover, William, Boston, Mass. (1823).

Goddard, George S., Boston, Mass. (1823).

Goddard, John, Newport, R. I. (1745–85). The celebrated cabinetmaker who, or with Townsend, created the blocked shell and applied it to clock cases of which some fifteen or more are known. These are the most individual, rare, and beautiful cases known. Found with Wheaton and other works.

Goddard, Nichols, Rutland, Vt. (?). Tall.

Godfrey, William, Philadelphia, Pa. (1750–63).

Godschalk, Jacob, Philadelphia, Pa. (1781).

Goff, Charles.

Goodfellow, William, Philadelphia, Pa. (1793–99).

Goodfellow, William, Philadelphia, Pa. (1813).

Goodfellow, William & Son, Philadelphia, Pa. (1796–99).

Goodhue, D. T., Providence, R. I. (1824).

Goodhue, Richard S., Portland, Me. (1834).

Gooding, Alanson, New Bedford, Mass.

Gooding, Henry, Boston, Mass. (1810–30).

Gooding, Josiah, Dighton, Mass., and Bristol, R. I. (1788–1867).

Goodrich, Chauncey, Bristol (village of Forestville), Conn. (1856).

Goodwin, Horace, Jr., Hartford, Conn. (1831–41 or longer). "Keeps constantly on hand for sale, watches, jewelry, fancy goods, etc."

Goodwin & Williams.

Gorden, Smyley, Lowell, Mass. (1832). "He was a maker of clock cases, and put his name on them."

Gordon, Thomas, New York (1759). Clockmaker.

Gorgas, Jacob (1760–1829). Began business in Cocalico, now Ephrata (b. Germany). About one hundred and fifty clocks known. Gorgas was perhaps the earliest maker in Lancaster Co.

Gorgas, Joseph (son of Jacob), Lancaster Co., Pa.

Gorgas, Solomon (son of Jacob), Lancaster Co., Pa.

Gorham, Charles L., Barre, Mass. Name on dial of hall.

Goron, Thomas, Boston, Mass. (1759). "From London, opposite the Merchant's Coffee House, sells all kinds of Timepieces."

Gould, Abijah, Rochester, N. Y. (1834).

Govett, George, Philadelphia, Pa. (1813–31).

Grant, James, Hartford and Wethersfield, Conn. (1794). "Watch and Clock Maker from London."

Grant, William, Boston (c. 1815). Banjo.

Graves, Alfred, Willow Grove, Pa. (1845).

Green, John, Carlisle, Pa.

Green, John, Philadelphia, Pa. (1794).

Greenleaf, David, Hartford, Conn. (1799). Watchmaker and jeweler.

Greenough, N. C., Newburyport, Mass. (1848).

Greer, John, Carlisle, Pa. (c. 1774). Clock and watchmaker.

Gridley, Timothy, Sanbornton, N. H. (1808–). He established a wooden clock manufactory, introducing two men from Conn., Messrs. Peck and Holcomb, to take charge of the business. Col. Simeon Cate bought out the clock business of Mr. Gridley. Mrs. James

Connor painted and lettered the faces of the clocks for them.

Griffin, Henry, New York City (1792–1818).

Griffith, Edward, Georgia (1796). Watchmaker.

Griffith, Owen, Philadelphia, Pa.

Griswold, Daniel White, Manchester, Conn. (b. 1767, d. 1844). Made a number of clocks, though his regular business was that of trader between Boston and New York.

Groppengerser, J. L., Philadelphia, Pa. (1840).

Grotz, Isaac, Easton, Pa. (1810–35).

Grove, William, Hanover, Pa. (1838). Tall clock.

Gruby, Edward L., Portland, Me. (1834).

Guild, Jeremiah, Cincinnati, O. (1831).

Guild, John (c. 1775).

Guild, John, Philadelphia, Pa. (1819).

Guinand, Frederick Edward, Baltimore, Md. (1814–27). Watch and clock maker.

Gunkle, John (fl. 1830–40), Ephrata, Pa., at Trout Run. (Name also spelled Kunkle.) Made good, but few, clocks.

H

Haas & Co., John, New York City (1825). "Musical Clockmakers."

Hahn, Henry, Reading, Pa. (1754–1845).

Haigh, Jefferson, Baltimore, Md. (1829–31). Watch and clock maker at 26½ West Pratt Street.

Hall, Asa. Name on dial, "Hall."

Hall, Christian, Lititz, Pa. (1775–1848).

Hall, John, Philadelphia, Pa. (1811–19).

Hall, Seymour & Co., Unionville, Conn. (c. 1820).

Ham, George, Portsmouth, N. H. (1810).

Ham, Supply, Portsmouth, N. H. One of the ancient and honorable clock and watchmakers of Portsmouth. Kidney-shaped, maple mantel clock. He owned a clock made by "J. Windmill, London" which bears this inscription of its owners: "1677, George Jaffrey; 1720 George Jaffrey, Jr.; 1749 George Jaffrey, 3rd; 1802, Timothy Ham; 1856, Supply Ham; 1862 Francis W. Ham."

Hamlen, Nathaniel, Augusta, Me. (1790–1820). Grandmother clock, 43½ x 10½.

Hamlin, William, Providence, R. I. (1797).

Hampton, Samuel, Chelsea, Mass. (1847).

Hanks, Benjamin, Litchfield, Conn. (1778–85). "Benjamin Hanks came from Mansfield, Conn., to Litchfield in 1778, remaining until 1785; returned to Mansfield. While here he was a clock and watchmaker, and contracted for and put up the first clock in the city of New York, on the old Dutch Church, Nassau and Liberty streets. This clock was unique, having a windmill attachment, his own patent, for winding itself up." Also cast bells.

Harden, James, Philadelphia, Pa. (1819).

Hardy, William, South Carolina (1773). Watch and clock maker.

Harland, Thomas, Norwich, Conn. (1773–1807). Made "watches; spring, musical and plain clocks; church clocks and regulators. Watchwheels and fusees of all sorts and dimensions cut and finished upon the shortest notice, neat as in London, and at the same prices." Taught apprentices from all parts of New England, the most famous of whom was Eli Terry. He also taught Daniel Burnap (which see). In 1790 ten or twelve hands were constantly employed, and it is stated that he made annually 200 watches and 40 clocks. His prices varied from £4 10s to £7 10s.

Harrison, James (brother of Lemuel), Waterbury, Conn. (1790–1830). Built a clock factory on Little Brook in 1802.

Harrison, John, Philadelphia, Pa.

Harrison, John Murray.

Harrison, Lemuel (brother of James), Waterbury, Conn. (1800). He and his brother made clocks by hand before 1800. Ephraim Downs worked for him in 1811.

Harrison, Wooster (son of Lemuel), Trumbull and Newfield, Conn. (1795–1800). Clock maker.

Hart, Alpha (brother of Henry), Goshen, Conn. (1820).

Hart, Eliphaz, Norwich on the Green, Conn. (1812). Worker in gold and silver, jewelry and timekeepers.

Hart, Henry (brother of Alpha), Hart Hollow, Goshen, Conn.

Hart, Judah, Norwich at the Landing, Conn. (1812). Timekeepers.

Hart, Orrin, Bristol, Conn. (1840).

Hart & Wilcox, Norwich, Conn.

Harwood, George, Rochester, N. Y. (1839). "Clocks, warranted to keep good time. 20 cases just received from Connecticut, which will be sold by the case or singly as low as any warranted clocks can be sold in this city."

Haselton & Wentworth, Lowell, Mass. (1832).

Hasle, James, of Derby, "Maryland" (1774).

Hatch, Geo. D., No. Attleboro, Mass. (1856). Striking banjo movement.

Hatton (Thomas), Connecticut (1773). "Every boy ought to be taught the art of hammering with great care; and to obtain which he should practice well on clock dials."

Hawxhurst (or Hauxhurst) & Demilt, New York City (1790).

Hawxhurst, Nathaniel, New York City (1786–98).

Hayes, Peter B. (or P.), Poughkeepsie, N. Y. (1831). "(Dealers in Watches, Clocks. . . .)"

Heath, Reuben, Scottsville, N. Y. (1791–1818). Clock maker and repairer; sold clocks of other makers.

Hedge, George, Buffalo, N. Y. (1831).

Hedsal, Joseph, Florida, N. Y. Inlaid tall, French foot, double arch, moon motion.

Heffords, ——, Middleboro (Titicut), Mass. Famous for clocks of superior quality, which he invented and manufactured.

Heilig, Jacob, Philadelphia, Pa. (1770–1824).

Heilig, John, Germantown, Pa. (1824–30).

Heintzelman, John Conrad (b. 1766, d. 1804). Business in Manheim, Pa. Grandfather of the celebrated General Heintzelman. Also had son Peter, clock maker. Very tall, beautiful fret clock.

Heisley, Frederick, Frederick, Md. (1786–1816). Advertisement appeared as "Frederick Heisley Clock and Watch Maker has removed his shop to his Dwelling House. . . ."

Hendrick, Barnes & Co., Forestville, Conn. (1845). In the old Ives shop, made the first marine clocks.

Hendricks, Uriah, New York City (1756). Was by trade a watchmaker. "At his store next door to the Sign of the Golden Key in Hanover Square has imported two fine repeating eight day clocks which strike every half hour and repeat."

Heppleman, John, Manheim, Pa. Probably late 18th or early 19th C.

Hepton, Frederick, Philadelphia, Pa. (1785).

Hequembourg, C., New Haven, Conn. (1818). Was in business many years. Sold gold and silver watches with gold or enamelled dials, and repaired clocks and watches.

Heron, Erskine, South Carolina (1765). Cleaned and mended all sorts of watches and clocks.

Heron, Isaac, New York City (1769–80). "Isaac Heron, watchmaker, facing Coffee House Bridge, has a musical clock noble and elegant, also a neat and extraordinary good chamber repeating clock."

Heron, James, New Town (?). Tall, quarter column, fret, double arch, rocking ship, brass face.

Herr, William, Jr., Providence, R. I. (1849).

Herwick, Jacob, Carlisle, Pa. (1779).

Heydorn & Imlay, Hartford, Conn. (1811). Bought the most extensive set of clock-making tools in the state from Nathan Allyn, but later sold them. The making of clocks in Hartford discontinued about this time.

Hibben, Andrew, South Carolina (1765). Repaired watches and clocks.

Hicks, Willet, New York City (1790).

Hildeburn, Samuel, Philadelphia, Pa. (1819).

Hildeburn & Watson, Philadelphia, Pa. (1832). "Manufacturers of Jewelry and Watch Case Makers, and Importers of Watches and Fancy Goods."

Hildeburn & Woodworth, Philadelphia, Pa. (1819).

Hildreth, Jonas, Salisbury, Vt. (1805).

Hill, D., Reading, Pa. (1820–40).

Hill, Joakin, Flemington, N. J. (1790–1800). Made long-case clocks and excellent workmanship, and charged a good price for them. Hepplewhite fret. One with American eagle inlay.

Hilldrop (or Hilldrup), Thomas, Hartford, Conn. (1774–94). Watchmaker, jeweler, and silversmith from London.

Hiller, Joseph, Salem, Mass. (1770). "1770. Joseph Hiller, moved from Boston, has taken a shop opposite the Court House, on the Exchange."

Hilliard, Christopher, Hagerstown, Md. Born in Fredericktown, 1802, died 1871. Made and repaired clocks and watches.

Hilliard, James, South Carolina (1738). Clock and watchmaker.

Hills, Amariah, New York City (1845).

Hitchcock, H., Lodi, N. Y. (c. 1800). "Scals, keys, chains, clocks and watches for sale by H. Hitchcock, Lodi, N. Y."

Hitchcock, Samuel R., Humphreysville, N. Y. (1810).

Hoadley, Samuel and Luther, Winsted (town of Winchester), Conn. (1807–13). In 1807 Samuel and Luther Hoadley with Riley Whiting opened works at Winsted, Conn., for making wood clocks. Luther died 1813, Samuel entered army, retiring from business.

Hoadley, Silas, Plymouth, Conn. (1808–49). Learned carpenter's trade from his uncle, Calvin Hoadley. Worked for Eli Terry, and in 1809 formed partnership with Eli Terry and Seth Thomas at Greystone. Terry withdrew 1810, Thomas 1812. Hoadley continued to make clocks, mostly cheap, here till 1849, when he retired.

Hockers, G. Made tall clock for the Ephrata Cloister in 1750.

Hodges & North, Wolcottville (now Torrington), Conn. (1830).

Hodgson, William, Philadelphia, Pa. (1785).

Hoffner, Henry, Philadelphia, Pa. (1791).

Hoffs, George, Lancaster, Pa. (1765–1816) (b. Westerberg, Germany, c. 1740). Watches and tall clocks.

Hoffs, John, son of George, with whom he was in business, but afterwards went into business alone, Lancaster, Pa. (d. 1816). Father and son made over one hundred known clocks, some with quarter and chime.

Holbrook, George, Brookfield, Mass. (1803). He made the clock and bell which were placed on the meetinghouse of Leicester, Mass., Jan. 13, 1803.

Holbrook, ——, Medway, Mass. (c. 1830). Made clock for Unitarian meetinghouse In Keene, N. H., a few years after 1829.

Hollinshead, Jacob, Salem, Mass. (? N. Y.) (1771).

Hollinshead, Morgan, Moorestown, N. J.

Holloway, Robert, Baltimore, Md. (1822–23). Watch and clock maker at 115 High Street. See Chandlee & Holloway.

Holman, Salem, Hartford, Conn. (1816).

Holway, Philip, Falmouth, Mass. (1800).

Homer, William, Moreland, Pa. (1849).

Hood, Francis, New York City (1810).

Hood, John, Philadelphia, Pa.

Hooker & Goodenough, Bristol, Conn. (1849).

Hopkins & Alfred, Harwinton, Conn. (1820), Hartford, Conn. (1827). They made excellent clocks, wood works.

Hopkins & Lewis, Litchfield, Conn. Inscription on enamel dial of walnut case tall clock in South Carolina.

Hopkins, Asa, Litchfield (parish of Northfield), Conn. (1820 and earlier). In 1813 he obtained a patent on an engine for cutting wheels.

Hopkins, Henry P., Philadelphia, Pa. (1832). "Dealer in Watches, Clocks. . . ."

Horn, Eliphalet, Lowell, Mass. (1832).

Horn, E. B., Boston, Mass. (1847).

Hotchkiss & Benedict, Auburn, N. Y. (c. 1820). Makers of shelf clocks.

Hotchkiss, Elisha, Burlington, Conn. (c. 1815).

Hotchkiss & Field, Burlington, Conn. (1820).

Hotchkiss, Hezekiah, New Haven, Conn. (1748).

Hotchkiss & Pierpont, Plymouth, Conn. (1811–). "Had been selling long clocks without the cases, in New Jersey." C. Jerome.

Hotchkiss, Robert & Henry, Plymouth, Conn. ("Prior to 1846").

Hotchkiss, Spencer & Co., Salem Bridge (now Naugatuck), Conn. (1832). "Manufacturer of Buttons and Eight Day Brass Clocks."

Hotchkiss, William, "Maryland" (1775).

Howard & Davis, Boston, Mass. (1847–56).

Howard, Edward, Roxbury, Mass. (1840–82). Apprentice to Aaron Willard, Jr. Started business for himself, 1840. David P. Davis became his partner, 1847, and they made clocks and scales. In 1849 Aaron L. Dennison joined them, and a watch factory was started in Roxbury. In 1854 they moved to Waltham, and watches made there were marked "Dennison, Howard & Davis." In 1857 the Waltham factory was sold to Royal E. Robbins. Howard returned to Roxbury, and 1861 started the Howard Clock & Watch Company. He retired 1882.

Howard, Thomas, Philadelphia, Pa. (1789–91).

Howe, Jubal, Boston, Mass. (1833).

Howell, Nathan (b. New Haven, Conn.) (mid. 18th C.)

Hoyt, George A., Albany, N. Y. (1830).

Hoyt, James A., Troy, N. Y. (1837).

Hubbard, Daniel, Medfield, Mass. (1820).

Hubbell, L.

Huckel, Samuel, Philadelphia, Pa. (1819).

Hughes, Edmund, Hampton and Middletown, Conn. (c. 1800).

Huguenail, Charles T., Philadelphia, Pa. (1799).

Humbert, Dross, Philadelphia, Pa. (1795).

Humphreys, Joshua, East Whiteland, Pa. (1771).

Hunt, ——, New York City (1789).

Hunt, John, Plainville and Farmington, Conn. Clock maker.

Hurtin & Burgi, Bound Brook, N. J. (1766).

Huston, James, Walnut Ward, Philadelphia Co. (1774).

Huston, William, Middle Ward, Philadelphia Co. (1774). Clock maker.

Hutchins, Abel, Concord, N. H. (1788–1819). Apprentice of Simon Willard. Was in partnership with his brother Levi. They were born in Harvard, Mass.

Hutchins, Levi, Concord, N. H. (1786–1819). Apprentice (3 yrs.) 9f Simon Willard. Learned art of repairing watches in Abington, Conn. About 1786 established business of brass clock making. In 1788 his brother Abel became partner. Made many hall, and some shelf clocks.

Hyman, Henry, Lexington, Ky. (1799).

Hyman, Samuel, Baltimore, Md. (1799). Watch and clock maker at 8 Market Space.

I

Inch, John, Annapolis, Md. (1745). Watch and clock maker.

Ingersoll, Daniel G., Boston, Mass. (1800–10).

Ingraham, E. & A., Bristol, Conn. (1848–55).

Ingraham, Elias, Bristol, Conn. (1835–85). Designer of the "Sharp Gothic" and other styles of clock cases. Originally a cabinet-maker. Made clock cases 1827–35 for George Mitchell, and learned clock making in his factory. In 1835 bought a shop in Bristol and began making clocks. In 1843 he and his brother formed a partnership with Elisha C. Brewster. Brewster & Ingraham was succeeded by E. & A. Ingraham & Co., 1856. A joint stock company was formed 1881.

Ingraham & Co., E., Bristol, Conn. (1856–81). Joint stock company formed 1881 and now called The E. Ingraham Co.

Ives & Birge, Bristol, Conn. (c. 1843).

Ives Brothers (five in number), Bristol, Conn. (1815–20 also 1822–37).

Ives, Charles G., Bristol, Conn. (c. 1810–20). Made wood clocks.

Ives, Chauncey, Bristol, Conn. (1827–36).

Ives, C. & L. C., Bristol, Conn. (1832). "Manufacturers of Eight Day Patent Brass and Thirty Hour Wood Clocks." About 1830 Chauncey and Lawson C. Ives built a factory in Bristol for making 8-day brass clocks — the kind invented by Joseph Ives. Business was closed 1836.

Ives, Ira, Bristol, Conn. (c. 1815–37).

Ives, Joseph, Bristol, Conn., and New York City (1811–25). "Joseph Ives made wood movements as early as 1811. In 1818 he invented a metal clock, with iron plates and brass wheels, and began its manufacture. This clock was large and clumsy and never became very successful."

Ives, Lawson C., Bristol, Conn. (1827–36).

J

Jacks, James, South Carolina (1784). Clock and watchmaker.

Jackson, Isaac, New Garden, Pa. (1766).

Jackson, John, E. Marlborough, Pa. (1769).

Jackson, Joseph H., Philadelphia, Pa. (1802–10).

Jackson, Thos., Portsmouth. Tall clock, pine, very slender. Baltimore Museum.

Jacob, Charles, Annapolis, Md. (1775). Watchmaker.

James, Joshua, Boston, Mass. (1823).

Jeffreys, Samuel, Philadelphia, Pa. (before the Revolution).

Jencks, John E., Providence, R. I. (1800).

Jenkins, Harman, Albany, N. Y. (1817).

Jenkins, Ira, Albany, N. Y. (1813).

Jerome, Chauncey, Plymouth, Bristol, and New Haven, Conn. (1816–60). Author of "American Clock Making," published 1860. Worked for Eli Terry winter of 1816; then began making clocks by himself. In 1821 moved to Bristol. In 1824 firm of Jerome & Darrow formed (Chauncey and Noble Jerome and Elijah Darrow). A little later Chauncey Jerome got up the "Bronze Looking Glass Clock." Did well with this until the panic of 1837. In 1838 he invented and began making the one-day brass clock, which drove out all wood clocks. By 1840 his business was very large. In 1842 began sending clocks to England. In 1844 moved his business to New Haven. His product was so good that many small manufacturers used Jerome labels for their poorer clocks. In 1850 a joint stock company was formed in New Haven — the Jerome Manufacturing Company. In 1855 the company failed and Jerome was ruined. P. T. Barnum was connected with the company during the last six months of its existence. The real difficulty was the previous indebtedness of the Terry & Barnum Co., which was assumed by the Jerome Mfg. Co. Jerome spent his last years almost in obscurity and died very poor.

Jerome, Chauncey & Noble, Richmond, Va., also Hamburg, S. C. (1835–36). They made the cases and parts at Bristol, Conn., packed and shipped them to Richmond, and took along workmen to put them together there.

Jerome & Darrow, Bristol, Conn. (1824–31). "Manufacturers of Fancy Thirty Hour and Eight Day Wood Clocks."

Jerome & Grant, Bristol, Conn.

Jerome Mfg. Co., New Haven, Conn. (1850–55). See Chauncey Jerome.

Jerome, Noble, Bristol, Conn. (1820–40). Brother of Chauncey, and in business with him.

Jewell, Jerome & Co., Bristol, Conn. (1849). Town clocks.

Job, John, Philadelphia, Pa. (1819).

Jocelyn, Nathaniel, New Haven, Conn. (1790).

Jocelyn, Simeon, New Haven, Conn. (1768–1823). Mathematician, music publisher. Important maker.

Johnson, Addison, Wolcottville (now Torrington), Conn. (1825). Pillar and scroll clocks, handsome cases and good works.

Johnson, Chauncey, Albany, N. Y. (1829). "Musical, ornamental and common clocks."

Johnson, David, Boston (1687). Watchmaker.

Johnson, Edward, "Maryland" (1774).

Johnson, John, South Carolina (1763). "Cleans and repairs watches in the best manner."

Johnson, Simon, Sanbornton, N. H. (1830–60). "A very superior quality of clocks has been produced from this establishment by the senior Mr. Johnson, and latterly by the Johnson Brothers."

Johnson, William S., New York City (c. 1830).

Johnston, John, South Carolina (1764). Makes and mends all sorts of watches.

Jonckheere, Francis, Baltimore, Md. (1807–24). Watch and clock maker on Bond Street, Fell's Point.

Jones, Abner, Weare, N. H. (1780). Made large old-fashioned 8-day brass clocks that sold for $50 each.

Jones, Ball & Poor, Boston, Mass. (1847).

Jones, Edward K., Bristol, Conn. (1825).

Jones, Ezekiel, Boston, Mass. (1823). Shelf clock.

Jones, George, Wilmington, Del. (1810–37).

Jones, George, Jr., Wilmington, Del. (1814).

Jones, Griffith G., Baltimore, Md. (1824–27). Watch and clock maker.

Jones, Jacob, Baltimore, Md. (1817–18). Watchmaker at 39 German Street.

Jones, Jacob, Pittsfield, N. H. (c. 1800). A grandfather clock made by him, which once belonged to Stephen Bachelor Crane, is now owned by Dr. —— Crane of Colrain, Mass.

Jones, Samuel G., Baltimore, Md. (1799–1829). Watch and clock maker at 93 Baltimore Street from 1815 to 1829. Advertises as "late of Patton & Jones," which firm had been at the same address since 1799.

Joseph, Isaac, Boston, Mass. (1823).

Joslin, Gilman, Boston. *See* Finley.

Joslyn, James, New Haven, Conn. (1798–1820).

Joyce, Robert, New York City (1794).

Judd, Henry, Torrington, Conn. Name on sticker of woodwork "Shell."

K

Kedzie, J., Rochester, N. Y. (1847).

Keeler, Joseph, Norwalk, Conn.

Keim, John, Reading, Pa. (1745–1819).

Kellogg, Daniel, Hebron, Conn. (1766–1855). Goldsmith and clock maker.

Kelly (or Kelley), Allen, Sandwich, Mass. (1810–30).

Kelly, Ezra, New Bedford, Mass. (1823–45).

Kelly, John, New Bedford, Mass. (1836).

Kemble, William, New York City (1786).

Kemlo, Francis, Chelsea, Mass. (1847).

Kennard, John, Newfields, N. H. (19th C.) Was brass worker and clock maker. Henry Wiggin, Jr., made cases for his clocks.

Kennedy, Elisha, Middletown, Conn. (1788). Clock and watch maker, and repairer.

Kennedy, Patrick, Philadelphia, Pa. (1795–99).

Kenney, Asa, West Millbury, Mass. (c. 1800).

Keplinger, Samuel, Baltimore, Md. (b. 1770, d. 1849), (fl. 1812–49 ?). Watch and clock maker at 60 North Howard Street.

Keplinger, William, probably son of Samuel. Baltimore, Md. (1829–31). Watch and clock maker, on Paca Street, near Baltimore.

Kerner & Paff, New York City (1796). "Musical clocks with figures and cuckoo clocks."

Kersey, Robert, Easton, Md. (1793). Watch and clock maker.

Ketcham & Hitchcock, New York City (1818).

Kimball, John, Jr., Boston, Mass. (1823).

Kimball, William, New York (1775).

Kincaird, Thomas, Christiana Bridge, Del. (1775).

King, Thomas R., Baltimore, Md. (1819–31). Watch and clock maker at 52½ or 54 North Howard Street.

Kinkead, James, Pennsylvania (1774). Watch and clock maker.

Kippen, George, Bridgeport, Conn. (1822). Kept a great variety of goods, and made and repaired clocks and watches.

Kirk, Charles, Bristol, Conn. (1823–33). In 1833 he sold his clock factory and business to Elisha C. Brewster, but conducted it for him until about 1838.

Kirk, Charles, New Haven, Conn. (1847). Brass marine clocks.

Kirkwood, Alexander, South Carolina (1761). Watch and clock maker.

Kirkwood, John, Wilmington, S. C. (before the Revolution).

Kline, B., Philadelphia, Pa. (1841).

Kline, John, Philadelphia, Pa. (1820).

Kline, John, Reading, Pa. (1820–40).

Klingman, Jacob, Reading, Pa. (1758–1806).

Knapp, William, Annapolis, Md. (1764–68). Knapp, who is said to have been a native of Cork, announced in the Maryland *Gazette* for March 27, 1764, the opening of a watchmaker's shop in Annapolis near the church.

Kneedler, Jacob, Horsham, Pa. (1791). Clock works.

Knowles, John, Philadelphia, Pa. (1784). Watchmaker and storekeeper.

Kohl, Nicholas, Willow Grove, Pa. (1830).

Koplin, Washington, Norristown, Pa. (1850).

Kreuzer, Fidel. Name on back of floral decorated dial on clock in Pennsylvania.

Kumbell, William, New York City (1775–89).

L

Labhart, W. I., New York City (1810).

Ladomus, Lewis, Philadelphia, Pa. (1846).

Lamb, Cyrus, Oxford, Mass. (1832). Probably not a regular clock maker. He was a millwright, and a skilful mechanic. It is said that he had in his shop at the time of the fire (Jan. 7, 1832) a remarkable clock of his own designing which it was supposed would run for several years with one winding.

Lamoine, A., Philadelphia, Pa. (1811).

Lampe, John, Annapolis, Md. (1779), Baltimore (1780–87). Watch and clock maker. Advertisement states that, "John Lampe, Clock and Watchmaker, late from Annapolis has his shop in part of . . . Isaiah Wagster's house." . . . .

Lamson, Charles, Salem, Mass. (1850). (With James Balch.)

Lane, Aaron, Eliz^th Town. This name is on a tall clock in the Sheldon-Bement house in Old Deerfield.

Lane, James, Philadelphia, Pa. (1813).

Lane, J., Southington, Conn.

Lane, Mark, Southington, Conn. (1831). "Manufacturer of Eli Terry's Patent Clocks."

Langdon, Edward, Bristol, Conn. (19th C.). In company with E. Emerson Root for a time.

Lanny, D. F., Boston, Mass. (1789).

Laquaine, Philadelphia, Pa.

Larkin, Joseph, Boston, Mass. (1841–47).

Latchow, John, Baltimore, Md. (1829). Watchmaker on Pearl and Saratoga streets.

Latham, ——, Marple. On dial of clock with mahogany inlaid case, in Pennsylvania. Marple is the name of a township in Delaware County, near Chester, Pa.

Latimer, James, Philadelphia, Pa. (1819).

Latournau, John B. M., Baltimore, Md. (b. 1796, d. 1853) (fl. c. 1820–53). Jeweler, watch and clock maker.

Latshar, John, York, Pa. (1779).

Launay, David, New York City (1801). "Had for sale at his watchmaking shop a highly finished clock which decorated the library of the late King of France."

Laundry, Alexander, Philadelphia, Pa.

Launey, David F., New York City (1793 and 1802).

Lawrence, George, Lowell, Mass. (1832).

Lawshe, John, in Amwell. Name on brass dial of tall walnut clock, having brass works also.

Lawson, William H., Waterbury, Conn.

Leach, Caleb, Plymouth, Mass. (1776–90).

Leach & Bradley, Utica, N. Y. (1832). "Dealers in Jewelry, Manufacturers of Silver Ware."

Leavenworth, Mark, Waterbury, Conn. (1810–30).

Leavenworth & Co., Mark, Waterbury, Conn. (1832).

Leavenworth & Sons, Albany, N. Y. (1817).

Leavenworth, William, Waterbury, Conn. (1802–15). Made clocks on Mad River about 1802. Col. William Leavenworth was in business in 1810, but failed, and moved to Albany, N. Y.

Leavitt, Dr. Josiah, Hingham, Mass. (1772). He made a clock which was placed in the attic story of the Old Meeting House (1772 or 73), and the dial appeared in a dormer window facing the street. Dr. Leavitt afterward removed to Boston, where he became somewhat noted as an organ builder.

Lee, William, Charlestown, S. C. (1717).

Lefferts, Charles, Philadelphia, Pa. (1819).

Lefferts & Hall, Philadelphia, Pa. (1819).

Le Huray, Nicholas, Jr., Philadelphia, Pa. (1832). "Clocks, Watches and Jewelry."

Leigh, David, Pottstown, Pa. (1849).

Leinbach, Elias and John, Reamstown, Pa. (fl. 1788–1810). Fine faces, but not good works.

Leinhardt, Christi, Carlisle, Pa. (1782).

Lemist, William King, Dorchester, Mass. (b. 1791). Apprentice of Simon Willard about 1806 or 1808. Died 1820, in shipwreck.

Lenhardt, Godfrey, York, Pa. (1779).

Leroy, Abraham, Lancaster, Pa. (fl. 1757–65). Father-in-law of Wilmer Atkinson.

Lescoiet, Lanbier, Hartford, Conn. (1796). (Clock and Watch maker from Paris). At the Sign of the Clock in King Street, Hartford.

Leslie & Price, Philadelphia, Pa. (1793–99).

Leslie, Robert, Philadelphia, Pa. (1745–91). "Robert Leslie, Clock and Watchmaker, on the north side of Market between Fourth and Fifth St., Philadelphia. Having obtained patents for several Improvements on Clocks and Watches, begs leave to inform his friends and the public that he is now ready to execute any work on the said constructions; which may be applied to Clocks and Watches already made or new ones, and on trial have been found superior to any heretofore brought into common use. He has so simplified the repeating part of a watch as to enable him to make it at two-thirds of the common price which will not only be an advantage in the first purchase, but ever after as it can be cleaned when necessary for two-thirds less than the common price. He has also simplified the striking parts of clocks, which enables him to reduce the price one-fourth, and repairs at the lowest prices, horizontal, repeating, plain and other watches, and musical, chiming and plain clocks, with punctuality and dispatch, and warrants all work done in his shop. An assortment of Clock-Watchmakers Tools and Materials for sale on Reasonable Terms. Two Journeymen and an Apprentice wanted." Gazette of the United States, Philadelphia, 1791.

Leslie, Robert, & Co., Baltimore, Md. (1795–96). This firm is listed at 119 Baltimore Street in 1796. Abraham Patton represented in Baltimore under this name, the firm of Leslie & Price, of Philadelphia.

Leslie & Williams, New Brunswick, N. J. (1780). Tall clocks.

Lester, Robert, Philadelphia, Pa. (1791–98).

Le Tilier, John, Philadelphia, Pa.

Levely, George, Baltimore, Md. (1774–96). Watch and clock maker from Philadelphia who had opened a shop on Market Street. Mr. Edgar G. Miller has a tall clock by him.

Levi, Isaac, Philadelphia, Pa. (1780). Watchmaker, "lately from London."

Levy, Michael, Philadelphia, Pa. (1813).

Levy, Michael and Isaac, Baltimore, Md. (1785). Advertised September 30, 1785, "Michael and Isaac Levy, Clock and Watchmakers Late from London . . . have for sale a large assortment of the most elegant and fashionable Clocks and Watches which they will dispose of for cash on the lowest terms;" . . . . An Isaac Levi and Michael Levy, "late from London" also advertised as watchmakers on Front Street near the coffee house, Philadelphia.

Lewis, Curtis, Reading, Pa. (1770–1847).

Lewis, Erastus, New Britain (later Waterbury), Conn. (c. 1800).

Lewis, Levi, Bristol, Conn. (1811–20).

Liebert, Henry, Norristown, Pa. (1849).

Limeburner, John, Philadelphia, Pa. (1791).

Lind, John (or Johannes), Philadelphia, Pa. (1791).

Lister, Thomas, Halifax, British North America (1760–1802). He was a maker of very choice long-case clocks, and in many of them which are still found going are the following lines, generally pasted on the door of the body;
"Lo! here I stand by thee
  To give thee warning day and night;
  For every tick that I do give
  Cuts short the time thou hast to live.
  Therefore, a warning take by me,
  To serve Thy God as I serve thee;
  Each day and night be on thy guard,
  And thou shalt have a just reward."

Little, Peter, Baltimore, Md. (b. 1775, d. 1830) (fl. 1796–1816). Watch and clock maker at 122 Baltimore Street from 1800 to 1816. He was born in Littletown, Adams County, Pa., on the Maryland border, December 11, 1775. He came to Baltimore in 1789, and learned his trade with Capt. George Leveley.

Littlejon, James, South Carolina (1761). Watch and clock maker.

Lockwood, Joshua, South Carolina (1757–71). Watchmaker.

Lockwood, Joshua, South Carolina (1781). Watchmaker.

Lockwood & Scribner, New York City (1847).

Lohse & Keyser, Philadelphia, Pa. (1832). "Importers of . . . Clocks. . . ."

Loomis, Wm. B., Middletown, Conn.

Lord & Goddard, Rutland, Vt. (1797–1830).

Lorton, William B., New York City (1810–25). "Manufacturer and wholesale dealer in American clocks in all their variety."

Lovis, Capt. Joseph, Hingham, Mass. (1775–1804).

Low & Co., John J., Boston, Mass. (1832). "Importers of Watches. . . ."

Lowens, David, Philadelphia, Pa. (1785).

Lownes, Hyatt, Hagerstown, Md. (1792). "carefully makes and repairs all kinds of Clock and Watchs. . . ."

Lowrey, David, Newington, Conn. (1740–1819). Blacksmith and clock maker.

Ludwig, John, Philadelphia, Pa. (1791).

Lufkin & Johnson, Boston, Mass. (1800–10).

Lukens, Isaiah, Philadelphia, Pa. (1790–1828).

Lukens, Seneca, Horsham Meeting, Pa. (1830).

Luscomb, Samuel, Salem, Mass. (1773). Made clock put in tower of East Meeting House, 1773.

Lyman, G. E., Providence, R. I. (1849).

Lyman, Roland, Lowell, Mass. (1832).

Lynch, John, Baltimore, Md. (1804–32). "Manufacturer of Silver Work, and Clock and Watch Maker."

M

M'Cabe, John, Baltimore, Md. (1774). Watch and clock maker from Dublin, advertised that he had opened a shop at the Sign of the Dial opposite the Coffee House in Market Street.

McClurg, John, Boston, Mass. (1823).

M'Cormick, Robert, Philadelphia, Pa.

M'Crow, Thomas, Annapolis, Md. (1767). Watchmaker from Edinburgh.

McDowell, James, Philadelphia, Pa. (1794–99 or later).

McDowell, James, Jr., Philadelphia, Pa. (1805–25).

MacFarlane, John, Boston, Mass. (1800–10).

M'Harg, Alexander, Albany, N. Y. (1817).

McIlhenny, Joseph E., Philadelphia, Pa. (1819).

McIlhenny & West, Philadelphia, Pa. (1819).

M'Keen, H., Philadelphia, Pa. (1832).

McMyers, John, Baltimore, Md. (1799). Clockmaker on Bond Street, Fell's Point.

Maas, or Manns, Frederick, name on a Pennsylvania clock.

Mackay, Crafts, Boston, Mass. (1789).

Mahve, Matthew, Philadelphia, Pa. (1761). Watchmaker.

Maker, Matthew, Charleston, S. C. (before 1776).

Manning, Richard, Ipswich, Mass. (1748–60).

Manross, Elisha, Bristol (village of Forestville), Conn. (1827–49). He occupied the Joseph Ives shop in Forestville. In 1845 he built a factory near the railroad.

Manross (brothers), Bristol, Conn. (1860). Made movements of brass marine clocks.

Marache, Solomon, New York City (1759).

Marand, Joseph, Baltimore, Md. (1804). Clock and watchmaker on Harrison St.

Marble, Simeon, New Haven, Conn. (1817).

Marks, Isaac, Philadelphia, Pa. (1795).

Marquand & Bros., New York City (1832). "Importers and Dealers in Watches and Jewelry, Manufacturers of Silver Ware, Clocks and Watches Repaired."

Marsh, George, Bristol, Conn.

Marsh, George C., Wolcottville (now Torrington), Conn. (1830).

Marsh, Gilbert & Co., Farmington, Conn. (1820).

Martin, George, Lancaster, Pa. (fl. 1780–). Made catgut ropes.

Martin, Samuel, New York (c. 1800). Tall mahogany, quarter columns, veneered. Arched dial, painted.

Martin, Thomas, Baltimore, Md. (1764). Watchmaker.

Masham, Samuel, of Wiltshire, "Maryland" (1774).

Masi & Co., F., Washington, D. C. (1833). "Manufacturers of Jewelry, Dealers in Watches. . . ."

Masi, Seraphim, Washington, D. C. (1832). "Dealer in Watches, Clocks. . . ."

Mason, H. G., Boston, Mass. (1844–49).

Mathey, Lewis, Philadelphia, Pa. (1797).

Matlack, White, Philadelphia, Pa.

Matlack, White C., New York City (1769–75).

Matlack, William, Philadelphia, Pa.

Matthewson, J., Providence, R. I. (1849).

Maurepas, ——, Bristol, Conn. (1855).

Maus, Frederick, Philadelphia, Pa. (1785–93).

Maus, Jacob, Trenton, N. J. (1780). "Clocks and Watches Made and Old Repaired."

Mayer, Elias, Philadelphia, Pa. (1832). "Manufacturer of Jewelry; keeps Watches and Materials."

Maynard, George, New York City (1702–30).

Mead, Adriance & Co., Ithaca, N. Y. (1832). "Dealers in Watches, Clocks. . . ."

Mead, Benjamin, Castine, Me. (1800–10).

Meeks, Edward, Jr., New York City (1796). "Makes and has for sale 8 day clocks and chiming timepieces."

Megar, Thomas J., Philadelphia, Pa. (1799). Dial by Patten & Jones, which see.

Melcher, ——, Plymouth Hollow (now Thomaston), Conn. (c. 1790).

Melly, "Brothers Melly," New York City (1829). "All kinds of watches and clocks."

Mendenhall, Thomas, Philadelphia, Pa.

Mends, Benjamin, Philadelphia, Pa.

Menzies, James, Philadelphia, Pa. (1800 and later).

Merchant, William, Philadelphia, Pa.

Meredith, Joseph P., Baltimore, Md. (1824–28). Watch and clock maker.

Merriam, Silas, ——, Conn. (1790).

Merriman & Bradley, New Haven, Conn. (1825).

Merriman, Reuben, Cheshire, Conn. Name given by Herbert S. Pratt, Westbury, N. Y.

Merriman, Silas, New Haven, Conn. (1734–1805). Made brass clocks.

Merriman, Titus, Bristol, Conn. (1810–30). About 1810 he was associated with Butler Dunbar making clocks.

Mery (or Merry), F., Philadelphia, Pa. (1799).

Meyer, J. A., New York City (1832). "Importer of . . . Clocks. . . ."

Meyers, John, Fredericktown, Md. (1793–1825).

Miler, Kennedy, Elizabethtown, N. J. The case shows the heights of craftsmanship of which the Jersey cabinetmakers were capable in the days of the young Republic. The case and the excellent brass works have come down through the years absolutely untouched, even the door glass being original.

Milk, Thomas, "Maryland" (1775).

Millard, Squire, Warwick, R. I. Maker of hall clocks.

Miller, Aaron, Elizabethtown, N. C. (?) (1747).

Miller, Abraham, Easton, Pa. (1810–30).

Miller, Edward F., Providence, R. I. (1824).

Miller, George, Germantown, Pa.

Miller, Henry. Tall clock.

Miller, John, Germantown, Pa. (1774).

Miller, Pardon, Providence, R. I. (1824–49).

Miller (or Millar), Thomas, Philadelphia, Pa. (1832). "Watch and Jewelry Store."

Millum, Moses, Baltimore, Md. (1819). Watchmaker at 25 Caroline Street, Fell's Point.

Milne, Robert, New York City (1798–1802).

Miner, Richardson, Stratford, Conn. (1736–97). Goldsmith and clock maker.

Mitchell & Atkins, Bristol, Conn. (1830).

Mitchell, George, Bristol, Conn. (1827–40).

Mitchell, Henry, New York City (1786–1802).

Mitchell, Hinman & Co., Bristol, Conn. (1831). "Manufacturers of Clocks, and dealers in Buttons, etc."

Mitchell & Mott, New York City (1793–1802). Hall, inlaid, moon dial.

Mitchell, Phineas, Boston, Mass. (1823).

Mitchelson, David, Boston, Mass. (1774) "Watches, Plain, Skeleton and Horizontal, in Gold, Silver and Pinchbeck cases, in particular a great variety of Silver Watches for 10 dollars to 10 guineas, some of which show the day of the month, and others with Seconds are very suitable for Physicians, likewise Spring and Pendulum Eight Day Clocks, also an assortment of Tools and Materials used by Clock and Watch-Makers."

Mohler, Jacob, Baltimore, Md. (b. 1744, d. 1773) (fl. 1773). Watch and clock maker, and had his shop "under the Printing Office in South Street near Market Street" in 1773. In the Maryland *Journal* he states that he "makes, sells and repairs all sorts of horizontal, musical, repeating and plain clocks and watches, . . ."

Mongin, David, South Carolina (1747). Clock and watchmaker.

Monkhouse, Thomas, London (1759–   ). —— John, London (c. 1770). —— John, & Son, Carlisle (1785–1810). High-class works brought over and installed in John Goddard block-and-shell case.

Monroe & Co., E. & C. H., Bristol, Conn. (1856).

Monroe, John, Barnstable, Mass.

Montgomery, Andrew, Baltimore, Md. (1774–79). Watch and clock maker at Calvert and Baltimore streets in 1822 and '23; at 46 Baltimore Street in 1824.

Montgomery, Robert, New York City (1786).

Moolinger, Henry, Philadelphia, Pa. (1794).

Morgan, Elijah, Poughkeepsie, N. Y. (1832). "Dealer in Watches, Clocks. . . ."

Morgan, Theodore, Salem, Mass. (1837).

Morgan, Thomas, Baltimore, Md. (1774–79). Watch and clock maker. In 1777 removed to Philadelphia.

Morrell, Benjamin, Boscawen, N. H. (1816–45).

Morrell, John, Baltimore, Md. (1822–23). Watch and clock maker at 27 S. Charles Street.

Morrell & Mitchell, New York City (1816–20).

Morris, Abel, Reading, Pa. (1774).

Morris, William, Grafton, Mass. (1765–76).

Morris, Sheldon, Litchfield, Conn.

Morris, Wollaston, "Maryland" (1774).

Morse & Co. (Myles Morse & Jeremiah Blakeslee), Plymouth Hollow (now Thomaston), Conn. (1841–49). Made clocks with brass works, one-day time and wire going.

Morse, Elijah (son-in-law of William Crane), Canton, Mass. (1819–).

Morse, Henry (son-in-law of William Crane), Canton, Mass. (1819–).

Morse, Miles (or Myles), Plymouth, Conn. (1849). With Jeremiah Blakeslee before 1849. Myles Morse and Gen. Thomas A. Davis of New York City built a clock factory on West Branch of Naugatuck, Plymouth, Conn., 1850–55.

Mosimann, Jacob, Baltimore, Md. (1810–12). Watchmaker at 21½ Baltimore Street.

Mosley, Robert E., Newburyport, Mass. (1848).

Mott, Jordan, New York City (1802–25). Advertised, 1810, "Jordan Mott (of the late firm of Mott & Morrel), at his store No. 247 Pearl Street, has on hand an extensive assortment of Clocks, Gold and Silver Watches, Jewelry and Silver Ware" (written in script).

Moulton, Edward, Rochester, N. H. (1807–25). Square top with fret above. Often inlaid. Tall clock. This sort of clock frequent around Rochester. Also Ed. G. Moulton, Saco, Me.

Moulton, Francis, Lowell, Mass. (1832).

Moulton, Thomas, Rochester (c. 1800).

Moulton, Thomas M. Dunbarton, N. H. Made very fine long-case clocks.

Mourgue, Peter, South Carolina (1735–36). Watch and clock maker.

Mowroue, Francis, New York City (1816).

Moyer, Joseph D., Skippackville, Pa. Name on dial, 30-hour hall clock, movement with chain.

Mulliken, Jonathan (son of Samuel), Newburyport, Mass. (1774–82). In 1774 bought land and buildings in Newburyport where he made and sold watches and clocks.

Mulliken, Joseph, Newburyport, Mass. (d. 1804).

Mulliken, Nathaniel, Lexington, Mass. (1751–89). His shop was burned by the British, April 19, 1775. Mulliken was with American troops. A British soldier carried off a brass musical clock in a sack.

Mulliken, Samuel, Newbury (now Newburyport), Mass. (1750–56). Removed to Newbury, 1750. Built house and shop where he made and repaired hall clocks until his death in 1756. Clock "Samuel Mulliken, Bradford," fine brass face with cherubs supporting crown in spandrels, and, flanking round brass name plate in arch, cornucopias. Probably Samuel was at Bradford before Newbury. This clock owned by Mrs. Eugene L. MacNair East Falls Church, Va., descended to her in direct line from Chase family in Newburyport. That the clock came from Newburyport bears out the evidence it was from the Newbury Samuel Mulliken.

Mulliken, Samuel, Jr., Newburyport, Salem, and Lynn, Mass. (1781–1807). Probably grandson of Samuel, son of John, nephew of Jonathan. Born 1761. Served apprenticeship with Jonathan Mulliken; then opened shop on State St. In 1783 he married Jonathan's widow. Several years later he removed to Salem, and then to Lynn. Was postmaster of Lynn 1803–07. "Samuel Mulliken will barter clocks for English and West India goods and country produce."

Munger, A., Auburn, N. Y. (1825). Made shelf clocks with pillars and looking-glass.

Munger & Benedict, Auburn, N. Y. (1833).

Munger & Pratt, Ithaca, N. Y. (1832). "Dealer in Clocks, Watches. . . ."

Munro, John, Charleston, S. C. (1785). Watchmaker from Edinburgh and London.

Munroe, Daniel, Concord, Mass. (1800–08), and Boston, Mass. (1808–). Brother of Nathaniel and in business with him in Concord.

Munroe, Daniel, Jr., Boston, Mass. (1823).

Munroe, Nathaniel (brother of Daniel), Concord, Mass. (1800–17). Baltimore, Md. (1817–). Served apprenticeship with Abel Hutchins. In business with brother Daniel, 1800–08, and with Samuel Whiting, 1808–17. Also had an extensive brass foundry, where he made bells, clock movements, etc.

Munroe & Whiting (Nathaniel Munroe and Samuel Whiting), Concord, Mass. (1808–17). Did a large business, chiefly eight-day clocks, with brass works, and had seven or eight apprentices and journeymen.

Myers, Frederick, Md. (17–). Tall.

Mygatt, Comfort Starr, Danbury, Conn. (1763–1832). Clock maker.

N

Narney, Joseph, Charles Town, S. C. (1753–61). Watchmaker and mender.

Neiser (or Neisser), Augustine (1737–80). He emigrated from his birthplace, Moravia, to Georgia in 1736; moved to Germantown, Pa., in 1739.

Nettleton, Heath & Co., Scottsville, N. Y. (1800–18). "Riley Whiting's model improved clocks, cased and sold by Nettleton, Heath & Co., Scottsville, N. Y."

Nettleton, W. K., Rochester, N. Y. (1834).

Newberry, James, Annapolis, Md. (1748). Advertised in the Maryland *Gazette* for July 20, 1748, as a watch and clock maker, and that he had just removed from the shop of John Inch to that of Samuel Soumaien.

Newberry, James, Philadelphia, Pa. (1819).

Newell, Thomas, Sheffield, Mass. (1810–20).

New Haven Clock Co. (1855–). Successor to the Jerome Mfg. Co. See Hiram Camp. Other men in this concern (1860) were: Hon. James English, H. M. Welsh, John Woodruff, Philip Pond (left two or three years before), Chas. L. Griswod (left), L. F. Root.

Newman, John, Boston, Mass. (1764) Boston *Gazette* July 23, 1764. "Clock and Watch Maker." "Shop opposite North Door of Court House in King Street, Boston."

Nicholls, George, New York City (1728–50).

Nichols, Walter, Newport, R. I. (1849).

Nicolet, Joseph Marci, Philadelphia, Pa. (1797).

Nicolet, Julian, Baltimore, Md. (1819–31). Watch and clock maker.

Nicolette, Mary, Philadelphia, Pa. (1793–99).

Ninde, James, Baltimore, Md. (1799–1835). Watch and clock maker.

Noble, Philander, Pittsfield, Mass.

Nolen & Curtis, Philadelphia, Pa. Dial painters. "Simon Willard and His Clocks" locates this firm in Boston.

Nolen, Spencer, Philadelphia, Pa. (1819). Clock dial manufacturer.

North, Norris, Wolcottville (now Torrington), Conn. (1820).

Northrop, R. E., New Haven, Conn. (c. 1820).

Northrop & Smith, Goshen, Conn. (c. 1820).

Norton, Samuel, Hingham, Mass. (1785).

Norton, Thomas, Philadelphia, Pa. (1811).

Noyes, Leonard W., Nashua, N. H. (1830–40).

Nutter, E. H., Dover, N. H.

O

Oakes, Frederick, Hartford, Conn. (1828). Watchmaker and goldsmith.

Oakes, Henry, Hartford, Conn. (1830). Henry Oakes & Co., dealers in watches, jewelry, cutlery, combs, fancy goods.

O'Hara, Charles, Philadelphia, Pa. (1799).

Oliver, Griffith, Philadelphia, Pa. (1785–93).

Oliver, John, South Carolina (1765). Watch and clock maker.

Oliver, Welden, Bristol, Conn. (c. 1820). Made shelf clocks, wood works, one-day time, bell strike.

Olmstead, Nathaniel, New Haven, Conn. (1826). Watches, jewelry, and silverware. Clocks and watches made and repaired.

O'Neil, Charles, New Haven, Conn. (1823). "Clock and watch repairer, informs his friends and the public he is at work at Messrs. Merriman and Bradley and solicits their patronage."

Orr, Thomas, Philadelphia, Pa. (1811).

Orton, Preston & Co., Farmington, Conn. (c. 1815).

Osgood, John, Haverhill, N. H. Was an early jeweler, also manufactured the old-fashioned high clocks.

Osgood, John, Boston, Mass. (1823). Probably also worked earlier. Tall, mahogany, brass decorated.

Owen, E. Name occasionally found cast in iron subframe of English hall clock dials, sometimes used in colonial hall clocks.

Owen, Griffith, Philadelphia, Pa. (1813). Bombé shape, tall clock.

Oyster, Daniel, Reading, Pa. (1764–1845).

P

Packard, Isaac, North Bridgewater (now Brockton), Mass. (18–). Associated with Rodney Brace.

Packard, J., Rochester, N. Y. (1819).

Packard & Schofield, Rochester, N. Y. (1819). "Perpetual Motion." "Packard & Schofield, Watch-makers, have at their shop, next door south of 'The Telegraph,' a handsome assortment of Gold, Silver and Plated ware which will be sold at a moderate profit, for no man can live by the loss. Clocks and watches of every description repaired and warranted to keep in motion merely by winding every day."

Paine & Heroy, Albany, N. Y. (1813).

Palmer, John, Philadelphia, Pa. (1795).

Park, Seth, Park Town, Pa. (1790).

Park, Solomon, Southampton Township, Pa. (1782).

Parke, Solomon, Philadelphia, Pa. (1791–1819).

Parke & Co., Solomon, Philadelphia, Pa. (1799).

Parker, Gardner, Westborough, Mass. (17–). Before the Revolutionary War, Gardner Parker was making clocks.

Parker, Isaac, Deerfield, Mass. (1780).

Parker, John, "Maryland" (1774). Watch movement maker.

Parker, Thomas, Philadelphia, Pa. (1785–1813).

Parker & Co., Thomas, Philadelphia, Pa. (1819).

Parker, Thomas, Jr., Philadelphia, Pa. (1819). Tall and shelf clocks.

Parmelee, Able (nephew and apprentice of Ebenezer). Bell founder, Guilford, Conn. (1720–).

Parmelee (or Parmilee), Ebenezer, Guilford, Conn. (1726–40). In 1726 he made a clock for the church in Guilford, which was used until 1893. It is now set up in the attic of the Henry Whitefield House, and is still in running order. In 1740 he made a clock with brass works for the New Haven Meeting-house. Born 1690. Probably first clock maker in Connecticut.

Parmier, John Peter, Philadelphia, Pa. (1793).

Parry, John J., Philadelphia, Pa. (1795–1813).

Patton, Abraham, Philadelphia, Pa. (1795–1815). Represented Leslie & Co., later with Patton & Jones of Baltimore.

Patton, David, Philadelphia, Pa. (1799).

Patton & Jones, Philadelphia, Pa. (1799.) Abraham Patton and Samuel G. Jones. Name cast in iron plate on back of white dial in Megear clock.

Payne, Lawrence, New York City (1732–55).

Peale, Charles Wilson, Annapolis, Md. (1764). "Makes, cleans and repairs clocks, and cleans and mends watches."

Pearsall & Embree, New York City (1786).

Pearsall, Joseph, New York City (1786–98).

Pearson & Grey, George-Town, S. C. (1768). "Clock and Watch-Makers, Cleans and Repairs all Kinds of Clock and Watches."

Pearson, Isaac, Burlington, N. J. (c. 1730).

Pearson, William, Jr., New York City (1775).

Pease, Isaac T., Enfield, Conn. (1818).

Peaseley, Robert, Boston (1735). Watchmaker.

Peck, Benjamin, Providence, R. I. (1824).

Peck, Edson C., Derby, Conn. (1827).

Peck, Elijah, Boston, Mass. (1789).

Peck & Co., Julius, Litchfield, Conn. (1820).

Peck, Moses, Boston, Mass. (1789).

Peck, Timothy, Litchfield, Conn. (1790).

Peckham & Knower, Albany, N. Y. (1814). "Have for sale 7 Willard's Patent Timepieces and 8 day clocks warranted of the best workmanship."

Penniman, John R., Roxbury and Boston (1806–28). Clock glass painter for Simon Willard.

Perkins, Robinson, Jaffrey, N. H.

Perkins, Thomas, Philadelphia, Pa. (1785–99).

Perkins, Thomas, Pittsburgh, Pa. (1815).

Perrigo, *see* Ferrigo.

Perry ——, E. Windsor (Conn.?). Name on hall clock.

Perry, Marvin, New York City (1769–80). "Repeating and Plain Clock and Watchmaker from London, where he has improved himself under the most eminent and capital artists in these branches, has opened shop in Hanover Square at the Sign of the Dial. He mends and repairs, musical, repeating, quarterly, chiming, silent, pull, and common weight clocks."

Perry, Thomas, New York City (1740–75). "Thomas Perry, watch-maker from London, at the Sign of the Dial, in Hanover Square, makes and cleans all sorts of clocks and watches in the best manner, and at a most reasonable rate."

Peters, James, Philadelphia, Pa. (1832). "Clock and Watch-maker, also Gold and Silver Ware." Tall clocks.

Pfaff, A., Philadelphia, Pa. (1820–35). A clock in Empire style, built above a cabinet with a pipe organ which plays two minutes before the hour. Musical part made by "Dominibus Nuhle." Clock owned by Mrs. J. M. Young, Chicago.

Pfaltz, J. William, Baltimore, Md. (1800–12). Was in partnership with Philip Sadtler, later in business alone.

Phillippe & LeGras, Baltimore, Md. (1796). Clock and watchmakers, and jewelers.

Phillips, Joseph, New York City (1713–35).

Pierret, Matthew, Philadelphia, Pa. (1795).

Pierson, Henry S., Portland, Me. (1834).

Pinkard, Jonathan, Philadelphia, Pa. (1773).

Piper, James, Chestertown, Md. (b. 1749, d. 1802) (fl. 1772–91). Watch and clock maker, also made surveying instruments.

Pitkin, Levi, East Hartford, Conn. (1795). "Jewelry, silversmith and clock-maker." Some of his clocks made before 1799.

Pitkins (four brothers), East Hartford, Conn. (1826–41 or later). In 1826 John O. Pitkin and Walter Pitkin. In 1836 Henry Pitkin and James F. Pitkin, watches. Theirs was the first watch made in America. Both industries were in the same building; their products were sold at Pitkins (H. & J. F.) in Hartford.

Pitman & Dorrance, R. I. (1800).

Pitman, Saunders, Providence, R. I. (1780).

Pitman, William R., New Bedford, Mass. (1836). "Manufacturers of gold and silverware, clocks and watches repaired and warranted."

Platt, ——, New Milford, Conn. (1793).

Platt, A. S., Bristol, Conn. (1849).

Platt, G. W. & N. C., New York City (1832). "Manufacturers of Silver Thimbles, Spectacles and spoons; also dealers in Jewelry, Silver Ware and Goods."

Pomeroy, Chauncey, Bristol, Conn. (c. 1835).

Pomeroy, Noah, Bristol, Conn. (1849–78). In 1849 bought out Chauncey Ives. Made clock movements only. Sold out to Hiram C. Thompson, 1878.

Pomeroy & Parker, Bristol, Conn. (1855).

Pond, Philip, Bristol, Conn. (1840).

Pope, Joseph, Boston, Mass. (1788).

Pope, Robert, Boston, Mass. (c. 1785). Very tall mahogany, quarter column, brass face, chime. Dainty fret over arch in addition to open fret at top.

Porter, Daniel, Williamstown, Mass. (1799). Three of his clocks are still running in or near Williamstown. They are eight-day clocks, with brass works and handsome cases.

Porter, William, Waterbury, Conn. (1814–20). Zenas Cook, Daniel Clark and William Porter owned a clock factory in Waterbury in 1814.

Post, Samuel, Jr., New London, Conn. (1760–94). In the clock and watch business.

Potter, Eli, Williamstown, Mass.

Potter, Ephraim, Concord, N. H. (1775–90).

Potter, H. J., Bristol, Conn. (1849).

Potter, J. O. & J. R., Providence, R. I. (1849).

Pound, John, South Carolina (1746). Clock and watchmaker.

Powell, John, Annapolis, Md. (1745). Powell was probably an indentured watch and clock maker. *See* William Roberts (*post*).

Praefelt, John, Philadelphia, Pa. (1797).

Pratt, Daniel, Jr., Salem, Mass. (1839).

Pratt, D., & Sons, Boston, Mass. (1849).

Pratt & Frost, Reading, Mass. (1832–35). Daniel Pratt, Jr., and Jonathan Frost.

Pratt, Phineas, Saybrook, Conn. (1747–1813). Clock maker by trade.

Pratt, William, & Brother, Boston, Mass. (1847).

Price, Isaac, Philadelphia, Pa. (1799).

Price, Joseph, Baltimore, Md. (1799). Watch and clockmaker, at 35 Baltimore Street. This may be an error for Joseph Rice.

Price, Philip, Philadelphia, Pa. (1819).

Price, W. L., Birmingham. Dial maker.

Prichard & Monson, Bristol, Conn. Maker of Connecticut shelf clock with wooden works.

Priest, Joseph, "Maryland" (1775). (Port of Bristol.)

Prince, Geo. W., Dover, N. H.

Prince, Isaac, Philadelphia, Pa. (1791–95).

Proctor, Cardan (or Carden), New York City (1737–60).

Proud, John, Newport, R. I. Very early Newport dealer. Name on brass hall clock dials. Cases and movements and style and age like William Clagget's.

Provaux,——, South Carolina (1775). Watchmaker.

Pulsifer, F. L., Boston, Mass. (1856).

Purse, Thomas, Baltimore, Md. (1796–1812). Watch and clock maker.

Q

Quandale, Lewis, Philadelphia, Pa. (1813).

Quare, Daniel, London. A Quaker (1648–1724). Inventor of the repeating watch. Celebrated clock maker.

Quimby, Phineas, Belfast, Me. (1830–50).

Quimby, William, Belfast, Me. (1821–50). Succeeded by Abel B. Eastman.

Quincy, Henry, Portland, Me. (1834). "Clocks, Watches, Jewelry, shell combs, all kinds of fancy articles repaired."

Quinn, Thomas, Philadelphia, Pa. (1775).

R

Racine, Daniel, Baltimore, Md. (1799). Watchmaker.

Ranlet, Noah, Gilmanton, N. H. Name on small grandmother's clocks. (Miller.)

Ranlet, Samuel, Monmouth, Me. (1800).

Rapp, William D., Philadelphia, Pa. (1831). Norristown, Pa. (1837).

Rea, Archelaus, Salem, Mass. (1789).

Read, Wm. H. J., Philadelphia, Pa. (1832). "Clock and Watchmaker, Ever-pointed Pencils, Spoons, . . . for sale."

Reed, Benjamin, Bristol, Conn. (c. 1775).

Reed, Ezekiel, North Bridgewater (now Brockton), Mass. (previous to 1800).

Reed, Isaac, Stamford, Conn. (before Revolution).

Reed, Simeon, Cummington, Mass. (c. 1770).

Reed, Stephen, New York City (1802–32). "Store of Watches and Clocks; Jewelry and Silver Ware."

Reed, Zelotus (son of Simeon), Goshen, Mass. (c. 1796).

Reed & Son, Isaac, Philadelphia, Pa. (1832). "Watch-makers and Importers. Manufacturers of Jewelry, etc."

Reeves, David S., Philadelphia, Pa. (1832).

Reiley, John, Philadelphia, Pa. (1785–95).

Reymond, ——, Charleston, S. C. (1785). "Clock and Watch Maker from Paris. Makes and mends all sorts of watches in his trade. . . ."

Reynolds, John, Hagerstown, Md. (c. 1790–1832). Watch and clock maker.

Rice & Barry, Baltimore, Md. (1785–87). Watch and clock makers.

Rice, Joseph T., Albany, N. Y. (1813–31).

Rice, Phineas, Charlestown, Mass. (1830).

Rich, John, Bristol, Conn. (1820).

Rich, Joseph, ——, Conn. (19th C.).

Rich, Joseph, Baltimore, Md. (1784–1801). Watch and clock maker.

Richards, B. & A. Bristol, Conn. (1820).

Richards & Co., Gilbert, Chester, Conn. (1832). "Manufacturers of Patent Clocks."

Richards & Morrell, New York City (1809–32).

Richardson, Francis, Philadelphia, Pa. (1736).

Richmond, Franklin, Providence, R. I. (1824–49).

Richmond, G. & A., Providence, R. I. (1810).

Richter, Joseph, Baltimore, Md. (1817).

Riddle, James, Fermanaugh Township, Pa. (1780).

Rider, Arthur, Baltimore, Md. (1822–24). Watch and clock maker.

Riggs, William H. C., Philadelphia, Pa. (1819).

Riley, John, Philadelphia, Pa. (1799).

Ritchie, Benjamin, "Maryland" (1774). Of Scotland.

Ritchie, George, Philadelphia, Pa. (1785–93).

Rittenhouse, Benjamin (younger brother of David and in partnership with him) (1760). Worcester, Pa., a township neighboring on Norriton.

Rittenhouse, David, Norristown, Pa. (1751–70). Philadelphia, Pa. (1770–77). Established his trade of clock making in Norristown, 1751. Moved to Philadelphia 1770. Was also a famous astronomer, and made mathematical instruments. Was Treasurer of Pennsylvania, 1777–89; professor of Astronomy in Pennsylvania University 1779–82; Director of U. S. Mint at Philadelphia, 1792–95; President of American Philosophical Society, 1790–96). (Norristown was Norriton.) Both long and short S found on dials. As a rule dials were engraved but some were bare. Very great variety in cases. Some extremely plain, others the finest known. Made one-day, eight-day, and astronomical clocks. Also various special clocks, a fourteen-day, a month clock, and that used by him in observing the transit of Venus. The Drexel Institute clock is two feet wide and more than nine feet high; has a planetarium, musical attachment with sixteen chimes, and records seconds, minutes, hours, days, and the moon's position, etc. Probably the richest and most elaborate antique American clock.

Roath, R. W., Norwich, Conn. (1832). "Manufacturer of Ever Pointed Pencil Cases and Window Springs; Dealer in Watches. . . ."

Roberts, E., & Co. (sons of Gideon), Bristol, Conn. (1815–30).

Roberts, Gideon, Bristol, Conn. (1780–1804). Pioneer of clock making in Bristol. "He made the columns and pinions on a small foot-lathe, cut out the wheels with his jack-knife and hand-saw, and painted the dial-face on a piece of white paper which he afterward pasted upon the clock. When he had finished a few, he mounted his horse, with the clocks fastened about him, and started out to peddle them. Many clocks made by him are known to have done good service."

Roberts, Jacob, Easton, Pa. (1810–30).

Roberts, John, Philadelphia, Pa. (1799).

Roberts, William, Annapolis, Md. (1745). Advertised in the Maryland *Gazette* for September 6, 1745, "to acquaint all Gentlemen and others who have any Watches and Clocks to repair, that they may have them done in the best manner," as "John Powell who was advertised last week in this paper as a Runaway" had only "gone into the County a Cyder-drinking" and "is returned to his Master's service."

Rockwell, Samuel, B., Middletown, Conn. (1742), Providence, R. I. (1750–54). Middletown (1762). Four fine clocks have been located, with "Samuel Rochwell, Providence" across face.

Rode, William, Philadelphia, Pa. (1785–95).

Rogers, Abner, Berwick, Me. (1820).

Rogers, Isaac, Marshfield, Mass. (1800–28).

Rogers, James, New York City (1822–78).

Rogers, Samuel, Plymouth, Mass. (1800–04).

Rogers, William, Boston, Mass. (1860).

Rogers, William, Hartford, Conn. (1837). "Dealer in watches, and timepieces of every description repaired in the best manner."

Rohr, John A., Philadelphia, Pa. (1811).

Root, S. Emerson, Bristol, Conn. (b. 1820, d. 1896). Orphaned when young, came to Bristol and lived with his uncle, Chauncey Ives. When a young man, engaged in clock business, at first with Edward Langdon, then alone. He was the inventor of the paper clock dial with brass sash.

Rose, Daniel, Reading, Pa. (1749–1827).

Rosset & Mulford (near the Stone Bridge in Elizabethtown, Pa., March 27, 1807). Cabinetmakers, veneered and inlaid clock with eagle and stars.

Roth, N., Utica, N. Y. (1779).

Roulstone, John, Boston, Mass. (1768). (Boston *News-Letter*, May 12, 1768). "Clock and Watch-Maker . . . removed from shop he lately improved to shop three doors Southward of that, and the third Door Northward of the White Horse Tavern."

Rouse

Russell, George, Philadelphia, Pa. (1832). "Clock and Watch-maker; also Dealer in Watches, Jewelry and Silver Ware."

Russell, Major John (son of John Russell), Deerfield, Mass. (1765). "Set up his trade of watchmaker," 1765.

Rutter, Moses, Baltimore, Md. (1804).

Sadd, Harvey, New Hartford, Conn. (1776–1840).

Sadd, Thomas, East Windsor, Conn. (1750).

Sadtler, P. B., Baltimore, Md. (1804).

Sallady, Jacob, Bedminster Township, Pa. (1782).

Samuels & Dunn, New York City (1844). Sold clocks with spurious labels (Chauncey Jerome).

Sandell, Edward, Baltimore, Md. (1817).

Sands, Stephen, New York City (1772–86).

Sanford, Eaton, Plymouth, Conn. (1760–76).

Sanford, Isaac, Connecticut.

Sanford, Ransom, Plymouth, Conn. (1840). Made brass pinions and barrels for Seth Thomas clock movements.

Sanford, Samuel, Plymouth, Conn. (1845–77).

Sargeant, Jacob (brother of Joseph), Hartford, Conn. (c. 1790–1838). One of the first jewelers and silversmiths in Hartford; also made clocks.

Sargeant, Joseph (brother of Jacob), Springfield, Mass. (1800).

Savoye, N., Boston, Mass. (1832).

Sawin & Dyer, Boston, Mass. (1800–20). Fine banjos.

Sawin, John, Boston, Mass. (1823–63). Apprentice of Aaron Willard; in clock making business in Boston; frequently employed by Simon Willard, Jr., & Son, to make clocks for them. "Manufacturer of all kinds of clocks for Church, Gallery, Bank, Inc. office, Factory, Watch-clocks and common House-Clocks, 33 Cornhill."

Sawin, John, Chelsea, Mass. (1847).

Sawyer, C. & H. S., Colebrook, Conn. (1849).

Saxton & Lukens, Philadelphia, Pa. (1828–40).

Sayre, Charles, East Town, Name on dial, hall clock.

Sayre, John, New York City (1800).

Sayre & Richards, New York City (1805).

Schmidt, John, of London, a Dane, patented clock "Father Time" made at Lakeport, Calif. At Essex Institute.

Schreiner, Charles W., Philadelphia, Pa. (1813).

Schriner, Martin, Lancaster, Pa. (1790–1830).

Schriner, M. &. P., Lancaster, Pa. (1830–40).

Schroeter, Charles, Baltimore, Md. (1817).

Schuyler, P. C., New York City (1802). "Begs leave to inform his friends and the public in general that he has again commenced business at 48 John Street, one door west of William street. From the knowledge he has of the above business he flatters himself he will give general satisfaction."

Scott, John, Peters Township, Pa. (1780).

Searson, John, New York City (1757).

Sedgwick & Bishop, Waterbury, Conn. (1820).

Sedgwick & Botsford, Watertown, Conn. Wood clocks.

Seward. Name on eight-day lyre. Said to be brother of Wm. H. Seward. Found in New York State.

Seymour, Robert, Waterbury, Conn. (1814).

Seymour, Williams & Porter, Unionville (on Roaring Brook), Conn. (c. 1835). Began making clocks about 1835, but a destructive fire in 1836 or 1837 seriously interrupted. The clock business seems never to have flourished in Unionville after the fire, though it was carried on in the screw factory after the abandonment of the screw business by Pierpont & Co. The above firm's name is also in clocks made at Farmington, Conn., probably after the fire.

Shaw, David, Plainfield, Mass. (b. 1792, d. 1882, approximately). Name given by Galen W. Johnson, Shelburne Falls, Mass.

Shaw, Seth W., Providence, R. I. (1856).

Shearman, Martin, Hingham, Mass. (1821).

Shearman, Robert, Wilmington, Del. (1760–70). (Some say Philadelphia.) Handsome, richly carved tall clock.

Shearman, Robert, Philadelphia, Pa. (1799).

Shepherd & Boyd, Albany, N. Y. (1813).

Shepherd, M., South Carolina (1774). Watchmaker.

Shepherd, Nathaniel, New Bedford, Mass.

Sherman, Robert, Philadelphia, Pa. (1799).

Shermer, John, Philadelphia, Pa. (1813).

Shields, Thomas, Philadelphia, Pa.

Shipman, Nathaniel, Norwich, Conn. (1789). Apprentice of Thomas Harland; offered for sale jewelry and time-keepers.

Shipman, N., & Son, Norwich, Conn. (1879). Clock makers and silversmiths.

Shreiner, Henry M. (grandson of the original Martin), Lancaster, Pa.

Shreiner, Martin (1767), in business till 1830. Made a great many fine clocks and numbered them, the highest known number being 356. Lancaster, Pa. Also with son made fire engines, the best of their time. Laid out Shreiner's cemetery. Burial place of Thaddeus Stevens.

Shreiner, Martin, 2d, Lancaster, Pa. Alive at 84, in 1917.

Shreiner, Martin & Philip, sons of original Martin, succeeded him in business in 1830.

Shroeter, Charles, Baltimore, Md. (1807–18). Watchmaker.

Sibley, Asa, Conn. (?).

Sibley, Gibbs, Canandaigua, N. Y. (1788).

Sibley, S., Great Barrington, Mass. (1790).

Simonton, Gilbert, New York City (1820).

Simpson, Alexander, Hagerstown, Md. (1799–1805). Clock, watch and mathematical instrument maker.

Sinnett, John, New York City (1774). He advertised clocks of all kinds and "Watches neat and plain, gold, silver, shagreen and metal. Some engraved and enamelled with devices new and elegant; also the first in this country of the small new-fashioned watches the circumference of a British shilling."

Sinnott, Patrick, Baltimore, Md. (c. 1761). Advertised in Maryland *Gazette* of Annapolis, April 16, 1761, that Patrick Sinnott, lately from Philadelphia "has taken a House next door to Mr. John Hart's, the Dutch Saddler, and opposite to Dr. John Stevenson's, where he carries on the Jewelry Business and . . . likewise makes and repairs Clocks and watches with all Sorts of Silversmith's work."

Smith, New York (early 19th C.). Bowery and Division streets. Name without initials on banjo. Lower glass with figure of Liberty placing wreath on head of an eagle supporting American coat of arms.

Smith, Aaron, Ipswich, Mass. (1825). "Smith's Clock Establishment, corner of the Bowery and Division St."

Smith, Charles, Pennsylvania.

Smith, Edmund, New Haven, Conn. (1817). He advertises that he always has cheap and handsome clock cases on sale.

Smith, Capt. Elisha, Sanbornton, N. H.

Smith, Elisha, Jr., Sanbornton (spelled Sandbornton on dial), N. H. Apprentice of Abel Hutchins. (Early 19th C.)

Smith, George, Carlisle, Pa. (1780).

Smith & Goodrich, Bristol, Conn. (1827–49).

Smith, Henry, Plymouth Hollow (now Thomaston), Conn. (1840).

Smith, Henry C., Waterbury, Conn. (1814).

Smith, I., Skippackville, Pa. Name on hall clock dial.

Smith, James, Philadelphia, Pa. (1846). "Wholesale clock establishment No. 82 North Third street where watch-makers and merchants will find the largest assortment ever offered at prices exceedingly low. Year, month, 8 day and 30 hour and alarm."

Smith, Jesse, Concord, Mass. (c. 1800). Apprentice of Levi Hutchins.

Smith, Jesse, Jr., Salem, Mass. (1837).

Smith, John, South Carolina (1754). "Makes and mends all sorts of Clocks and Watches."

Smith, Josiah, Reading, Pa. (1778–1860).

Smith, Luther, Keene, N. H. (c. 1785–1840). In 1794 he made town clock for Keene.

Smith, L., and Blakesley, A., Bristol, Conn. Empire shelf. Style of 1802.

Smith, Lyman, Stratford, Conn. (1802). "Clock and Watch Maker, Silver Smith and Jeweler."

Smith, Philip, Marcellus, Onondaga County, N. Y.

Smith, Sml [sic], New York (late 18th C.). Tall.

Smith & Sill, Waterbury, Conn. (1831).

Smith, Stephen.

Snelling, Henry, Philadelphia, Pa. (1776). Watchmaker.

Snyder, Peter, Jr., Exeter Township, Pa. (1779).

Solledy, John, Richland Township, Pa. (1782).

Solliday, D. H., Sy. Town, Pa. Tall clock.

Solliday, John N., Reading, Pa. (adv. Aug. 31, 1816).

Souers, Christopher, Philadelphia, Pa. (1724–). A very gifted man. Was author, printer, paper-maker, doctor, and farmer. In these callings he spelled his name Sower, but on his clocks Souers.

Southworth, Elijah, New York City (1793–1810).

Souza, Samuel, Philadelphia, Pa. (1819).

Spalding & Co., Providence, R. I. Makers of hall clocks.

Spaulding, Edward, Providence, R. I. (1770–97).

Sparck, Peter, Philadelphia, Pa. (1797).

Spence, John, Boston, Mass. (1823).

Spencer, Noble, Wallingford and Stratford, Conn. (1796). Clock and watchmaker and repairer.

Spencer, Wooster & Co., Salem Bridge (now Naugatuck), Conn. (1828–37).

Sperry, Anson, Waterbury, Conn. (c. 1810).

Sperry, T. S., 25 St. John St., New York. Made only a few clocks.

Sperry & Shaw, New York City (1844). Sold clocks with spurious labels (Chauncey Jerome).

Splangler, Rudolph, York, Pa. (1780).

Sprogell, John, Philadelphia, Pa. (1791).

Sprogell, John, Jr., Philadelphia, Pa. (1771). Watchmaker.

Spruck, Peter, Philadelphia, Pa.

Spurch, Peter, Philadelphia, Pa. (1795–99).

Spycher, Peter, Jr., Tulpehocom, Pa. (1784).

Squire & Bros., New York City (1847).

Stanton, Job, New York City (1810).

Stanton, Wm., Providence, R. I. (1816).

Stanton, W. P. & H., Rochester, N. Y. (1838).

Staples, John L., Jr., New York City (1793).

Starr, Frederick, Rochester, N. Y. (1834). "Cabinet and Clock Factory."

Stauffer, Samuel C., in business early in the 1800s, Manheim, Pa., also in partnership with Christian Eby. Made many good tall clocks.

Stebbins & Howe, New York City (1832). "Store and Watches, Jewelry, Silver Ware and Fancy Goods."

Stebbins, Lewis, Waterbury, Conn. (1811). "A Singing master." Chauncey Jerome worked for him, making dials for old-fashioned long clocks.

Steckell (or Stickell), Valentine, Frederick, Md. (1793–96). Watch and clock maker.

Steikleader, John, Hagerstown, Md. (1791–93). Clock and Watchmaker. "Makes and repairs all kinds of Watches, clocks, and silverwork."

Stein, Abraham, Philadelphia, Pa. (1799).

Stein, Albert H., Norristown, Pa. (1837).

Stevens, George M., Boston, Mass. (1890). Repairer.

Stevenson, Howard & Davis, Boston, Mass. (1845).

Stever & Bryant, Burlington (village of Whigville), Conn. (1830).

Stewart, Arthur, New York City (1832).

Stickney, Moses O., Boston, Mass. (1823).

Stillas, John, Philadelphia, Pa. (1785–93).

Stillman, William, Burlington, Conn. (1789–95).

Stillson, David, Rochester, N. Y. (1834).

Stoddard & Kennedy, New York City (1794).

Stokel, John, New York City (1820–43).

Stollenwerck, P. M., New York City (1820 and earlier). In 1816 he advertises: "P. M. Stollenwerck's Mechanical Panorama. This ingenious piece of mechanism . . . presents on a scale of 340 square feet a view of a commercial and manufacturing City. . . . Admission 50 cents; children half price. To see the mechanism, 25 cents additional. Mr. Stollenwerck, inventor and proprietor of the Mechanical Panorama, continues his profession of Clock and Watch-maker, at No. 157 Broadway and also repairs all kinds of Mechanical, Mathematical and Musical Instruments." (Clock and Watch-maker written in script.)

Stollenwerck, P. M., Philadelphia, Pa. (1813). (Same as namesake, N. Y.?)

Storrs, N., Utica, N. Y. (early 19th C.?). Inlaid curly maple tall clock. Metropolitan Museum.

Stover & Kortwright, New York City. Name on dial, hall.

Stow, D. F., New York City (1832). "Dealer in Clocks, Watches, Jewelry, etc."

Stow, Solomon, Southington, Conn. (1828–37). Came to Southington 1823 and began cabinetmaking. In 1828 began clock making. In 1834 built dam and shop near depot. In 1837 entered employ of Seth Peck & Co., tinners' machines. "Manufacturer of Eli Terry's Patent Clocks."

Stowell, Abel, Worcester, Mass. (1790–1800). Abel Stowell carried on a very extensive manufacture of tower and church clocks. The town clock in the Old South Meetinghouse, Worcester, was made by Abel Stowell in 1800.

Stowell, Abel, Boston, Mass. (1823–56).

Stowell, John, Boston, Mass. (1825–36).

Stowell, John, Medford, Mass. (1815–25).

Stowell, John J., Charlestown, Mass. (1831).

Stoy, Gustavus, Lebanon, Pa.

Stratton, Charles, Worcester, Mass. (1820).

Stretch, Peter, Philadelphia, Pa. (1670–1746). Did work on the town clock. It is believed in Philadelphia that this celebrated maker was the first in America. It is stated that there is a clock of his dating from 1702, and another in 1710. They have handsome brass faces and very early cases, not specially elaborate. Stretch was a friend of William Penn. Cf. with dates of Joseph Bagnall and Will Claggett.

Stretch, Samuel, Philadelphia, Pa. (1717). Watchmaker.

Stretch, Thomas, Philadelphia, Pa. (1697–1765). Watchmaker.

Studley, David, Hanover, Mass. (1806–35). He learned the trade of John Bailey.

Studley, David F., North Bridgewater (now Brockton), Mass. (1834). He came from Hanover, Mass., in September, 1834, and made watches and jewelry, also repaired all kinds of clocks. Later became associated with his brother Luther in the business, and afterwards sold out to Luther.

Studley, Luther (brother of David F.), North Bridgewater (now Brockton), Mass. (18–).

Stump, Joseph, Pennsylvania (?).

Suley, John, Baltimore, Md. (1810–12). Watchmaker.

Sutton, Robert, New Haven, Conn. (1825).

Swan, Benjamin, Haverhill, Mass., and Augusta, Me. (1810–40).

Syberberg, Christian, New York City (1755–75).

Syberberg, Christopher (1757). South Carolina *Gazette*. Clock and watchmaker.

Syderman, Philip, Philadelphia, Pa. (1785–94).

T

Taber, S., & Co., Providence, R. I. (1849).

Taber, Elnathan, Roxbury, Mass. (1784–1854). Native of Dartmouth, Mass., in 1768, of Quaker parentage. Came to Rcxbury at age of 16 or 19, served as apprentice to Simon Willard, and afterwards engaged in clock making on his own account. When Simon Willard retired, Taber bought most of his tools and the good will of the business, his clocks being as good as Simon Willard's. He made clocks for Simon Willard, Jr., & Son (1838–54).

Taber, S. M., Providence, R. I. (1824). Maker of hall clocks.

Taber, Stephen, New Bedford, Mass. (1798–1802). See article in Boston *Transcript*, July 21, 1928. (b. 1777, d. 1862).

Taber, Thomas (son of Elnathan), Boston, Mass. (1852–57). Continued his father's business.

Taf, John James, Philadelphia, Pa. (1794).

Tappan, William B., Philadelphia, Pa. (1819).

Tarbox, H. & D., New York City (1832). "Importers of Watches, Clocks, Watch and Clock-Makers' Tools and Materials, and keep constantly on hand a general assortment of Goods suitable for Country Watch and Clock-Makers. Also Manufacturers of Watch Cases and Jewelry."

Taylor, Samuel, Philadelphia, Pa. (1799).

Taylor, Samuel, Worcester, Mass. (1855).

Tenney, William, Nine Corners, Dutchess Co., N. Y. (1790).

Terry & Andrews, Bristol, Conn. (1735–40).

Terry & Barnum, East Bridgeport, Conn. (1855) Merged their company and the Jerome Co. into one, thus causing the failure of the latter in fall of 1855.

Terry, Burnham, Connecticut (19th C.). Balance escapement.

Terry Clock Co., Pittsfield, Mass. (1880). It was through efforts of George H. Bliss in 1880 that the Terry Clock Co. was organized, and that the three brothers Terry were persuaded to come to Pittsfield from Connecticut. In 1885 C. E. Terry (grandson of Eli) was superintendent and manager. In 1888 the business was reorganized under title The Russell & Jones Clock Co., and soon afterwards it was discontinued.

Terry Clock Co., Waterbury, Conn. (Alarm Patent Applied for Grandfather's Clock.)

Terry, Downs & Co., Bristol, Conn. (1851–57).

Terry, Eli, Plymouth, Conn. (1793–). Learned clock making and engraving of Daniel Burnap in Hartford; also received instruction from Thomas Harland. In 1792 he made his first tall wooden clock, which is now owned by his descendants and is still going. In 1792 or '93 he went to Northbury (then a part of Watertown, now Plymouth), Conn., and began making hang-up clocks. His first clocks were made by hand, but soon he began using water power. By 1800 he had some help but was able to make and sell only a few each year, at about $25 apiece (for movement and dial alone). In 1807 he sold to Heman Clark, an apprentice, and bought an old mill, with water-power, in the southern part of Plymouth, now called Greystone. Seth Thomas and Silas Hoadley joined him, forming the firm Terry, Thomas and Hoadley. In 1810 Terry sold out to his partners and removed to Plymouth Hollow. Before this, he had made several different forms of shelf clock. Finally, in 1814, he devised what he called his "perfected wood clock," with the "pillar scroll top case." In construction it was radically different from all previous clocks, and it became popular at once. Seth Thomas paid $1000 for the right to manufacture it, and he and Terry each made about six thousand the first year. The same year Terry began to teach two of his sons, Eli, Jr., and Henry, the clock business. Although his fame and fortune were made with the improved wood shelf clock, he also made fine clocks with brass works, and some tower clocks. He died at Terryville, 1852.

Terry, Eli, Jr., Plymouth Hollow (now Thomaston), Conn. (1814–24), Terryville, Conn. (1824–41). In 1814 he began working with his father. When twenty-five years old he built a shop of his own on the Pequabuck, and the village where he lived was called Terryville in his honor.

Terry, Eli, 3rd, Plymouth, Conn. (1862).

Terry, Henry (son of Eli 1st), Plymouth Hollow (now Thomaston), Conn. (1814–30). He continued the business in his father's factory, but finally gave up clock making for the woolen business.

Terry, L. B., Albany, N. Y. (1831).

Terry, R. & J. B., Bristol, Conn. (1828–35). Probably later than this. Sons of Samuel?

Terry, Samuel (brother of Eli), Bristol, Conn. (1820–35). Came to Bristol about 1825 and began making Jerome's "Bronze Looking-Glass Clock." "Manufacturer of Patent Thirty Hour Wood Clocks with various Patterns of Fancy Cases, and Eight Day Church Steeple Clocks, also Brass Founder."

Terry, Silas Burnham (son of Eli), Plymouth Hollow (now Thomaston), Conn. (1823–76). Had a shop at junction of Pequabuck and Poland brooks in 1831. After 1852 was in employ of Wm. L. Gilbert at Winsted, and of

Waterbury Clock Co. Then he and his sons organized the Terry Clock Co., and he continued as head of this firm till his death.

Terry, Theodore, Ansonia, Conn. (1860).

Terry, Thomas, Boston, Mass. (1823).

Thibault & Brother, Philadelphia, Pa. (1832). "Manufacturers and Importers of . . . Watches. . . ."

Thomas & Hoadley, Greystone (town of Plymouth), Conn. (1810). In 1810 Seth Thomas and Silas Hoadley bought out the Terry factory and continued the manufacture of works for tall cases.

Thomas, Isaac, Williston, Md. (1768). (Some say Pennsylvania.)

Thomas, Joseph, Philadelphia, Pa. (1830).

Thomas, Seth, Plymouth Hollow (now Thomaston), Conn. (1809–50). Worked for Eli Terry as a joiner. In 1809 formed partnership with Eli Terry and Silas Hoadley at Greystone. In 1810, after buying out Terry's interest, Thomas and Hoadley continued the manufacture of tall clocks. In 1812 Thomas sold to Hoadley and went to Plymouth Hollow. Began clock making on his own account and was successful, though he was not inventive. In 1853 incorporated the Seth Thomas Clock Company, which is still in business. He died in 1859. Soon after that part of Plymouth was named Thomaston in his honor.

Thomas Co. (Seth), Thomaston (formerly Plymouth Hollow), Conn. (1853 to present time).

Thompson, James, Baltimore, Md. (1796). Watchmaker.

Thompson, William, Baltimore, Md. (1795–1824). Watch and clock maker.

Thompson, William, Carlisle, Pa. (1780).

Thomson, James, Pittsburgh, Pa. (1815).

Thornton, Joseph, Philadelphia, Pa. (1819). Clock and watchmaker.

Thownsend, Charles, Philadelphia, Pa. (1819).

Thownsend, John, Jr., Philadelphia, Pa. (1819).

Tiebout, Alexander, New York City (1798).

Timby, Baldwinsville, N. Y. Shelf clock "Solar Time Piece." Another apparently same pattern by "Gilman Joslin, Boston, 1860." Has a terrestrial globe (six inches) "containing the latest discoveries." Essex Institute.

Tinges, Charles, Baltimore, Md. (1796–1815, perhaps earlier and later). Watchmaker.

Tobias, S. & I., & Co., New York City (1829).

Todd, Richard J., New York City (1832).

Tolford, Joshua, Kennebunk (also Portland), Me. (1815, before and after). Watch and clock maker, offers for sale "rich jewelry." He moved to Portland, whence he came, after remaining in this town about a year.

Tolles, Nathan, Plymouth, Conn. (prior to 1836). Made parts of clocks.

Tompkins, George S., Providence, R. I. (1824). Made clocks, watches, and silverware.

Tompkion, Thomas, "father of English watch making," London (b. 1638, d. 1713). Made for the Court of Charles II. Invented many improvements in clock and watch movements. Buried at Westminster Abbey. His pupil was George Graham.

Torrey, Benjamin B., Hanover, Mass.

Tower, Reuben, Plymouth and Hingham, Mass. (1813–20). (Spelled Rubin occasionally.) (Hanover?)

Townsend, Charles, Philadelphia, Pa. (1799–1811). (cf. Thownsend.)

Townsend, Christopher, Newport, R. I. (1773).

Townsend, David, Philadelphia, Pa. (1789).

Townsend, Isaac, Boston, Mass. (1790).

Townsend, John, Newport, R. I. (1769). Case maker. Fine example with block front with shell, in Metropolitan Museum marked John Townsend, Newport, R. I., 1769. Brother-in-law of John Goddard and son of John Townsend, cabinetmaker of Newport.

Townsend, John, Jr., Philadelphia, Pa. (1813).

Tracy, Erastus, Norwich, Conn. (1768–96). Clock and watchmaker.

Tracy, Gurdon (brother of Erastus), New London, Conn. (1767–92). Watch and clock maker.

Treadway, Amos, Middletown, Conn. (1787). "stole two china faced watches from Amos Treadway."

Troth, James, Pittsburgh, Pa. (1815).

Trott, Andrew C., Boston, Mass. (1800–10).

Trott & Cleveland, New London, Conn. (1792). Bought out the stock and equipment of Gurdon Tracy.

Trott, Jonathan, Jr., New London, Conn. (1771–1813). Clock maker and silversmith.

Tuller, William, New York City (1831).

Turell, Samuel, Boston, Mass. (1789).

Tustin, Septimus, Baltimore, Md. (1814). Watchmaker.

Tuthill, Daniel M., Saxton's River, Vt. (1842). Both brass and wooden clocks. Brass works were purchased in Connecticut, wooden works made by him. He made all the cases, and put the finished product on the market.

Twiss, B. & H. (Benjamin, Ira, and Hiram), Meriden, Conn. (1820–32). "Benjamin & Hiram Twiss began manufacture of clocks in 1828." "Manufacturers of the Improved Clocks." Ira removed to Montreal, Canada, about 1829.

U

Uhreledig, Valentine, Reading, Pa. (1779).

Union Mfg. Co., Bristol, Conn. Made brass clocks.

Universum Clock Co., Boston (19th C.). Astronomical clock, Salem Institute.

Upjohn, James (came to America in 1802). Was a member of the London Clock-makers' Company.

Upson, Merrimam & Co., Bristol, Conn. (1830).

Urick, Valentine, Reading, Pa. (1760).

Urletig, Valentine, Reading, Pa. (1767–83). (See Uhreledig. The same person evidently.)

V

Van Vleit, B. C., Poughkeepsie, N. Y. (1832). Watch and clock maker and silversmith. "Dealer in Watches, Clocks, . . .; Repairer of Clocks and Watches; Manufacturer of Silver Spoons, etc."

Van Wagenen, John, Oxford, N. Y. (1843). "Fine Pieces, Brass and Wood Clocks of the best kind warranted to keep correct time, for sale lower than ever offered before, at the cheap store."

Veazie, Joseph, Providence, R. I. (1805).

Vinton, David, Providence, R. I. (1792).

Vogt, John, New York City (1758).

Voight, Henry, Philadelphia, Pa. (1775–93).

Voight, Sebastian, Philadelphia, Pa. (1775–99).

Voight, Thomas (son of Henry), Philadelphia, Pa. (1811–35).

Vuille, Alexander, Baltimore, Md. (1766).

W

Wade, Nathaniel, Newfield & Stratford, Conn. In 1796 went into partnership with Hall. "Clocks and watches made and repaired."

Wadsworth, Lounsbury & Turner, Litchfield, Conn. (1830). Made Terry's Patent clocks.

Wadsworths & Turners, Litchfield, Conn. (1832). "Terry's Patent."

Wady, James, Newport, R. I. (1750–55).

Wagstaff, Thomas, London (1766–94). Quaker, celebrated maker, supplied clocks frequently to American Quakers who had them cased in Philadelphia or Newport. A lacquered clock by him is known.

Wales, Samuel H., Providence, R. I. (1849–56).

Walker, A., Brockport, N. Y. (1832).

Wall & Almy, New Bedford, Mass. (1820–23).

Wall, William A., New Bedford, Mass.

Walsh, ——, Forestville (town of Bristol), Conn. (c. 1825).

Walter, Jacob, Baltimore, Md. (b. 1782, d. 1865) (fl. 1815–c. 1860). Watch and clock maker and silversmith.

Walters, Henry, South Carolina *Gazette* (1757). Clock and watchmaker.

Ward, Anthony, New York City (1724–50).

Ward, Anthony, Philadelphia, Pa. (1717). Clock maker.

Ward & Govett, Philadelphia, Pa. (1813).

Ward, Isaac, Philadelphia, Pa. (1813).

Ward, John & William L., Philadelphia, Pa. (1832). "Watches, Jewelry and Silver Ware."

Ward, Joseph, New York City (1735–60).

Ward, Lauren, Salem Bridge (now Naugatuck), Conn. (1832–40).

Ward, Lewis, Salem Bridge (now Naugatuck), Conn. (1829–40).

Ward, Macock, Wallingford, Conn. (1702–83). Apprentice of Ebenezer Parmelee (fl. 1724–83). Master of many trades. Politically active. Made all kinds of clocks and cases.

Ward, Nathan, Fryeburg, Me. (1801).

Ward, Richard, Salem Bridge (now Naugatuck), Conn. (1832–40).

Ward, Thomas, Baltimore, Maryland (1755). Advertised as watch and clock maker in Baltimore Town.

Ward, William, Salem Bridge (now Naugatuck), Conn. (1832–40).

Warfield, J. H., Baltimore, Md. (c. 1827). Watchmaker.

Warner, Cuthbert, Baltimore, Md. (c. 1780–1838). Watch and clock maker.

Warner, George J., New York City (1795 and later).

Warner, John, New York City (1790–1802).

Warner (George J.) & Reed, New York City 1802).

Warner (George J.) & Schuyler, New York City (1798).

Warrington, John, Philadelphia, Pa. (1811).

Waterbury Clock Co. (successor to Benedict & Burnham Co.). Included: Deacon Aaron Benedict, Mr. Burnham of New York, Noble Jerome (making movements), Edward Church (making cases), Arad W. Welton (1855).

Watson, J., Chelsea, Mass. (1847).

Watson, Lumas, Cincinnati, O. (1816–21). Ephraim Downs made clocks for him.

Way, John, Waggon Town. Grandfather clock. There is a Wagontown in Chester County, Pa.

Weatherly, David, Philadelphia, Pa. (1813).

Weaver, Holmes. "Cabinet and chair maker Meeting-Street NewPort" from label in 18th C. tall clock owned by Henry A. Hoffman, Barrington, R. I.

Weaver, N., Utica, N. Y. (1844).

Webb, Isaac, Boston, Mass. (1708). (Boston *News-Letter*, Mar. 29/Apr. 5, 1708). "Watch-Maker and Clock-Maker, that formerly lived next door to the Royal-Exchange Tavern near East End of Town-House in Boston, is now removed over against the West-End of said Town-House in High Street two Doors from Prison Lane."

Weidemeyer, John M., Fredericksburg, Va.

Welch, Elisha N., Bristol, Conn. (1855–). In 1855 he bought the property and business of J. C. Brown. In 1864 he organized The E. N. Welch Manufacturing Company.

Welch Mfg. Co., The E. N., Bristol, Conn. (1864). Organized by Elisha N. Welch. This is now the Sessions Clock Company.

Weldon, Oliver, Bristol, Conn. (1820).

Weller, Francis, Philadelphia, Pa. (1777). "Watch-Maker. Repairs all sorts of clocks and watches."

Welsh, Alexander, Baltimore, Md. (1800–01). Watchmaker.

Welton, Hiram & Heman, Plymouth, Conn. (1841–44). They bought the "upper shop" of Eli Terry, Jr., in Terryville, and used it for many years. They underwrote some firm that failed; this caused their failure also, in 1845.

West, James L., Philadelphia, Pa. (1832). "Fillagree Worker; orders for jewelry, watches Plate and Fancy Articles promptly attended to."

West, Thomas G., Philadelphia, Pa. (1819).

Weston, J., Boston, Mass. (1849–56).

Wetherell, Nathan, Philadelphia, Pa. (1830–40).

Wharfe, Joseph, Frederick-Town, Md. (1819). Watchmaker and silversmith.

Wheaton, Caleb, Providence, R. I. (1784–1827). Reputed best maker of his time in Rhode Island. A bill relating to Goddard cases is displayed, signed by Wheaton, in this work. Wheaton's works were generally silver faces engraved by him personally. He engraved plates for Rhode Island paper money.

Wheaton, Caleb, & Son, Providence, R. I. (1824).

Wheaton, Calvin, Providence, R. I. (1790).

Wheaton, Godfrey, Providence, R. I. (1824).

Whetcroft, William, Baltimore, Md. (1778). "To be sold by the subscriber, at Elkridge Landing, a great variety of material for the clock, Watch and Jewelry business."

Whipple, Arnold, Providence, R. I. (1810).

Whitaker, George, Providence, R. I. (1805).

Whitaker, Gen. Josiah, Providence, R. I. Partner of Nehemiah Dodge.

Whitaker (Josiah) & Co., Providence, R. I. (1824).

Whitaker, Thomas, Providence, R. I. He and George Dana bought out Nehemiah Dodge.

White, Peregrine, Woodstock, Conn. (1774–). Made "tall clocks, with full moons and elaborate appurtenances." David Goodell of Pomfret made cases for his clocks. (Some err in supposing he was the Peregrine born in the "Mayflower.")

White, Sebastian, Philadelphia, Pa. (1795).

Whitear, John, Fairfield, Conn. (1738–62).

Whitear, John (son of John) (1762–73). Succeeded his father.

Whitehead, John, Philadelphia, Pa. (1831).

Whiting, Riley, Winsted (town of Winchester), Conn. (1807–35). In 1807, with Samuel and Luther Hoadley, he started making clocks at Winsted. When Luther died and Samuel retired, Mr. Whiting continued business. He died in 1835. (See Lucius Clark.) "The machinery (of these wood clocks) was carried by a tin wheel on an upright iron shaft. The cog-wheels were of cherry, the pinion was of ivy, or calmia (mountain laurel), and the face of white-wood, all home products. These, with a little wire, a very little steel, brass, tin, and cordage, made up the staples of material of the old one-day shelf clocks which they produced and scattered all over the United States and Canada."

Whiting, Samuel, Concord, Mass. (1808–17). In partnership with Nathaniel Munroe, 1808–17; worked for himself, 1817.

Whitman, Ezra, Bridgewater, Mass. (1790–1840).

Whittaker, William, New York City (1731–55).

Whittemore, J., Boston, Mass. (1856).

Wiedemeyer, J. M., Baltimore, Md. (1800–01). Watchmaker.

Wiggin, Henry, Jr., Newfields, N. H. (19th C.) He made cases for John Kennard's clocks.

Wiggins, Thomas, & Co., Philadelphia, Pa. (1832).

Wilbur, Job B., Newport, R. I. (1815–49).

Wilcox, A., New Haven, Conn. (1827).

Wilcox, Cyprian, New Haven, Conn. (1827). Clock and watchmaker and silversmith.

Wildbahm, Thomas, Reading, Pa. (1763–1805).

Wilder, Ezra (son of Joshua), Hingham, Mass. (1800–70).

Wilder, Joshua, Hingham, Mass. (1780–1800). Did not die until near 1860.

Willar, ——, Philadelphia, Pa. (1778). Removed to New York.

Willard, Aaron (son of Benjamin and Sarah Willard), Roxbury, Mass. (1780–90). Boston, Mass. (1790–1823). Born in Grafton, Mass., 1757. Probably learned clock making from one of his brothers. In 1780 opened a shop near his brother Simon's in Roxbury. Was a better business man than his brothers. About 1790 he moved to Washington Street, Boston, and established a factory connected with his house. Employed twenty or thirty workmen. A little colony of clock makers and the allied trades grew up here. Retired, 1823. Died, 1844.

Willard, Aaron, Jr. (son of Aaron and Catherine Willard), Boston, Mass. (1806–50), (b. 1783). Learned trade in his father's factory. For short time was in partnership with Spencer Nolan as clock and sign painters. In 1823 took over his father's business. The lyre clock was originated by him. He closed out business and removed to Newton, 1850, where he died 1864.

Willard, Alexander T. (brother of Philander, and third cousin of Simon Willard), Ashburnham, Mass. (1796–1800), and Ashby, Mass. (1800–40). (*See* Philander.)

Willard, Benjamin (son of Benjamin and Sarah Willard), Grafton, Lexington, and Roxbury, Mass. (1764–1803). Was the first of this family to engage in clock making. Probably started about 1764. Learned trade of Benjamin Cheney, East Hartford. Removed to Lexington about 1768, and to Roxbury, 1771. Advertised in the Boston *Gazette* February 22, 1773, "Musical clocks playing different tunes, a new tune every day in the week, and on Sunday a Psalm tune. These tunes perform every hour." One of his clocks has a large sweep hand to turn to tunes the names of which appear around the main dial. In 1790 he was living in Worcester. In 1803 he went to Baltimore, Md., where he died the same year. His clocks are marked Grafton, Lexington, or Roxbury.

Willard, Benjamin F. (son of Simon and Mary Willard), Roxbury, Mass. (b. 1803). Was skilled mechanic and inventor. Learned clock making from his father. Did not engage in business for himself, but worked for others and for a time for his father. In last year of his life conducted jewelry and silversmith business in Boston under name Rich & Willard. Died in 1847.

Willard, Ephraim (son of Benjamin and Sarah Willard), Medford, Mass. (1777), Roxbury, Mass. (1798), Boston, Mass. (1801), and New York City (1805). Born in Grafton, 1755. Though he appears to have been in clock-making business over twenty years, clocks made by him are rare.

Willard, Henry (son of Aaron and Mary (2nd wife) Willard), Boston, Mass. (b. 1802). Was apprentice of William Fisk, a noted cabinet-maker. Made clock cases for his father, Aaron Willard, his brother, Aaron Willard, Jr., William Cummens, Elnathan Taber, Simon Willard, Jr., and Son, but not for Simon Willard. In 1847 removed to Canton, Mass. In 1887 returned to Boston and died there same year.

Willard & Nolan, Boston, Mass. (1806–09). Dial and sign makers. (The Willard was Aaron, Jr.)

Willard, Philander J. (brother of Alexander, and third cousin of Simon Willard), Ashburnham, Mass., and Ashby, Mass. (1772–1840). Made clocks in Ashburnham till 1825; then moved to Ashby and was associated with his brother in clock-making business. Both were ingenious and skilful, and did a large business, mostly on orders. Philander made a gravity clock, very curious, still in existence.

Willard, Simon (son of Benjamin and Sarah Willard), Roxbury, Mass. (1770?–1839). Born in Grafton, Mass., 1753. Was the most famous of this clock-making family. Apprenticed to an English clock maker named Morris, also helped by his brother Benjamin. At age of 13 he made without assistance a tall clock far superior to those of his master. Probably started in business for himself in Grafton, but moved to Roxbury, 1780, and set up his shop at 2196 Washington Street, where he lived until his retirement, 1839. In 1802 he brought out his Patent Timepiece, an instant success, later called the banjo clock. No improvement has since been made on the original design. He also made regular clocks, gallery clocks, and tower clocks. Among them are two clocks which he presented to Harvard College, the large clock in the Capitol at Washington, made at the age of 82, and that on the Old State House, Boston. Simon Willard died in Boston, 1848. (After he retired from business, 1839, Elnathan Taber, his best apprentice, bought most of his tools and the good will of the business, and received permission to put the name Simon Willard on his dials. Simon Willard, Jr., took these clocks and sold them at his store in Boston. All clocks sold from there had name "Simon Willard, Boston" or "Simon Willard & Son, Boston." As early as 1780 his reputation was so high that other clock makers put the name Willard on their clock-dials).

Willard, Simon, Jr. (son of Simon and Mary Willard), Boston, Mass. (1828–70). At West Point, 1813–15. Resigned from army in 1816. Crockeryware business in Roxbury, 1817–24. In his father's clock-making shop, 1824–26. In New York learned chronometer and watch business from D. Eggert in eighteen months. Set up in business for himself in 1828 at No. 9 Congress Street, Boston, and remained till 1870. Made the astronomical clock now in observatory of Harvard University. His astronomical regulator was standard time for all railroads in New England.

Willard, Zabdiel, A. (son of Simon, Jr., and Eliza Willard), Boston, Mass. (1841–70), (b. 1826). Apprentice in father's store, 1841. Admitted as partner, 1850.

Williams, David, Newport, R. I. (before 1800 to 1824). Also Providence?

Williams, Orton, Prestons & Co., Farmington, Conn. (1820). "Improved Clocks with Brass Bushings."

Williams, Stephen, Providence, R. I. (1799). In 1799 associated with Nehemiah Dodge. In 1800 in business by himself.

Williamson, Henry, Baltimore, Md. (1808). Watch and clock maker.

Willmott, Benjamin, Easton, Md. (1797–1816). Watch and clock maker.

Wills, Joseph, Philadelphia, Pa.

Wilmirt, John J., New York City (1793–98).

Wilmurt, Stephen M., New York City (1802).

Wilson, Hosea, Baltimore, Md. (1817).

Wilson & Osborn, Birmingham, England (1722–85). After 1775 made independently till 1812. From 1812 to 1825, Mrs. Osborn and a son made under name of Osborn & Co. Dials imported in large numbers. Sometimes movements also English. Much confusion due to finding of name in iron subdial back of the white dial and on many colonial clocks.

Wing, Moses, Windsor, Conn. (1760–1809). Made brass clocks.

Wingate, Frederick B., Augusta, Me. (1800). Made good tall clocks in large numbers.

Wingate, George, Baltimore, Md. (1816). Watch and clock maker.

Wingate, Paine, Newburyport, Mass. (1803), in Boston directory (1789), in Augusta, Me., directory (1811). (*See* Frederick B.)

Winship, David, Litchfield, Conn. (1832). "Clock Case Maker and Dealer in Clocks."

Winslow, Ezra, Westborough, Mass. (1860). A brass worker, he made and repaired brass clocks.

Winslow, Jonathan. "This clock made by Jonathan Winslow, purchased before 1800 by Moses Shaw of Palmer, Mass., whose wife was Mary McMaster. He died in 1835 and she died in 1837. The clock was given to Linda McMaster Forbes, wife of Capt. Henry Forbes of Enfield — a niece of Mrs. Shaw. At the death of Mrs. Forbes, the clock was given to her nephew, Livy McMaster of Fitchburg, and has been doing good service in this city since 1873."

Winston, A. L. & W., Bristol, Conn. (1849). Makers of brass clocks.

Winterbottom, T., Philadelphia, Pa. (1750). Clock maker.

Witman, Benjamin, Reading, Pa. (1774–1857).

Witmer, Able, Ephrata, Pa. (fl. late in 18th C.). Was a member of the Cloister. Twenty-four-hour type.

Wood, David, Newburyport, Mass. (c. 1790–1824). Had a shop in 1792 in Market Square. In 1824, he advertised "new and second-hand clocks for sale." Some of his cases had brass rosettes at the ends of the scrolls on hood. He was a notable maker of hall and shelf clocks.

Wood & Hudson, Mt. Holly, Vermont.

Wood, John, Philadelphia, Pa. (1770–93). "Clocks, watches, gold and silver work made, mended and sold at the sign of the Dial, the corner of Front and Chestnut streets." Good maker of hall clocks. A clock by him in old Barracks, Trenton, N. J.

Wood, Josiah, New Bedford, Mass. (1800–10).

Woodcock, William, Baltimore, Md. (1819–29). Watch and clock maker.

Woolson, Thomas, Jr., Amherst, N. H. (1805).

Wriggins, Thos., & Co., Philadelphia, Pa. (1831). "Watch and Jewelry Store, Manufacturers of Silver Plate, Spoons, etc."

Wright, Charles Cushing, New York City. After 1812 settled in Utica.

Wright, John, New York City (1712–35).

Wright, Samuel, Lancaster, N. H. (1808–   ). Did well here for some years.

Wright, William, Baltimore, Md. (1802–03). Watchmaker.

Y

Yeaden, Richard, South Carolina (1772). Watch and clock maker.

Yeomans, Elijah, Hadley, Mass. (1771–83). Goldsmith and clock maker.

Young, David, Hopkinton, N. H.

Young, Francis, Philadelphia, Pa. (1777). Watch and clock maker. "Repairs all sorts of watches and clocks."

Young, Jacob, North Ward, Philadelphia Co. (1769). Watchmaker.

Young, Joseph, Newburgh, N. Y. Inlaid tall, French feet, double arch, moon motion.

Young, Stephen, New York City (1810–16).

Youngs, Ebenezer (son of Seth), Windsor, Conn., and New York State (1736–1818). Clock and watchmaker.

Youngs, Ebenezer, Hebron, Conn. (1778).

Youngs, Seth, Hartford, Conn. (fl. 1711–35). Later removed to Windsor.

Z

Zahm, G. M., Lancaster, Pa. (1843).

Zimmerman, Anthony, Reading, Pa. (1768–88).

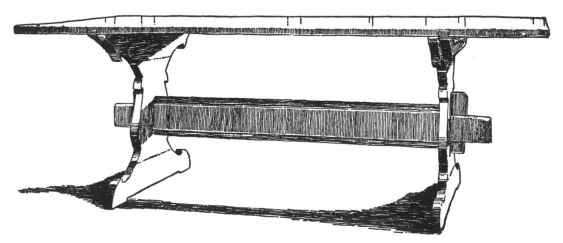

A fine type of a Swedish trestle and board. The base ends and the deep truss with its wedges, and the mortise shoe base are salient and good features.

The close resemblance to Pennsylvania types of construction is striking. The early Swedish settlements gave a cast to some early Pennsylvania styles. Size of top is 37 by 86 inches.

An all original "Brewster" settee, whose exportation I wish the Swedish government had prevented. Yet for merit and style and remarkable design it is excellent. (*See* Page 392.)

The great Johnson four-gate table, perhaps unique in America in having the swing from the center which greatly increases the beauty and the convenience of the table, because thus there are wedge-shaped openings which prevent the legs from interfering with the knees. Size of top is 72 by 78 inches. (*See* Page 396.)

INDEX

VOLUME III FURNITURE TREASURY

The index for Volumes I and II is at the end of Volume II. This index refers only incidentally to Volumes I and II, and the numbers refer to the pages in this volume. In the other index the numbers refer to the legends under the pictures, as those volumes have no page numbers.

INDEX

collections, 132; methods in and rules for, 133; inventories for, 138; small collections, hope in, 138; simple pieces, 139; lack of it, like amnesia, 141; where and what, 142; danger of buying in private houses, 144; Victorian era to be avoided, 145; rules for, 270; chapter on What and Where, 142; educative influence, 336; reactions of, 399; sure means of avoiding errors, 411.

Collecting late Empire, 148.

Collectors. *See* Collecting.

Collectors' yarns, 388.

Color, in furniture, 229.

Concord Antiquarian Society, rooms in, 310, 311, 312, 320, 326.

Connecticut block and shell, weak attachment of foot, 444. *See also* Feet, and Goddard I, 444.

Connecticut, mantels, 21, 22.

Connecticut River work, 29.

Constructional features. *See* chapters on Cabinetmaking and descriptions of measured drawings through the volume.

Convertible furniture, 220, 221. *See also* Beds.

Corner chair, 160.

Corrections and Comments on Volumes I and II, 109 and following.

Correlation of furniture with architecture, 261.

Couch, 124, 238.

Couch chair, 220, 221.

Court cupboard table, 396.

Cradle, barrel, 167; finest example of, 397.

Crane. *See* Iron, under finials.

Crestings, 161, 168, 175, 178, 179, 180, 181, 187, 192, 193, 197; of cabinet pieces, 260.

Crowding the stair, 413.

Cupboards, wall or corner, 26; corner, 120; open corner, 75, right; domes of, 231, 233; oak, 254; shell top, 256; demi-dome, plastered, 257, 258; court, pine, story of, 392.

Currans, Philadelphia, 120, 124.

D

Davenport, 238.

Day bed, 124, 238. *See also* Couch, and Chaise longue.

Dealers, becoming repairers, 20, 137, 262.

Decorating, interior, 9; avoidance of clutter, 26; the profession of, 135; commissions in, 135; need of training for, 135; must make a living, 137.

Definitions. *See* Glossary, 338.

Design, modern, 6; inferior if modern, 7; limited number of possible forms, 7. *See* chapter on Cabinetmakers, 153.

Desks, 120; Washington, 120, bottom; Sheraton, 299; English designs of, 153.

Details, measured. *See* Measured drawings.

Detection of fraud, 262.

Dining room, equipment of, 412.

Directoire styles, 14.

Disbrowe, 429.

Document drawers, carved fronts, 89.

Dog, fire, 222.

Donnelly, Ernest John, the artist who has done all the sketching for this book, title page, Introduction, 192.

Dough trough, 300

Dovetail, blind, 278, 386.

Drawings, measured. *See* Measured drawings.

Dressers, 120, bottom, 223.

(538)

330, and following; manipulation of, 331; rubbing down, 331; special care in August, 332; testing wood for dryness, 332.

Fire carrier, 131.

Firelighter, 131.

Fireplaces, 17; with tile, 20, 22, 29; center of early history, 129, 314, 320, 326.

Fireplace utensils, 230.

Flemish scrolls, 161, 179, 181, 192.

Floors, narrow boards, bad, 26.

Fluting, on Chippendale chairs, which see; also beds, which see.

Foliated rosettes. *See* Rosettes.

Forks, iron, 14.

Frets, 260.

Fuller, Samuel, 123.

Furniture, American; most of the articles shown in this work are American; if otherwise, the fact is so stated.

Furniture, arrangement of, 24, 26, 266; the right things together, 410.

Furniture, books on. *See* Glossary 338; also Lyon, Lockwood, Nutting.

Furniture catalogs, tend to name American origins, 265.

Furniture drops. *See* Drops.

Furniture fakes, 236, 262; ordered by the consumer, 266.

Furniture finials, 60; Greek origin, 60; simple, 62; Philadelphia, 64, 67; for beds, 62, 63; Goddard, John, 69, 76; Chapin, 65, 66; flame, 63, 64, 67, 68, 69, 70, 71, 74, 75, 76, 77, 84, 85, 86; New England flame, 16 on page 67; auger or spiral, 68; ball, 68, 84; fluted, 69, 70, 72, 74, 76, 77, 79; foliations on urn, 69, 75; animal, 70; cock, 70; owl, 70; brass, for clocks, 69 and 70 on page 70, 30 to 33 on page 72; clocks, wood, page 72 bottom, also

74, 75, 76, 79, 84; pierced flame, 40 on page 74; eagle, 79; pheasant, 80; heron, 81; pineapples, 8, 79; spiral with button, 82; vases with flowers, 82; draped urns, 82; wreath, 83; Winthrop's bust, 83; cross stretchers, 85, bottom.

Furniture, foreign, 416.

Furniture, modern, makers fail, if reproductions good, 266.

Furniture, moving of and exhibition of, 225.

Furniture origins. *See* Cabinetmaking, also 217, 264; foreign, 149; chapter on Pitfalls, 262.

Furniture, Pilgrim, 230.

Furniture, pine, 24.

Furniture refinishing, 225. *See* Finishing.

Furniture repair or restoration, 224.

Furniture reproductions. *See* Reproductions.

Furniture, upholstered, to be restored, 225.

G

Gaming table, 302.

Garvan Collection, 119, 120, 487.

Georgian style, 23, 26, 258. *See* Glossary, 356; period of 1714–45 about, resembles Queen Anne, but often richer, 356.

Gibbons, Grinling, 417.

Gillingham chairs, 216, 430.

Glossary, 338.

Glue, old, now disguised, 14.

Glue, unsafe dependence on, 227.

Goddard, John I., 23; long article concerning, 431; conclusions regarding, 445.

Goddard, John, grandson of John I, label, 113.

Goddard specimens, 120; remarkable stonetop table, recently discovered, 431; bill, earliest date, 431; other Goddard notations, 432; will of, 433; inventory,

434; comparison of values with other commodities, 434; shell-and-block furniture, 435.

Goddard, Stephen, son of John I. *See* Glossary.

Goddard, Thomas, son of John I. *See* Glossary.

Goodwin, William B., Hartford, 388, 491.

Goosenecks, 97, 100.

Gostelowe, Jonathan, very celebrated maker. *See* Glossary.

Gothic styles, 15, 238. *See* Chippendale Gothic.

Guilford, 301.

Gwinnett, Button, 388.

Gumwood, 419.

H

Hands, clock; illustrations and chapter on, 469–86.

Hardware, 25, 129, 130, 290; full showing, volume II, 409, 410.

Hard words, 236.

Hartford, Connecticut, probable source of some block-front furniture; also in earlier volumes; principal source of American oak, 491.

Heart motive, in furniture, 183.

Hepplewhite, 24; type, 120, 169–74, 176; oval back, 176; intersecting scrolls, 177; draped back, 177; reverse feathers, 178; tambour, 288.

Hergesheimer, 146.

Hickory, used in furniture, 419.

Highboys, bonnet top, 119; scroll top, 119; blocks on, 486.

Highboys, restoration of legs, 231; drawings of, 274–76.

Highboys, shells, 8.

Hinges, L, 192.

Hogarth, ramp on chair back, called after him, 358.

Holly, 419.

Hope for the small collector, 138.

Horse, trestle, 22, bottom left.

Humbugs, 236.

I

Illustration for novels, etc., 408.

Imitation, 262, 403.

Individuality, in style, 23.

Inlay, 307; herringbone, 308; repairing, 308; William and Mary, 309; modern, 309.

Interchangeability, no such thing in old days, 12.

Interior decorating, 9; modern degradation of, 9.

Interiors, kitchen, 167; Queen Anne parlor, 182, 223, 228, 230, 272, 310, 311, 312; dining room, gate-leg period, 314, 320, 326, 381.

Iron, utensils, 14; combined knocker latch, 115; fireplace utensils, 129.

Isham, student of Goddard, 483

J

Jacks, clock work, 20.

Jaffrey house, now destroyed, 27; mantel, 206.

Joiner, often same as carpenter, 16.

Joints of leaves, kinds of, 268.

Joints. *See* Mortises.

Joint stools, 230.

Jones, Inigo; work similar to that of Wren, 445.

Jumel mansion, 261.

INDEX

INDEX

New art, 149.

New London, Connecticut, probable source of furniture, 491.

Newport type or school, principally Goddard I, 436; not to be confounded with later Newport productions, 436; the term refers to Goddard and John Townsend and Job Townsend, father-in-law of Goddard, but not to Stephen or Thomas, sons of John Goddard, Sr., nor to John, the grandson, whose work was of the later period.

Nigrosine, for black, 227.

Nineteenth century, reason for decline in, 3.

Nulling, 15.

Nutting, Wallace, books by, flyleaf; room of, 205; furniture of, 175, 184, 185–88, 196–201, 202. *See also* Glossary.

O

Oak, fine for solidity of effect, 23, 24.

Oak, in furniture, 421; English oak, 421; quartering, 332.

Old houses, 261.

Overstuffed furniture, always bad, 5.

P

Painted furniture, 184.

Palladio, the Italian adaptor of Greek designs to the arch and the Renaissance. *See* Cabinetmaking and 445.

Paneling, 272. *See also* Interiors.

Parlors, 182, 228.

Patina, 266. *See* chapter on Finishing, 316, 317.

Pear wood, 422.

Periods in furniture, table of, 382.

Pheasant. *See* under Finials.

Phyfe, Duncan, 14, 23, 270, 450. *See* chapter on Cabinetmaking.

Pig, 222, top left; a warming foot stool.

Pilgrim Hall, Plymouth, 397.

Pineapple, 8, 79.

Pine furniture. *See* Furniture, pine.

Pine, in furniture, 422.

Pitfalls for the collector, 262.

Pole-screens. *See* Screens.

Poplar, 423.

Prices, fluctuation of, 265, 268; of furniture, 334; foolish to predict, 336.

Publications of Old America Company, flyleaf.

Q

Quality in furniture, 18.

Quartering lumber, cut of, 332.

Queen Anne, 9, 23.

R

Radiates, numbers of, in shells, 485. *See also* Shells.

Ram's-horn arm, 196.

Randolph, Benjamin. *See* Glossary, 451; *see* Chairs, also 145.

Redundant ornament, 149.

Refinishing, 225.

Reifsnyder sale, high prices obtained at, 120.

Repairing furniture, 16; long delayed, 20.

Repairs, 224; omit all possible, 224; broken parts, 224.

Replacements, how far wise, 229.

Reproductions, 4, 233; no real demand for, 6; evil of standardizing, 139; must be honest, 234; not feasible if cheap, 234, 266; by dealers, 137, 270; English, posing as old, 137.

INDEX

APPENDIX

CRUDE HOMEMADE FURNITURE

The frontier was once, of course, the Atlantic Coast, and steadily moved west. The General Court of Massachusetts once voted to build a road twelve miles west into the wilderness, "that being as far," so the act recited, "as any one could ever wish to go." On the frontier, wherever it may be, crude furniture must always be made.

The bench is the crudest article on the frontier, which is now some mountain region far from the railway. The bench was a puncheon, that is, a log split in the middle, roughly smoothed on the flat side, and supplied with four hewn straddling legs set into holes bored on the rounded side. Later, when good workmen specialized on furniture, this bench became a wash bench for the men, who washed out of doors or in the shed. Also, tables were made in the same manner, from a larger log. They resembled, in the size of their tops, the trestle and board of the Middle Ages, being two feet wide, or more. The tops of the benches and tables were made tolerably good by a short smoothing plane.

Stools were done in the same manner, and were made in sizes adapted for children or adults. Such stools, benches, and tables are still in use in certain mountain sections of our country.

Sawing, while common with the first settlers, was not thought necessary, as riven lumber was more quickly prepared and is even found on drawer bottoms and insides of panels on richly carved seventeenth-century furniture.

A broadax man of experience could hew so as to leave no ax cuts showing. The beams now set up with ax cuts, supposed to be old fashioned, are a reflection on our fathers, who would have been ashamed of such a job. One had only to watch the hewers of ship timbers at Bath in this generation to see finished work on which no tool but an ax was ever lifted up.

The floors were, of course, made of the same puncheons.

Chairs with rush seats can be, and often were, made with no other tools but an ax and a pod auger. The "backs," or two slats, were split and drawshaved so that only careful examination can detect that the ax and the drawshave and the auger were the only tools used. Further, this method of making slats continued into the really fine period twenty years each side of 1700. I have seen some of these chairs found by Dr. Irving W. Lyon of Buffalo. As the first beds required only two hewn side rails and one post, also hewn, the settler had all his necessary articles of furniture except his chests with three tools, the ax, the drawshave, and the auger. To make his chest he must add a chisel, for fitting the joinings, and the smoothing plane.

If he wished, he added the pit saw (one man in a pit, one above). It is true he soon wished to make molding planes, which he could grind himself, and set in a handmade block of wood.

If he wished luxury, he filed a V chisel and a gouge, and everything necessary and beautiful was possible to him.

He found growing in the marshes a certain rush with a rasping stock. He tied these in bundles and had sandpaper!

Thus, the rush (reed, flag), abundant by brooks or marshes, supplied him with
1. Sandpaper (a special rush).
2. Thatch for his roof.
3. Cover for his floor.
4. Seats for his chair.
5. Lights (rush soaked in fat).
6. Rush (cat-tails shredded) for stuffing his bed tick.
7. The pen (the earliest scribes' pen was from *calamus*, a reed).

So that he slept under, walked on, sat on, slept on, read by, and wrote by the marsh rush. And he *ate* the root!

The old settler was not so slow. With an ax *alone* he built his log house. He chinked the cracks with moss, built his chimney with stones and mud, or fine lime mortar from oyster shells. Stick chimneys, as liable to burn, were early forbidden in town. He ate from homemade trenchers, made wooden spoons, cut his food with his clasp knife, and used no fork, even were he a king. His appetizer was mustard greens or peppers, the cranberries he found growing, the turkeys flying, and he ploughed the sea and reaped cod fish (called "Cape Ann turkey").

The window means the wind hole, and no glass appeared in simple cottages, even in England, but a battened or paneled shutter closed the hole. Later pretentious people used oiled paper sash. But that was new-fangled and luxurious.

With the maple and pine tree, the adjacent sea, the marsh and the borrowed Indian corn, he had a complete physical civilization. His dwelling soon rivaled those of England. The thrifty man speedily became forehanded because the resources in fisheries, lumber, and marsh grass gave him, as he cleared the forest, a better background of wealth than the old world. He also had a Bible, which he kept in a carved box, and Brewster had a hundred books in the learned tongues, which he could not only read — he could print them and bind them!

All the smaller appurtenances of the home he had from head and fingers — loom, linen, wheels, reels, bone buttons, thorn needles, deer hide, feathers from the wild goose breast, and — Priscilla!